ALLUSIONS IN
ULYSSES

ALLUSIONS IN

ULYSSES

AN ANNOTATED LIST
BY WELDON THORNTON

THE UNIVERSITY OF NORTH CAROLINA PRESS · CHAPEL HILL

Copyright © 1961, 1968 by
The University of North Carolina Press
Manufactured in the United States of America
Library of Congress Catalog Card Number 68–14359
Printed by Heritage Printers, Inc., Charlotte, North Carolina

This book is dedicated
to my parents
MARGIE M. THORNTON
ELBERT E. THORNTON

ACKNOWLEDGMENTS

Writing this book has necessarily involved help from many sources; I wish to acknowledge and thank the persons and institutions listed here.

I should like to thank the staffs of the following libraries: the library of the State University of New York at Buffalo, especially Miss Anna Russell and Mr. David Posner; the library of Cornell University; the library of Trinity College, Dublin; and the National Library of Ireland, especially Miss Margaret Deignan. I have relied most heavily of all on the Louis Round Wilson Library of The University of North Carolina at Chapel Hill, and I owe thanks to every department of that library. I should like particularly to acknowledge the help of the staff of the Humanities Reference Room, and especially Miss Louise McG. Hall and Mrs. Pattie McIntyre.

I should like to thank and acknowledge the help of the University of North Carolina Research Council for two grants to finance travel, gathering of research materials, student assistance, and secretarial costs; the University of North Carolina Library Research Fund Committee for funds for microfilming; the University of North Carolina English Department for student assistants to aid in proof reading; and the American Philosophical Society for a grant that made it possible for me to spend several weeks in Dublin, Ireland.

I wish to thank Mr. Oliver D. Gogarty of Dublin, Ireland, for his permission to publish excerpts from letters from his father, Oliver St. John Gogarty, to James Joyce, now in the Cornell Joyce collection. I thank the Society of Authors, literary representatives of the Joyce Estate, for permission to publish passages from Joyce's "Alphabetical Notebook," now in the Cornell collection. And I thank the *James Joyce Quarterly* (Copyright, The University of Tulsa, Tulsa, Oklahoma), and especially editor Thomas F. Staley, for permission to reprint portions of this book which appeared in an earlier form in that journal.

While it is impossible to recall all the persons who have helped me in this study, I do wish to give thanks to the following: Father James Devereux, S.J., and Professors Alfred Engstrom, David Hayman, C. Hugh Holman, Vivian Mercier, Daniel W. Patterson, Ulrich Schneider, and Fritz Senn. In addition, almost every member of the English Department of the University of North Carolina has helped me at one time or another, as have many of my colleagues in other departments; to all of them, my thanks.

For the last, I have reserved my special thanks to the following people who gave me assistance in various ways that will put me forever in their debt: Professor Richard M. Kain, Professor Oscar Maurer, Father William T. Noon, S.J., and Professor Harry K. Russell.

W.T.

CONTENTS

ALLUSIONS IN
ULYSSES

INTRODUCTION

The purpose of allusion in a literary work is essentially the same as that of all other types of metaphor—the development and revelation of character, structure, and theme—and, when skillfully used, it does all of these simultaneously. An allusion achieves its purposes through inviting a comparison and contrast of the context in which it is used with its original context. Allusion is distinguished from other varieties of metaphor or analogy by the greater complexity and potential its context necessarily brings with it; it is a metaphor with an almost inexhaustible number of points of comparison. No matter how skillfully an author uses an ordinary image, such as a rose, there are only limited points of comparison to be developed—color, beauty, length of life, etc. But an allusion to Lucifer, for example, provides a framework of relations among characters, qualities of personality, themes, structural patterns, all of which may be put to use if the author has the desire and the genius to do so. Such a context is always present in historical allusions and allusions to the arts, and may be found even in philosophical concepts and theological doctrines. Often the doctrine itself involves a context—Arius' doctrine concerning the Trinity, for example—but even if it does not, there is always the personal and historical context in which the doctrine was formulated. Arius' struggle to develop and defend his doctrine would provide a complex basis for allusive use even if his doctrine did not.

Joyce's use of allusion is distinguished from other authors' not by its purposes, but by its extent and thoroughness. *Ulysses* involves dozens of allusive contexts, all continually intersecting, modifying, qualifying one another. Here again Joyce's uniqueness and complexity lie not in his themes or characters, nor in his basic methods of developing them, but in his accepting the challenge of an Olympian use of his chosen methods. I hope this list will provide a fuller appreciation of the vastness of the task Joyce assumed and will serve as the basis for many new insights into how allusions function in the novel.

In compiling this list, I have aimed at completeness in the areas of literature, philosophy, theology, history, the fine arts, and popular and folk music. Inadequately as this aim may be realized, such an attempt is now possible because of the prior work of such scholars as Stuart Gilbert, Joseph Prescott, William Schutte, William York Tindall, M. J. C. Hodgart and Mabel Worthington, and Robert M. Adams. My debt to these and to many others is obvious. The present list, however, is more than a compilation of previously discovered allusions, for it attempts to be complete, and consequently it contains many allusions never listed before as well as some which have been only partially or mistakenly identified by earlier scholars.

Although its bulk may at first belie it, this list does not provide a complete and exhaustive annotation of everything in *Ulysses* which may need annotating. It is a list of *allusions*, and by so calling it, I intend to suggest certain limits to the material I have chosen to include. These limits are not always clear-cut, and they have often been difficult to decide upon, but there are limits. My general principle, although even this may at times be set aside, has been to include only those words and phrases that are allusions in the sense that they necessarily bring some *context* with them. For example, difficult or archaic words are not annotated, nor are slang phrases, nor foreign phrases, nor clichés, unless these are part of an allusion. As an illustration, the Gaelic tag *sliante* (*Ulysses*, p. 43.4/44.2) may for some readers need annotation, but since it is not to my knowledge a part of an allusion, it is not included; the word *gamp* (*Ulysses*, p. 37.37/38.37) does involve an allusion, and it is included. The list also excludes geographical references (such as those to Dublin streets and businesses) unless they seem to involve an allusion. Further, references to actual persons of Joyce's day, or appearances of such persons as characters in the novel, are not ordinarily included, although they may be commented upon if they seem potentially misleading to the reader. Neither A. E., who appears as a character, nor Padraic Colum, who is mentioned, is included in the list, since they were actual men of Joyce's day; any allusions to their works, however, are included in the list. The main purpose behind this policy is to prevent the necessity of listing every appearance of a character in *Ulysses* who was an actual person (or, as Buck Mulligan, clearly based on a person), and to avoid the lengthy and perhaps less than worthwhile witch hunt into the backgrounds of each character in the novel. This, to say the least, is the province of another study.

One insoluble problem about the limits of the list has been situational parallels between *Ulysses* and other works. The reader is sometimes aware of a similarity between a situation in *Ulysses* and in some other work, but the similarity may not emerge clearly enough in any word or phrase to be considered an allusion. No clear-cut rule has been possible in such cases, and I have perhaps been too conservative, but, since this is a list of allusions and not a study of possible literary parallels, I have included only those situational similarities that emerge in specific words and phrases. The "Circe" episode is in some ways a special case, as a prefatory note to that section explains.

I hope that the foregoing guidelines will serve to clarify the limits of the list. The inclusion of proverbs, however, raises some questions that call for more specific statements. Although I am not sure how convincingly it can be argued that all proverbs involve a context of some sort, I have included proverbs in the list. Here again the line between a proverb and a cliché or an ordinary turn of phrase is difficult, often impossible, to draw. My aim has been to include proverbs, but to exclude clichés or mere familiar turns of phrase or idioms. Usually, my criterion in this matter has been whether or not I have located the phrase in question in some collection of proverbs, although sometimes I have gone beyond this to include a phrase that seems to me clearly proverbial even though I could not find it in such a collection. In instances where the proverb occurs in the Bible or in Shakespeare, or in some proverb collection that we know Joyce used (such as Swift's *Polite Conversation*), I call attention to its occurrence there. This is done not necessarily in the implication that Joyce got the proverb from that source, but because these sources are of special importance in *Ulysses* and need always to be considered.

Biblical quotations in the list are usually taken from the King James version of the Bible rather than the Douay. This is done since there is evidence that Joyce used and even studied the King James version. The spelling of biblical proper names in *Ulysses* generally follows the King James version, and there are some allusions that clearly show its use (see for example entry 197.17). Also, the Cornell Joyce Collection contains a notebook in which Joyce copied the book of Revelation from the King James version (see Scholes's *Catalogue*, item 9). In the event that biblical allusion is questionable, I have consulted concordances to both the King James and Douay versions.

It will be noticed that some of the quotations from songs contain slash marks to indicate line breaks, while others do not. When the text I have followed has made it possible to indicate line endings, I have done so; when it has not, I have not inferred them.

Even though the format of the list is, hopefully, clear enough in itself, there are some rules of procedure of which the reader should be aware. The numbers at the beginning of each entry indicate the page and line on which the allusion begins in the 1961 and 1934 Random House (or Modern Library) editions, respectively. The phrase in small capital letters which immediately follows the numbers presents the allusion to be commented upon. This phrase, which always follows the 1961 edition, is not so much a quotation from the novel as it is a signaling device. I have not, that is, indicated in the phrase itself whether it occurs in dialogue or in authorial exposition, nor have I indicated whether the phrase does or does not end in terminal punctuation, nor is the type face of the phrase in *Ulysses* indicated (e.g., italicizing is not shown). These rules were adopted since it is clear that this book must be used with *Ulysses* in hand, and nothing is lost by regarding the words in small capitals as a signaling phrase rather than an exact quotation, while the possibility of many trivial errors is thus eliminated. In some instances ellipses follow the signaling phrase; this is to indicate that the allusion continues beyond what is given. It is usually quite clear to the reader where the allusion ends, but, in some cases where there may be doubt, I have included a word or two after the ellipsis to specify the end of the allusion. The list contains many cross references from one entry to another. Generally, allusions that recur often in *Ulysses* are most fully annotated in their first appearance, and subsequent instances simply refer the reader to the entry where the allusion is explained. If an allusion occurs twice within a relatively few lines, or if it occurs very frequently over several pages, separate entries are not provided for each instance of the allusion; rather, each of its occurrences is listed in the initial entry (see entries 5.5 and 282.40 for examples). I use only the first page and line number (that of the 1961 edition) to make cross references between entries of this book, since it is immaterial for this purpose which edition of *Ulysses* the reader is using. Cross references are always preceded by the word "entry." Reference to the text of *Ulysses* are always preceded by "p.," and the page numbers of both the 1961 and the 1934 editions are given. One inconvenient aspect of the system of citation is that there are in some instances two successive entries with identical page and line numbers, as a result of two allusions occurring in the same line. This should be kept in mind to prevent possible confusion when following up a cross reference, or when using the index.

I have not adopted any strict policy about giving credit to those who first pointed out an allusion. Generally, no credit is given unless the allusion is unordinary or esoteric. It should be recognized that I have made use of all of the sources cited in the list, and my failure to credit anyone with the discovery of an allusion is not to be taken as a suggestion that I am its discoverer.

In certain chapters of the list—"Scylla and Charybdis," "Oxen of the Sun," and "Circe"—special circumstances have required brief prefatory notes. The list proper is preceded by a list of the abbreviations that have been used and is followed by an appendix containing the words of three songs that are alluded to pervasively in certain sections of *Ulysses*, and by the Bibliography and Index, both of which are preceded by brief explanatory notes.

ABBREVIATIONS
USED IN THE LIST

(Full publication information can be found in the Bibliography.)

AJJ	*The Art of James Joyce*, by Walton Litz
CW	*The Critical Writings of James Joyce*
DAB	*The Dictionary of American Biography*
DNB	*The Dictionary of National Biography* (British)
ELH	*ELH: A Journal of English Literary History* (periodical)
FV	*Fabulous Voyager: James Joyce's* Ulysses, by Richard M. Kain
JA	*Joyce and Aquinas*, by William T. Noon, S.J.
JJ	*James Joyce*, by Richard Ellmann
JJM II	*A James Joyce Miscellany, Second Series*, ed. by Marvin Magalaner
JJM III	*A James Joyce Miscellany, Third Series*, ed. by Marvin Magalaner
JJMU	*James Joyce and the Making of* Ulysses, by Frank Budgen
JJQ	*The James Joyce Quarterly* (periodical)
JJR	*The James Joyce Review* (periodical)
JJU	*James Joyce's* Ulysses, by Stuart Gilbert

JS   *Joyce and Shakespeare: A Study in the Meaning of* Ulysses,
           by William Schutte
MBK   *My Brother's Keeper*, by Stanislaus Joyce
MLN   *Modern Language Notes* (periodical)
MLQ   *Modern Language Quarterly* (periodical)
ODEP   *The Oxford Dictionary of English Proverbs*
ODNR   *The Oxford Dictionary of Nursery Rhymes*
OED   *The Oxford English Dictionary*
PMLA   *Publications of the Modern Language Association* (period-
           ical)
RG   *A Reader's Guide to James Joyce*, by William York Tindall
SoC   "Stream-of-Consciousness Technique in James Joyce's *Ulys-
           ses*," by Erwin Ray Steinberg (unpublished Ph.D. disserta-
           tion)
SS   *Surface and Symbol: The Consistency of James Joyce's*
           Ulysses, by Robert M. Adams

The following works are referred to by the author's last name; full publication information can be found in the Bibliography.

Apperson   G. L. Apperson, *English Proverbs and Proverbial
                Phrases*
Brandes   George Brandes, *William Shakespeare: A Critical
                Study*
Butler   Alban Butler, *Butler's Lives of the Saints*
Chambers   E. K. Chambers, *William Shakespeare: A Study of Facts
                and Problems*
Harris   Frank Harris, *The Man Shakespeare and His Tragic
                Life-Story*
Hoagland   Kathleen Hoagland, *1000 Years of Irish Poetry*
Hodgart and   Matthew J. C. Hodgart and Mabel Worthington, *Song
   Worthing-   in the Works of James Joyce*
   ton
Lee   Sidney Lee, *A Life of William Shakespeare*
Scholes   Robert E. Scholes, *The Cornell Joyce Collection: A
                Catalogue*

TELEMACHUS

3.5/5.5 INTROIBO AD ALTARE DEI   The beginning of the Ordinary
of the Mass: "I will go unto the altar of God." This is also found in
Psalms 43:4. Mulligan parodies the Mass in many ways on this page.
Cf. p. 599.21/583.33.

3.8/5.8 COME UP, KINCH. COME UP, YOU FEARFUL JESUIT   Edmund
Epstein suggests that this is derived from Friar Laurence's words
to Romeo in *Romeo and Juliet*, III, iii, 1: "Romeo, come forth,
come forth, thou fearful man" (*JJR*, I, 43).

3.22/5.22 FOR THIS, O DEARLY BELOVED, IS THE GENUINE CHRISTINE: BODY
AND BLOOD AND SOUL AND OUNS   Mulligan's statement seems to be
a general parody of lesson 26 of the *Maynooth Catechism* ("On the
Blessed Eucharist") and to relate especially to the first question
of that lesson: "What is the Blessed Eucharist?" to which the reply
is "The Blessed Eucharist is the sacrament of the body and blood,
soul and divinity of Jesus Christ, under the appearances of bread
and wine." The version cited is that of 1882, which was in use
throughout Joyce's lifetime. Farmer and Henley's *Slang and Its
Analogues* lists "blood-an'-ouns" and explains it as "an abbreviated

form of an old and blasphemous oath—'God's blood and wounds!' "
Cf. the use on p. 658.19/642.25.

3.28/5.28 CHRYSOSTOMOS   Chrysostomos, "golden mouthed," is a
common epithet for orators. The best-known by this title are Dion
C., the Greek rhetorician (*ca.* 50–*ca.* 117), and St. John C., one of
the fathers of the Greek church (347?–407). Neither here nor in
the only other use of Chrysostomos in *Ulysses* (p. 494.31/484.31)
does the context indicate which of these is alluded to. Perhaps the
name of Mulligan's prototype, Oliver St. John Gogarty, suggests
St. John C. as the more likely.

3.34/5.34 A PRELATE, PATRON OF ARTS IN THE MIDDLE AGES   Though
this reference is very general, an earlier use of this phrase by Joyce
may suggest which patron, if any, Stephen has in mind. In his essay
on Galway, "The City of the Tribes" (1912), Joyce said, "The
parish house of Saint Nicholas still preserves a record of another
Italian prelate of the Middle Ages—an autograph letter of the notorious Borgia" (*CW*, p. 230). Mason and Ellmann explain that this
refers to Pope Alexander VI (Roderigo Lanzol Borgia). Alexander
VI was pope from 1492 through 1503. Born a Spaniard, he was
elected by a corrupt conclave, and his name has long represented
the worst qualities of the corrupt Renaissance popes. He was a great
patron of the arts and was the father of Cesare and Lucrezia Borgia.
In his "Alphabetical Notebook," now at Cornell (Scholes, item 25),
Joyce has written, *s.v.* Gogarty, (Oliver Saint John), "The plump
shaven face and the sullen oval jowl recall some prelate, patron of
arts in the middle ages."

4.23/6.21 A BLACK PANTHER   As A. M. Klein points out in his article
on this chapter of *Ulysses* ("The Black Panther, a Study in Technique," *Accent*, X, 139–55), the panther was long used as a symbol
of Christ. See entry 412.33.

5.2/6.40 SNOTGREEN   W. Y. Tindall suggests that this may come
from Rimbaud's "morves d'azur" (*RG*, p. 139). The phrase occurs
in l. 76 of Rimbaud's poem "Le Bateau Ivre."

5.5/7.1 WHAT ALGY CALLS IT: A GREY SWEET MOTHER   Algy is Alger-
non Charles Swinburne. In stanza 33 of his poem "The Triumph
of Time," he says, "I will go back to the great sweet mother,/
Mother and lover of men, the sea./ I will go down to her, I and
no other,/ Close with her, kiss her and mix her with me." This is
also alluded to on pp. 5.9/7.5 and 5.37/7.32. (The *Little Review*
version of this passage reads "great sweet mother.")

5.7/7.3 EPI OINOPA PONTON   This phrase, "Over the wine-dark sea,"
recurs in Homer. See for example the *Odyssey*, I, 183; II, 421;
III, 286; IV, 474.

5.8/7.4 THALATTA! THALATTA   This is Attic Greek for "The sea! The sea!" which is the cry of the Ten Thousand when they sight the sea in Xenophon's *Anabasis*, IV, vii, 24.

5.13/7.9 OUR MIGHTY MOTHER   This alludes to a phrase that Irish poet A. E. frequently uses in his poetry to designate the physical world, or, more specifically, the Earth. For instance, in "To One Consecrated," the second stanza reads "The Mighty Mother nourished you;/ Her breath blew from her mystic bowers;/ Their elfin glimmer floated through/ The pureness of your shadowy hours." See also "The Place of Rest," "The Face of Faces," "The Message of John," and "In the Womb" for other instances of this phrase. Gogarty used it in a parody of A. E. called "Hymn of Brahma," the third line of which says, "Awhile the Mighty Mother's Voice said 'OM' " (letter to Joyce, *ca.* March 18, 1903, now at Cornell; Scholes, item 526, p. 2).

5.20/7.16 I'M HYPERBOREAN AS MUCH AS YOU   The Hyperboreans in Greek legend were a race believed to live in a land of sunshine and plenty beyond the north wind. More important in this context is Nietzsche's use of the term in sec. 1 of *The Antichrist* to indicate those "above the crowd."

5.27/7.23 THE LOVELIEST MUMMER OF THEM ALL   Edmund Epstein (*JJR*, I [June, 1957], 47) points this out as an allusion to Antony's words about Brutus in *Julius Caesar*, V, v, 68: "This was the noblest Roman of them all." In the light of statements a few lines earlier about Stephen's killing his mother, Mulligan's allusion may compare two noble murderers—Brutus and Stephen.

5.31/7.27 PAIN, THAT WAS NOT YET THE PAIN OF LOVE   The idea that the pain of love is pleasure is a poetic commonplace, and I have not located a specific source for this phrase. Perhaps, as Fritz Senn has suggested to me, Stephen is thinking of Damilcar's song in Dryden's *Tyrannic Love*: "Pains of love be sweeter far/ Than all the other pleasures are" (IV, i). But Damilcar is speaking of romantic, physical love. Probably Stephen has the generality rather than a specific quotation in mind. For a sampling of quotations on this theme, see *Stevenson's Book of Quotations*, pp. 1195–97, *s.v.* Love: Pain or Pleasure.

6.28/8.22 AS HE AND OTHERS SEE ME   This echoes the line in Burns's "To a Louse," "O wad some power the giftie gie us/ To see oursel's as ithers see us."

6.33/8.27 LEAD HIM NOT INTO TEMPTATION   This alludes to the Pater Noster or Lord's Prayer, which occurs in the gospels and regularly in the Mass. "Lead us not into temptation" is found in Matthew 6:13 and Luke 11:4.

6.33/8.27 AND HER NAME IS URSULA   Richard M. Kain has suggested
to me that this alludes to St. Ursula, the leader of the eleven thousand virgins. Although the story is still disputed and the sources
and dates are vague, Ursula was supposedly a Cornish princess who
led eleven thousand virgins from the British Isles, up the Rhine river
to Basel, and later to Cologne, where they were slaughtered by the
Huns. Various dates from 238 to *ca.* 451 have been given to the
incident. Mulligan's amusement seems more appropriate when we
read Alban Butler's statement that "St. Ursula, who was the mistress
and guide to heaven to so many holy maidens, whom she animated
to the heroic practice of virtue, conducted to the glorious crown
of martyrdom, and presented spotless to Christ, is regarded as a
model and patroness by those who undertake to train up youth
in the sentiments and practice of piety and religion" (*The Lives
of the Saints* [New York, 1846], X, 250; Oct. 21). St. Ursula and
her virgins are mentioned on p. 339.40/333.32.

6.37/8.31 THE RAGE OF CALIBAN AT NOT SEEING HIS FACE IN A MIRROR
In the Preface to *Dorian Gray*, Oscar Wilde says "The nineteenth
century dislike of Realism is the rage of Cailban seeing his own
face in a glass. The nineteenth century dislike of Romanticism is
the rage of Caliban not seeing his own face in a glass." Wilde is
mentioned on p. 6.38/8.32.

6.40/8.34 THE CRACKED LOOKINGGLASS OF A SERVANT   As S. Gilbert
points out (*JJU*, p. 101), this is from Oscar Wilde's *Intentions*. In
the dialogue "The Decay of Lying," Cyril says to Vivian, "I can
quite understand your objection to art being treated as a mirror.
You think it would reduce genius to the position of a cracked
looking-glass." In the "Alphabetical Notebook" now at Cornell
(Scholes, item 25), Joyce has, *s.v.* Ireland, the statement that "Irish
art is the cracked looking-glass of a servant," without any indication of source.

7.15/9.8 BEG FROM THESE SWINE   This alludes to the parable of the
Prodigal Son, where we are told, "And he would fain have filled
his belly with the husks that the swine did eat; and no man gave
unto him" (Luke 15:16). This parable is alluded to several times
in *Ulysses*.

7.23/9.15 BREAK THE NEWS TO HER GENTLY   This seems to allude to
one of several slightly different songs. Hodgart and Worthington
list it as an allusion to "Break the News to Mother," a very popular
American ballad written in 1897 by Charles K. Harris—over one
million copies of sheet music were sold. The chorus begins, "Just
break the news to Mother; She knows how dear I love her, And

tell her not to wait for me, For I'm not coming home." For words and music see Boni, *Fireside Book of Favorite American Songs* (New York, 1952). *The Christy Minstrel Song Books* (London: Boosey and Co., n.d.) prints what is clearly an adaptation of this song (Book V, p. 36), and the Irish *Favorite Songster* (Dublin, n.d.) gives a somewhat different song entitled "Break It Gently to My Mother" (p. 210).

7.27/9.19 A SCARED CALF'S FACE GILDED WITH MARMALADE   Though it is unlikely, this may recall the golden calf that Aaron and the people of Israel made while Moses was on the mountain, described in Exodus 32 and Deuteronomy 9:7 ff. For another context involving gold and castration, see p. 77.1/75.39.

7.30/9.22 MATTHEW ARNOLD'S FACE   W. T. Noon has suggested that the gardener is masked with Arnold's face because his " 'lawn-mowing,' or attempt to tidy up and eliminate all the differences between religion, poetry, and philosophy, is one of the motifs of *Ulysses*" (*JA*, p. 8). Joyce himself took a cut at Arnold in his early essay, "The Study of Languages" (1898/99?), where, after stressing the importance of mathematics, he said, "In this we are supported by the great lights of our age, though Matthew Arnold has his own little opinion about the matter, as he had about other matters" (*CW*, p. 26).

7.33/9.25 TO OURSELVES   Stephen is probably thinking of "Sinn Fein," the Irish nationalistic group whose name means "We Ourselves," or "By Ourselves," though if so, this seems to be an anachronism. See entry 163.38.

7.33/9.25 OMPHALOS   *Omphalos* is a Greek word meaning "navel" or "central point." The navel has long been an important religious symbol in Greek, Asiatic, and esoteric lore. S. Gilbert discusses the *omphalos* at some length, emphasizing its importance as a symbol of birth and the interconnectedness of all life (*JJU*, pp. 51–56). In esoteric lore the navel is considered the seat of the soul and is gazed on at length by the devotee. I am not certain which association Stephen has in mind here, but the immediate context suggests that the self-contemplating Irish nationalists, in their desire for independence and their assumption of Ireland's great importance, are mistakenly turning in upon themselves, and away from the larger European society. For other uses of *omphalos*, see entries 17.37, 38.3, and 402.31.

8.11/10.1 I REMEMBER ONLY IDEAS AND SENSATIONS   Although Locke would have disagreed with Mulligan's saying he remembers sensations (since, strictly speaking, only ideas are the objects of memory), this is apparently an allusion to Locke's theory of knowledge. On the relationship between sensations and ideas in Locke's philosophy, see *An Essay Concerning Human Understanding*, Book IV, chap. xi. This allusion links Mulligan with the sense-data empiricism of Locke's philosophy; there are numerous allusions later in *Ulysses* linking Stephen with Bishop Berkeley, the idealist who argued against Locke and Hume.

8.34/10.23 SIR PETER TEAZLE   Sir Peter and Lady Teazle are characters in Dublin-born Richard Brinsley Sheridan's play *School for Scandal* (1777).

9.14/11.4 LOYOLA   St. Ignatius of Loyola (1491 1556) founded the Society of Jesus (Jesuits) in 1534.

9.19/11.8 GIVE UP THE MOODY BROODING   S. Gilbert suggests (*JJU*, p. 103) that this recalls Telemachus' brooding in Book I of the *Odyssey*. Telemachus broods over his father's absence and the suitors' abuse and usurpation of his substance until the goddess Athene, in the guise of Mentes, encourages him.

9.22/11.12 AND NO MORE TURN ASIDE AND BROOD . . .   This is from Yeats's poem "Who Goes with Fergus?" which first appeared in his play *The Countess Cathleen*. Ellmann says that Joyce attended the *première* of the play on May 8, 1899, and was "moved by the lyric, 'Who Goes with Fergus?', which Florence Farr sang; its feverish discontent and promise of carefree exile were to enter his own thought, and not long afterwards he set the poem to music and praised it as the best lyric in the world" (*JJ*, p. 69). Stephen's thought of "woodshadows" (p. 9.25/11.15) is prompted by "the shadows of the wood" in the poem, even though that line is not quoted in *Ulysses*. Further allusions to the poem are found on pp. 9.28/11.18, 9.33/11.22, 9.37/11.26, and 10.8/11.37.

9.33/11.22 A BOWL OF BITTER WATERS   An earthen vessel of bitter water is referred to several times in the fifth chapter of Numbers in describing the ritual performed to try a woman suspected of adultery. The woman drinks water containing dust from the floor of the tabernacle (referred to as "bitter water"); if she has committed adultery, the water will cause her belly to swell and her thigh to rot; if she has not, it will have no harmful effects. Probably the specific test is not so important to the present context as that the bowl of bitter water is used to test the person's purity. Cf. p. 46.4/46.42.

10.2/11.31 SHE HEARD OLD ROYCE SING   Edward William Royce (b. 1841) was a member, along with Nellie Farren, Edward Terry, and Kate Vaughan, of one of the most famous teams of the Gaiety

Theatre in London. W. MacQueen-Pope discusses them in the chapter "The Great Quartet" in his book *Gaiety: Theatre of Enchantment* (London, 1949?). See the following entry.

10.2/11.31   THE PANTOMIME OF TURKO THE TERRIBLE   The Christmas pantomime *Turko the Terrible* was the first of the famous Gaiety pantomimes staged at the Gaiety Theatre, Dublin. It was done in December, 1873; the words were by Irish editor and writer Edwin Hamilton (1849–1919). *The Irish Playgoer* ran a series of articles on the Dublin pantomimes beginning in their Christmas, 1899, issue. In that issue they say, "It was at Christmas 1873 that the first pantomime was tried at the Gaiety and the famous 'Turko the Terrible'—a pantomime never excelled in Dublin—was the work selected. Mr. Edwin Hamilton was accountable for the words of the songs and the one sung by King Turko in the throne room while anticipating the delights to be derived from his magic rose, where he thinks 'Invisibility is just the thing for me,/I am the boy that can enjoy/Invisibility' was the most successful in the whole book. Mr. E. W. Royce enacted the title role as only his lively self at that time could" (I, no. 7 [Christmas, 1899], 19). Most of the Dublin pantomimes were localized rewritings of earlier pantomimes. I suspect that this one was based on an "extravaganza" by William Brough, listed in Allardyce Nicoll's *Hist. of Eng. Drama* (Cambridge, 1959), V, 280: "Turko the Terrible; or, The Fairy Roses," which was first done at Holborn, December 26, 1868. R. M. Adams has suggested that what Joyce had in mind here was not a performance of *Turko the Terrible* itself, but of *Sindbad the Sailor*, begun on December 26, 1892, which included Royce as Turko the Terrible, a role inserted into *Sindbad* because of its Dublin popularity (*SS*, pp. 76ff.). Adams' suggestion may be supported by the presence of typed copies of reviews of this pantomime from Dublin newspapers for December, 1892–January, 1893, in the Buffalo Joyce collection (Speilberg catalogue, IX. A. 4). For use of these reviews later in *Ulysses*, see entry 678.32.

10.9/11.38   THE MEMORY OF NATURE   S. Gilbert (*JJU*, p. 189) quotes a passage from A. P. Sinnett's *The Growth of the Soul* (1896), which uses this phrase as an esoteric term. See entry 143.31.

10.23/12.13   LILIATA RUTILANTIUM . . .   E. R. Steinberg has identified this as coming from the "Ordo Commendationis Animae," a prayer for the dying, which can be found in most Roman Catholic *Rituals* in Tit. V, Cap. 7. The *Ritual* says this prayer is said by the bedside of the dying "during the death agony." In the Irish *Ritual* of the time, this passage is translated, "may the lilied throng of radiant Confessors encompass thee; may the choir of rejoicing Virgins welcome thee."

10.32/12.22   LIKE A GOOD MOSEY   At least two critics have seen this as an allusion to Moses, but this seems to me unlikely. *Mosey* is a dialect word meaning idiot, fool, or person of soft intellect; Bloom uses it on p. 160.1/157.31. See Wright's *English Dialect Dictionary*, *s.v.* mosey.

11.6/12.35   THE DRUIDY DRUIDS   The druids were the priests of the ancient religion of the Celts in Gaul, Britain, and Ireland. P. W. Joyce discusses them in his *Short History*, Pt. II, chap. iii, pp. 137–42.

11.10/12.39   O, WON'T WE HAVE A MERRY TIME . . .   This alludes to "De Golden Wedding," a song written in 1880 by American Negro James A. Bland (1854–1911), who also wrote "Carry Me Back to Ol' Virginny," "Golden Slippers," and others. Hodgart and Worthington mistakenly describe the song as a spiritual. The chorus says "All the darkies will be there, Don't forget to curl your hair; Bring along your damsels fair, For soon we will be treading; Won't we have a jolly time, Eating cake and drinking wine? All the high toned darkies will be at the golden wedding." For words and music see Henry R. Waite's *College Songs* (Boston, 1918), p. 36. Hodgart and Worthington cross list this song with the alternate title "On Coronation Day," but the copy I examined shows no basis for such an alternate title. I suspect that there is another song entitled "On Coronation Day"—perhaps one based on Bland's—but I have not found such a song.

11.23/13.10   A SERVER OF A SERVANT   This alludes to Noah's curse on Canaan (the descendants of Ham) after waking from his wine. Ham was the only one of his sons to see him naked in his drunkenness, and when Noah awoke, he said "Cursed be Canaan; a servant of servants shall he be unto his brethren" (Gen. 9:25).

12.27/14.15   IN NOMINE PARTIS ET FILII ET SPIRITUS SANCTI   The blessing of the Holy Trinity: "In the name of the Father and of the Son and of the Holy Ghost." Too common in Catholic prayers and liturgy to specify a single source.

12.33/14.21   OLD MOTHER GROGAN   Although Mother Grogan seems from the context to be from Irish literature or folklore, I have not yet located her.

12.42/14.30   FIVE LINES OF TEXT AND TEN PAGES OF NOTES ABOUT THE FOLK AND THE FISHGODS OF DUNDRUM   This seems to be a general allusion to the work of the antiquarians who were editing, explaining, and annotating early Irish literature and folklore at this time. There are several towns named Dundrum in Ireland, but I do not think Mulligan is actually alluding to lore about one of them. He probably chose it because the Dun Emer press was located at Dundrum in county Dublin. See entry 13.1.

13.1/14.31   PRINTED BY THE WEIRD SISTERS IN THE YEAR OF THE BIG WIND "Weird sisters" is from *Macbeth*, I, iii, 32. Marion Witt has pointed out the allusion here to the colophon of Yeats's book *In the Seven Woods* ("A Note on Joyce and Yeats," *MLN*, LXIII, 552). The book was printed in 1903 by the press of the Dun Emer Guild, in which both Lily and Elizabeth Yeats were then working. The colophon says "Here ends In the Seven Woods, written by William Butler Yeats, printed, upon paper made in Ireland, and published by Elizabeth Corbet Yeats at the Dun Emer Press, in the house of Evelyn Gleeson at Dundrum in the county of Dublin, Ireland, finished the sixteenth day of July, in the year of the big wind, 1903." The colophon makes it clear that here "in the year of the big wind" means 1903, in allusion to "the gale" of that year, on which see entry 396.38. But traditionally for an Irishman, "the big wind" refers to a terrible storm that began on the night of January 6, 1839. *Thom's* for 1904 says, in its "Dublin Annals," *s.v.* 1839: "Dublin visited by an awful storm on the night of the sixth January, causing great destruction of life and property; the river Liffey rose many feet, overflowing the quay walls in several places. On the same night the Bethesda church and surrounding houses in Dorset-street, were consumed by fire. Calamitous fire in Mary-street, by which six persons lost their lives. The destruction of property was estimated at £70,000" (p. 2099). Walsh's *Handy-Book of Literary Curiosities*, *s.v.* Wind, The Big, has a description of the storm and points out that events came to be dated by reference to "the big wind."

13.6/14.36   THE MABINOGION   The *Mabinogion* is a collection of Welsh tales translated into English by Lady Charlotte Guest in 1838–49. The four true *mabinogi* (Welsh for "instructions to young bards") in Lady Guest's collection deal with old Celtic mythology, including stories of the children of Llyr, the sea god. The *Mabinogion* is mentioned again on p. 13.11/14.41.

13.6/14.36   THE UPANISHADS   The Upanishads are parts of the Vedas, the ancient Hindu scriptures. They deal particularly with mystical, speculative topics. The "Dublin mystics" were much interested in the Eastern scriptures, and in 1896 Charles Johnston, one of the leaders of the group, had translated *From the Upanishads*. See E. A. Boyd's *Ireland's Literary Renaissance* (1916), chap. X, "The Dublin Mystics."

13.20/15.8   FOR OLD MARY ANN . . .   Hodgart and Worthington list

this as an allusion to an Irish song "McGilligan's Daughter Mary
Ann." Although I know such a song exists, and have heard lines
from it sung by a Dubliner, I have not yet located a printed version. The closest I have come is a song by Louis A. Tierney entitled "Mick McGilligan's Daughter, Mary Anne," printed in *Walton's 132 Best Irish Songs and Ballads*, pp. 34–35, but Tierney's
song is obviously a more modern rewriting of the one Mulligan
sings.

13.33/15.20 COLLECTOR OF PREPUCES   The old milkwoman has just
said "Glory be to God," and Mulligan alludes to God here through
his commandment to circumcise all male children (Gen. 17:10–14).
The Cornell collection contains a letter from Gogarty to Joyce
in which Gogarty uses the phrase "Jehovah who collects fore-
skins" (Scholes, item 531, p. 2).

14.2/15.30 SILK OF THE KINE AND POOR OLD WOMAN   These were, as
Stephen's statement indicates, traditional names for Ireland. In
Yeats's play *Cathleen Ni Houlihan* the old woman says, "Some call
me the Poor Old Woman." Of such names Seumas MacManus says,
"During our many dark ages when it was treason for our singers to
sing of Ireland, the olden poets sang of, and to, their beloved, under
many such endearing and figurative titles" (*Story of Irish Race*,
p. 712). However, Donal O'Sullivan says such a theory is "non-
sensical" (*Songs of the Irish*, p. 130). But it is obvious from Stephen's statement (and from Yeats's) that many an Irishman who
is not a Gaelic scholar does regard these terms as traditional for
Ireland. In his notes on Nora's dreams, apparently made in 1916
(see Scholes, item 52), Joyce speaks in passing of "the old poetic
name of Ireland 'Silk of the Kine' " (reprinted in Ellmann, *JJ*, p.
451; Ellmann's transcription of this paragraph contains an error: the
manuscript reads "the music of romance," not "the magic of romance"). "Silk of the Kine" occurs as the second line of the Irish
song "Druimfhionn Donn Dilis," for words and music of which,
see O'Sullivan, *op. cit.*, p. 143. "Poor old woman" probably alludes
to the "Shan Van Vocht"; see entry 17.36.

14.3/15.31 A WANDERING CRONE, LOWLY FORM OF AN IMMORTAL   The
idea of a goddess walking the earth as an old woman is fairly common in myth and folklore, but in the light of entry 14.2, Stephen
is probably thinking specifically of Yeats's *Cathleen Ni Houlihan*.

14.22/16.9 WOMAN'S UNCLEAN LOINS, OF MAN'S FLESH MADE NOT IN
GOD'S LIKENESS, THE SERPENT'S PREY   Stephen is alluding to the
inferior position allotted woman in the biblical story of the Creation and the Fall. "Unclean loins" also suggests an allusion to the

description of woman as "unclean" after giving birth (Lev. 12) and during the menstrual period (Lev. 15:19–33). And Willis E. McNelly points out that this also refers with striking accuracy to the administration of extreme unction. He says "The techniques of the actual annointing [*sic*] with olive oil in the administration of extreme unction include annointing the eyes, the ears, the nostrils, the mouth, the hand, the feet, and the loins. Yet the annointing of the feet may be omitted for any good reason, and the unction of the loins is always to be omitted if the subject is a woman" (*JJQ*, II, 297).

15.7/16.35 WELL, IT'S SEVEN MORNINGS A PINT AT TWOPENCE IS SEVEN TWOS . . .   J. Mitchell Morse has suggested (*JJQ*, III, 163) that this owes something to the passage in the Witch's Kitchen in Goethe's *Faust*, Book I, in which the Witch declaims for the benefit of Faust and Mephistopheles: "This you must ken!/ From one make ten,/ And two let be,/ Make even three,/ Then rich you'll be./ Skip o'er the four!/ From five and six,/ The Witch's tricks,/ Make seven and eight,/ 'Tis finished straight;/ And nine is one,/ And ten is none,/ That is the witch's one-time-one!" (ll. 2540–52, George Madison Priest's translation). As Morse points out, Mephistopheles compares the Witch's nonsense to the "Three and One, and One and Three" of the Christian Trinity, which makes the allusion more fitting to this chapter.

15.20/17.6 ASK NOTHING MORE OF ME, SWEET. ALL I CAN GIVE YOU I GIVE   These are the opening lines of Swinburne's short poem "The Oblation" (from *Songs Before Sunrise*). The third and fourth lines are quoted on p. 15.27/17.13. The poem was set to music by English poet and composer Theophile Marzials (1850–1920).

15.32/17.18 IRELAND EXPECTS THAT EVERY MAN THIS DAY WILL DO HIS DUTY   A parody of Lord Nelson's famous signal to his fleet at Trafalgar, October 21, 1805. There are several versions of Nelson's statement. Robert Southey (*Life of Nelson*, chap. 9) gives "England expects every man will do his duty." This is probably an allusion to the song "The Death of Nelson" by Arnold and Braham, since except for the substitution of Ireland for England, Mulligan's exact phrase occurs there; see entry 225.19.

16.7/17.32 AGENBITE OF INWIT   *Ayenbite of Inwyt* (Remorse of Conscience) is the title of a moral treatise which Dan Michel of Northgate translated from the French about 1340. In the Preface to the Early English Text Society edition of the work (London, 1866), Richard Morris explains that the *Ayenbite of Inwyt* is a literal translation of a French treatise entitled *Le Somme des Vices et de Virtues*, composed in 1279 by Frère Lorens (Laurentius Gallus) for the use of Philip II of France. The allusion is repeated on p. 17.3/18.28.

16.8/17.33 YET HERE'S A SPOT   An allusion to Lady Macbeth's words during the sleepwalking scene in *Macbeth*, V, i, 35.

16.9/17.34 THE CRACKED LOOKINGGLASS OF A SERVANT   See entry 6.40.

16.39/18.22 MULLIGAN IS STRIPPED OF HIS GARMENTS   This alludes to the tenth of the fourteen Stations of the Cross, "Christ is stripped of his garments." This station has a scriptural basis, clearest in Matthew 27:28 and John 19:23–24. The phrase is also used in the Old Testament, just before Aaron's death: "And Moses stripped Aaron of his garments" (Num. 20:28).

17.5/18.30 DO I CONTRADICT MYSELF? VERY WELL THEN, I CONTRADICT MYSELF   These exact words occur in Whitman's *Song of Myself*, sec. 51.

17.36/19.17 BILLY PITT HAD THEM BUILT   William Pitt (1759–1806) had the Martello towers built along the coasts of England and Ireland in 1803–6 as one of the defensive measures the British took against a possible invasion by France. The name *Martello* comes from Cape Mortello, Corsica, where a similar tower was located which the British had great difficulty in taking in 1794.

17.36/19.17 WHEN THE FRENCH WERE ON THE SEA   In addition to referring to the futile French attempts to help the Irish rebels in 1796 and 1798, this alludes to the "Shan Van Vocht," an anonymous Irish ballad of the close of the eighteenth century. The song begins "Oh! the French are on the sea,/Says the Shan Van Vocht." "Shan Van Vocht" is Irish for "The Poor Old Woman." For the text of the song, see Hoagland, pp. 297–98. See also entry 14.2.

17.37/19.18 THE OMPHALOS   On the *omphalos*, see entry 7.33. This context suggests that Mulligan is using *omphalos* in reference to the navel-shaped stone used in Greek religious rites. The most famous of these was the *omphalos* at Delphi, which supposedly marked the center of the earth. See also entries 38.3 and 402.31.

18.9/19.31 WE HAVE GROWN OUT OF WILDE AND PARADOXES   Mulligan is thinking of Oscar Wilde's love of the paradoxical, so evident in his bon mots and epigrams. See entries 6.37 and 6.40.

18.11/19.33 HAMLET'S GRANDSON IS SHAKESPEARE'S GRANDFATHER   Mulligan is here parodying Stephen's theory of *Hamlet*, which is developed in "Scylla and Charybdis."

18.17/19.39 JAPHET IN SEARCH OF A FATHER   This may allude to the biblical Japheth, son of Noah (Gen. 9:18–27). Certainly it alludes to Frederick Marryat's novel, *Japhet in Search of a Father* (1836), which deals with a foundling's search for his father. Early in the novel the foundling says, "... and if I saw a nose upon any man's face, at all resembling my own, I immediately would wonder and surmise whether that person could be my father. This constant dwelling upon the subject at last created a species of monomania, and a hundred times a day I would mutter to myself, 'Who is my father? Indeed the very bells, when they rung a peal, seemed, as in the case of Whittington, to chime the question" (chap. IV). Japhet does finally find his father.

18.25/20.5 ELSINORE. THAT BEETLES O'ER HIS BASE INTO THE SEA   Horatio warns Hamlet against being led by the ghost to "the dreadful summit of the cliff/ That beetles o'er his base into the sea" in *Hamlet*, I, iv, 71.

18.33/20.13 THE SEAS' RULER   The idea that England is the seas' ruler is too common to specify a single source, though the song "Rule, Brittania" is a good possibility; see entry 329.15. For a sampling of quotations on this topic, see *Stevenson's Book of Quotations*, s.v. England: Brittania Rules the Waves, pp. 547–48.

18.37/20.17 THE FATHER AND THE SON IDEA. THE SON STRIVING TO BE ATONED WITH THE FATHER   I have not found any such interpretation of *Hamlet* as Haines describes here. Ironically, the theory of the play which Stephen develops in "Scylla and Charybdis" has its basis in Stephen's ideas about the relationship between the Father and the Son in the Trinity. For a thorough discussion of this, see W. T. Noon, *JA*, chap. VI. See entries 21.7 ff.

19.3/20.25 I'M THE QUEEREST YOUNG FELLOW THAT EVER YOU HEARD ... (Further stanzas begin on pp. 19.8/20.30 and 19.16/20.38.) These stanzas reproduce almost verbatim some stanzas in a poem actually written by Oliver St. John Gogarty. In a letter to Joyce in 1905 (printed in Ellmann, JJ, pp. 212–14) Vincent Cosgrave included nine four-line stanzas of a poem by Gogarty entitled "The Song of the Cheerful (but slightly sarcastic) Jesus." The first two stanzas here reproduce the first two stanzas of that poem almost word for word. The stanza on p. 19.16/20.38 is a freer adaptation of the last stanza of Gogarty's poem. Joyce used the first two lines of the third stanza on p. 591.18–19/576.9–10. W. Litz prints an early draft of *Ulysses* in which Doherty (who later became Mulligan) sang these lines (*AJJ*, pp. 135, 137).

19.21/21.4 MERCURY'S HAT   Mulligan's fluttering hands, apparently held near his head, remind Stephen of the winged hat which is one of the chief attributes of Mercury or Hermes. Perhaps deeper matters of personality also influence the identification. In Howe and

Harrer's *Handbook of Classical Mythology*, we read of Hermes, "He is conceived as an energetic youth having incredible agility and speed, cunning and mischievous not only to the point of playing practical jokes but even of lying and thieving, a faithful and reliable aid and messenger of Zeus, and a benefactor of man in the various arts of human intercourse" (*s.v.* Hermes). Also, under the heading Mercury, Howe and Harrer point out that though the name Mercury came to be used merely as a Latin equivalent for Hermes, ". . . in the worship of Mercury the emphasis continued to be placed upon his function as god of trade."

19.29/21.11 JOSEPH THE JOINER   Haines's suggested title alludes to Joseph's being a carpenter. In Matthew 13:55 Jesus is referred to as "the carpenter's son."

20.20/21.40 NOW I EAT HIS SALT BREAD   In canto xvii of "Paradiso," Cacciaguida predicts to Dante, "Thou shall leave each thing/Belov'd most dearly: this is the first shaft/Shot from the bow of exile. Thou shalt prove/How salt the savour is of other's bread,/How hard the passage to descend and climb/By other's stairs. But that shall gall thee most/Will be the worthless and vile company,/With whom thou must be thrown into these straits" (ll. 55–62, H. F. Cary's translation).

20.42/22.21 ET UNAM SANCTAM CATHOLICAM ET APOSTOLICAM ECCLESIAM "And in one holy, catholic, and apostolic church," from the Nicene Creed, which is a part of the Mass on Sundays and major feast days.

21.3/22.23 SYMBOL OF THE APOSTLES IN THE MASS FOR POPE MARCELLUS Palestrina wrote a *Missa Papae Marcelli* for Pope Marcellus II (1501–55), although it was not composed until after the Pope's death. As W. T. Noon explains, *symbol* here means *creed*, and this refers simply to the Apostles' Creed in the Mass (*JA*, pp. 109–10). F. Budgen quotes Joyce as saying that in writing this Mass, Palestrina saved music for the church (*JJMU*, p. 182).

21.7/22.28 PHOTIUS   According to the *Catholic Encyclopedia*, Photius was "one of the worst enemies the Church of Christ ever had, and the cause of the greatest calamity that ever befell her." It was Photius (*ca.* 815–97) who, after the refusal of Pope Nicholas I to confirm his election to the Patriarchate of Constantinople (862), became leader of what developed into the Greek schism that finally separated the Greek Church from the Roman in 1054. Probably Photius is called a mocker because of his refusal to accept the *Filioque* clause of the Nicene Creed, which says that the Holy Spirit proceeds from the Father *and the Son.*

21.8/22.29 ARIUS, WARRING HIS LIFE LONG UPON THE CONSUBSTANTIALITY
Arius (d. 336) was an important heresiarch who denied the consubstantiality of the Father and the Son. In his view the Son was
not of the same substance as the Father (*homoousios*), but merely
of a similar substance (*homoiousios*). The first Nicene Council
(325) was called to settle the questions raised by Arius' opinion,
and the creed it formulated explicitly denies the Arian heresy. See
entry 21.10.

21.9/22.30 VALENTINE, SPURNING CHRIST'S TERRENE BODY Valentinus
(d. 160 or 161) was the most important of the Gnostic heretics. He
held that Christ did not have a real body and did not actually suffer.

21.10/22.31 THE SUBTLE AFRICAN HERESIARCH SABELLIUS Little is
known about the man from whom the Sabellian (or Modalist or
Monarchian) heresy takes its name. Apparently he was born in
Africa, and he was teaching in Rome about A.D. 215. His heresy,
which seems to have arisen out of an attempt to maintain orthodoxy
against the Gnostic heresies, consisted of an essential identification
of the Father and the Son. In his view the three persons of the
Trinity are simply different modes of a single divine substance.
Arius' and Sabellius' heresies are complementary, and they are
frequently paired, as by Dante in "Paradiso," canto xiii, ll. 127–30,
and by St. Thomas in his discussion of the Trinity in *Summa Theologica*. In his discussion of "Whether the Son is other than the
Father," St. Thomas says, "Now, in treating of the Trinity, we
must beware of two opposite errors, and proceed cautiously between them—namely, the error of Arius, who placed the Trinity
of substance with the Trinity of persons; and the error of Sabellius,
who placed unity of person with the unity of essence" (Part I,
ques. xxxi, art. 2).

21.13/22.34 THE VOID AWAITS SURELY ALL THEM THAT WEAVE THE WIND
See entry 24.7.

21.15/22.36 MICHAEL'S HOST Michael is traditionally the leader of
Christian armies against the heathens. Revelation 12:7 says "Michael
and his angels fought against the dragon." Milton describes him
as "of celestial armies prince" in *Paradise Lost*, VI, 44. "Blessed
Michael the Archangel" is invoked during the Confiteor in the
Mass. There is also a prayer invoking him which is often said
after low Mass, which is given in full on p. 83.22–27/82.13–18.

21.28/23.6 THERE'S FIVE FATHOMS OUT THERE Hodgart and Worthington list this as an allusion to Ariel's song "Full Fathom Five" in
The Tempest, but the boatman who says these words is certainly

unaware of this. This is probably the germ of Stephen's later
thought of the song; see entry 50.4. I have seen several maps of the
Dublin Bay area which include a "Five Fathom Line."

22.27/24.3 UEBERMENSCH   This is a reference to the "Superman"
philosophy of Nietzsche. See entries 5.20, 23.7, and 50.36.

23.7/24.24 HE WHO STEALETH FROM THE POOR LENDETH TO THE LORD
This is Mulligan's version of Proverbs 19:17. "He that hath pity
upon the poor lendeth unto the Lord." William S. Walsh gives the
following anecdote: "Dean Swift, so the story runs, once preached
a charity sermon at St. Patrick's, Dublin, the length of which disgusted many of his auditors; which coming to his knowledge, and
it falling his lot soon after to preach another sermon of the like
kind in the same place, he took special care to avoid falling into
the former error. His text on the second occasion was, 'He that
hath pity upon the poor lendeth unto the Lord, and that which
he hath given will he pay him again.' The Dean, after repeating
his text in a more than commonly emphatic tone, added, 'Now,
my beloved brethren, you hear the terms of this loan; if you like
the security, down with your dust' " (*Handy-Book of Literary
Curiosities, s.v.* Dust; "Dust" here, as the context suggests, means
"money").

23.7/24.24 THUS SPAKE ZARATHUSTRA   Zarathustra (Zoroaster, born
ca. 600 B.C.) was the founder of Zoroastrianism, a religion of ancient Persia. Nietzsche used these words as the title of a book
(1883) in which Zarathustra became the mouthpiece of Nietzsche's
philosophy of the *Uebermensch.*

23.12/24.29 HORN OF A BULL, HOOF OF A HORSE, SMILE OF A SAXON
Although I have not located the exact proverb Stephen thinks of,
I have found proverbs similar enough to his to be its source. P. W.
Joyce, in his *English As We Speak It* gives: "Three things not to
be trusted—a cow's horn, a dog's tooth, and a horse's hoof" (p. 110),
and a proverb in Thomas F. O'Rahilly's *A Miscellany of Irish
Proverbs* (Dublin, 1922) comes even closer to the content of
Stephen's: "Four things which an Irishman ought not to trust,—a
cow's horn, a horse's hoof, a dog's snarl, and an Englishman's
laugh" (Proverb 232). Padraic Colum says the proverb in *Ulysses*
is a seventeenth-century proverb telling of three things to beware
of, but he cites no source (*Our Friend James Joyce*, p. 63).

23.16/24.33 LILIATA RUTILANTIUM   See entry 10.23.

24.2/25.2 TARENTUM   Tarentum (Greek Taras; modern Taranto)
was a Greek city in southern Italy that sent for Pyrrhus, King of
Epirus, to defend its citizens against the Roman threat in 281 B.C.
See also the other allusions to Pyrrhus on this page.

24.7/25.7 FABLED BY THE DAUGHTERS OF MEMORY . . .   This paragraph seems to blend several ideas and phrases from William Blake.
Perhaps the main source is Blake's notes on "A Vision of the Last
Judgment." At several places in these notes Blake discusses "Fable"
and uses images of fire concerning the Last Judgment. The passages
in the notes which seem most pertinent to the present context are
the following (all page references are to the 1957 Keynes edition):
"The Last Judgment is not Fable or Allegory, but Vision. Fable
or Allegory are a totally distinct & inferior kind of Poetry. Vision
or Imagination is a Representation of what Eternally Exists, Really
& Unchangeably. Fable or Allegory is Form'd by the daughters of
Memory. Imagination is surrounded by the daughters of Inspiration, who in the aggregate are call'd Jerusalem" (p. 604); ". . . they
Assert that Jupiter usurped the Throne of his Father, Saturn &

brought on an Iron Age & Begat on Mnemosyne, or Memory, The
Greek Muses, which are not Inspiration as the Bible is. Reality was
Forgot, & the Vanities of Time and Space only Remember'd and
call'd Reality. Such is the Mighty difference between Allegoric
Fable & Spiritual Mystery" (p. 605); "The Earth beneath these
falling Groupes of figures is rocky & burning, and seems as if
convuls'd by Earthquakes; a Great City on fire is seen in the distance; the armies are fleeing upon the Mountains" (p. 608); "Truth
is Eternal. Error, or Creation, will be Burned up, & then, & not till
Then, Truth or Eternity will appear. It is Burnt up the Moment
Men cease to behold it" (p. 617). Also, in light of the focus on
history in this episode and the proximate references to weaving (p.
21.13/22.34 and p. 25.20/26.19), a statement that Blake makes in
Jerusalem seems important: "the Daughters of Albion Weave the
Web/ Of Ages and Generations" (p. 698; I feel however that there
is some other more specific source for the weaving allusions which
I have not found). In Blake's works the "Daughters of Memory"
(often called the Daughters of Albion) are usually contrasted un-
favorably with the "Daughters of Inspiration" (the Daughters of
Beulah). In his book on Blake, Arthur Symons explains, "To him
observation was one of the daughters of memory, and he had no
use for her among his Muses, which were all eternal, and the children of the imagination. 'Imagination,' he said, 'has nothing to do
with memory' " (*William Blake* [London: Jonathan Cape, 1928,
p. 65; first published in 1907]). And one further passage from these
notes must be quoted for its general relevance to Stephen's views
throughout *Ulysses*: "Thinking as I do that the Creator of this
World is a very Cruel Being, & being a Worshipper of Christ, I
cannot help saying: 'the Son, O how unlike the Father!' First God
Almighty comes with a Thump on the Head. Then Jesus Christ
comes with a balm to heal it" (p. 617).

24.9/25.9 THUD OF BLAKE'S WINGS OF EXCESS   This recalls several
passages in Blake about Excess, but a definite source is hard to find.
In "The Proverbs of Hell" Blake says, "The road of excess leads
to the palace of wisdom," and "Excess of sorrow laughs. Excess of
joy weeps" (1957 Keynes ed., pp. 150 and 151). Morton D. Paley
suggests that this passage telescopes the first proverb I have quoted
with one which follows later in the same section of "Proverbs of
Hell": "No bird soars too high, if he soars with his own wings"
(*JJM III*, pp. 176–77).

24.9/25.9 I HEAR THE RUIN OF ALL SPACE, SHATTERED GLASS AND TOPPLING
MASONRY   I think this sentence has at least part of its origin in

the passages from Blake quoted in entry 24.7. But perhaps it also owes something to a statement Blake made in a letter to William Hayley, May 6, 1800: ". . . every Mortal loss is an Immortal Gain. The Ruins of Time builds Mansions in Eternity" (1957 Keynes ed., p. 797). Stephen alludes to this statement later in *Ulysses*, p. 391.18/385.4.

24.13/25.13 ASCULUM   Pyrrhus won a costly victory over the Romans at Asculum in Apulia in 279 B.C.

24.15/25.15 ANOTHER VICTORY LIKE THAT AND WE ARE DONE FOR   According to Plutarch (*Lives*, "Pyrrhus"), Pyrrhus made such a statement after his victory at Asculum.

24.21/25.21 WHAT WAS THE END OF PYRRHUS   On Pyrrhus' death, see entry 25.14. Pyrrhus is also referred to on pp. 24.23/25.23, 24.26/25.25, and 24.32/25.32.

24.31/25.31 VICO ROAD, DALKEY   S. Gilbert sees this occurrence of the name "Vico" as significant to this episode, the "art" of which is history (*JJU*, p. 110). A. M. Klein uses this as evidence for his argument that the structure of this episode is closely based on the four-step cycle of history proposed by Italian philosopher Giambattista Vico (1668–1744). Though Vico was of great importance to Joyce, I am skeptical of Mr. Klein's arguments concerning this episode ("Shout in the Street: An Analysis of the Second Chapter of Joyce's *Ulysses*," in *New Directions 13*, pp. 327–45). There is a Vico Road in Dalkey.

25.14/26.14 HAD PYRRHUS NOT FALLEN BY A BELDAM'S HAND IN ARGOS   Plutarch records (*Lives*, "Pyrrhus") that Pyrrhus was stunned by a roof-tile thrown by an old woman during a battle in Argos in 272 B.C., and Zopyrus took advantage of Pyrrhus' stupor to cut his head off.

25.14/26.14 OR JULIUS CAESAR NOT BEEN KNIFED TO DEATH   This is primarily a reference to the murder of Julius Caesar in 44 B.C., but may of course be seen as an allusion to any account of the event, such as Shakespeare's *Julius Caesar*.

25.20/26.19 WEAVE, WEAVER OF THE WIND   See entry 24.7.

25.25/26.25 WEEP NO MORE   This is from line 165 of Milton's "Lycidas." Lines 165–67 of the poem are quoted on p. 25.32–34/26.32–34, although the poem reads *shepherds*, not *shepherd*.

25.35/26.35 IT MUST BE A MOVEMENT THEN, AN ACTUALITY OF THE POSSIBLE AS POSSIBLE. ARISTOTLE'S PHRASE   Aristotle discusses motion in such terms in several places in his works, most explicitly in *Physica*, where he formally defines motion: "*The fulfillment of what exists potentially, in so far as it exists potentially, is motion*"

(201a 10). For similar statements, see *Physica* 202a 7 and 251a 9 and *Metaphysica* 1065b 20 ff.

26.2/27.2 SHIFTING HER DRAGON SCALY FOLDS   A. M. Klein (*op. cit.,* entry 24.31) sees this as an allusion to the Cadmus myth. Klein makes this suggestion on the basis of Vico's discussing the Cadmus myth in the paragraph following his mentioning the scales of a dragon (*The New Science,* paras. 540, 541). Stephen may be thinking of Vico's dragon image here, but I still see no Cadmus allusion in his phrase. Cadmus is alluded to later in *Ulysses*; see entry 598.33.

26.3/27.2 THOUGHT IS THE THOUGHT OF THOUGHT . . . THE SOUL IS THE FORM OF FORMS . . .   As E. R. Steinberg has pointed out (*SoC,* p. 137), this is from *De Anima,* III, 432a, where Aristotle says, ". . . as the hand is the instrument of instruments, so the mind [*nous*] is the form of forms and sensation the form of sensibles." *De Anima* is also alluded to several times on p. 37/38.

26.7/27.7 THROUGH THE DEAR MIGHT OF HIM THAT WALKED THE WAVES . . . From Milton's "Lycidas," l. 173. Christ's walking on the water is described in Matthew 14:24–33; Mark 6:47–52; and John 6:16–21. The allusion is repeated on p. 26.12/27.12.

26.15/27.15 TO CAESAR WHAT IS CAESAR'S, TO GOD WHAT IS GOD'S Christ makes this statement in Matthew 22:21; Mark 12:17; and Luke 20:25. Paul paraphrases it in Romans 13:7.

26.19/27.19 RIDDLE ME, RIDDLE ME, RANDY RO . . .   Hodgart and Worthington consider this a part of the riddle that follows on p. 26.33/27.33, but these lines are from an entirely different riddle. Archer Taylor prints the following riddle from South Antrim: "Riddle me, riddle me, randy-bow,/ My father gave me seed to sow,/ The seed was black and the ground was white./ Riddle me that and I'll give you a pipe (variant: pint).———Writing a letter" (*English Riddles from Oral Tradition* [Berkeley, 1951], p. 439). Stephen simply suppresses the final lines of this riddle, as he suppresses parts of other things he alludes to (see entry 45.31, for example). Probably he does so here because the riddle and its solution remind him of his failure to justify himself as an author.

26.33/27.33 THE COCK CREW/ THE SKY WAS BLUE . . .   Joseph Prescott points out ("Notes on Joyce's *Ulysses,*" MLQ, XIII, 142–62) that this riddle occurs in P. W. Joyce's *English As We Speak It,* p. 187. The riddle P. W. Joyce gives is "Riddle me riddle me right:/ What did I see last night?/ The wind blew/ The cock crew,/ The bells of heaven/ Struck eleven/ Tis time for my poor *sowl* to go to heaven. Answer: The fox burying his mother under a holly tree." In his brief discussion of the riddle, P. W. Joyce in-

dicates that the answer is a nonsense solution and that no one could
be expected to solve it. Perhaps the riddle once had an answer
that has been lost. If this is the riddle Stephen knows, it is significant, especially since Mulligan has suggested that Stephen killed
his mother (p. 5.16/7.12), that he substitutes grandmother for
mother as the object of the murder that he assumes took place. See
also p. 559.12/545.22.

27.38/28.37   HIS MOTHER'S PROSTRATE BODY THE FIERY COLUMBANUS IN
HOLY ZEAL BESTRODE   Columbanus (543–615) was an Irish saint
and writer. Most of his work was done on the European mainland.
H. E. Rogers discusses several important similarities between
Stephen and St. Columbanus in "Irish Myth and the Plot of
Ulysses," ELH, XV, 306–27. Joyce mentioned "fiery Columbanus"
in his "Ireland, Island of Saints and Sages" (CW, p. 157).

28.2/28.42   A POOR SOUL GONE TO HEAVEN   This is from the riddle
recited earlier. See entry 26.33.

28.2/28.42   AND ON A HEATH BENEATH WINKING STARS A FOX . . . SCRAPED
IN THE EARTH . . .   William Schutte points out two passages from
plays by Renaissance dramatist John Webster which this passage
resembles and to which it may owe something. The first is a passage from Webster's The White Devil in which Cornelia speaks
of various animals friendly to buried men, but then says of the
wolf, "But keepe the wolfe far thence, that's foe to men,/ For
with his nailes hee'l dig them up again" (V, iv, 97–98). The second
is a passage from Webster's The Duchess of Malfi, in which Frederick says of his sister, whom he has murdered, "The wolfe shall
finde her grave, and scrape it up:/ Not to devoure the corpse, but
to discover/ The horrid murther" (IV, ii, 332–34). Schutte also
cites Webster's editor F. L. Lucas as saying that " 'Superstition
believed that it was murdered bodies that were dug up' by wolves"
(JS, pp. 102–3 fns.). There is also a proverbial saying that may be
related to this passage and to Stephen's answer to the riddle: "Nails
long enough to scratch her Granum out of her grave." In Swift's
Polite Conversation, the third conversation, Miss Notable says of
an acquaintance, "O, the hideous Creature! Did you observe her
Nails. They were long enough to scratch her Granum out of her
Grave" (p. 162). Partridge explains that Granum is Grandmother
and says the proverb is "probably 17th–20th centuries, but mostly
rural in the 19th–20th."

28.7/29.5   SHAKESPEARE'S GHOST IS HAMLET'S GRANDFATHER   Stephen
is thinking of Mulligan's mimicry of his theory of Hamlet. See
entry 18.11.

28.11/29.9 IN GRAVE MORRICE   Stephen, as the following lines suggest, may be basing this notion on the fact that our numerals are Arabic in origin and the morrice dance is, etymologically, Moorish. W. W. Skeat says, ". . . it is clear that the word meant 'Moorish dance,' though the reason for it is not quite certain" (*An Etymological Dictionary*, s.v. *morris, morris-dance*). Stephen's phrase may also echo Milton's "Comus," l. 116: "Now to the Moon in wavering morrice move"; cf. entry 49.14.

28.14/29.12 AVERROES   Averroes (Ibn Rushd, 1126–98) was an Arabian philosopher, best known for his commentaries on Aristotle. His Neo-Platonic view of Aristotle gave rise to several doctrines that were formally anathematized in 1270.

28.14/29.12 MOSES MAIMONIDES   Maimonides (1135–1204) was a Jewish philosopher who was chiefly concerned with synthesizing the Jewish revelation and Aristotle's philosophy. He influenced thinkers of the Middle Ages, especially Albert the Great and St. Thomas Aquinas. See entry 687.21.

28.16/29.14 A DARKNESS SHINING IN BRIGHTNESS WHICH BRIGHTNESS COULD NOT COMPREHEND   A paradoxical play on light and darkness is common to both secular and sacred literature, but this allusion most likely reverses the roles of light and darkness in John 1:5, which says "And the light shineth in darkness; and the darkness comprehended it not." Compare John 3:19–21 and Isaiah 5:20. E. Epstein says that Dionysius the Areopagite made some "comment on the doctrine of the brightness of God looking like darkness to some exalted spirits," but Epstein does not elaborate: (*JJR*, I, ii, 45–in Epstein's review of Schutte's *JS*). Dionysius' system was concerned with the ascent of the soul by the negative way (i.e., leaving behind sense perceptions and reasoning), in which the soul passes into "the darkness of unknowing" and is enlightened by "the ray of divine darkness." Probably Henry Vaughan had this in mind in his poem "The Night," when he says, "There is in God —some say—/ A deep but dazzling darkness" (ll. 49–50).

29.24/30.20 AS IT WAS IN THE BEGINNING, IS NOW . . . AND EVER SHALL BE . . . WORLD WITHOUT END   These words conclude the very common Gloria Patri, or lesser doxology.

29.25/30.21 TRAY OF STUART COINS, BASE TREASURE OF A BOG   "Base treasure" here alludes to James II's debasement of Irish currency in 1689 by coining money out of copper, brass, and pewter (see R. Bagwell's *Ireland Under the Stuarts*, III, 276–78). In his "Alphabetical Notebook," Joyce refers to this incident, saying "Irish wits follow in the footsteps of King James the Second who struck off base money for Ireland which the hoofs of cattle have trampled into her soil." This statement seems particularly appropriate to the "Nestor" episode, for it blends Deasy's concern with money, his interest in cattle (especially hoof and mouth disease), and his "wit" about the Jews not being permitted in Ireland; see especially the language of p. 36.18–19/37.15–16. Stephen's reference to a "bog" may allude to a folk tradition mentioned in the anonymous ballad "Lillibullero": "Dere was an old prophecy found in a bog,/ *Lillibullero, etc.*/ Dat our land would be ruled by an ass and a dog./ *Lillibullero, etc.*/ So now dis old prophecy's coming to pass,/ *Lillibullero bullen a la,*/ For James is de dog and Tyrconnel's de ass./ *Lillibullero, etc.*" (from O'Lochlainn's *Irish Street Ballads*, p. 73).

29.27/30.22 THE TWELVE APOSTLES HAVING PREACHED TO ALL THE GENTILES   In Matthew 10:5–6 Christ says, "Go not into the way of the Gentiles, and into any city of the Samaritans enter ye not: But go rather to the lost sheep of the house of Israel." But, as we know from Acts 10 and 11, the early church did decide to preach to the Gentiles. Probably Stephen simply means that it was the Gentiles who accepted the Christian revelation and now consider the apostles their own. See also entry 333.20.

29.39/30.35 THE SCALLOP OF ST. JAMES   A scallop was commonly worn by pilgrims as a sign of their having been to the shrine of St. James the Greater at Compostella, Spain.

30.24/31.19 IF YOUTH BUT KNEW   Deasy is alluding to the old proverb "If youth but knew what age would crave, it would both get and save." This is in the *ODEP* and was already proverbial in 1670 when John Ray included it in his *Collection of English Proverbs.*

30.25/31.20 PUT BUT MONEY IN THY PURSE   This is Iago's advice to Roderigo in *Othello*, I, iii, 345 ff.

30.35/31.29 THAT ON HIS EMPIRE . . . THE SUN NEVER SETS . . . A FRENCH CELT SAID THAT   This has been said, in one form or another, of every great empire since that of Alexander the Great. But R. M. Adams sees Deasy's attributing it to a French Celt as an error, for, he says, ". . . its origin has never been assigned to one of that interesting breed" (*SS*, p. 23).

31.15/32.11 ALBERT EDWARD, PRINCE OF WALES   Albert Edward (1841–1910), son of Queen Victoria, reigned as Edward VII from 1901 through 1910. He is referred to frequently in *Ulysses* and appears in the "Circe" episode on pp. 590/575 ff.

31.18/32.11 O'CONNELL'S TIME . . . THE FAMINE . . . THE ORANGE LODGES AGITATED FOR REPEAL OF THE UNION . . . FENIANS   Daniel O'Connell (1775–1847), "The Liberator," was a Catholic and a fervent worker for the repeal of the Act of Union, which had been bribed through the Irish Parliament in 1800. The Famine occurred in 1846–47. The Orange Lodges were Protestant organizations dedicated to maintaining the Protestant religion and the Protestant control of Irish politics. R. M. Adams says that Deasy's statement about them is another instance of his ignorance, for "the Orange lodges were pro-Union and could not rationally have been anything else. They were founded 'to support and defend her Majesty Queen Victoria, the Protestant religion, the laws of the country, the legislative union, and the succession to the throne.' They were proud to proclaim that 'Orangeism is now what it ever has been, an organization for the maintenance of British authority in Ireland,' and they could not conceivably have retained this objective while agitating against the Union" (*SS*, p. 22). But Phillip L. Marcus corrects Adams by quoting several sources to show that in the early years of the Orange lodges they were indeed anti-Union (*JJQ*, IV [Fall, 1966], 49). The Fenians were a secret revolutionary society, founded about 1858, whose purpose was to achieve Irish independence from England.

31.23/32.19 GLORIOUS, PIOUS AND IMMORTAL MEMORY   This phrase is the Orange toast to the memory of William III. Joyce had earlier used the phrase in his lecture on Defoe (see "Daniel Defoe" by James Joyce, ed. by Joseph Prescott, *Buffalo Studies* I, i [Dec., 1964] p. 8). Prescott cites D. A. Chart's *Story of Dublin* for the full toast. Chart gives, "To the glorious, pious and immortal memory of the Great and Good King William III., who saved us from popery, slavery, arbitrary power, brass money and wooden shoes" (p. 264).

31.23/32.19 THE LODGE OF DIAMOND IN ARMAGH THE SPLENDID BEHUNG WITH CORPSES OF PAPISHES   On September 21, 1795, old antipathies between Protestant and Catholic erupted in the "Battle of the Diamond" in Armagh, in which twenty or thirty "Defenders" (an organization of Catholic tenants) were killed. Following the battle, the Orange Society was founded by the Protestants (on these incidents, see Curtis, *Hist. of Ire.*, pp. 336–37). (Apparently the only use of Orange Lodge before 1795 was in reference to Masonic groups; see *OED s.v.* orange.) "Armagh the splendid" is a set phrase that goes back at least as far as Mangan's translation of "Prince Alfrid's Itinerary through Ireland"; see entry 293.38.

31.25/32.21 THE PLANTERS' COVENANT. THE BLACK NORTH AND THE TRUE BLUE BIBLE   Throughout this paragraph Stephen is thinking of history in terms of the conflict between Catholic and Protestant in Ireland, but I am not certain what he means by the "planters' covenant." Probably he is thinking of what is usually called "Plantation," i.e., the confiscation and redistribution of the lands of "rebel" Irishmen to loyal Englishmen, usually with some requirement that the receivers take an oath recognizing the English king as head of the Church. Though the practice is common in Irish history, the most notorious Plantations occurred under James I (in 1609) and Cromwell (in 1652). The "black north" refers to Northern Ireland, which is predominantly Protestant. John J. Marshall, in his *Popular Rhymes and Sayings of Ireland* (Dungannon, 1924) says, "The Northern and Southern portions of Ireland have in later days been characterized as 'the Black North,' and the 'Sunny South'" (p. 7).

31.26/32.22 CROPPIES LIE DOWN   In an earlier version of this list, I printed a song included by T. C. Croker in his *Popular Songs of Ireland*, entitled "When the Paddies of Erin," and to be sung to the tune of "Croppies Lie Down." But I expressed doubt then that the song was the original "Croppies Lie Down." Since then I have found another song that is much more likely to be the original song. It is entitled "Croppies Lie Down" and was printed in *The Vocal Library; being the Largest Collection of English, Scottish, and Irish Songs, ever Printed in a Single Volume* . . . (London: G. B. Whittaker, 1824), p. 512. *The Vocal Library* prints words only and records nothing about author or source. The allusions in the song to a possible French invasion, and the date of publication of *The Vocal Library*, date the song between about 1798 and 1824. Since the song is so difficult of access, I print here all the *Vocal Library* gives:

"Croppies Lie Down"

We soldiers of Erin, so proud of the name,
We'll raise upon rebels and Frenchmen our fame;
We'll fight to the last in the honest old cause,
And guard our religion, our freedom, and laws;
We'll fight for our country, our King, and his crown,
And make all the traitors and croppies lie down.

The rebels so bold, when they've none to oppose,
To houses and hay-stacks are terrible foes;
They murder poor parsons and likewise their wives
At the sight of a soldier they run for their lives:

Whenever we march through country and town,
In ditches and cellars the croppies lie down.

United in blood to their country's disgrace,
They secretly shoot those they dare not to face;
But whenever we catch the sly rogues in the field,
A handful of soldiers make hundreds to yield:
The cowards collect but to raise our renown,
For as soon as we fire the croppies lie down.

While thus in this war so unmanly they wage,
On women, dear women, they turn their damn'd rage;
We'll fly to protect the dear creatures from harms,
They'll be sure to find safety when clasp'd in our arms:
On love in a soldier no maiden will frown,
But bless the brave troops that made croppies lie down.

Should France e'er attempt by force or by guile,
Her forces to land on old Erin's sweet isle,
We'll shew that they ne'er can make free soldiers slaves,
They shall only possess our green fields for their graves:
Our country's applauses our triumphs will crown,
Whilst with their French brothers the croppies lie down.

When wars and when dangers again shall be o'er,
And peace with her blessings revisit our shore;
When arms we relinquish, no longer to roam,
With pride will our families welcome us home;
They'll drink in full bumpers, past troubles to drown,
A health to the lads that made croppies lie down.

The word *croppy* is usually explained as referring to the close-cropped hair of the Wexford rebels in 1798. It came to be a general term for rebel Irishmen.

31.29/32.25 SIR JOHN BLACKWOOD WHO VOTED FOR THE UNION *Burke's Landed Gentry of Ireland* (4th ed., 1958, p. 83) lists a Blackwood family from county Down which has as its motto *per via rectas*, but Deasy is mistaken about his ancestor's political attitudes. According to *Complete Baronetage* (Exeter, 1906, V, 371), Sir John Blackwood was an M.P. for Killyeagh and Bangor (both in county Down) at various times from 1761 until his death on February 27, 1799, but he was "a firm opponent of proposed

Union." Notice that Sir John died before the vote came up in the Irish Parliament. But Joyce knew all of this and put the error into Deasy's mouth intentionally. In August, 1912, Henry N. Blackwood Price, a descendant of the Blackwoods of county Down, wrote Joyce a letter asking for aid in his fight against foot and mouth disease in Ireland. In this letter he said, "Be energetic. Drop your lethargy. Forget Leinster for Ulster. Remember that Sir John Blackwood died in the act of putting on his topboots in order to go to Dublin to vote against the Union" (quoted in Ellmann, *JJ*, p. 336; Price is mentioned in *Ulysses*, p. 33.14/34.9, and is discussed by Ellmann, *JJ*, pp. 336–38). For a thorough discussion of this error through different sources than those cited above, see R. M. Adams, *SS*, pp. 20–22. In addition Adams cites an unpublished letter in the Cornell collection from James Joyce to Stanislaus in which James quotes from the passage in Price's letter cited above.

31.30/32.26 ALL IRISH, ALL KING'S SONS   Though I have been told there is a proverb saying "All Irishmen are king's sons," I have not yet located such a proverb in print. Richard M. Kain explains that the proverb derives from the fact that areas of Ireland were named for families, as, for instance, "Joyce's country."

31.35/32.31 LAL THE RAL THE RA/ THE ROCKY ROAD TO DUBLIN   "The Rocky Road to Dublin" is an anonymous Irish ballad. Words and music may be found in O'Lochlainn's *Irish Street Ballads*, p. 102. The allusion is continued four lines later in "Dangling on to Dublin. . . ."

32.15/33.11 LORD HASTINGS' REPULSE, THE DUKE OF WESTMINSTER'S SHOTOVER, THE DUKE OF BEAUFORT'S CEYLON, PRIX DE PARIS, 1866   The Lord Hastings who owned "Repulse" was Henry Weysford Rawdon-Hastings, Marquis of Hastings (1842–68). In the Irish peerage he held the titles Earl of Moira and Baron Rawdon of Moira, both of which became extinct when he died without issue. "Repulse" won the One Thousand Guineas in 1866. Hugh Lupus Grosvenor, first Duke of Westminster (1825–99) is described by the *DNB* as the "most successful breeder of racehorses of his generation." Among his many winning horses was his filly, "Shotover," which won the Derby and the Two Thousand Guinea Stakes in 1882. Henry Charles Fitzroy Somerset, eighth Duke of Beaufort 1824–99) was a well-known English sportsman. He was Master of the Horse during 1858–59 and 1866–68. As the allusion indicates, his "Ceylon" won the Prix de Paris in 1866. Cf. entry 50.20

32.25/33.21 EVEN MONEY FAIR REBEL   R. M. Adams has pointed out Joyce's accuracy in this allusion in that Stephen "not only recol-

lects the name of the horse, but the precise odds prevailing on
June 4, 1902, when Fair Rebel (by Circassian out of Liberty,
owned by Mr. W. P. Cullen) won the Curragh Plate of fifty
sovereigns" (*SS*, p. 176 fn.).

33.3/33.41 LIVERPOOL RING WHICH JOCKEYED THE GALWAY HARBOUR
SCHEME   R. M. Adams explains this as a reference to the futile
attempts to establish Galway as a trans-Atlantic port; however,
Adams says he can find no evidence of any "Liverpool ring," and
that Deasy is mistaken again (*SS*, p. 23). Joyce briefly discussed
later attempts to revive the idea of Galway as a trans-Atlantic port
in his "The Mirage of the Fisherman of Aran" (*CW*, pp. 234–37).
For a fuller discussion of such schemes and their failures, see entry
639.31.

33.7/34.3 CASSANDRA   Cassandra was the daughter of Priam and
Hecuba whose prediction of the downfall of Troy was disregarded.
Because she refused the love of Apollo, he condemned her to speak
true prophecies that no one would believe.

33.7/34.3 BY A WOMAN WHO WAS NO BETTER THAN SHE SHOULD BE
The proverbial phrase that Deasy here applies to Helen of Troy
(see entry 34.41) is listed in the *ODEP* under "No better than she
(they) should be," and several instances are cited, from 1604 on.
This also occurs in Swift's *Polite Conversation*, first conversation,
where the women are discussing an old acquaintance, Mrs. Cloudy,
and Miss Notable says, "I'm told for certain, she's no better than
she should be." Partridge says of this, "a loose free-loving woman
('Elle ne vaut pas grand chose'): 17th–20th centuries. One of the
most famous of all euphemisms" (p. 116).

33.11/34.7 KOCH'S PREPARATION   Robert Koch (1843–1910), the
great bacteriologist, was one of the first to use inoculation as a
means of preventing disease.

33.16/34.12 TAKE THE BULL BY THE HORNS   "To take the bull by
the horns," meaning "to meet a difficulty rather than to evade it,"
is proverbial. The *ODEP* lists four instances from 1816 on.

33.38/34.34 THE HARLOT'S CRY FROM STREET TO STREET . . .   From
Blake's "Auguries of Innocence," ll. 115–16.

34.4/35.1 AND THAT IS WHY THEY ARE WANDERERS ON THE EARTH TO THIS
DAY   This alludes to the legend of the Wandering Jew and to
the general situation of the Jewish people. On the Wandering Jew,
see entry 217.35.

34.8/35.5 THEY SWARMED LOUD, UNCOUTH ABOUT THE TEMPLE   This
may recall the description of the moneychangers in the temple in
Matthew 21:12; Mark 11:15; Luke 19:45; and John 2:13.

34.22/35.19 HISTORY . . . IS A NIGHTMARE FROM WHICH I AM TRYING TO

AWAKE   J. Prescott has pointed out ("Notes on Joyce's *Ulysses*," *MLQ*, XII, 149–62) that this is a variation of a line by Jules Laforgue (1860–87) in *Melanges posthumes* (Paris, 1903, p. 279). Laforgue there says, "La vie est trop triste, trop sale. L'histoire est un vieux cauchemar bariolé qui ne se doute pas que les meilleures plaisanteries sont les plus courtes" ("Life is too sad, too coarse. History is a gaudy old nightmare who does not suspect that the best jokes are the shortest").

34.27/35.24 ALL HISTORY MOVES TOWARD ONE GREAT GOAL, THE MANIFESTATION OF GOD   Though it seems unlikely that Deasy's commonplace alludes directly to either of them, I have come across two passages in Victorian poetry which are so similar in thought and diction that they deserve printing here. One of these is the final stanza of Tennyson's *In Memoriam*, where he speaks of "That God, which ever lives and loves,/ One God, one law, one element,/ And one far-off divine event,/ To which the whole creation moves." The other is Matthew Arnold's "Westminster Abbey," where he says "For this and that way swings/ The flux of mortal things,/ Though moving inly to one far-set goal" (ll. 160–62).

34.33/35.30 A SHOUT IN THE STREET   Stephen's remark vaguely resembles several passages in the Old Testament. Proverbs 1:20 says, "Wisdom crieth without; she uttereth her voice in the streets." Isaiah 42:2 says, "He shall not cry, nor lift up, nor cause his voice to be heard in the street." S. Gilbert says (*JJU*, p. 49 fn.) that this is Stephen's formula for the "voice of God: Jupiter tonans" (i.e., Jupiter the Thunderer—a phrase used several times by Ovid in *Metamorphoses*). But there is probably an allusion here to something more specific than these suggestions point to.

34.39/35.36 A WOMAN BROUGHT SIN INTO THE WORLD   An allusion to the fall of man through Eve. Deasy goes on to list other instances of evil brought about by women.

34.40/35.37 A WOMAN WHO WAS NO BETTER THAN SHE SHOULD BE   See entry 33.7.

34.41/35.38 HELEN, THE RUNAWAY WIFE OF MENELAUS, TEN YEARS THE GREEKS MADE WAR ON TROY   An allusion to the well-known story of Helen's leaving her husband for Paris, and to the Trojan War, which it brought about. S. Gilbert points out (*JJU*, p. 113) the similarity of Deasy's criticism of women and Nestor's telling of the treachery of Clytemnestra (*Odyssey*, III, 239–312).

34.42/35.39 A FAITHLESS WIFE FIRST BROUGHT THE STRANGERS TO OUR SHORE HERE, MACMURROUGH'S WIFE AND HER LEMAN O'ROURKE, PRINCE OF BREFFNI   This allusion involves a mistake about Irish history. It was Devorghil, the wife of Tiernan O'Rourke, Prince

of Breffni, who in 1152 deserted her husband for Dermot Mac-
Murrough, King of Leinster. Supposedly because of this "abduc-
tion," Roderick O'Connor, High King of Ireland, joined with
O'Rourke to rout MacMurrough in 1167 or 1168 (note the lapse
of fifteen years since the wife's departure). MacMurrough fled to
Henry II for aid and thus became the means by which the English
first invaded Ireland in 1169. The presence of this same error about
the identity of Devorghil's spouse in Joyce's notes to *Exiles* (1951
ed., p. 175) might suggest that this is Joyce's error, not Deasy's.
But this is not the case since, as R. M. Adams points out, Joyce
had the relationship right in the *Little Review* version (*SS*, pp.
21–22, 266). This may also be considered an allusion to a song
Thomas Moore wrote about this incident, entitled "The Song of
O'Rourke, Prince of Breffni."

35.2/35.41 A WOMAN TOO BROUGHT PARNELL LOW   It was his love
for Kitty O'Shea, wife of Captain Patrick O'Shea, that provided the
opponents and enemies of Irish statesman Charles Stewart Parnell
(1846–91) with the means by which to destroy him. Parnell loved
Mrs. O'Shea for many years, had two children by her, and married
her shortly before his death. When their love was brought to public attention through Captain O'Shea's bringing a divorce suit
against his wife, Parnell's enemies took the opportunity to turn
the Irish people against him. Joyce concluded his essay "The Shade
of Parnell" (1912) with the following statement: "In his final
desperate appeal to his countrymen, he begged them not to throw
him as a sop to the English wolves howling around them. It redounds
to their honour that they did not fail this appeal. They did not
throw him to the English wolves; they tore him to pieces themselves" (*CW*, p. 228).

35.6/36.3 FOR ULSTER WILL FIGHT/ AND ULSTER WILL BE RIGHT   In a
letter dated May 7, 1886, Lord Randolph Churchill (1849–95)
said, "Ulster will fight; Ulster will be right." Only a few months
earlier Lord Churchill, who was a vehement opponent of Gladstone and of Home Rule for Ireland, had gone to Belfast where he
had made a speech to excite the Loyalists there into action against
the Home Rule Bill. In his biography of his father, Lord Churchill,
Winston S. Churchill says of the slogan, "The jingling phrase,
'Ulster will fight, and Ulster will be right,' was everywhere caught
up. It became one of the war-cries of the time and sped with spirit-
speed all over the country" (*Lord Randolph Churchill* [New
York, 1906], II, 65).

PROTEUS

37.1/38.1 INELUCTABLE MODALITY OF THE VISIBLE   Aristotle discusses the forms of the visible and the audible in Books II and III of *De Anima*, but nowhere have I found this exact phrase. Perhaps it has its origin in Victor Cousin's translation, which Ellmann says Joyce read (*JJ*, p. 124). Almost all of the allusions to Aristotle on pages 25, 26, and 37 (26, 27, and 38) of *Ulysses* are allusions to Books II and III of *De Anima*. This allusion is repeated on p. 37.15/ 38.15. See Joseph Duncan, "Modality of the Audible in Joyce's *Ulysses*," *PMLA*, LXXII (March, 1957), 286–95; and John Killham, " 'Ineluctable Modality' in Joyce's *Ulysses*," *University of Toronto Quarterly*, XXXIV, 269–89

37.2/38.2 SIGNATURES OF ALL THINGS   Jacob Boehme (or Behmen), German shoemaker and theologian (1575–1624), wrote a work called *The Signature of All Things*. Joyce had a copy of it in his library (R. Ellmann, *JJ*, p. 794). Hugh Kenner sees this as a reference to St. Thomas' idea that *signate* matter and substantial form are combined in created things (*Dublin's Joyce* [London, 1955], p. 138).

37.4/38.4 SNOTGREEN   See entry 5.2.

37.4/38.4 LIMITS OF THE DIAPHANE. BUT HE ADDS: IN BODIES   This alludes to Aristotle's *De Anima*, II, 418b–19a. The word Stephen translates *diaphane* (Greek *diaphanes*) is usually translated *transparent*. Aristotle explains that what is visible is color, but the color must always be in some substratum which, while not visible *per se*, is visible by reason of its color. Aristotle calls this substratum the *transparent*. E. R. Steinberg points out (*SoC*, p. 136) that St. Thomas also discusses this in his commentary on *De Anima*, Lectio Fifteen, par. 428, on Book II. This allusion is repeated on p. 37.8/ 38.8.

37.6/38.6 BY KNOCKING HIS SCONCE AGAINST THEM   R. M. Adams says that Stephen has Aristotle repeat with his head Dr. Johnson's famous experiment with his foot to refute Berkeley (*SS*, p. 134). Since Berkeley is of considerable importance in this episode, I give Boswell's account of the incident: "After we came out of the church, we stood talking for some time together of Bishop Berkeley's ingenious sophistry to prove the non-existence of matter, and that every thing in the universe is merely ideal. I observed, that though we are satisfied his doctrine is not true, it is impossible to refute it. I never shall forget the alacrity with which Johnson answered, striking his foot with mighty force against a large stone, till he rebounded from it, 'I refute it thus'" (Boswell, *Life*, Aug. 6, 1763).

37.7/38.7 BALD HE WAS AND A MILLIONAIRE   These ideas were part of a medieval tradition about Aristotle. J. Duncan discusses this briefly (*op. cit.*, entry 37.1).

37.8/38.8 MAESTRO DI COLOR CHE SANNO   "Master of those who know," Dante's description of Aristotle in "Inferno," canto iv, ll. 131–32.

37.14/38.14 NACHEINANDER . . . NEBENEINANDER   Fritz Senn has suggested (*JJQ*, II, 134–36) that this alludes to Gotthold Ephraim Lessing's famous work on aesthetics, *Laokoon* (1766), and particularly to Lessing's distinction (see esp. chap. XVI) between poetry, which deals with objects one after another in time (*nacheinander* or *aufeinander*), and sculpture and painting, which deal with objects next to one another in space (*nebeneinander*). Senn also points out that Lessing remarks on the different impressions received through the eye and through the ear. For more details, see Senn's article. See also entry 559.10.

37.16/38.16 A CLIFF THAT BEETLES O'ER HIS BASE   From *Hamlet*, I, iv, 70–71. See entry 18.25.

37.20/38.20 MADE BY THE MALLET OF LOS DEMIURGOS   E. R. Steinberg has shown by reference to the Buffalo MS of this episode
that the allusion here is to Blake's Los (*SoC*, pp. 140–41). Steinberg
also cites several passages in Blake's works which refer to Los and
his hammer:" Book of Los," chap. iv; "Book of Urizen," chap. v,
70–71. In his lecture on Blake (1912), Joyce said of him, "To him,
all space larger than a red globule of human blood was visionary,
created by the hammer of Los" (*CW*, p. 222). This statement is
from Blake's *Milton*, I, sec. 29: "For every Space larger than a
red globule of Man's blood/ Is visionary, and is created by the
Hammer of Los." The demiurge in Platonic and Neo-Platonic philosophy and Gnostic philosophy was a subordinate deity who was
creator of the physical world. See also entries 24.7 and 186.16.

37.21/38.21 AM I WALKING INTO ETERNITY ALONG SANDYMOUNT STRAND
M. D. Paley says that here and in the preceding allusion to Los,
Stephen seems to have in mind the epiphanal moment that follows
Milton's entering through Blake's left foot in *Milton*, I, sec. 21:
"And all this Vegetable World appear'd on my left Foot/ As a
bright sandal form'd immortal of precious stones & gold./ I stoop'd
down & bound it on to walk forward thro' Eternity" ("Blake in
Nighttown," *JJM III*, p. 177).

37.22/38.22 DOMINIE DEASY KENS THEM A'   This suggests a Scottish
song, but Hodgart and Worthington take no note of it, and I have
not been able to identify it. D. Daiches is probably right in saying
that "Stephen is putting Deasy into a mock-Scottish folk song."
Though "Dominic" is a common name for a schoolmaster, there
may be some allusion here to Dominie Sampson, the schoolmaster
in Scott's *Guy Mannering*.

37.24/38.24 WON'T YOU COME TO SANDYMOUNT,/ MADELINE THE MARE
This seems to be an Irish song or poem, or a parody of one, but I
have not been able to locate it. D. Daiches calls it "popular verse,"
but does not identify it.

37.31/38.31 AND EVER SHALL BE, WORLD WITHOUT END   From the
Gloria Patri. See entry 29.24.

37.35/38.35 LIKE ALGY, COMING DOWN TO OUR MIGHTY MOTHER   Algy
is A. C. Swinburne. See entries 5.5 and 5.13.

37.37/38.37 THE OTHER'S GAMP POKED IN THE BEACH   In light of the
proximate mention of a "midwife's bag," it is likely that Stephen
uses *gamp* because of Mrs. Gamp, the umbrella-carrying monthly
nurse in Dicken's *Martin Chuzzlewit*. Dickens tells us that Mrs.
Gamp's sign-board proclaimed her "Midwife," and that at her
first appearance in the novel she has just been up all night help-

ing another "professional lady" deliver a child (chap. 19). This character's name is the source of the word *gamp* to mean *umbrella*. That Mrs. Gamp had an imaginary friend named Mrs. Harris makes the allusion more appropriate to this Protean chapter.

37.41/38.41 CREATION FROM NOTHING A reference to the Hebrew-Christian idea of creation *ex nihilo*, as described in Genesis 1.

38.3/39.3 WILL YOU BE AS GODS In Genesis 3:5 the serpent says to Eve, ". . . ye shall be as gods, knowing good and evil." In Milton's *Paradise Lost*, IX, 709–10, Satan also says to Eve, "ye shall be as Gods,/ Knowing both Good and Evil as they know."

38.3/39.3 GAZE IN YOUR OMPHALOS This alludes to the posture of contemplation in Eastern religions in which the devotee gazes fixedly at his navel. Stephen has just referred to "mystic monks." The close juxtaposition of "omphalos" and Eve's "belly without blemish" suggests an allusion to Philip Henry Gosse's book on geology and evolution, entitled *Omphalos: An Attempt to Untie the Geological Knot* (1857). The book took its title from Sir Thomas Browne's discussion of whether painters who depict Adam and Eve with navels are in error. Edmund Gosse discusses his father's book in *Father and Son* (1907), chap. 5.

38.4/39.4 EDENVILLE An allusion to the Garden of Eden, or perhaps to heaven. See p. 394.20/388.3.

38.6/39.6 ADAM KADMON Adam Kadmon is the archetypal or primordial man of the Kabalah. He includes all of the ten Sephiroth or intelligences which emanated from the En Soph. According to the Kabalistic book Sohar, the earthly Adam of the Garden of Eden was created by the ten Sephiroth.

38.6/39.6 HEVA, NAKED EVE Heva was an early name for Eve. A character named Heva appears as the wife of Har in Blake's early prophetic poem, "Tiriel."

38.7/39.7 SHE HAD NO NAVEL. GAZE. BELLY WITHOUT BLEMISH See entry 38.3 on *omphalos*.

38.7/39.7 A BUCKLER OF TAUT VELLUM S. Gilbert says "The image of the 'buckler of taut vellum' is derived from an Homeric association, for the Achaean shields were adorned with 'whiteheaped' *omphaloi* (bosses)" (*JJU*, p. 52). Gilbert then quotes a passage from the *Iliad* describing Agamemnon's shield: "Thereon were twenty white bosses of tin, and one in the midst of black cyanus" (XI, 34; Leaf, Lang, and Myers translation).

38.8/39.8 WHITEHEAPED CORN Solomon's Song 7:2 says, "Thy navel is like a round goblet, which wanteth not liquor: thy belly is like an heap of wheat set about with lilies."

38.8/39.8 ORIENT AND IMMORTAL, STANDING FROM EVERLASTING TO EVER-
LASTING   This alludes to Thomas Traherne's *Centuries of Meditations,* Century III, sec. 3: "The Corn was Orient and Immortal
Wheat, which never should be reaped, nor was ever sown. I
thought it had stood from everlasting to everlasting." Though
Traherne is here describing the child's world, he explicitly links
it with Stephen's subject, Paradise: "Certainly Adam in Paradice
had not more sweet and Curious Apprehensions of the World,
than I when I was a child" (sec. 1). Throughout this beautiful
section of the *Meditations,* Traherne's language is very suggestive
of Joyce's idea of the epiphany. At one point he says, "Eternity
was Manifest in the Light of Day, and something infinit Behind
every thing appeared" (sec. 3). See S. Gilbert, *JJU,* pp. 52–53, for
a fuller quotation from this section. W. Y. Tindall has pointed out
that the allusion to Traherne is anachronistic, since *Centuries of
Meditations* was not published until 1908 (*RG,* p. 148). The phrase
"everlasting to everlasting" is common in the Bible; see Psalms
41:13, 90:2, 103:17, and 106:48.

38.10/39.10   MADE NOT BEGOTTEN   This is a reversal of the essential
part of the Nicene Creed, which says that Christ was "begotten not
made; consubstantial with the father." See entry 21.8.

38.11/39.11   THE MAN WITH MY VOICE   J. Prescott (*op. cit.,* entry
34.22) points out that this recalls the similarity of the voices of
Telemachus and Odysseus, which is commented on by Nestor
and by Helen and Menelaus in the *Odyssey.* Father William T.
Noon has suggested to me that, especially in light of p. 43.10/44.7,
there is an allusion here to Jacob's deceiving Isaac by pretending to
be Esau (Gen. 27). This would fit in well with the theme of pre-
tense and assumed identity in this episode (see particularly p. 45.25/
46.22 ff.).

38.14/39.14   LEX ETERNA   St. Thomas discusses the various types of
law in the *Summa Theologica,* and important among these is the
lex eterna, or Eternal Law. See *Summa Theologica,* Part II (First
part), question xci ("Of the Various Kinds of Law"), and question xciii ("Of the Eternal Law"). Of God and the Eternal Law,
St. Thomas says, "His law is not distinct from Himself" (question
xci, art. 1).

38.15/39.15   THE DIVINE SUBSTANCE WHEREIN FATHER AND SON ARE
CONSUBSTANTIAL   The doctrine of consubstantiality was first
given formal statement in the Nicene Creed in A.D. 325. See entries
21.8 and 38.10.

38.16/39.16   ARIUS   See entries 21.8 and 38.18.

38.16/39.16   TO TRY CONCLUSIONS   In talking to his mother after he has slain Polonius, Hamlet ironically advises her, "like the famous ape,/ To try conclusions, in the basket creep/ And break your own neck down" (*Ham.*, III, iv, 194). And William Schutte also lists another passage from Shakespeare which may be alluded to here. In *The Merchant of Venice*, Launcelot Gobbo meets his father on the street. He says "Oh heavens, this is my true-begotten father! Who, being more than sand-blind, high-gravel blind, knows me not. I will try confusions with him" (II, ii, 36–9; see *JS*, p. 23).

38.18/39.18   IN A GREEK WATERCLOSET HE BREATHED HIS LAST   This refers to the mode of Arius' death. Sozomen gives the following account in his *Ecclesiastical History*, Book II, chap. xxix: "Late in the afternoon, Arius, being seized suddenly with pain in the stomach, was compelled to repair to the public place set apart for emergencies of this nature. As some time passed without his coming out, some persons, who were waiting for him outside, entered, and found him dead and still sitting on the seat." Athanasius gives substantially the same account in his epistle *Ad Serapionem de Morte Arrii*. Arius' death occurred in Constantinople.

38.22/39.22   NIPPING AND EAGER AIRS   In *Hamlet*, I, iv, 2, when they are on the platform awaiting the ghost, Horatio says to Hamlet "It is a nipping and an eager air."

38.24/39.24   MANANAAN   Mananaan is the Irish god of the sea, the equivalent of Proteus in the Greek myth. H. E. Rogers (*op. cit.*, entry 27.38) calls him the "great shape-shifter of Irish myth." The waves are Mananaan's "whitemaned seahorses." D. Daiches explains that "white horses" is still the British name for the white foam on top of waves.

38.31/39.31   COULDN'T HE FLY A BIT HIGHER THAN THAT   This alludes to the legend of Daedalus and Icarus in Greek myth. Icarus' death came about because he flew too high and the sun melted the wax holding together the wings his father had made.

38.35/39.35   HIGHLY RESPECTABLE GONDOLIERS   The phrase "highly respectable gondoliers" occurs several times in a song by Don Alhambra in act one of Gilbert and Sullivan's *The Gondoliers*. Stephen's thought of his uncle John's being a cornet player (see p. 237.24/234.10) probably prompts this allusion, since a cornet player is referred to several times in *The Gondoliers*.

38.36/39.36   JESUS WEPT   John 11:35 consists only of these two words, "Jesus wept." This occurs when Mary and Martha are leading him to the tomb of their brother, Lazarus.

38.39/39.39   COIGN OF VANTAGE   As Duncan's company approaches

Macbeth's castle, Banquo says of the martlets, "No jutty, friezc,/ Buttress, nor coign of vantage but this bird/Hath made his pendent bed and procreant cradle" (*Mac.*, I, vi, 6–8).

39.2/40.2 NUNCLE RICHIE   Although *nuncle* was at one time a rather common variant of uncle (see *OED*), the word occurs in only one of Shakespeare's plays, *King Lear*, but there it occurs sixteen times.

39.9/40.9 WILDE'S REQUIESCAT   Oscar Wilde wrote his short poem "Requiescat" after the death of his sister, Isola.

39.27/40.27 ALL'ERTA   "On guard!" These are the opening words of Verdi's *Il Trovatore*, and they are also the first words of Ferrando's *aria di sortita* in that opera.

39.28/40.28 FERRANDO'S ARIA DI SORTITA   (The *de* of the 1961 Random House edition is an error.) Ferrando's *aria di sortita* (song of entry) opens Verdi's *Il Trovatore*.

39.35/40.35 COME OUT OF THEM   This may allude to Christ's statement "Come out of them," which he said on two occasions in exorcising a demon. See Mark 1:25 and 9:25.

39.35/40.35 NOR IN THE STAGNANT BAY . . . LAID FIRE TO THEIR BRAINS   J. Prescott (*op. cit.*, entry 34.22) says, "These thoughts echo Stephen's reading of Yeats's story *The Tables of the Law*, in which Joachim and Swift figure. Stephen's reading of the story is recorded in *Stephen Hero* (N.Y., 1944), pp. 176–77, 178." Yeats's stories "The Tables of the Law" and "The Adoration of the Magi" do reveal some striking parallels with the opening sections of *Ulysses*, both in the characters' situations and in the authors and works alluded to. See entry 48.26.

39.37/40.37 JOACHIM ABBAS   Joachim of Flora (*ca.* 1145–1202) was an Italian mystic theologian who divided history into three ages, those of the Father, the Son, and the Holy Spirit (developed in his *Expositio in Apocalypsim*, I, v). His system is discussed in Yeats's story "The Tables of the Law."

39.37/40.37 THE HUNDREDHEADED RABBLE   E. R. Steinberg (*SoC*, p. 148) suggests an allusion here to the statement of one of the citizens in *Coriolanus*, II, iii, 17–18: ". . . he himself stuck not to call us the manyheaded multitude." However, the similarity between the two is so slight that the allusion seems unlikely.

39.38/40.38 A HATER OF HIS KIND RAN FROM THEM TO THE WOOD OF MADNESS   As the context suggests, this is an allusion to Jonathan Swift, and particularly to his madness.

39.40/40.40 HOUYHNHNM   The Houyhnhnms were a race of horses in *Gulliver's Travels*. They had the power of reason and ruled over Yahoos, a brutish race in human form.

40.1/41.1 DESCENDE, CALVE, UT NE NIMIUM DECALVERIS   "Come down, bald one, lest you become even balder." (W. Y. Tindall gives "Come down, bald priest, lest you be deballed." *RG*, p. 149). This is probably a modification of II Kings 2:23. In II Kings 2:23–24, we are told that Elisha was mocked by some children and that he cursed them in the name of the Lord, whereupon two bears came out of the woods and ate forty-two of the children. In the Vulgate the children's taunt is "Ascende calve, ascende calve" ("Go up, thou bald head; go up, thou bald head"). On the basis of the records of Marsh's Library, Dublin, R. M. Adams shows that Joyce's immediate source for this specific phrase was Joachim Abbas' *Vaticinia Pontificum* (Venice, 1589). The opening sentence of the first part of the work is "Ascende, calve, ut ne amplius decalveris." Adams points out that *amplius* was the reading in the *Little Review* version (*SS*, pp. 125–26). Though the *Vaticinia Pontificum* is spurious, and Joyce probably knew this, Adams' evidence of its use is convincing. On Joachim's canon, see Henry Bett, *Joachim of Flora* (London, 1931), chap. II. For Stephen's jocular translation of this Latin, see p. 243.3/239.23.

40.5/41.5 THE ALTAR'S HORNS   The horns of the altar are mentioned frequently in the Old Testament; see any concordance.

40.7/41.6 FAT WITH THE FAT OF KIDNEYS OF WHEAT   As Ulrich Schneider has pointed out to me, this alludes to the "Song of Moses," in which Moses tells of God's blessings to Jacob, and says, "And he made him to suck honey out of the rock, and oil out of the flinty rock; Butter of kine, and milk of sheep, with fat of lambs, and rams of the breed of Bashan, and goats, with the fat of kidneys of wheat . . ." (Deut. 32:13–14).

40.13/41.12 DAN OCCAM . . . THE IMP HYPOSTASIS TICKLED HIS BRAIN   William of Occam (d. 1349?) was an English scholastic philosopher and theologian who is best known for his principle of methodological simplicity known as "Occam's razor." "Dan" is an archaic title meaning "Mr." or "Sir." Occam was a member of the Franciscan order. Stephen's use of *hypostasis* here is misleading since hypostasis refers to the union of God and man in Christ, not to Christ's real presence in the Eucharist (the single word *hypostasis* was added to the text sometime after the *Little Review* version). What Stephen is thinking about is the problem of multilocation, i.e., how Christ's body can be wholly present on many altars at the same time. Occam, and other contemporary scholastic theologians, felt this to be one of the most crucial problems of Christ's real presence in the Eucharist. (See *Reportatio Occam*, book 4, question 4, marginal letter H: "Ideo ad videndum quomodo corpus Christi existit sub specie panis apparent . . . difficultates: . . . quomodo idem corpus numero potest coexistere pluribus locis secundum se totum.") Occam argued that for God it is possible to effect such a mode of existence for a corporeal substance (the body of Christ) that it can be wholly present to many contiguous parts of a place, in this case the host, or the many hosts throughout the world. See *Reportatio Occam*, book 4, question 4, marginal letter I; also *De Corpore Christi*, chap. 6; and *Quaestiones quodlibetales*, quodlibeta 4, question 36; and *De Sacramento Altaris*, question 3. For a fuller discussion see Gabriel Buescher, *The Eucharistic Teaching of William Occam* (Washington, D.C., 1950), chap. IV.

40.19/41.18 COUSIN STEPHEN, YOU WILL NEVER BE A SAINT   This is an adaptation of a remark Johnson attributed to Dryden: "Cousin Swift, you will never be a poet" (*Lives of the Poets: Swift*).

40.19/41.18 ISLE OF SAINTS   *Insula Sanctorum* was a medieval name for Ireland. In April of 1907, Joyce delivered a lecture in Trieste entitled "Irland, Isola del Santi e dei Savi" ("Ireland, Island of Saints and Sages"; the lecture is reprinted in *CW*, pp. 153–74). The phrase is also used on p. 337.39/331.35.

40.35/41.34 ALL THE GREAT LIBRARIES OF THE WORLD, INCLUDING ALEXANDRIA   Alexandria was the site of the greatest library of antiquity.

40.37/41.36 MAHAMANVANTARA   This is a Hindu term meaning "great year," i.e., an immense span of time. S. Gilbert sees an allusion here to the esoteric doctrines of *manvantara* and *pralaya*, "alternate periods of activity and repose" (*JJU*, p. 35). Gilbert also quotes the following from A. J. Sinnett's *Esoteric Buddhism*: "Man has a manvantara and pralaya every four-and-twenty hours, his periods of waking and sleeping; vegetation follows the same rule from year to year as it subsides and revives with the seasons. The world too has its manvantaras and pralayas, when the tide-wave of humanity approaches its shore, runs through the evolution of its seven races, and ebbs away again, and such a manvantara has been treated by most exotic religions as the whole cycle of eternity" (*JJU*, p. 123).

40.37/41.36 PICO DELLA MIRANDOLA   Pico (1463–94) was an Italian humanist and scholar who tried to blend pre-Christian religion with Christianity. In *Witchcraft Magic and Alchemy*, Grillot de Givry lists Pico, along with Jacob Boehme (see entry 37.2), among those who "may be regarded as the chief innovators who intermixed Christian theology with principles which were foreign to it and which it refused to admit officially" (Frederick Publications, n.p., 1954, p. 208). Probably Stephen was introduced to Pico through Pater's *The Renaissance*. See entry 40.38.

40.38/41.36 AY, VERY LIKE A WHALE   In his attempt to agree with Hamlet's protean description of a cloud, Polonius agrees that it is "Very like a whale" in *Hamlet*, III, ii, 399.

40.38/41.36 WHEN ONE READS THESE STRANGE PAGES OF ONE LONG GONE ONE FEELS THAT ONE IS AT ONE WITH ONE WHO ONCE   This is probably a parody of Walter Pater's style, particularly in his essay "Pico della Mirandola" in *The Renaissance*. At one point in the essay, Pater says "He will not let one go; he wins one on, in spite of oneself, to turn again the pages of his forgotten books." Fritz Senn has suggested that Stephen's phrase may dimly recall a sentence of Oscar Wilde's about Kipling. The sentence first appeared in *Nineteenth Century* for September, 1890, and later in the essay "The Critic as Artist" in *Intentions*: "As one turns over the pages of his *Plain Tales from the Hills*, one feels as if one were seated under a palm-tree reading life by superb flashes of vulgarity" (*JJQ*, I [Summer, 1964], 65).

41.1/41.41 THAT ON THE UNNUMBERED PEBBLES BEATS   In convincing his blind father that they are on the brink of Dover cliff, the disguised Edgar says to Gloucester, "The murmuring surge/ That on the unnumbered idle pebbles chafes/ Cannot be heard so high" (*King Lear*, IV, vi, 20).

41.2/41.42 LOST ARMADA   The reference here is probably to the Spanish Armada, which the English defeated in 1588. In his "The Mirage of the Fisherman of Aran" (1912), Joyce, speaking of Galway Bay, said, "Beneath the waters of this bay and along its coast lie the wrecks of a squadron of the unfortunate Spanish Armada. After their defeat in the English Channel, the ships set sail for the North, where the storms and waves scattered them" (*CW*, p. 234).

41.5/42.3 ISLE OF DREADFUL THIRST   S. Gilbert says of this "Compare the 'isle of dreadful hunger' of Pharos; such isles of hunger and thirst were only too familiar to Egyptian and Phoenician mariners" (*JJU*, p. 124). Menelaus does describe the great hunger of himself and his men during their stay on Pharos while searching for Proteus (*Odyssey*, Book IV).

41.14/42.12 QUI VOUS A MIS DANS CETTE FICHUE POSITION   As M. Magalaner shows (*Time of Apprenticeship*, pp. 50 ff.) this question and its answer are from Léo Taxil's blasphemous book, *La vie de Jesus* (Paris, 1884). Léo Taxil was the pseudonym of G. S.

Jogand-Paqes. Magalaner discusses Taxil at length. In light of the theme of the Mary-Joseph-Holy Ghost triangle that Magalaner discusses, an Irish folk song that Douglas Hyde prints is very interesting. In his *Religious Songs of Connacht* (Dublin, 1906) he gives a song entitled "Mary and St. Joseph" in which Mary (then with child) asks Joseph to pick some cherries for her. In Hyde's literal translation, "Then spake St. Joseph with utterance that was stout, 'I shall not pluck thee the jewels [cherries], and I like not thy child. Call upon his father, it is he you may be stiff with' " (I, 279). Alan Dundes ("Re: Joyce—No In at the Womb," *Modern Fiction Studies*, VIII [Summer, 1962], 137–47) points out a similar story of Joseph's being jealous in the lost book "Protevangelion." The "Protevangelion" account also describes Joseph demanding of Mary how she became pregnant. This apocryphal book may be found in *The Lost Books of the Bible* (New York: Alpha House, Inc., 1926).

41.17/42.15 THE WILD GOOSE   The first "wild geese" were those Irishmen who left Ireland for the continent after the defeat of James II's forces at the Battle of the Boyne in 1690. The term is now more generally applied to any Irishman who goes to the continent, though it applies more particularly to political exiles.

41.18/42.16 MY FATHER'S A BIRD   A line from "The Ballad of Joking Jesus." See entry 19.3.

41.20/42.18 ABOUT THE NATURE OF WOMEN HE READ IN MICHELET   Jules Michelet (1798–1874) was a French historian who wrote works entitled *La Femme*; *Les Femmes de la revolution*; and *L'Amour*. He also wrote *Oeuvres Choises de Vico* and a multi-volume *Historie de France*, which was his greatest work.

41.21/42.19 LA VIE DE JESUS BY M. LEO TAXIL   See entry 41.14.

41.34/42.30 FLESHPOTS OF EGYPT   In Exodus 16:3 the children of Israel lament their following Moses and wish they had stayed "in the land of Egypt, when we sat by the fleshpots, and when we did eat bread to the full." Bloom thinks of "Fleshpots of Egypt" on p. 86.15/85.2

41.38/42.36 LUI, C'EST MOI   D. Daiches suggests that this is a parody of Louis XIV's remark "L'etat c'est moi" ("I am the state"). M. Jacques Aubert has suggested that this may owe something to Montaigne's famous remark about his friendship with Estienne de la Boetie, in his essay "On Friendship" (Book I, essay xxviii): "Si on me presse de dire pourquoy je l'aymois, je sens que cela ne se peut exprimer, qu'en respondant: 'Par ce que c'estoit luy; par ce que c'estoit moy' " ("If I am required to say why I loved him, I feel that it cannot be explained except by saying, 'Because he was he, because I was I' ").

42.8/43.6 FIERY COLUMBANUS   St. Columbanus was an Irish missionary and writer. See entry 27.38.

42.8/43.6 FIACRE   St. Fiacre was an Irish saint of the seventh century. He built a monastery in France and died in that country. Joyce mentioned Fiacre in his "Ireland, Island of Saints and Sages" (*CW*, p. 158). *Fiacre* also means *hackney* or *cab*. P. Colum explains the derivation from the saint's name in *Our Friend James Joyce*, pp. 127–28 (for this use of the word in *Ulysses*, see p. 397.8/390.30). See also the next entry.

42.8/43.6 SCOTUS   "Scotus" could refer either to John Duns Scotus (1266–1308) or to John Scotus Erigena (830–880?). In my opinion it is the former, though others disagree with me on this. Both men were supposedly of Irish birth, and both are discussed by Joyce in his lecture "Ireland, Island of Saints and Sages" (*CW*, pp. 153–74, esp. pp. 160–61). What inclines me toward Duns Scotus is a section in Joyce's "Alphabetical Notebook" which is clearly an early version of this passage in *Ulysses*, and in which he specifically mentions Duns Scotus in conjunction with Fiacre and Columbanus: "Duns Scotus has won a poorer fame than S. Fiacre, whose legend sown in French soil, has grown up in a harvest of hackney-cabs. If he and Columbanus the fiery, whose fingertips God illumined, and Fridolinus [?—or Frigidian] Viator can see as far as earth from their creepy-stools in heaven they know that Aquinas, the lucid sensual Latin, has won the day" (the passage quoted is under the heading Ireland).

42.10/43.7 EUGE! EUGE   As Father W. T. Noon has pointed out to me, these words occur in the Litany of Saints and in several places in the Bible. See Psalms 35:21, 35:25, 40:15, 70:3, and Ezekiel 25:3. In each of these contexts the words "Euge! Euge!" (Translated "Aha! Aha!" or "Well done! Well done!") are the words of an enemy or mocker, and God is called on to chastise the mocker. These words also occur occasionally in Roman drama (see for example Plautus' *Aulularia*, IV, vi, 11), but the allusion here is clearly to the scriptural context.

42.12/43.10 LE TUTU   Although Stephen could have brought *le tutu* (a kind of short muslin drawers worn by ballet girls) back from Paris, the reference here is probably to the Parisian magazine *Le Tutu*. The *Annuaire de la Presse Francaise* for 1904–5 lists this magazine in its "Humoristiques" section and describes it as a weekly that began publication in 1901.

42.13/43.11 PANTALON BLANC ET CULOTTE ROUGE   Although the context clearly indicates that this is a magazine, I have not been able to identify it. The *Annuaire de la Presse Francaise* for 1904–5 lists no such title, although it does list a weekly called "La Vie en Culotte Rouge" in its "Humoristiques" section. In reply to a request for information, the Department of Periodicals of the Bibliotheque Nationale said that no such periodical as *Pantalon blanc et culotte rouge* is listed in any of the catalogues or bibliographies at their disposal. In view of the relationship between this title and *Le Tutu* (entry 42.12), it is possible that Joyce is either making up or slightly adapting the names of periodicals to bring in the theme of women's drawers with Stephen, since it is later important for Bloom. On Joyce's own feelings about drawers, see R. Ellmann, *JJ*, p. 452.

42.18/43.16 THEN HERE'S A HEALTH TO MULLIGAN'S AUNT . . . Hodgart and Worthington identify this as an allusion to "Matthew Hannigan's [*sic*] Aunt," by French. Percy French (1854–1920) was an Irish poet, song writer, and parodist. The chorus of "Matthew Hanigan's Aunt" begins, "So here's a health to Hanigan's aunt!/ I'll tell you the reason why,/ She always had things dacent/ In the Hanigan family. . . ." Words may be found in *Prose, Poems and Parodies of Percy French*, pp. 155–56.

43.7/44.5 THE DALCASSIANS   The Dalcassians were one of the families of the Munster dynasty. The Dal Cais were descendants of Cormac Cas, grandson of the famous Eoghan Mor. P. W. Joyce mentions the Dalcassians frequently in his *Short History*.

43.8/44.5 ARTHUR GRIFFITH   Arthur Griffith (1872–1922), editor of *The United Irishman* and of its successor *Sinn Fein* (see entry 72.41), was one of the most forceful and influential workers for Irish freedom. He founded the Sinn Fein movement in November, 1905 (see entry 163.38) and was for a brief time president of the Irish Free State in 1922. Padraic Colum has written a biography of Griffith entitled *Ourselves Alone! The Story of Arthur Griffith and the Origin of the Irish Free State* (New York, 1959).

43.10/44.7 YOU'RE YOUR FATHER'S SON. I KNOW THE VOICE   See entry 38.11.

43.12/44.9 M. DRUMONT, FAMOUS JOURNALIST   Edouard Adolphe Drumont (1844–1917) was a journalist who was probably best known as a bitter anti-Semite. His paper, *La Libre Parole* (founded

1892), was a chief organ of anti-Jewish feeling. He and Leo Taxil
were violent opponents (see entry 41.14 and Magalaner, *op. cit.*).

43.13/44.11 VIEILLE OGRESSE WITH THE DENTS JAUNES   "Old hag with
the yellow teeth." According to the context, this is what Drumont
called Queen Victoria, but I have not located the statement.

43.14/44.12 MAUD GONNE   Maud Gonne (1866–1953) was a beautiful, chauvinistic Irish woman whom Yeats loved and tried for
years to marry, unsuccessfully. Joyce was to have met her during
his Paris stay in 1902–3, but he didn't. Bloom thinks of her later;
see entry 72.40.

43.15/44.12 LA PATRIE   *La Patrie* was a well known French political
periodical, founded in 1841. See also the following entry.

43.15/44.13 M. MILLEVOYE   Lucien Millevoye (1850–1918), grandson of the French poet Charles Millevoye, became editor-in-chief
of *La Patrie* in 1894.

43.15/44.13 FELIX FAURE   François Félix Faure (1841–99), French
statesman who was elected president of France in 1895, died suddenly of a cerebral hemorrhage at the Elysee in 1899. M. Jacques
Aubert has added another dimension to this by explaining that
Faure is supposed to have died while in the arms of his mistress.

43.20/44.18 GREEN EYES, I SEE YOU. FANG, I FEEL   E. R. Steinberg
(*SoC*, p. 147), suggests an allusion here to Iago's words to Othello,
"Oh, beware, my lord, of jealousy./ It is the green eyed monster
which doth mock/ The meat it feeds on" (*Oth.*, III, iii, 165–67).

43.24/44.22 PEEP OF DAY BOY'S HAT   The "Peep o' Day Boys" was
an organization of Ulster Protestants who, beginning about 1785,
staged early morning raids on Catholic cottages to search for and
seize arms. They were opposed by a Catholic group called the
"Defenders." Later the "Peep o' Day Boys" merged with the
Orangemen. See entry 31.23.

43.25/44.23 HOW THE HEAD CENTRE GOT AWAY, AUTHENTIC VERSION. GOT
UP AS A YOUNG BRIDE, MAN, VEIL, ORANGEBLOSSOMS   On November 11, 1865, James Stephens, "Head Centre" of the Fenians, was
imprisoned in Richmond Jail in Dublin. On November 24 his escape was effected by John Devoy and Colonel Thomas Kelly, with
the help of two of the guards who were sympathizers. Stephens
was kept in hiding in a house in Ballybough for seven months. In
June, 1866, he and several others drove through Dublin in an open
carriage in broad daylight, finely dressed and in silk hats. The
carriage took Stephens out the Malahide road along the sea to a
rendezvous with a small boat that took him to a ship close by and
thus to his escape (from *Adventures of an Irish Bookman*, by M. J.

McManus, Dublin, 1952, pp. 24–28). Apparently the disguise as a bride is apocryphal. In his essay "Fenianism," Joyce himself says that Stephens' disguise is "according to legend" (*CW*, p. 189).

43.26/44.24 DROVE OUT THE ROAD TO MALAHIDE   The proximate reference to the "young bride" suggests that Hodgart and Worthington are right in saying this is an allusion to Gerald Griffin's (Irish poet, 1803–40) poem "The Bridal of Malahide," although there is no line in the poem exactly like this one. For the poem see *Dublin Book of Irish Verse*, p. 116. See also entry 43.25.

43.27/44.25 OF LOST LEADERS   This probably alludes to Robert Browning's poem "The Lost Leader," in which he criticizes Wordsworth for his betrayal of the liberal cause.

43.31/44.29 COLONEL RICHARD BURKE ... UNDER THE WALLS OF CLERKENWELL   On December 13, 1867, an attempt was made to release several Fenian prisoners, including Colonel Richard Burke, from Clerkenwell Prison in London. The rescuers blew down the wall of the prison with a keg of gunpowder and killed and injured several people in the process. Joyce refers to this event in "Fenianism" (*CW*, p. 190).

43.34/44.31 SHATTERED GLASS AND TOPPLING MASONRY   See entry 24.9.

43.38/44.36 LOVELESS, LANDLESS, WIFELESS   This may echo a line from Euripides' *Iphigenia in Tauris* in which Iphigenia speaks of herself as "husbandless, childless, countryless, loveless" (l. 220). Very similar lines occur in *Helen* (l. 690), and in *Orestes* (ll. 205–6).

44.2/44.41 THE BOYS OF KILKENNY ...   "The Boys of Kilkenny" is an anonymous Irish song. Its first verse says, "Oh! the boys of Kilkenny are stout roving blades, And if ever they meet with their nice little maids, They kiss them and coax them, they spend their money free, Oh! of all towns in Ireland, Kilkenny for me, Oh! of all towns in Ireland, Kilkenny for me!" Words and music may be found in Moffatt's *Minstrelsy of Ireland*, 3rd ed., p. 192. This song is also alluded to on p. 44.5/45.2 and p. 44.6/45.4. Stephen's thought of Kilkenny leads him to think of St. Canice and of Strongbow's castle; see the following entries.

44.4/45.1 SAINT CANICE   Canice (or Kenny) was an Irish saint (died *ca.* 599) who preached in Ireland and Scotland. He was a friend of St. Columba (or Columkille) and accompanied him on his mission to Brude, king of the Picts. Kilkenny, which means cell or church of Kenny, takes its name from St. Canice.

44.4/45.1 STRONGBOW'S CASTLE ON THE NORE   With the arrival of

Strongbow (Richard FitzGilbert de Clare, Earl of Pembroke, d. 1176) in Ireland on August 23, 1170, the English conquest of Ireland began in earnest. Strongbow had been called on by Dermot MacMurrough, King of Leinster and last of the provincial kings of Ireland, to help him in his fight against Tiernan O'Rourke and Roderick O'Connor (see entry 34.42). Strongbow, who married Dermot's daughter, Eva, became king of Leinster when Dermot died. Strongbow had a castle built at Kilkenny (on the Nore) for the protection of his domain, and this explains Stephen's association of him with Kilkenny.

44.5/45.2 HE TAKES ME, NAPPER TANDY, BY THE HAND   This adapts a line from "The Wearin' of the Green," an anonymous Irish ballad dating from about 1798. The song contains the lines, "I met wid Napper Tandy, and he took me by the hand,/ And he said, 'How's poor ould Ireland, and how does she stand?'" For words, see Hoagland, pp. 300–1. Napper Tandy (1740–1803) was one of the co-founders, along with Wolfe Tone, Rowan Hamilton, and others, of the "Society of United Irishmen" in October, 1791. In "Ireland, Island of Saints and Sages," Joyce mentions Tandy as one of the "heroes of the modern movement" (*CW*, p. 162).

44.9/45.7 REMEMBERING THEE, O SION   An echo of the Jews' lament for their homeland. Psalms 137:1 says, "By the rivers of Babylon, there we sat down, yea, we wept, when we remembered Zion."

44.23/45.20 A SHUT DOOR OF A SILENT TOWER ENTOMBING THEIR BLIND BODIES   H. E. Rogers (*op. cit.*, entry 27.38) says this suggests the Tower of Death that occurs many times in Irish myth.

44.26/45.24 FORM OF FORMS   From Aristotle. See entry 26.3.

44.28/45.26 IN SABLE SILVERED   In *Hamlet*, I, ii, 242, Horatio describes the beard of the ghost as "a sable silvered."

44.28/45.26 ELSINORE'S TEMPTING FLOOD   In *Hamlet*, I, iv, 69, Horatio warns Hamlet against the ghost by saying, "What if it tempt you toward the flood, my lord."

44.34/45.32 UN COCHE ENSABLÉ, LOUIS VEUILLOT CALLED GAUTIER'S PROSE   Veuillot (1813–83) was a French journalist and editor of the Paris *Univers*. Theophile Gautier (1811–72) was a French poet, critic, and novelist. He was one of the principal Parnassians and was influential in the symbolist and imagist movements. I have not located the remark Stephen ascribes to Veuillot, calling Gautier's prose "a coach stuck in the sand."

44.39/45.37 SIR LOUT'S TOYS   Frank Budgen records the following conversation with Joyce about Sir Lout: " 'Who are Sir Lout and his family?' I said. 'The people who did the rough work at the beginning?' 'Yes,' said Joyce. 'They were giants right enough, but weak reproductively. Fasolt and Fafner in *Das Rheingold* are of the same breed, sexually weak as the music tells us. My Sir Lout has rocks in his mouth instead of teeth. He articulates badly' " (*JJMU*, p. 52). This conversation indicates that Sir Lout may have been Joyce's own creation, but this cannot be taken for granted.

45.1/45.39 FEEFAWFUM. I ZMELLZ DE BLODZ ODZ AN IRIDZMAN   In *King Lear*, III, iv, 187, Mad Tom says, "Child Rowland to the dark tower came./ His word was still,—'Fie, foh, and fum,/ I smell the blood of a British man.' " But this is not the origin of the statement, for it goes back to an earlier folk tale and rhyme.

45.7/46.4 THE TWO MARIES   The two Marys (Mary Magdalene and Mary the mother of James and Joses) are mentioned together in several places in the Bible: Matthew 27:56 and 61; Matthew 28:1; Mark 15:47; and Mark 16:1. In Australian slang, a Mary is a native woman (*OED*).

45.7/46.4 THEY HAVE TUCKED IT SAFE AMONG THE BULRUSHES   An allusion to the hiding of Moses by his mother. According to Exodus 2:3, "And when she could not longer hide him, she took for him an ark of bulrushes, and daubed it with slime and with pitch, and put the child therein; and she laid it in the flags by the river's brink."

45.8/46.5 PEEKABOO. I SEE YOU   Hodgart and Worthington list this as an allusion to "Peekaboo," by Scanlan. American songwriter William J. Scanlan, (b. 1856) did write a song by this title which first appeared in his show *Friend and Foe* in 1881 and which became quite popular. But these words begin several common children's songs and nursery rhymes and could allude to them.

45.10/46.7 GALLEYS OF THE LOCHLANNS RAN HERE TO BEACH   In the latter part of the eighth century (*ca.* 795) Ireland was besieged by successive waves of Teutonic invaders, mainly from Norway and Denmark. Apparently, in strict usage, the Lochlanns were the earlier invaders, who came from Norway; the later invaders, from Denmark, were called Danars. However, the invaders were commonly lumped together as Danars. "Danevikings" are mentioned on p. 45.12/46.9.

45.12/46.9 WHEN MALACHI WORE THE COLLAR OF GOLD   This is an exact quotation from a song by Thomas Moore entitled "Let Erin Remember the Days of Old." The song begins, "Let Erin remember the days of old/ Ere her faithless sons betrayed her;/ When Malachi wore the collar of gold/ Which he won from the proud invader." Malachi II (948–1022), King of Meath and High King, was, along with Brian Boru, one of the two men who did most to free

Ireland from the Norse oppression in the tenth century. Mabel Worthington explains ("Irish Folk Songs in Joyce's *Ulysses*," *PMLA*, LXXI, 325) that after Malachi took Dublin from the Danes in 996, he "took the collar of the Norwegian prince Tomar as part of his booty."

45.13/46.10 A SCHOOL OF TURLEHIDE WHALES STRANDED IN HOT NOON ... As John V. Kelleher has pointed out ("Joyce Digested," *Accent*, V [Spring, 1945], 181–86), this alludes to a historical event. During a famine in 1331, a school of whales was caught in the shallows of Dublin Bay. The Dubliners killed and ate the whales, temporarily relieving the famine. Walter Harris, in his *The History and Antiquities of the City of Dublin* (1766) says, *s.v.* 1331, "A great famine afflicted all Ireland in this and the foregoing year, and the city of Dublin suffered miserably. But the people met with an unexpected and providential relief. For about the 24th of June a prodigious number of large sea fish, called Turlehydes, were brought into the bay of Dublin, and cast on shore at the mouth of the river Dodder. They were from 30 to 40 feet long, and so bulky, that two tall men placed one on each side of the fish could not see one another. The lord justice, sir Anthony Lucy, with his servants, and many of the citizens of Dublin, killed above 200 of them, and gave leave to the poor to carry them away at their pleasure" (pp. 264–65). Harris' book provided the basis of the "Dublin Annals" section of *Thom's Directory*, and it might be thought that Joyce got this from the *Directory* for 1904. But R. M. Adams (*SS*, pp. 141–42) argues, on the basis of the word *cagework*, which occurs in another section of Harris, but not in *Thom's*, that Joyce used the serial reprinting of Harris' book which was appearing in the *Dublin Penny Journal* in 1904. In light of p. 49.12/50.4, this passage may also suggest the capture of Proteus by Menelaus at high noon. See entry 49.12.

45.18/46.15 I MOVED AMONG THEM ON THE FROZEN LIFFEY ... Harris' *History* (see entry 45.13) records, *s.v.* 1338, "So great a frost was this year from the 2d of December to the 10th of February, that the river Liffey was frozen over so hard as to bear dancing, running, playing foot-ball, and making fires to broil herrings on" (p. 266).

45.20/46.17 I SPOKE TO NO-ONE: NONE TO ME   Hodgart and Worthington list this as an allusion to the English folk song "The Miller of the Dee" (also "There Was a Jolly Miller Once" and "The Jolly Miller"), but there is no line in the song closely similar to Stephen's statement. Perhaps they consider this an allusion to "I care for nobody, no, not I, if nobody cares for me." For words and music, see G. Bantock, *One Hundred Songs of England*, p. 36.

45.22/46.19 I JUST SIMPLY STOOD PALE, SILENT, BAYED ABOUT   This alludes to the legend of Acteon, who, transformed by Diana into a deer, was pursued and slain by his own dogs. R. Ellmann (*JJ*, p. 150) points out other instances of this image in Joyce's writings. Joyce used it in the early essay-sketch entitled "A Portrait of the Artist" in 1904 (included in Scholes and Kain, *The Workshop of Daedalus*, pp. 56–74), and he used it later that year in "The Holy Office."

45.22/46.19 TERRIBILIA MEDITANS   If this phrase is an allusion, I have not identified it.

45.23/46.20 FORTUNE'S KNAVE   In *Anthony and Cleopatra*, V, ii, 2, Cleopatra says, "'Tis paltry to be Caesar./ Not being Fortune, he's but Fortune's knave,/ A minister of her will."

45.25/46.22 THE BRUCE'S BROTHER   Following Robert Bruce's defeat of the English at Bannockburn in 1314, his brother, Edward Bruce, invaded Ireland and spent the next several years trying to establish himself as king of Ireland. Although his early campaigns were successful, his forces were defeated and he was slain at Faughart on October 14, 1318.

45.26/46.22 THOMAS FITZGERALD, SILKEN KNIGHT   Lord Thomas Fitzgerald, tenth Earl of Kildare (d. 1537), was called "Silken Thomas." He raised a rebellion against the English and was executed after it failed.

45.26/46.23 PERKIN WARBECK, YORK'S FALSE SCION   Perkin Warbeck (1474–99), a commoner, pretended for several years to be Richard, Duke of York, the son of Edward IV, who was one of the two young sons of Edward IV supposedly murdered by order of Richard III in 1483.

45.28/46.24 LAMBERT SIMNEL   Lambert Simnel (*ca.* 1475–*ca.* 1537) was a commoner who was trained from childhood to play the part of a prince by a priest named William Symonds. Simnel claimed to be Edward, Earl of Warwick, son of the Duke of Clarence, and was actually crowned Edward VI in Dublin in 1487. His forces were defeated by those of Henry VII, after which Henry used Simnel as a scullion in the royal kitchen.

45.29/46.26 ALL KING'S SONS   See entry 31.30.

45.31/46.27 THE COURTIERS WHO MOCKED GUIDO IN OR SAN MICHELE WERE IN THEIR OWN HOUSE. HOUSE OF . . .   Guido Cavalcanti (*ca.* 1259–*ca.* 1300) was a Florentine poet and a friend of Dante. As Edmund Epstein has pointed out ("Cruxes in *Ulysses*: Notes Toward an Annotated Edition," *JJR*, I, 25–36), the story of Guido's walking in the Orto San Michele is told in the *Decameron*, the ninth story of the sixth day. While he was in a cemetery his friends came to mock him about his pensiveness. He told them that they could say to him what they pleased since they were in their own house. One of them realized he meant they were in the house of Death. *Death* is the word Stephen hesitates to say here.

46.30/47.24   MOVES TO ONE GREAT GOAL   See entry 34.27.

46.39/47.33   THE SIMPLE PLEASURES OF THE POOR   As E. R. Steinberg suggests (*SoC*, p. 146), this line echoes "The short and simple annals of the poor" from Thomas Gray's "Elegy Written in a Country Churchyard."

46.40/47.34   SOMETHING HE BURIED THERE, HIS GRANDMOTHER   This alludes to the riddle Stephen recited to his class earlier. See entry 26.33.

47.2/47.37   A FURY OF HIS CLAWS . . . A PARD, A PANTHER, GOT IN SPOUSE-BREACH   This passage blends several old bestiary traditions. Under *spousebreach* (which means adultery) the *OED* quotes the following from John de Trevisa's *Bartholomeus (de Glanvilla) De Proprietatibus Rerum*, XVIII, lxvi: "Leopardus is a cruel beeste and is gendered in spowsebreche of a parde and of a lionas" (trans. 1398; Bodl. MS). T. H. White's *The Bestiary* has the same lore under Leopard. Wm. Schutte has suggested that part of this comes from Brunetto Latini's *Il Tesoro*, which Stephen later directly quotes from (see entry 194.21). Schutte quotes and translates a passage from *Il Tesoro* which says, "And know that the female panther bears young only once. And hear why. The young when they have grown within the mother's body will not suffer themselves to remain there until the time of proper birth; rather they force nature so that they mutilate their mother's womb and issue forth from it in such a way that it can never bear her more young" (*JS*, pp. 100–1; Schutte cites *Il Tesoro*, II, 260).

47.5/47.40   HAROUN AL RASCHID   Haroun al Raschid (763–809) was a caliph of Bagdad who was renowned for the splendid court he kept. He is known primarily through his role in several of the *Arabian Nights* tales. "Sindbad the Sailor" is set during his caliphate.

47.10/48.3   THE RED EGYPTIANS   Wm. Schutte feels that Stephen's use of this term probably owes something to a description of Gypsies in Richard Head's *The Canting Academy*, which Stephen alludes to a few lines later. The passage Schutte quotes from Head does involve the notion that the Gypsies are descended from the

Egyptians, and says they color their faces with a "tawney hue" (see *JS*, p. 61).

47.13/48.6 THE RUFFIAN AND HIS STROLLING MORT   This is the first of several allusions in the following lines to a seventeenth-century canting song, "The Rogue's Delight in Praise of His Strolling Mort." This song was printed in Richard Head's *The Canting Academy* (London, 1673). Wm. Schutte reproduces the pertinent stanzas and discusses them; see *JS*, pp. 60–61. Further allusions to the song occur on pp. 47.16/48.9, 47.20/48.13, 47.23/48.16, and 47.29/48.22.

47.23/48.16 WHITE THY FAMBLES, RED THY GAN . . .   These four lines reproduce verbatim the second stanza of "The Rogue's Delight" as it appears in Head's *The Canting Academy*. See entry 47.13.

47.27/48.20 MOROSE DELECTATION AQUINAS TUNBELLY CALLS THIS, FRATE PORCOSPINO   *Delectatio morosa* is one of the three internal sins, and consists of "the pleasure taken in a sinful thought or imagination even without desiring it" (*Cath. Encyc.*, XIV, 5). St. Thomas discusses this sin in the *Summa Theologica, Part II (First part)*, question xxxi, art 2; question lxxiv, art. 6; and question lxxxviii, art. 5. Tunbelly refers to the proportions of St. Thomas' stomach. According to an apocryphal story, he was so fat that a special place had to be cut out for him at the table where he ate.

47.33/48.26 MY HAMLET HAT   In light of p. 50.25/51.14, this is clearly an allusion to Ophelia's song in *Hamlet*, IV, v, 25. See entry 50.25.

47.33/48.26 IF I WERE SUDDENLY NAKED HERE AS I SIT   In view of the context, this may owe something to Hamlet's being "set naked" on the kingdom of King Claudius. The letter Hamlet sends Claudius upon his return to Denmark from the sea voyage says "'High and mighty, you shall know I am set naked on your kingdom'" (*Ham.*, IV, vii, 43–44).

47.35/48.28 THE SUN'S FLAMING SWORD   Ulrich Schneider has suggested that this alludes to the flaming sword that God placed outside the garden of Eden after he evicted Adam and Eve. Genesis 3:24 says, "So he drove out the man; and he placed at the east of the garden of Eden Cherubims, and a flaming sword which turned every way, to keep the way of the tree of life."

47.35/48.28 TO EVENING LANDS   Though this is a very ordinary phrase, it may allude to the subtitle of J. W. Boddham-Whetham's *Western Wanderings: a Record of Travel in the Evening Land*

(London, 1874), in which the author describes his travels in the United States.

47.38/48.31 OINOPA PONTON, A WINEDARK SEA   This phrase is common in Homer. See entry 5.7.

47.39/48.32 BEHOLD THE HANDMAID OF THE MOON   A variation of Luke 1:38 in which Mary says to the announcing angel, "Behold the handmaid of the Lord." These same words also occur in the Angelus.

47.39/48.32 IN SLEEP THE WET SIGN CALLS HER HOUR   Wm. Schutte lists this as an allusion to Horatio's calling the moon "the moist star/ Upon whose influence Neptune's empire stands" (*Ham.*, I, i, 118–19).

48.1/48.34 OMNIS CARO AD TE VENIET   This is recited in the Introit of the Requiem Mass. It is from Psalms 65:2, which says, "O thou that hearest prayer, unto thee shall all flesh come."

48.3/48.36 MOUTH TO HER MOUTH'S KISS   J. Prescott has shown (*op. cit.*, entry 34.22) that this is very similar to a line in "My Grief on the Sea," a song translated by Douglas Hyde in his *Love Songs of Connacht* (Dublin, 1904). The sixth stanza of Hyde's translation says "And my love came behind me—/ He came from the South;/ His breast to my bosom,/ His mouth to my mouth" (p. 21).

48.4/48.37 MY TABLETS   In *Hamlet*, I, v, 107, Hamlet, thinking of Claudius, says "My tables—meet it is I set it down/ That one may smile, and smile, and be a villain."

48.7/48.40 MOUTH TO HER WOMB. OOMB, ALLWOMBING TOMB   S. Gilbert (*JJU*, p. 133) points out the following similar passages in Shakespeare and Blake: "The earth that's Nature's mother is her tomb:/ What is her burying grave, that is her womb" (*Rom. and Jul.*, II, iii, 9–10); "The Door of Death I open found/ And the Worm Weaving in the Ground/ Thou'rt my Mother from the Womb,/ Wife, Sister, Daughter, to the Tomb,/ Weaving to dreams the sexual strife/ And weeping over the Web of Life" ("The Gates of Paradise," ll. 43–48).

48.18/49.9 DARKNESS SHINING IN THE BRIGHTNESS   This reverses John 1:5: "And the light shineth in darkness; and the darkness comprehended it not." See entry 28.16.

48.19/49.10 AUGUR'S ROD   One of the insignias of the augur's office was his *lituus*, a staff free from knots and bent at the top, which he used to mark out the templum or consecrated space within which his observations for augury were to be made. See the eleventh edition of the *Encyclopaedia Britannica*, II, 903–4, for further information on augury.

48.19/49.10 IN BORROWED SANDALS   Wm. Schutte lists this (*JS*, p. 182) as an allusion to Ophelia's song in *Hamlet*, IV, v, 26, but this is questionable. See entry 50.25.

48.23/49.14 FORM OF MY FORM   An allusion to what Aristotle said of the mind. See entries 44.26 and 26.4.

48.26/49.17 BISHOP OF CLOYNE   George Berkeley (1685–1753), Irish idealist philosopher, became Protestant Bishop of Cloyne in 1734. Father W. T. Noon suggests that Stephen's allusion to Berkeley "grows out of his own optical experiments as he walks beside the sea, and suggests some familiarity on Joyce's part with Berkeley's 'Essay toward a New Theory of Vision,' in which Berkeley sets out to establish that the sense qualities of all things are 'inside the head' " (*JA*, p. 113). Stephen's remark about the bishop does seem to go to the core of Berkeley's philosophy. The veil of the temple, which separated the holy from the most holy (see next entry), probably refers to Berkeley's going beyond Locke in saying that not only secondary qualities, but reality itself is mental. Stephen's statement about the veil and the shovel hat means that Berkeley found reality inside his head. Compare Mulligan's earlier allusion to Locke on p. 8.11/10.1.

48.26/49.17 THE VEIL OF THE TEMPLE   The veil of the temple is described in detail in Exodus 26:31–35. Its purpose was to "divide unto you between the holy place and the most holy" (26:33). In Matthew 27:51 we are told that when Christ died, "the veil of the temple was rent in twain from the top to the bottom." W. Y. Tindall (*RG*, p. 148) says this suggests Mallarmé's "veil of the temple," and Yeats refers to "That inquietitude of the veil of the Temple, which M. Mallarmé considers a characteristic of our times" in his story "The Adoration of the Magi." See entry 39.35.

48.27/49.18 SHOVEL HAT   "Shovel hat" is a term used to describe the hat of Protestant clergymen, but its use here may suggest that Stephen is thinking of Richard Whately (1787–1834), archbishop of Dublin (appointed 1831), who was known as "Shovel Hat" Whately. "Shovel Hat" Whately was mentioned, for example, in the *United Irishman* of November 28, 1903, p. 3, col. a.

48.37/49.28 THE INELUCTABLE MODALITY OF THE INELUCTABLE VISUALITY   See entry 37.1.

49.10/50.1 ET VIDIT DEUS. ET ERANT VALDE BONA   Genesis 1:31: "And God saw everything that he had made, and, behold, it was very good."

49.11/50.2 WELCOME AS THE FLOWERS IN MAY   "As welcome as the flowers in May" is proverbial and is listed in the *ODEP*. Hodgart and Worthington list this as an allusion to a song by Sullivan entitled "You're As Welcome as the Flowers in May," but I have not located the song. The *Christy Minstrel Song Book* (London: Boosey and Co., n.d.) prints a song by Frederick Buckley entitled "The Flowers of May," which contains the line "And welcome with the young year The blithesome flowers of May" (Book IV, p. 47).

49.12/50.4   I AM CAUGHT IN THIS BURNING SCENE. PAN'S HOUR, THE FAUNAL NOON   This suggests the capture of Proteus by Menelaus at high noon in Book IV of the *Odyssey*. W. Y. Tindall points out that it suggests Mallarmé's "Afternoon of a Faun" (*RG*, p. 149).

49.14/50.5   WHERE ON THE TAWNY WATERS LEAVES LIE WIDE   Though I suspect this phrase of containing an allusion, I have not been able to discover it. There is a passage in Milton's "Comus" which has general similarities with this episode of *Ulysses*, but which lacks specific verbal parallels. At Comus' first appearance, he comes in "with a charming-rod in one hand," and speaks a passage that includes the following: "The sounds and seas with all their finny drove/ Now to the moon in wavering morrice move,/ And on the tawny sands and shelves/ Trip the pert fairies and the dapper elves" (ll. 115–18).

49.16/50.7   AND NO MORE TURN ASIDE AND BROOD   From Yeats's poem "Who Goes with Fergus?" There are many allusions to this poem on p. 9/11. See entry 9.22.

49.23/50.13   WILDE'S LOVE THAT DARE NOT SPEAK ITS NAME   Oscar Wilde's friend Lord Alfred Douglas wrote a poem entitled "The Debate of Two Loves" which uses the phrase "I am the love that dare not speak its name." See H. Howarth, "The Joycean Comedy: Wilde, Jonson, and Others," *JJM II*, p. 184. Howarth quotes a statement that Wilde made at his trial when asked about this passage: "The 'Love that dare not speak its name' in this century is such a great affection of an elder for a younger man as there was between David and Jonathan. . . . It is that deep, spiritual affection that is as pure as it is perfect. . . . There is nothing unnatural about it. It is intellectual, and it repeatedly exists between an elder and a younger man, when the elder man has intellect, and the younger man has all the joy, hope and glamour of life before him."

49.23/50.14   HE NOW WILL LEAVE ME. AND THE BLAME? AS I AM. AS I AM. ALL OR NOT AT ALL   John Z. Bennett has suggested that this, too, involves an allusion to Oscar Wilde. In *The Picture of Dorian Gray*, soon after the death of Sibyl Vane, Dorian says to Basil Hall-

ward, "Don't leave me, Basil, and don't quarrel with me. I am what
I am. There is nothing more to be said" (chap. IX).

49.36/50.26 HISING UP THEIR PETTICOATS   This is from "McGilligan's Daughter Mary Ann." See entry 13.20.

49.39/50.29 SAINT AMBROSE   Saint Ambrose (340?–397) was the
Bishop of Milan and one of the four great Doctors of the Western
Church. See the following entry, and compare Bloom's charac-
teristically general reference to "the doctors of the church" on p.
83.18/82.10.

49.41/50.31 DIEBUS AC NOCTIBUS INIURIAS PATIENS INGEMISCIT   "Days
and nights it patiently groans over wrongs." Father W. T. Noon
has pointed out to me that this is from St. Ambrose's *Commentary
on Romans*. It occurs in the last sentence of Ambrose's comment
on Paul's statement in Romans 8:22, "For we know that the whole
creation groaneth and travaileth in pain together until now." Ambrose's statement may be found in J. P. Migne's *Patrologia Latina*
(1879), XVII, 131, col. 1. As Father Noon suggests, Joyce probably came across this in some choir manual or sodality manual.

50.4/50.36 FULL FATHOM FIVE THY FATHER LIES   The first line of
Ariel's song in *The Tempest*, I, ii, 397. See entry 50.19.

50.5/50.37 FOUND DROWNED   This phrase is a common newspaper
heading, deriving from the fact that "found drowned" is the official
coroner's jury's verdict when a person is so found and no foul play
is suspected. Such an instance occurs in the *Freeman's Journal* for
March 29, 1904, p. 5, col. e, headed "Found Drowned in the Dodder." It tells of the finding of the body of a twenty-five-year-old
girl, and the last paragraph says, "Evidence of the recovery of the
body from the Dodder having been given, the jury returned a
verdict, 'Found drowned.' "

50.8/50.40 A PACE A PACE   I suspect this of being an allusion to the
nursery rhyme "This is the way the ladies ride," but the ODNR
does not list "a pace a pace" among the variants of that rhyme (pp.
257–58). Cf. entry 534.24.

50.9/50.41 SUNK THOUGH HE BE BENEATH THE WATERY FLOOR   This is
line 167 of Milton's "Lycidas," in which he affirms Lycidas' immortality in spite of his drowning.

50.13/51.3 GOD BECOMES MAN BECOMES FISH BECOMES BARNACLE GOOSE
BECOMES FEATHERBED MOUNTAIN   S. Gilbert says this is "a variant
of the kabalistic axiom of metempsychosis (as well as an allusion
to the protean ebb and flow of living matter): 'a stone becomes a
plant, a plant an animal, an animal a man, a man a spirit, and a spirit

a god'" (*JJU*, p. 128). Stephen's thought here is very similar to
Hamlet's when he traces the noble dust of Alexander until he finds
it stopping a bunghole (*Ham.*, V, i, 225 ff.).

50.19/51.8 A SEACHANGE THIS   In his song in *The Tempest*, I, ii, 397,
Ariel sings, "Nothing of him that doth fade/ But doth suffer a sea-
change/ Into something rich and strange." Ariel sings this song
about Alonso, who is thought to have drowned, but who has actually come to no harm at all.

50.20/51.9 OLD FATHER OCEAN. PRIX DE PARIS: BEWARE OF IMITATIONS
Fritz Senn says that the Paris here may be Paris of Troy, whose
prize was Helen. Senn says, "According to a version of the Greek
myths attributed to Stesichorus, only a phantom of Helen accompanied Paris to Troy, while she herself, faithful, stayed with King
Proteus in Egypt" (*JJQ*, I, 64). Stesichorus (*ca.* 632–*ca.* 522 B.C.)
was a Greek poet, of whose works we now possess only about
thirty fragments, none longer than six lines. The best-known account of his story about Helen—and the only one I know—is Plato's
Phaedrus, 234a, but the version given there does not contain all of
the details Senn mentions. In that dialogue, Socrates says, "I bethink
me of an ancient purgation of mythological error which was de-
vised, not by Homer, for he never had the wit to discover why
he was blind, but by Stesichorus, who was a philosopher and knew
the reason why; and, therefore, when he lost his eyes, for that was
the penalty which was inflicted upon him for reviling the lovely
Helen, he at once purged himself. And the purgation was a recantation, which began thus,—'False is that word of mine—the truth is
that thou didst not embark in well-benched ships, nor ever go to
the citadel of Troy;' and when he had completed his poem, which
is called 'the recantation,' immediately his sight returned to him"
(*Dialogues of Plato*, trans. B. Jowett [Oxford, 1953], p. 149).

50.23/51.12 I THIRST   These are the words of Christ on the cross,
John 19:28.

50.24/51.13 ALLBRIGHT HE FALLS, PROUD LIGHTNING OF THE INTELLECT,
LUCIFER, DICO, QUI NESCIT OCCASUM   Father John P. Lahey of Le
Moyne College has pointed out the probable origin of this phrase
in the service for Holy Saturday. In the "Exsultet" in that service
(the "Exsultet" is a hymn in praise of the paschal candle, sung by
the deacon), the deacon praises the continued light of the candle
and says, "Flammus ejus lucifer matutinus inveniat. Ille, inquam,
lucifer qui nescit occasum" ("May the rising star of morning find
it burning still—that morning star that knows no setting"). (The
"Exsultet" is traditionally ascribed to St. Augustine or St. Ambrose,

but its authorship is not known.) But Stephen's phrase, which may be translated "Lucifer, I say, who knows no fall," clearly applies to Lucifer-Satan and owes something to Isaiah 14:12 ("How art thou fallen from heaven, O Lucifer, son of the morning . . .") and to Luke 10:18 ("I beheld Satan as lightning fall from heaven").

50.25/51.14 MY COCKLE HAT AND STAFF AND HIS MY SANDAL SHOON In *Hamlet*, IV, v, 25, Ophelia sings, "How should I your truelove know/ From another one?/ By his cockle hat and staff/ And his sandal shoon."

50.26/51.15 TO EVENING LANDS See entry 47.35.

50.29/51.18 ALL DAYS MAKE THEIR END This recalls the proverb known in several languages. The *ODEP* lists "The longest day hath an end," and lists nine instances from *ca.* 1340 to 1841, including John Ray's *Proverbs* (1670). Compare Brutus' statement in *Julius Caesar*, V, i, 125: "But it sufficeth that the day will end."

50.31/51.20 OF ALL THE GLAD NEW YEAR, MOTHER, THE RUM TUM TIDDLEDY TUM. LAWN TENNYSON, GENTLEMAN POET This alludes to Lord Tennyson's poem "The May Queen," the third line of which reads, "Of all the glad New-year, mother, the maddest merriest day." The poem was set to music by Dempster under the title "Call Me Early, Mother Dear," as Hodgart and Worthington point out.

50.33/51.22 THE OLD HAG WITH THE YELLOW TEETH See entry 41.13.

50.33/51.22 MONSIEUR DRUMONT, GENTLEMAN JOURNALIST See entry 43.12.

50.36/51.25 TOOTHLESS KINCH, THE SUPERMAN This combines Stephen's dental problems with an allusion to Nietzsche's *Uebermensch*. See entry 22.27.

56.12/56.10 LICKING THE SAUCER CLEAN   In light of Bloom's many allusions to nursery rhymes, this probably echoes the statement in "Jack Sprat" that he and his wife "licked the platter clean." For the text of the rhyme and a brief discussion of its origins, see *ODNR*, p. 238.

56.18/56.16 THIN BREAD AND BUTTER   The nursery rhyme "Little Tommy Tucker" begins "Little Tommy Tucker,/ Sings for his supper:/ What shall we give him?/ White bread and butter" (*ODNR*, pp. 416–17). Though I have not located it in print, I believe there is a variant reading "Thin bread and butter."

56.32/56.30 AT PLEVNA THAT WAS   Plevna (or Pleven) is a northern Bulgarian city famous for having undergone a siege of 143 days in the Russo-Turkish War of 1877–78. Under Osman Pasha the Turkish garrison resisted the assaults of the Russians from July 20 until December 10, 1877. This is the first of many allusions in this episode which suggest that Bloom's early morning thoughts are somewhat oriented around the books on his bookshelf (see pp. 708/693 ff.). Two questions on p. 710/694 call attention to Plevna's being discussed in Hozier's *History of the Russo-Turkish War*, which Bloom has on his shelf.

57.13/57.11 DELIVERING WITH TRAYS OUR DAILY   This alludes to "Give us this day our daily bread" from the Pater Noster or Lord's Prayer (Matt. 6:11 and Luke 11:3). Stephen alluded to the Pater Noster on p. 6.33/8.27.

57.18–32/57.16–30. WALK ALONG A STRAND . . . DULCIMERS. I PASS   E. R. Steinberg quotes this passage (*SoC*, pp. 91–92) and points out many correspondences with Coleridge's "Kubla Khan." Although some of the parallels are quite striking (e.g., "A damsel with a dulcimer" and "a girl playing one of those instruments what do you call them: dulcimers"), I do not see any clearly identifiable use of phrases or lines from the poem.

57.22/57.20 TURKO THE TERRIBLE   Turko the Terrible was a character in a pantomime of the same title by Edwin Hamilton; Stephen thought of the pantomime on p. 10.2/11.31, *q.v.* Bloom's thought of Turko is apparently prompted by his remembering "Tweedy's big moustaches," for on p. 596/581 "Major Tweedy, moustached like Turko the Terrible" appears. In W. MacQueen Pope's *Gaiety: Theatre of Enchantment* there is a picture of William Royce (see entry 10.2) dressed in near-Eastern garb and with huge moustaches (facing p. 220). MacQueen Pope does not say what role Royce is dressed for, but it is tempting to see him as Turko. R. M. Adams says that Turko the Terrible could have been found in Dublin's comic newspaper, *Zoz* (*SS*, p. 98), but my examination of almost two years of the paper, which ran from 1876–78, yielded only one depiction of Turko, so he was certainly not a regular feature of the paper.

57.33/57.31 KIND OF STUFF YOU READ: IN THE TRACK OF THE SUN. SUN-BURST ON THE TITLEPAGE   A book entitled *In the Track of the Sun* is on Bloom's bookshelf (p. 709/693). *In the Track of the Sun: Diary of a Globe Trotter* by Frederick Diodati Thompson was published by Heineman in 1893. It is a first-person description of the author's trip around the world, in which he left New York on October 14, 1891, going west, and arrived back in New York from England on May 18, 1892. Only a relatively small part of the book is devoted to the U.S. and Europe; most of it describes Thompson's travels in the Orient—Japan, India, and the Near East. Probably this book is the source of some of Bloom's thoughts about Eastern lore. For example, on p. 114.29/113.10 Bloom thinks, "Where is that Parsee tower of silence? Eaten by birds." Such a tower, with vultures perched around it, is pictured on p. 156 of Thompson's book.

Also, on p. 368.40/362.23 Bloom's mind moves from a phrase involving "on the track of" directly to thoughts of the East. In the present entry, Bloom's thought "Sunburst on the titlepage" seems to apply to *In the Track of the Sun*, but on p. 709/693 we are told that the title page of his copy is missing. Interestingly, the title page of neither the British nor the American edition bears a sunburst; rather they both depict something Bloom referred to only two lines earlier: an Oriental girl playing a stringed instrument. Possibly the thought of the sunburst comes from the *Freeman* headpiece (see entry 57.35). Certainly the stream of consciousness is moving on several levels here, and Bloom's subconscious memory of the missing title page seems truer than his conscious.

57.35/57.33 WHAT ARTHUR GRIFFITH SAID ABOUT THE HEADPIECE OVER THE *Freeman* LEADER: A HOMERULE SUN RISING UP IN THE NORTHWEST . . .   Griffith, founder of Sinn Fein and the newspaper *United Irishman*, was mentioned by Stephen on p. 43.8/44.6. I have not located the specific remark Bloom attributes to Griffith, but the reference is probably to the emblem of the *Freeman's Journal*, which depicts the Bank of Ireland with the sun rising behind it, and underneath the inscrolled motto "Ireland a Nation." Since the Bank of Ireland on College Green (which once housed the Irish parliament) faces slightly east of south, the sun rising behind it is rising in the northwest. The remark also expresses Griffith's attitude toward the *Freeman's Journal*, which he felt was only pseudo-nationalistic.

58.7/58.5 MY BOLD LARRY   In view of the reference to Larry O'Rourke as "bold Larry O" on p. 281.38/277.17, I suspect that this alludes to an Irish ballad entitled "Bold Traynor O." The ballad is mentioned by title by John Hand in an article entitled "Street Songs and Ballads and Anonymous Verse," in *Irish Literature*, III, 3265–71. Hand lists "Bold Traynor O" among several songs that "had an immense run in their day" (p. 3270). I have not located a copy of the song.

58.11/58.9 THE RUSSIANS, THEY'D ONLY BE AN EIGHT O'CLOCK BREAKFAST FOR THE JAPANESE   This is one of the few allusions to the Russo-Japanese War in *Ulysses*, though the war, which lasted from February, 1904, to September, 1905, was in progress on the day of the novel. Richard M. Kain sees the lack of discussion of the war as an example of the inertia of Dublin society (*FV*, pp. 175–76).

58.23/58.21 ADAM FINDLATERS OR DAN TALLONS   Daniel Tallon was Lord Mayor of Dublin in 1899 and 1900. Adam Findlater was apparently a small-time politician in DunLaoghaire (Kingstown). Perhaps Bloom learned of him from Arthur Griffith's *United Irish-*

man, which mentions Findlater on occasion, characterizing him as kowtowing to the English in hope of some preferment. For example, an article in the August 29, 1903, issue concludes, "This evident design of Mr. Adam Findlater to encourage foreign manufacture in Ireland should meet with some recognition from the powers that be. For years past Mr. Findlater has been begging for a knighthood, and there is no reason on earth when Mr. Brown of Dunleary has received one that Mr. Adam Findlater should be considered ineligible" (p. 4, col. d). A similar comment appears in the issue for September 19, 1903, p. 5, col. d.

59.16/59.13 KINNERETH ON THE LAKESHORE OF TIBERIAS Although Kinnereth is not mentioned in the Bible, at the present time Kinneret is a small town on the southwest side of Lake Tiberias (the Sea of Galilee). In John 6:1 the Sea of Tiberias is given as another name for the Sea of Galilee.

59.37/59.34 MAKE HAY WHILE THE SUN SHINES This is a common proverbial phrase. The *ODEP* lists seven instances, dating back as far as 1509.

60.3/59.41 O PLEASE, MR POLICEMAN, I'M LOST IN THE WOOD Hodgart and Worthington list this as an allusion to a music hall song entitled "O Please, Mr. Policeman, I'm Lost in the Wood." I have not located this song, but there were many music hall songs about policemen at this time.

60.39/60.35 MUST BE WITHOUT A FLAW As Joseph Prescott has pointed out ("Notes on Joyce's *Ulysses*," *MLQ*, XIII, 150), Bloom's thought about the necessity for perfect citrons is from a Jewish precept. Prescott quotes a long passage from the *New Edition of the Babylonian Talmud* which specifically discusses citrons. Prescott also points out that Bloom's bookshelf contains *Philosophy of the Talmud* (p. 709/693). This is another of Bloom's thoughts in this episode which centers around his bookshelf. Earlier Stephen thought of his dream in which a melon was associated with the Near East and with some ceremony of entrance (p. 47.7/47.42).

61.3/60.40 HIS BACK IS LIKE THAT NORWEGIAN CAPTAIN'S R. Ellmann briefly recounts the story John Joyce told of a hunchbacked Norwegian captain who berated Dublin tailor J. H. Kerse for being unable to fit him, and who was berated in turn by Kerse for being impossible to fit (*JJ*, pp. 22–23). Joyce uses the story more fully in *Finnegans Wake*, especially pp. 311 ff.

61.5/60.42 ON EARTH AS IT IS IN HEAVEN Another allusion to the Pater Noster. See entry 57.13.

61.12/61.6 BRIMSTONE THEY CALLED IT RAINING DOWN: THE CITIES OF THE PLAIN: SODOM, GOMORRAH, EDOM The cities of the plain are referred to in Genesis 14:2 as Sodom, Gomorrah, Admah, Zeboiim, and Zoar. In Genesis 19:24–25 God's raining down brimstone on the cities is described. Bloom is mistaken in including Edom as one of the cities. Edom was the name given in Genesis 25:30 to Esau, who became father of the Edomites (Gen. 36:9).

61.25/61.19 MUST BEGIN AGAIN THOSE SANDOW'S EXERCISES   This is another allusion involving a book on Bloom's shelf, for he has a book by Eugene [*sic*] Sandow entitled *Physical Strength and How to Obtain It* (p. 709/694). Eugen Sandow (real name Frederick Muller, 1867–1925) was a famous strong man. In *Old Pink 'Un Days* (New York, 1925), J. B. Booth says, "it was at the aquarium [the Royal Aquarium in London] that Eugene [*sic*] Sandow leapt into fame during a 'strong man' boom by challenging Samson from the audience and defeating him" (pp. 308–9). Sandow gives his version of this challenge in his *Strength and How to Obtain It* (London, 1897, pp. 93 ff.). The contest occurred on Saturday, November 2, 1889. Samson gives his own quite different story in the London *Times*, Monday, November 4, 1889, p. 9, col. f. I have found no book by Sandow with the exact title given on p. 709/694. *Strength and How to Obtain It* is probably the book referred to. It does contain instructions for exercises, as well as the "chart of measurements" Bloom mentions on p. 721/706. Sandow did perform at the Empire Palace in Dublin from May 2 until May 14, 1898, but R. M. Adams' reference to this is puzzlingly inaccurate (*SS*, p. 73): The *Freeman's Journal* of May 7, 1898, does not "report" Sandow's performance beyond the usual advertisement on p. 4 (though his performance was reviewed in the issue of May 3, p. 5, col. a), and there is no page nine in the newspaper.

62.36/62.30 SEASIDE GIRLS   This song is alluded to in more detail on p. 67.6/66.35 and p. 67.11/67.1. Although I have not located any song with these exact words, as Hodgart and Worthington point out, "There were innumerable late 19th cent. MH [music hall] songs about seaside girls." Christopher Pulling devotes an entire chapter to them (chap. LV: "They Did Like to be by the Seaside") in his *They Were Singing and What They Sang About* (London, 1952). Pulling quotes a song entitled "All the Girls are Lovely by the Seaside," which begins, "All the girls are lovely by the seaside,/ All the girls are lovely by the sea" (p. 61).

63.1/62.36 O, MILLY BLOOM, YOU ARE MY DARLING ...   The valentine verse Bloom calls to mind is very similar to a quatrain sent to Joyce himself by Eileen Vance (actually written by her father). Stanislaus Joyce (*MBK*, p. 5) and R. Ellmann (*JJ*, p. 31) give slightly different versions of the verse sent to Joyce. In any event the quatrain goes back to one Samuel Lover (1797–1868) printed in the chapter "Ballads and Ballad Singers" in his *Legends and Stories of Ireland* (Philadelphia, 1835), II, 206. The quatrain Lover gives is, "Oh Thady Brady you are my darlin,/ You are my looking-glass from night till morning/ I love you betther without one fardin/ Than Brian Gallagher wid house and garden."

63.31/63.24 LA CI DAREM   This is the first of many allusions in *Ulysses* to the duet by Don Giovanni and Zerlina in act I, scene 8 of Mozart's *Don Giovanni*. The duet begins "La ci darem la mano" ("There we shall join hands"). In the course of the duet Don Giovanni prevails on Zerlina to accept his love. For the text of the duet and a discussion of Joyce's use of *Don Giovanni* in *Ulysses*, see Vernon Hall, Jr., "Joyce's use of Da Ponte and Mozart's *Don Giovanni*," *PMLA*, LXVI (March, 1951), 78–84.

63.31/63.24 LOVE'S OLD SWEET SONG   This very popular song was first published in England in 1884. As we are told in *Ulysses*, p. 706/691, the words are by G. Clifton Bingham (1859–1913), the music by Irish lawyer James Lyman Molloy (1837–1909). The words of this song can be found in Ralph L. Woods, *A Treasury of the Familiar*, p. 620.

64.4/63.38 VOGLIO E NON VORREI . . . VOGLIO   As V. Hall points out, this is a slight misquotation of a line Zerlina sings in her duet with Don Giovanni (see entry 63.31). Bloom's "Voglio e non vorrei" ("I want to, yet I shouldn't") should be "Vorrei e non vorrei" ("I should like to, yet I shouldn't"). R. M. Adams suggests that Bloom's *voglio* comes from his thinking of Leporello's aria earlier in the opera in which he says "non voglio piu servir" ("I will no longer serve"), and that this is picked up in Bloom's statement to Molly's apparition, "At your service," on p. 439/432 (SS, p 71). Bloom recalls the quotation in this entry correctly on p. 93.25/92.19.

64.18/64.10 METEMPSYCHOSIS   *Metempsychosis* is a Greek word meaning transmigration of the soul. The belief in transmigration or reincarnation goes back in Indian thought at least as far as the Upanishads, and it was a part of the early Orphic teachings in Greece. Pythagoras is probably the best-known exponent of the idea. It was also discussed by early Jewish philosophers. In the Kaballah it first emerges in the book *Bahir*, and it came to play an important role in Hadisic belief and literature. According to C. D. Ginsberg, the doctrine was propounded among the early Christians. See his *The Essenes; the Kaballah* (London, 1955), pp. 124–25 and p. 125 fn.

64.25/64.17 RUBY: THE PRIDE OF THE RING   I have not located a book with this exact title. A check of the *Catalogue of Printed Books* in the British Museum, *The Library of Congress Catalogue*, and *The English Catalogue of Books*, vols. I–X (1800–1920) reveals no such title. Still it is very possible that there was a book by this title since the volume of 1 d. and even ½ d. circus literature at this time was great. See for instance the list of English Circus Dime Novels in the *Circus and Allied Arts: A World Bibliography* (Derby, England, 1962), III, 89–105. Many of the titles listed there are very similar to this one—e.g., the anonymous *Circus Tom; or, The Pride of the Ring* (item 5118); or Henry T. Johnson's *The Pride of the Ring, A World Famous Circus Story of Fun, Frolic and Adventure* (item 5199); or Guy Rayner's *Pride of the Ring* (item 5423).

64.29/64.21 TRAPEZE AT HENGLER'S   Hengler's Circus was one of the most popular nineteenth-century English circuses. It was begun about 1857 by the Hengler family, who had long been circus performers. The circus played lengthy runs in Dublin every year. For more information see Ruth Manning-Sanders, *The English Circus* (London, 1952), especially pp. 84–87.

64.31/64.22 BREAK YOUR NECK AND WE'LL BREAK OUR SIDES   J. F. Killeen suggests ("James Joyce's Roman Prototype," *Comparative Literature*, IX [Summer, 1957], 193–203) that this recalls "cuis cervices fractas lebenter vidissent" (*sic*—the quote should be "cuius etiam cervices fractas libenter vidissent," which means, "Whose neck we would have been happy to see broken") from chap. 54 of Petronius' *Satyricon*. But this seems unlikely, especially in Bloom's mind, and the present context is in no way similar to that of the *Satyricon*. More likely, if he did not make the phrase up, Bloom is simply repeating a common circus saying.

64.39/64.30 PAUL DE KOCK'S   Charles-Paul de Kock (1793–1871) was a French author of many novels. He is mentioned on p. 465/457 as the author of *The Girl with the Three Pairs of Stays*. W. Y. Tindall says, "Paul de Kock's novel is actually *The Girl with the Three Skirts*" (*RG*, p. 210), but Joyce is right, for de Kock wrote both. An eleven-volume collection of de Kock's work published by Mathieson and Co., London, n.d., has *The Girl with the Three Pairs of Stays* in vol. 4 and *The Girl with the Three Petticoats* in vol. 9. De Kock was mentioned by Joyce in his notes for *Exiles* (1952 ed., p. 175), and Ellmann lists de Kock's *Le Cocu* among Joyce's books in Trieste (*JJ*, p. 794).

65.12/65.1 PHOTO BITS   According to the *British Union-Catalogue of Periodicals*, *Photo Bits* was first published on July 9, 1898. *Willing's Press Guide . . . 1905* (for 1904) lists it as appearing on Tuesdays at a price of one pence.

65.15/65.4   NAKED NYMPHS: GREECE   In Greek myth, nymphs were inferior female deities, distinguished by the spheres of nature with which they were associated. They were usually associated with groves, springs, rivers, mountains, valleys, or cool grottoes. Many of Homer's heroes have nymphs as lemans. In their translation of the *Odyssey*, Butcher and Lang frequently refer to Calypso as "that fair goddess" or "the nymph Calypso."

66.8/65.38   BEEF TO THE HEELS   Fritz Senn has pointed out (*JJQ*, II, 136–37) that this phrase is included in P. W. Joyce's *English As We Speak It*, p. 136, where we read, "When a woman has very thick legs, thick almost down to the feet, she is 'like a Mullingar heifer, beef to the heels.'" The *ODEP* lists this phrase and includes an instance from Samuel Lover's *Rory O'More* (1837). Senn suggests, I think correctly, that Milly has heard the phrase from her boy friend, Bannon, who uses it on p. 397.20/390.41 of Milly herself.

66.15/66.4   SONG ABOUT THOSE SEASIDE GIRLS   See entry 62.36.

67.6/66.35   ALL DIMPLED CHEEKS AND CURLS . . .   From the song about the seaside girls; see entry 62.36. Other lines are quoted on p. 67.11/67.1.

67.39/67.29   TITBITS   *Titbits from all the most interesting books, periodicals, and contributors in the world* began publication on October 22, 1881, and is still being published. *Willing's Press Guide . . . 1905* (for 1904) describes it as being published on Thursday for Saturday at a price of one pence. See entry 68.39.

68.7/67.37   THE MAID WAS IN THE GARDEN   An allusion to the nursery rhyme "Sing a Song of Sixpence." For the full text of the rhyme and interesting comments on its origin and suggested meanings, see *ODNR*, pp. 394–95.

68.26/68.15   CHAP IN THE WAXBOX THERE GOT AWAY JAMES STEPHENS THEY SAY   Apparently Bloom is alluding to James Stephens' celebrated escape from Richmond Jail, Dublin, in 1865. Stephen thought of this event earlier (see entry 43.25). In the source cited in the earlier entry, MacManus mentions that Stephens had to hide in an empty sentry-box at one point in his escape.

68.27/68.16   O'BRIEN   Probably Bloom is here alluding to William Smith O'Brien whom he thinks of later in "Hades" (entry 93.11). O'Brien (1803–64) was an Irish landowner in county Clare and a leader in the Repeal Movement. In 1846 O'Brien and others seceded from Daniel O'Connell's Repeal Association to form the Irish Confederation. On July 29, 1848, O'Brien and some peasants engaged a garrison of police at Ballingary in Tipperary and several people were killed in the skirmish. O'Brien was found guilty of high trea-

son and sentenced to death, but the sentence was later commuted to
penal servitude. Later he was unconditionally pardoned. James
Stephens was also involved in the Ballingary affair as an aide to
O'Brien, which is probably why Bloom thinks of them together.
Stephens was slightly wounded, but escaped by shamming death.

68.32/68.21 THE LOW LINTEL   In his "Inscription for a Friend's
House," Henry Van Dyke (1852–1933) writes of "The lintel low
enough to keep out pomp and pride." While the allusion seems
perhaps unlikely, Joyce's saying, "He went in, bowing his head
under the low lintel" in depicting Bloom's defecation (which he
spares Stephen), contributes importantly to our impression of
Bloom as a man without "pomp and pride."

68.35/68.24 THE KING WAS IN HIS COUNTING HOUSE   From "Sing a
Song of Sixpence." See entry 68.7.

68.39/68.27 MATCHAM'S MASTERSTROKE. WRITTEN BY MR PHILIP BEAU-
FOY   *The Catalogue of Printed Books* in the British Museum
lists one book by Philip Beaufoy, entitled *The Dosing of Cuthbert
and Other Stories for Boys* (London: Thos. Nelson & Sons, 1927).
(According to information from the publisher, only one of the
stories in the book—the title story—was written by Beaufoy.) Of
Beaufoy, Stanislaus Joyce says, ". . . if I am not greatly mistaken
he was, and I hope still is, a real person who had various stories accepted by *Titbits* in those years" (*MBK*, pp. 91–92). *Titbits* did
include a "Prize Tit-bit" in each issue, with the statement "Payment at the rate of One Guinea per column has been sent to the
author." A check of an incomplete file of the periodical for 1903–4
revealed one story by "Mr. P. Beaufoy, 6, Clement's Inn, W.C."
entitled "A Mysterious Post-Card" (Nov. 7, 1903, pp. 157–58), but
probably a fuller file would turn up a story bearing the address
Joyce uses. However, the lines from "Matcham's Masterstroke"
quoted on p. 69.12/68.41 ff. are probably not Beaufoy's since Stanislaus says that James Joyce himself wrote a story using the words
"laughing witch" which he intended to send to *Titbits* (*MBK*, p.
91). Beaufoy is mentioned again on p. 69.16/69.3.

69.28/69.14 PONCHIELLI'S DANCE OF THE HOURS   The very popular
"Dance of the Hours" occurs in act three of Amilcare Ponchielli's
La Gioconda (1876). It is a "ballet suite which, in costume changes,
light effects, and choreography represents the hours of dawn, day,
evening, and night. It is also intended to symbolize, in its mimic
action, the eternal struggle between the powers of darkness and
light" (*Kobbe's Complete Opera Book* [rev. ed.; London, 1954]).
The allusion is continued on p. 69.38/69.24.

71.16/70.16   MET HER ONCE IN THE PARK. IN THE DARK. WHAT A LARK . . .
If Bloom's memory of Corny Kelleher's singing represents an actual
song, I have not yet located it. Perhaps it is the same song Bloom
sings on p. 491.5/481.13. The "tooraloom" refrain occurs several
times in *Ulysses*, not always in association with any lyrics. Hodgart and Worthington have no note on Bloom's lilting, either here
or on p. 491/481.

71.40/70.40   FLOWERS OF IDLENESS   W. Y. Tindall sees this as alluding to Byron (*RG*, p. 158). One of Byron's earliest collections of
poems was entitled *Hours of Idleness* (1807).

71.41/70.41   BOTANIC GARDENS   W. Y. Tindall (*RG*, p. 158) lists this
as an allusion to Erasmus Darwin (1731–1802), who wrote a long
poem entitled *The Botanic Garden* (1791). However, this seems
unlikely; there are botanic gardens in Dublin. See p. 108.29/107.12.

71.42/70.41   SENSITIVE PLANTS   W. Y. Tindall lists this as an allusion
to Shelley (*RG*, p. 158). Shelley wrote a sentimental poem entitled
"The Sensitive Plant."

72.40/71.39   MAUD GONNE'S LETTER   The problem of British soldiers

on the Dublin streets was being discussed via letters to the newspapers in May and June, 1904. The *Freeman's Journal* of June 3,
1904, had a letter from Mr. Alfred Webb to Mrs. Maud Gonne
MacBride, complimenting her for her effort concerning the problem (p. 3, col. f). However, I have not yet located a letter from
Mrs. MacBride herself on the topic.

72.41/71.40 GRIFFITH'S PAPER   Arthur Griffith's (see entry 43.8)
paper was *The United Irishman*, which he and poet William
Rooney (1873–1901) founded in 1899. It ran from March 4, 1899,
through April 14, 1906, and was superseded by *Sinn Fein*.

73.39/72.38 HANDSOME IS AND HANDSOME DOES   The saying Bloom
misquotes is proverbial; the *ODEP lists* "Handsome is that handsome does" and cites four instances from 1580 onwards, including
John Ray's *Proverbs* (1670) and *The Vicar of Wakefield* (1776),
chap. 1.

73.41/72.40 AND BRUTUS IS AN HONORABLE MAN   Mark Antony repeats this ironic statement several times in his oration over Caesar
in *Julius Caesar*, III, ii.

74.6/73.5 VEILED EYELIDS   This and other references to eyelids in
this episode (p. 71.28/70.28 and p. 75.8/74.6) may echo Tennyson's
distinctive line "tir'd eyelids upon tir'd eyes" in "The Lotus-
Eaters." Also, in *Hamlet*, Queen Gertrude says to Hamlet, "Do not
forever with thy vailèd lids/ Seek for thy noble father in the dust."
I, ii, 70–71).

74.30/73.28 PARADISE AND THE PERI   "Paradise and the Peri" is the
title of the second section of Thomas Moore's very popular *Lalla
Rookh* (1817). It has been set to music several times, probably best
known in Robert Schumann's "Das Paradies und die Peri," a work
for solos, chorus, and orchestra, first performed in Dublin on February 10, 1854. The peri, in Persian mythology, are creatures descended from the fallen angels and excluded from paradise until
their penance is done.

75.14/74.12 QUEEN WAS IN HER BEDROOM EATING BREAD AND   From
the nursery rhyme "Sing a Song of Sixpence." See entry 68.7.

75.18/74.16 LOVE'S/ OLD/ SWEET/ SONG . . .   An allusion to "Love's
Old Sweet Song"; the allusion is repeated on p. 75.24/74.22. See
entry 63.31.

76.23/75.19 LEAH   There were several plays by this title in the nineteenth century; apparently the one Bloom is referring to is *Leah,
the Jewish Maiden*, which was written by American dramatist and
theater manager Augustin Daly (1838–99). The play first opened
in Boston in December, 1862, under the title *Leah the Forsaken*.

It first played in England at the Adelphi Theatre in London on
October 1, 1863, with Kate Bateman in the leading role. Daly's play
was one of several current adaptations of S. H. Mosenthal's play,
Deborah, which was first performed in Hamburg on January 15,
1849, and first published in Budapest the same year. For further
information on Mosenthal's play and the use Joyce makes of it,
see J. Prescott's "Mosenthal's *Deborah* and Joyce's *Ulysses*," *MLN*,
LXVII, 334–36. See also the following entries.

76.23/75.19   MRS. BANDMAN PALMER . . . HAMLET SHE PLAYED LAST NIGHT
Mrs. Bandmann-Palmer (nee Millicent Palmer; died 1905) was a
well-known actress of the period. She made her London debut as
Pauline in Charles Dance's *Delicate Ground* in November, 1864.
W. D. Adams says that "in 1892 she appeared for the first time as
Hamlet, a *role* which she has since performed very frequently both
in London and in the English provinces" (*Dictionary of Drama*,
London, 1904, p. 106). According to newspapers of the day, *Leah*
was playing at the Gaiety at this time; see R. M. Kain, *FV*, p. 57.
See also entry 198.24.

76.25/75.21   PERHAPS HE WAS A WOMAN   The theory that Hamlet
was a woman dressed and educated as a man was proposed by Ed
ward Payson Vining (who is mentioned by name on p. 198.25/
196.9) in his book *Mystery of Hamlet: An Attempt to Solve an Old
Problem* (Philadelphia, 1881). Vining seems to have had a penchant
for the exotic; he also wrote a book entitled *An Inglorious Columbus; or, Evidence that Hwui Shan and a Party of Buddhist Monks
from Afghanistan Discovered America in the Fifth Century, A.D.*

76.25/75.21   WHY OPHELIA COMMITTED SUICIDE   Bloom suggests that
Ophelia's learning that Hamlet was a woman might provide an
explanation for her suicide (*Ham.*, IV, vii). See the preceding entry.

76.26/75.22   KATE BATEMAN . . . THE ADELPHI   Kate Bateman (1842–
1917) was born in Baltimore and achieved fame as an actress in the
U.S. and in England. Her best-known roles were Leah, Juliet, Lady
Macbeth, and Medea. The opening of *Leah* on October 1, 1863,
at the Adelphi in London with Kate Bateman in the leading role
(see entry 76.23) is described in Charles Lamb Kenney's pamphlet
The New Actress and the New Play at the Adelphi Theatre (Lon-
don, 1863). Kenney discusses Mosenthal's play briefly and praises
Bateman highly. Interestingly, he compares her with Ristori and
Rachel (see following entries).

76.29/75.24   RISTORI   Adelaide Ristori (The Marchessa Capranica
del Grillo, 1821–1906) was a famous Italian actress. L. D. Ventura
in his *Memoirs and Artistic Studies of Adelaide Ristori* (New York,

1907) lists Mosenthal's *Deborah* as one of the "plays in which Ristori shone" (pp. 236–37).

76.29/75.25 MOSENTHAL   Solomon Hermann Von Mosenthal (1821–77) was a German dramatist, novelist, and librettist. His *Deborah* was popular in Germany and was adapted in English by several dramatists.

76.30/75.26 RACHEL   Here Bloom is trying to remember the name of Mosenthal's play, *Deborah*. The name Rachel may have been suggested by her being Leah's sister (Gen. 29) or, though the difference in pronunciation makes this less likely, by the famous French actress, Rachel (Elisa Felix, 1821–58).

76.30/75.26 THE SCENE HE WAS ALWAYS TALKING ABOUT WHERE THE OLD BLIND ABRAHAM RECOGNIZES THE VOICE AND PUTS HIS FINGERS ON HIS FACE. NATHAN'S VOICE . . .   This refers to a scene in Mosenthal's *Deborah*, act II, scene xiv. Prescott (*op. cit.*, entry 76.23) quotes from the German text to show its similarity. Since Bloom's father seems to have seen both Mosenthal's German original, *Deborah* (done by Ristori in Vienna), and Daly's English adaptation, *Leah* (with Kate Bateman at the Adelphi), I examined the text of both at this point and found the German closer to what Bloom remembers.

77.4/75.41 ELDORADO   Eldorado was a legendary South American treasure city sought by the Spaniards. The implication is that the horses have no unfulfilled desires. *Eldorado* means "the gilded," and there are interesting associations of sound and meaning among *Eldorado*, the *gilded* oats the horses eat, and their being *gelded*.

77.15/76.11 VOGLIO E NON . . . LA CI DAREM LA MANO   These are lines from a duet by Don Giovanni and Zerlina in act I of Mozart's *Don Giovanni*. See entries 63.31 and 64.4.

77.25/76.21 A BLINKING SPHINX   The Sphinx has been an art object, object of veneration, and symbol of wisdom in Middle Eastern and Greek culture for thousands of years. In ancient Egypt the Sphinx frequently symbolized the Pharaoh in his divine role as the sun-god, Ra. In the Oedipus legend the Sphinx had confounded all men with her riddle, "What walks on four feet in the morning, on two at noon, and on three in the evening?" and she killed all who failed to answer it. Finally Oedipus solved it by saying that man first crawls, then walks upright, and later uses a cane.

77.26/76.22 MOHAMMED CUT A PIECE OUT OF HIS MANTLE NOT TO WAKE HER   Though I have not verified it personally, I have been told on good authority that the story of Mohammed's cutting his mantle to prevent waking a cat is told in the *Sahīh* of Bukhari (d. 870). Bukhari (Mohammed ibn Ismail al-Bukhari) was a scholar and a

Moslem saint. The *Sahīh*, his collection of traditions concerning the Prophet, is second only to the *Koran* in importance for Moslems.

78.35/77.30 NO ROSES WITHOUT THORNS This is proverbial; the *ODEP* lists nine instances from the fifteenth to the nineteenth centuries.

78.38/77.33 O, MARY LOST THE PIN OF HER DRAWERS . . . Hodgart and Worthington list "O, Mary Lost the Pin of Her Drawers" as a song, but give no author, nationality, or source. I have not been able to trace the song. The allusion is continued on p. 79.5/78.3 and p. 79.10/78.7.

79.6/78.4 MARTHA, MARY. I SAW THAT PICTURE SOMEWHERE . . . Martha and Mary were the sisters of Lazarus (John 11). There have been many paintings depicting this scene, but I have not yet found one that conforms with the details Bloom gives. The National Gallery of Ireland now has two paintings of this subject—one by Eustache LeSueur (1616–55) and one by Peter Paul Rubens (*fl.* 1577–1640)—but only the Reubens was in the Gallery in 1904, and neither painting is similar to Bloom's description.

79.24/78.21 LORD IVEAGH . . . LORD ARDILAUN . . . Edward Cecil Guinness (1847–1927) was raised to the peerage as Baron Iveagh in 1891; his brother, Arthur Edward Guinness (1840–1915), was raised to the peerage as Baron Ardilaun in 1880. Both were sons of Sir Benjamin Lee Guinness (1798–1868).

80.4/79.1 SAINT PETER CLAVER AND THE AFRICAN MISSION A Spanish Jesuit saint (*ca.* 1581–1654), Claver left Spain forever in 1610 to become the "slave of the Negroes" in the New World. He ministered to them as soon as they were taken off the ships in Cartagena, Colombia. According to Butler's *Lives of the Saints* (III, 524; Sept. 9), Claver was "declared by Pope Leo XIII patron of all missionary enterprises among Negroes, in whatever part of the world." He was canonized in 1888.

80.5/79.1 THE HEATHEN CHINEE Bret Harte wrote a poem entitled "The Heathen Chinee" (sometimes "Plain Language from Truthful James"). S. Spaeth points out that the poem has been twice set to music, once by Henry Tucker, and once in 1870 by F. Boott (*Hist. of Pop. Music in Amer.*, pp. 173, 176).

80.7/79.4 PRAYERS FOR THE CONVERSION OF GLADSTONE THEY HAD TOO William E. Gladstone (1809–98) was for many years the British prime minister. Though I have not verified that prayers were held for Gladstone's conversion, Bloom's proximate reference to Dr. William Walsh makes interesting the following excerpt from a letter from Walsh to his diocese requesting prayers for the dying

Gladstone (it is also stylistically interesting for any reader of the "Eumaeus" episode): "Withdrawn for ever from the connections of public life, Mr. Gladstone in his present state of patient suffering attracts the sympathy not only of those who in his years of energetic public service venerated him as a political leader, but also, and perhaps even more especially, of others who in public offices were his strenuous opponents. From a respected Irish Catholic gentleman the thoughtful suggestion has come within the last few days that if any opportunity presented itself I should ask the faithful of the diocese to discharge some portion of the debt of gratitude which we owe to Mr. Gladstone by now remembering him in our prayers before the Throne of Mercy. I feel grateful for the suggestion. Doubtless through this letter it will be the means of obtaining for our venerable benefactor of former years many prayers, and in particular a prayer that God in whom he always trusted may now in his hour of suffering be pleased to send him comfort and relief to lighten his heavy burden, and to give him strength and patience to bear it, in so far as in the designs of Providence it may have to be borne for his greater good" (quoted in David Williamson's *William Ewart Gladstone: Statesman and Scholar* [New York, 1898], pp. 416–17; Williamson doesn't date the letter, but it appears to have been written in the spring of 1898, a short time before Gladstone's death on May 19, 1898).

80.9/79.6 DR. WILLIAM J. WALSH D.D.   Walsh (1841–1921) was Roman Catholic Archbishop of Dublin. Joyce mentioned Walsh in his satiric poem "Gas from a Burner" (1912): "For everyone knows the Pope can't belch/ Without the consent of Billy Walsh" (*CW*, p. 243).

80.10/79.7 BUDDHA THEIR GOD LYING ON HIS SIDE IN THE MUSEUM The Oriental Collection of the National Museum now contains several statues depicting Buddha recumbent in the traditional posture. The largest of these statues, which is approximately fifty-four inches long, came into the Museum in 1891, so it could have been available to Bloom. Molly later mentions such a statue on p. 771.34/756.36.

80.12/79.9 ECCE HOMO. CROWN OF THORNS AND CROSS   "Ecce Homo" ("Behold the man") were the words of Pilate in John 19:5 when Christ was brought before him wearing the crown of thorns and the purple robe. Joyce may also have had in mind the painting "Ecce Homo" by the Hungarian painter Michael Munkacsy (1844–1900), which was on display at the Royal Hibernian Academy in

1899, and about which Joyce wrote an essay. See "Royal Hibernian Academy 'Ecce Homo,'" *CW*, pp. 31–37.

80.12/79.9 CLEVER IDEA ST. PATRICK THE SHAMROCK   According to legend, St. Patrick (*ca.* 389–*ca.* 461), the patron saint of Ireland, used the three-in-one structure of the shamrock leaf to explain the doctrine of the Trinity to the Irish king Laoghaire. But P. Colum doubts that St. Patrick would have made use of so inadequate an illustration. Colum says that the Irish wore the shamrock because it resembled the cross, and the association with the Trinity is an afterthought (*Treasury of Irish Folklore*, pp. 119, 395).

80.24/79.21 WHO IS MY NEIGHBOR   This is the lawyer's question to Christ in Luke 10:29, in answer to which Christ tells the parable of the Good Samaritan.

80.26/79.23 SEVENTH HEAVEN   While this may allude to the Ptolemaic cosmology, it more likely alludes to the Jewish (and Moslem) "heaven of heavens." The *OED* says (*s.v.* heaven, 5.c) "By the Jews (at least in later times) seven heavens were recognized; the highest, called also 'heaven of heavens,' being the abode of God and the most exalted angels. Thence also the seven heavens of Mohammed."

80.34/79.30 SHUT YOUR EYES AND OPEN YOUR MOUTH   Hodgart and Worthington list this as an allusion to the nursery rhyme "Close your eyes and open your mouth," which seems likely, although I have not been able to locate a printed text of the rhyme.

81.7/80.3 HOKYPOKY PENNY A LUMP   The *OED* defines hokeypokey as "a cheap kind of ice cream, sold by street vendors," and mentions an article in the *Pall Mall Gazette*, September 25, 1888, which explains the origin of "Hokey pokey, a penny a lump" through an incident tending to identify the phrase with the Italian "O che poco!" ("O how little"). Apparently this was a street vendor's song. Hodgart and Worthington list this as an allusion to a nursery rhyme and street song and list several variants. I. and P. Opie print a rhyme beginning "Hokey, pokey, whisky thum" in the *ODNR*, p. 211.

81.12/80.7 LOURDES CURE   Lourdes is a town in southwestern France where visions of the Virgin Mary appeared to a peasant girl, Bernadette Soubrious, February 11, 1858, and other times. It has long been famous for the miraculous cures effected there.

81.12/80.8 WATERS OF OBLIVION   Though I have not found a source for this exact phrase, the association of water with oblivion is common and traditional. Recall, for instance, Shakespeare's "swallowing gulf/ Of blind forgetfulness and dark oblivion" (*Richard III*, III, vii, 128–29), and Milton's "Lethe, the river of oblivion . . . whereof who drinks/ Forthwith his former state and being forgets" (*Paradise Lost*, II, 583–85).

81.12/80.8 THE KNOCK APPARITION   An appearance of the Virgin Mary with St. Joseph and St. John the Evangelist was seen by a number of people at Knock, county Mayo, on August 21, 1879. Other visions were seen in January and February, 1880, and many miraculous cures were effected there.

81.14/80.10 SAFE IN THE ARMS OF KINGDOM COME   This alludes to a gospel funeral hymn entitled "Safe in the Arms of Jesus" (or "Safety in Jesus"), written about 1868 by Frances J. Van Alstyne (nee Crosby) and set to music by W. H. Doane. Bloom's alteration of this well-known title is probably another instance of his aversion to speaking the name of *Jesus*, which S. Gilbert has noted (*JJU*, p. 154 fn.).

81.18/80.14 SUPPOSE HE LOST THE PIN OF HIS   Another allusion to the "Mary" song; see entry 78.38.

81.20/80.16 I.N.R.I.   This stands for *Iesus Nazarenus, Rex Iudaeorum* (Jesus of Nazareth, King of the Jews), which John says was the inscription Pilate had placed on Christ's cross (John 19:19).

81.20/80.16 I.H.S.   This originally came from the first three letters of the Greek word for *Jesus* (iota, eta, sigma), but it has popularly become regarded as the abbreviation for various phrases, among them *Iesus Hominum Salvator*—Jesus, Saviour of Men; *In Hoc Signo* (*Vinces*)—In this sign (thou shalt conquer); and *In Hac Salus*—In this (cross) is salvation. See *OED, s.v.* IHS.

81.26/80.22 THAT FELLOW THAT TURNED QUEEN'S EVIDENCE ON THE INVINCIBLES . . . DENIS CAREY   The Invincible Society was a small secret organization formed in Dublin about December, 1881. It contained approximately twenty members, all Fenians, and their aim was the assassination of Irish government officials who supported and implemented England's policy of coercion. On May 6, 1882, some members of the Invincibles assassinated the newly appointed Chief Secretary, Lord Frederick Cavendish, and an undersecretary at Dublin Castle named T. H. Burke. The murder took place in Phoenix Park, Dublin. Apparently Burke, an Irishman who had been supporting English policy, was their real target, and Lord Cavendish was slain because he was with Burke and could have identified the assassins. The murders were a serious blow to Ireland's hopes for Home Rule and self-determination, since the new Chief Secretary, Lord Cavendish, was much more sympathetic to Ireland's

cause than was the man he replaced, William E. (Buckshot) Forster
(on whom see entry 656.39). When the assassins were tried in
1883, one of the main sources of evidence against them was James
Carey (1845–83), a member of the group who turned Queen's
evidence. Carey was a respected Dublin builder and Town Coun-
cilor and was known as a very religious man. He was among the
leaders of the Invincibles and was an accomplice in the assassina-
tions. After his testimony helped win the conviction of several
members of the group, Carey and his family secretly shipped out
on the *Kinfauns Castle,* using the name Power. However, he was
slain on shipboard on the high seas on July 29, 1883, by a man
named Patrick O'Donnell, who was an agent of the Invincibles.
(Further information on Carey's murder can be found in the day-
by-day reports in the London *Times* from July 31 to Aug. 10,
1883). Bloom's thought that Carey had six children when the
murder was being plotted is amazingly accurate: in a London *Times*
interview of February 20, 1883, Mrs. Carey says that they have
seven children, and that the youngest is a baby two months old
(*Times,* Feb. 20, 1883, 10 c). Bloom's confusion about Carey's
name is partly due to his having a brother named Peter, who was
also involved in the Phoenix Park slayings. Bloom gets James' name
right on p. 163.19/161.5, but forgets it again in the fatigue of early
morning on p. 642.9/626.16.

81.29/80.25 PETER CLAVER   See entry 80.4.

82.9/81.3 THE STABAT MATER OF ROSSINI   The *Stabat Mater* ("The
Mother was standing") is a medieval poem and hymn on the Virgin
at the cross. The original author is not known, but the work is
usually attributed to Innocent III (d. 1216) or to Jacopone da
Todi (d. 1306). The Italian composer Rossini (1792–1868) did one
of the best-known settings.

82.15/81.8 QUIS EST HOMO   These are the opening words of a
soprano duet that occurs early in Rossini's setting of the *Stabat
Mater.* For information about an April, 1904, concert in Dublin
in which this was sung by a woman named Mollie, see R. M. Adams,
SS, p. 68.

82.16/81.9 MERCADANTE: SEVEN LAST WORDS   Though Italian composer Saverio Mercadante (1795–1870) was prolific—he wrote sixty
operas—he apparently did not write a version of the Seven Last
Words. Bloom's knowledge of composers and their works is often
erroneous and inconsistent; see, for example, entries 661.8 ff.

82.17/81.10 MOZART'S TWELFTH MASS: THE GLORIA IN THAT   As
Hodgart and Worthington point out, Bloom is probably thinking

of the spurious work still often called "Mozart's Twelfth Mass." It was the twelfth Mass in the collection published by Vincent Novello in the early nineteenth century. This spurious Mass was numbered by Kochel K. Anh. 232; the true Twelfth Mass is K. 262 (Einstein's no. 246a).

82.19/81.12 PALESTRINA   Giovanni Pierluigi Palestrina (1524–94) was a master of polyphonic sacred music. Since this reference occurs immediately after Bloom has thought of the popes as patrons of the arts, he may be thinking specifically of the Mass for Pope Marcellus, which Stephen thought of on p. 21.3/22.23. Pope Julius III, Pope Marcellus II, and Pope Pius IV all were patrons of Palestrina.

82.40/81.32   GLORIA AND IMMACULATE VIRGIN. JOSEPH HER SPOUSE. PETER AND PAUL   Bloom is thinking of a familiar passage in Catholic prayers: "by the intercession of the glorious and immaculate virgin Mary, Mother of God, of saint Joseph her spouse, of thy blessed apostles Peter and Paul. . . ." This passage occurs in a prayer frequently used after low Mass. The *gloria* in this phrase may be a misprint for *glorious*; R. M. Adams says that it is (*SS*, p. 166) and points out that both the Rosenbach MS and the *Little Review* versions read *glorious*. But this evidence is not conclusive, for Joyce made many changes in the *Little Review* version, even on occasion introducing errors into it (see, for example, entry 34.42), and Bloom's *gloria* could be a vague echo of p. 82.17/81.10.

83.6/81.40   WALLS HAVE EARS   This proverbial saying occasionally occurs alone, but more often in combination with some other. The *ODEP* lists many instances of "Fields (Hedges) have eyes, and woods (walls) have ears." In Swift's *Polite Conversation*, third conversation, Miss Notable says to Lady Smart, "Ay, Madam, but they say Hedges have Eyes, and Walls have Ears" (p. 167). Partridge's note traces the origin and development of the phrase.

83.16/82.7   THE PRIEST IN THE FERMANAGH WILL CASE IN THE WITNESS BOX   Bloom is apparently thinking of a recent trial, probably reported in the *Freeman's Journal*, but I have not located the incident referred to.

83.18/82.10   THE DOCTORS OF THE CHURCH   As Bloom is perhaps aware, "doctor of the church" is an official title, bestowed on those distinguished for their eminence in theology and their holiness. The title was first conferred by Pope Boniface VIII in 1295 on St. Gregory the Great, St. Ambrose, St. Augustine, and St. Jerome, who are known as the "four doctors." The title has been conferred on only a few even to this day; see *Catholic Encyclopedia*, V, 75.

83.22/82.13 BLESSED MICHAEL, ARCHANGEL . . .   This entire paragraph gives verbatim a prayer that is often said after low Mass.

83.36/82.27 GLIMPSES OF THE MOON   In his first encounter with the
ghost, Hamlet says, "What may this mean/ That thou, dead corse,
again, in complete steel,/ Revisit'st thus the glimpses of the moon
. . ." (*Ham.*, I, iv, 51–53). Bloom's use of the phrase is typically
unlike that in its original context.

84.15/83.5 QUEST FOR THE PHILOSOPHER'S STONE. THE ALCHEMISTS
One of the main goals of the alchemists was the discovery of the
"Philosopher's Stone," which would enable them to transmute base
metals into gold.

85.1/83.32 ONE OF THE OLD QUEEN'S SONS, DUKE OF ALBANY WAS IT? HAD
ONLY ONE SKIN. LEOPOLD YES   Apparently this is Bloom's interpretation of the fact that Leopold, Duke of Albany (1853–84), the
youngest of Victoria's sons, suffered from hemophilia. He died as
a result of the breaking of a blood vessel in his head. See Hector
Bolitho, *The Reign of Queen Victoria* (New York, 1948), pp.
197, 314.

86.15/85.2 FLESHPOTS OF EGYPT   From Exodus 16:3. See entry 41.32.

86.19/85.7 CYCLIST DOUBLED UP LIKE A COD IN A POT   Hodgart and
Worthington list this as an allusion to "Johnny I hardly Knew Ye,"
an anonymous Irish Ballad about a man who returns from battle
without eyes, arms, legs, or nose. One line in the fourth stanza says
"Like a cod you're doubled up head and tail." For full words and
several parodies, see K. Hoagland, pp. 271–74. Since the only allusions to the song in *Ulysses* are to the phrase "doubled up like a
cod in a pot," the allusion seems conjectural.

86.30/85.18 AND THE SKULLS WE WERE ACRACKING WHEN M'CARTHY
TOOK THE FLOOR   Hodgart and Worthington list this as an allusion to "When McCarthy took the flute at Inniscorthy," and say
"Constantine Curran, in a BBC broadcast on Joyce, spoke of Joyce
singing 'When McCarthy took the flute at Inniscorthy.' The transcription of the broadcast contains many errors, and it is likely that
Curran and *Ulysses* have reference to the same song, which remains
unidentified." R. Ellmann lists a song entitled "The Man Who
Played the Flute at Inniscorthy" as "among the Irish songs Joyce
swaggered or sighed" (*JJ*, p. 53). I have not identified the song.

86.32/85.20 WHICH IN THE STREAM OF LIFE WE TRACE IS DEARER THAN
THEM ALL   This is a misquote from the ballad "In Happy Moments Day by Day" in act II of W. Vincent Wallace's (1814–65)
opera *Maritana* (text by Edward Fitzball; *première* at Drury Lane
in London, Nov. 15, 1845). In this ballad, the words of which are

by Alfred Bunn, the unscrupulous courtier Don Jose de Santarem is recalling his first sight of the Queen of Spain. The ballad ends, "Some thoughts none other can replace,/ Remembrance will recall;/ Which in the flight of years we trace,/ Is dearer than them all,/ Which in the flight of years we trace,/ Is dearer than them all."

86.35/85.23 THIS IS MY BODY   This is said in the Consecration of the Host in the Mass and occurs in the Bible in Matthew 26:26, Mark 14:22, and Luke 22:19.

86.41/85.29 THE LIMP FATHER OF THOUSANDS   E. C. McAleer has pointed out the following passage from Thomas Inman's *Ancient Faiths Embodied in Ancient Names*, I, 80: "Whilst attending hospital practice in London, I heard a poor Irishman apostrophise his diseased organ as 'You father of thousands.'" McAleer suggests that Inman may have been Joyce's source, or this may simply be "a descriptive term current among his countrymen" ("The 'Father of Thousands' Image in *Ulysses*," *Notes and Queries*, IX [Aug., 1962], 306–7). McAleer incorrectly cites the author's name as Thomas Ingram; it is Thomas Inman. The book McAleer cites was published in two volumes in 1868–69. And while McAleer's suggestion is sound, the emphasis on plants and botany in this episode prompts me to point out that "father of thousands" is a slight variation of the name of a common house plant, known as "mother of thousands" (*Saxifraga sarmentosa*).

87.18/86.18 SLOP ABOUT IN SLIPPERSLAPPERS   Old Mother Slipper Slopper is a character in a nursery rhyme printed in *ODNR*, pp. 173–75. The rhyme, whose first line is "A fox jumped up one winter's night," is about a fox's stealing a goose and taking it home to his family. The fourth stanza begins "Old Mother Slipper Slopper jumped out of bed,/ And out of the window she popped her head." The *ODNR* says, "This rollicking song is traditional both in England and America, the fourth verse being a particular favorite and sometimes appearing alone." Mother Slipperslapper is referred to on p. 475.19/466.24, and woman's slipperslappers on p. 586.16/571.7.

87.36/86.34 THE WHEELS RATTLED ROLLING OVER THE COBBLED CAUSE-WAY   As Hodgart and Worthington explain, this is an allusion to the song "The Pauper's Drive," which is alluded to several times in this episode (e.g., p. 96.12/95.2). The words are by Englishman Thomas Noel, music by J. J. Hutchinson. According to Helen K. Johnson, the idea of the song was suggested to Noel by his "seeing a funeral where the body was borne upon a cart at full speed." The refrain of the song goes "Rattle his bones over the stones:/ He's only a pauper whom nobody owns!" For words, music, and commentary, see Helen K. Johnson, *Our Familiar Songs*, pp. 630–32.

88.15/87.13 FIDUS ACHATES   The loyal or faithful Achates was a friend of Aeneas, and this phrase recurs in the *Aeneid* (e.g., VI, 158; VIII, 521; XII, 384). (The phrase is now often used ironically.) For our purposes the most important use of the phrase is that in Book VI of the *Aeneid* (l. 158), which describes Aeneas and his "faithful Achates" just before Aeneas' descent into Hades. This prepares for other allusions to Book VI of the *Aeneid* which occur later in this episode.

88.19/87.17 THE WISE CHILD THAT KNOWS HER OWN FATHER   This is an adaptation of Launcelot's statement in *The Merchant of Venice*, II, ii, 80, to his father, old Gobbo, that "It is a wise father that knows his own child." Old Gobbó, who is nearsighted, has just failed to recognize Launcelot as his son.

88.36/87.34 I'LL TICKLE HIS CATASTROPHE   In *II Henry IV*, II, i, 66, Falstaff's page says to Mistress Quickly, "I'll tickle your catastrophe."

90.21/89.19 THY WILL BE DONE   Another allusion to the Pater Noster or Lord's Prayer. See entries 57.11 and 60.42.

91.1/89.40 THE CROPPY BOY   This well-known Irish song by Caroll Malone (pseudonym of poet William B. McBurney, *ca.* 1844–*ca.* 1892) is alluded to repeatedly in the "Sirens" episode. For the words of this song, see the Appendix. R. M. Adams discusses a singing of the ballad in June, 1897, which was described in the *Freeman's Journal* in terms that may have given Joyce some hints for Ben Dollard's performance of it (*SS*, p. 65; the source cited is *Freeman's Journal*, June 10, 1897, p. 6).

92.5/90.41 EUGENE STRATTON   Eugene Stratton was an American blackface comedian. He was born Eugene Augustus Ruhlmann (1861–1918) in Buffalo, New York, of Alsatian parents (see his obituary in the London *Times*, Sept. 16, 1918, p. 5, col. d). Stratton is praised very highly by W. J. MacQueen Pope in *The Melodies Linger On*, where he says that Stratton, who went to England with a minstrel troupe and "joined the Moore and Burgess Minstrels at the old St. James hall in Picadilly," was a song writer and performer and was a master of the soft-shoe dance. MacQueen Pope goes on to call Stratton a "tremendous star of Music Hall . . . one of the most artistic of them all" (p. 411). Both the *Freeman's Journal* and the *Evening Telegraph* for June 16, 1904, advertise "Eugene

Stratton, the World Renowned Comedian" at the Theatre Royal.

92.5/90.41 MRS. BANDMAN PALMER   Mrs. Bandmann-Palmer was an English actress. See entry 76.23 and associated entries.

92.6/91.1 LEAH   This refers to the play *Leah, the Jewish Maiden*. See entry 76.23 and associated entries.

92.6/91.1 LILY OF KILLARNEY   *The Lily of Killarney* is a three-act opera written by John Oxenford (1812–77) and Dion Boucicault (1820?–90), music by J. Benedict. It was based on Boucicault's play *The Coleen Bawn*. The opera was first performed at Covent Garden Opera House, in February, 1862. The Dublin newspapers of the day advertised as a "Tremendous Success" *The Lily of Killarney*, being done at the Queen's Royal Theatre by the Elster-Grime Grand Opera Company.

92.7/91.1 ELSTER GRIMES OPERA COMPANY   There was at this time an opera company called the Elster-Grime (not Grimes) Grand Opera Company, which was currently playing in Dublin (see entry 92.6), but I have not been able to find any information on the Company.

92.8/91.3 FUN ON THE BRISTOL   Allardyce Nicoll lists "Fun on the Bristol; or, A Night at Sea" as an anonymous farce (*Hist. of Eng. Drama*, V, 682). It was first performed at Manchester on May 15, 1882, and, in a revised version, at the Gaiety Theatre, London, on September 5, 1887. The Dublin newspapers of June 16, 1904, advertised "the New Musical Comedy Version of Fun on the Bristol" at the Theatre Royal, along with Eugene Stratton.

92.12/91.7 SIR PHILIP CRAMPTON'S MEMORIAL FOUNTAIN BUST   Sir Philip Crampton (1777–1858) was a Dublin surgeon. His memorial fountain and bust was located at the junction of College Street with Great Brunswick Street (now Pearse Street) and D'Olier Street. It has since been removed. The inscription proclaimed that Sir Philip was "Surgeon-General to Her Majesty's Forces." W. Y. Tindall has a picture of the bust in *The Joyce Country*, p. 38.

93.11/92.6 SMITH O'BRIEN   This Irish protestant leader in the Repeal Movement was alluded to earlier; see entry 68.27. Bloom thinks of O'Brien here because the carriage has just passed his statue, which was then at the south end of O'Connell bridge, but has since been moved north of the river. The inscription says, "William Smith O'Brien/ born/ 17th October 1803/ sentenced to death for/ high treason/ on the/ 9th October 1848/ died/ 16th June 1864," so Bloom is right in surmising that this is his "deathday." For a picture of the statue, See *Dublin and Cork*, p. 79.

93.13/92.8 FARRELL'S STATUE   The statue of Smith O'Brien which Bloom has just seen was done by Dublin sculptor Sir Thomas Farrell (1827–1900) in 1869.

93.20/92.15 HAS THAT SILK HAT EVER SINCE. RELICS OF OLD DECENCY Hodgart and Worthington list this as an allusion to "The Hat Me Father Wore," by "Ferguson; McCarthy." I have not located a version of this song by these writers, but *Walton's Treasury of Irish Songs and Ballads* prints a song by Johnny Patterson entitled "The Hat My Father Wore," which must be substantially the same. Patterson's song begins, "I am Paddy Miles, an Irish boy," and the first verse ends "But on St. Patrick's Day I love to wear/ The hat my father wore." The chorus says, "It's old, but it's beautiful,/ The best was ever seen,/ 'Twas worn for more than ninety years/ In that little isle so green./ From my father's great ancestors/ It's descended with galore,/ 'Tis the relic of old decency,/ The hat my father wore" (*Walton's*, p. 105).

93.25/92.19 VOGLIO E NON VORREI .... MI TREMA UN POCO IL   These are lines from the Don Giovanni-Zerlina duet in Mozart's *Don Giovanni*. See entries 63.24 and 63.38.

93.31/92.25 A SMILE GOES A LONG WAY   Hodgart and Worthington list this as an allusion to "A Smile Will Go a Long Long Way," an American popular song by Davis and Akst. But according to *Variety Cavalcade*, this song by Benny Davis and Harry Akst was not copyrighted until 1923. If there was an earlier song by this title, I have not located it. The phrase "A smile will go a long, long way" is certainly very common, but it is not listed in the *ODEP* or in Apperson.

93.39/92.33 THE HUGECLOAKED LIBERATOR'S FORM   The Liberator is Daniel O'Connell, on whom see entry 31.18. A bronze statue of O'Connell twelve feet high, on a limestone pedestal twenty-eight feet high, stands at the north end of O'Connell bridge. O'Connell is depicted wrapped in his cloak. For a picture of the statue, see *Dublin and Cork*, p. 78.

93.41/92.35 THE TRIBE OF REUBEN   Reuben was the eldest child of Jacob and Leah (Gen. 29:32). The tribe of Reuben was one of the twelve tribes of Israel and is frequently referred to in the Bible (e.g., Num. 1:5; 1:21). Dodd was a Jew, and his first name was Reuben. For background on Dodd and on the event Bloom relates (which actually happened in 1911), see Ellmann, *JJ*, pp. 38–39.

94.8/93.2 GRAY'S STATUE   The statue is that of Sir John Gray (1816–75), best known as main procurer for Dublin of its supply of fine

"Vartry water." He was also editor and proprietor of the *Freeman's Journal* at one time. His statue is depicted in *Dublin and Cork*, p. 79, and the statue is briefly discussed by Richard M. Kain in his *Dublin in the Age of Yeats and Joyce*, p. 17.

94.23/93.16 HOBBLEDEHOY   Hobbledehoy, meaning an adolescent boy, is used by Swift in his *Polite Conversation*. See entry 548.26.

94.27/93.20 DROWN BARABBAS   Barabbas was the seditionist and murderer whom the Jewish multitude wished to have released rather than Jesus. See Matthew 27:16–26; Mark 15:11–15; Luke 23:18–25; and John 18:40. There is no reference to drowning in any of these contexts.

95.9/94.1 NELSON'S PILLAR   Nelson's Pillar was a 134-foot monument to admiral Viscount Horatio Nelson (1758–1805) which stood in the middle of O'Connell street near the Post Office. The two old women in Stephen's story in "Aeolus" climb this monument. The Pillar is no longer standing, having been blown up in an explosion set by unknown hands in the early hours of March 8, 1966.

95.20/94.12 AS DECENT A LITTLE MAN AS EVER WORE A HAT   Another allusion to "The Hat My Father Wore." See entry 93.20.

95.39/94.30 FATHER MATHEW   Bloom has just seen the statue of Father Theobald Mathew (1790–1856), who campaigned long and fervently for temperance in Ireland. A picture of the statue can be found in *Dublin and Cork*, p. 84. The *DNB* contains an article on Father Mathew.

95.39/94.30 FOUNDATION STONE FOR PARNELL   The foundation stone for the statue of Parnell which now stands at the north end of O'Connell street was laid on October 8, 1899, but the completed statue was not unveiled until October 1, 1911. The statue is depicted in *Dublin and Cork*, p. 86.

96.12/95.2 RATTLE HIS BONES. OVER THE STONES. ONLY A PAUPER. NOBODY OWNS   This alludes to "The Pauper's Drive." See entry 87.36.

96.14/95.3 IN THE MIDST OF LIFE   This alludes to the First Anthem in the Burial of the Dead service in the *Book of Common Prayer*: "In the midst of life we are in death. . . ." The phrase has no direct biblical source; it is said to derive from a ninth-century anthem. The Irish *Book of Common Prayer*, which differs only slightly from the English, contains this same phrase.

96.29/95.18 THEY USED TO DRIVE A STAKE OF WOOD THROUGH HIS HEART IN THE GRAVE   Brewer's *Dictionary of Phrase and Fable* explains that suicides "were formerly buried ignominiously on the high-road, with a stake thrust through their body, and without Christian rites" (*s.v.* suicides). In his *The Neighborhood of Dublin* (Dublin, 1912), Weston St. John Joyce describes an old burial ground for suicides at Ballybough (in NE Dublin): "Down to a hundred years ago Ballybough was a noted burial place for suicides, the bodies being interred in the time-honoured fashion, transfixed with stakes, in a waste plot of ground adjoining the cross roads at the bridge [Ballybough bridge]" (p. 247).

96.35/95.24   WEAR THE HEART OUT OF A STONE, THAT. MONDAY MORNING START AFRESH. SHOULDER TO THE WHEEL   This may allude to the never-ending task of Sisyphus, who appears in Hades in the *Odyssey* and who is explicitly mentioned in *Ulysses*, p. 587.30/572.23. See entry 587.30.

96.40/95.29   AND THEY CALL ME THE JEWEL OF ASIA . . .   "The Jewel of Asia" is a song sung by O Mimosa San in act II of the light opera *The Geisha*. According to Mark Lubbock's *The Complete Book of Light Opera*, *The Geisha* was first produced on April 25, 1896, at Daly's Theatre, London. The book was by Owen Hall, lyrics by Harry Greenbank, music by Sidney Jones. Edmund Epstein prints the whole of "The Jewel of Asia" in *JJR*, III (1959), 47–49, where he explains that it was a supplementary number and was written by Harry Greenbank and composed by James Philp (*sic*—S. Spaeth, *Hist. of Pop. Music in Amer.*, p. 290, says the composer was James Philip). R. M. Adams has pointed out that *The Geisha* was reviewed in the *Weekly Freeman* for December 28, 1901, p. 9 (*SS*, p. 74).

97.1/95.32   RATTLE HIS BONES   Another allusion to "The Pauper's Drive." See entry 87.36. Allusions to this song also occur on p. 97.9/95.40 and p. 97.10/96.1

97.14/96.5   A GREAT RACE TOMORROW IN GERMANY. THE GORDON BENNETT The Gordon Bennett cup race was instituted by American journalist and sportsman James Gordon Bennett (1841–1918). The race was first run in 1900; from 1900 to 1903 it was run on various circuits in France; in 1903 it was held in Ireland and in 1904 it was run on the Salzburg circuit in Germany. A list of locations and winners for the 1900–1905 races can be found in the 1905 *World Almanac and Encyclopedia*, p. 266. The Dublin newspapers of the day carried long spreads on the race. Joyce interviewed one of the French drivers for the 1903 race (see *CW*, pp. 106–8), and drew on this material in the *Dubliners* story "After the Race."

97.20/96.11   HAS ANYBODY HERE SEEN KELLY? KAY EE DOUBLE ELL WY The original "Has Anybody Here Seen Kelly?" was an English song by C. W. Murphy and Will Letters, but the only version I have found is an American adaptation done in 1909 by William J. Mc-Kenna. The words of McKenna's song are printed in S. Spaeth's *Read 'Em and Weep*, pp. 258–59. In Spaeth's discussion of the English original, he explains that the couplet Bloom thinks of on p. 97.21/96.12 was in the original "Kelly" song. Spaeth says the original "dealt with an Irishman from the Isle of Man, who was taken in hand by a lady of leisure, only to leave her for a rival. Its forerunner had been a song about one Antonio, a hokey-pokey ice-cream merchant, who played his benefactress a similar trick. When Emma Carus sang the original *Kelly,*, it contained the lines: 'He's as bad as old Antonio,/ He left me on my ownio.' " Spaeth goes on to say that this couplet and the Isle of Man references were a "wow" in England, but they meant nothing to an American audience and were changed in McKenna's adaptation. But McKenna's chorus must have some of the original in it, for it begins, "Has anybody here seen Kelly?/ K E double L Y." Apparently the earlier song about Antonio which Spaeth mentions was entitled "Oh, Oh, Antonio," for C. Pulling mentions both this and "Has Anybody Here Seen Kelly" as among the best-remembered songs of music hall performer Florrie Ford (*They were Singing*, p. 207). I have not located the original of either of these songs.

97.21/96.12   DEAD MARCH FROM SAUL   The Dead March occurs in act III of Handel's famous oratorio *Saul* (1738). But apparently the song was a common music hall number, as the present context suggests. In *Weep Some More, My Lady* (New York, 1927), Sigmund Spaeth prints a song called "Awfully Clever," after the third verse of which the following is spoken: "I give them *Hail, Columbia*, you know, or else I give them the *Dead March in Saul* on the flute. Oh, it's awfully jolly, they do laugh, it completely doubles them up" (p. 56).

97.21/96.12   HE'S AS BAD AS OLD ANTONIO. HE LEFT ME ON MY OWNIO   See entry 97.20.

97.42/96.33   ROAST BEEF FOR OLD ENGLAND   "The Roast Beef of Old England" is a well-known English song, one version of which goes back at least as far as Henry Fielding's *Don Quixote in England* (1734). For words, music, and discussion, see William Chappell's *Popular Music of the Olden Time* (London, n.d.), II, 636–38.

98.27/97.18   GORDON BENNETT CUP   See entry 97.14.

99.9/97.42   A MAN STOOD ON HIS DROPPING BARGE   This recalls the ferryman Charon, who transports Aeneas across the river Styx

during his visit to Hades. This is the most explicit of several situational correspondences in this episode which show that Joyce is
drawing on Aeneas' visit to Hades in Book VI of the *Aeneid* as well
as on Ulysses' in Book XI of the *Odyssey*.

99.11/98.2 ABOARD OF THE BUGABU   Hodgart and Worthington list
this as an allusion to "Aboard the Bugaboo," alternate titles "On
Board the Bugaboo," "The Cruise of the Bugaboo," an Irish song
by Rooney. *Nugent's Bohemian Songster* (Dublin, n.d.; 16 pp.)
prints a song by J. P. Rooney entitled "Wreck of the Bug-a-Boo."
The first of its six stanzas goes, "Come all you tender-hearted blokes
and listen unto me—/ I'll tell you of the dangers I have passed upon
the briny sea!/ Many's the hardships I have seen and dangers I
went through/ Since I shipped as cook and steward on board of the
Bug-a-boo" (p. 12).

99.18/98.9 JAMES M'CANN'S HOBBY TO ROW ME O'ER THE FERRY
Though I suspect these words allude to something, I have not
identified the allusion. James M'Cann must be James McCann who
was chairman of the Grand Canal Company, the purpose of which
was to encourage use and development of the canals. McCann is
depicted and discussed in *Modern Ireland: Men of the Period . . .*
(London: The Biographical Publishing Co. [1899?]), pp. 52–54.

99.25/98.16 BRIAN BOROIMHE HOUSE   Brian Boru (or Boroimhe)
(926–1014) was a king of Ireland, best known for his victory over
the Danish forces at Clontarf in 1014 (Clontarf is in NE Dublin).
After the battle, Boru was slain in his tent. Thom's *Dublin Directory* (1904) lists this house in Glasnevin: "Ryan, J. M. family
grocer, tea, wine and spirit merchant, Brian-boroihm house" (p.
1700). The house, which still stands, is so called because over its
door there is a vivid painting depicting Brian Boru in battle.

99.31/98.22 THOUGH LOST TO SIGHT . . . TO MEMORY DEAR   Though
this phrase is much older and its origin is disputed (see Walsh,
Handy-Book of Literary Curiosities, p. 705), its popularity was
increased by its use in a song by English verse writer and composer
George Linley (1798–1865). Linley wrote the song about 1830–40
for Augustus Braham, who sang it. The song, "Though lost to
Sight, to Memory Dear," begins, "Though lost to sight, to memory
dear/ Thou ever wilt remain;/ One only hope my heart can
cheer,—/ The hope to meet again." W. H. Grattan Flood discussed
the origin of the song in an article in *Ireland's Own*, August 7, 1907,
p. 3. In his essay he points out that the title phrase was a frequent
motto on tombstones, mortuary cards, etc., during the eighteenth
and nineteenth centuries, and he says that Linley was born in Leeds
of Irish parents.

100.2/98.35 THAT IS WHERE CHILDS WAS MURDERED   This alludes to
the murder of seventy-six-year-old Thomas Childs on September
2, 1899; the murder took place at 5 Bengal Terrace, Glasnevin. As
subsequent conversation in the carriage indicates, Thomas' brother
Samuel was charged with the murder. He was tried and acquitted
in October, 1899, with Seymour Bushe as the defense counsel. See
the following entry.

100.4/98.37 SEYMOUR BUSHE GOT HIM OFF   This continues the allusion to the Childs's murder trial, noted in the preceding entry.
Though Seymour Bushe did defend Childs, and though Childs was
acquitted, the remarks made about Bushe's speech on p. 139/137
are not accurate. Bushe did speak on evidence, but did not mention the Mosaic or the Roman codes. The closest he came was in
contrasting English procedure, which would have allowed Mrs.
Childs to testify in her husband's behalf, with Irish procedure,
which apparently prohibited it. The closing arguments and Bushe's
speech are given in great detail in the *Evening Telegraph* of Saturday, October 21, 1899, p. 5 cols. g and h, and p. 6 col. a. Ellmann
says that Joyce attended the trial and took notes on Bushe's speech
(*JJ*, p. 95).

100.8/98.41 BETTER FOR NINETYNINE GUILTY TO ESCAPE THAN FOR
ONE INNOCENT PERSON TO BE WRONGFULLY CONDEMNED   Sir William Blackstone (1723–80), English jurist and legal writer, said in
his *Commentaries*, vol. IV, chap. 27, "It is better that ten guilty
persons escape than that one innocent suffer." Perhaps Cunningham's exaggeration of the number owes something to Christ's statement in Luke 15:7: "Joy shall be in heaven over one sinner that
repenteth, more than over ninety and nine just persons, which need
no repentance." Matthew 18:12–14 uses very similar language.

100.16/99.7 MURDER WILL OUT   The *ODEP* includes "Murder will
out (cannot be hid)" and lists nine instances from *ca.* 1300 on.
Among the best-known instances of this phrase are those in Chaucer's "Prioress' Tale" and "Nun's Priest's Tale."

101.8/99.39 GOT HERE BEFORE US, DEAD AS HE IS   This recalls Elpenor,
one of Ulysses' men in the *Odyssey*, who died in a fall from Circe's
housetop at the end of book IX of the poem and is the first shade
Ulysses sees in Hades in book XI. Ulysses is surprised and says,
"Elpenor, how hast thou come beneath the darkness and the
shadow? Thou hast come fleeter on foot than I in my black ship"
(Butcher and Lang translation).

102.9/100.40 THERE ARE MORE WOMEN THAN MEN IN THE WORLD
Hodgart and Worthington list this as an allusion to "Three Women
to Every Man," a song by Murray and Leigh. Apparently this is a

music hall song, but I have not located a copy of it. S. Gilbert, in reference to this line in *Ulysses*, quotes the following from "a comic song" (Gilbert gives no title): "That's why some girls/ Are single all their lives,/ Six women to every man,/ Say, girls, say if you can/ Why can't every man/ Have six wives?" (*JJU*, p. 344).

102.11/100.42   I HOPE YOU'LL SOON FOLLOW HIM. FOR HINDU WIDOWS ONLY   Bloom is probably thinking of the Hindu custom of *suttee*, by which a widow was expected to sacrifice herself on the funeral pyre of her husband. The custom was once widely practiced in India. Though the practice was outlawed in the early nineteenth century, isolated voluntary instances have occurred in the twentieth.

102.13/101.2   WIDOWHOOD NOT THE THING SINCE THE OLD QUEEN DIED   Queen Victoria died on January 22, 1901. Her husband, Prince Albert, had died on December 14, 1861, and the old Queen had spent the last forty years of her life in conscientious widowhood. For example, Lytton Strachey says that the Queen visited the Frogmore Memorial (the mausoleum where Albert, and later Victoria herself, was buried) almost daily when the court was at Windsor (*Queen Victoria* [New York, 1921], p. 404).

102.16/101.5   IN HER HEART OF HEARTS   In *Hamlet*, III, ii, Hamlet says to Horatio, "Give me that man/ That is not passion's slave, and I will wear him/ In my heart's core—aye, in my heart of heart,/ As I do thee" (76–79).

102.23/101.12   CORK'S OWN TOWN   Joseph Prescott has pointed out the allusion here to an Irish song entitled "Cork's Own Town." For words, notes, and a discussion of authorship, see T. C. Croker, *Popular Songs of Ireland*, pp. 165–71. The phrase "Cork's Own Town" occurs only as the title, not in the lyrics of the song.

103.23/102.11   WHO'LL READ THE BOOK? I, SAID THE ROOK   This alludes to the nursery rhyme "Who Killed Cock Robin," which is printed in *ODNR*, pp. 130–33. One stanza of the rhyme reads, "Who'll be the parson?/ I said the Rook/ With my little book,/ I'll be the parson."

103.27/102.15   DOMINENAMINE   This is an echo of the words Bloom hears the priest speaking, though not a direct quotation. Probably the priest said "Domine" and Bloom is here trying to form "in nomine Domini" ("in the name of the Lord").

103.30/102.18   THOU ART PETER   In Matthew 16:18 Christ says to Peter, "And I say also unto thee, That thou art Peter, and upon this rock I will build my church; and the gates of hell shall not prevail against it."

103.34/102.21 NON INTRES IN JUDICIUM CUM SERVO TUO, DOMINE
This is the beginning of the prayer of absolution which is said over
the dead before burial: "Enter not into judgment with thy servant,
O Lord."

104.12/102.42 ET NE NOS INDUCAS IN TENTATIONEM   After the prayer
of absolution (entry 103.34), the priest says part of the Pater
Noster in silence and then begins to speak aloud with this phrase:
"And lead us not into temptation."

104.25/103.13 IN PARADISUM   This is the beginning of the anthem
that is said or sung as the coffin is carried to the grave: *In paradisum
deducant te Angeli* ("May the angels lead you into paradise").

104.41/103.28 THE O'CONNELL CIRCLE   The O'Connell circle in Glasnevin Cemetery has at its center a 165-foot replica of an old Irish
round tower, in the base of which is Daniel O'Connell's body (on
O'Connell, see entry 31.18).

105.31/104.18 I AM THE RESURRECTION AND THE LIFE   Mr. Kernan
is thinking of the opening of the Burial of the Dead service in the
Book of Common Prayer. The service begins with John 11:25: "I
am the resurrection and the life, saith the Lord: he that believeth in
me, though he were dead, yet shall he live" (the Irish *Book of Common Prayer* is identical here). On p. 105.40/104.26 Bloom repeats
Mr. Kernan's phrase and thinks of the raising of the dead at the
Last Judgment.

105.42/104.28 COME FORTH, LAZARUS! AND HE CAME FIFTH AND LOST
THE JOB   In John 11:43 we are told "And when [Jesus] thus
had spoken, he cried with a loud voice, Lazarus, come forth."
Though I know that Bloom's joke is not original with Joyce, I
have not located a copy of it in print.

107.42/106.24 SILVER THREADS AMONG THE GREY   This is Bloom's
variation on a line from the very popular song "Silver Threads
among the Gold." The song, with words by Eben E. Rexford and
music by Hart Pease Danks, appeared in 1873. Words and music
can be found in Boni, *Fireside Book of Favorite American Songs*,
pp. 231–33.

108.5/106.29 WHEN CHURCHYARDS YAWN   This recalls Hamlet's
statement in soliloquy in *Hamlet*, III, ii: " 'Tis now the very witching time of night,/ When churchyards yawn and Hell itself
breathes out/ Contagion to this world" (406–8). Bloom thinks of
another part of this statement on p. 445.21/438.6.

108.5/106.30 DANIEL O'CONNELL   Daniel O'Connell has been alluded
to several times earlier. See entry 31.18.

108.15/106.39 LOVE AMONG THE TOMBSTONES. ROMEO   This probably alludes to the popular song "Love Among the Roses," written by William H. Delehanty in 1869 (see S. Spaeth, *Hist. of Pop. Music in Amer.*, p. 202). Words and music of the song can be found in S. Spaeth's *Weep Some More*, pp. 83–84. Spaeth says that the title phrase, "Love among the Roses," has "become practically universal." The song is a sentimental love ballad, the chorus of which ends, "And how we met, I'll ne'er forget, 'Twas love among the roses." Bloom is also thinking of Romeo and Juliet's each thinking the other dead and committing suicide.

108.21/107.4 HOLY FIELDS   While the context suggests that Bloom is thinking of burial grounds, there may be an allusion here to Elysium, the Fields of the Blest, which Aeneas visits in book VI of the *Aeneid*. Perhaps this is complementary to the "dismal fields" Bloom thinks of later, on p. 111.29/110.10.

108.21/107.4 MORE ROOM IF THEY BURIED THEM STANDING   S. Gilbert comments on this thought of Bloom, "Thus kings and warriors were buried in pagan Ireland" (*JJU*, p. 174). Edmund Curtis says of Laoghaire, king of Ireland of the time of St. Patrick, "Laoghaire died like a pagan fighting against Leinster in 463, and by his own orders was buried upright in his armour facing the hereditary foes" (*Hist. of Ireland*, p. 11).

108.30/107.13 THOSE JEWS THEY SAID KILLED THE CHRISTIAN BOY   Bloom is probably thinking here not so much of any specific accusation as of the general allegation of ritual murder which is sometimes made against the Jews. This is usually known as the "blood accusation" or "blood libel." Though Josephus deals with a similar charge, the accusation that Jews killed Christian children and used their blood for ritual purposes did not appear widely before about the twelfth century. According to such charges the Jews drained the blood from their victim and used it in various rituals such as the *seder* rites. One of the most famous such stories is that of Little St. Hugh of Lincoln, mentioned by Chaucer in the "Prioress' Tale" (cf. p. 690.17/674.28). Such accusations have occasionally appeared even in the twentieth century. See *Jewish Encyclopedia*, III, 260–67, *s.v.* blood accusation.

108.38/107.20 THE LEAN OLD ONES TOUGHER   In light of the proximate reference to the gravediggers in Hamlet (p. 109.14/107.36), Bloom may be thinking here of the conversation between Hamlet and the gravedigger about how long a man will lie in the earth before he rots. The gravedigger says some corpses "will scarce hold the laying in," but that "a tanner will last you nine year," since "his hide is so tanned with his trade that a' will keep out water a great while" (*Ham.*, V, i, 179 ff.).

109.4/107.27   YOUR HEAD IT SIMPLY SWURLS. THOSE PRETTY SEASIDE GURLS Bloom is thinking again of Boylan's song. See entry 62.36.

109.8/107.31   WARMS THE COCKLES OF HIS HEART   "To warm the cockles of one's heart" is proverbial and is listed in the *ODEP*. P. W. Joyce, in *English As We Speak It*, lists "takes the cockles off your heart" to mean "cheers one up." He explains that "cares and troubles clog the heart as cockles clog a ship" (p. 194).

109.8/107.31   THE ONE ABOUT THE BULLETIN . . .   I have not located the joke Bloom thinks of.

109.14/107.36   GRAVEDIGGERS IN HAMLET   The gravediggers appear in *Hamlet*, V, i. See entry 108.38.

109.16/107.38   DE MORTUIS NIL NISI PRIUS   As E. C. McAleer has suggested ("Ignorance of Bloom," in *Studies in Honor of Hodges and Thaler*, p. 125), this seems to be Bloom's version of *De mortuis nihil* (or *nil*) *nisi bonum* ("Of the dead speak nothing but good"). But in the context Bloom's variation is not sheer nonsense; he perhaps knows that *prius* means *before* and is following up his thought about how much time must elapse before we can joke about the dead.

109.27/108.8   WE COME TO BURY CAESAR   In *Julius Caesar*, III, ii, 79, Antony says, "I come to bury Caesar, not to praise him."

109.27/108.8   HIS IDES OF MARCH OR JUNE   Bloom is still thinking of *Julius Caesar*; this alludes to the soothsayer's statement to Caesar "Beware the ides of March" (*Jul. Cae.*, I, ii, 18, 23), and to Caesar's later being slain on the ides of March. In the Roman (Julian) calendar, the ides was one of the days of the month used as references to fix the other days. The ides was the fifteenth day of March, May, July, and October, the thirteenth of the other months. Dignam's death, occurring on Monday, June 13 (p. 111.17/109.40), did occur on the ides of June.

109.36/108.16   SAY ROBINSON CRUSOE WAS TRUE TO LIFE. WELL THEN FRIDAY BURIED HIM   I do not understand this statement, for it suggests that Bloom mistakenly thinks that Robinson Crusoe died on his island, though Bloom has apparently read the book (see entry 153.16).

109.38/108.19   O, POOR ROBINSON CRUSOE . . .   The *ODNR* prints the following rhyme: "Poor old Robinson Crusoe!/ Poor old Robinson Crusoe!/ They made him a coat,/ Of an old nanny goat,/ I wonder how they could do so!/ With a ring a ting tang,/

And a ring a ting tang,/ Poor old Robinson Crusoe!" (pp. 373–74).
Hodgart and Worthington also list "Poor Old Robinson Crusoe"
as a song by Hatton, but I have not identified the song.

110.3/108.25 LAY ME IN MY NATIVE EARTH   Hodgart and Worthington list this as an allusion to "Jug of Punch," an Irish folk song,
and to "When I am Laid in Earth," by Purcell, from *Dido and
Aeneas.* Any allusion to "The Jug of Punch" seems to me unlikely;
for words and music, see A. P. Graves and Charles Wood's *Irish
Folk Songs* (London: Boosey and Co., 1897), pp. 114–19. "When
I am Laid in Earth," by Nahum Tate and Henry Purcell, is from
the opera *Dido and Aeneas* (the song is sometimes called "Dido's
Song"). The song says, "When I am laid in earth, may my wrongs
create No trouble in thy breast. . . ." Words and music can be
found in G. Bantock, *One Hundred Songs of England*, pp. 124–26.

110.4/108.26 BIT OF CLAY FROM THE HOLY LAND   J. Prescott (*MLQ*,
XIII, 151) quotes from the *Universal Jewish Encyclopedia* (New
York, 1940): "Atoning power (also a sort of special holiness)
was attributed in popular belief to the soil of Palestine; hence the
longing of many Jews to be buried in the Holy Land or, if that
were not possible, to have a handful of soil from Palestine put into
the coffin, usually under the head of the deceased" (II, 596); and
"Often, especially in Palestine, earth from Palestine was placed
in the coffin" (II, 600).

110.4/108.26 ONLY A MOTHER AND DEADBORN CHILD EVER BURIED IN THE
ONE COFFIN   J. Prescott (*MLQ*, XIII, 151–52) cites a passage
from *Laws and Customs of Israel* (London, 1940), translated by
Gerald Friedlander, to show that Bloom is wrong about this and
that Jewish custom does permit burying people of certain kinships
in the same grave. But Bloom's statement specifies coffin, not
grave, and the passage Prescott quotes deals only with burial in the
same grave. I have not been able to learn of specific regulations
governing burial within a single coffin.

110.7/108.29 THE IRISHMAN'S HOUSE IS HIS COFFIN   This is Bloom's
variation on a well-known proverb. The *ODEP* lists "A man's
(Englishman's) house is his castle," and gives seven instances from
1581 on.

110.25/109.6 A DONKEY . . . NEVER SEE A DEAD ONE, THEY SAY   P. W.
Joyce, in his *English As We Speak It*, lists "Three things no person
ever saw:—a highlander's kneebuckle, a dead ass, a tinker's funeral"
p. 111). Joyce gives no information about the proverb. The *ODEP*
lists "You never see a dead donkey nor a dead post boy," and cites

Dickens' *Pickwick Papers*, chap. 51, as the only instance of the proverb.

110.33/109.14 FEEL NO MORE Hodgart and Worthington list this as an allusion to the song "Fear no more the heat o' the sun" in *Cymbeline*, IV, ii, but, even though that song about death would be appropriate to the "Hades" context, allusion to it seems unlikely. William Schutte does not include it in his list of Shakespearean allusions in *JS*.

110.42/109.23 DEVIL IN THAT PICTURE OF SINNER'S DEATH SHOWING HIM A WOMAN If Bloom has some specific painting in mind here, I have not found it. Holbein's famous *Dance of Death* series contains nothing very close to what Bloom describes.

111.2/109.24 LAST ACT OF LUCIA. SHALL I NEVERMORE BEHOLD THEE? BAM! EXPIRES This alludes to Gaetano Donizetti's (1797–1848) opera *Lucia di Lammermoor* (1835). Bloom is thinking of the final scene of the opera, and of words spoken by Edgar after Lucia's death and before his own suicide. But no text of the opera which I have examined has any phrase similar to the one Bloom uses. I suspect that, knowingly or unknowingly, Bloom is remembering the refrain from Stephen Foster's popular song "Gentle Annie." The chorus of that song begins, "Shall we never more behold thee; never hear thy winning voice again. . . ." The phrase "Shall we never more behold thee" is sometimes listed as an alternate title of the song.

111.5/109.27 EVEN PARNELL. IVY DAY DYING OUT Ivy day, depicted in Joyce's "Ivy Day in the Committee Room," was October 6, the anniversary of Charles Stewart Parnell's death. On this day his followers commemorated Parnell by wearing a sprig of ivy in their lapels.

111.8/109.31 OUT OF THE FRYINGPAN OF LIFE INTO THE FIRE OF PURGATORY Another Bloom variation on a proverbial phrase. The *ODEP* lists "Out of the frying-pan into the fire" and lists five instances from 1514 on.

111.11/109.34 WHEN YOU SHIVER IN THE SUN. SOMEONE WALKING OVER IT This alludes to the old superstition that Swift brings into his *Polite Conversation*. In the first conversation, Miss Notable shudders and then says, "Lord, there's some Body walking over my Grave" (p. 102). In his note on this passage Partridge says this is "Still said when one shivers for no apparent reason."

111.23/110.4 OUT OF SIGHT, OUT OF MIND The *ODEP* lists many instances of this well-known proverb.

111.29/110.10 THE DISMAL FIELDS   This may be the complement to the "holy fields" Bloom thought of on p. 108.21/107.4 (*q.v.*), and may therefore allude to Tartarus, which Aeneas visits in book VI of the *Aeneid*.

111.42/110.23 CHARLEY, YOU'RE MY DARLING   "Charlie Is My Darling" is a Jacobite song in celebration of the Young Pretender, Charles Stuart (1720–88). It exists in several versions (both words and music), the best known being that set down by Lady Caroline Nairne (1766–1845). The refrain is "Oh! Charlie is my darling, My darling, my darling, Oh! Charlie is my darling, The young Chevalier." For words, music, and a biographical sketch of Lady Caroline, see Helen K. Johnson, *Our Familiar Songs*, pp. 484, 486–87.

112.14/110.37 HAS ANYBODY HERE SEEN? KAY EE DOUBLE ELL   See entry 97.20.

112.30/111.11 HIS NAVELCORD   This recalls Stephen's earlier thoughts of the *omphalos*, and specifically of the navel cord as the "strand-entwining cable of all flesh" (p. 38.2/39.2). See entry 7.33 and associated entries.

112.35/111.16 THE CHIEF'S GRAVE   "The chief" is Charles Stewart Parnell, who is buried in Glasnevin Cemetery. On the traditions about Parnell mentioned in the following lines, see entries 648.43 ff.

113.5/111.28 OLD IRELAND'S HEARTS AND HANDS   Hodgart and Worthington list this as an allusion to the song "Old Ireland's Hearts and Hands," by Harvey. I have not identified Harvey, but I did find a copy of a song of this title by W. T. Parkes in *Erin's Call Song Book*. The Parkes song begins, "O Erin, home of lovely scenes,/ O land of love and song,/ In joy once more my fond heart leans/ On thee, so true and strong. . . ." I also quote the entire chorus: "O sweetheart, Erin, good old land!/ Tho' near or far I stray,/ I love them all, each heart and hand,/ I love thy shamrock spray./ Old Ireland's hearts and hands!/ Old Ireland's hearts and hands!/ O sweetheart, Erin, good old land!/ I love thy hearts and hands" (p. 8).

113.18/111.40 EULOGY IN A COUNTRY CHURCHYARD . . .   Bloom is trying to think of "Elegy Written in a Country Churchyard" by Thomas Gray (1716–71), but mistakenly ascribes it to two English poets of a later period. Stephen earlier alluded to this poem; see entry 46.39.

113.21/112.2 GOD'S ACRE   This has long been a set phrase for a churchyard. The earliest examples the *OED* cites say the phrase is of German origin. Henry Wadsworth Longfellow wrote a poem entitled "God's Acre," in which he says, "I like that ancient Saxon phrase, which calls the burial-ground God's-Acre."

113.34/112.15 HEART ON HIS SLEEVE   The *ODEP* lists "He wears his heart on his sleeve" (*s.v.* Wears), and cites two instances of it, the first being Iago's statement in *Othello*, "But I will wear my heart upon my sleeve/ For daws to peck at" (I, i, 64–65).

113.37/112.18 WOULD BIRDS COME THEN AND PECK LIKE THE BOY WITH THE BASKET OF FRUIT . . .   Bloom is thinking of the fifth century B.C. Greek painter Zeuxis, who was famed for his realistic depictions. Pliny, in his *Natural History*, tells several stories of his realistic work, including two about grapes. The first involves a competition with Parrhasius, in which Zeuxis painted grapes so realistically that birds tried to eat them; but he still lost to Parrhasius, who painted a curtain so skillfully that it deceived Zeuxis himself. Then Pliny says, "It is said that Zeuxis also subsequently painted a Child Carrying Grapes, and when birds flew to the fruit with the same frankness as before, he strode up to the picture in anger with it and said, 'I have painted the grapes better than the child, as if I had made a success of that as well, the birds would inevitably have been afraid of it'" (Book XXXV, sec. xxxvi). Bloom probably thinks of Apollo because of Apollodorus, an earlier realistic painter, of whom Zeuxis was a more brilliant successor.

113.42/112.23 AS YOU ARE NOW SO ONCE WERE WE   Several people have pointed out to me that this alludes to a tombstone inscription, more common in the past than now, of which there are several versions. From the line Bloom thinks of here and from a line spoken by Bello on p. 535.22/523.25, we can guess that the inscription Joyce had in mind was something like the following: "Passengers, as ye pass by,/ Behold the place where now we lie;/ As you are now, so once were we,/ As we are now, so will you be."

114.18/112.41 ROBERT EMMET WAS BURIED HERE BY TORCHLIGHT, WASN'T HE   Robert Emmet (1778–1803) was an Irish patriot, member of the United Irishmen and leader of a furtive rebellion and march on Dublin Castle in the summer of 1803. He escaped and fled Dublin, but returned, partly to see his sweetheart, Sarah Curran. He was captured, tried, and executed for treason. The exact circumstances of his execution and burial are hazy, and for many years the place of his burial was unknown. According to Helen Landreth's *The Pursuit of Robert Emmet* (New York, 1948), Emmet was hanged and beheaded, the beheading done with a common knife, and apparently while Emmet's heart was still beating

(p. 352). The severed head was taken by the artist George Petrie, to make a death mask, and the body was coffined and buried in the public burying ground known as the Hospital Fields, though it was soon removed (pp. 352–53). Concerning its burial, Landreth says, "Many places in Dublin claim the honor of holding Emmet's body: the graveyards of St. Michan's, St. Peter's and the vaults of St. Ann's. The quiet little burying-ground in the shadow of the church at Glasnevin, made famous by its association with Dean Swift, has a stone which is said to cover Emmet's body. But when investigations were made at these places about a hundred years after Emmet's death, nothing was found to confirm the rumors. In 1904 the vault of Dr. Trevor's family, in St. Paul's Church, King Street, Dublin, was opened. For a long time there had been a story that a headless body rested there. The Parish Registry had entries for only four bodies for this vault. The remains of five were found. One, enclosed in a thin penal shell, was the headless skeleton of a young man about Emmet's build" (p. 353). See also p. 290.34/286.3. Bloom may be aware that during much of 1903 (the centennial of Emmet's death), the *United Irishman* had carried stories of the renewed attempts to locate Emmet's burial place.

114.24/113.5 VOYAGES IN CHINA   Bloom's bookshelf (p. 708/693) contains "*Voyages in China* by 'Viator.'" *Viator* is a fairly common pseudonym, especially for authors of travel books, but none of the catalogues I have consulted has turned up a book entitled *Voyages in China.*

114.28/113.9 ASHES TO ASHES   This alludes to the Burial of the Dead service in the *Book of Common Prayer*: "Earth to earth, ashes to ashes, dust to dust, in sure and certain hope of the resurrection to eternal life, through our Lord Jesus Christ." The Irish *Book of Common Prayer* is identical. Though the phrase "ashes to ashes, dust to dust" echoes several biblical passages (e.g., Gen. 18:27; Job 30:19; and Job 42:6), it apparently has no direct biblical source.

114.29/113.10 PARSEE TOWER OF SILENCE? EATEN BY BIRDS   The Towers of Silence, or Dakhmas, are the means of disposing of the dead in the Zoroastrian (Parsi) religion. The remains of the dead are taken into the Tower and left, and the flesh is soon devoured by vultures. Towers in large communities may have a constant attendance of birds. Bloom may have learned of such towers in his *In the Track of the Sun*, which depicts one. See entry 57.33.

114.42/113.23 THE LOVE THAT KILLS   Though the idea of a love that kills is quite common, there may be some echo here of the well-known lines in Oscar Wilde's "The Ballad of Reading Gaol" (1898): "Yet each man kills the thing he loves . . ." (stanza 7).

115.15/113.38 THE TANTALUS GLASSES   Tantalus, mythical king of Lydia, was one of those whom Ulysses saw in torment during his trip to Hades (*Odyssey*, book XI). Tantalus' punishment for his various sins against the gods was that, though he stood chin deep in water, he was tortured by thirst, for whenever he tried to drink, the water fled him. Also, the trees around him were filled with fruit, but when he reached for it, the wind tossed the boughs away. The *OED* defines a tantalus as a stand containing cut-glass decanters which, though apparently free, cannot be removed until the grooved bar which engages the stoppers is raised.

115.18/113.42 HATE AT FIRST SIGHT   This is Bloom's variation on the well-known proverbial expression "Love at first sight." The *ODEP* lists several instances of this phrase.

116.3/115.3 NELSON'S PILLAR   See entry 95.9.

117.28/116.26 OUR SAVIOUR: BEARDFRAMED OVAL FACE: TALKING IN THE
DUSK MARY, MARTHA   Bloom is again thinking of some artistic
depiction of Christ in the house of Mary and Martha. See entry
79.6.

117.30/116.28 MARIO THE TENOR   This alludes to the popular Italian
tenor Giovanni Matteo, Cavaliere di Candia (1810–83), whose stage
name was Mario. He did several times sing Lionel in Flotow's
Martha, including a performance of it at Covent Garden during
his final season, 1871. R. M. Adams (*SS*, p. 169) points out that
Mario retired in 1871, when Bloom was only five years old, and
that Bloom's remembering him is impossible.

117.34/116.33 MARTHA   *Martha, oder der Markt von Richmond*
is an opera in four acts by German composer Friedrich von Flotow
(1812–83), libretto by Friedrich Wilhelm Riese, based on an earlier
ballet-pantomime by Flotow and others. It was first produced in
Vienna on November 25, 1847 and was first done in England at
Drury Lane Theatre, June 4, 1849 (in German). The opera is

also well known in Italian and English translations. For comments on the specific aria Bloom thinks of, see entry 256.26.

118.33/117.33 QUEEN ANNE IS DEAD   This is a traditional example of stale news, and is listed in *ODEP*. A similar phrase occurs in Swift's *Polite Conversation* when Lady Smart says, "And, pray what News Mr. *Neverout*?" and Neverout replies, "News, why Madam, Queen Elizabeth's dead." In his note, Partridge says that this is "the prototype of 'Queen Anne's dead,' the latter occurring earliest in 1722 (Apperson), a mere eight years after Queen Anne died" (p. 56).

119.4/118.5 PHIL BLAKE'S WEEKLY PAT AND BULL STORY. UNCLE TOBY'S PAGE FOR TINY TOTS   The context here makes it clear that these are features of some newspaper or magazine, but I have never seen either of them in any of the Irish papers I have examined.

119.11/118.12 MORE IRISH THAN THE IRISH   This proverbial phrase, sometimes occurring in the Latin form "Hibernicis ipsis Hibernior," has long been applied to those newcomers to Ireland who show themselves more chauvinistic than the natives. The *ODEP* lists the proverb, the earliest instance it cites being Riley's *Dictionary of Latin Quotations* (1860).

120.30/119.29 THE HOUSE OF KEYS . . . MANX PARLIAMENT   "The "House of Keys" is the name of the twenty-four-man elective branch of the legislature of the Isle of Man. The origin of the term is not certainly known. Since the 1820's this island in the Irish Sea has been under the British crown but not subject to the acts of the English parliament, so its use by the Irish as a symbol of home rule is natural.

120.35/119.33 VOGLIO   This alludes to Mozart's *Don Giovanni*. See entries 63.31 and 64.4.

122.10/121.9 FOUND DROWNED   See entry 50.5.

122.15/121.14 AND IT WAS THE FEAST OF THE PASSOVER   Passover (probably from the Hebrew verb *pasach* or *pessach*, to pass over) is celebrated by the Jews to commemorate the destroying angel's passing over the Israelites' houses, marked with the blood of a lamb, and slaying the first born of the Egyptians only. This occurred the night before the Israelites' departure from Egypt. See Exodus 12:1–13:16. The following lines of *Ulysses* contain several allusions to the Passover ritual, which is contained in the Haggadah book Bloom mentions on p. 122.20/121.18.

122.21/121.20 NEXT YEAR IN JERUSALEM   This phrase is the traditional conclusion to the Seder service on Passover eve; the celebrants exclaim, "Next year in Jerusalem" in expression of their joyous hope of return to the Holy Land.

122.22/121.21 THAT BROUGHT US OUT OF THE LAND OF EGYPT . . . This is Bloom's mistake for the very common Old Testament phrase that says that the Lord God "brought you out of the land of Egypt, out of the house of bondage." The phrase occurs frequently in the Old Testament, as in Exodus 13:3 and 13:14. Bloom is thinking here specifically of the "haggadah" or "telling" portion of the Passover ritual, in the course of which the story of the Jews' going into Egypt, their persecution, the plagues, their deliverance, etc., are told, and this phrase or a very similar phrase is used several times. The story is punctuated by an occasional "Alleluia!"

122.23/121.22 SHEMA ISRAEL ADONAI ELOHENU   This is the beginning of the best-known Hebrew prayer, usually called the *Shema*. It is from Deuteronomy 6:4 and says, "Hear, O Israel: the Lord our God is one Lord." It is Judaism's confession of faith, which proclaims the absolute unity of God. It is recited twice daily—in the morning and in the evening. As Bloom's "No, that's the other" indicates, this daily prayer is not a part of the Passover ritual.

122.24/121.23 THEN THE TWELVE BROTHERS, JACOB'S SONS   In the course of the "haggadah" or "telling" portion of the Passover ritual, the Israelites' going into Egypt is described and the sons of Jacob are referred to.

122.25/121.24 THEN THE LAMB AND THE CAT . . .   Bloom is thinking of the "Had Gadya" (One Kid), an Aramaic song that is sung at the conclusion of the Passover festival. It is a cumulative rhyme similar in form to the well-known "Old Woman and her Pig" or "The House that Jack Built." The last and most inclusive verse says "Then came the Most Holy—blessed be He!—and destroyed the angel of death that slew the slaughterer that killed the ox that drank the water that quenched the fire that burned the stick that beat the dog that bit the cat that ate the kid which my father bought for two zuzim. One only kid, one only kid." Bloom's statement "Justice it means but it's everybody eating everybody else" is similar to a comment that the *Jewish Encyclopedia* makes about the rhyme: "It was for a long time regarded as an allegorical version of the principle of 'jus talionis,' a sort of commentary upon Exod. 21:24–25" (VI, 127). For complete words, a musical setting, and commentary, see the *Jewish Encyclopedia*, VI, 127–30.

122.30/121.29 PRACTICE MAKES PERFECT   This proverbial saying is listed in the *ODEP* under "Use (later Practice) makes perfect," and seven instances are cited, dating back to 1560.

123.17/122.17   ERIN, GREEN GEM OF THE SILVER SEA   Hodgart and Worthington list this as an allusion to Thomas Moore's song "Let Erin Remember the Days of Old," the first stanza of which ends, "Ere the emerald gem of the western world/ Was set in the crown of a stranger." This, of course, is not the exact phrase in *Ulysses*, and I have not located a source for this exact phrase, but another possible source worth noting is an earlier song by Irish poet, political writer, and physician William Drennan (1754–1820), entitled "When Erin First Rose." The song has six eight-line stanzas, the first of which begins, "When Erin first rose from the dark swelling flood,/ God bless'd the green island and saw it was good;/ The em'rald of Europe, it sparkled and shone,/ In the ring of the world the most precious stone." Stanza five of the song uses the phrase "the Emerald Isle." Moore is said to have admired the song, and it is generally accepted as the earliest use of "the Emerald Isle." For full words, see *The Cabinet of Irish Literature*, I, 309–10. The phrase in *Ulysses* may also owe something to John of Gaunt's description of England as "This precious stone set in the silver sea" in *Richard II*, II, i, 46. Cf. entry 186.34.

123.18/122.18   THE GHOST WALKS   The probable allusion here to the ghost of King Hamlet is confirmed by William S. Walsh's explanation of this as "a bit of theatrical and journalistic slang for 'salaries are paid.' " Walsh explains the meaning as follows: "During a rehearsal of 'Hamlet' by a company of English strolling players whose salaries had been long in arrears, the Ghost, in answer to Hamlet's exclamation, 'Perchance 'twill walk again,' shouted, emphatically, 'No! I'm d———d if the Ghost walks any more until our salaries are paid!' " (*Handy-Book of Literary Curiosities, s.v.* Ghost walks, The).

124.1/122.38   AND XENOPHON LOOKED UPON MARATHON . . .   This is an adaptation of the well-known lines in Byron's poem "The Isles of Greece," which occurs in *Don Juan*, canto III, following stanza 86: "The mountains look on Marathon—/ And Marathon looks on the sea." The poem is alluded to by title later in *Ulysses* (entry 734.28), and Mulligan earlier alluded to Xenophon's *Anabasis* (entry 5.8).

124.20/123.19   A RECENTLY DISCOVERED FRAGMENT OF CICERO'S   Professor MacHugh probably chose Cicero to compare Dawson with because Cicero was the greatest of Roman orators and because his pure style set the standard for Latin oratory and was imitated for centuries.

125.14/124.14 REAPING THE WHIRLWIND   Though the whirlwind is repeatedly mentioned in the Bible, only in one place is the image of reaping explicitly used. In Hosea 8:7 we read of the idolatrous Israelites, "For they have sown the wind, and they shall reap the whirlwind."

125.16/124.16 BRAINS ON THEIR SLEEVE   This is Bloom's variation of the proverbial "He wears his heart upon his sleeve"; see entry 113.34.

125.21/124.20 HOT AND COLD IN THE SAME BREATH   This phrase is listed by William S. Walsh, who says it means to be hypocritical or to veer about. Walsh cites a poem occasioned by an experimental attempt to ventilate Parliament by alternate blasts of hot and cold air (*Handy-Book of Literary Curiosities, s.v.* Hot and cold, To blow). But the phrase has its origin in Aesop's fable "The Man and the Satyr" (sometimes "The Saytr and the Traveller"), in which a satyr becomes frightened of a man who first blows on his hands to warm them and then on his soup to cool it. The satyr refuses the man his friendship, saying he will have nothing to do with one who can blow hot and cold with the same breath.

126.2/125.2 THE MOON . . . HE FORGOT HAMLET   Wm. Schutte lists this as an allusion to *Hamlet*, without reference to any specific scene. He also points out that the Rosenbach MS reads, "The Moon . . . He forgot the moon," and Schutte says it is not clear why, in the final version, MacHugh associates the moon with Hamlet (*JS*, pp. 28, 188).

126.17/125.17 FEATHERED HIS NEST WELL   This proverbial phrase is listed in seven instances by the *ODEP*, going back as far as 1553 and including James Kelly's *Scottish Proverbs* (1721).

126.26/125.26 THE SHAM SQUIRE   "The Sham Squire" was Francis Higgins (1746–1802), an Irish huckster who was perhaps the informer on Lord Edward Fitzgerald. Higgins defrauded a respectable Dublin woman into believing he was a country gentleman and married her, for which he was prosecuted and imprisoned. Higgins was also editor of the *Freeman's Journal* at one time (several editors of the paper are alluded to in this episode). The *DNB* has a short sketch of Higgins.

127.2/126.2 NORTH CORK MILITIA . . .   I have been unable to make any sense of these remarks of Crawford. R. M. Adams thinks they indicate Crawford's mental decay and says, ". . . it would be a shrewd dialectician indeed who could make much sense out of the editor's crowings about North Cork militia with Spanish officers in Ohio" (*SS*, pp. 160–61). The North Cork militia was notorious for its severity with the Irish people before and during the 1798 rebellion in Wexford and Wicklow.

127.28/126.28 IS THAT CANADA SWINDLE CASE ON TODAY? There was such a case being tried in Dublin at this time. It is alluded to more fully on p. 322.3/316.19; see entry 322.3 for details.

129.13/128.5 WE ARE THE BOYS OF WEXFORD ... These lines are from the chorus of the song "The Boys of Wexford," by Irish physician and poet R. Dwyer Joyce (1830–83). The chorus goes, "We are the boys of Wexford,/ Who fought with heart and hand,/ To burst in twain the galling chain,/ And free our native land!" For full words, see H. Halliday Sparling's *Irish Minstrelsy* (London, n.d.), pp. 55–56, or O'Lochlainn's *Irish Street Ballads*, pp. 96–97.

129.22/128.14 BEGONE! ... THE WORLD IS BEFORE YOU Though this is a very ordinary phrase and there may be no allusion here at all, this is much like the closing lines of *Paradise Lost*, in which Milton says of Adam and Eve, "The world was all before them, where to choose/ Their place of rest, and Providence their guide" (XII, 646–47). Or compare Byron's "Epistle to August," the eleventh stanza of which begins "The world is all before me. . . ."

130.17/129.8 BUT IT IS NOT ALWAYS AS IT SEEMS Here again is a phrase that is probably too common to have a specific source. But two quite different passages which come to mind as possible analogues are Henry Wadsworth Longfellow's "A Psalm of Life," which says "For the soul is dead that slumbers,/ And things are not what they seem" (ll. 1–4), and the duet by Captain Corcoran and Buttercup in act II of Gilbert and Sullivan's *H.M.S. Pinafore* (1878) which begins "Things are seldom what they seem. . . ."

130.28/129.19 'TWAS RANK AND FAME THAT TEMPTED THEE ... This alludes to a ballad sung by Manuel in act III of Balfe's *The Rose of Castille* (on which see entry 134.19). The song is sung to Elvira, who has just learned that her husband is a muleteer and appears ready to leave him. It begins, " 'Twas rank and fame that tempted thee, 'Twas empire charm'd thy heart,/ But love was wealth—the world to me—/ Then, false one, let us part."

130.37/129.24 FAT IN THE FIRE This is proverbial, being listed in the *ODEP* in six instances, dating back to *ca.* 1374 and including Heywood's 1546 collection of proverbs.

131.4/129.28   THE CHANCE OF A SNOWBALL IN HELL   Though I am sure this phrase is proverbial, I have not found it in any of the collections of proverbs I have examined.

131.5/129.33   THE GRANDEUR THAT WAS ROME   This alludes to the well-known lines from Edgar Allan Poe's "To Helen," in which he refers to "the Glory that was Greece/ And the grandeur that was Rome."

131.12/130.4   THE JEWS IN THE WILDERNESS AND ON THE MOUNTAINTOP SAID: IT IS MEET TO BE HERE. LET US BUILD AN ALTAR TO JEHOVAH Though the Jews did frequently build altars to Jehovah, I have not located this precise phrase anywhere in the Bible. For examples of their building an altar to God, see Genesis 12:7 and 22:9.

131.16/130.7   ON OUR SHORE HE NEVER SET IT   The question of the extent of Roman dominion over Ireland has frequently been discussed by Irish historians. Keating, in his *History of Ireland*, concludes, "it is not alone that the Romans did not come to Ireland, but even that it is there the people of other countries were protected from the Romans" (Irish Text Society ed., IV, 17, 19).

131.16/130.8   CLOACAL OBSESSION   Using this phrase to describe the English, Joyce is ironically echoing H. G. Wells's use of it to describe Joyce himself in his review of *A Portrait of the Artist*. Wells said, "It is no good trying to minimize a characteristic that seems to be deliberately obtruded. Like Swift and another living Irish writer, Mr. Joyce has a cloacal obsession. He would bring back into the general picture of life aspects which modern drainage and modern decorum have taken out of ordinary intercourse and conversation" ("James Joyce," *New Republic*, X [March 10, 1917], 159).

131.20/130.11   AS WE READ IN THE FIRST CHAPTER OF GUINNESS'S, WERE PARTIAL TO THE RUNNING STREAM   Though no running stream is mentioned in the first chapter of Genesis, the rivers of the garden of Eden are described in Genesis 2:10–14.

131.24/130.15   PONTIUS PILATE IS ITS PROPHET   This parodies the famous Moslem statement of belief "There is no god but God and Mohammed is his prophet." The reference to Roman law implies some phrase such as "There is no law but Roman law and Pontius Pilate is its prophet."

131.26/130.17   THAT STORY ABOUT CHIEF BARON PALLES   Christopher Palles (1831–1920) was Lord Chief Baron of the Exchequer. He was a graduate of Clongowes and of Trinity College, Dublin. The *DNB* has a short article on him. I have not located the story about Palles to which O'Molloy refers.

132.12/131.1 ON SWIFT SAIL FLAMING . . .   Stephen is recalling the
poem he thought of earlier. See entry 48.3.

132.26/131.15 A WOMAN BROUGHT SIN INTO THE WORLD. FOR HELEN . . .
O'ROURKE, PRINCE OF BREFFNI   Stephen is recalling some of his
conversation with Deasy. See entries 34.39, 34.41, and 34.42.

132.31/131.24 HABSBURG. AN IRISHMAN SAVED HIS LIFE ON THE RAM-
PARTS OF VIENNA . . . MAXIMILIAN KARL O'DONNELL, GRAF VON TIR-
CONNEL IN IRELAND   Though I have not been able to verify, or
even fully to make sense of, this statement, there may be some fact
in it. At least there was a branch of the O'Donnell family which
settled in Austria, and one of its best-known members was General
Karl O'Donnell, count of Tyrconnel (1715–71), who held important commands during the Seven Years' War. See *Encyclopaedia Britannica*, 11th ed., XX, 8.

132.35/131.24 WILD GEESE   Stephen earlier used this phrase which
refers to exiled Irishmen; see entry 41.17. The context here shows
that Crawford is thinking specifically of the O'Donnell family,
several of whom left Ireland after the Battle of the Boyne, some set-
tling in Spain and others in Austria.

133.6/131.31 HUNGARIAN IT WAS ONE DAY   R. M. Adams (*SS*, p. 63)
sees this as a prediction by Crawford of the beginning of the First
World War, which was precipitated by the assassination of Archduke Francis Ferdinand of Austria-Hungary by a Serbian nationalist on June 28, 1914. Perhaps Adams is right; this entire
passage is obscure to me. But for all I can tell, Crawford may still
be referring to the episode he mentioned on p. 132 31/131.20.

133.14/132.3 TIME IS MONEY   Apparently Joyce is having Professor
MacHugh fall into an ironic error in ascribing this proverb to the
Romans. The *ODEP* lists "Time is money" and cites the Greek
philosopher Theophrastus, pupil and successor to Aristotle, as its
earliest instance. The *ODEP* cites no Latin version, nor is one given
in any of the several dictionaries of classical quotations I have
looked at. Joyce may well have gotten his information from Diogenes Laertius' *Lives of Eminent Philosophers*. In his life of Theophrastus, Laertius says "a very favorite expression of his was, that
time was the most valuable thing that a man could spend" (London,
1853, p. 196).

133.16/132.4 LORD JESUS! LORD SALISBURY   Mainly interested in contrasting uses of "Lord," MacHugh seems to have chosen his example well, for the Lord Salisbury referred to here was a minor anti-
Christ for the Irish. Robert Arthur Talbot Gascoyne-Cecil, 3rd

Marquess of Salisbury (1830–1903), was a British member of Parliament from 1853 to 1903 who set himself sternly against parliamentary and franchise reforms and who constantly opposed Gladstone's attempts to grant Home Rule to Ireland.

133.18/132.6 KYRIE ELEISON   The litany "Kyrie, eleison" ("Lord, have mercy") is sung regularly in the Mass.

133.25/132.13 THE CATHOLIC CHIVALRY OF EUROPE THAT FOUNDERED AT TRAFALGAR   At Trafalgar, off the southwest coast of Spain, Lord Nelson defeated a combined French and Spanish fleet on October 21, 1805. Nelson was himself killed in the battle.

133.27/132.14 THE EMPIRE OF THE SPIRIT, NOT AN IMPERIUM, THAT WENT UNDER WITH THE ATHENIAN FLEETS AT AEGOSPOTAMI   MacHugh is continuing his contrast between Greece and Rome. Aegospotami was a small river and a town on what is now the Gallipoli Peninsula of Turkey. The area of the river's mouth was the scene of the decisive victory of the Spartans under Lysander over the Athenians under Conon in 405 B.C. This defeat led to the close of the Peloponnesian War and the decline of Athens.

133.29/132.16 PYRRHUS, MISLED BY AN ORACLE, MADE A LAST ATTEMPT TO RETRIEVE THE FORTUNES OF GREECE   Plutarch, whose *Life* of Pyrrhus is our chief source of information about him, does not describe anything that exactly fits the implications of this phrase. Perhaps this refers to an incident that resulted in Pyrrhus' death. During the attack on Argos in which he died, Pyrrhus saw in the market place brass statues of a wolf and a bull, poised to attack one another. Pyrrhus became terrified, recollecting an oracle that had said fate had determined his death when he should see a wolf fighting with a bull. As a result of his fear, Pyrrhus ordered a retreat, but the orders miscarried, separate parts of Pyrrhus' own army clashed, and Pyrrhus' death resulted (see entry 25.14). But Plutarch, as if to show Pyrrhus' error in responding to these statues as a fulfillment of the oracle, goes into some detail to explain the very ordinary course of events which caused the statues to be there.

133.32/132.20 THEY WENT FORTH TO BATTLE . . . BUT THEY ALWAYS FELL   This probably alludes to the original title of Yeats's poem "The Rose of Battle." In *The Countess Kathleen and Various Legends and Lyrics* (1892) this poem was entitled "They went forth to the Battle, but they always fell" (*Variorum Poems*, p. 113). In later collections it was always entitled "The Rose of Battle." Yeats's early title may derive from a line in Ossian's poem *Cath-loda*, duan ii: "His race came forth, in their years; they came forth to war, but they always fell." (I have seen this line from *Cath-loda* quoted by others as, "They went forth to battle, but they always fell," but every copy of the poem I have examined has the slightly different phrase I have given.)

134.9/132.31 ... I CAN'T SEE THE JOE MILLER, CAN YOU?   "Joe Miller" has become slang for a joke, in allusion to Joseph Miller (1684–1738), an actor and reputed humorist in the Drury Lane company. *Joe Miller's Jests* was published in 1739. I have not located a limerick similar to Lenehan's.

134.10/132.32   IN MOURNING FOR SALLUST   Sallust (86–35 B.C.) was a Roman historian and supporter of Caesar in the Civil War.

134.19/133.4   THE ROSE OF CASTILLE   *The Rose of Castille* is an opera by Irish composer Michael William Balfe (1808–70). It was first done at the Lyceum in London on October 29, 1857.

134.31/133.15   LIKE FELLOWS WHO HAD BLOWN UP THE BASTILLE   The Bastille was destroyed by the people of Paris on July 14, 1789.

134.32/133.16   OR WAS IT YOU SHOT THE LORD LIEUTENANT OF FINLAND ... GENERAL BOBRIKOFF   This alludes to the shooting of General Bobrikoff, the Russian governor-general of Finland, by Finnish aristocrat Eugen Schaumans on June 16, 1904. The shooting occurred in Helsinki at 11:00 A.M., and it has been questioned whether the incident could have been known about in Dublin at this time (see R. M. Adams, *SS*, pp 203–4). But in view of the fact that Central European time was one hour and twenty-five minutes ahead of Dublin time, and that this scene is set in a newspaper office, it seems entirely possible that the news had reached Dublin by this time. It certainly arrived in time to be printed up briefly in the *Evening Telegraph* (Last Pink) for this day (see the "Very Latest" column, p. 3).

135.16/133.34   IN THE LEXICON OF YOUTH ...   The context suggests that Crawford is quoting from Sir Edward Bulwer-Lytton's play *Richlieu: or, The Conspiracy* (produced 1839). In that play Richlieu says to his page François, whom he is sending on an important errand, "In the lexicon of youth, which fate reserves/ For a bright manhood, there is no such word/ As fail! (II, ii).

135.23/134.4   FATHER SON AND HOLY GHOST AND JAKES M'CARTHY   Though this seems to be a popular catch phrase, I have not located it in any of the dictionaries I have used.

136.3/134.17   IN EIGHTYONE, SIXTH OF MAY, TIME OF THE INVINCIBLES, MURDER IN THE PHOENIX PARK   On the Phoenix Park murders, which occurred May 6, 1882—not 1881—see entry 81.26; see also the entries following this one.

136.11/134.26 TIM KELLY, OR KAVANAGH I MEAN, JOE BRADY . . . SKIN-
THE-GOAT DROVE THE CAR   Tim Kelly, Michael Kavanagh, Joe
Brady, and James ("Skin-the-Goat") Fitzharris were all involved
in the Phoenix Park murder. Kelly and Brady were both executed
for their part in the crime; Kavanagh and Fitzharris were accom-
plices, both having driven cabs to transport the men who committed the murders. Kavanagh's cab contained four of the principals
in the murder—Pat Delaney, Tom Caffrey, Joe Brady, and Tim
Kelly—but Kavanagh turned Queen's evidence and escaped prosecution. Fitzharris' cab contained fewer important men and to some
extent served as a decoy. Fitzharris was first charged with murder,
but was acquitted and was then charged with being an accomplice
after the fact, found guilty, and sentenced to life imprisonment.
(This information comes from *Report of the Trials at the Dublin
Commission Court April and May, 1883, of the Prisoners Charged
with the Phoenix Park Murder* . . . [Dublin, 1883], and from various
accounts of the trial in the London *Times* during the first six months
of 1883.) William J. Feeney also discusses several of these details
in his "*Ulysses* and the Phoenix Park Murder," *JJQ,* I, 56–58.

136.26/135.1 WEEKLY FREEMAN OF 17 MARCH   R. M. Adams (*SS,*
pp. 162–63) has pointed out the problems in knowing *which* March
17 Crawford is speaking of. No *Weekly Freeman* appeared on
March 17 in 1904 (it appeared on March 19 that year), and if
Crawford is thinking of 1883—the year of the trial, and the year
the news broke—the news would have been stale, as Adams points
out, by March 17 that year, because Kavanagh's testimony about
the route the cabs followed was given on February 10 (see entry
137.5). And Crawford's "Take page four, advertisement for Brans-
come's coffee, let us say," appears very casual and offhand and
suggests that he was not referring to an actual advertisement.
And the National Library of Ireland holdings of the *Weekly Freeman* for 1883 begin with the April 28 issue, so we may never know
whether the March 17, 1883, issue had an advertisement for Brans-
come's coffee on page 4.

137.5/135.18 THE ROUTE SKIN-THE-GOAT DROVE THE CAR FOR AN ALIBI . . .
Though Crawford is right that Skin-the-Goat's cab served to some
extent as a decoy (see entry 136.11), the route he describes is that
taken by the cab of Michael Kavanagh, which carried four of the
principals in the murder. The route is described in some detail
by Kavanagh himself in his testimony as Queen's evidence (London
Times, Feb. 12, 1883, p. 7, cols. a–c). Kavanagh specifically men-

tioned Inchicore, Roundtown, Palmerston Park, and a pub in Lee-
son park where his passengers got off.

137.17/135.30 NIGHTMARE FROM WHICH YOU WILL NEVER AWAKE
See entry 34.22.

137.19/135.32 THE LORD EVER PUT THE BREATH OF LIFE IN   This
phrase and the name Adam suggest the account of God's creation
of Adam in Genesis 2:7: "And the Lord God formed man of the
dust of the ground, and breathed into his nostrils the breath of
life."

137.22/135.35 MADAM, I'M ADAM. AND ABLE WAS I ERE I SAW ELBA
Both of these palindromes are listed in William S. Walsh's *Handy-
Book of Literary Curiosities*, *s.v.* Palindrome. They are, naturally,
attributed to Adam and Napoleon respectively.

137.23/135.36 THE OLD WOMAN OF PRINCE'S STREET   This refers to
the *Freeman's Journal*, whose offices had an entrance on Prince's
Street. The phrase is a parody of the designation of the Bank of
England as "the Old Lady in Threadneedle Street," which goes
back to an eighteenth-century caricature.

137.24/136.1 WEEPING AND GNASHING OF TEETH   This phrase occurs
several times in Matthew and once in Luke to describe the fate of
those who are not a part of the kingdom of God. See, for example,
Matthew 8:12 and 22:13.

137.27/136.4 TAY PAY WHO TOOK HIM ONTO THE STAR . . . BLUMENFELD
"Tay Pay" is Irish politician and journalist Thomas Power O'Connor (1848–1929), who was popularly known by his first two initials. He founded the *Star* in 1887, described by the *DNB* as "an
evening journal noted for its radicalism and for its inauguration
of 'the new journalism,' characterized by what was called the
'human touch' " (*s.v.* O'Connor, Thomas Power). Blumenfeld is
Ralph David Blumenfeld (1864–1948), editor of the *Daily Mail*
from 1900 to 1902 and of the *Daily Express* from 1904 to 1932.
The *DNB* has an article on him.

138.1/136.17 THE INVINCIBLES   See entry 81.26.

138.3/136.19 LADY DUDLEY WAS WALKING HOME THROUGH THE PARK . . .
Lady Dudley was the wife of William Humble Ward, second Earl
of Dudley, who was appointed lord lieutenant of Ireland in 1902
(for information on both Lord and Lady Dudley, see *DNB, 1931–
1940, s.v.* Ward, W. H.). But the incident referred to here does not
seem to have actually occurred. The cyclone mentioned is probably the gale of February 26–27, 1903 (on which see entry 396.38),
but a check of the papers of that week turned up nothing on Lady

Dudley. R. M. Adams has suggested that the episode described in *Ulysses* was probably suggested to Joyce by an item in the June 9, 1904, *Freeman's Journal* (*SS*, p. 230). The paper of that day had a news item headed "Hawking in Phoenix Park," which described the prosecution the day before in Police Court of several hawkers who were selling mementoes of the Phoenix Park murders. The news item says the hawkers were given repeated warnings, and they were prohibited from their practice as far back as November, 1903 (p. 2, col. j). No mention is made of Lady Dudley.

138.11/136.27 WHITESIDE, LIKE ISAAC BUTT, LIKE SILVERTONGUED O'HAGAN   James Whiteside (1804–76) was lord chief justice. He defended O'Connell in state trials in 1844 and Smith O'Brien at Clonmel in 1848. He was a member of Parliament from Enniskillen and attained a high position in the House of Commons. Crone calls him "one of the great orators of the century." For a picture of a statue of Whiteside in St. Patrick's, see *Dublin and Cork*, p. 47. Isaac Butt (1813–79) was the father of Home Rule. He founded the Home Rule Association in 1870. He was a member of Parliament and a professor of political economy at Trinity College, Dublin. Crone calls him "a great orator." Thomas O'Hagan (1812–85) was a member of Parliament, became lord chancellor in 1868, and was raised to the peerage in 1870. The *DNB* praises O'Hagan for his power of speech and capacity as a trial lawyer. He defended Gavan Duffy in a libel action in 1842 and on state trial in 1844.

138.16/136.32 WOULD ANYONE WISH THAT MOUTH FOR HER KISS   Here and on p. 138.30/137.8 Stephen is again thinking of the poem he remembered on p. 132.12/131.1. See entry 48.3.

138.18/136.34 RHYMES AND REASONS   The *ODEP* lists the proverbial "Neither rhyme nor reason" and cites eight instances, including three from Shakespeare.

138.23/137.1 LA TUA PACE . . .   Most of these quotations illustrating rhyme come from the speech of Paolo and Francesca to Dante in canto v of "Inferno." I quote lines 89–96, italicizing the passages quoted in *Ulysses*: "O animal grazioso e benigno,/ Che visitando vai *per l'aer perso*/ Noi che tingemmo il mondo di sanguigno:/ Se fosse amico il re dell' universo,/ Noi pregheremmo lui per *la tua pace*/ Poiche hai pieta del nostra mal perverso./ Di quel che udire e *che parlar ti piace*/ Noi udiremo e parleremo a vui/ *Mentre che il vento, come fa, si tace*" ("O gracious creature and benign! who go'st/ Visiting, *through this element obscure*,/ Us, who the world with bloody stain imbru'd;/ If for a friend the King of all we own'd,/ Our prayer to him should for *thy peace arise,*/ Since thou hast pity on our evil plight./ Of whatso'er to hear *or to discourse/ It pleases thee,* that will we hear, of that/ Freely with thee discourse, *while e'er the wind,/ As now, is mute.*") The other quotations, "quella pacifica oriafiamma" ("so burn'd the peaceful oriflamb") and "Che i miei *di rimirar fe' piu ardenti*" ("That he made mine eyes more ardent to regaze"), are from "Paradiso," canto xxxi, lines 127 and 142. At that point in the poem, Dante is gazing up at the Virgin. First he compares her with the oriflamb (or oriflamme) which Gabriel gave to the ancient kings of France. It was a flame on a golden ground; no one who fought under it could be defeated. In the second line quoted (l. 142), Dante sees St. Bernard gazing at the Virgin in such a way that it makes him "more ardent to regaze." (The translation here is that of H. F. Cary, except for line 142 of "Paradiso," canto xxxi, which is taken from the Carlyle-Wicksteed translation, since Cary obscures the literal meaning of that line.)

138.29/137.8 TOMB WOMB   See entry 48.7.

139.1/137.14 THE THIRD PROFESSION   The three learned professions traditionally have been divinity, law, and medicine, usually listed in that order. But in this instance, the context indicates that law is the "third profession."

139.2/137.14 YOUR CORK LEGS   As Joseph Prescott has pointed out, this alludes to an Irish song entitled "The Cork Leg" (or "The Runaway Cork Leg"). Prescott printed a ten-stanza version of the song in his "Local Allusions in Joyce's *Ulysses*" (reprinted in *Exploring James Joyce*, 1964). There are several versions of the song in circulation, all of which tell the story of a Dutch merchant who loses a leg and has a cork one made to replace it, only to learn that he cannot keep his new leg from traveling. I found a version in a paperback song book entitled *Harding's Nightingale Song Book*, which has thirteen stanzas and ends in a pun on "L.E.G." and "elegy."

139.3/137.15 HENRY GRATTAN AND FLOOD AND DEMOSTHENES AND EDMUND BURKE   Henry Grattan (1746–1820) was an Irish statesman and orator, best known for his part in gaining for Ireland the independent parliament known as "Grattan's Parliament." Henry Flood (1732–91) was another famous Irish statesman and orator. Both Grattan and Flood contributed occasional papers on Irish politics to the *Freeman's Journal*. Demosthenes (*ca.* 383–22

B.C.) was a famous Athenian orator. Edmund Burke (1729–97) was born in Dublin and graduated from Trinity College, Dublin, and went on to become one of the greatest orators of his time.

139.5/137.17 HARMSWORTH OF THE FARTHING PRESS   This is Alfred C. Harmsworth (1865–1922), who was born in the Dublin suburb of Chapelizod. M. Magalaner briefly discusses Harmsworth in connection with the periodicals mentioned at the beginning of the *Dubliners* story "An Encounter" (*Time of Apprenticeship*, p. 149). Harmsworth published several popular magazines for boys during the 1890's. The *DNB* article on Harmsworth points out that he was created a baronet in 1903 and raised to the peerage as Baron Northcliffe in 1905. In 1908 he became chief proprietor of the London *Times*.

139.6/137.19 PADDY KELLY'S BUDGET, PUE'S OCCURRENCES AND OUR WATCHFUL FRIEND THE SKIBBEREEN EAGLE   There were actual Irish newspapers by these titles. *Paddy Kelly's Budget* is described in some detail by B. P. Bowen in "Dublin Humorous Periodicals of the 19th Century," in the *Dublin Historical Record*, XIII (March–May, 1952), 2–11. Bowen refers to the journal as "the Budget," and says, ". . . it was published in November, 1832, and continued to January, 1834, when it was succeeded by Young Paddy Kelly's Budget which continued to December, 1835, or perhaps later" (p. 3). Bowen also describes it as "a topical journal with a tendency to vulgarity" (p. 3). The magazine is also described in Stephen J. Brown's *Ireland in Fiction*, p. 342. *Pue's Occurrences* was among the earliest newspapers in Ireland. J. T. Gilbert in his *A History of the City of Dublin* (Dublin, 1861; 3 vols.) says that Richard Pue (d. 1758), printer, and owner of Dick's Coffee House, began publishing a newspaper called *Pue's Occurrences* about 1700. Gilbert briefly describes the paper, which was still running at the time of Pue's death (Gilbert, I, 174–75). Gilbert says, however, that Robert Thornton, also of Skinner's-row, issued the first newspaper in Dublin in 1685 (I, 178). The *Skibbereen Eagle* (later the *West Cork Eagle*, still later by other names) was a county Cork newspaper in the 1860's (Skibbereen is a town in county Cork). E. C. Brewer's *Dictionary of Phrase and Fable* explains that the phrase now refers to "a type of newspaper that, without having any sort of influence, seeks by threats to direct political affairs; because an insignificant sheet of this name once solemnly warned Lord Palmerston that it had 'got its eyes both on him and on the Emperor of Russia.' "

139.8/137.21   A MASTER OF FORENSIC ELOQUENCE LIKE WHITESIDE   See entry 138.11.

139.9/137.21   SUFFICIENT FOR THE DAY IS THE NEWSPAPER THEREOF   This is a parody of Christ's statement in the sermon on the mount, "Sufficient unto the day is the evil thereof" (Matt. 6:34).

139.11/137.24   GRATTAN AND FLOOD WROTE FOR THIS VERY PAPER   See entry 139.3.

139.13/137.26   DR. LUCAS   Charles Lucas (1713–71), said by Grattan to have "laid the groundwork of Irish liberty," was among the earliest contributors to the *Freeman's Journal*. The *DNB* article on Lucas says that he contributed to the newspaper from its commencement in 1763, sometimes anonymously, but more often under the signature of "A Citizen," or "Civis."

139.13/137.26   JOHN PHILPOT CURRAN . . .   John Philpot Curran (1750–1817) was an eminent Irish orator and patriot. Wilmot Harrison calls him "the most famous member of the Irish bar" (*Memorable Dublin Houses*, p. 76). While a student at Trinity College, Dublin, Curran cured himself of stuttering. He made his greatest speech, on "universal emancipation," at the trial of Hamilton Rowan in 1794. Kendal Bushe is Charles Kendal Bushe (1767–1843), who was educated at Trinity, was a member of Parliament, and was chief justice. Grattan said of him, "Bushe spoke with the lips of an angel." On Seymour Bushe, see entry 100.4.

139.24/137.35   THAT CASE OF FRATRICIDE . . .   See entries 100.2 and 100.4.

139.26/138.1   AND IN THE PORCHES OF MINE EAR DID POUR   This alludes to the ghost's explanation to Hamlet about the manner of his death, from *Hamlet*, I, v, 63 (though the text reads *my ears*, not *mine ear*). Stephen goes on to wonder how the ghost knew this since King Hamlet died in his sleep. See also entry 139.28, and cf. entry 196.38.

139.28/138.2   OR THE OTHER STORY, BEAST WITH TWO BACKS   In *Othello*, I, i, 118, Iago tells Brabantio that ". . . your daughter and the Moor are now making the beast with two backs." But the "other story" Stephen refers to is the love of Claudius and Gertrude (see entry 139.26).

139.31/138.6   HE SPOKE ON THE LAW OF EVIDENCE . . .   These statements about Bushe's speech are not accurate; see entry 100.4. The *lex talionis*, or law of retaliation, is described in Exodus 21:23–25. And the famous statue of Moses by Michelangelo is not at the Vatican, but in the church of San Pietro in Vincoli.

140.29/139.4   THE OPAL HUSH POETS   The context shows that this refers to the Dublin theosophical group, on which see chap. X of E. A. Boyd's *Ireland's Literary Renaissance.* But I have not found an earlier use of this phrase to describe the group, and if this is an allusion, I am unaware of it.

140.30/139.5   THAT BLAVATSKY WOMAN   Madame Helena Petrovna Blavatsky (1831–91) was a Russian spiritualist who was one of the founders of the Theosophical Society (1875).

140.31/139.6   A. E. HAS BEEN TELLING SOME YANKEE INTERVIEWER THAT YOU CAME TO HIM . . .   Richard M. Kain has suggested that the interviewer was University of Pennsylvania professor Cornelius Weygandt, who visited Dublin in 1902, and that Weygandt mentions Joyce, though not by name, in his *Irish Plays and Playwrights* (1913). See "The Yankee Interviewer in *Ulysses*," *JJM III*, 155–57.

141.3/139.15   A SPEECH MADE BY JOHN F. TAYLOR   Taylor was an actual person, and on October 24, 1901, he made the speech on the Irish language which was the basis for the speech described in *Ulysses.* Ellmann describes Taylor as a "patriotic barrister" and an orator whom Joyce admired (see *JJ*, pp. 94–95).

141.17/139.29   THE VIALS OF HIS WRATH BUT POURING THE PROUD MAN'S CONTUMELY UPON THE NEW MOVEMENT   The first phrase here alludes to Revelation 16:1: "And I heard a great voice out of the temple saying to the seven angels, Go your ways, and pour out the vials of the wrath of God upon the earth." Hamlet says "For who would bear . . . the proud man's contumely" during his "To be or not to be" soliloquy (*Ham.*, III, i, 71).

142.13/140.24   AND LET OUR CROOKED SMOKES   This is from *Cymbeline.* In the concluding speech of the play, Cymbeline says, "Laud we the gods,/ And let our crooked smokes climb to their nostrils/ From our blest altars" (V, v, 476–78). This full statement is quoted on p. 218.10/215.19.

142.21/140.32   IT WAS REVEALED TO ME THAT THOSE THINGS ARE GOOD . . .   This is a verbatim quotation from St. Augustine's *Confessions*, Book VII, section 12.

142.35/141.6   BY THE NILEBANK THE BABEMARIES KNEEL, CRADLE OF BULRUSHES: A MAN SUPPLE IN COMBAT: STONEHORNED, STONEBEARDED, HEART OF STONE   Stephen here combines allusions to the discovery of Moses by the Pharaoh's daughter, described in Exodus 2:1–9, and to Michelangelo's statue of Moses, mentioned earlier on p. 139.33/138.8. On "stonehorned," see entry 470.26.

142.39/141.10   ISIS AND OSIRIS, OF HORUS AND AMMON RA   Isis and Osiris, daughter and son of Geb, god of the earth, and Nut, god of the sky, were among the most important Egyptian deities. Their marriage produced their son, Horus. Ammon Ra was the supreme god of the Egyptians.

143.11/141.21   FOLLOWED THE PILLAR OF THE CLOUD   This refers to the pillar of cloud which led the Israelites by day. Exodus 13:21 says, "And the Lord went before them by day in a pillar of cloud, to lead them the way." The pillar of cloud is mentioned several other times in the Old Testament. It is alluded to again on pp. 210.25/208.1 and 727.20/712.10.

143.20/141.30   AND YET HE DIED WITHOUT HAVING ENTERED THE LAND OF PROMISE   Moses' viewing the promised land from atop Mt. Pisgah, his death without entering that land, and his succession by Joshua are described in Deuteronomy 34.

143.24/141.33   AND WITH A GREAT FUTURE BEHIND HIM   J. Prescott has suggested (MLQ, XIII, 153) that this recalls an exchange in Oscar Wilde's Lady Windermere's Fan, act III: Lord Augustus. [Puffing a cigar.] "Mrs. Erlynne has a future before her." Dumby. "Mrs. Erlynne has a past before her."

143.28/141.38   GONE WITH THE WIND   This alludes to the well-known line from Ernest Dowson's (1867–1900) poem "Non Sum Qualis Eram Bonae Sub Regno Cynarae" ("I am no longer the same man I was under the kind reign of Cynara"—which is a quotation from Horace's Odes, Book IV, ode 1, lines 3–4). The third stanza of Dowson's poem begins, "I have forgot much, Cynara! gone with the wind. . . ." This line is an adaptation of Psalms 103:16: "For the wind passeth over it, and it is gone. . . ."

143.28/141.38   HOSTS AT MULLAGHMAST AND TARA OF THE KINGS   Though both Mullaghmast and Tara are known in ancient Irish history (Tara as the seat of the high kings of Ireland), Stephen is here thinking of modern history and oratory. He is alluding to the series of vast repeal meeting held by Daniel O'Connell in 1843 and called by the Times the "Monster meetings." The crowds at these meetings numbered in the hundreds of thousands. The two largest meetings were held at Tara on August 15, 1843, and at Mullaghmast on October 1, 1843. The Tara crowd was said to be 750,000 to 1,000,000. See P. S. O'Hegarty, Ireland Under the Union, pp. 144, 147.

143.29/141.39   MILES OF EARS OF PORCHES   Stephen is still thinking of the monster meetings described in the preceding entry, but he does so in terms of a Hamlet allusion he thought of earlier. See entry 139.26.

143.31/142.2   AKASIC RECORDS OF ALL THAT EVER ANYWHERE WHEREVER

WAS   S. Gilbert discusses Akasic records and quotes from A. P. Sinnett's *The Growth of the Soul* (1896) to explain that the *Akasa* (from Sanskrit for *sky*) is the all-embracing medium in which thoughts, indeed all consciousness, are preserved. Gilbert quotes Sinnett as saying, "consciousness is in indirect relations with the all but infinite memory of Nature, which is preserved with imperishable perfection in the all-embracing medium known to occult science as the Akasa" (quoted in *JJU*, p. 189). See Stephen's use of "the memory of nature" on p. 10.9/11.38.

144.10/142.20 LAY ON, MACDUFF   From Macbeth's challenge to Macduff in *Macbeth*, V, viii, 33.

144.11/142.21 CHIP OFF THE OLD BLOCK   The *ODEP* lists four instances of this proverbial phrase from 1642 on.

144.25/142.33 FUIT ILIUM   "Fuit Ilium" (literally "Troy has been") is from the passage in the *Aeneid* when Panthus replies to Aeneas' question about how the battle is going by saying, "Fuimus Troes, fuit Ilium et ingens/ gloria Teucrorum" ("We Trojans, with Ilium and all its Teucrian glory, Are things of the past"; Book II, ll. 325–26, C. Day Lewis' translation).

144.26/142.34 KINGDOMS OF THIS WORLD   This probably alludes to Christ's statement to Pilate in John 18:36: "My kingdom is not of this world: if my kingdom were of this world, then would my servants fight, that I should not be delivered to the Jews: but now is my kingdom not from hence."

145.3/143.9 TWO DUBLIN VESTALS   In the Roman religion, the vestal virgins were the attendants of the sacred fire in the worship of Vesta, goddess of the fire on the hearth of the home and the state. They were from patrician families and took an oath of virginity for thirty years. They enjoyed many privileges, including immunity from the laws, but those who broke the vow were immured alive in an underground room and left to die.

145.9/143.14 AKASIC RECORDS   See entry 143.31.

145.10/143.16 LET THERE BE LIFE   Though this exact phrase does not occur in the account of the creation, Stephen's statement is obviously patterned on God's statement "Let there be light" (Gen. 1:3) and similar statements also in Genesis 1.

145.12/143.18 NELSON'S PILLAR   See entry 95.9. Nelson's Pillar is mentioned several times in the course of Stephen's story.

145.18/143.24 WISE VIRGINS   Christ tells the parable of the wise and foolish virgins in Matthew 25:1–13.

145.32/144.2 LOURDES WATER   Lourdes water is water from the shrine at Lourdes, France, about which see entry 81.12.

146.1/144.6   VESTAL VIRGINS   See entry 145.3.

146.27/144.32   HOUSE OF KEYS   See entry 120.30.

146.33/145.3   STRAIGHT FROM THE STABLE   This phrase, and a similar one Stephen uses on p. 504.5/493.18, seems to be a variation on the well-known "Straight from the horse's mouth," but I have not located these phrases in any dictionary of proverbs or sayings I have consulted.

147.30/146.3   OUT FOR THE WAXIES' DARGLE   Joseph Prescott has explained this as referring to an annual shoemaker's picnic that was held in the glen of the Dargle river near Dublin (see "Local Allusions in Joyce's *Ulysses*," reprinted in *Exploring James Joyce*, pp. 51–58).

148.9/146.15   THE ONEHANDLED ADULTERER   Horatio Nelson, Viscount Nelson (1758–1805), British naval hero, lost his right arm in the attempt to capture Santa Cruz on July 24, 1797. Nelson did commit adultery with and have a child by Lady Emma Hamilton (*ca.* 1765–1815), wife of Sir William Hamilton (1730–1803).

148.25/147.1   SOPHIST WALLOPS HAUGHTY HELEN . . .   These headline statements are developed by more specific statements about these women in the following lines. See the next entries.

148.29/147.5   ANTISTHENES . . .   Antisthenes was a fifth century B.C. Athenian who founded the Cynic school of philosophy. Most of our information about him comes from the description in Diogenes Laertius' *Lives of Eminent Philosophers*. Laertius describes Antisthenes as a pupil of Gorgias and as the founder of the Stoic and Cynic schools of philosophy. Laertius says that Antisthenes used to lecture in the Gymnasium called Cynosarges, and some say that his sect took the name of Cynics from that (Greek *kynikos* means *dog-like*). And Laertius adds that Antisthenes himself was called Haplocyon ("downright dog"). Laertius catalogues Antisthenes' works, and in the ninth volume of them he includes "an essay on Helen and Penelope," but he says no more, and I have not been able to find further information on the treatise.

149.5/147.11   POOR PENELOPE. PENELOPE RICH   The first of these Penelopes is the wife of Ulysses. On Penelope Rich, see entry 201.38.

149.24/147.29   DEUS NOBIS HAEC OTIA FECIT   At the opening of Virgil's first Eclogue, Tityrus says to Meliboeus, "O Meliboee, deus nobis haec otia fecit" ("O Meliboeus, god made us these comforts") (Eclogue I, l. 6).

149.25/148.1   A PISGAH SIGHT OF PALESTINE   This alludes to Thomas Fuller's (1608–61) huge descriptive geography of the Holy Land,

A Pisgah-Sight of Palestine and the Confines Thereof, with the History of the Old and New Testament (1650). Stephen's use of "Parable" recalls Christ's parables and suggests that MacHugh may have been right in observing that the story is about "wise virgins" (p. 145.18/143.24). See also the following entry.

149.29/148.5   MOSES AND THE PROMISED LAND   This follows up the reference to Pisgah a few lines later, since Moses viewed the promised land from Mt. Pisgah. See entry 143.20.

150.6/148.12   SIR JOHN GRAY'S PAVEMENT ISLAND   This refers to the statue of Sir John Gray which stands in the middle of O'Connell Street. See entry 94.8.

150.12/148.18   ONEHANDLED ADULTERER   This alludes to Nelson. See entry 148.9.

LESTRYGONIANS

151.4/149.4 GOD. SAVE. OUR   This alludes to the English national anthem, "God Save the King." The origins of the song and its author are not fully known. For words and music, see Alfred H. Miles, *Our National Songs*, p. 48. See also entry 597.6.

151.11/149.11 BLOOD OF THE LAMB. . . . ALL ARE WASHED IN THE BLOOD OF THE LAMB   The Blood of the Lamb is mentioned several times in the Bible; most significant for this context is Revelation 7:14 where the saved are described as follows: "These are they which came out of great tribulation, and have washed their robes, and made them white in the blood of the Lamb." But Bloom is probably thinking more immediately of the hymn "Washed in the Blood of the Lamb," by Elisha A. Hoffman (b. 1839). The hymn begins, "Have you been to Jesus for the cleansing power?" and is sometimes entitled "Holiness Desired."

151.14/149.14 FOUNDATION OF A BUILDING . . .   Leonard Albert sees this as one of the many allusions to Masonic lore in this episode. See his essay "Ulysses, Cannibals, and Freemasons," *A.D.*, II, 265–83.

151.15/149.15 DRUID'S ALTARS   The druids, priests of the ancient religion of the Celts in Gaul, Britain, and Ireland, were mentioned earlier on p. 11.6/12.35. Apparently some druids did perform human sacrifices, but authorities question whether the practice occurred among Irish druids. P. W. Joyce says he does not believe the ancient Irish practiced human sacrifice (*Short History*, p. 141). Douglas Hyde points out the late date of sources attesting druid sacrifices (e.g., the Book of Leinster) and says he doubts that it ever took place, and that if so, it had fallen into abeyance before the coming of Christianity (*Lit. Hist. of Ireland*, pp. 92–93).

151.15/149.15   ELIJAH IS COMING. DR. JOHN ALEXANDER DOWIE, RESTORER OF THE CHURCH IN ZION, IS COMING   The second coming of Elijah is to precede the day of judgment. Malachi 4:5–6 says, "Behold, I will send you Elijah the prophet before the coming of the great and dreadful day of the Lord: And he shall turn the heart of the fathers to the children, and the heart of the children to their fathers, lest I come and smite the earth with a curse." *Restorer* refers to Matthew 17:10–11: "And his disciples asked him, saying, Why then say the scribes that Elias must first come? And Jesus answered and said unto them, Elias truly shall first come and restore all things." John Alexander Dowie (1847–1907) was an Edinburgh-born fanatical evangelist. He founded his own church and Zion City, Illinois, and both the town and the church were under his sole control. In 1902 he proclaimed himself Elijah the Restorer, and two years later consecrated himself the First Apostle. In 1903 Dowie and three thousand of his followers made a $300,000 attempt to convert New York City. Undaunted by his failure, he immediately began a Round the World salvation campaign, costs defrayed by required deposits of Zion City residents to the Zion City bank (which Dowie owned). Dowie was later deposed by one of his disciples, Wilbur Glenn Voliva (a firm believer in the flatness of the earth), for "polygamous teaching and other grave charges" (from the *DAB*, q.v. for a fuller account of Dowie). As R. M. Adams has pointed out (*SS*, p. 8), Dowie was not in Dublin at this time. According to accounts in the London *Times* of that week, Dowie arrived in London on Saturday, June 11; had trouble finding accommodations there because of some statements he had reportedly made about the King; left London for Boulogne on Monday, June 14; arrived back in London from Boulogne on Friday, June 17; and sailed from Liverpool for New York on the *Lucania* on Saturday, June 18.

151.19/149.19   ALL HEARTILY WELCOME   In view of the considerable use of Swift's *Polite Conversation* in this episode, this phrase probably echoes that work. The phrase "heartily welcome" occurs four times in the second conversation (the dining scene), which is the one most drawn on in this episode. In its first occurrence, Lady Smart says, "Well, you are all heartily welcome, as I may say" (p. 124; the other occurrences are on pp. 127, 131–32, and 147 of Partridge's edition).

151.20/149.20 TORRY AND ALEXANDER   The *United Irishman* of March 26, 1904, mentions that a Dr. Torrey from America is then conducting a mission in Dublin and refers to it as the "Torrey-Alexander mission." Torrey is probably American evangelist Reuben Archer Torrey (1856–1928). The *National Cyclopaedia of American Biography* says of him, "While on a visit to Great Britain during 1903–05, he held meetings in the principal English and Scotch cities, including one of five months' duration at the Royal Albert hall in London, during which he was reported to have converted a total of 17,000 people" (XXI, 428). I have not identified Alexander.

151.24/149.23 PEPPER'S GHOST IDEA   Pepper's ghost seems to have been a character of a dramatic company that specialized in presenting plays involving a spectral effect, probably through the use of some phosphorescent substance on their costumes. My information about Pepper's ghost is derived solely from an advertisement in *Zoz*, announcing a performance of "The original Pepper's Ghost! and Spectral Opera Company" at the Rotunda on April 2, 1877, and from a *Zoz* comment on the performance a few days later.

151.24/149.24 IRON NAILS RAN IN   See entry 81.20.

151.40/149.39 EAT YOU OUT OF HOUSE AND HOME   The *ODEP* lists five instances of this proverbial saying, dating back to *ca.* 1410, and including one from Shakespeare. In *II Henry IV*, II, 1, 80, Mistress Quickly says of Falstaff, "He hath eaten me out of house and home."

151.41/149.40 LIVING ON THE FAT OF THE LAND   In Genesis 45:18, Pharaoh tells Joseph to tell his brethren, "I will give you the good of the land of Egypt, and ye shall eat the fat of the land."

152.1/149.41 THE BLACK FAST YOM KIPPUR   Yom Kippur, the Day of Atonement, is the holiest day of the Jewish religious year. It is celebrated on the tenth of Tishri (middle of September to the beginning of October), and its purpose is to gain atonement for sins committed during the year. "It is the earnest and consecrating close of the ten Penitential Days, which begin with the judgment of God on Rosh Hashanah" (*Universal Jewish Encyclopedia* [New York, 1940]). Though fasting is a part of this ritual, Bloom seems to be blending Jewish and Catholic elements here. P. W. Joyce (*English As We Speak It*, p. 215) has "Blackfast: among Roman Catholics, there is a 'black fast' on Ash Wednesday, Spy Wednesday, and Good Friday, i.e. no flesh meat or whitemeat is allowed—no flesh, butter, eggs, cheese, or milk."

152.10/150.9 PROOF OF THE PUDDING   This proverbial phrase, which is listed in the *ODEP*, occurs in Swift's *Polite Conversation*, second conversation, where Neverout says "the Proof of the Pudden, is in the eating" (p. 129). Partridge says it is "17th–20th centuries."

152.28/150.25 ELIJAH . . . IS COM   See entry 151.15.

152.37/150.33 SHAKESPEARE HAS NO RHYMES: BLANK VERSE   Probably this is Bloom's observation about a particular passage rather than a generalization about the whole of Shakespeare's work. It seems unlikely that anyone who can quote *Hamlet* as correctly as Bloom does would be unaware of the many ɹhymed lines in Shakespeare. Cf. entry 152.39.

152.39/150.36 HAMLET, I AM THY FATHER'S SPIRIT/ DOOMED FOR A CERTAIN TIME TO WALK THE EARTH   The actual words of the Ghost to Hamlet are, "I am thy father's spirit,/Doomed for a certain term to walk the night" (*Ham.*, I, v, 9–10). Stephen later errs similarly in quoting the first line of this passage; see entry 188.35.

153.9/151.7 FROM THEIR HEIGHTS, POUNCING ON PREY   W. Y. Tindall (*RG*, p. 169) says this suggests the Lestrygonians' attack upon the enharbored ships in the *Odyssey*, book IX. We are told that Ulysses' ships (except his own) were penned in a close, steep-cliffed harbor when the Lestrygonians attacked from the heights, and at one point the Lestrygonians' attack is compared to men spearing fish. See also entry 170.40.

153.12/151.10 MANNA   Manna, frequently mentioned in the Bible, was the food from heaven which miraculously fed the Israelites during their journey to the Promised Land. See Exodus 16:11–36.

153.15/151.13 NO ACCOUNTING FOR TASTES   This proverbial saying is listed in the *ODEP*. In light of the many allusions in this episode to Swift's *Polite Conversation*, this may owe something to Col. Atwit's "Why; every one as they like; as the good Woman said, when she kiss'd her Cow." See entry 380.34.

153.16/151.14 ROBINSON CRUSOE HAD TO LIVE ON THEM   Though he had other types of food as well, Robinson Crusoe several times mentions killing sea birds, though he did not know what kind they were and not all of them were edible. See, e.g., Crusoe's "Journal" entries for November 3 and November 14, 15, 16.

153.30/151.27 WHICH IN THE STREAM OF LIFE WE TRACE This is from W. V. Wallace's opera *Maritana*; see entry 86.32.

154.5/152.2 FASCINATING LITTLE BOOK THAT IS OF SIR ROBERT BALL'S Sir Robert Ball (1840–1913), who was born in Dublin, was astronomer royal of Ireland, Lowdean professor of astronomy, and director of the observatory at Cambridge. He was a popular lecturer and author of several works on astronomy. Since he has it on his bookshelf (p. 708/693), Bloom is probably thinking of Ball's *The Story of the Heavens*. Perhaps this is the same book M'Coy describes on p. 233.33/230.18.

154.7/152.4 MET HIM PIKEHOSES Metempsychosis; see entry 64.18.

154.23/152.19 WE HAVE SINNED: WE HAVE SUFFERED Bloom is recalling his thoughts about the letters I.H.S. See entry 81.20.

154.36/152.31 HAVE A FINGER IN THE PIE The *ODEP* lists this proverbial phrase and includes citations from John Ray's *Proverbs* (1678) and from Shakespeare. In *Henry VIII*, the Duke of Buckingham says of Cardinal Wolsey, "The Devil speed him! No man's pie is freed/ From his ambitious finger" (I, i, 52–53).

154.37/152.32 PILLAR OF SALT This alludes to the story of Lot's wife, who was turned into a pillar of salt because her curiosity forced her to disobey God and turn around to view the destruction of the cities of the plain. See Genesis 19.

155.9/153.4 FEAST OF OUR LADY AT MOUNT CARMEL The thought of the Carmelite convent at Rathmines (the Tranquilla Convent) makes Bloom think of this Feast. The Feast of Our Lady of Mount Carmel was instituted by the Carmelites between 1376 and 1386. It is celebrated on July 16, or the Sunday following, or on some Sunday in July. According to the *Catholic Encyclopedia*, " . . . the object of the feast is the special predilection of Mary for those who profess themselves her servants by wearing her scapular."

155.15/153.10 IT WAS A NUN THEY SAY INVENTED BARBED WIRE This is another of Bloom's fancies. Though there is some uncertainty about it, the inventor of barbed wire was probably Joseph Farwell Glidden, a De Kalb, Illinois, farmer. He invented it in 1873, first sold it in 1874 (see Walter Prescott Webb, *The Great Plains* [Boston, 1931]).

155.22/153.17 THE BIG FIRE AT ARNOTT'S In the "Dublin Annals" section of Thom's *Dublin Directory* (1904), the following occurs: "1894. May 4.–the block of buildings owned by the firm of Arnott &co. (Lim.), which extends from Henry-street to Prince's-street, totally destroyed by fire" (p. 2105).

155.26/153.21   FOR WHAT WE HAVE ALREADY RECEIVED MAY THE LORD
MAKE US   This is from a common prayer after meals; on p.
169.35/167.17 Bloom thinks of "Grace after meals."

155.42/153.37   STREAM OF LIFE   This probably alludes to W. V.
Wallace's opera *Maritana*, which Bloom alluded to on p. 153.30/
151.27. See entry 86.32.

156.3/153.39   PENDENNIS   Bloom thinks of Thackeray's *Pendennis*
(1848-50) while trying to remember the name of someone beginning with Pen. On p. 181.32/179.6 Bloom recalls the name as
"Penrose."

156.8/154.3   WINDS THAT BLOW FROM THE SOUTH   Hodgart and
Worthington list this song, but they have a question mark by it,
indicating that they have not identified it. They assume that this is
the same song as the one quoted on p. 525.3/513.19 (and in *Stephen
Hero*, p. 165), but it is not clear why they assume this. I have not
been able to identify the song.

156.17/154.11   MAY BE FOR MONTHS AND MAY BE FOR NEVER   This
misquotes a line from the song "Kathleen Mavourneen," by Mrs.
Julia Crawford and Frederick Crouch. The chorus of the song
says, "It may be for years and it may be forever; Oh! why are thou
silent, thou voice of my heart? It may be for years and it may be
forever; Then why are thou silent, Kathleen Mavourneen?" For
words and music, see *Songs That Never Grow Old*, pp. 112-13.

156.40/154.33   ALL ON THE BAKER'S LIST   In his chapter "Proverbs,"
P. W. Joyce (*English As We Speak It*, p. 109) lists "I'm *on the
baker's list* again" as meaning "I am well and have recovered my
appetite."

157.10/155.3   YOUR FUNERAL'S TOMORROW/ WHILE YOU'RE COMING
THROUGH THE RYE   Hodgart and Worthington point out that
this blends allusions to a music hall song entitled "His Funeral Is
Tomorrow" and to Burns's "Comin' thro' the Rye." Words and
music of "His Funeral Is Tomorrow," by Felix McGlennon, can
be found in the *Song Dex Treasury of Humorous and Nostalgic
Songs*; it is called an Irish comic song. It begins, "I will sing of
Mick McTurk," and the chorus says, "And his funeral's to-morrow,
My poor heart aches with sorrow" (II, 67).

157.34/155.26   RAISE CAIN   This saying, meaning to make a distur-
bance, is proverbial and is listed in the *ODEP*.

158.25/156.16   THE UNFAIR SEX   This is Bloom's variation on the
common description of woman as "the fair sex."

158.37/156.27   PHILIP BEAUFOY . . . MATCHAM OFTEN THINKS OF . . .

Bloom is remembering the story he read earlier; see entry 68.39.

161.6/158.36 METHOD IN HIS MADNESS   In *Hamlet*, Polonius says of Hamlet's cryptic but satirical remarks, "Though this be madness, yet there is method in it" (II, ii, 207).

161.15/159.3 DOG IN THE MANGER   This alludes to Aesop's fable about the selfish dog in the manger who prevented the cattle from eating the straw placed for them, even though he had no use for it himself.

161.28/159.16 TWILIGHTSLEEP IDEA: QUEEN VICTORIA WAS GIVEN THAT. NINE SHE HAD   Bloom is probably thinking of the administration of chloroform to Victoria during the birth of Prince Leopold in April, 1853. Since the use of anesthesia in childbirth was then in its pioneer stages, the Queen's use of it attracted considerable attention. Victoria did have nine children.

161.29/159.17 OLD WOMAN THAT LIVED IN A SHOE . . .   Bloom is thinking of the nursery rhyme that begins, "There was an old woman who lived in a shoe." For text and comment, see *ODNR*, pp. 434–35.

162.4/159.33 OLD MRS THORNTON WAS A JOLLY OLD SOUL   This, one of Bloom's several allusions to nursery rhymes in this episode, alludes to the well-known rhyme "Old King Cole," which begins, "Old King Cole/ Was a merry old soul." For text and comment, see *ODNR*, pp. 134–35; the *ODNR* lists one variant that has *jolly* instead of *merry*.

162.18/160.5 MACKEREL THEY CALLED ME   Several critics have said that this suggests Christ. The fish was used as a symbol of Christ among the early Christians since the Greek word *ichthos* (fish) forms an acronym on the phrase *Iesos Christos, Theou Uios Soter* ("Jesus Christ, Son of God, Saviour"). I have found nothing specifically on the mackerel as a symbol of Christ.

162.22/160.9 POLICEMAN'S LOT IS OFT A HAPPY ONE   This parodies "A Policeman's Lot is Not a Happy One," sung by the Sergeant of Police in act II of Gilbert and Sullivan's *The Pirates of Penzance* (1880).

162.29/160.16 TOMMY MOORE'S ROGUISH FINGER   This alludes to the statue of Irish writer Thomas Moore which stands opposite the east front of the Bank of Ireland. The statue, which is located over a public urinal, depicts Moore with a finger upraised. W. Y. Tindall has a picture of the statue in his *The Joyce Country*, p. 100.

162.30/160.17 MEETING OF THE WATERS   Here and two lines later Bloom alludes to Moore's song on the vale of Avoca (county

Wicklow) entitled "The Meeting of the Waters." It begins, "There is not in the wide world a valley so sweet/ As that vale in whose bosom the bright waters meet."

162.34/160.21 MICHAEL BALFE   Balfe (1808–70) was a well-known Irish composer and singer, best known for his opera *The Bohemian Girl* (1843), which is alluded to often in *Ulysses*.

162.36/160.23 COULD A TALE UNFOLD   In *Hamlet*, the Ghost says to Hamlet, "But that I am forbid/ To tell the secrets of my prison house,/ I could a tale unfold . . ." (I, v, 13–15).

162.40/160.26 THE DAY JOE CHAMBERLAIN WAS GIVEN HIS DEGREE IN TRINITY   Joseph Chamberlain (1836–1914), British statesman, was Colonial Secretary from 1895 until 1903. His negotiations with Transvall president Kruger were not successful, and he was wrongly blamed for the aggressive act that precipitated the Boer War. After the war he went to South Africa to try to effect reconciliation with the Boers. He was granted an honorary degree of LL.D. by Trinity College, Dublin, on December 18, 1899, at which time a group of students demonstrated against him and against the Boer War.

163.7/160.36 WHEELS WITHIN WHEELS   The *ODEP* and Apperson list several instances of this proverbial phrase, and both list the King James version of Ezekiel 1:16 as the earliest example. The *ODEP* explains that it means "A complexity of forces or influences." The wheels appear to Ezekiel as a part of his vision, and he says of them, " . . . and their appearance and their work was as it were a wheel in the middle of a wheel." Ezekiel 10:10 is similar.

163.10/160.39 UP THE BOERS   "Up ———" is a common phrase said in support of a person or thing. The *OED* lists several instances, though it does not list this one. The Irish were naturally sympathetic with the Boer cause and even fielded brigades on the South African side in the war. For a full expression of the Irish feeling for the Boers, see Michael Davitt's *The Boer Fight for Freedom* (1902).

163.11/160.40 THREE CHEERS FOR DE WET   Christian Rudolph De Wet (1854–1922) was a Boer general and statesman who was particularly successful in guerrilla fighting. Following the war he first favored amity with the British, but later supported a separate Boer state.

163.12/160.41 WE'LL HANG JOE CHAMBERLAIN ON A SOURAPPLE TREE   On Joe Chamberlain, see entry 162.40. As Hodgart and Worthington point out, this phrase alludes to a song entitled "We'll Hang

Jeff Davis," by Turner, which is a parody of "The Battle Hymn of the Republic." Though I know such a song exists, I have not been able to find a printed copy of it.

163.13/160.42 VINEGAR HILL   Vinegar Hill, county Wexford, was the site of an Irish insurgent stronghold in the Wexford uprising of 1798. The insurgents were defeated in the Battle of Vinegar Hill, June 21, 1798, by British forces under General Lake. This may also be considered an allusion to R. D. Joyce's "The Boys of Wexford," which mentions Vinegar Hill; see entry 129.13.

163.14/161.1 THE BUTTER EXCHANGE BAND   I have not identified this, but the context suggests that it refers to a group of young patriots. Perhaps it has some association with the butter market or butter exchange in Cork, which was a large and well-known market.

163.16/161.3 WHETHER ON THE SCAFFOLD HIGH   This alludes to the very popular Irish song "God Save Ireland," by Timothy Daniel Sullivan (1827–1914), who was editor of the *Nation* and Lord Mayor of Dublin. The refrain of the song says, " 'God save Ireland,' said the heroes; 'God save Ireland,' said they all;/ 'Whether on the scaffold high, or the battle-field we die,/ O what matter, when for Erin dear we fall!' " For complete text, see Hoagland, pp. 522–23.

163.18/161.4 HAS HARVEY DUFF IN HIS EYE   This alludes to Harvey Duff, the police informer in Dion Boucicault's play *The Shaughran* (1875). Duff, who is disliked by all, is described in the Dramatis Personae as "a Police Agent in disguise of a peasant, under the name of Keach."

163.19/161.5 PETER OR DENIS OR JAMES CAREY THAT BLEW THE GAFF ON THE INVINCIBLES   James Carey is the correct name of the man who informed on the Invincibles; see entry 81.26.

163.27/161.13 PEEPING TOM   Peeping Tom was the tailor who peeked at Lady Godiva, wife of Leofric, earl of Mercia, during her ride naked through the streets of Coventry in order to get her husband to remit a tax he had imposed on the people. As a result of his peeping, Tom was struck blind.

163.33/161.19 THERE ARE GREAT TIMES COMING . . .   There may be some allusion here to one of several songs having titles similar to this. American songwriter Stephen Foster wrote one entitled "There's a Good Time Coming" in 1846, but English composer Henry Russell's song by the same title is probably better known. Two of the cheap paperback song books I examined in the National Library of Ireland contained copies of this song. According to the version in *The Favorite Songster* (Dublin, n.d.), the song begins, "There's a good time coming, boys,/ A good time coming," and the chorus says, "There's a good time coming, boys,/ A good time coming;/ There's a good time coming, boys,/ Wait a little longer." Every stanza ends with the phrase "Wait a little longer."

163.36/161.22 JAMES STEPHENS' IDEA . . . CIRCLES OF TEN . . .   Bloom is correct about the Fenians' being organized in circles of ten; see P. S. O'Hegarty, *Ireland Under the Union*, p. 424. On Stephens' escape from Richmond jail, see entry 43.25. But I have not found a story of his escape which involves the turnkey's daughter.

163.38/161.24 SINN FEIN   Sinn Fein (Gaelic for "Ourselves Alone") was the name of the political group founded by Arthur Griffith in 1904–5 and dedicated to achieving Irish independence. The phrase *Sinn Fein* is used several times in *Ulysses* and clearly refers to this political group, but this is apparently an anachronism, for I can find no evidence of Sinn Fein being used to designate this group before about November of 1904. Apparently Grffith had used it in a letter to William Rooney several years earlier, but it was not publicly used until late in 1904. Padraic Colum (*Ourselves Alone* [New York, 1959]) says, ". . . at the end of 1904 an enthusiastic lady, Miss Mary Butler, suggested the name 'Sinn Fein' which Arthur Griffith, forgetting that he had used it in a letter from Africa, instantly adopted" (p. 87; see also p. 32). Apparently Joyce felt Sinn Fein to be so important to his purpose that he disregarded the small anachronism involved in using it.

163.38/161.24 HIDDEN HAND   This may allude to the play *The Hidden Hand* (1864) by Victorian editor and playwright Tom Taylor (1817–80). The play is a melodrama of mystery and intrigue involving a murder by arsenic poisoning. For a brief comment and plot summary, see M. Willson Disher, *Melodrama*, p. 51.

163.41/161.27 GARIBALDI   Giuseppe Garibaldi (1807–82) was a famous Italian patriot and soldier who fought for the unification of Italy. As D. Daiches has pointed out, in this and in the following paragraphs "Bloom is thinking of a variety of nationalist conspirators who escaped from danger."

163.42/161.28 PARNELL. ARTHUR GRIFFITH   Both of these Irish statesmen are frequently alluded to in *Ulysses*; see entries 35.2 and 43.8 and the Index.

164.2/161.30 GAMMON AND SPINACH   This may allude to a line in the refrain of the nursery rhyme "A Frog he Would A-Wooing Go." The refrain says, "With a rowley, powley, gammon and spinach,/ Heigh ho! says Anthony Rowley." See *ODNR*, pp. 177–

81. Another well-known and distinctive use of the phrase is in Dickens' *David Copperfield*, when Miss Mowcher, the dwarf who comes to dress Steerforth's hair, says, "What a world of gammon and spinage it is, though, ain't it?" (chap. XXII).

164.14/161.41   HOME RULE SUN RISING IN THE NORTHWEST   See entry 57.35.

164.24/162.10   ALL ARE WASHED IN THE BLOOD OF THE LAMB   See entry 151.11.

164.33/162.18   PYRAMIDS . . . SLAVES. CHINESE WALL   Bloom is thinking of great edifices and cities of the past, and especially those built by slave labor.

164.33/162.19   BUILT ON BREAD AND ONIONS   Bloom means to indicate cheap food. "A crust of brown bread and an onion" are used to represent a spare diet in *Don Quixote*, Part I, chap. 11, but I do not think any allusion to that passage is involved here. I have not found this exact phrase in any of the dictionaries of quotations, phrases, or idioms I have consulted.

164.34/162.20   ROUND TOWERS   This refers to the many round towers that still dot the Irish landscape. These towers, about seventy of which yet remain, were apparently built during the ninth through the thirteenth centuries, and seem to have been built in connection with cathedrals and abbey churches and to have served as belfries and as places of refuge from the attacks by Scandinavian invaders.

165.17/163.3   MAD FANNY AND HIS OTHER SISTER MRS DICKINSON   Parnell did have a sister named Fanny Parnell (1854–82) and another who was Mrs. E. M. Dickinson. Fanny Parnell emigrated to America and there wrote Fenian poems that brought her a reputation as a minor poet.

165.19/163.5   DAVID SHEEHY BEAT HIM FOR SOUTH MEATH   This alludes to David Sheehy's defeat of John Howard Parnell for the parliamentary seat from South Meath in the October, 1903, election. The *United Irishman* followed the contest with a "plague on both your houses" attitude, and the October 17, 1903, issue reported Sheehy's defeat of Parnell by approximately 2,200 votes to 1,000. John Howard Parnell was the brother of Charles Stewart Parnell.

165.20/163.5   THE CHILTERN HUNDREDS   A "hundred" is simply a legal subdivision of a county or shire. "Applying for the Chiltern hundreds" is an accepted device used by members of Parliament who wish to resign. As the *OED* explains (*s.v.* Chiltern hundreds), "No member of Parliament is by law at liberty to resign his seat, so long as he is duly qualified; on the other hand, a member who accepts an office of profit under the Crown must vacate his seat, subject to re-election. A member desiring to resign therefore applies for the *Stewardship of the Chiltern Hundreds*, or other similar appointment, which is, by a legal figment, held to be such an office; the appointment necessitates his resignation, and, having thus fulfilled its purpose, is again resigned, so as to be ready for conferment upon the next member that wishes to make the same use of it."

165.25/163.11   OF THE TWOHEADED OCTOPUS . . .   A. E. seems to be referring to some occult lore, but I have not found anything like this in any of the books on the occult which I have consulted. Probably this is a Joycean parody of occultism.

165.31/163.17   COMING EVENTS CAST THEIR SHADOWS BEFORE   This alludes to Thomas Campbell's poem "Lochiel's Warning," in which the Wizard says to Lochiel, " . . . coming events cast their shadows before" (l. 56). The Wizard is trying to dissuade Lochiel from going into battle for Charles the Pretender. (*Lochiel* is the title of the chief of the Clan Cameron; the Lochiel of this poem was Donald Cameron [1695?–1748], "The Gentle Lochiel.")

165.34/163.20   ALBERT EDWARD, ARTHUR EDMUND, ALPHONSUS EB ED EL ESQUIRE   Bloom's set of variations on A. E.'s initials seems to involve only one clear allusion: Albert Edward is Edward VII, who was known for sixty years as Albert Edward, Prince of Wales. If the other names involve specific allusions, I have not identified them.

166.36/164.20   THE TIP OF HIS LITTLE FINGER BLOTTED OUT THE SUN'S DISK   John Killham has pointed out (*University of Toronto Quarterly*, XXXIV, 288) the possible parallel here with a passage in Bishop Berkeley's *A New Theory of Vision* (1709), in which Berkeley conjectures about the lack of perspective in a person with newly acquired vision. Berkeley says of such a person, ". . . it is evident one in those circumstances would judge his thumb, with which he might hide a tower, or hinder its being seen, equal to that tower; or his hand, the interposition whereof might conceal the firmament from his view, equal to the firmament" (sec. LXXIX).

166.39/164.23   SUNSPOTS WHEN WE WERE IN LOMBARD STREET WEST   Bloom is probably thinking of 1893; in that year sunspot activity reached one of its periodic highs, being greater that year than any year since 1870.

166.40/164.24   THERE WILL BE A TOTAL ECLIPSE THIS YEAR: AUTUMN

SOME TIME   Thom's *Dublin Directory* (1904) lists two eclipses for 1904, one on March 17, and one on September 9. Of the latter it says, "A total Eclipse of the Sun, September 9, 1904, invisible at Dublin" (p. 2). The *Directory* then goes on to give precise times for the eclipses.

167.8/164.33   CAP IN HAND GOES THROUGH THE LAND   Though I have not located this in any dictionary of proverbs, *Stevenson's Book of Quotations* lists the similar "Cap in hand never did anyone harm" as an Italian proverb.

167.21/165.5   THE YOUNG MAY MOON SHE'S BEAMING, LOVE . . .   This alludes to the opening lines of Thomas Moore's song "The Young May Moon," which begins "The young May moon is beaming, love./ The glow-worm's lamp is gleaming, love."

167.32/165.16   AS SOBER AS A JUDGE   This phrase, or some slight variation of it, is proverbial; the *ODEP* lists "as grave as a judge."

167.36/165.19   BROTH OF A BOY   Wm. Walsh (*Handy-Book of Literary Curiosities*, p. 121) says of this "a phrase much affected by the Irish, yet not unknown in England and America. As broth is the essence of beef, a broth of a boy is the essence of what a boy should be, the right sort of a boy. . . ." Walsh then goes on to quote from Byron's *Don Juan*, canto viii, where Byron uses this phrase. Byron begins stanza 24 of that canto by saying, "But Juan was quite 'a broth of a boy,' " and in the preceding stanza he has described this as an Irish phrase.

167.36/165.19   DION BOUCICAULT BUSINESS WITH HIS HARVESTMOON FACE IN A POKY BONNET   Dion Boucicault was an Irish dramatist; he is mentioned in entry 92.6. Bloom seems to be alluding to some scene from a Boucicault play, but I have not been able to identify it.

167.38/165.21   THREE PURTY MAIDS FROM SCHOOL   This refers to the trio "Three Little Maids from School," sung by the sisters Yum-Yum, Pitti-Sing, and Peep-Bo in act I of Gilbert and Sullivan's *The Mikado* (1885).

168.1/165.26   THE HARP THAT ONCE DID STARVE US ALL   Bloom is parodying the opening line of Thomas Moore's "The Harp That Once through Tara's Halls," which begins "The harp that once through Tara's halls/ The soul of music shed,/ Now hangs as mute on Tara's walls,/ As if that soul were fled."

168.14/165.38   ALL THE BEEF TO THE HEELS   See entry 66.8.

168.20/166.2   THE HUGUENOTS BROUGHT THAT HERE   Ward, Lock and Company's *A Pictorial and Descriptive Guide to Dublin* (18th ed.; London, n.d.) says, "One of the specialties of Dublin, made nowhere else in the world, though even here it now employs but few people, is the making of Poplin. This industry was introduced by the Huguenots in 1693" (p. 25). Grace Lawless Lee, in *The Huguenot Settlements in Ireland* (London, 1936), discusses this in some detail and says, ". . . to the La Touche family is attributed the establishment of the silk and poplin weaving industry in Dublin" (p. 237).

168.20/166.2   LA CAUSA È SANTA! TARA. TARA. GREAT CHORUS THAT. TARA. . . . MEYERBEER . . .   This alludes to German operatic composer Giacomo Meyerbeer's (1791–1864) opera *Les Huguenots*. The opera was first produced in Paris, in French, in 1836. It has been translated and performed in several languages, but is probably most widely known in Italian. This lengthy opera was composed in five acts, but it is often shortened and presented in three. I am puzzled by Bloom's phrase ("The cause is sacred"), because no copy of the opera which I have seen contains this exact phrase, though there is talk throughout the opera of the "holiness" of the cause. Perhaps Bloom is thinking of the "Benediction of Swords" scene (usually in act IV), in which St. Bris sings an aria beginning "D'un sacro zel l'adore." The chorus Bloom recalls with his "Tara tara" is probably the well-known "Rataplan" chorus of the Huguenot soldiers which usually opens act III.

168.26/166.8   HER BIRTHDAY . . . SEPTEMBER EIGHTH   As W. Y. Tindall has pointed out (*RG*, p. 172), September 8 is the birthday of the Virgin Mary as well as of Molly Bloom; the Feast of the Birthday of Our Lady is celebrated on September 8.

168.28/166.10   WOMEN WON'T PICK UP PINS. SAY IT CUTS LO   This refers to the proverb that says "A pin cuts love." In Swift's *Polite Conversation*, first conversation, Miss Notable says to Col. Atwit, "Pray, Colonel, make me a Present of that pretty Knife," to which Col. Atwit replies, "Not for the World, dear Miss, it will cut Love" (p. 71). Partridge says this alludes to "the very old superstition that one should never give anything sharp to one's beloved—at least, before marriage."

169.22/167.3   SEE OURSELVES AS OTHERS SEE US   An allusion to Robert Burns's "To a Louse." Stephen alluded to the same line earlier; see entry 6.28.

169.22/167.4   HUNGRY MAN IS AN ANGRY MAN   The *ODEP* lists "A hungry man, an angry man," and traces it back to Howell's *English Proverbs* (1659). Swift uses this in *Polite Conversation*, second conversation, when Miss Notable says, "To say the Truth, I'm hungry," and Neverout replies, "And I'm angry, so let us both go fight" (p. 123).

169.23/167.5 THAT LAST PAGAN KING OF IRELAND CORMAC IN THE SCHOOL POEM . . . This alludes to "The Burial of King Cormac," by Sir Samuel Ferguson (1810–86), which says of Cormac, "He choked upon the food he ate,/ At Sletty, Southward of the Boyne." Cormac was a third-century Irish king who, according to tradition and to Ferguson's poem, provoked the enmity of the pagan priests by declaring his belief in the "One, Unseen, Who is God alone." For the poem, see Hoagland, pp. 459–63. For more information on Cormac, his death, and his conversion, see entry 666.38.

169.36/167.18 LOOK ON THIS PICTURE THEN ON THAT While confronting his mother in her bedchamber, Hamlet holds before her a picture of his father and of Claudius, and says, "Look here upon this picture, and on this" (*Ham.*, III, iv, 53).

170.4/167.28 BORN WITH A SILVER KNIFE IN HIS MOUTH The phrase Bloom is parodying, "Born with a silver spoon in his mouth," is proverbial and is listed in the *ODEP*.

170.13/167.37 TABLE TALK Several writers have written works entitled *Table Talk*, Hazlitt's probably being the best known, but allusion to any of them seems unlikely. The phrase is quite ordinary and may involve no allusion at all. But perhaps Joyce had in mind a passage in *Merchant of Venice* which uses this phrase in conjunction with several gustatory images. Lorenzo and Jessica are preparing to go to dinner when the following exchange occurs:

LOR. . . . First, let us go to dinner.
JES. Nay, let me praise you while I have a stomach.
LOR. No, pray thee, let it serve for table talk. Then howsoe'er thou speak'st, 'mong other things I shall digest it.
Jes. Well, I'll set you forth. (III, v, 91–95)

170.23/168.5 TOOTH AND NAIL "To fight tooth and nail," is proverbial and is listed in the *ODEP*.

170.30/168.12 DON'T TALK OF YOUR PROVOSTS AND PROVOST OF TRINITY This alludes to the song "Father O'Flynn," by Alfred Percival Graves and Sir Charles Villiers Stanford. The second verse of the song begins, "Don't talk of your Provost and Fellows of Trinity,/ Famous for ever at Greek and Latinity,/ Dad and the divels and all at Divinity,/ Father O'Flynn'd make hares of them all." Bloom continues the allusion on p. 170.38/168.19. For the text of the poem, see Hoagland, pp. 555–56.

170.36/168.17 SIR PHILIP CRAMPTON'S FOUNTAIN See entry 92.12.

170.40/168.22 WANT A SOUP POT AS BIG AS THE PHOENIX PARK. HARPOON-

ING FLITCHES AND HINDQUARTERS OUT OF IT   S. Sultan (*Argument of Ulysses*, p. 123) sees this as an analogue to Homer's description of "the Lestrygonians decimating the harbor-bound Achaean fleet" in book IX of the *Odyssey*. Cf. entry 153.9.

171.31/169.12 HAM AND HIS DESCENDANTS MUSTERED AND BRED THERE In this gustatory pun-parody, Bloom refers to Ham, the son of Noah who saw his father naked. Ham was the father of Canaan, and for his sin, Canaan was cursed with being the servant of the houses of the other sons, Shem and Japheth (Gen. 9:22–27). The progeny of Ham are described in Genesis 10:6–20.

171.38/169.19 THERE WAS A RIGHT ROYAL OLD NIGGER . . .   (Further parts of this limerick are given on p. 172.30/170.10 and p. 172.36/170.16.) I have not located any source for Bloom's limerick, but it can be reconstructed almost completely from what Bloom remembers of it.

171.42/169.23 KOSHER. NO MEAT AND MILK TOGETHER . . . YOM KIPPUR FAST SPRING CLEANING OF INSIDE   The phrase "spring cleaning" suggests that Bloom mistakenly thinks that Yom Kippur occurs in the spring, but perhaps he is simply using the phrase metaphorically. For his earlier thought of Yom Kippur, see entry 152.1.

172.3/169.26 SLAUGHTER OF INNOCENTS   The slaughter of the Holy Innocents is described in Matthew 2:16–18. Herod ordered all the male children two years old or under in Bethlehem to be killed, in an attempt to do away with the recently born "King of the Jews," the infant Jesus.

172.4/169.26 EAT, DRINK AND BE MERRY   This phrase, or one very similar, is common in the Bible. The closest instances are in Ecclesiastes 8:15 and in the Parable of the Rich Fool in Luke 12:19. A similar phrase, followed by "for tomorrow we die," occurs in Isaiah 22:13 and I Corinthians 15:32. Bloom uses this phrase again on p. 526.27/515.8.

172.5/169.27 CHEESE DIGESTS ALL BUT ITSELF   This proverbial saying occurs in Swift's *Polite Conversation*, second conversation, in which Lady Answerall says, "They say, Cheese digests every Thing but itself" (p. 150). Partridge says the saying is sixteenth through twentieth centuries, but is rarely heard in the twentieth except in the country.

172.11/169.33 COOL AS A CUCUMBER   This proverbial phrase is listed in the *ODEP* and occurs in Swift's *Polite Conversation*, second conversation. Lady Smart offers Miss Notable some cucumbers, to which Miss replies, "Madam, I dare not touch it; for they say,

Cucumbers are cold in the third Degree" (p. 129). Partridge says "perhaps compare the simile, 'as cool as a cucumber,' " P. W. Joyce (*English As We Speak It*, p. 141) says, "A person who is cool and collected under trying circumstances is 'as cool as a cucumber.' "

172.13/169.35 GOD MADE FOOD, THE DEVIL THE COOKS   This also occurs in Swift's *Polite Conversation*, second conversation. Lord Smart says, "This Goose is quite raw. Well; God sends Meat, but the Devil sends Cooks" (p. 142).

173.14/170.36 THAT BOXING MATCH MYLER KEOGH WON   As R. M. Adams has shown (*SS*, p. 70), some of the facts about this bout are taken from an actual bout that occurred in Dublin on April 29, 1904. The bout, which was between M. L. Keogh and Garry of the Sixth Dragoons, was advertised in the *Freeman's Journal* for April 28 and 29, 1904, and the result was reported in the April 30 issue. Keogh won by a knockout in the third round. On p. 251.1/247.17, young Dignam observes that the Keogh-Bennet fight was on May 22, but the Dublin papers tell of no similar match at about that time.

173.24/171.5 HERRING'S BLUSH   Though I strongly suspect that these words involve an allusion, and probably relate in some way to the immediately following phrase, my efforts to pin this down have been unsuccessful.

173.24/171.5 WHOSE SMILE UPON EACH FEATURE PLAYS WITH SUCH AND SUCH REPLETE   This seems to allude to some song of the day—perhaps from popular opera—but Hodgart and Worthington do not list it, and I have not been able to identify it.

173.40/171.21 HEADS I WIN TAILS YOU LOSE   This is proverbial. The *ODEP* lists several instances under "Heads (Cross) I win, tails (pile) you lose," and explains that the phrase refers to spinning a coin in the air.

174.11/171.34 ROTHSCHILD'S FILLY   R. M. Adams discusses the detail and accuracy of Nosey Flynn's horse lore. Among the many details he verifies are the facts that in the Derby run on June 2, 1904, "St. Amant was owned by M. de Rothschild, and won the Derby in the manner described, in the midst of a violent rainstorm" (*SS*, p. 175). But, Adams points out, in the midst of the correct details, Flynn is puzzlingly wrong about one important fact: St. Amant was not a filly, but a colt. The *Freeman's Journal* of June 2 carried a full account of the race (p. 7, col. e), and it does make it clear that St. Amant was a colt.

174.19/171.42   FOOL AND HIS MONEY   "A fool and his money are soon parted" has been proverbial for centuries, and its origin is uncertain. The *ODEP* lists several instances of the phrase.

174.37/172.17   JOHNNY MAGORIES   Though this seems to refer to a person, it does not. P. W. Joyce (*English As We Speak It*, p. 278) lists "Johnny Magorey; a hip or doghaw; the fruit of the dog rose. (Central and Eastern counties.)"

174.41/172.22   YES BUT WHAT ABOUT OYSTERS . . . WHO FOUND THEM OUT   In view of the many allusions to the second conversation of Swift's *Polite Conversation* in this episode, this probably derives from Col. Atwit's statement in that conversaton: "He was a bold Man that first eat an Oyster" (p. 123). Partridge says this is a "mid17th-mid19th century proverb."

175.9/172.31   THAT ARCHDUKE LEOPOLD WAS IT? NO. YES, OR WAS IT OTTO ONE OF THOSE HABSBURGS? OR WHO WAS IT USED TO EAT THE SCRUFF OFF HIS OWN HEAD   Bloom's allusion to popular lore about one of the Hapsburgs may have some basis in fact, but I have not been able to confirm it. Of all the Hapsburgs, Leopold I (1640–1705) seems to be the one whose personal life and habits have attracted most popular attention, but I have not found a story such as this about him.

175.19/172.41   ROYAL STURGEON   The sturgeon has been legally designated a "royal fish" since the time of Edward II. Legally, royal fish are those "which, when taken in territorial waters, belong to the crown or its grantee, though caught by another person. These are whales, sturgeons and porpoises; and grampuses are also sometimes added (whales, porpoises and grampuses being 'fishes' only in a legal sense)" (*Encyc. Brit.*, 11th ed., X, 434d).

175.37/173.16   A KISH OF BROGUES   Literally, this means a basket of boots. But there may be an allusion here to a book by Irishman William Boyle (1853–1922) which was published in 1899 and entitled *A Kish of Brogues*. Though it is probably coincidence rather than allusion, the name Micky Hanlon, which Bloom thought of a few lines earlier, blends the names of two characters in Boyle's book—Michael Duffy and Larry Hanlon.

176.6/173.27   O WONDER   Perhaps there is an echo here of Miranda's phrase in *The Tempest*, when she sees the sailors and noblemen gathered, "O, wonder!/ How many goodly creatures are there here!" (V, i, 181–82), or of Ferdinand's words on seeing Miranda, "My prime request,/ Which I do last pronounce, is, O you wonder!/ If you be maid or no?" (I, ii, 425–27).

176.25/174.3 SHAPELY GODDESSES, VENUS, JUNO   Bloom is thinking of statues of these goddesses in the National Museum. There are more specific allusions to both of these goddesses elsewhere in *Ulysses*; see the Index.

176.30/174.8 PYGMALION AND GALATEA   According to Greek myth, Pygmalion, King of Cyprus, fell in love with a beautiful statue, prayed to Aphrodite for such a wife, Aphrodite brought the statue to life, and Pygmalion married her. According to some versions, the statue was made by Pygmalion himself and was named Galatea. Bloom probably knows of this through W. S. Gilbert's play, *Pygmalion and Galatea* (1871), which played at the Queen's Royal Theatre, Dublin, in November, 1891. In that play, Pygmalion, a sculptor, is married to a woman named Cynisca, who is jealous of the animated statue, Galatea; after considerable trouble, Galatea voluntarily returns to her original state.

176.42/174.20 TO MEN TOO THEY GAVE THEMSELVES . . . A YOUTH EN-JOYED HER   Bloom is thinking of goddesses who lay with human men. Though such stories are not uncommon, Venus and Adonis immediately comes to mind, because of its importance in the "Scylla and Charybdis" episode. And Bloom has referred to Venus on p. 176.26/174.4.

177.28/175.6 THE CRAFT   "The craft" is Freemasonry. The allusion is continued on p. 177.30/175.8, where Nosy speaks of the "Ancient free and accepted order," i.e., the Order of Free and Accepted Masons. For an essay arguing that the imagery and lore of Free-masonry pervade this chapter, see Leonard Albert, "Ulysses, Cannibals, and Freemasons," *A.D.*, II, 265–83.

177.40/175.18 THERE WAS ONE WOMAN . . .   I have found several sources which confirm that Elizabeth, the daughter of Arthur St. Leger, first Viscount Doneraile, was the only female Freemason, but I have not found any account that contains the detail of her hiding in a clock. Wm. Walsh's *Handy-Book of Curious Information* says that the story was originally contained in "a rare tract published in Cork in 1811" (*s.v.* "Freemason, Female"). When Elizabeth (*ca.* 1693–1773) was about seventeen years old, she witnessed unseen the ceremonies of Freemasonry at her father's house. When she was apprehended, death was first thought to be the only possible issue, but her father, Lord Doneraile, prevailed and she was sworn in. It is said that she afterwards took part in Freemason's processions and that portraits of her in her masonic apron exist (see also Cokayne, *Complete Peerage*, IV, 397, *s.v.* Doneraile)

178.15/175.33   GIVE THE DEVIL HIS DUE   The *ODEP* lists several instances of the proverbial "Give the devil his due," including two
from Shakespeare, both of which indicate that the saying was proverbial even in Shakespeare's time. In *I Henry IV*, Prince Hal says
of Falstaff, "he was never yet a breaker of proverbs. He will give
the Devil his due" (I, ii, 131–32), and in *Henry V*, the Duke of
Orleans cites this saying in the proverb capping contest (III, vii,
125).

179.35/177.11   DON GIOVANNI, A CENAR TECO/ M'INVITASTI   This is
from the final scene of Mozart's opera *Don Giovanni*, in which the
statue of the Commendatore arrives to have supper with Don
Giovanni. The full line the Commendatore sings is, "Don Giovanni!
a cenar teco m'invitasti! e son venuto! ("Don Giovanni! by thee
invited, Here behold me as thou directed"). Bloom thinks of this
again on p. 180.6/177.23 and mistakenly translates *teco* as *tonight*.
There are many other allusions to *Don Giovanni* in *Ulysses*; see
entry 64.4 and the Index.

180.21/177.38   THOSE LOVELY SEASIDE GIRLS   See entry 62.36.

180.26/178.3   WHY I LEFT THE CHURCH OF ROME? BIRD'S NEST. WOMEN
RUN HIM   R. M. Adams has shown (*SS*, p. 206), by drawing on
the Rosenbach MS and the *Little Review*, that this passage should
read, "*Why I Left the Church of Rome?* Bird's nest women run
him." None of the catalogues I have examined list the exact title
Why I Left the Church of Rome, though titles beginning *Why I
Left . . .* are quite common. "Bird's nest," as Adams explains, is
Dublin slang for a Protestant proselytizing center. *Dignam's Dublin Guide* (Dublin, [1891]) describes a "bird's nest" in the Coombe
and says, "Mistaken philanthropists support the latter institute for
the purpose of snatching poor Catholic children from their parents,
or as orphans" (p. 38).

182.28/180.1   ALL THOSE WOMEN AND CHILDREN EXCURSION BEANFEAST
BURNED AND DROWNED IN NEW YORK   This refers to the *General
Slocum* disaster; see entry 239.22.

182.30/180.3   KARMA . . .   The concept of Karma is central to
Hinduism and Buddhism. It is the idea that acts in previous exis-
tences in the cycle of rebirths will inevitably lead to a good or bad
reincarnation in later lives. Thus evil acts in one life lead to an
inferior state in the next, good acts lead to an improved state.

182.31/180.4   MET HIM PIKEHOSES   Metempsychosis; see entry 64.18.

182.37/180.10   ANNALS OF THE BLUECOAT SCHOOL   For a Dubliner,
"the bluecoat school" is not Christ's Hospital, London, but King's
Hospital, Dublin. Sir Frederick Richard Falkiner wrote a book

entitled *The Foundation of the Hospital and Free School of King Charles II., Oxmantown, Dublin, commonly called the Blue Coat School*, but apparently the book was not published until 1906. Sir Frederick, whom Bloom has just seen, was chairman of the board of the school.

183.7/180.22   THE MESSIAH WAS FIRST GIVEN FOR THAT. YES. HANDEL Bloom is correct. Handel's oratorio was given its first performance in the Music Hall, Fishamble Street, Dublin, for the benefit of the Society for relieving Prisoners, the Charitable Infirmary, and Mercer's Hospital, on April 13, 1742.

183.19/180.34   SIR THOMAS DEANE DESIGNED   Sir Thomas Deane (1792–1871) was an architect and the mayor of Cork. He did design the National Library and the National Museum in Dublin.

SCYLLA AND CHARYBDIS

The great concentration of Shakespearean material in this episode has made me more willing to see phrases, or even individual words, as Shakespearean allusions than I otherwise would be, especially if the words are unordinary or the context particularly suggests an allusion. I have also made frequent reference to certain books in the list for this episode. Although these books are all included in the List of Abbreviations and are cited more fully in the Bibliography, I note them briefly here for the reader's greater convenience.

GEORGE BRANDES, *William Shakespeare: A Critical Study* (1899)—cited as Brandes

E. K. CHAMBERS, *William Shakespeare: A Study of Facts and Problems* (1930)—cited as Chambers

FRANK HARRIS, *The Man Shakespeare and His Tragic Life-Story* (1909)—cited as Harris

SIDNEY LEE, *A Life of William Shakespeare* (1898)—cited as Lee

WILLIAM M. SCHUTTE, *Joyce and Shakespeare: A Study in the Meaning of* Ulysses (1957)—cited as Schutte, *JS*

The books by Brandes, Harris, and Lee are works Joyce himself used in writing the "Scylla and Charybdis" episode; Chambers is a convenient source of information and writings about Shakespeare; Schutte is a study of Joyce's use of Shakespearean material.

---

184 2/182.2 THOSE PRICELESS PAGES OF WILHELM MEISTER? A GREAT POET ON A GREAT FELLOW POET   Lyster is referring to Book IV, chap. 13, of Goethe's *Wilhelm Meister's Apprenticeship* (1796), in which *Hamlet* is interpreted in terms of the inadequacy of Hamlet's character to meet the challenge facing him. Wilhelm says the play presents "the effects of a great action laid upon a soul unfit for the performance of it," and he says of Hamlet, "A lovely, pure, noble, and most moral nature, without the strength of nerve which forms a hero, sinks beneath a burden it cannot bear and must not cast away" (Carlyle's translation).

184.3/182.3 A HESITATING SOUL TAKING ARMS AGAINST A SEA OF TROUBLES ...   This alludes to Hamlet's "To be or not to be" soliloquy in *Hamlet*, III, i, in which he considers whether to "take arms against a sea of troubles/ And by opposing end them" (ll. 59–60). The word *hesitating* probably implies Goethe's judgment, mentioned in entry 184.2.

184.6/182.6 HE CAME A STEP A SINKAPACE FORWARD ...   As Wm. Schutte points out (*JS*, p. 183), this alludes to *Twelfth Night*, in which Sir Toby tells Sir Andrew, "My very walk should be a jig; I would not so much as make water but in a sink-a-pace" (I, iii, 139). This is the only occurrence of *sinkapace* in Shakespeare, though he does refer to the dance under the spelling *cinquepace* in *Much Ado*, II, i, 77, but allusion to that context seems unlikely; see entry 184.14. According to the *OED*, s.v. *cinque pace*, this is a lively dance involving steps regulated by the number five.

184.6/182.6 NEATSLEATHER   Wm. Schutte (*JS*, p. 185) follows B. J. Morse in listing this as an allusion to *Julius Caesar*, in the opening scene of which the cobbler says to the tribunes, "As proper men as ever trod upon neat's leather have gone upon my handiwork" (I, i, 29). The context in *Ulysses* does make a Shakespearean allusion likely, but it seems the allusion might equally as well be to Stephano's statement on discovering Caliban: "If I can recover him, and keep him tame, and get to Naples with him, he's a present for any emperor that ever trod on neat's leather" (*Tempest*, II, ii, 70–73). These are the only occurrences of the word in Shakespeare. Neat's leather is oxhide.

184.10/182.10   THE BEAUTIFUL INEFFECTUAL DREAMER   This continues to present Goethe's view of Hamlet (see entry 184.2), but it does so through a phrase from Matthew Arnold. The final sentence of Arnold's essay "Shelley" (in *Essays in Criticism: Second Series*) says, describing Shelley, "And in poetry, no less than in life, he is 'a beautiful *and ineffectual* angel, beating in the void his luminous wings in vain.'" (The phrase is in quotation marks because Arnold had himself used it to describe Shelley in the final paragraph of his essay on Byron.)

184.12/182.12   GOETHE'S JUDGMENTS   See entry 184.2.

184.14/182.14   HE CORANTOED OFF   In light of entry 184.6, Wm. Schutte is probably right (*JS*, p. 183) in seeing this as another allusion to Sir Toby's spiel to Sir Andrew in *Twelfth Night*, I, iii, in which he says, "why dost thou not go to church in a galliard and come home in a coranto" (l. 137).

184.18/182.18   MONSIEUR DE LA PALISSE . . . WAS ALIVE FIFTEEN MINUTES BEFORE HIS DEATH   Wm. Schutte explains this allusion. Marechal de la Palisse was killed while fighting valiantly at the Battle of Pavia in 1525, and his men reportedly said, "Un quart d'heure avant sa mort il est en vie," to try to show how heroic his death was. Schutte says, "This naive statement gave Bernard de la Monnaye the idea of writing a whole series of ridiculously obvious truths about the hero," and Schutte then goes on to quote one of the fifty-one stanzas (*JS*, pp. 33–34).

184.22/182.22   THE SORROWS OF SATAN   *The Sorrows of Satan; or, the Strange experience of one Geoffrey Tempest, millionaire* (1895) was a popular novel by Marie Corelli. R. M. Adams cites a letter from James Joyce to Stanislaus of February 28, 1905 (now in the Cornell collection; Scholes catalogue item 122) saying he had read the novel. The book was dramatized in several versions by different playwrights, the best known being that of Herbert Woodgate and Paul M. Berton, first done at the Shaftesbury Theatre, London, January 9, 1897. Eglinton's phrase about getting students "to write *Paradise Lost* at your dictation" seems to allude to the doctrines of "Electric Christianity" which Corelli propounded in an earlier book, *A Romance of Two Worlds* (1886). Perhaps the Dublin group became familiar with the ideas of "Electric Christianity" through George Bernard Shaw's review of the Woodgate and Berton dramatization of *The Sorrows of Satan*, for in that review Shaw discussed some of its "miraculous powers," including "seeming to improvise on the pianoforte by playing at the dictation of angels." For this review, which appeared on January 17, 1897, in the *Saturday Review*, see the Ayot St. Lawrence edition of Shaw's works, XXV, 15–22.

184.24/182.24 FIRST HE TICKLED HER . . .   I have found no original for this bawdy rhyme and presume it to be Joyce's own.

184.29/182.29 SEVEN IS DEAR TO THE MYSTIC MIND   Seven is, of course, a highly valued number in esoteric lore. For instance, in his *Esoteric Buddhism*, A. P. Sinnett devotes much of his second chapter to the "Seven Principles of Man." Cf. entry 185.29.

184.30/182.30 THE SHINING SEVEN W. B. CALLS THEM   "W. B." here is not William Blake, but W. B. Yeats, for this alludes to a line in his poem "A Cradle Song" (which appeared first in book form in *The Countess Kathleen and Various Legends and Lyrics*, 1892). Though he revised the line several times, in one version that he used from 1895 through 1924, Yeats described the planets as "the Shining Seven" (see the *Variorum* edition of Yeats's poems, p. 118).

184.35/182.35 ORCHESTRAL SATAN, WEEPING MANY A ROOD/ TEARS SUCH AS ANGELS WEEP   Wm. Schutte (*JS*, p. 49) points out that these lines resemble two lines from book I of *Paradise Lost*: line 196, where we are told that Satan "lay floating many a rood," and line 620, where we read that "Tears such as angels weep, burst forth."

184.37/182.37 ED EGLI AVEA DEL CUL FATTO TROMBETTA   This is a verbatim quotation from Dante's "Inferno." In canto xxi, Dante and Virgil are led along the edge of the Fifth Chasm by demons, under the captaincy of Barbaricca, and we are told, "each of them had pressed his tongue between his teeth toward their captain, as a signal; *and he of his arse had made a trumpet*" (ll. 137–39; the italicized passage—my italics—translates Stephen's phrase).

184.39/182.39 GAPTOOTHED KATHLEEN   I cannot satisfactorily explain this phrase. The most famous gap-toothed personage is Chaucer's Wife of Bath, but I see no basis for an allusion to her. Perhaps Stephen is vaguely thinking of Mangan's poem "Kathaleen-Ny-Houlihan," which concerns awaiting the "Young Deliver of Kathaleen-Ny-Houlihan," and the second stanza of which begins "Think her not a ghastly hag, too hideous to be seen;/ Call her not unseemly names, our matchless Kathaleen."

184.40/182.40 HER FOUR BEAUTIFUL GREEN FIELDS, THE STRANGER IN HER HOUSE   In Yeats's play *Cathleen Ni Houlihan* (1902), Bridget Gillane asks The Poor Old Woman (a personification of Ireland), "What was it put you wandering?" and the Old Woman replies, "Too many strangers in the house" (*Collected Plays* [New York, 1953], p. 53). Shortly thereafter, Michael Gillane asks her, "What hopes have you to hold to?" and the Old Woman replies, "The hope of getting my beautiful fields back again; the hope of putting the strangers out of my house" (p. 55). But neither of these phrases originated with Yeats: the enemy has long been called "the stranger" (as in Moore's "Let Erin Remember the Days of Old"), and the four green fields has long stood for Ireland, presumably in allusion to the original four provinces of Ulster, Connacht, Munster, and Leinster.

185.2/183.2   IN THE SHADOW OF THE GLEN   This alludes to a one-act play by John M. Synge, entitled "In the Shadow of the Glen," which was first performed at Molesworth Hall, Dublin, October 8, 1903. The play is set in county Wicklow, where Tinahely is, but beyond that I can find no connection between the play and the context in *Ulysses*.

185.9/183.9   THOUGH I ADMIRE HIM, AS OLD BEN DID, ON THIS SIDE IDOL-ATRY   In his *Timber: or, Discoveries; Made Upon Men and Matter* (a miscellaneous collection of notes and reflections, first published in 1640) Ben Jonson said of Shakespeare: "I lov'd the man, and doe honour his memory (on this side Idolatry) as much as any." This may be found in Chambers, II, 210.

185.12/183.12   WHETHER HAMLET IS SHAKESPEARE OR JAMES I OR ESSEX   The idea that the character of Hamlet was based on Robert Devereux, second Earl of Essex (1567–1601) occurs frequently in *Hamlet* criticism. The argument for James I as a pattern for Hamlet, though less common, has been made. One extended example is William Preston Johnson's *The Prototype of Hamlet and Other Shakespearean Problems* (New York: Belford Company [1890?]). In his Preface, Johnson says that in his book "the theory is maintained that, in his original conception of Hamlet, Shakespeare found the prototype of the Prince in James VI of Scotland" (p. 18).

185.16/183.16   GUSTAVE MOREAU   French painter Gustave Moreau (1826–98) is known for his weird, mystical paintings.

185.21/183.21   A. E. HAS BEEN TELLING SOME YANKEE INTERVIEWER   Stephen is remembering O'Molloy's earlier statement to him; see entry 140.31. The next sentence is Stephen's idea of Yankee lingo.

185.23/183.23   THE SCHOOLMEN WERE SCHOOLBOYS FIRST   This probably echoes Emerson's statement in "The American Scholar," "Meek young men grow up in libraries, believing it their duty to accept the views which Cicero, which Locke, which Bacon, have given; forgetful that Cicero, Locke, and Bacon were only young men in libraries when they wrote these books." And it may perhaps owe something to a statement of Eglinton's in his essay "The Breaking of the Ice," which appeared in *Dana* in May, 1904: "But we are men conversing with men when we read Sophocles and Horace, while we have to conjure up our own past selves when we read

Augustine and the Angelic Schoolman (or, to keep up the metaphor, schoolboy), Thomas Aquinas" (p. 14).

185.24/183.24 ARISTOTLE WAS ONCE PLATO'S SCHOOLBOY   It is of
course true that Aristotle was a pupil of Plato.

185.29/183.29 FATHER, WORD AND HOLY BREATH . . . HEAVENLY MAN.
HIESOS KRISTOS, MAGICIAN OF THE BEAUTIFUL, THE LOGOS . . .   This
and the following paragraph contain many references to theosophical lore and to persons involved in the theosophical movement.
Several of those referred to were members of the Dublin Lodge of
the Theosophical Society. Most important among these is A. E., and
these paragraphs also contain allusions to his poetry, though his
poetry is so infused with theosophical imagery that it is hard to
separate allusions to his poems from allusions to theosophical lore
itself. For background on the Dublin Lodge, see the chapter "The
Dublin Mystics" in E. A. Boyd's *Ireland's Literary Renaissance*.
Almost all of the theosophical lore in *Ulysses* seems to derive either
from Mme Blavatsky's *Isis Unveiled* or from A. P. Sinnett's *Esoteric
Buddhism*. On Mme Blavatsky, see entry 185.38; her book is com-
prehensive and has a thorough index. Sinnett's book went through
several editions (I have used the 5th ed., annotated and enlarged;
it has no index, but has a detailed table of contents). Mme Blavatsky's more concise *The Key to Theosophy* (1889), which contains "a Copious Glossary of General Theosophical Terms," is also
helpful. In the words quoted in this entry Stephen is thinking of
theosophical interpretations of the Christian Trinity; on this see
Key to Theosophy, pp. 61, 164–67, and *Isis Unveiled*, II, 576.
Heavenly man may refer specifically to the "Heavenly Man" or
"Protogonos," "the first born of God, or the Universal Form and
Idea" who engendered Adam (*Isis Unveiled*, II, 276). There may
also be allusions here to A. E.'s poems "The Great Breath" (*Homeward*, p. 24) and "The Message of John" (*The Earth Breath*, pp.
74–79); in the latter poem, Christ is asked, "Art thou the Christ
for whom we hope?/ Art thou a magian . . .?" (p. 77).

185.31/183.31 THIS VERILY IS THAT   Though *verily* has biblical connotations, since, in the King James translation, Christ frequently
uses the word, the monistic identification of all things here is
clearly theosophical. Cf. the preceding entry.

185.32/183.31 I AM THE FIRE UPON THE ALTAR. I AM THE SACRIFICIAL
BUTTER   Stephen is probably thinking of A. E. and his poetry.
The phrase "I am one with . . ." begins a refrain in his poem "By
the Margin of the Great Deep," and in "The Message of John,"
Christ twice says, "I am . . ." (*Homeward*, p. 14, and *The Earth*

Breath, pp. 74–79). And his poem "Dawn" uses the phrase "Fire on the Altar" (*Homeward*, p. 27). The "sacrificial butter" is probably Stephen's ironic joining of A. E.'s interests in theosophy and dairying; one of the primary concerns of *The Irish Homestead*, which A. E. edited, was dairy management, and every issue had a section entitled "Creamery Management." Cf. entry 510.23.

185.33/183.33 DUNLOP, JUDGE, THE NOBLEST ROMAN OF THEM ALL . . . In *Julius Caesar*, Antony says of Brutus, "This was the noblest Roman of them all" (V, v, 68). Examination of issues of *The Irish Theosophist* reveals that the following were among the members of the Dublin Lodge of the Theosophical Society: Daniel N. Dunlop, William J. Judge, Mrs. Cooper-Oakley, and of course, George Russell. "K. H." apparently refers to a Mahatma named Koot Hoomi who is mentioned in several issues, and from whom A. P. Sinnett derived some of his lore.

185.35/183.35 BROTHERS OF THE GREAT WHITE LODGE   This refers to the Great White Brotherhood believed in by Theosophists. This is a group of adepts set apart from the rest of mankind by their superior knowledge of and powers in things spiritual. The members of this brotherhood, while they do not dwell together, are in constant communication with one another in various countries. They are also called Mahatmas.

185.36/183.36 THE CHRIST WITH THE BRIDESISTER . . .   Though I have found nothing precisely like this in theosophical lore, Mme Blavatsky does discuss Christ and Sophia as a male-female pair in *Isis Unveiled*, II, 42.

185.38/183.38 THE PLANE OF BUDDHI . . . BAD KARMA . . . H. P. B'S ELEMENTAL   H. P. B. is Helena Petrovna Blavatsky (1831–91), Russian-born founder of the Theosophical Society (1875). After some dissension within the society, Mme Blavatsky went to India and disseminated her theosophical ideas from there. Her most important book is *Isis Unveiled*, which is mentioned on p. 191.37/189.28. The words and phrases quoted in this entry are technical terms in theosophy. See the "Glossary" in *Key to Theosophy* or the Index of *Isis Unveiled* (both cited in entry 185.29).

186.4/184.5 THAT MODEL SCHOOLBOY . . .   Stephen is referring to Aristotle (see entry 185.24), and he goes on to allude to Hamlet's "To be or not to be" soliloquy in *Hamlet*, III, i, 56 ff.

186.11/184.11 WOULD HAVE BANISHED ME FROM HIS COMMONWEALTH Stephen has elevated himself to the rank of poet, and is alluding to Plato's judgment, expressed in *The Republic*, X (sec. 606–7), that for the health of the state the poet should be banished.

186.13/184.13 UNSHEATHE YOUR DAGGER DEFINITIONS   Arthur Heine lists this as an allusion to *III Henry VI*, II, ii, 59, 80, 123, but this seems unlikely (and Schutte's *JS* does not list this allusion). If there is any allusion involved here, it is probably to Brutus' words to Cassius in *Julius Caesar*: "Sheathe your dagger./ Be angry when you will, it shall have scope" (IV, iii, 107–8).

186.13/184.13 HORSENESS IS THE WHATNESS OF ALLHORSE   Though there may be some more specific allusion here, this seems to describe Aristotle's theory of universals in scholastic terms (*whatness*, for example, seems to be the scholastic *quidditas*). Aristotle held that universals have no separate existence, but are immanent in things that are similar.

186.14/184.14 EONS   S. Sultan points out (*Argument of Ulysses*, p. 154) the probable pun here on the original form of A.E.'s pen name: Æon.

186.15/184.14 GOD: NOISE IN THE STREET   See entry 34.33.

186.16/184.16 THROUGH SPACES SMALLER THAN RED GLOBULES OF MAN'S BLOOD . . .   M. D. Paley explains this as an allusion to a passage in Blake's *Milton* ("Blake in Nighttown," *JJM III*, p. 178). In Book I, sec. 29 of *Milton*, Blake says, "For every Space larger than a red Globule of Man's blood/ Is visionary, and created by the Hammer of Los:/ And every Space smaller than a Globule of Man's blood opens/ Into Eternity of which this Vegetable Earth is but a shadow" (1957 Keynes ed.; *Complete Writings*, pp. 516–17). Joyce had used this same passage earlier in his lecture on Blake (*CW*, p. 222). Blake also used the adjective "vegetable" to describe this world in his notes on "A Vision of the Last Judgment," which Joyce knew. See entries 37.20 and 24.7.

186.24/184.23 JUBAINVILLE'S BOOK   Marie Henri d'Arbois de Jubainville (1827–1910), an authority on Celtic language and literature, was professor of Celtic at the College de France. He wrote many books on the subject, but the one referred to here is almost certainly, as Wm. Schutte suggests (*JS*, p. 37), the one which Richard Best himself translated: *The Irish Mythological Cycle and Celtic Mythology* (Dublin, 1903). Schutte points out that the book became one of the texts of the Revival, and that Eglinton had reviewed it when it appeared. There was also a review-summary of the book in the *Freeman's Journal* of March 4, 1904 (p. 2, cols. d–e).

186.25/184.24 HYDE'S LOVESONGS OF CONNACHT   Dr. Douglas Hyde (1860–1949), Irish scholar and president of Ireland (1938–45), was one of the prime movers in the revival of Irish literature and language. His *The Love Songs of Connacht* (1893) and *Literary History of Ireland* (1899) were particularly important. His role in the Revival is discussed in P. S. O'Hegarty's *Ireland Under the Union*, chap. LVI, and in Richard M. Kain's *Dublin in the Age of Yeats and Joyce*. Joyce briefly discussed some of Hyde's works in his review of Lady Gregory's *Poets and Dreamers* (*CW*, p. 104). *The Lovesongs of Connacht* is mentioned or alluded to several times in *Ulysses*; see, for example, entry 48.3.

186.28/184.27 BOUND THEE FORTH, MY BOOKLET, QUICK . . .   The reference to Hyde makes Stephen think of a stanza of a poem Hyde wrote to illustrate a meter commonly used by Irish bards. Wm. Schutte identifies this and prints the original stanza by Hyde, which Stephen varies here (*JS*, p. 72). The stanza is the first in a six stanza poem that Hyde says illustrates "the great official" meter of the Irish bards, "the celebrated Deibhidh." Hyde gives the stringent metrical rules of the stanza and says the meter was lost in the seventeenth or eighteenth century, and that his poem is the first composed in it in more than 150 years. The poem concludes Hyde's little volume *The Story of Early Gaelic Literature* (London, 1895). I give the first stanza of the poem (but omit to follow Hyde's use of capitals and bold face type to focus on points of metrical interest): "Bound thee forth my booklet quick/ To greet the polished public./ Writ—I ween't was not my wish—/ In lean unlovely English" (p. 174).

186.35/184.33 AN EMERALD SET IN THE RING OF THE SEA   This is an exact quotation from John Philpot Curran's (see entry 139.13) song "Cushla-ma-Chree" ("Pulse of my Heart"), which begins "Dear Erin, how sweetly thy green bosom rises,/ An emerald set in the ring of the sea. . . ." For words and music, see Moffat's *Minstrelsy of Ireland*, 3rd ed., pp. 42–43. See also entry 123.17.

186.40/184.37 FOR THEM THE EARTH IS . . . THE LIVING MOTHER   A. E. is probably thinking of Dana, one of the goddesses of the Tuatha De Danann whom he describes as an earth-mother in his poem "Dana." And A. E.'s thought is also similar to that of Douglas Hyde when Hyde says, ". . . everything around him recalled to the early Gael the traditional history of his own past. The two hills of Slieve Luachra in Kerry he called the paps of Dana . . ." (*Lit. Hist. of Ireland*, p. 47). Hyde goes on to enumerate other landmarks that are infused with legend.

187.3/184.40 FRANCE PRODUCES THE FINEST FLOWER OF CORRUPTION IN MALLARMÉ   French poet Stéphane Mallarmé (1842–98) was a symbolist and an experimentalist whose work became more obscure as he developed. His comments about *Hamlet* are referred to in the following paragraphs.

187.5/185.1 THE POOR OF HEART   This phrase may perhaps combine and echo parts of the Beatitudes: "Blessed are the poor in spirit: for theirs is the kingdom of heaven" and "Blessed are the pure in heart: for they shall see God" (Matt. 5:3 and 5:8).

187.5/185.2 THE LIFE OF HOMER'S PHAEACIANS   The Phaeacians were the inhabitants of the island of Scheria, where Ulysses was cast after the boat in which he left Calypso's island was wrecked by the storm. Their king was Alcinous, whose daughter was Nausicaä. They lived an idyllic existence. It was to the Phaeacians that Ulysses related his adventures after the fall of Troy.

187.10/185.7 IL SE PROMÈNE, LISANT AU LIVRE DE LUI-MÊME ...   The three references to Mallarmé's comments about *Hamlet* in this and the following lines all derive from a single short statement that first appeared as a letter, "Hamlet et Fortinbras," in the *Revue Blanche* of July 15, 1896. The letter is reprinted in Mallarmé's *Oeuvres Complètes* (Paris: Gallimard, 1945), p. 1564 (in a note to Mallarmé's essay *"Hamlet"*). Mr. Best's phrase reproduces Mallarmé's exactly.

187.15/185.12 HAMLET OU LE DISTRAIT   For the source of this in Mallarmé, see entry 187.10. In his letter Mallarmé does refer to a provincial playing of *Hamlet* in which it was billed as *"Hamlet, ou le Distrait"* ("Hamlet, or the Absent-Minded One"). But *piece* is not a part of this quaint title; rather, that word is Mallarmé's own, and it occurs a few lines later, in his serious discussion of the play.

187.22/185.19 THE ABSENTMINDED BEGGAR   Rudyard Kipling wrote a poem entitled "The Absent-Minded Beggar" which is alluded to several times in *Ulysses*. Kipling's statement about the poem in *Something of Myself* (chap. VI) indicates that the poem was written "to procure small comforts for the troops at the Front" in the Boer War, but the poem is actually an appeal for funds for families left behind by the soldiers. Wm. Schutte (*JS*, p. 116) says that the poem was first published on October 31, 1899, in the *Daily Mail* and that it was set to music by Sir Arthur Sullivan. Perhaps, in light of the theme of sonship in this episode, the lines most relevant are "Cook's son—Duke's son—son of a belted Earl—/ Son of a Lambeth publican—it's all the same today!" (this line is alluded to on p. 589.8/574.3). The phrase "Khaki Hamlets" on p. 187.31/185.28 probably also alludes to this poem, for it says "Will you kindly drop a shilling in my little tambourine/ For a gentleman in khaki ordered South?" (ll. 3–4).

187.26/185.23 SUMPTUOUS AND STAGNANT EXAGGERATION OF MURDER
For the source of this phrase in Mallarmé, see entry 187.10. Mallarmé's phrase is "cette somptueuse et stagnante exagération de
meurtre" (p. 1564).

187.27/185.24 A DEATHSMAN OF THE SOUL ROBERT GREENE CALLED HIM
R. M. Adams points out (*SS*, p. 128) that Stephen "makes very
casual use" of his source here, for Greene uses this phrase not of
Shakespeare, but of Lust. Two paragraphs after his statement about
Shakespeare (see entry 210.4), Greene says, "Flie lust, as the
deathsman of the soule, and defile not the Temple of the holy
Ghost" (*Groats-Worth of Witte*, p. 46).

187.28/185.25 NOT FOR NOTHING WAS HE A BUTCHER'S SON WIELDING THE
SLEDDED POLEAXE AND SPITTING IN HIS PALM. NINE LIVES ARE TAKEN
OFF . . .   John Aubrey, in his sketch of Shakespeare in *Brief
Lives*, says "his father was a Butcher" (Chambers, II, 252). Wm.
Schutte points out that all three of Joyce's main sources mention
Aubrey's statement (*JS*, p. 170). "Sledded poleaxe" alludes to the
disputed passage in *Hamlet* in which Horatio describes King Hamlet: "So frowned he once when, in an angry parle,/ He smote the
sledded Pollax on the ice" (*Ham.*, I, i, 62–63). This is the Folio
reading; the first and second quartos give "sleaded Pollax." Some
editors take it to mean *poleaxe*, others *Polacks*. R. M. Adams points
out (*SS*, p. 129) that only eight lives are taken off in the play,
so Stephen has exaggerated the murder.

187.30/185.27 OUR FATHER, WHO ART IN PURGATORY   This parody
of the Pater Noster alludes to the condition of Hamlet's father's
ghost, who says he is "doomed for a certain term to walk the
night/ And for the day confined to fast in fires/ Till the foul
crimes done in my days of nature/ Are burnt and purged away"
(*Ham.*, I, v, 10–13).

187.31/185.28 KHAKI HAMLETS DON'T HESITATE TO SHOOT   On "Khaki
Hamlets," probably from Kipling's "The Absent-Minded Beggar,"
see entry 187.22. Adaline Glasheen says that " 'Don't hesitate to
shoot' was an Irish byeword, being a quotation from the notorious
Captain ('Pasha') Plunkett when he was helping to coerce the
Irish" ("Another Face for Proteus," *JJR*, I, ii, 8). I have not located
this Captain Plunkett.

187.31/185.28 THE BLOODBOLTERED SHAMBLES IN ACT FIVE   Stephen
refers to the bloody final scene of *Hamlet*, in which four people
die, through an allusion to Macbeth's description of Banquo in the
vision the witches show him: "the blood-boltered Banquo smiles
upon me" (*Mac.*, IV, i, 123).

187.32/185.29 THE CONCENTRATION CAMP SUNG BY MR SWINBURNE . . . WHELPS AND DAMS . . .   As Wm. Schutte explains, this alludes to Swinburne's sonnet "On the Death of Colonel Benson." The poem was first printed in Frank Harris' *Saturday Review*, November 9, 1901, and was followed the next week by letters about the poem from Duncan C. McVarish, Swinburne, and Stephen Gwynn. Swinburne's letter is reprinted in *The Swinburne Letters* (New Haven, 1962), VI, 154–55. The poem was reprinted in Swinburne's *A Channel Passage and Other Poems* (1904). (See Schutte's detailed note, *JS*, p. 116, fn.) The second quatrain of the sonnet reads, "Nor heed we more than he what liars dare say/ Of mercy's holiest duties left undone/ Toward whelps and dams of murderous foes, whom none/ Save we had spared or feared to starve and slay." English officer Colonel George Elliott Benson (1861–1901) was killed when a column he was commanding was attacked by a Boer force under General Botha, on November 3, 1901. Some of the newspaper accounts called the attack an "ambush."

187.37/185.34 THE DEVIL AND THE DEEP SEA   "Between the devil and the deep sea" is proverbial. The *ODEP* lists five instances from 1637 to 1859, but does not explain the origin of the phrase.

188.1/185.37 LIKE THE FAT BOY IN PICKWICK HE WANTS TO MAKE OUR FLESH CREEP   This refers to Joe, the fat boy in Dickens' *Pickwick Papers*, of whom it is frequently said "Damn that boy, he's gone to sleep again." When Joe begins to tell old Mrs. Wardle of his having seen Mr. Tupman kiss Rachel Wardle's hand in the arbor, he says to her, "I wants to make your flesh creep" (chap. VIII).

188.3/185.39 LIST! LIST! O LIST! . . . IF THOU DIDST EVER   Before he makes his revelation to Hamlet, the Ghost says to him "List, list, oh, list!/ If thou didst ever thy dear father love—" (*Ham.*, I, v. 22–23).

188.10/186.7 LIMBO PATRUM   *Limbo Patrum* occurs only once in Shakespeare's works: in *Henry VIII*, the Porter, speaking of some rioters, says, "I have some of 'em in Limbo Patrum, and there they are like to dance these three days" (V, iv, 66–67). In this case, the phrase is apparently slang for *jail*. But *Limbus Patrum* is a term in Catholic theology. It designates the temporary place or state of souls of the just who, though purified from sin, are excluded from the beatific vision until Christ's ascension. This is distinguished from *Limbus Infantum*, a permanent place of the unbaptized, excluded by their original sin.

188.14/186.11 IT IS THIS HOUR . . .   Wm. Schutte has shown (*JS*, pp. 158–59) that the material in this paragraph comes largely from Brandes, pp. 101 and 303. Consider, for example, the following paragraphs from Brandes' chapter on the theaters and audiences: "The days of performance at these theatres were announced by the hoisting of a flag on the roof. The time of beginning was three o'clock punctually, and the performance went straight on, uninterrupted by entr'actes. It lasted as a rule, for only two hours or two hours and a half.

"Close to the Globe Theatre lay the Bear Garden, the rank smell from which greeted the nostrils, even before it came in sight. The famous bear Sackerson, who is mentioned in *The Merry Wives of Windsor,* now and then broke his chain and put female theatregoers shrieking to flight" (p. 101).

188.17/186.14 CANVASCLIMBERS WHO SAILED WITH DRAKE   Sir Francis Drake (1540?–96) is most famous for being the first Englishman to circumnavigate the globe (1577–80), but he took part in many expeditions and was vice-admiral in the fleet that defeated the Spanish Armada in 1588. His last expedition was in 1595–96, against the West Indies; he died and was buried at sea during this trip. *Canvasclimber* occurs only once in Shakespeare's works. In *Pericles,* Marina tells Leonine that at her birth "Never was waves nor wind more violent,/ And from the ladder tackle washes off/ A canvasclimber" (IV, i, 60–62).

188.18/186.15 AMONG THE GROUNDLINGS   This alludes to Hamlet's criticism of poor acting to the company of actors: "Oh, it offends me to the soul to hear a robustious periwig-pated fellow tear a passion to tatters, to very rags, to split the ears of the groundlings, who for the most part are capable of nothing but inexplicable dumb shows and noise" (*Ham.,* III, ii, 8–14).

188.21/186.17 SHAKESPEARE HAS LEFT THE HUGUENOT'S HOUSE IN SILVER STREET . . .   Wm. Schutte has shown (*JS,* p. 173) that Stephen's knowing this information is anachronistic, since it was not known until 1910, when Charles W. Wallace published an article in *Harper's Monthly Magazine* entitled "New Shakespeare Discoveries: Shakespeare as a Man Among Men" (CXX [March, 1910] 489–510). Wallace discovered, through records in the Public Record Office in London, that Shakespeare lived for a time with a family named Mountjoy whose house was at the corner of Silver and Maxwell streets. Wallace says, "They were French, possibly Huguenots" (p. 490). Stephen's description seems loosely based on one paragraph in Wallace: "By reference to a map of London you will see that the Globe theatre, situated on the south side of the

Thames just between the Bankside and Maiden Lane, was almost
directly south of Silver Street. You can see Shakespeare start out
from Silver Street for the theatre. Sometimes he stops on the way
for Hemings and Condell. A brisk walk of ten minutes, with lively
talk, down Wood Street past the old city prison called the Counter,
across Cheapside near where the Cheapside Cross stood, then
through Bread Street past the Mermaid tavern takes them to the
river, where a waterman ferries them across" (p. 508). Throughout
the article, Wallace depicts Shakespeare as congenial and gregar-
ious, which of course is the opposite of Stephen's depiction of him.

188.24/186.20 THE SWAN OF AVON   In line 71 of his poem to Shakespeare printed in the First Folio, Ben Jonson refers to him as "Sweet
Swan of Avon" (Chambers, II, 209).

188.25/186.21 COMPOSITION OF PLACE. IGNATIUS LOYOLA   Composition of place (also called mental representation) is a term used by
St. Ignatius Loyola in his *Spiritual Exercises*. It is the first prelude
to the first exercise and involves envisioning or imagining the physical counterpart of the thing being meditated upon. The term is
effectively defined by the priest who preaches the retreat sermon
in *A Portrait of the Artist*: "This morning we endeavoured, in our
reflection upon hell, to make what our holy founder calls in his
book of spiritual exercises, the composition of place. We endeavoured, that is, to imagine with the senses of the mind, in our
imagination, the material character of that awful place and of
the physical torments which all who are in hell endure" (p. 127).

188.30/186.25 THE PLAYER IS SHAKESPEARE   Both Brandes and Lee
refer to Shakespeare's playing the Ghost in *Hamlet*. This tradition
goes back to a statement by Nicholas Rowe in his sketch of
Shakespeare's life in his edition of the *Works* (1709), see Chambers,
II, 265.

188.32/186.28 HE SPEAKS THE WORDS TO BURBAGE   Schutte (*JS*, p.
162) quotes Lee as saying, "Burbage created the title-part in *Hamlet*" (Lee, p. 222). Actor Richard Burbage (*ca.* 1567–1619) is
mentioned in the "Names of the Principall Actors" prefixed to
the First Folio.

188.35/186.31 HAMLET, I AM THY FATHER'S SPIRIT   In *Hamlet*, I, v,
9, the Ghost says, "I am thy father's spirit," but he does not call
Hamlet by name. Bloom quoted this line with exactly this same
error on p. 152.39/150.36.

188.36/186.32 BIDDING HIM LIST   An allusion to *Hamlet*, I, v, 22;
see entry 188.3.

188.37/186.33 THE SON OF HIS BODY, HAMNET SHAKESPEARE, WHO HAS

DIED IN STRATFORD THAT HIS NAMESAKE MAY LIVE   Shakespeare did have a son named Hamnet (1585–96). Schutte says that of Joyce's three main sources, Brandes alone suggests a connection between the names Hamnet and Hamlet (*JS*, p. 159). There is also an echo here of Christ's dying so that man might live.

189.2/186.37   IN THE VESTURE OF BURIED DENMARK   In the opening scene of *Hamlet*, Horatio asks the Ghost, "What art thou that usurp'st this time of night,/ Together with that fair and warlike form/ In which the majesty of buried Denmark/ Did sometimes march?" (46–49).

189.8/187.3   ANN SHAKESPEARE, BORN HATHAWAY   Anne Hathaway (1555/56–1623), eight years Shakespeare's senior, became his wife in 1582.

189.12/187.6   ART THOU THERE, TRUEPENNY   When Hamlet is adjuring Horatio and Marcellus to swear to keep silent about the Ghost, he hears the Ghost from beneath say "Swear," and says "Ah, ha, boy! Say'st thou so? Art thou there, truepenny?" (*Ham.*, I, v, 149–50).

189.15/187.9   AS FOR LIVING, OUR SERVANTS CAN DO THAT FOR US, VILLIERS DE L'ISLE HAS SAID   This alludes to a line in the play *Axel* (1890) by Philippe-Auguste de Villiers de l'Isle-Adam (1838–89). A. E. probably knows the line through its use by W. B. Yeats as an epigraph in his *The Secret Rose* (1897), which was dedicated to A. E. In that book, the following epigraph appears on p. vi, facing the dedication on p. vii: "As for living, our servants will do that for us. Villiers de l'Isle Adam." Yeats had seen *Axel* in Paris in 1894 and wrote a generally favorable review of the play which appeared in *The Bookman* for April, 1894.

189.20/187.14   FLOW OVER THEM WITH YOUR WAVES AND WITH YOUR WATERS . . .   In A. E.'s play *Deirdre* (1903), Cathvah, the Druid magician whose spell brings about the downfall of Naisi and Deirdre, says, "Let thy waves rise,/ Mananaun Mac Lir./ Let the earth fail/ Beneath their feet,/ Let thy waves flow over them,/ Mananaun:/ Lord of Ocean!" (act III). (According to Alan Denson's bibliography of A. E., *Deirdre* first had publication in book form in 1903, but had previously appeared in the *All-Ireland Review* in 1901–2 and in the *Celtic Christmas* issue of the *Irish Homestead* in Dec., 1902.)

189.27/187.22   AGENBITE OF INWIT   See entry 16.7.

189.34/187.29   HE'S FROM BEYANT BOYNE WATER   Hodgart and Worthington identify this as an allusion to "The Battle of the Boyne (Boyne Water)," an "Orange ballad with various versions."

The allusion here seems to be simply to the title "The Boyne Water" rather than to any line in the song; "beyant the Boyne" does not occur in any of the versions I have seen. This song is included in most collections of Irish songs. See Hoagland, pp. 249–50, or Moffat, *Minstrelsy of Ireland*, 3rd. ed., pp. 128–29.

189.38/187.33 BUZZ. BUZZ   To Polonius' stale news that the actors have arrived, Hamlet replies, "Buzz, buzz!" (*Ham.*, II, ii, 412).

189.39/187.34 ENTELECHY, FORM OF FORMS   This alludes to Aristotle. Stephen earlier mentioned "form of forms"; see entry 26.3. Aristotle used *entelechy* to describe that which realizes or makes actual the otherwise merely potential. Stephen here sees it as the over-all pattern into which all other processes fit—the process of processes. Since some of Stephen's other information about Aristotle comes from Diogenes Laertius' *Lives and Opinions of Eminent Philosophers* (see entry 204.6), it is interesting that that work includes a long paragraph on Aristotle's concept of entelechy which says, in part, that for Aristotle, "the soul is incorporeal, being the first entelechy" (p. 193). Cf. entry 432.20.

190.3/187.39 A.E.I.O.U.   On one level, this listing of the vowels simply acknowledges Stephen's debt to A. E. But these letters also were stamped on coins and medals and inscribed on public buildings by Frederick III, Emperor of the Holy Roman Empire (1415–93). The motto these letters stood for is variously given, usually as "Archidux Electus Imperator Optime Vivat." See *Stevenson's Book of Quotations, s.v.* "Proverbs: A."

190.8/188.3 SHE DIED . . . SIXTY-SEVEN YEARS AFTER SHE WAS BORN . . .   Anne Hathaway (see entry 189.8) died on August 6, 1623, seven years after Shakespeare's death. Schutte (*JS*, p. 162) quotes Lee as saying Shakespeare's widow died on August 6, 1623, "at the age of sixty-seven" (Lee, p. 286).

190.15/188.9 LILIATA RUTILANTIUM   See entry 10.23.

190.17/188.11 GLOWWORM OF HIS LAMP   This alludes to Thomas Moore's song "The Young May Moon." See entry 167.21.

190.27/188.19 WHAT USEFUL DISCOVERY DID SOCRATES LEARN FROM XANTHIPPE? DIALECTIC . . . AND FROM HIS MOTHER HOW TO BRING THOUGHTS INTO THE WORLD   Although almost nothing is known of her, Socrates' wife, Xanthippe, has become emblematic of the shrewish wife. Stephen may owe part of the idea he expresses here to Steele's *Spectator* essay 479 (Tues., Sept. 9, 1712), "Causes of Unhappiness in Married Life." There Steele says, "Socrates, who is by all accounts the undoubted head of the sect of the henpecked, owned and acknowledged that he owed great part of his virtue to the exercise which his useful wife constantly gave it. . . . At several times, to different persons, on the same subject, he has said, 'My dear friend, you are beholden to Xanthippe, that I bear so well your flying out in a dispute' " (cf. entry 432.25). On Socrates' mother, who was a midwife, see entry 202.26.

190.30/188.22 HIS OTHER WIFE MYRTO . . . SOCRATIDIDION'S EPIPSYCHI-DION   Stephen probably learned of Socrates' second wife from Diogenes Laertius, who says in his *Lives of Eminent Philosophers* in the essay on "Socrates," that Socrates had two wives, one named Xanthippe and the other Myrto (*Lives*, p. 66). "Epipsychidion" ("a soul in complement to a soul") is the title of a poem Shelley wrote to Emilia Viviani, whom he felt to be in perfect harmony with himself.

190.33/188.25 THE ARCHONS OF SINN FEIN AND THEIR NOGGIN OF HEM-LOCK   Stephen's allusion to the nationalistic Sinn Fein organization (see entry 163.38) identifies it with those rulers of Athens (archons) who sentenced Socrates to die by drinking the hemlock.

190.41/188.33 HE HAD A GOOD GROATSWORTH OF WIT   Greene's *Groats-Worth of Witte* (1592) was the title of a pamphlet by Robert Greene which contains one of the earliest known references to Skakespeare. Cf. entries 187.27, 210.4, and 211.21.

190.41/188.33 NO TRUANT MEMORY   This phrase may echo Horatio's statement to Hamlet that he is away from the university at Wittenberg because of his "truant disposition" (*Ham.*, I, ii, 169).

190.42/188.34 HE TRUDGED TO ROMEVILLE   As Hodgart and Worthington suggest, this probably alludes to the canting song "The Rogue's Delight in Praise of his Strolling Mort." See entry 47.13.

191.1/188.35 THE GIRL I LEFT BEHIND ME   There are at least two very different versions of a song by this title, one an "English" version, the other an "Irish." The English version is anonymous and begins, "I'm lonesome since I cross'd the hills . . . ," and words and music may be found in Hatton and Faning, *Songs of England*, I, 101. The Irish version is sometimes attributed to Samuel Lover or to Thomas Osborne Davis, but it too is apparently anonymous. It begins, "The dames of France are fond and free, And Flemish lips are willing. . . ." Words and music can be found in Chapple, *Heart Songs*, pp. 66–67.

191.1/188.35 IF THE EARTHQUAKE DID NOT TIME IT   Wm. Schutte lists this as an allusion to *Venus and Adonis*, and, in light of the references to the poem later in this paragraph, this seems correct. Shakespeare describes an earthquake in lines 1046–48 of the poem. Schutte says that Stephen's implication that the poem can be dated or has been dated by some scholars through this earthquake reference, is erroneous. Schutte points out that ". . . no scholar of all those whose conclusions about the date of the work are carefully summarized by Rollins in the New Variorum edition of the poems [Philadelphia, 1938] attempts to fix the date by Shakespeare's reference to the earthquake" (*JS*, p. 177).

191.3/188.36 POOR WAT   As Wm. Schutte has pointed out, this alludes to Shakespeare's *Venus and Adonis*, in which "Poor Wat," the hare, listens "To hearken if his foes pursue him still" (ll. 697–99).

191.3/188.37 THE STUDDED BRIDLE AND HER BLUE WINDOWS   These phrases combine two allusions to *Venus and Adonis*. In lines 37–38 we are told of Venus, "The studded bridle on a ragged bough/ Nimbly she fastens," and later Shakespeare says of her, "Her two blue windows faintly she upheaveth,/ Like the fair sun" (ll. 482–83).

191.4/188.38 VENUS AND ADONIS, LAY IN THE BEDCHAMBER OF EVERY LIGHT-OF-LOVE IN LONDON   Wm. Schutte (*JS*, p. 61) points out that this comes from Brandes' book, where he says of *Venus and Adonis*, "It is an entirely erotic poem, and contemporaries aver that it lay on the table of every light woman in London" (p. 56). Schutte quotes a contemporary poem that may be one of the bases of Brandes' statement (*JS*, p. 159). "Light of Love" was also the title of a popular sixteenth-century song, now lost, which Shakespeare refers to occasionally (see *Two Gent. of Verona*, I, ii, 83, and *Much Ado*, III, iv, 44 and 47). For discussion of this song, see Chappell's *Popular Music of the Olden Time*, pp. 221–25, and his *Old English Popular Music*, I, 82–84.

191.6/188.39 IS KATHERINE THE SHREW ILLFAVOURED? HORTENSIO CALLS HER YOUNG AND BEAUTIFUL   In *The Taming of the Shrew*, Hortensio describes Katherina to Petruchio as "young and beauteous" (I, ii, 86).

191.8/188.41 A PASSIONATE PILGRIM   *The Passionate Pilgrim* is the title of a collection of poems published in 1599 with Shakespeare listed on the title page as author, though only a few of the poems were by Shakespeare.

191.8/188.42 HIS EYES IN THE BACK OF HIS HEAD   "He has an Eye behind him (or in the back of his head)" is listed in the *ODEP*, and one of the instances cited is J. Kelly's *Scottish Proverbs* (1721), which says the phrase is "Spoken of wary and cautious people." But Stephen, strangely, uses the phrase to mean just the opposite.

191.10/189.1 HE LEFT HER AND GAINED THE WORLD OF MEN

Wm. Schutte sees this as an allusion to Browning's poem "Parting at Morning," and briefly discusses its aptness for Stephen's situation (*JS*, p. 62). This brief poem, a sequel to "Meeting at Night," ends with "the need of a world of men for me."

191.13/189.4 IF OTHERS HAVE THEIR WILL ANN HATH A WAY   This pun on Anne Hathaway's name is not original with Stephen. As Wm. Schutte points out, it occurred in print at least as early as 1792 in the poem "A Love Dittie," in Charles Dibdin's novel *Hannah Hewit; or the Female Carusoe.* Schutte quotes the poem, *JS*, p. 62, fn. Stephen's phrase also echoes the opening lines of Shakespeare's "Sonnet 135": "Whoever hath her wish, thou hast thy 'Will,'/ And 'Will' to boot, and 'Will' in overplus." Arthur Heine also suggests (*Shakespeare Association Bulletin*, XXIV, 60) an allusion to "Sonnet 143," which ends, "So will I pray that thou mayst have thy 'Will,'/ If thou turn back and my loud crying still."

191.13/189.5 BY COCK, SHE WAS TO BLAME   This alludes to Ophelia's song in *Hamlet* IV, v: "Young men will do 't, if they come to 't,/ By cock, they are to blame" (ll. 61–62).

191.14/189.6 SWEET AND TWENTY-SIX   In *Twelfth Night*, Feste sings a song which ends, "In delay there lies no plenty,/ Then come and kiss me, sweet and twenty,/ Youth's a stuff will not endure" (II, iii, 51–53). Twenty-six refers to Shakespeare's age at the time his supposed seduction by Anne Hathaway took place.

191.15/189.6 THE GREYEYED GODDESS WHO BENDS OVER THE BOY ADONIS   In *Venus and Adonis*, Venus says, "Mine eyes are gray" (l. 140).

191.16/189.7 STOOPING TO CONQUER   This alludes generally to the situation of Venus and Adonis and also alludes to Goldsmith's comedy, *She Stoops to Conquer* (1773), in which Kate Hardcastle wins young Marlow by pretending to be a servant girl.

191.16/189.7 AS PROLOGUE TO THE SWELLING ACT   After Ross and Angus inform Macbeth that he is now Thane of Cawdor as well as Thane of Glamis, he says in an aside, "Two truths are told/ As happy prologues to the swelling act/ Of the imperial theme" (*Mac.*, I, iii, 127–29).

191.17/189.8 A BOLDFACED STRATFORD WENCH WHO TUMBLES IN A CORN-FIELD . . .   In *Venus and Adonis*, Venus is described as "like a bold-faced suitor" (l. 6). "Tumbles" is probably another allusion to Ophelia's song that Stephen alluded to earlier (entry 191.13). Immediately after the words quoted there, Ophelia says, "Quoth she, before you tumbled me,/ You promised me to wed" (*Ham.*, IV, v, 63–64). Since *cornfield* occurs only once in Shakespeare, the word probably alludes to the Pages' song in *As You Like It*: "It

was a lover and his lass . . . That o'er the green cornfield did pass"
(V, iii, 17–19). See the following entry for a continuation of this
allusion.

191.24/189.15 BETWEEN THE ACRES OF THE RYE . . .   In *As You Like
It*, the Pages sing a song for Audrey and Touchstone which has
the lines "Between the acres of the rye,/ With a hey, and a ho, and
a hey nonino,/ These pretty country folks would lie" (V, iii, 23–
25).

191.26/189.17 PARIS: THE WELL PLEASED PLEASER   This seems to
allude to Paris' role in judging the beauty contest between Juno,
Minerva, and Venus. Paris pleased Venus and was well pleased
with his reward, Helen. Heine lists this as a general allusion to
Troilus and Cressida (*Shakespeare Association Bulletin*, XXIV,
60).

191.29/189.20 THE HOMESTEAD   *The Irish Homestead* was an Irish
agricultural and industrial magazine, edited by A. E. It ran from
1895 to 1923. Though Stephen later calls it "the pigs' paper" (p.
193.2/190.35), Joyce published three of the *Dubliners* stories in it
in 1904.

191.34/189.25 PETER PIPER PICKED A PECK . . .   This is a play on the
well-known children's rhyme and tongue twister "Peter Piper
picked a peck of pickled peppers." For the text of the rhyme and
a brief comment, see *ODNR*, p. 347.

191.37/189.28 ISIS UNVEILED   This refers to Mme Blavatsky's best-
known book. See entries 185.29 and 185.38.

191.38/189.29 CROSSLEGGED UNDER AN UMBREL UMBERSHOOT   This
and the following sentence contain several technical terms from
theosophy. See entries 185.29 and 185.38 and the sources cited there.

191.41/189.32 LOUIS H. VICTORY   Victory was a minor Irish poet,
author of the verse quoted a few lines later. See entry 192.6.

192.1/189.33 T. CAULFIELD IRWIN   Irwin (1823–92) was another
minor Irish poet, author of several books of poetry (for titles see
the British Museum *Catalogue*). But I can find no evidence that
Irwin deserves inclusion among the theosophists. William Rooney
(on whom see entry 72.41) had a long, laudatory article entitled
"Thomas Caulfield Irwin" in the *New Ireland Review*, VII (1897),
86–100. He says nothing of Irwin's having an interest in theosophy;
rather, he praises his down-to-earth, unobscure writing.

192.1/189.33 LOTUS LADIES TEND THEM I' THE EYES   In describing
Cleopatra and her retinue, Enobarbus says to Agrippa, "Her gentlewomen, like the Nereides,/ So many mermaids tended her i' the
eyes,/ And made their bends adornings" (*Ant. and Cleo.*, II, ii, 211–

13). The meaning of the phrase is disputed, but probably it means the handmaids were responsive even to glances from Cleopatra's eyes. This is one of the most discussed passages in the play. The Variorum has more than five pages of comments on it.

192.2/189.34   FILLED WITH HIS GOD HE THRONES   Wm. Schutte (*JS*, p. 185) lists this as an allusion to Menenius' statement about Coriolanus: "He wants nothing of a god but eternity and a Heaven to throne in" (*Corio.*, V, iv, 25–26).

192.3/189.34   BUDDHA UNDER PLANTAIN   Stephen must be thinking of Buddha's sitting under the sacred bo tree or pipal, sacred to the Buddhists because the Buddha received enlightenment under such a tree; it is not, however, a plantain.

192.6/189.38   IN QUINTESSENTIAL TRIVIALITY . . .   These lines misquote the opening lines of a poem by Louis H. Victory (see entry 191.41) entitled "Soul-Perturbating Mimicry." The poem begins, "In quintessential triviality/ Of flesh, for four fleet years, a she-soul dwelt . . . ," and it goes on to a total of thirty-two lines. It is included in Victory's *Poems* (London, 1895), pp. 54–55.

192.9/190.1   MR RUSSELL . . . IS GATHERING TOGETHER A SHEAF OF OUR YOUNGER POETS' VERSES   This refers to a fifty-six page collection of lyric poems by such Irish poets as Padraic Colum, Eva Gore-Booth, Thomas Keohler, Susan Mitchell, Seumas O'Sullivan, and others, which A. E. edited. The first edition of *New Songs* appeared in April of 1904 and was reviewed by Oliver Gogarty in the May, 1904, issue of *Dana*, so that, as Wm. Schutte points out (*JS*, pp. 69–70) Joyce's customary accuracy slips here in his referring to the book as being presently compiled. Neither Joyce nor Gogarty had any verse in the volume. Cf. entry 192.23.

192.16/190.8   MY CASQUE AND SWORD   The words *casque* and *sword* occur in close connection only once in Shakespeare's works. In *Troilus and Cressida*, Troilus, after seeing Cressida and Diomedes dallying with one another, says of Diomedes helm, "Were it a casque composed by Vulcan's skill,/ My sword should bite it" (V, ii, 170–71).

192.16/190.8   TOUCH LIGHTLY WITH TWO INDEX FINGERS. ARISTOTLE'S EXPERIMENT . . .   Wm. Schutte (*JS*, p. 70) explains this as a reference to a problem Aristotle raises in *Problemata*, XXXV, 10: "Why is it that an object which is held between two crossed fingers appears to be two? Is it because we touch it at two sentient points? For when we hold the hand in its natural position we cannot touch an object with the outer sides of the two fingers" (*Works of Aristotle*, ed. W. D. Ross [Oxford, 1927], VII, 965a, ll. 36–39).

A textual note to this problem says that "two crossed fingers" is a possibly doubtful reading. Perhaps Stephen's use of "index fingers" might enable us to trace which translation of Aristotle he used, but I have not done so.

192.18/190.10 NECESSITY IS THAT IN VIRTUE OF WHICH IT IS IMPOSSIBLE THAT ONE CAN BE OTHERWISE   Aristotle says this during his discussion of necessity in the *Metaphysics*, sec. 1015b. In W. D. Ross's translation the pertinent statement is "necessity is that because of which the thing cannot be otherwise."

192.19/190.11 ARGAL   "Argal" is the gravedigger's word for "ergo" in *Hamlet*, V, i. The three uses of the word in this scene are the only instances of its use in Shakespeare, and they are the source of all the instances listed in the *OED*.

192.23/190.15 COLUM'S DROVER   The poem "A Drover," by Padraic Colum appears in *New Songs* (see entry 192.9). The thirty-six-line poem is on page 42 of the collection.

192.25/190.16 YEATS ADMIRED HIS LINE: AS IN WILD EARTH A GRECIAN VASE   This is the final line in Padraic Colum's poem "A Portrait (A poor scholar of the 'Forties)." This was the first poem in the *New Songs* collection (see entry 192.9).

192.28/190.19   MISS MITCHELL'S JOKE ABOUT MOORE AND MARTYN . . . Miss Mitchell is Susan Mitchell, contemporary Dublin satirist and parodist, who wrote a book entitled *Aids to the Immortality of Certain Persons in Ireland, Charitably Administered* (1908), directed mainly at Moore, Martyn, and Yeats. The joke referred to arises from the very different personalities of Moore and Martyn, and it alludes to the proverbial "To sow one's wild oats," which is listed in the *ODEP* and Apperson.

192.30/190.21 DON QUIXOTE AND SANCHO PANZA . . . A KNIGHT OF THE RUEFUL COUNTENANCE   Cervantes refers to Don Quixote as "The Knight of the Rueful Countenance" in *Don Quixote*, Pt. I, chap. 19. Sancho Panza is the squire of the knight. For evidence that Joyce based some of the conversation in this scene on a post-Bloomsday essay by John Eglinton entitled "Irish Books" (1911), see Wm. Schutte, *JS*, pp. 45–47. In that essay Eglinton speculates on a Knight of the Rueful Countenance coming out of Dublin's back streets. Among other things, he says, ". . . we can conceive him issuing forth, fresh hearted as a child at the age of fifty, with glib and saffron-coloured kilt, to realize and incidentally to expose the ideals of present-day Ireland. . . . His Dulcinea would be— who but Kathleen ni Houlihan herself."

192.30/190.22 OUR NATIONAL EPIC HAS YET TO BE WRITTEN, DR. SIGERSON

SAYS   Dr. George Sigerson (1838–1925), Irish physician, poet, and translator, was another of those who aided the revival of Irish literature during the last decade of the nineteenth century. His *Revival of Irish Literature* (1894) and *Bards of the Gael and Gall* (1897) were important. Sigerson does discuss the general topic of the epic and early Irish verse forms in his lecture "Irish Literature: Its Origin, Environment, & Influence," but nowhere in his works have I found the precise thought here attributed to him.

192.32/190.24   WITH A SAFFRON KILT   This alludes to what was at the time believed to be a traditional item of Irish garb, though later opinion on the matter is less certain. In his *Old Irish and Highland Dress*, H. F. McClintock argues that, contrary to popular opinion, the kilt was not a traditional Irish garment, though he points out that many earlier commentators thought that it was. Among these was P. W. Joyce, who firmly held this opinion in his *Social History of Ancient Ireland* (1903), but of Joyce's book, McClintock says, "There is no doubt that this work, which was widely read and carried much weight at the time, did a great deal to popularize the idea and to bring about its wide acceptance by the public, so much so that the adoption of a saffron kilt as a form of national uniform and dress for Irish pipe bands followed almost as a matter of course. For this the leaders in the movement had what seemed ample authority to point to, and cannot be blamed" (p. 123). Cf. entry 192.30.

192.33/190.24   O'NEILL RUSSELL   Since I have not found any O'Neill Russell in the Dublin circle at this time, I presume that this facetiously alludes to A. E. (George Russell) as an Irish hero. O'Neill is an appropriate name for such an allusion since the O'Neills were one of the most important and renowned families in early Ireland. Irish kings were drawn from this family from the twelfth to the seventeenth century.

192.34/190.25   AND HIS DULCINEA   This continues the Don Quixote allusion of entry 192.30. Dulcinea del Toboso is the name Don Quixote gives to the peasant girl Alonza Lorenzo, whom he imagines to be a beautiful noblewoman.

192.36/190.28   CORDELIA   Cordelia is the faithful youngest daughter of Lear in *King Lear*; see also the following entry. *Cordoglio* is not an allusion but an Italian word meaning "deep sorrow, grief, affliction."

192.36/190.28   LIR'S LONELIEST DAUGHTER   Thomas Moore's song "The Song of Fionnuala" begins, "Silent, O Moyle, be the roar of thy water,/ Break not, ye breezes, your chain of repose,/ While, murmuring mournfully, Lir's lonely daughter/ Tells to the night star her tale of woes." Fionnuala was the only daughter of Lir, a Danaan deity and the father of the sea god Mananaan. She was one of the four children Lir had by his first wife, Aebh. His second wife, Aeife, became jealous of these children and had them turned into swans for nine hundred years. They died soon after their return to human form. Cf. entry 211.38.

192.37/190.29 NOOKSHOTTEN   The *OED* lists only one instance of *nookshotten* prior to 1688, and that one is in Shakespeare's *Henry V*. In testifying to his willingness to fight the English, the Duke of Bourbon says, "If they march along/ Unfought withal, but I will sell my dukedom/ To buy a slobbery and a dirty farm/ In that nook-shotten isle of Albion" (III, v, 11–14). The *OED* says the word means "running out into corners or angles."

193.2/190.35 GOD ILD YOU   (The Bodley Head and the 1961 Random House editions of *Ulysses* read "Good ild you," but this is apparently an error.) The phrase "God 'ild you" ("God reward you") occurs three times in Shakespeare. Touchstone says it in *As You Like It*, III, iii, 75, and V, iv, 56, and Ophelia says it in *Hamlet*, IV, v, 41.

193.2/190.35 THE PIGS' PAPER   This refers to *The Irish Homestead*; see entry 191.29. According to Ellmann, Stanislaus said that Joyce forebore to sign his name to a story published in *The Irish Homestead* because he was ashamed of publishing in it (*JJ*, p. 170).

193.3/190.36 SYNGE HAS PROMISED ME AN ARTICLE FOR DANA TOO   Synge is, of course, dramatist John M. Synge (1871–1909). *Dana* was a magazine edited by John Eglinton, which ran from May, 1904, until April, 1905. It was subtitled "An Irish Magazine of Independent Thought." Joyce published one of the *Chamber Music* poems in the August, 1904, issue, over his own name.

193.4/190.37 THE GAELIC LEAGUE   The Gaelic League was founded in 1893 by Douglas Hyde, Father Eugene O'Growney, and John MacNeill. Its aims were: "1. The preservation of Irish as the National Language of Ireland, and the extension of its use as a spoken tongue. 2. The study and publication of existing Gaelic literature, and the cultivation of a modern literature in Irish" (O'Hegarty, *Ireland Under the Union*, p. 616—see the whole of chap. LVI).

193.11/191.1 HE CREAKED TO AND FRO, TIPTOEING UP NEARER HEAVEN BY THE ALTITUDE OF A CHOPINE   Hamlet, in addressing the company of players which is visiting Elsinore, says to one of the young ones, "By 'r Lady, your ladyship is nearer to Heaven than when I saw you last, by the altitude of a chopine" (*Ham.*, II, ii, 443–45). A chopine was a lady's shoe with a thick cork sole.

193.15/191.5 AN INWARD LIGHT   The phrase "inward light" occurs often in poetry; see, for example, Wordsworth's "Character of the Happy Warrior," l. 6, or Milton's *Paradise Lost*, III, 51–52. But in view of the recent reference to Lyster's being a "quaker librarian" (p. 193.8/190.40), this refers to a Quaker tenet. George Fox (1624–91), founder of the Society of Friends (Quakers), taught that every person could receive whatever understanding and guidance in divine truth he needed from the "inward light" supplied in his own heart by the Holy Spirit.

193.20/191.10 CHRISTFOX IN LEATHER TREWS   This phrase apparently ascribes to Shakespeare the qualities of Christ and of a fox, but if it is an allusion, I have not identified its source.

193.21/191.11 WALKING LONELY IN THE CHASE   Wm. Schutte suggests (*JS*, p. 65) that this phrase alludes to the opening of the forty-second Psalm in the translation of Nahum Tate and Nicholas Brady, both of whom were Irishmen: "As pants the hart for cooling streams/ When heated in the chase. . . ." But Stephen's phrase is not very close to that in the Psalm, and I am doubtful of the allusion.

193.22/191.12 A WHORE OF BABYLON   In Revelation, Babylon is used figuratively for Rome, and represents a city of wickedness. See, for example, Revelation 17:5, which speaks of "Babylon the great, the mother of harlots and abominations of the earth." The only use of the phrase in Shakespeare's works is in *Henry V*, where, in her report of Falstaff's death, the Hostess (Mistress Quickly) says of him, "A' did in some sort, indeed, handle women, but then he was rheumatic, and talked of the whore of Babylon" (II, iii, 39–41). Wm. Schutte says (*JS*, p. 66) that Stephen's phrase may be a reflection of Frank Harris' comment that "Shakespeare's 'universal sympathy'—to quote Coleridge—did not include the plainly-clad tub-thumper who dared to accuse him to his face of serving the Babylonish Whore" (Harris, p. 380). Harris says this while developing his idea that Shakespeare did not know the common people and the puritans of his day, and that he lost thereby.

193.23/191.13 BULLY TAPSTERS' WIVES   Wm. Schutte (*JS*, p. 65) explains this as an allusion to Mrs. Davenant of Oxford. John Aubrey (1626–97), in his sketch of Shakespeare in his *Brief Lives*, says that John Davenant, husband of the woman in question, was a vintner. See entry 202.1.

193.23/191.13 FOX AND GEESE   A. B. Gomme, in her *Traditional Games*, lists two children's games by this name. Both involve pursuit and capture, one played among children, the other played with markers. But Stephen may have in mind the exchange between Lysander, Theseus, and Demetrius in *A Midsummer Night's Dream*:

> Lys. This lion is a very fox for his valor.
> The. True, and a goose for his discretion.
> Dem. Not so, my lord, for his valor cannot carry his discretion, and the fox carries the goose.
> The. His discretion, I am sure, cannot carry his valor, for the goose carries the fox.
>
> (V, i, 234–40)

193.25/191.15 ONCE AS SWEET, AS FRESH AS CINNAMON, NOW HER LEAVES FALLING, ALL, BARE   Wm. Schutte has pointed out the allusion here to an Irish song entitled "Fair Maidens' Beauty Will Soon Fade Away" (*JS*, p. 66). P. W. Joyce prints the words and music of the song in his *Ancient Irish Music* and in his *Old Irish Folk Music and Songs*. The copy of the song which I have seen was in the 1906 printing of *Ancient Irish Music*. The song begins, "My love she was born in the north counterie," and the second stanza (which is what Stephen alludes to) says, "My love is as sweet as the cinnamon tree;/ She clings to me as close as the bark to the tree:/ But the leaves they will wither and the roots will decay,/ And fair maidens' beauty will soon fade away!" (p. 68).

193.26/191.16 FRIGHTED OF THE NARROW GRAVE AND UNFORGIVEN   Wm. Schutte points out that Brandes discusses Anne Shakespeare's growth in religiosity late in her life (*JS*, pp. 159–60).

193.31/191.21 A VESTAL'S LAMP   On the vestal virgins, see entry 146.1

193.32/191.22 WHAT CAESAR WOULD HAVE LIVED TO DO HAD HE BELIEVED THE SOOTHSAYER   In his *Julius Caesar*, Shakespeare follows Plutarch's account and depicts Caesar as being warned by a soothsayer whose advice he disregards.

193.34/191.24 POSSIBILITIES OF THE POSSIBLE AS POSSIBLE   Earlier Stephen has thought of history as an "actuality of the possible as possible" (see entry 25.35). His present phrase describes in Aristotelian terms those things that did not come about.

193.35/191.25 WHAT NAME ACHILLES BORE WHEN HE LIVED AMONG WOMEN   In *Urn Burial*, chap. V, Sir Thomas Browne says, "What song the Syrens sang, or what name Achilles assumed when he hid himself among women, though puzzling questions, are not beyond all conjecture." Achilles hid himself among women because his mother, Thetis, knowing that he was fated to die at Troy, disguised him as a woman and hid him among the women of the court of King Lycomedes of Skyros. Ulysses, however, discovered him there and persuaded him to go to Troy, where he was killed by Paris. See also entry 640.35.

193.38/191.27   THOTH, GOD OF LIBRARIES, A BIRDGOD, MOONYCROWNED Thoth, in Egyptian religion, was god of wisdom and magic and a patron of learning. He invented writing and was messenger and scribe of the gods. The Greeks identified him with Hermes and gave him the name Hermes Trismegistus. Perhaps originally a moon god, he is often represented as an ibis-headed man. The statuette in the Louvre depicts Thoth as an ibis-headed man crowned with the moon (see *Larousse Encyclopedia of Mythology* [New York, 1959], p. 25).

193.39/191.28   AND I HEARD THE VOICE OF THAT EGYPTIAN HIGHPRIEST . . . Stephen is apparently remembering John F. Taylor's speech, which he heard earlier (p. 142/140). But either Stephen misremembers the speech or he is embellishing it.

194.5/191.35   OTHERS ABIDE OUR QUESTION   Mathew Arnold's sonnet on Shakespeare begins, "Others abide our question. Thou art free."

194.12/192.1   TA AN BAD AR AN TIR. TIAM IMO SHAGART   These Gaelic sentences say, "The boat is on the land. I am a priest." As J. Prescott explains (*MLQ*, XIII, 154), the first sentence occurs almost verbatim in the Reverend Eugene O'Growney's *Simple Lessons in Irish*, Part I, p. 22. O'Growney's exact sentence is "Atá an bád ar tír" ("There is a boat on the land"). In *Stephen Hero* we are told that Stephen "bought the O'Growney's primers published by the Gaelic League" (p. 61).

194.21/192.10   A BASILISK. E QUANDO VEDE L'UOMO L' ATTOSCA. MESSER BRUNETTO   The basilisk is a fabulous beast, hatched by a serpent from a cock's egg. It is said to have a poisonous bite, a suffocating breath, and the power to kill with its glance. Wm. Schutte has pointed out (*JS*, p. 49) that Brunetto is Brunetto Latini (d. 1294?), Italian diplomat and writer, and that Stephen's phrase is from Latini's *Il Tesoro*. The edition Schutte cites is *Il Tesoro de Brunetto Latini volgarizzato da Bono Giamboni*, ed. P. Chabaille (4 vols.; Bologna, 1887), II, 137–38. Stephen's incomplete phrase is a paraphrase from a clause in Brunetto: "e col suo vedere attosca l'uomo quando lo vede" ("and with his sight he destroys the man who sees him"). As Schutte points out, Shakespeare makes frequent use of the basilisk.

194.23/192.12 MOTHER DANA, WEAVE AND UNWEAVE OUR BODIES
Dana, who is called Mother of the Irish Gods, was the greatest
of the Danaan deities. She is mentioned in A. E.'s play *Deirdre*,
which was alluded to earlier in this episode (see entry 189.20). J.
Prescott (*MLQ*, XIII, 154) points out an allusion here to a statement in the "Conclusion" to Walter Pater's *The Renaissance*: "It is
with this movement, with the passage and dissolution of impressions, images, sensations, that analysis leaves off—that continual
vanishing away, that strange, perpetual weaving and unweaving
of ourselves" (para. two of the "Conclusion").

194.30/192.19 THE MIND, SHELLEY SAYS, IS A FADING COAL   Shelley,
in his *Defense of Poetry*, develops the idea that poetry is something
divine or inspired, and says, "Poetry is not like reasoning, a power
to be exerted according to the determination of the will. A man
cannot say, 'I will compose poetry.' The greatest poet even cannot
say it; for the mind in creation is as a fading coal, which some invisible influence, like an inconstant wind, awakens to transitory
brightness; this power arises from within, like the color of a flower
which fades and changes as it is developed, and the conscious portions of our natures are unprophetic either of its approach or its
departure" (*Defense of Poetry*, ed. by Albert S. Cook [New York,
1890], p. 39).

194.35/192.23 DRUMMOND OF HAWTHORNDEN HELPED YOU AT THAT
STILE   William Drummond of Hawthornden (1585–1649) was a
Scottish poet. R. M. Adams says that this reference to Drummond
is "unnecessary—the things which Stephen has been saying bear
no such intimate relation to anything in William Drummond as to
require acknowledgement" (*SS*, p. 142). I have not found any
basis for Stephen's statement.

194.41/192.29 THAT MOLE IS THE LAST TO GO   Stephen earlier referred to a mole on his right breast (p. 194.26/192.15), but that is
not what he means here; nor is he referring, as some have said, to
Hamlet's "old mole" under the floor in *Hamlet*, I, v, 161. Rather,
this alludes to Hamlet's conversation with Horatio and Marcellus
earlier in the play where he spoke of "some vicious mole [blemish]
of nature" in a man that causes his downfall (*Ham.*, I, iv, 24). According to Stephen, Shakespeare's mole is an interest in women.
Perhaps this idea comes, at least in part, from Frank Harris. After
a list of Shakespeare's virtues and faults, Harris says, "But none of
these faults would have brought him to ruin; he was snared again
in full manhood by his master-quality, his overpowering sensuality, and thrown in the mire" (p. 381). And a few pages later

Harris refers to Shakespeare's "ungovernable sensuality . . . which in his maturity led him to worship Mary Fitton" (p. 383).

195.2/192.32 THE PLAYS OF SHAKESPEARE'S LATER YEARS WHICH RENAN ADMIRED SO MUCH   I have found no evidence, either through Shakespeare bibliography or in Renan's own essays, for his having expressed great admiration for Shakespeare's late plays, and I suspect that this statement is based largely, or solely, on Renan's having written an adaption of *The Tempest*, entitled *Caliban, Suite de La Tempete* (1878). For scholarly opinion that, of Shakespeare's works, "Renan only read *The Tempest* and knew the other plays merely at second hand," see Colin Smith's "Introduction" to Renan's *Caliban* (Manchester, Eng., 1954), pp. 10–11. Cf. p. 205.6/202.30, where Stephen refers more specifically to "the play Renan admired."

195.14/192.42 LIKE ANOTHER ULYSSES, PERICLES, PRINCE OF TYRE   Wm. Schutte (*JS*, p. 160) quotes a comparison of Ulysses and Pericles which Brandes makes: "Pericles is a romantic Ulysses, a far-travelled, sorely tried, much enduring man."

195.16/193.2 A CHILD, A GIRL PLACED IN HIS ARMS, MARINA   In *Pericles*, III, i, the nurse Lychordia presents his new-born daughter, Marina, to Pericles and says, "Take in your arms this piece/ Of your dead Queen" (ll. 17–18).

195.17/193.3 THE BYPATHS OF APOCRYPHA   As Wm. Schutte suggests (*JS*, p. 48), Eglinton is referring to the doubtful position of *Pericles*, the play Stephen has just cited, in Shakespeare's canon. The play was not included in the First Folio, and it is now generally agreed to be only in part by Shakespeare. See Stephen's reply in defense of taking the play as Shakespeare's, p. 195.28/193.14.

195.18/193.4 THE HIGHROADS ARE DREARY BUT THEY LEAD TO THE TOWN   Though this sounds proverbial, I have not located it in any of the proverb collections I have used. The closest I have found is "Keep the common road and thou'rt safe," from Thomas Fuller's *Gnomologia*, listed in Stevenson's *Home Book of Proverbs*, p. 1999.1.

195.20/193.6 SHAKESPEARE BACON'S WILD OATS   Stephen is blending a thought of the theory of the Baconian authorship of Shakespeare's plays with his memory of the joke told earlier about Martyn being Moore's wild oats. See entry 192.28.

195.21/193.7 CYPHERJUGGLERS   This alludes to the attempts of some scholars to prove Bacon's authorship of Shakespeare's plays by means of a cipher or code contained in certain passages in the plays. Schutte points out (*JS*, p. 165) that both Brandes and Lee discuss the Baconians and both mention Ignatius Donnelly's *The Great*

Cryptogram: Francis Bacon's Cipher in the So-Called Shakespeare Plays (1888). See also entry 210.4.

195.23/193.9 EAST OF THE SUN, WEST OF THE MOON: TIR NA N-OG
Both of these phrases refer to "The Land of Heart's Desire." "East of the Sun and West of the Moon" is the title of a well-known Scandinavian fairy story; it can be found in Andrew Lang's *Blue Fairy Book.* "Tir na n-og" is the Land of Youth, the Celtic otherworld, a land of complete happiness and timelessness.

195.25/193.11 HOW MANY MILES TO DUBLIN . . . Stephen's variation on the well-known nursery rhyme "How many miles to Babylon?" See *ODNR*, pp. 63–64, for a text of the rhyme and comments on it.

195.28/193.14 MR. BRANDES Stephen here explicitly mentions Shakespearean scholar George Brandes, whose *William Shakespeare: A Critical Study* (1898) Wm. Schutte has shown to be one of the main sources of the Shakespearean knowledge in this chapter. See *JS*, Appendix A.

195.30/193.16 MR SIDNEY LEE, OR MR SIMON LAZARUS AS SOME AVER HIS NAME IS Sidney Lee's biography, *A Life of William Shakespeare* (1898) was another of the main sources Joyce used in writing this chapter; see Wm. Schutte, *JS*, Appendix A. Ellmann says that Joyce learned that Lee's name was Lazarus from Karl Bleibtreu and cites a letter from Bleibtreu to Joyce, November 28, 1918, now at Cornell (*JJ*, p. 425). Bleibtreu's letter is item 429 in Scholes's catalogue of the Cornell Joyce collection.

195.32/193.18 MARINA . . . A CHILD OF STORM, MIRANDA, A WONDER, PERDITA, THAT WHICH WAS LOST Marina, Miranda, and Perdita are, respectively, the daughters of Pericles in *Pericles*, Prospero in *The Tempest*, and Leontes in *The Winter's Tale*. Wm. Schutte points out (*JS*, p. 160) that these three girls, and Imogen (Cymbeline's daughter in *Cymbeline*), are mentioned in a very similar context by Brandes, pp. 572–73. Stephen next goes on to suggest that in his granddaughter Elizabeth Hall, "what was lost is given back" to Shakespeare.

195.34/193.20 MY DEAREST WIFE, PERICLES SAYS, WAS LIKE THIS MAID Pericles says of his unrecognized daughter, Marina, "My dearest wife was like this maid, and such a one/ My daughter might have been" (*Pericles*, V, i, 108–9).

195.35/193.21 WILL ANY MAN LOVE THE DAUGHTER IF HE HAS NOT LOVED THE MOTHER? Stephen seems here to be parodying some biblical phrase on the Father and the Son, perhaps some such phrase as "Will any man love the Father if he has not loved the Son?" But the closest parallel I can find is in John 8:19, when Christ says,

"... if ye had known me, ye should have known my Father also."
John 14:7 is similar, and this idea runs through the entire gospel
of John.

195.37/193.23 THE ART OF BEING A GRANDFATHER . . . L'ART D'ETRE
GRAND . . .   *L'Art d'etre grand-pere (The Art of Being a Grandfather)* was the title of a book of poems which Victor Hugo (1802–
85) published in 1877. It consisted largely of poems written for
the enjoyment, entertainment, and instruction of his grandchildren.

196.8/193.35 MR FRANK HARRIS . . .   This, along with the earlier
references to George Brandes (p. 195.28/193.14) and Sidney Lee
(p. 195.30/193.16), makes explicit reference to all three of the men
whose works on Shakespeare provided Joyce's main sources for this
chapter. A series of articles by Harris had appeared intermittently
in the *Saturday Review* between March 19 and December 10, 1898,
and were later published in book form as *The Man Shakespeare
and his Tragic Life-Story* (1909). See Wm. Schutte, *JS*, Appendix
A.

196.11/193.37 THE FAVOURED RIVAL IS WILLIAM HERBERT, EARL OF PEM-
BROKE   Frank Harris does develop the idea of William Herbert,
third earl of Pembroke (1580–1630) as Shakespeare's rival for the
love of Mary Fitton. In speaking of Shakespeare's "Sonnets," Harris says, "These, then, are the personages of the drama, and the
story is very simple: Shakespeare loved Mistress Fitton and sent
his friend, the young Lord Herbert, to her on some pretext, but
with design that he should commend Shakespeare to the lady. Mistress Fitton fell in love with William Herbert, wooed and won
him, and Shakespeare had to mourn the loss of both friend and
mistress" (p. 202).

196.16/194.2 AUK'S EGG, PRIZE OF THEIR FRAY   If the auk has any
special mythological or symbolic meaning, I have not discovered
it. The great auk became extinct about 1844, and Stephen is probably using this simply to represent something exceedingly rare.
The *Encyclopaedia Britannica*, 11th ed., says, "A special interest
attaches to the great auk (*Alca impennis*), owing to its recent ex-
tinction and the value of its eggs to collectors" (II, 916, *s.v.* Auk).

196.17/194.3 DOST LOVE, MIRIAM? DOST LOVE THY MAN   This passage
is misleading and enigmatic because it clearly suggests that Lyster,
the quaker librarian, is married to a woman named Miriam. In reality Lyster remained a bachelor until very late in life—until after his
retirement from the National Library—and when he did marry, it
was to a woman named Jane Campbell from Galway.

196.19/194.5 A SAYING OF GOETHE'S . . . BEWARE OF WHAT YOU WISH
FOR IN YOUTH BECAUSE YOU WILL GET IT IN MIDDLE LIFE   This
refers to the motto of Part II of Goethe's *Wahrheit und Dich-
tung*: "Was man in der Jugend wunscht, hat man im Alter die
Fulle" ("What one wishes for in youth, one has in abundance in
old age").

196.21/194.7 WHY DOES HE SEND TO ONE WHO IS A BUONAROBA, A BAY
WHERE ALL MEN RIDE . . . A LORDLING TO WOO FOR HIM   The
phrase "bona roba" (to mean "showy girl") occurs only twice in
Shakespeare, both times in the dialogue of Shallow, in *II Henry
IV*, III, ii, ll. 26 and 217. Neither instance has any direct relevance
for the present context. The second quatrain of Shakespeare's
"Sonnet 137" says, "If eyes, corrupt by overpartial looks,/ Be
anchored in the bay where all men ride,/ Why of eyes' falsehood
hast thou forged hooks?" Wm. Schutte (*JS*, p. 164) quotes a passage from p. 200 of Harris' book which raises substantially the
same question Stephen is raising here. On the whole interpretation
of the "Sonnets" which this implies, see entry 196.11.

196.24/194.10 A LORD OF LANGUAGE   Tennyson's poem "To Virgil"
describes Virgil as "Landscape-lover, lord of language" (l. 5). But
E. Epstein (*JJR*, I, 32), while recognizing this passage from Tennyson, feels that Oscar Wilde's description of himself by this phrase
in *De Profundis* is a more likely source. I agree that Wilde is a
likely source, even though this involves an anachronism, since *De
Profundis* was not published until 1905. Also, it should be noted
that the pertinent passage occupied a much more prominent position in the 1905 edition than it does in the current one. In 1905
the passage was in the third paragraph of the work, whereas Wilde's
successive additions and revisions cause it to fall near the middle
of the current standard edition (that of Vyvyan Holland, published in 1949). I quote from the 1905 edition: "A week later, I am
transferred here [Reading Gaol]. Three months go over and my
mother dies. No one knew how deeply I loved and honoured her.
Her death was terrible to me; but I, once a lord of language, have
no words in which to express my anguish and my shame" (p. 3).

196.26/194.12 HE WAS OVERBORNE IN A CORNFIELD FIRST (RYEFIELD I
SHOULD SAY)   See entries 191.17 and 191.24.

196.29/194.14 THE GAME OF LAUGH AND LIE DOWN   The *ODEP* lists
"Laugh and lay (lie) down," explains it as "An obsolete game at
cards," and lists five instances of its use, including Skelton (1522),
Florio (1591), and Chapman (1606). But Wm. Schutte explains

(*JS*, p. 61) that this probably alludes to a poem entitled "The Art of Loving" which appeared in Head's *The Canting Academy*: "She'l smile, and she'l frown/ She'l laugh and lie down,/ At every turn you must tend her" (Head, p. 180). On Head's book, see Schutte, *JS*, p. 160.

196.29/194.15 ASSUMED DONGIOVANNISM   Stephen's reference to Don Giovanni recalls Bloom's many allusions to Mozart's opera *Don Giovanni*. See entries 63.31 and 197.5.

196.31/194.16 THE TUSK OF THE BOAR HAS WOUNDED HIM THERE This alludes to Shakespeare's *Venus and Adonis*, in which we are told that "nuzzling in his [Adonis'] flank, the loving swine/ Sheathed unaware the tusk in his soft groin" (ll. 1115–16). This wound was the cause of Adonis' death. Ulysses, too, was wounded in the thigh by a boar in his youth, as we are told in book XIX of the *Odyssey*.

196.32/194.17 WHERE LOVE LIES ABLEEDING   "Love Lies Ableeding" is the subtitle of Beaumont and Fletcher's play *Philaster* (1611). Wm. Schutte observes the similarity between the heroine of the play and the "psychologically castrated Shakespeare" (*JS*, p. 107).

196.35/194.21 DARKENING EVEN HIS OWN UNDERSTANDING OF HIMSELF These words seem to echo a phrase from the *Catechism* which Stephen explicitly refers to later. See entry 212.14.

196.38/194.23 THEY LIST   An allusion to the Ghost's words to Hamlet; see entry 188.3.

196.38/194.23 AND IN THE PORCHES OF THEIR EARS I POUR   The Ghost explains that, in his murder, Claudius took "juice of cursed hebenon in a vial,/ And in the porches of my ears did pour/ The leperous distillment" (*Ham.*, I, v, 62–64). Stephen repeats the allusion in the next line. See also entry 139.26.

196.40/194.25 BUT THOSE WHO ARE DONE TO DEATH IN SLEEP CANNOT KNOW THE MANNER OF THEIR QUELL . . .   Stephen's thoughts here are following the same lines they did earlier on p. 139.26/138.1 ff. Here he is referring to King Hamlet's Ghost's knowledge of how he was murdered. Wm. Schutte sees the word *quell* as suggesting Lady Macbeth's words to Macbeth while they plot to kill Duncan: "What cannot you and I perform upon/ The unguarded Duncan? What not put upon/ His spongy officers, who shall bear the guilt/ Of our great quell?" (*Mac.*, I, vii, 69–72).

197.1/194.28 THE POISONING AND THE BEAST WITH TWO BACKS THAT URGED IT . . .   Stephen suggests a sensual motive for Claudius' slaying King Hamlet through an allusion to Iago's words to Desdemona's father, Brabantio: "Your daughter and the Moor are now making the beast with two backs" (*Oth.*, I, i, 117–18).

197.4/194.30 HIS LEAN UNLOVELY ENGLISH   This alludes to a poem by Douglas Hyde; see entry 186.28.

197.5/194.32 WHAT HE WOULD BUT WOULD NOT   R. M. Adams has suggested (*SS*, p. 98) that this parallels Bloom's "voglio e non vorrei" allusions to *Don Giovanni;* see entry 64.4. Stephen's specific meaning is developed in the following lines: see the next two entries.

197.6/194.33 FROM LUCRECE'S BLUECIRCLED IVORY GLOBES   In "The Rape of Lucrece," Lucrece's breasts are described as "like ivory globes circled with blue" (l. 407), as Tarquin gazes on her just before raping her. See also the preceding and following entries.

197.7/194.33 TO IMOGEN'S BREAST, BARE, WITH ITS MOLE CINQUESPOTTED Iachimo sees on Imogen's "left breast/ A mole cinque-spotted" when he spies on her asleep in order to gain personal knowledge of her with which to convince Posthumus that he has been intimate with her (*Cymbeline*, II, ii, 37–38). Earlier in the scene Iachimo has referred to Tarquin's rape of Lucrece (ll. 12–14). These two assaults—Tarquin's on Lucrece, Iachimo's on Imogen—the first carried out, the second only thought about, correspond to Stephen's "would but would not" in the preceding line.

197.12/194.38 HIS BEAVER IS UP   Horatio tells Hamlet that they saw the Ghost's face because "he wore his beaver up" (*Ham.*, I, ii, 229). Stephen's language in the following sentence echoes the scene in *Hamlet.*

197.15/194.41 THE SON CONSUBSTANTIAL WITH THE FATHER   An allusion to the doctrine of the consubstantiality of the Father and Son; see entry 21.8.

197.17/195.2 HAST THOU FOUND ME, O MINE ENEMY   In I Kings 21:20, Ahab says to Elijah, "Hast thou found me, O mine enemy?" Wm. Schutte, after explaining Ahab's treachery to Naboth, says, "Stephen has reason to think of himself as Ahab and Mulligan as Elijah; Mulligan has accused him of murdering his mother" (*JS*, p. 73). (This is one instance in which Joyce is clearly following the King James' version of the Bible rather than the Douay, for this verse in the Douay has the quite different "Hast thou found me thy enemy?")

197.26/195.11 WAS DU VERLACHST WIRST DU NOCH DIENEN   Though this statement, which says, "What you laugh at, you will still serve," certainly seems proverbial, I have not located it in any of the dictionaries of proverbs I have consulted. Wm. Schutte refers to it as "proverbial" and a "German aphorism" (*JS*, p. 74).

197.28/195.13 BROOD OF MOCKERS: PHOTIUS, PSEUDOMALACHI, JOHANN MOST   On Photius, see entry 21.7. Pseudomalachi apparently refers to the conjectured author of the book of Malachi. Many authorities feel that Malachi is not the proper name of the author, but rather that Malachi 1:1 is a superscription added later, and *Malachi* means simply "the messenger of the Lord." (See entry 213.31.) Johann Joseph Most (1846–1906) was a German anarchist. Wm. Schutte explains that Most "attacked, violently and cynically, all conventional beliefs" and says, "his radical paper *Freiheit*, which was published in London, was suppressed in 1882 by the British government for its enthusiastic approval of the Phoenix Park murders" (*JS*, p. 74). But R. M. Adams finds these poor examples of mockers, and he concludes, "These three names are so ill-sorted, so diverse in their connotations or lack of connotation, and so obscurely connected (if they are connected at all) that their juxtaposition as 'mockers' seems altogether perverse" (*SS*, p. 138).

197.29/195.14 HE WHO HIMSELF BEGOT . . .   This is Stephen's version of what the Apostle's Creed would be if the heresy of Sabellius (see entry 21.10) were accepted. See W. T. Noon, *JA*, chap. VI, esp. p. 115.

197.30/195.15 AGENBUYER   While this does recall Stephen's phrase "agenbite of inwit" (see entry 16.7), the word *agenbuyer* for *redeemer* is quite common in Middle English. See the *Middle English Dictionary*, s.v. *agenbuyer*.

197.34/195.22 GLORIA IN EXCELSIS DEO   The "Gloria in excelsis Deo" ("Glory be to God on high") is a regular part of the beginning of the Mass except during the penitential season and in masses for the dead. It follows the Kyrie.

198.14/195.32 THE CHAP THAT WRITES LIKE SYNGE   Wm. Schutte explains (*JS*, p. 75) that this alludes to a contemporary Dublin quip. Yeats had said of the newly discovered Synge that he was another Aeschylus, so that Gogarty and others began to describe Aeschylus as the man who writes like Synge. As Schutte says, the quip is briefly recounted in P. Colum, *Road Round Ireland*, pp. 358–59, and Gogarty, *As I Was Going Down Sackville Street*, pp. 299–300.

198.18/196.2 HYDE'S LOVESONGS OF CONNACHT   See entry 186.25.

198.24/196.8 AN ACTRESS PLAYED HAMLET FOR THE FOURHUNDRED-ANDEIGHTH TIME LAST NIGHT IN DUBLIN   This refers to Mrs. Bandmann-Palmer; see entry 76.23. The *Irish Daily Independent* of June 16, 1904, in its brief review of the performance says that Mrs.

Bandmann-Palmer "made her 405th appearance in the character of Hamlet last night" (p. 4). But the 5 is so badly printed that it looks like an 8, and this is probably Joyce's source.

198.25/196.9   VINING HELD THAT THE PRINCE WAS A WOMAN   See entry 76.25.

198.27/196.10   JUDGE BARTON   This is Sir Dunbar Plunket Barton (1853–1937), M.R.I.A., who in 1919 published a book called *Links Between Ireland and Shakespeare*. The book systematically investigates Irish materials in many of the plays. Barton does discuss the theory that Hamlet was a Danish prince of Dublin (chap. V). A statement in the Preface indicates that the work was "planned and begun" by 1894.

198.27/196.11   HE SWEARS (HIS HIGHNESS NOT HIS LORDSHIP) BY SAINT PATRICK   When Hamlet is discussing the Ghost with Horatio and Marcellus, he apologizes for offending them, to which Horatio says, "There's no offense, my lord," and Hamlet replies, "Yes, by Saint Patrick, but there is, Horatio,/ And much offense too" (*Ham.*, I, v, 135–37). "He swears by" may also recall Hamlet's repeated demand, later in this same scene, that Horatio and Marcellus *swear*.

198.29/196.13   THAT STORY OF WILDE'S . . . PORTRAIT OF MR W. H. . . . Oscar Wilde's *The Portrait of Mr. W. H.* first appeared in *Blackwell's Magazine*, July, 1889, in a version less than half the length of the work as we now have it. In it Wilde supported for the Mr. W. H. of the dedication to the "Sonnets" his own version of the Willie Hewes or Hughes first suggested by Thomas Tyrwhitt in 1766. According to Wilde, Willie Hewes was a young actor whose talent Shakespeare was trying to encourage and protect. Since Wilde presents the theory in story form, and the main character loses his belief in it after convincing a friend, it is difficult to know Wilde's own attitude toward the theory.

198.32/196.16   A MAN ALL HUES   This alludes to "Sonnet 20," where Shakespeare speaks of the man he is writing to as "A man in hue, all hues in his controlling." Oscar Wilde quotes this in his *Portrait of Mr. W. H.* (London, 1958), p. 14.

199.5/196.30   YOU WOULD GIVE YOUR FIVE WITS FOR THE YOUTH'S PROUD LIVERY HE PRANKS IN   The phrase "youth's proud livery" occurs in "Sonnet 2," l. 3. The word *pranks* may allude to Coriolanus' statement about Sicinius and Brutus: "Behold, these are the Tribunes of the people,/ The tongues o' the common mouth. I do despise them,/ For they do prank them in authority/ Against all noble sufferance" (*Corio.*, III, i, 21–24; an allusion to *Twelfth Night*, II, iv, 89, seems unlikely to me). Man's five wits (i.e., common wit, imagination, fantasy, estimation, and memory) are mentioned several times in Shakespeare, but not in any context similar to the present one.

199.6/196.31 LINEAMENTS OF GRATIFIED DESIRE   This is a line from an epigram in Blake's *Note-Book,* called "The Question Answer'd": "What is it men in women do require?/ The lineaments of Gratified Desire./ What is it women do in men require?/ The lineaments of Gratified Desire" (1957 Keynes ed., p. 180).

199.7/196.32 JOVE, A COOL RUTTIME SEND THEM   In *The Merry Wives of Windsor,* Falstaff says, "Send me a cool rut time, Jove" (V, v, 15).

199.9/196.35 EVE. NAKED WHEATBELLIED SIN   See entries 38.6 through 38.8.

199.21/197.4 THE SENTIMENTALIST IS HE . . .   This alludes to a statement in George Meredith's *Richard Feverel,* chap. XXVIII: " 'Sentimentalists,' says THE PILGRIM'S SCRIP, 'are they who seek to enjoy Reality, without incurring the Immense Debtorship for a thing done.' "

199.30/197.13 IT'S WHAT I'M TELLING YOU, MISTER HONEY   Mulligan is here parodying Synge, whom he mentions on p. 200.2/197.26, but apparently the parody is general rather than of any specific passage in Synge. The Cornell Joyce collection contains a letter Gogarty wrote to Joyce, *ca.* March 18, 1903, in similar "Kiltartan." It begins, "It is myself that write to answer the letter you kindly sent me and I waiting for it in Ireland" (Scholes, item 526). See also entry 205.27.

200.12/197.36 OISIN WITH PATRICK   Apparently Stephen is comparing his meeting Synge in Paris with the meeting between Oisin and St. Patrick. The Irish story of a dialogue between Oisin and St. Patrick, or of Oisin in the Land of Youth, goes back at least as far as a Gaelic poem by Michael Comyn written about 1750 and entitled "The Lay of Oisin on the Land of Youth." Brian O'Looney wrote an English adaptation of the poem, and this formed the basis of P. W. Joyce's "Oisin in Tirnanoge." Yeats probably drew on O'Looney's or Joyce's story for his poem "The Wanderings of Oisin," though in his notes to the poem he mentions "the Middle Irish dialogues of St. Patrick and Oisin." In this dialogue Oisin always represents a hearty paganism in opposition to St. Patrick's Christianity. See for example Yeats's poem or the brief dialogue from Standish O'Grady's *A History of Ireland, Critical and Philosophical,* printed in *Irish Literature,* VII, 2752–56.

200.14/197.38 I MET A FOOL I' THE FOREST   In *As You Like It,* II, vii, 12, Jaques says, "A fool, a fool! I met a fool i' the forest."

200.17/197.41 MR JUSTICE MADDEN IN HIS DIARY OF MASTER WILLIAM
SILENCE   The Right Honorable Dodgson Hamilton Madden
(1840–1928) was Judge of the High Court of Justice of Ireland and
Vice-Chancellor of Dublin University. He wrote *The Diary of
Master William Silence: A Study of Shakespeare and of Elizabethan Sport* (London, 1897), in which he claims (unseriously)
to present a journal by Master William Silence (really William
Shakespeare), telling of hunting experiences in Goucestershire. In
this way Madden provides an exposition of Elizabethan sport
which, amply interlarded with quotations from the plays, illustrates and illuminates Shakespeare's great knowledge of hunting
and field sports. As he says in his Preface, he hopes "a description
of the various incidents of the chase might serve to illustrate and
to connect the scattered passages in which Shakespeare has recorded his recollections of the harbouring, the unharbouring, the
hunting, the baying, and the breaking up of the hart" (p. vi). See
entry 248.34.

200.27/198.10 BRISK IN A GALLIARD HE WAS OFF AND OUT   Sir Toby
mentions a galliard three times in quick succession in his conversation with Sir Andrew in *Twelfth Night*, I, iii, 127, 137, and 142. A
galliard was a lively dance. Cf. entry 184.14.

200.29/198.12 BROADBRIM   This alludes to the broadbrim hat that
is one of the traditional items of Quaker dress.

201.3/198.28 JEHOVAH, COLLECTOR OF PREPUCES   See entry 13.33

201.4/198.29 THE FOAMBORN APHRODITE   In most myths Aphrodite
(or Roman Venus), the Greek goddess of love and beauty, is said
to have risen from the foam of the sea at the spot where Uranus'
genitals fell after he was mutilated by Cronus.

201.6/198.31 LIFE OF LIFE, THY LIPS ENKINDLE   In Shelley's *Prome-
theus Unbound*, Asia and Panthea hear Voices in the Air singing a
song that begins, "Life of Life! thy lips enkindle/ With their love
the breath between them" (II, v, 48–49).

201.10/198.33 HE IS GREEKER THAN THE GREEKS   This is apparently
Mulligan's variation on the proverbial "More Irish than the Irish"
(on which see entry 119.11), but it may owe something as well to
Eramus' description of Rudolphus Agricola (Roelof Huysmann)
as "Most Greek among the Greeks, most Latin among the Latins"
(*Adagia: Dissimilitudo*). Mulligan's insinuation, here and on p.
217.36/215.5, is based upon the commonness of homosexuality
among the Greeks.

201.10/198.34 PALE GALILEAN EYES   Swinburne's "Hymn to Proserpine" says of Christ "Thou hast conquered, O pale Galilean; the world has grown gray from thy breath" (l. 35). These words, and the poem's introductory epigraph, allude to the deathbed statement of the Roman emperor Julian the Apostate in A.D. 363: "Vicisti, Galilaee." W. Y. Tindall says, "Bloom's 'Galilean eyes' combine Jesus with Galileo, who also observed Venus" (*RG*, p. 178).

201.11/198.35 VENUS KALLIPYGE   The Callipygian Venus (Venus of the shapely buttocks) is the statue of Venus found in the Domus Aureo of Nero at Rome and now in the Museo Nazionale at Naples. The *Encyclopaedia Britannica*, 11th ed., calls it "a specimen of the most sensual type."

201.11/198.35 O, THE THUNDER OF THOSE LOINS   The context here suggests that this phrase comes from Swinburne, but I have not been able to locate it.

201.12/198.36 THE GOD PURSUING THE MAIDEN HID   This alludes to the first chorus in Swinburne's *Atalanta in Calydon*, in which the following lines occur: "The laughing leaves of the trees divide,/ And screen from seeing and leave in sight/ The god pursuing, the maiden hid" (First Chorus, stanza 6).

201.15/198.39 A PATIENT GRISELDA   Griselda is the wife of Walter in Chaucer's "Clerk's Tale." She endures her husband's trials of her with complete patience and submission, and she has become known as a paradigm of the patient wife.

201.15/198.39 A PENELOPE STAYATHOME   This alludes to Penelope's staying faithfully in Ithaca during Ulysses' absence of twenty years. It may also recall the scene in *Coriolanus* in which Valeria tries to get Coriolanus' wife, Virgilia, to "play the idle huswife" with her. When Virgilia refuses, Valeria says, "You would be another Penelope" (*Corio.*, I, iii, 77, 92).

201.17/198.41 ANTISTHENES,PUPIL OF GORGIAS . . . TOOK THE PALM OF BEAUTY . . .   On Antisthenes, see entry 148.29. Stephen's statement alludes to several well-known details of the Trojan War. "Poor Penelope" is used on p. 202.7/199.30 to describe Anne Hathaway.

201.21/199.3 HE DREW A SALARY EQUAL TO THAT OF THE LORD CHANCEL-LOR OF IRELAND   Wm. Schutte (*JS*, p. 176) says that none of Joyce's main sources for this episode draw this comparison. Schutte conjectures that Joyce found the salary of the lord chancellor of Ireland in a book on Irish history and compared it with accounts given by Brandes and Lee.

201.23/199.4 HIS ART, MORE THAN THE ART OF FEUDALISM, AS WALT

WHITMAN CALLED IT   In many of his comments on Shakespeare, Whitman associates him with feudalism. For example, in his "Notes on British Literature," Whitman says, "[Shakespeare] seems to me of astral genius, first class, entirely fit for feudalism. . . . But there is much in him ever offensive to democracy. He is not only the tally of feudalism, but I should say Shakespeare is incarnated, uncompromising feudalism, in literature" (*Complete Writings* [New York, 1902], V, 275–76; see also the Index to this collection, *s.v.* Shakespeare).

201.24/199.6 HOT HERRINGPIES, GREEN MUGS OF SACK . . .   Some, though not all, of the items in this list have some referent in Shakespeare. In *As You Like It*, Touchstone says that "honesty coupled to beauty is to have honey a sauce to sugar" (III, iii, 31); and in *I Henry IV*, King Henry tells Prince Hal that when a king is seen too much among his people, they become "surfeited with honey" and begin to "loathe the taste of sweetness" (III, ii, 71–72). Marchpane is mentioned only once in Shakespeare: in *Romeo and Juliet* one of the servants of Capulet says to another, "Good thou, save me a piece of marchpane" (I, v, 9). Ringocandies probably alludes to Falstaff's statement when he sees Mistress Ford: "Let it thunder to the tune of 'Green Sleeves,' hail kissing comfits, and snow eringoes" (*Merry Wives*, V, v, 21–22). Eringoes were a candied root, supposed to increase potency in love.

201.26/199.8 SIR WALTER RALEIGH, WHEN THEY ARRESTED HIM . . .   Wm. Schutte (*JS*, p. 160) shows that this comes from Brandes' study. Brandes says of Raleigh, "When he was arrested in 1603, he had gems to the value of £4000 (about £20,000 in modern money) on his breast" (p. 417).

201.28/199.10 ELIZA TUDOR HAD UNDERLINEN ENOUGH TO VIE WITH HER OF SHEBA   Wm. Schutte (*JS*, p. 176) lists this as one item he can find no source of in Brandes, Lee, or Harris. Stephen is apparently referring to the Queen of Sheba. None of the biblical passages about the Queen of Sheba makes any reference to her underlinen, though her great wealth is described. Her famous visit to King Solomon is described in I Kings 10:1–13 and II Chronicles 9:1–12.

201.29/199.11 TWENTY YEARS HE DALLIED   Shakespeare's twenty years of dalliance parallels Ulysses' twenty years' absence from Ithaca in the *Odyssey*.

201.31/199.13 MANNINGHAM'S STORY . . .   Stephen repeats the substance of the anecdote from the diary of John Manningham. For a full presentation of the diary account, see Chambers, II, 212. Wm.

Schutte (*JS*, p. 160) says that all three of Joyce's sources deal with the anecdote, but only Brandes presents Manningham's account in full.

201.34/199.15   MORE ADO ABOUT NOTHING   An obvious variation on *Much Ado About Nothing*.

201.34/199.16   TOOK THE COW BY THE HORNS   A variation on the proverbial "take the bull by the horns," on which see entry 33.16.

201.35/199.17   KNOCKING AT THE GATE   This immediately recalls the famous "knocking at the gate" scene in *Macbeth*, II, iii, but it may also echo Petruchio's words to his servant, Grumio: "Villain, I say, knock me at this gate,/ And rap me well, or I'll knock your knave's pate" (*Taming of the Shrew*, I, ii, 11–12).

201.37/199.19   MISTRESS FITTON   (The *Fitten* of the 1961 Random House is an obvious error.) Mistress Fitton was a maid of honor to Queen Elizabeth. Brandes and Harris identify her as the Dark Lady of the sonnets, and Harris goes so far as to say that "the story of [Shakespeare's] idolatrous passion for Mary Fitton is the story of his life" (p. 212). See entry 196.11.

201.37/199.19   MOUNT AND CRY O   In *Cymbeline*, Posthumus thinks of the ease with which Iachimo supposedly prevailed on Imogen for her love: "perchance he spoke not, but/ Like a full-acorned boar, a German one,/ Cried 'Oh!' and mounted, found no opposition . . ." (II, v, 15–17). Bloom later alludes to a line from this soliloquy; see entry 492.30.

201.38/199.19   LADY PENELOPE RICH   Lady Penelope Rich 1562?–1607), daughter of Walter Devereux, first earl of Essex, was celebrated by Sir Philip Sidney in his "Astrophel and Stella" series of sonnets. Wm. Schutte says that Stephen's inclusion of her in the list of Shakespeare's presumed mistresses "is hardly a gallant gesture" on his part, since "she has never been a serious candidate for that honor" (*JS*, p. 177). But the Variorum *Sonnets*, edited by Hyder Edward Rollins (1944), does mention several critics who have discussed the idea that Lady Penelope is the subject of the Sonnets (see esp. II, 260–61).

202.1/199.24   AND SIR WILLIAM DAVENANT OF OXFORD'S MOTHER   John Aubrey suggests that Sir William Davenant of Oxford was Shakespeare's illegitimate son. Brandes and Harris accept the story; Lee does not. For Aubrey's statement, see Chambers, II, 254. See also entry 193.23.

202.2/199.25   HER CUP OF CANARY FOR EVERY COCKCANARY   This apparently alludes to Sir Toby's statement to Sir Andrew: "O knight, thou lackest a cup of canary" (*Twelfth Night*, I, iii, 85).

202.4/199.27 BLESSED MARGARET MARY ANYCOCK   M. Magalaner (*Time of Apprenticeship*, pp. 152–53) has pointed this out as an allusion to Blessed Margaret Mary Alacoque (1647–90; now St. Margaret Mary Alacoque—she was canonized in 1920), who is mentioned in the *Dubliners* story "Eveline." She was a member of the Visitation Order, Apostle of the Devotion to the Sacred Heart of Jesus, and was known for her strict mortification of self. She experienced visions from the age of twenty, in one of which she was directed to establish widespread devotion to the Sacred Heart of Jesus.

202.5/199.28 AND HARRY OF THE SIX WIVES' DAUGHTER   Henry VIII is the Harry of six wives; Queen Elizabeth, Harry's daughter by Anne Boleyn, is the daughter alluded to.

202.6/199.29 FROM NEIGHBOR SEATS, AS LAWN TENNYSON, GENTLEMAN POET, SINGS   In the "Prologue" to Tennyson's *The Princess*, we are told that the gathering included "lady friends/ From neighbor seats" ("Prologue," ll. 97–98).

202.9/199.32 DO AND DO   In *Macbeth*, the witches say, "I'll do, I'll do, and I'll do" (I, iii, 10).

202.9/199.32 IN A ROSERY OF FETTER LANE OF GERARD, HERBALIST   John Gerard (1545–1612) was the author of *The Herball or Generall Historie of Plantes* (1597). Wm. Schutte discusses the problem of how Joyce knew that Gerard had a rosery in Fetterlane (*JS*, p. 176). Marcus Woodward, in his Introduction to his 1927 edition of Gerard's work, confirms that he did actually have a rosery in Fetterlane, but Woodward cites no source for this information and his edition was, of course, too late for Joyce to have used it.

202.10/199.33 HE WALKS, GREYEYEDAUBURN   Wm. Schutte (*JS*, pp. 169–70) quotes both Lee and Harris as saying that the Stratford bust gives Shakespeare hazel eyes and auburn hair and beard.

202.10/199.33 AN AZURED HAREBELL LIKE HER VEINS   This alludes to Arviragus' statement about the apparently dead Fidele (Imogen in disguise): "Thou shalt not lack/ The flower that's like thy face, pale primrose, nor/ The azured harebell, like thy veins . . ." (*Cymbeline*, IV, ii, 220–22).

202.11/199.34 LIDS OF JUNO'S EYES, VIOLETS   In *The Winter's Tale*, Perdita, speaking of various flowers, refers to "violets dim,/ But sweeter than the lids of Juno's eyes . . ." (IV, iv, 120–21).

202.17/199.40 THE COURT WANTON SPURNED HIM FOR A LORD   This refers to Mary Fitton and William Herbert. See entries 196.11 and 201.37.

202.19/199.42 LOVE THAT DARE NOT SPEAK ITS NAME   Stephen's suggestion of homosexuality couches itself in an allusion to a poem by Lord Alfred Douglas. See entry 49.23.

202.20/200.1 AS AN ENGLISHMAN . . . HE LOVED A LORD   "An Englishman loves a lord" is proverbial and is listed in the *ODEP*, though the first occurrence it lists is 1909. F. Budgen quotes Joyce as saying of Clutton Brock's criticism of his writing, "He is stating the English preference for tawdry grandeurs. Even the best Englishman seems to love a lord in literature" (*JJMU*, p. 75).

202.25/200.6 UNEARED WOMBS   Shakespeare's "Sonnet 3" says, "For where is she so fair whose uneared womb/ Disdains the tillage of thy husbandry" (ll. 5–6).

202.26/200.7 MAYBE, LIKE SOCRATES, HE HAD A MIDWIFE TO MOTHER AS HE HAD A SHREW TO WIFE   Diogenes Laertius begins his discussion of Socrates by saying, "Socrates was the son of Sophroniseus, a statuary, and of Phaenarete, a midwife" (*Lives of Eminent Philosophers*, p. 63), and he discusses the shrewish nature of Socrates' wife Xanthippe in section xvii of his essay (pp. 70–71). But I can find no evidence in Brandes, Lee, Harris, or Chambers that Mary Arden Shakespeare was a midwife; Schutte makes no comment about this. R. M. Adams says, "The parallel between Shakespeare and Socrates is urged on the grounds that both had shrews to wife and midwives as mothers; but Mary Arden, who married about the age of twenty and had plenty to occupy her after that, is most unlikely to have practiced the midwife's art, and there is no evidence that she did" (*SS*, p. 129).

202.27/200.8 BUT SHE . . . DID NOT BREAK A BEDVOW   The phrase "In act thy bed vow broke" occurs in "Sonnet 152," l. 3.

202.39/200.19 MARY, HER GOODMAN JOHN . . .   All of these were relatives of Shakespeare. Mary, his mother, died after John, his father; Anne Hathaway outlived Shakespeare; Judith, Shakespeare's daughter, outlived her husband and children; and Elizabeth, Susanna's daughter, married a second husband two years after the death of her first. The only questionable item in the list is whether Joan, Shakespeare's sister, survived all four of her brothers. Authorities differ about the date of Gilbert's death, though some (e.g., Chambers, II, 7) feel that he died many years before his sister, and perhaps Stephen, for the sake of his theory, does the same.

203.1/200.23 WED HER SECOND, HAVING KILLED HER FIRST   This alludes to the player queen's words in the play within the play:

"None wed the second but who killed the first" (*Ham.*, III, ii, 190). See also the preceding entry.

203.4/200.26 SHE HAD TO BORROW FORTY SHILLINGS   Wm. Schutte (*JS*, p. 170) shows that both Lee and Harris discuss Anne's borrowing forty shillings from Thomas Whittington, her father's former shepherd. The debt was still unpaid at Whittington's death in 1601, and he directed the executor of his will to collect it from William Shakespeare. For the item in the will, see Chambers, II, 42.

203.6/200.27 THE SWANSONG TOO WHEREIN HE HAS COMMENDED HER TO POSTERITY   This refers to Shakespeare's will, which Eglinton and Stephen discuss. Schutte (*JS*, pp. 165–66) says that both Brandes and Lee discuss at length the terms of the will, and both support all of Stephen's statements. For the text of the will, see Chambers, II, 169 ff. The will does contain all the provisions Eglinton mentions on p. 203.16/200.38 ff.

203.22/201.5 HE LEFT HER HIS SECONDBEST BED   In his will, Shakespeare's only reference to his wife is "Item, I gyve unto my wief my second best bed with the furniture." These words were added interlineally to the original will; see Chambers II, 173, and plate xxi; and for a defense of the "second best bed" clause based on contemporary legal grounds, see Chambers, II, 176–77, and the sources cited there. Wm. Schutte (*JS*, pp. 164–65) quotes a statement from Harris that Shakespeare's daughters begged the dying man to mention Anne and thus he wrote in the second best bed (Harris, p. 362).

203.31/201.14 WOA   W. Y. Tindall says (*RG*, p. 178) that this word suggests Wagner's Rheinmaidens, but he does not specify what he thinks it alludes to—perhaps to the maiden's onomatopoetic river song which recurs through act I of *Das Rheingold*, or perhaps to their cry of "Weh'!" (Woe!) at the end of act I when Alberich steals the gold. But in any event the allusion seems doubtful; the word is probably used here much as it is on p. 231.31/228.18—to mean "pull up," or "stop."

203.32/201.15 PRETTY COUNTRYFOLK   "Pretty countryfolk" is from a song in *As You Like It*. See entry 191.24.

203.35/201.18 A HOUSE IN IRELAND YARD   Wm. Schutte (*JS*, p. 163) has shown that Joyce took this detail from Lee. R. M. Adams is mistaken in saying that Ireland Yard is named only once as the location of the house, "in a footnote on p. 457" (*SS*, p. 127): the statement Schutte quotes is on p. 267 of Lee's book.

204.1/201.24 SEPARATIO A MENSA ET A THALAMO   Apparently this is

Mulligan's version of the legal phrase "separatio a mensa et thoro" ("separation from board and bed"); Mulligan's phrase means "separation from board and bedchamber." The Catholic Church has always regarded marriage as a sacrament and therefore indissoluble. This doctrine became established in English law and remained long after the Reformation. Until the statute of 20 and 21 Victoria (1857) c. 85 and amendments, a marriage in England could not be dissolved except by the "omnipotent power of Parliament." What the courts granted instead of a divorce was a *separatio a mensa et thoro.*

204.5/201.28 THAT STAGYRITE SCHOOLURCHIN AND BALD HEATHEN SAGE Aristotle, who was born in Stageira in Macedon. Stephen has earlier alluded to Aristotle's being "Plato's schoolboy" (p. 185.23/183.23), and to his baldness (p. 37.7/38.7).

204.6/201.29 WHEN DYING IN·EXILE FREES AND ENDOWS HIS SLAVES As R. M. Adams has pointed out (*SS,* p. 141), this material on Aristotle's will comes from Diogenès Laertius' *Lives of Eminent Philosophers,* which quotes from Aristotle's will at some length. The will does include provisions freeing and endowing some of his slaves, asking for a statue of his mother, asking that his wife's bones be reinterred with his, and asking that his concubine, Herpyllis, be provided for and allowed to live in whichever of his houses she chooses (*Lives,* pp. 181–94, esp. p. 186).

204.9/201.32 NELL GWYNN HERPYLLIS   Nell Gwynn (1650–87) was an actress and mistress of Charles II. Charles's dying request to his brother was, supposedly, "Don't let poor Nelly starve." Herpyllis was a hetaira or concubine whom Aristotle is supposed to have taken after the death of his wife, Pythias. Stephen blends the names because Charles II's last words about Nell Gwynn are similar to Aristotle's statement about Herpyllis in his will. See entry 204.6.

204.13/201.36 HE DIED DEAD DRUNK   Mulligan is alluding to the story, first told by John Ward, that Shakespeare died as a result of a drinking bout with Drayton and Jonson. Ward (1629–81) was vicar of Stratford. In his *Diary* he says, "Shakespear, Drayton, and Ben Jhonson, had a merry meeting, and itt seems drank too hard, for Shakespear died of a feavor there contracted" (*Diary of John Ward; see* Chambers II, 249–50).

204.19/202.2 WHAT HE THOUGHT OF THE CHARGE OF PEDERASTY BROUGHT AGAINST THE BARD   If Dowden ever in print discussed any such charge against Shakespeare, or made the comment Mulligan quotes on p. 204.20/202.3, I have not discovered it. In his *Shakspere: A Critical Study of his Mind and Art* (New York: Harper, 1905, 3rd ed.), during his discussion of the "Sonnets," Dowden does admit that Shakespeare had moral flaws (pp. 351–52), but he does not discuss pederasty, nor does he use the flippant tone Mulligan implies.

204.26/202.9 YOU CANNOT EAT YOUR CAKE AND HAVE IT   This proverbial phrase is listed in the *ODEP*, and was included in John Heywood's *Proverbs* (1546).

204.30/202.13 HE DREW SHYLOCK OUT OF HIS OWN LONG POCKET   Wm. Schutte (*JS*, p. 160) quotes Brandes as saying, "Shakespeare's impulse to present a Shylock on the stage took effect upon his mind because it was at that moment preoccupied with the ideas of acquisition, property, money-making, wealth" (Brandes, p. 151).

204.31/202.14 THE SON OF A MALTJOBBER . . . FAMINE RIOTS   This sentence blends facts drawn from Brandes and Lee; see Schutte, *JS*, pp. 161, 163, 166.

204.35/202.17 CHETTLE FALSTAFF WHO REPORTED HIS UPRIGHTNESS OF DEALING   Henry Chettle (d. 1607?) was a playwright and the editor of Greene's *Groats-Worth of Witte* (1592), but in December of the same year, Chettle prefixed to his own *Kind Hartes Dreame* an apology for Greene's insults to Shakespeare. Lee, Brandes, and Harris all quote Chettle's apology. Chettle was also said to have been the original of Falstaff. Brandes simply records the idea; Harris accepts it. See Schutte, *JS*, pp. 168, 171. For Chettle's apology, see Chambers, II, 189.

204.35/202.18 HE SUED A FELLOWPLAYER FOR THE PRICE OF A FEW BAGS OF MALT   As Wm. Schutte shows (*JS*, p. 166), both Brandes and Lee mention Shakespeare's suing, not a fellow actor, but a Stratford resident named Philip Rogers for 35s. 10d. he owed Shakespeare for malt (Brandes, p. 155; Lee, p. 206). R. M. Adams points out that Joyce had the facts of this incident correct in his notebook and suggests that "Stephen simplifies irrelevant details, and alters the relation in order to show Shakespeare's sense of property as stronger than his sense of good fellowship" (*SS*, pp. 126–27).

204.37/202.19 EXACTED HIS POUND OF FLESH IN INTEREST   The pound of flesh alludes to the forfeit Shylock asks of Antonio in *The Merchant of Venice*; see I, iii, 146–52 and IV, i, *passim*. Wm. Schutte (*JS*, p. 161) quotes a statement in Brandes that Shakespeare apparently did lend money and "seems to have charged the current rate, namely, ten percent" (Brandes, pp. 154–55).

204.38/202.20 AUBREY'S OSTLER AND CALLBOY   Wm. Schutte (*JS*, 171) points out that "Aubrey does not say that Shakespeare was either ostler or callboy; he mentions only that prior to his acting career he followed his father's profession of butcher ('in a high style') and was once a schoolmaster." For Aubrey's account, see Chambers, II, 252–54. All three of Joyce's sources—Brandes, Lee, and Harris—discuss the tradition that Shakespeare did hold horses for the playgoers.

204.39/202.21 GRIST TO HIS MILL   This proverbial phrase is listed in the *ODEP.*

204.40/202.22 THE HANGING AND QUARTERING OF THE QUEEN'S LEECH LOPEZ   In 1594 Elizabeth's Jewish doctor, Roderigo Lopez, was tried for treason, convicted, and executed. A man named Antonio Perez was a principal in the case. Lee, pointing to the name Antonio, argues that Lopez was the source of Shylock. Lee also points out that Lopez' trial and execution evoked an anti-Semitic display. See Schutte, *JS*, p. 163, and Lee, p. 68. On his note sheets for this episode, Joyce had, under the heading 1594, "February: . . . Roderigo Lopez, Queen's jew doctor, tried. Anti-semitism," and "June: Execution of Lopez for attempting to poison Antonio Perez" (see R. M. Kain, "James Joyce's Shakespeare Chronology," *Massachusetts Review*, V, 349–50).

205.1/202.25 A SCOTCH PHILOSOPHASTER WITH A TURN FOR WITCH ROASTING   James I, who came to the throne in 1603, was a believer in witchcraft and demonology and caused many witches to be burnt at the stake. Wm. Schutte points out (*JS*, pp. 166–67) that both Brandes and Lee discuss this aspect of James's character.

205.2/202.26 THE LOST ARMADA IS HIS JEER IN LOVE'S LABOUR LOST   Stephen is suggesting that Don Adriano de Armado, the "fantastical Spaniard" of *Love's Labor's Lost*, is a gibe at the failure of the Spanish Armada. Armado is depicted as vain, ridiculous, and boastful. Wm. Schutte (*JS*, p. 167) quotes similar statements by Brandes and Lee about the meaning of Armado's name.

205.4/202.28 MAFEKING ENTHUSIASM   Mafeking is a town in NE Cape of Good Hope Province, South Africa, which was besieged in the Boer War. The British garrison under Lord Baden-Powell withstood a siege of 217 days (Oct. 12, 1899–May 17, 1900) until relief arrived. The *Encyclopaedia Britannica*, 11th ed., says, "The fate of the town had excited the liveliest sympathy in England, and the exuberant rejoicings in London on the news of its relief led to the coining of the word *Mafficking* to describe the behavior of crowds on occasions of extravagant demonstrations of a national kind" (XVII, 299). "Mafeking enthusiasm" is also a set phrase for the same thing.

205.4/202.28 WARWICKSHIRE JESUITS ARE TRIED AND WE HAVE A POR-
TER'S THEORY OF EQUIVOCATION   During the trial for his part in
the Gunpowder Plot (a plot by English Catholics to blow up the
British houses of Parliament on Nov. 5, 1605), Henry Garnett,
provincial of the English jesuits, made a defense of the doctrine of
equivocation which became notorious. Stephen is following Sidney
Lee here in the idea that the porter's comments about an equivo-
cator in *Macbeth*, II, iii, 8 ff., stem from Garnett's trial (see Schutte,
JS, p. 163). Joyce's notes for this episode contain entries about the
Gunpowder Plot, Garnett's execution, and the staging of *Macbeth*;
see Kain, *op. cit.*, entry 204.40, p. 352.

205.5/202.29 THE SEA VENTURE COMES HOME FROM BERMUDAS AND THE
PLAY RENAN ADMIRED IS WRITTEN   Stephen is referring to *The
Tempest*. Wm. Schutte says that Lee alone among Joyce's main
sources mentions the *Sea Venture*, a ship that was driven to the
hitherto unknown Bermuda Islands by a storm in the summer of
1609 (*JS*, p. 163). On Renan's admiration for *The Tempest*, see
entry 195.2.

205.7/202.31 PATSY CALIBAN, OUR AMERICAN COUSIN   This apparently alludes to the title of Victorian editor and playwright Tom
Taylor's (1817–80) popular play *Our American Cousin* (1858),
but I do not understand the use of *Patsy* here, unless it is for its
generally Irish connotations. There is no character in Taylor's play
named Patsy.

205.7/202.31 THE SUGARED SONNETS FOLLOW SIDNEY'S   "Sugared son-
nets" is a phrase used by Francis Meres in *Palladis Tamia: Wit's
Treasury* . . . (1598) in describing Shakespeare's "Sonnets." Wm
Schutte (*JS*, p. 167) shows that both Brandes and Lee cite the
source of the phrase, and both mention Sidney as a forerunner of
Shakespeare. For Mere's statement, see Chambers, II, 194.

205.9/202.33 THE GROSS VIRGIN WHO INSPIRED THE MERRY WIVES
According to a tradition first found in the dedicatory epistle to
John Dennis' (1657–1734) play *The Comical Gallant* (1702) (a
rewriting of *Merry Wives*), Shakespeare wrote *Merry Wives* at
Queen Elizabeth's "command and by her direction, and she was so
eager to see it acted that she commanded it to be finished in fourteen days; and was afterward, as tradition tells us, very well pleased
at the representation." The story is often repeated by eighteenth-
century editors. For Dennis' statement, see Chambers, II, 263.

205.12/202.36 A MIXTURE OF THEOLOLOGICOPHILOLOLOGICAL   S. Gilbert (*JJU*, p. 221) sees in this an echo of Polonius' "tragical-com-
ical-historical-pastoral" description of the players' capacities

(*Ham.*, II, ii, 417), and of Swift's *An Analytical Discourse upon Zeal, Histori-theo-physilogically Considered*, which is among the list of other "Treatises writ" by the same author, facing the title page of *A Tale of a Tub* (see the Guthkelch and Smith edition [2nd ed.; Oxford, 1958], p. 2).

205.15/202.39 YOUR DEAN OF STUDIES HOLDS THAT HE WAS A HOLY RO- MAN   This refers to an article written by Father Joseph Dar- lington, S.J., and published in two parts in *The New Ireland Review*, VIII (1897–98), 241–49 and 304–10. Though Father Darlington hedges a bit about whether Shakespeare was a practicing Roman Catholic, and though he occasionally equivocates on the meaning of *Catholicity*, his burden is to argue that the plays reflect and embody "the ancient ideals of Chivalry and Christian faith, which have bequeathed to us the magnificent cathedrals in Eng- land, and which covered all Europe with proofs of a creative power, that seemed to dwindle when disruption and unreality set in" (p. 241). For further information about Father Darlington, see K. Sullivan, *Joyce Among the Jesuits.*

205.16/202.40 SUFFLAMINANDUS SUM   Stephen's phrase is a varia- tion of a statement Ben Jonson made about Shakespeare in his *Timber: or, Discoveries Made Upon Men and Matter*: "Hee flow'd with that facility, that sometime it was necessary he should be stop'd: *Sufflaminandus erat*; as *Augustus* said of *Haterius*" (see Chambers, II, 210). The phrase means, "He should have been checked"; Stephen's variation says "I ought to be checked." Q. Haterius was a senator and rhetorician during the reign of Augus- tus and Tiberius; Augustus made the remark about Haterius' volu- bility.

205.19/203.1 A MYRIADMINDED MAN . . . COLERIDGE CALLED HIM MYRIAD- MINDED   In the opening paragraph of chap. XV of *Biographia Literaria*, Coleridge speaks of "our *myriad-minded* Shakespeare." In this chapter Coleridge undertakes an analysis of *Venus and Adonis* and *The Rape of Lucrece* to learn something about the "characteristics of original poetic genius." One of his observations is that one "promise of genius is the choice of subjects very remote from the private interests and circumstances of the writer himself," which he finds in *Venus and Adonis*. Very early in his book—p. 5— Frank Harris cites Coleridge's description of Shakespeare as " 'the myriad-minded man.' "

205.21/203.3 AMPLIUS. IN SOCIETATE HUMANA . . .   The context here suggests that this phrase ("Furthermore, in human society it is of the utmost necessity that there be friendship among the many")

occurs in a passage by St. Thomas dealing with incest, but if this
is so, I have not located the passage. St. Thomas does say something vaguely similar to the point Stephen goes on to develop (p.
205.30/203.11 ff.), in his discussion of incest in *Summa Theologica*,
II (Second Part), question 154, art. 9. There he says that one objection to incest is that it hinders a man from having many friends,
for when one marries a stranger, all of the wife's relatives are
joined to him in a special kind of friendship.

205.24/203.6 ORA PRO NOBIS   "Pray for us"—common in Catholic
prayers and liturgy.

205.27/203.8 ACUSHLA MACHREE   This refers to John Philpott Curran's song "Cushla-ma-Chree" ("Pulse of My Heart"); see entry
186.35.

205.27/203.8 IT'S DESTROYED WE ARE FROM THIS DAY! IT'S DESTROYED
WE ARE SURELY   This alludes to John M. Synge's play *Riders
to the Sea*. After Maurya envisions her son Michael dead, Cathleen
keens, "It's destroyed we are from this day. It's destroyed surely."
The play was first performed at Molesworth Hall, Dublin, on February 25, 1904.

205.30/203.11 SAINT THOMAS . . . WRITING OF INCEST   See entry
205.21.

205.32/203.13 THE NEW VIENNESE SCHOOL MR MAGEE SPOKE OF   Apparently Stephen is referring to Freud and his group, but R. M.
Adams says (*SS*, p. 129) that Magee has not spoken of them, and
I can find no reference to them by Magee. W. Y. Tindall (*RG*, p.
179) takes "the doctor" on p. 204.26/202.9 to be the earlier reference meant, but this cannot be, since the *Little Review* version
of this episode contains Stephen's statement, but lacks Magee's reference to "the doctor."

205.39/203.20 AS FOR THE LOLLARDS, STORM WAS SHELTER   The Lollards were adherents to a fourteenth- and fifteenth-century English
religious movement that grew from the followers of John Wy-
cliffe. They were persecuted and attempts were made to extermi-
nate the movement, but in many instances the Lollards simply
became stronger and more adamant. See the *Encyclopaedia Britannica*, 11th ed., XVI, *s.v.* Lollards.

205.40/203.21 BOUND THEIR AFFECTIONS TOO WITH HOOPS OF STEEL   In
his parting advice to his son Laertes, Polonius tells him, "Those
friends thou hast, and their adoption tried,/ Grapple them to thy
soul with hoops of steel" (*Ham.*, I, iii, 62–63).

205.41/203.22 OLD NOBODADDY   This refers to Blake's Nobodaddy,
a figure who embodies the worst aspects of an anthropomorphic

god, and whom Stephen sees as another example of the *dio boia* or
"lord of things as they are" (p. 213.22/210.37). He is characterized
quite clearly in Blake's poem that begins, "Let the Brothels of
Paris be opened," where Blake says, "Then old Nobodaddy aloft/
Farted & belch'd & cough'd,/ And said, 'I love hanging & drawing
& quartering/ Every bit as well as war & slaughtering'" (1957
Keynes ed., p. 185; see also "To Nobodaddy," p. 171).

206.3/203.25 NO SIR SMILE NEIGHBOR   In *The Winter's Tale*, Leontes
thinks of how many men are cuckolded "by his next neighbor,
by/ Sir Smile, his neighbor" (I, ii, 195–96).

206.3/203.26 COVET HIS OX OR HIS WIFE . . .   Exodus 20:17 says,
"Thou shalt not covet thy neighbor's house, thou shalt not covet
thy neighbor's wife, nor his manservant, nor his maidservant, nor
his ox, nor his ass, nor any thing that is thy neighbor's." Deuteronomy 5:21 is almost identical.

206.6/203.29 GENTLE WILL   This probably alludes to Jonson's depiction of Shakespeare as "gentle Shakespeare." He used the term
twice, once in the verses "To the Reader" (l. 2) facing the portrait in the First Folio, and in "To the Memory of Shakespeare"
(l. 56) also printed on a preliminary leaf of the Folio.

206.13/203.36 WHAT OF ALL THE WILL TO DO . . .   These are the
opening lines of A. E.'s poem "Sung on a By-Way." The first
of the poem's four stanzas says, "What of all the will to do?/
It has vanished long ago./ For a dream-shaft pierced it through/
From the Unknown Archer's bow."

206.15/203.38 THAT SECONDBEST BED   See entry 203.22.

206.16/203.38 THE MOBLED QUEEN   In *Hamlet*, the player refers to
Hecuba as "the mobled Queen," and the word is commented upon
by Hamlet and Polonius (II, ii, 525–27).

206.19/203.41 GOSPELLERS (ONE STAYED AT NEW PLACE . . .   A traveling preacher stayed at Shakespeare's house in 1614, while Shakespeare was in London. Wm. Schutte shows (*JS*, pp. 161–62) that
Brandes, Lee, and Harris all mention this, though Stephen's account
follows Brandes most closely. For the original entry in the Stratford town records, see Chambers, II, 153.

206.24/204.5 HOOKS AND EYES FOR BELIEVERS' BREECHES AND THE MOST
SPIRITUAL SNUFFBOX TO MAKE THE MOST DEVOUT SOULS SNEEZE   R.
M. Adams (*SS*, p. 127) says that these titles are anachronistic to
the seventeenth century and that Joyce got them from a review
article based on Octave Delepierre's *History of the Literature of
Lunatics*, which appeared in the *Irish Independent*, June 15, 1904,
p. 4, and that Joyce used nothing else from the article. I quote

the pertinent paragraph from the article: "Medical experts on insanity are inclined to encourage this literary inclination of their patients, finding that it affords them mental belief [*sic—relief?*] and distraction during the brief intervals of sanity. Indeed from a remote period the insane have constantly turned to writing as an occupation even while mentally afflicted. The number of works on theology and religious subjects written by known lunatics is immense. A mere catalogue of the titles of these books would occupy many pages. The very names of the volumes are often absurdly fantastical, such as 'Hooks and Eyes for Believers' Breeches,' and 'The Spiritual Snuffbox to make the Most Devout Souls Sneeze' " (*Irish Daily Independent and Nation*, June 15, 1904, p. 4, col. h). Richard M. Kain has also found these same absurd titles, with minor variations, cited in C. C. Bombaugh's *Gleanings for the Curious from the Harvest Fields of Literature*; see his note in *JJQ*, IV (Winter, 1967), 160.

206.26/204.8 AGENBITE OF INWIT: REMORSE OF CONSCIENCE   See entry 16.7.

206.27/204.8 AN AGE OF EXHAUSTED WHOREDOM   Wm. Schutte (*JS*, p. 161) points out that Brandes discusses James's court in these terms at some length.

206.30/204.11 WE HAVE IT ON HIGH AUTHORITY THAT A MAN'S WORST ENEMIES SHALL BE THOSE OF HIS OWN HOUSE AND FAMILY   There are several passages in the Bible which express this idea. Eglinton is probably thinking of Christ's words to his disciples in Matthew 10:35–36: "For I am come to set a man at variance against his father, and the daughter against her mother, and the daughter in law against her mother in law. And a man's foes shall be they of his own household." Luke 12:51–53 and Micah 7:6 are very similar.

206.34/204.15 I FEEL THAT THE FAT KNIGHT IS HIS SUPREME CREATION   Falstaff is described as "the fat knight" several times in Shakespeare's works. See, e.g., *Henry V*, IV, vii, 50, and *Merry Wives*, IV, ii, 29, 233.

206.36/204.17 DENY THY KINDRED   In the balcony scene, Juliet says to Romeo, "Deny thy father and refuse thy name . . ." (*Rom. and Jul.*, II, ii, 34).

206.36/204.17 THE UNCO GUID   This alludes to the title of Robert Burns's poem "Address to the Unco Guid or the Rigidly Righteous."

206.37/204.18 A SIRE IN ULTONIAN ANTRIM   Information about Eglinton's father is not easy to find, but the idea that he was a peasant is mistaken. According to the obituary published in the

Irish Independent on May 11, 1961, after Eglinton's death, his father was the Reverend Hamilton Magee, a Presbyterian minister and a North of Ireland man. A biographical note on Eglinton (*s.v.* Magee) in Alan Denson's *Letters from A. E.* says that his father was a Presbyterian minister in Dublin (p. 259).

206.40/204.21 WORDSWORTH. ENTER MAGEE MOR MATTHEW   Wm. Schutte (*JS*, p. 45) says, "For describing the arrival of the essayist's peasant father at the library to see his son, Stephen finds Wordsworth the appropriate model," and goes on to note that Eglinton admired Wordsworth, "whose portrait had been drawn at length in *Two Essays on the Remnant.*" *Mor* is a Gaelic word meaning "great"; here it means Magee senior, or Magee the elder (cf. the use on p. 231.26/228.13). Stephen is thinking that the elder Magee would be the type of Wordsworth's Matthew, the old schoolmaster who appears in many of Wordsworth's early poems, such as "The Two April Mornings," alluded to on p. 207.3/204.24.

207.1/204.22 A RUGGED ROUGH RUGHEADED KERN   In *Richard II*, Richard says, "Now for our Irish wars./ We must supplant those rough, rugheaded kerns/ Which live like venom where no venom else/ But only they have privilege to live" (II, i, 155–58).

207.1/204.22 IN STROSSERS   In *Henry V*, the Dauphin, speaking to the Constable of France about the latter's horse, says, "Oh, then belike she was old and gentle, and you rode like a kern of Ireland, your French hose off and in your strait strossers" (III, vii, 55–57).

207.2/204.23 HIS NETHER STOCKS BEMIRED   "Nether stocks" occurs only twice in Shakespeare, and neither instance seems particularly appropriate to the present context. In *I Henry IV*, II, iv, 130, Falstaff says, "Ere I lead this life long, I'll sew netherstocks and mend them and foot them too"; and in *King Lear*, when the Fool sees the disguised Kent in the stocks, he says, "When a man's overlusty at legs, then he wears wooden netherstocks" (II, iv, 10–11).

207.2/204.23 CLAUBER OF TEN FORESTS   Wm. Schutte has pointed out (*JS*, p. 50) that this is an exaggeration of a line that was in an early version of Yeats's play *The Countess Cathleen*. In the version alluded to, Shemus uses the phrase ". . . Though the dead leaves and clauber of four forests cling to my footsole." According to the *Variorum* edition of Yeats's plays, p. 11, this was the reading from the 1895 *Poems* until the 1908 *Collected Works*.

207.3/204.24 A WAND OF WILDING IN HIS HAND   This alludes to the final stanza of Wordsworth's poem "The Two April Mornings": "Matthew is in his grave, yet now,/ Methinks, I see him stand,/ As at that moment, with a bough/ Of wilding in his hand." Cf. entry 206.40.

207.10/204.31 HE WROTE THE PLAY IN THE MONTHS THAT FOLLOWED
HIS FATHER'S DEATH   Wm. Schutte (*JS*, pp. 161–62) shows that
Brandes calls attention to Shakespeare's beginning to write *Hamlet*
shortly after his father's death (Brandes, p. 341). John Shakespeare
was buried on September 8, 1601.

207.12/204.33 NEL MEZZO DEL CAMMIN DI NOSTRA VITA This is an
exact quotation of the opening line of Dante's "Inferno": "In the
middle of the journey of our life. . . ."

207.15/204.36 THE CORPSE OF JOHN SHAKESPEARE DOES NOT WALK THE
NIGHT   John Shakespeare was the poet's father; see entry 207.10.
In *Hamlet*, the Ghost tells Hamlet, "I am thy father's spirit,/
Doomed for a certain term to walk the night . . ." (I, v, 9–10).

207.16/204.37 FROM HOUR TO HOUR IT ROTS AND ROTS   In *As You
Like It* Jaques quotes the fool he met in the forest as saying,
" 'And so, from hour to hour, we ripe and ripe,/ And then, from
hour to hour, we rot and rot,/ And thereby hangs a tale' " (II,
vii, 27).

207.18/204.39 BOCCACCIO'S CALANDRINO WAS THE FIRST AND LAST MAN
WHO FELT HIMSELF WITH CHILD   In the third story of the ninth
day of the *Decameron*, Boccaccio tells how Calandrino is gulled by
his friends into believing he is with child and is then cured at considerable cost.

207.22/204.42 FROM ONLY BEGETTER TO ONLY BEGOTTEN   This blends
allusions to the dedication to Shakespeare's "Sonnets" and to the
Nicene Creed. The "Sonnets" are addressed "To the onlie begetter of these insuing sonnets"; the Creed calls Christ "the only-
begotten Son of God." The phrase "only begotten Son" also
occurs several times in the Bible; see, e.g., John 1:18 and 3:16.

207.23/205.1 THE MADONNA WHICH THE CUNNING ITALIAN INTELLECT
FLUNG TO THE MOB OF EUROPE   Stephen's point here is that the
core of Christian theology is contained in the relationships within
the Trinity rather than in the beliefs about Mary, such as that of her
sinlessness, her perpetual virginity, and her being the Mother of
God. He implies that the doctrines about Mary are products of the
Italian mind, given to men as a sort of intellectual-emotional sop.
Perhaps Stephen is thinking specifically of the declaration of Pope
Pius IX in 1854 that the dogma of the Immaculate Conception of
Mary was an article of faith (Pius IX was born an Italian, Giovanni
M. Mastai-Ferretti).

207.38/205.16 LOVES THAT DARE NOT SPEAK THEIR NAME   See entries
49.23 and 202.19.

207.40/205.18 QUEENS WITH PRIZE BULLS   This alludes to Queen
Pasiphae, wife of King Minos of Crete. Daedalus made for the

queen an artificial cow, by means of which she attracted a beautiful white bull, to which she bore the Minotaur. See also entries 411.28 and 569.8.

208.7/205.26 SABELLIUS, THE AFRICAN   See entry 21.10.

208.7/205.26 SUBTLEST HERESIARCH OF ALL THE BEASTS OF THE FIELD Genesis 3:1 says, "Now the serpent was more subtle than any beast of the field which the Lord God had made." Stephen has earlier called Sabellius "the subtle African heresiarch" (p. 21.10/22.31).

208.9/205.27 THE BULLDOG OF AQUIN . . . REFUTES HIM   W. Y. Tindall (*RG*, p. 174) says, "Aquinas is a dog because he was a Dominican or, according to a medieval pun, *Domini canis*, dog of God." St. Thomas discusses Sabellius' heresy in many places, but the one most relevant to this context is probably *Summa Theologica*, Part I, ques. xxxi, esp. art. 2; see entry 21.10.

208.12/205.30 RUTLANDBACONSOUTHAMPTONSHAKESPEARE This word fuses the names of some of those who have been suggested as the author of Shakespeare's plays—Roger Manners, fifth earl of Rutland (1576–1612); Francis Bacon (1561–1626); and Henry Wriothesley, third earl of Southampton (1573–1624).

208.12/205.31 ANOTHER POET OF THE SAME NAME IN THE COMEDY OF ERRORS   Stephen is alluding to the pairs of twins with identical names in *Comedy of Errors*, apparently suggesting that if one William Shakespeare did not write the plays, another did.

208.17/205.36 FOR NATURE, AS MR MAGEE UNDERSTANDS HER, ABHORS PERFECTION   This alludes to a statement made by Eglinton in his essay "Apostolic Succession" in his *Pebbles from a Brook* (1901). Wm. Schutte (*JS*, p. 45) quotes the pertinent passage: "Nature abhors perfection. Things perfect in their way, whether manners, poetry, painting, scientific methods, philosophical systems, architecture, ritual, are only so by getting into some backwater or shoal out of the eternal currents, where life has ceased to circulate. The course of time is fringed with perfections but bears them not upon its bosom" (*Pebbles*, p. 45).

208.20/205.40 THROUGH THE TWISTED EGLANTINE   In Milton's "L' Allegro," he speaks of seeing the lark "Through the sweet-briar, or the vine,/ Or the twisted eglantine" (ll. 47–48).

208.23/205.42 HIMSELF HIS OWN FATHER   This alludes again to the Sabellian heresy; Sabellius was mentioned on p. 208.7/205.26. See entry 21.10.

208.24/205.42 I AM BIG WITH CHILD   This may allude to the statement in Luke 2:5 that Mary was "great with child."

208.24/206.1 I HAVE AN UNBORN CHILD IN MY BRAIN. PALLAS ATHENA
Athena was born from the head of Zeus; but this may also allude
to the birth of Sin from the head of Satan, which Milton describes
in *Paradise Lost*, II, 747 ff.

208.25/206.2 THE PLAY'S THE THING   In *Hamlet*, II, ii, 632, Hamlet
says, "The play's the thing/ Wherein I'll catch the conscience of
the King."

208.28/206.4 HIS MOTHER'S NAME LIVES IN THE FOREST OF ARDEN
Shakespeare's mother was born Mary Arden. Stephen suggests that
the forest of Arden in *As You Like It* is so named for this reason.
But Lodge's *Rosalynde* (Shakespeare's source for *As You Like It*)
had a forest of Arden, and there was a forest so called in Warwickshire as well as in Europe. But for Stephen's reply to this kind of
objection, see p. 211.28/209.4 ff.

208.29/206.5 HER DEATH BROUGHT FROM HIM THE SCENE WITH VOLUM-
NIA IN CORIOLANUS   Mary Arden Shakespeare died in September,
1608. Wm. Schutte (*JS*, pp. 168–69) points out that both Brandes
and Harris suggest a connection between the poet's mother and
Volumnia, mother of Coriolanus.

208.30/206.6 HIS BOYSON'S DEATH IS THE DEATHSCENE OF YOUNG ARTHUR
IN KING JOHN   Wm. Schutte (*JS*, p. 160) shows that both
Brandes and Harris suggest a relationship between Hamnet's death
(he was buried Aug. 11, 1596) and the depiction of Arthur, nephew
of the King, in *King John*.

208.32/206.8 WHO THE GIRLS IN THE TEMPEST, IN PERICLES, IN WINTER'S
TALE ARE WE KNOW   See entry 195.32.

208.33/206.9 WHO CLEOPATRA . . . AND CRESSID AND VENUS ARE WE MAY
GUESS   Stephen suggests that these three demanding, seductive
women are all patterned on Anne Hathaway.

208.33/206.9 FLESHPOT OF EGYPT   From Exodus 16:3; see entry
41.32.

208.40/206.16 THEY LIST   From *Hamlet*; see entries 188.3 and
196.38.

209.2/206.20 GILBERT IN HIS OLD AGE TOLD SOME CAVALIERS . . .   Lee
says, "One of Shakespeare's younger brothers, presumably Gilbert,
often came, wrote [William] Oldys, to London in his younger
days to see his brother act in his own plays; and in his old age, when
his memory was failing, he recalled his brother's performance of
Adam in 'As You Like It' " (Lee, p. 44; quoted in Schutte, *JS*, p.
164). R. M. Adams (*SS*, p.127) quotes Lee's statement and says,
"Stephen, attracted by younger and more active roles or desirous
of giving the Bard a better part, allows him to play Orlando, or at

least to take part in the play's wrestling scene." The wrestling scene in *As You Like It* occurs in I, ii, and the contestants are Orlando and the wrestler, Charles.

209.10/206.28 WHAT'S IN A NAME   Juliet asks Romeo this in the balcony scene in *Romeo and Juliet* (II, ii, 43). The question is repeated on p. 210.5/207.20.

209.18/206.36 THEN OUTSPOKE MEDICAL DICK . . .   These lines are from a scurrilous poem written by Oliver St. John Gogarty. Four stanzas plus pseudo-erudite annotations (in parody of the annotators of folk literature) are to be found in a letter Gogarty wrote Joyce *ca.* 1902–3, now in the Cornell collection (Scholes, item 523). The second stanza begins, "Then out spoke medical Dick/ To his comrade medical Davy. . . ." Dick is characterized as having prodigious sexual apparatus, Davy as possessing a fortune, and their dialogue turns on the relative advantages of each.

209.23/207.4 THAT LAST PLAY WAS BEING WRITTEN WHILE HIS BROTHER EDMUND LAY DYING IN SOUTHWARK . . .   According to Lee, Edmund Shakespeare was buried on December 31, 1607. None of Joyce's three sources links Edmund with the villain in *King Lear*. Evidence from the Stationers' Register, November 26, 1607, indicates that "Master William Shakespeare his historye of Kinge Lear" was acted before the court of King James during the Christmas season of 1606. For the Stationers' Register entry, see Chambers, I, 463.

209.30/207.11 BUT HE THAT FILCHES FROM ME MY GOOD NAME   In *Othello*, Iago says to Othello, "Who steals my purse steals trash . . . But he that filches from me my good name/ Robs me of that which not enriches him/ And makes me poor indeed" (III, iii, 157–61).

209.32/207.13 HE HAS HIDDEN HIS OWN NAME, A FAIR NAME, WILLIAM, IN THE PLAYS . . .   No major Shakespearean character is named William; it is the name of a clown in *As You Like It*, and a cook in *II Henry IV*. But Stephen is alluding specifically to an exchange in *As You Like It* between Touchstone and William:

      Touch. Is thy name William?
      Will.   William, sir.
      Touch. A fair name.   (V, i, 23–25)

210.1/207.16 WILL IN OVERPLUS   This alludes to "Sonnet 135," where the phrase " 'Will' in overplus" occurs; see entry 191.13.

210.1/207.16 LIKE JOHN O'GAUNT HIS NAME IS DEAR TO HIM . . .   See *Richard II*, II, i, 73–83, for a speech by John of Gaunt in which he repeatedly puns on his own name.

210.2/207.17 THE COAT OF ARMS HE TOADIED FOR   In 1596 the poet's

father, John Shakespeare, made application for a coat of arms, probably at William's behest. As Wm. Schutte shows (*JS*, pp. 171–72),
all three of Joyce's sources discuss this, and Harris says that Shakespeare "stooped as low to get the coat of arms and crest as man
could stoop" (Harris, p. 378).

210.3/207.18   ON A BEND SABLE A SPEAR OR STEELED ARGENT   Wm.
Schutte (*JS*, p. 167) shows that both Brandes and Lee quote a de-
scription of Shakespeare's coat of arms which is similar to Stephen's.
For the description in the Grant of Arms, see Chambers, II, 19.

210.4/207.19   HONORIFICABILITUDINITATIBUS   This word, a curiosity
since it was supposedly the longest Latin word, occurs in *Love's
Labor's Lost*, V, i, 44; it means "in the condition of being loaded
with honors." Sir Edwin Durning-Lawrence, in chap. X of his
Bacon Is Shakespeare (1910), makes much of this word, finding it
to be an anagram of a Latin sentence which says that Bacon wrote
the plays.

210.4/207.19   GREATEST SHAKESCENE IN THE COUNTRY   In his *Groats-
Worth of Witte* (1592) Robert Greene says of Shakespeare that
he is "in his owne conceit the onely Shake-scene in a countrey." For
the full passage, see Chambers, II, 188–89. See also entry 187.27.

210.5/207.20   WHAT'S IN A NAME   See entry 209.10.

210.7/207.22   A FIREDRAKE ROSE AT HIS BIRTH   The firedrake, or
nova, which Stephen mentions actually did not appear until Shakespeare was eight-and-a-half years old. Wm. Schutte discusses
Stephen's great liberties with the facts about this nova and the possible sources of his information in some detail (*JS, passim*, esp. pp.
174–75).

210.13/207.28   AND FROM HER ARMS (Repeated on p. 210.16/207.31)
Hodgart and Worthington list this as an allusion to "The Moon
Hath Raised Her Lamp Above," from the *Lily of Killarney*, but
no copies of the song which I have seen have such a line. Context
makes an allusion to "Goodbye, Sweetheart, Goodbye" more likely
(on this song, see entry 256.13 and Appendix). In "Goodbye,
Sweetheart, Goodbye," the lover who is departing remarks on
the fading of the stars and says, "time doth tear me from thine
arms." The line is repeated in the song just as the phrase is repeated
here in *Ulysses*.

210.17/207.32   WAIT TO BE WOOED AND WON   This is probably an
allusion to Suffolk's words to Regnier in *I Henry VI*: "Thy daughter shall be wedded to my King/ Whom I with pain have woo'd
and won thereto" (V, iii, 137–38).

210.19/207.33   AUTONTIMERUMENOS. BOUS STEPHANOUMENOS   *Au-*

tontimerumenos is probably more precisely *Heauton-timorou-menos,* which means "self-tormentor" (see Liddell and Scott, *Greek-English Lexicon,* II, 1795, col. a), and is the title of a play by Roman comic poet Terence (*ca.* 185–*ca.* 159 B.C.) based on a play of the same title by Greek comedian Menander (342?–291 B.C.; only fragments of Menander's play now exist). E. Bernhardt-Kabisch has annotated the phrase "*Bous Stephanoumenos*" (which occurs at the end of chapter four of *A Portrait of the Artist*). He explains it as referring to a bull that is "wreathed" or "crowned" for various occasions, and, after explaining the importance of the bull as an emblem of divinity, he says, "It is, therefore, quite probable that the phrase 'Bous stephanoumenos' alludes to certain rites in which a bull was killed" (*Explicator,* XVIII [Jan., 1960], item 24).

210.20/207.34   STEPHEN, STEPHEN, CUT THE BREAD EVEN   In a list of children's doggerel rhymes based on various names, the following occurs: "Stephen, Stephen,/ Cut the loaf even" (Opie, *Lore and Language of Schoolchildren,* p. 160).

210.25/208.1   A PILLAR OF THE CLOUD BY DAY   This is from Exodus; see entry 143.11.

210.35/208.11   FABULOUS ARTIFICER, THE HAWKLIKE MAN . . . ICARUS This alludes to the artist Daedalus who fabricated wings of wax and feathers so that he and his son, Icarus, could escape from the island of Crete. Icarus' wings melted when he flew too close to the sun, and he fell into the sea and drowned. Shakespeare briefly recounts the story in *III Henry VI,* V, vi, 18–25. In "Father, he cries" Stephen is imagining Icarus' cry as he falls. W. Y. Tindall (*RG,* p. 179) sees the phrase as suggesting Jesus, another forsaken son, calling to his Father in extremity.

210.36/208.12   LAPWING   Wm. Schutte (*JS,* pp. 117–19) discusses the lapwing at some length. In addition to pointing out four references to the bird in Shakespeare's works (*Meas. for Meas.,* I, iv, 30–33; *Com. of Errors,* IV, ii, 25–28; *Much Ado,* III, i, 23–25; *Ham.,* V, ii, 193), he also says Stephen may have had in mind a verse from Blake: "O Lapwing, thou fliest around the heath,/ Nor seest the net that is spread beneath./ Why canst thou not fly among the corn-fields?/ They cannot spread nets where a harvest yields" ("Poems and Fragments from the Note-Book written about 1793," no. 15; 1957 Keynes ed., p. 168). Schutte also quotes from Robert Graves's *The White Goddess* on the nature of the lapwing and its use in poetic myth. Its characterizing trait is that it conceals its nest very carefully, and, on anyone's approach, it flutters or makes short, sporadic flights away from its nest, hoping to lead the person away and thereby to protect its brood.

210.40/208.16 THAT BROTHER MOTIVE . . .   Though the motif of the third brother who succeeds where the other two fail is common in folklore, it does not occur in "The Sleeping Beauty." For an example of this motif in Irish folklore, see the story "The Well of D'yerree-in-Dowan" in Douglas Hyde's *Beside the Fire: A Collection of Irish Gaelic Folk Stories* (London, 1910), pp. 129–41.

211.16/208.34 TWO NOBLE KINSMEN NUNCLE RICHIE AND NUNCLE EDMUND   Shakespeare is thought to have had a hand in writing the play *Two Noble Kinsmen*, by John Fletcher. *Nuncle* occurs in only one of Shakespeare's plays—*King Lear*—where it occurs sixteen times; cf. entry 39.2. Shakespeare did have brothers named Richard and Edmund.

211.21/208.39 MY WHETSTONE   Stephen is probably thinking of a statement in Robert Greene's *Groats-Worth of Witte*. In the story of the brothers Roberto and Luciano, Greene says of Luciano, "But beeing of a simple nature, hee served but for a block to whet Robertoes wit on" (G. B. Harrison's ed., 1923, p. 36).

211.25/209.1 THE VOICE OF ESAU   In Genesis 27 Jacob deceives his blind father, Isaac, into believing that he is Esau, and thus gains his father's blessing. Verse 22 says, "And Jacob went near unto Isaac his father; and he felt him, and said, The voice is Jacob's voice, but the hands are the hands of Esau." See also the following entry.

211.25/209.1 MY KINGDOM FOR A DRINK   In *Richard III*, Richard, his army routed at Bosworth Field, twice cries, "A horse! A horse! My kingdom for a horse!" (V, iv, 7, 13). In light of the preceding reference to Esau, this also alludes to Esau's sale of his birthright to his brother, Jacob, for a meal of bread and a potage of lentils (Gen. 25:27–34).

211.31/209.7 WHAT'S IN A NAME   See entry 209.10.

211.32/209.7 WOOS HER AND WINS HER   See entry 210.17.

211.32/209.8 RICHARD THE CONQUEROR, THIRD BROTHER, CAME AFTER WILLIAM THE CONQUERED   See Manningham's story, entry 201.31. On "third brother," see entry 210.40.

211.35/209.11 SHAKESPEARE'S REVERENCE, THE ANGEL OF THE WORLD This alludes to Belarius' statement in *Cymbeline*: "Though mean and mighty, rotting/ Together, have one dust, yet reverence,/ That angel of the world, doth make distinction/ Of place 'tween high and low" (IV, ii, 246–49).

211.36/209.12 THE UNDERPLOT OF KING LEAR . . . LIFTED OUT OF SIDNEY'S

ARCADIA   Wm. Schutte (*JS*, pp. 167–68) shows that both Brandes and Lee comment on the source of the Gloucester subplot of *King Lear* being Sidney's *Arcadia*.

211.38/209.14   A CELTIC LEGEND OLDER THAN HISTORY   While Holinshed's *Chronicles* does place the Lear story in English prehistory ("Leir the son of Baldud was admitted ruler over the Britons, in the year of the world 3105, at what time Joash reigned in Judah"), he says nothing of its being Celtic (see *Shakespeare's Holinshed*, ed. W. G. Boswell-Stone [London, 1896], pp. 1 ff.). But as Schutte shows (*JS*, p. 162), Brandes does ascribe a Celtic origin to the story. I quote the entire paragraph in Brandes: "The story was old and well known. It was told for the first time in Latin by Geoffrey of Monmouth in his *Historia Britonum*, for the first time in English by Layamon in his Brut about 1205. It came originally from Wales and bears a distinctly Celtic impress, which Shakespeare, with his fine feeling for all national peculiarities, has succeeded in retaining and intensifying" (p. 452).

211.41/209.16   AN EXCERPT FROM A NOVEL BY GEORGE MEREDITH   A passage from a Meredith novel was mentioned on p. 199.21/197.4.

211.42/209.17   QUE VOULEZ-VOUS? MOORE WOULD SAY   This probably alludes generally to George Moore's habit of using French tags, rather than to any specific passage or incident.

211.42/209.17   HE PUTS BOHEMIA ON THE SEACOAST AND MAKES ULYSSES QUOTE ARISTOTLE   In *The Winter's Tale*, Antigonus asks, "Thou art perfect, then, our ship hath touched upon/ The deserts of Bohemia?" (III, iii, 1–2). Wm. Schutte (*JS*, p. 168) shows that both Brandes and Lee call attention to this error as being in Greene's *Pandosto* and being followed by Shakespeare. But in *Troilus and Cressida*, it is Hector, not Ulysses, who cites Aristotle (II, ii, 166).

212.5/209.21   WHAT THE POOR IS NOT, ALWAYS WITH HIM   In Matthew 26:11, Christ says, "For ye have the poor always with you; but me ye have not always." Substantially the same statement occurs in Mark 14:7 and John 12:8.

212.6/209.21   THE NOTE OF BANISHMENT . . . THE TWO GENTLEMEN OF VERONA ONWARD TILL PROSPERO BREAKS HIS STAFF . . .   Stephen is thinking specifically of the banishment of Valentine by Sylvia's father, the Duke of Milan, in *The Two Gentlemen of Verona* and of Prospero's banishment from Milan by his brother Antonio in *The Tempest*.

212.8/209.24   TILL PROSPERO BREAKS HIS STAFF, BURIES IT CERTAIN FATHOMS IN THE EARTH AND DROWNS HIS BOOK   In *The Tempest*,

Prospero says that as soon as his purposes are fulfilled, "I'll break
my staff,/ Bury it certain fathoms in the earth,/ And deeper than
did ever plummet sound/ I'll drown my book" (V, i, 54–57).

212.13/209.28 HIS MARRIED DAUGHTER SUSAN . . . IS ACCUSED OF ADUL-
TERY   According to Wm. Schutte, Lee is the only one of Joyce's
three sources who mentions this incident (*JS*, p. 164). Lee says,
"On July 15, 1613, Mrs. Hall preferred, with the help of her father's
assistance, a charge of slander against one Lane in the ecclesiasical
[*sic*] court at Worcester; the defendant, who had apparently
charged the lady with illicit relations with one Ralph Smith, did
not appear, and was excommunicated" (Lee, pp. 226–27).

212.13/209.29 CHIP OF THE OLD BLOCK   On this common saying, see
entry 144.11.

212.14/209.30 DARKENED HIS. UNDERSTANDING, WEAKENED HIS WILL,
AND LEFT IN HIM A STRONG INCLINATION TO EVIL   In the Irish
Catechism of Joyce's day (*The Catechism Ordered by the National
Synod of Maynooth*), the following occurs in Lesson 6 ("On
Original Sin, etc."): "Q. What other particular effects follow from
the sin of our first parents? A. Our whole nature was corrupted by
the sin of our first parents—it darkened our understanding, weak-
ened our will, and left in us a strong inclination to evil."

212.19/209.34 IT IS PETRIFIED ON HIS TOMBSTONE UNDER WHICH HER
FOUR BONES ARE NOT TO BE LAID   Shakespeare's gravestone inscription reads, "Good frend for Iesus sake forbeare,/ To digg
the dust encloased heare!/ Bleste be yᵉ man yᵗ spares thes stones,/
And curst be he yᵗ moves my bones." P. W. Joyce (*English As We
Speak It*, p 127) records Instances of "four bones," but does little
to explain it. He records, " 'You care for nothing in the world but
your own four bones' (i.e. nothing but yourself). 'Come on then,
old beef-swiller, and try yourself against the four bones of an
Irishman' (R. D. Joyce: The House of Lisbloom.) *Four bones*
in this sense is very common."

212.20/209.36 AGE HAS NOT WITHERED IT. . . . INFINITE VARIETY
When Maecenas says of Cleopatra, "Now Antony must leave her
utterly," Enobarbus replies, "Never. He will not./ Age cannot
wither her, nor custom stale/ Her infinite variety" (*Ant. and Cleo.*,
II, ii, 238–41).

212.22/209.38 IN MUCH ADO ABOUT NOTHING, TWICE IN AS YOU LIKE
IT . . .   The referent of Stephen's *it* does not remain clear through
this paragraph, but he seems to be referring to banishment as a
theme in Shakespeare's plays (see entry 212.6). However, his in-

clusion of *Much Ado About Nothing* and *Measure for Measure* suggests that he is thinking of banishment in a general or metaphorical sense.

212.28/210.1   HE IS THE GHOST AND THE PRINCE. HE IS ALL IN ALL   In *Hamlet*, Horatio says about King Hamlet, "He was a man, take him for all in all" (I, ii, 187). This allusion is repeated two lines later, and again on p. 213.24/210.38.

212.33/210.6   LIKE JOSÉ HE KILLS THE REAL CARMEN   In the final scene of Georges Bizet's *Carmen* (1875), Don José kills the gypsy girl Carmen when she spurns him and tells him their love is over.

212.36/210.9   CUCKÓO! CUCKOO! . . . O WORD OF FEAR   Mulligan's words are from Spring's song at the end of *Love's Labor's Lost*: "Cuckoo, Cuckoo! Oh, word of fear,/ Unpleasing to a married ear" (V, ii, 911–12, 920–21).

212.38/210.11   DARK DOME RECEIVED, REVERBED   Shakespeare used *reverb* only once—in Kent's statement to Lear, "Thy youngest daughter does not love thee least,/ Nor are those empty-hearted whose low sound/ Reverbs no hollowness" (*King Lear*, I, i, 154–56). Contextually, however, a passage from *Troilus and Cressida* seems much more appropriate here. In explaining to Achilles what he is reading, Ulysses says that the author holds "That no man is the lord of anything,/ Though in and of him there be much consisting,/ Till he communicate his parts to others./ Nor doth he of himself know them for aught/ Till he behold them formed in the applause/ Where they're extended, who, like an arch, reverberates/ The voice again, or like a gate of steel/ Fronting the sun, receives and renders back/ His figure and his heat" (III, iii, 115–23). This passage has some interesting relationships to the context in *Ulysses*: not only is the subject appropriate, the passage is spoken by Ulysses, and the image of the sun is used to represent the author. On the sun image, see the following entry; *Ulysses*, p. 505.3/494.15; and Schutte, *JS*, p. 150.

212.40/210.13   DUMAS FILS (OR IS IT DUMAS PÈRE?) IS RIGHT. AFTER GOD SHAKESPEARE HAS CREATED MOST   Wm. Schutte has shown (*JS*, p. 150) that this refers to a comment by Alexandre Dumas *père* in an essay entitled "Comment Je Devins Auteur Dramatique" ("How I Became a Dramatist"). Dumas' statement is worth quoting in detail, for even its imagery seems to be made use of in *Ulysses* (see the preceding entry and *Ulysses*, p. 505.3/494.15): "I saw thus Romeo, Virginius, Shylock, Guillaume Tell, Othello; I saw Macready, Kean, Young. I read, I devoured, the strange repertoire, and I recognized that, in the theatrical world, everything has come from Shakespeare, as, in the real world, all comes from the sun; that no one could be compared with him, because he was a playwright such as Corneille, a comedian such as Molière, an original such as Calderón, a thinker such as Goethe, and a man of passion such as Schiller. I recognized that his works, his alone, included as many types as the works of all the others put together. I recognized finally that he was the man who had, after God, created the most" (*Théatre Complet*, I, 15). S. Gilbert says of this passage in *Ulysses*, " . . . this confusion of substance, of the Dumas *père-et-fils*, is a recall of Stephen's and Sabellius' hypothesis" (*JJU*, p. 220). Cf. the "Hamlet *père* and Hamlet *fils*" of p. 213.5/210.20.

212.42/210.15 MAN DELIGHTS HIM NOT NOR WOMAN NEITHER   In *Hamlet*, II, ii, 320, Hamlet says to Rosencrantz and Guildenstern, "Man delights not me—no, nor woman neither."

213.3/210.18 HE PLANTS HIS MULBERRY TREE   This refers to the old tradition that Shakespeare himself planted a mulberry tree in the garden at New Place, Stratford. As Wm. Schutte points out (*JS*, p. 168), both Brandes and Lee mention the story. On this tradition, see Chambers, II, 240, 273, 286, 296, and 298.

213.4/210.19 THE MOTION IS ENDED   Believing from the Nurse's fragmentary report that Romeo is dead, Juliet says, "Vile earth to earth resign, end motion here . . ." (*Rom. and Jul.*, III, ii, 59).

213.10/210.25 PROSPEROUS PROSPERO   Though this alludes to the happy ending of *The Tempest*, Prospero here represents Shakespeare, retired at Stratford; Lizzie is his granddaughter Elizabeth, and Richie is his brother Richard.

213.11/210.25 LIZZIE, GRANDPA'S LUMP OF LOVE   This is Elizabeth, Shakespeare's granddaughter (born 1608), daughter of Susanna Shakespeare and John Hall. Stephen used "lump of love" earlier in context with another Richie; see p. 39.14/40.14 and cf. p. 88.19/87.17. The expression had its origin in Joyce's family (*Ellmann*, *JJ*, p. 46).

213.11/210.26 NUNCLE RICHIE   See entries 39.2, 211.16, and 213.10.

213.12/210.27 THE PLACE WHERE THE BAD NIGGERS GO   This probably alludes to American songwriter Stephen Foster's song "Uncle Ned," which says, "Dere's no more hard work for poor old Ned/ He's gone whar de good niggers go." Recent reprintings of the song often bowdlerize *niggers* to *darkies*, but earlier printings have *niggers*; see, e.g., *Christy Minstrel Song Book* (London: Boosey and Co., n.d.), Book III, pp. 19–21.

213.14/210.29 MAETERLINCK SAYS: IF SOCRATES LEAVE HIS HOUSE TODAY   This alludes to a passage in Maurice Maeterlinck's *Wisdom and*

Destiny, sec. 10: "If Judas go forth to-night, it is towards Judas his steps will tend, nor will chance for betrayal be lacking; but let Socrates open his door, he shall find Socrates asleep on the threshold before him, and there will be occasion for wisdom" (Alfred Sutro's trans. [New York, 1901], pp. 31–32). On Maeterlinck, see entry 215.34.

213.21/210.36 HE GAVE US LIGHT FIRST AND THE SUN TWO DAYS LATER Stephen's statement is not precisely correct. According to Genesis, God created light on the first day, but the sun was created on the fourth, not the third day (Gen. 1:1–19).

213.24/210.38 ALL IN ALL IN ALL OF US   See entry 212.28.

213.25/210.40 IN THE ECONOMY OF HEAVEN, FORETOLD BY HAMLET, THERE ARE NO MORE MARRIAGES   While Claudius and Polonius are eavesdropping, Hamlet says to Ophelia, "I say we will have no more marriages. Those that are married already, all but one, shall live; the rest shall keep as they are" (*Ham.*, III, i, 154–56). Mr. Best completes the quotation on p. 213.34/211.7.

213.28/211.1 EUREKA! . . . EUREKA   These were supposedly the words of Archimedes when, while in his bath, he realized a method of testing the purity of the gold crown of King Hiero II.

213.31/211.4 THE LORD HAS SPOKEN TO MALACHI   This apparently alludes to the opening statement of the book of Malachi: "The burden of the word of the Lord to Israel by Malachi" (1:1). Perhaps Mulligan's penchant for such statements generated Stephen's interest in Pseudomalachi; see entry 197.28.

213.34/211.7 THOSE WHO ARE MARRIED . . .   See entry 213.25.

213.39/211.12 HIS VARIORUM EDITION OF THE TAMING OF THE SHREW On a literal level, the most recent variorum edition of *The Taming of the Shrew* in 1904 was that in the Third Variorum edition of 1821, edited by Boswell, since there was no New Variorum edition of the play.

214.3/211.18 THE PLATONIC DIALOGUES WILDE WROTE   Oscar Wilde cast "The Decay of Lying" and "The Critic as Artist" as dialogues. Both of these were included in *Intentions* (1891).

214.9/211.24 HERR BLEIBTREU   R. M. Adams says, "Herr Karl Bleibtreu, the German faddist who identified Shakespeare with the Earl of Rutland, did not publish his book on the subject until 1907; he was in Berlin over the summer of 1904, playing chess in the Café Kaiserhof, but if I read correctly his letter to Joyce (in the Cornell Library, dated 28 November, 1918), he had not yet created his theory about Shakespeare, and so was most unlikely to have been consulted on the matter by Piper (an historical figure) in 1904"

(SS, p. 8). In the letter Adams cites (Scholes, item 429), Bleibtreu is obviously replying to a series of questions Joyce had asked in his letter, some of them (which Bleibtreu is puzzled by) about his location and his progress on his Shakespeare theory in the summer of 1904.

214.10/211.25 THAT RUTLAND THEORY   Roger Manners, fifth earl of Rutland (1576–1612) has been suggested as a candidate for the authorship of Shakespeare's plays. See entry 214.9 and cf. entry 208.12.

214.15/211.29 I BELIEVE, O LORD, HELP MY UNBELIEF   In Mark 9:24, the father of the possessed boy says to Christ, "Lord, I believe; help thou mine unbelief."

214.18/211.32 DANA . . . THE NEXT NUMBER. FRED RYAN WANTS SPACE FOR AN ARTICLE ON ECONOMICS   On Dana, see entry 193.3. Frederick Ryan frequently contributed essays on politico-economic topics to the magazine. The "next number" is probably the August, 1904, issue, in which Ryan had an essay entitled "Empire and Liberty" (pp. 111–17). Joyce's poem "My love is in a light attire" appeared in this same issue on p. 124. Neither Ryan nor Joyce had anything in the July number.

214.18/211.32 PIECES OF SILVER   This alludes to Judas's betrayal of Christ for thirty pieces of silver (Matt. 27:3–10).

214.29/212.1 SUMMA CONTRA GENTILES   St. Thomas' Summa de Veritate Catholicae Fidei contra Gentiles ("Treatise on the Truth of the Catholic Church, against Unbelievers"), written 1261–64 at the request of St. Raymond of Pennafort, is intended to show that no demonstrated truth is opposed to revealed truth. It was a philosophical defense of Christian belief to be used against the Jews and Moors in Spain.

214.30/212.2 FRESH NELLY AND ROSALIE, THE COALQUAY WHORE   These were apparently characters created by Oliver Gogarty, the original of Buck Mulligan. In his essay which is printed as a Foreword to Gogarty's Selected Poems (1933), Horace Gregory refers to Gogarty as "the creator of that robustious company, Fresh Nelly, Mrs. Mack, Rosalie the Coal-Quay Whore . . ." (p. xxii). But I have not found any poems about these characters in any of Gogarty's books of poems which I have seen, nor are they mentioned in the letters from Gogarty to Joyce which are now in the Cornell Library. Gogarty does briefly mention Fresh Nellie in the opening lines of the prologue to the poem "The Old Woman of Beare" in his Collected Poems, p. 105: "(This to-day had been Fresh Nellie,/ For she had as wild a belly . . .)."

214.33/212.4 WANDERING AENGUS OF THE BIRDS   In Irish myth Angus
Og (Angus the Young), one of the Tuatha De Danann, is the god
of love and beauty and the special deity of youth and maidens.
Bright birds always hover about his head. Probably Mulligan has
in mind Yeats's poem "The Song of Wandering Aengus," which
appeared in *The Wind Among the Reeds* (1899). Mulligan's prototype, Gogarty, actually called Joyce by this phrase.

214.38/212.9 NOTRE AMI MOORE   Wm. Schutte has pointed out (*JS*,
p. 77) that this alludes to a private joke between George Moore
and Edward Martyn, in which Martyn referred to Moore as "*Mon
ami* Moore." Schutte quotes the pertinent passage from Moore's
Salve and cites several references by Martyn to this joke in *Salve*
and *Ave*. See *Salve* (London, 1912), p. 96 for the explanatory
passage that Schutte quotes, and *Salve*, p. 147, and *Ave* (New York,
1914), pp. 203–4 and 279 for later references to the joke.

215.4/212.16 IRISH NIGHTS' ENTERTAINMENT   This is apparently a
variation of *Arabian Nights' Entertainment*, which is one of the
common titles of this variously titled collection of stories. This
title is used in *Ulysses* on p. 659.28/643.32. But it may also owe
something to Patrick J. McCall's volume of stories, *The Fenian
Night's Entertainment* (1897). For a note on McCall and his work
and a story from this collection, see *Irish Literature*, VI, 2117–22.

215.8/212.20 I GALL HIS KIBE   In the graveyard scene, Hamlet says
to Horatio, "the age is grown so picked that the toe of the peasant
comes so near the heel of the courtier, he galls his kibe" (*Ham.*,
V, i, 151–53).

215.9/212.21 ALL AMORT   "All amort," a common Elizabethan saying meaning "completely dejected," occurs twice in Shakespeare's
works. In *I Henry VI*, Talbot asks, "But where is Pucelle now?/
I think her old familiar is asleep./ Now where's the Bastard's braves,
and Charles his gleeks?/ What, all amort?" (III, ii, 121–24); and
in *The Taming of the Shrew*, Petruchio says to Katherina "How
fares my Kate? What, sweeting, all amort?" (IV, iii, 36). Wm.
Schutte (*JS*, p. 77) mentions these two instances of the phrase and
also points to its occurrence in Greene's *Friar Bacon and Friar Bungay* (I, i), a play alluded to later in *Ulysses* (see entry 617.27).

215.25/212.37 SMOOTHSLIDING MINCIUS   This alludes to Milton's
"Lycidas," where he says, "O fountain Arethuse, and thou honored
flood,/ Smooth-sliding Mincius, crowned with vocal reeds,/ That
strain I heard was of a higher mood" (ll. 85–87). The Mincius is
an Italian river, best known because Virgil was born near it and
mentions it in his *Eclogues* and *Georgics*.

215.26/212.38 PUCK MULLIGAN   Puck, or Robin Goodfellow, is a
fairy in *A Midsummer Night's Dream*. Originally, Puck designated
an evil or malicious spirit or demon of popular superstition.

215.28/212.40 JOHN EGLINTON, MY JO, JOHN . . .   This parodies
Burns's poem "John Anderson," which begins "John Anderson,
my jo, John. . . ."

215.31/213.2 THE CHINLESS CHINAMAN! CHIN CHON EG LIN TON   This
alludes to "Chin, chin, Chinaman," a well-known song from the
opera *The Geisha* (on which see entry 96.40). The song is sung by
Wun Hi, proprietor of the tea shop, in act II of the opera.

215.34/213.5 M. MAETERLINCK   Maurice Maeterlinck (1862–1949),
Belgian poet and dramatist and winner of the Nobel prize for
literature in 1911, was an experimentalist who did much to bring
symbolism to the stage. Cf. entry 213.14.

215.37/213.8 THE WHIPPING LOUSY LUCY GAVE HIM   As Wm. Schutte
shows (*JS*, p. 172), all three of Joyce's main sources mention the
story told by Richard Davies (1688–1708) and Nicholas Rowe
(1674–1718) that Shakespeare stole deer from Sir Thomas Lucy's
park at Charlecote. Davies' statement avers that Lucy had Shakespeare "oft whipt and sometimes imprisoned." Rowe mentions a
ballad Shakespeare is said to have written on Lucy (for Davies'
and Rowe's accounts, see Chambers, II, 255–57 and 264–69). A
ballad traditionally said to be the one Shakespeare wrote has survived; E. Epstein quotes it in his review of Schutte's *JS* in *JJR*,
I, ii, 47. For various opinions on the authenticity of the ballad, see
Schutte, *JS*, p. 172. The reference to "the dozen white luces" on
Justice Shallow's coat of arms in *The Merry Wives of Windsor*,
I, i, 16, is generally thought to be a cut at Sir Thomas Lucy, whose
coat of arms bore luces (a fish), in a pun on the family name.

215.42/213.13 MINION OF PLEASURE   In "Sonnet 126" Shakespeare
warns the youth about Nature: "Yet fear her, O thou minion of
her pleasure!" (l. 9).

215.42/213.13 PHEDO'S TOYABLE FAIR HAIR   This alludes to Socrates'
toying with the hair of Phaedo while arguing with Simmias and
Cebes about the immortality of the soul. See Plato's *Phaedo*, sec. 89.

216.3/213.16 PUCK MULLIGAN FOOTED FEATLY   In Ariel's song with
which he leads Ferdinand to Prospero, he says, "Foot it featly here
and there" (*The Tempest*, I, ii, 380). See also entry 215.26.

216.4/213.17 I HARDLY HEAR THE PURLIEU CRY . . .   This parodies
quite closely the opening stanza of W. B. Yeats's poem "Baile and
Aillinn," which appeared in *In the Seven Woods* (1903). The poem
begins, "I hardly hear the curlew cry,/ Nor the grey rush when

the wind is high,/ Before my thoughts begin to run/ On the heir of
Uladh, Buan's son. ...."

216.14/213.27 JEST ON   Since Stephen consistently regards Mulligan as a mocker, this probably alludes to Blake's poem "Mock On,"
the first stanza of which says, "Mock on, Mock on Voltaire, Rousseau:/ Mock on, Mock on: 'tis all in vain!/ You throw the sand
against the wind,/ And the wind blows it back again" (1957 Keynes
ed., p. 418).

216.14/213.27 KNOW THYSELF   "Know thyself" comes down from
Greek antiquity; it was the first of the three maxims inscribed on
the Temple of Apollo at Delphi.

216.20/213.33 LONGWORTH IS AWFULLY SICK . . . ABOUT THAT OLD HAKE
GREGORY   This refers to a critical review of Lady Gregory's
Poets and Dreamers which Joyce himself wrote for the *Daily Express* (Dublin), March 26, 1903. As Mulligan says, E. V. Longworth, editor of the *Express*,·was persuaded by Lady Gregory to
take Joyce on as a reviewer. See *CW*, pp. 102–5.

216.27/213.39 THE MOST BEAUTIFUL BOOK THAT HAS COME OUT OF OUR
COUNTRY IN MY TIME   Yeats begins his "Preface" to Lady Gregory's *Cuchulain of Muirthemne* (London, 1902) with the statement "I think this book is the best that has come out of Ireland in
my time" (p. vii). However, Mulligan's next sentence does not
have its origin in the "Preface." Yeats does compare Lady Gregory's book to the *Mabinogion*, the *Morte D'Arthur*, and the *Ni-
belungenlied*, but only inadvertently does he mention the Greeks
("the Irish stories make one understand why the Greeks called
myths the activities of the daemons," p. xiv), and nowhere does he
mention Homer.

216.32/214.2 GONE THE NINE MEN'S MORRICE WITH CAPS OF INDICES
In *A Midsummer Night's Dream*, Titania says to Oberon, "The
nine men's morris is filled up with mud" (II, i, 98). "Nine men's
morris" was a game like checkers played by two players using a
square diagram and moving pegs or stones about so as to capture
the opponent's men. For a fuller description, see A. B. Gomme,
Traditional Games, I, 414–19. P. W. Joyce (*English As We Speak
It*, p. 294) briefly describes the game and recalls playing it in his
youth. See also entry 28.11.

216.34/214.4 BUCK MULLIGAN READ HIS TABLET   This probably alludes to Hamlet's statement after the Ghost has spoken to him:
"My tables—meet it is I set it down/ That one may smile, and smile,
and be a villain" (*Ham.*, I, v, 107–08).

217.7/214.18 MEDICAL DICK . . . MOTHER GROGAN . . . FRESH NELLY AND
ROSALIE   On Medical Dick and Medical Davy, see entry 209.17;
on Mother Grogan, see entry 12.33; on Fresh Nelly and Rosalie,
see entry 214.30. S. Gilbert (*JJU*, p. 224) says that Mulligan's cast
is not completely original, since "The 'ruined Pole' and most of
his companions were known to Oxford men of the period."

217.24/214.33 IF SOCRATES LEAVE HIS HOUSE TODAY   See entry
213.14.

217.31/214.40 AENGUS OF THE BIRDS   See entry 214.33.

217.35/215.4 THE WANDERING JEW   According to tradition, the
Wandering Jew is a Jew who, as Christ was carrying the cross to
Calvary, bade him to go faster (or in some versions, refused to
allow Christ to rest). Christ told him to "tarry till I come," and so
the Jew must wander the earth until the second coming. See Joseph
Gaer, *The Legend of the Wandering Jew* (New York, 1961).

217.36/215.5 HE LOOKED UPON YOU TO LUST AFTER YOU   In the Sermon on the Mount, Christ says, "whosoever looketh on a woman
to lust after her hath committed adultery with her already in his
heart" (Matt. 5:28).

217.37/215.6 I FEAR THEE, ANCIENT MARINER   These are the words
of the Wedding Guest to the Mariner in Coleridge's "The Rime
of the Ancient Mariner" (Pt. IV, stanza 1; Pt. V, stanza 13).

218.5/215.14 KIND AIR   In light of the allusion to *Cymbeline*, V, v,
476, only a few lines later, W. Y. Tindall's suggestion (*RG*, p. 177),
that this derives from a passage in *Cymbeline*, V, v, seems correct.
In that scene the soothsayer interprets an oracle about "tender air"
by an etymology linking it with *mollis aer* and *mulier*, so that
Cymbeline's daughter is seen to fulfill the oracle (*Cym.*, V, v,
435–52). But see also the reference to "delicate" air in the following entry.

218.5/215.14 COIGNS OF HOUSES . . . NO BIRDS   This recalls Banquo's
statement as King Duncan and his company approach Macbeth's
castle. Observing the many martlets (swallows), he says "No jutty,
frieze,/ Butress, nor coign of vantage but this bird/ Hath made
his pendant bed and procreant cradle./ Where they most breed
and haunt, I have observed/ The air is delicate" (*Mac.*, I, vi, 6–10).

218.8/215.17 CEASE TO STRIVE   Hodgart and Worthington list this
as an allusion to Yeats's "Who Goes with Fergus" (see entry 9.22),
but no version of the poem has ever contained the words *cease*
or *strive* (according to the *Variorum Poems*). Nowhere does
Shakespeare use this exact phrase, but in *Cymbeline*, V, v (which is

alluded to on p. 218.5/215.14 and p. 218.10/215.19), Cymbeline, wanting to know about his daughter, urges Iachimo "Strive, man, and speak" (l. 152).

218.8/215.17   PEACE OF THE DRUID PRIESTS OF CYMBELINE, HIEROPHANTIC This probably alludes to the final scene of *Cymbeline* in which the soothsayer or priest, Philarmonus, interprets the oracle and says that its "issue/ Promises Britain peace and plenty," and a few lines later adds that "The fingers of the powers above do tune/ The harmony of this peace" (*Cym.*, V, v, 457–58, 466–67).

218.10/215.19   LAUD WE THE GODS . . .   Cymbeline speaks these lines in the concluding scene of *Cymbeline* (V, v, 476–78). W. Y. Tindall suggests (*RG*, p. 177) that the closely following lines in the play (*Cym.*, V, v, 479–81), "Let/ A Roman and a British ensign wave/ Friendly together," foreshadow Father Conmee and William Humble, earl of Dudley, lord lieutenant of Ireland—representatives of Rome and Britain—in the immediately following "Wandering Rocks" episode.

WANDERING ROCKS

219.4/216.4 VERE DIGNUM ET JUSTUM EST   These words, "It is indeed fitting and right," begin the various Prefaces which are said in the Consecration in the Mass. The most common Prefaces, "the Preface of the Holy Trinity" (used on ordinary Sundays) and "The Common Preface" (used on ordinary weekdays), begin, "It is indeed fitting and right, our duty and our salvation, always and everywhere to give thanks to you, Lord, Holy Father, almighty and eternal God. . . ."

219.12/216.12 BLESSED HIM IN THE SUN   This may allude to the proverbial "Out of God's blessing into the warm sun," which the *ODEP* lists and explains as meaning "from better to worse." Among the instances listed in the *ODEP* are *King Lear*, II, ii, 167–69, and Swift's *Polite Conversation*. In the first conversation of Swift's work, Neverout says of Mrs. Nice, "Well, she's got out of God's Blessing into the warm Sun." Partridge repeats the explanation in the *ODEP* and says the proverb is sixteenth to twentieth centuries (p. 99).

219.17/216.17 CARDINAL WOLSEY'S WORDS . . .   According to Wm.

Walsh, (*Handy-Book of Literary Curiosities, s.v.* God. Had I served), Cardinal Thomas Wolsey (1473?–1530) said to Sir William Kingston, "Had I served God as diligently as I have the king, he would not have given me over in my gray hairs." In Shakespeare's *Henry VIII*, Cardinal Wolsey says to his servant, "Had I but served my God with half the zeal/ I served my King, he would not in mine age/ Have left me naked to mine enemies" (III, ii, 455–57).

219.41/216.40 PILATE! WY DON'T YOU OLD BACK THAT OWLIN MOB Though there is no similar statement in the Bible, this alludes to Pilate's capitulation before the Jewish mob when he turned Christ over to them. See Mark 15:1–15; Luke 23:1–25; and John 18:28–19:22. Apparently Father Vaughan dramatized his presentation.

220.4/217.3 O, LEST HE FORGET The ultimate source of this is the Bible, though Father Conmee may also be thinking of Kipling's "Lest we forget—lest we forget" in "Recessional." The poem, written for Victoria's Diamond Jubilee, first appeared in the London *Times*, July 17, 1897. The phrase "Lest . . . forget" is common in the Bible, usually as a part of an admonition to remember one's duty to God. See, e.g., Deuteronomy 4:23 and 6:12.

220.24/217.22 MR DENIS J. MAGINNI, PROFESSOR OF DANCING . . . WALKING WITH GRAVE DEPORTMENT The repeated description of Maginni, who is a dancing master, in terms of "deportment" recalls the Turveydrops, father and son, from Charles Dickens' *Bleak House*. The son, Mr. Prince Turveydrop, is a dancing master, and the elder Mr. Turveydrop is continually described as having "Deportment" (see esp. chap. XIV of the novel, entitled "Deportment").

220.34/217.31 LIKE MARY, QUEEN OF SCOTS Mary Queen of Scots (Mary Stuart, 1542–87), Catholic daughter of James V of Scotland, was imprisoned by Queen Elizabeth and beheaded on the charge of conspiring against Elizabeth's life. She is said to have been a woman of great beauty, charm, courage, and religious devotion.

220.41/217.38 INVINCIBLE IGNORANCE This is a technical term in Catholic theology. The *Catholic Encyclopedia* divides ignorance into two types, vincible and invincible, and says "Ignorance is said to be invincible when a person is unable to rid himself of it notwithstanding the employment of moral diligence, that is, such as under the circumstances is, morally speaking, possible and obligatory" (VII, 648, *s.v.* Ignorance). St. Thomas defines and discusses invincible ignorance in the *Summa Theologica*, Part II (First part), ques. LXXVI, art. 2.

221.5/218.03   SATCHELLED SCHOOLBOYS   This may recall Jaques' description of the schoolboy in the "seven ages of man" passage in *As You Like It*: "Then the whining schoolboy, with his satchel/ And shining morning face, creeping like snail/ Unwillingly to school" (II, vii, 145–47).

221.13/218.11   NEAR ALDBOROUGH HOUSE FATHER CONMEE THOUGHT OF THAT SPENDTHRIFT NOBLEMAN   Aldborough House was built by Lord Aldborough in 1797 at a cost of £40,000, but the location proved to be too damp and Lady Aldborough refused to live in it. D. A. Chart, in his *Story of Dublin*, calls the house "A 'sermon in stone' on the extravagance which ruined Irish nobility" (p. 326), and goes on to describe the house.

221.20/218.18   A DREADFUL CATASTROPHE IN NEW YORK   This refers to the *General Slocum* disaster, which is alluded to several times in *Ulysses*; see entry 239.22.

222.41/219.36   MR EUGENE STRATTON   See entry 92.5.

223.2/219.39   SAINT PETER CLAVER S.J. AND THE AFRICAN MISSION Claver is patron of missionary work among Negroes; see entry 80.4.

223.6/220.2   THAT BOOK BY THE BELGIAN JESUIT, LE NOMBRE DES ELUS John R. Elliott, Jr., has suggested ("Father Conmee and the Number of the Elect," *JJR*, III [1959], 62–64) that the book alluded to here is *Le rigorisme, le nombre des elus et la doctrine du salut*, by Father A. Castelein, S.J., published in Brussels and Paris in 1899. As Elliott explains, this book was a statement of liberal opinion on the controversial and doctrinally dangerous question of the number of the elect and the number of the damned. For further information, see the article "Elus (Nombre des)" in *Dictionnaire de Theologie Catholique* (Paris, 1939), esp. columns 2355, 2377–78.

223.16/220.11   THE JOYBELLS WERE RINGING IN GAY MALAHIDE . . . This alludes to the opening lines of Irish author Gerald Griffin's (1803–40) poem "The Bridal of Malahide": "The joy-bells are ringing/ In gay Malahide." The statement "she was maid, wife and widow in one day" also alludes to the poem, for in stanza fourteen, we are told of Maud that "she sinks on the meadow/ In one morning-tide,/ A wife and a widow,/ A maid and a bride!" But the ultimate source for the maid-wife-widow idea may be Duke Vincentio's question of Mariana in *Measure for Measure*, V, i: "Why, you are nothing, then—neither maid, widow, nor wife?"

(l. 178). Griffin's poem may be found in *Dublin Book of Irish Verse*, pp. 116–22. But there is some confusion concerning the historical events behind Griffin's poem, both in Father Conmee's statement and in the note to the poem in *Dublin Book*, pp. 762–63, by "C. G. D." (Charles Gavan Duffy?). Both of these imply that it was the death of Lord Talbot that made Maud "maid, wife, and widow in one day," but that is not the case. Maud Plunkett married Thomas Hussy, son of the Baron of Galtrim, and the bridal party was attacked and Hussy killed (Griffin specifically mentions Hussy in stanza eighteen of his poem). Only later did Maud marry Richard Talbot, Lord of Malahide.

223.22/220.17 OLD TIMES IN THE BARONY   Father John Conmee actually wrote a short book entitled *Old Times in the Barony* (Dublin: Catholic Truth Society of Ireland, n.d.). Kevin Sullivan discusses the book briefly in *Joyce Among the Jesuits* and describes it as "a nostalgic but unsentimental recall of an older way of life, rural and uncomplicated, around the neighborhood of Luainford" (p. 17). I have not been able to date Conmee's book precisely, but it must have appeared *ca.* 1902.

223.24/220.19 MARY ROCHFORT, DAUGHTER OF LORD MOLESWORTH, FIRST COUNTESS OF BELVEDERE . . .   Mary Rochfort, wife of Colonel Robert Rochfort, first earl of Belvedere, was accused of an intrigue with her brother-in-law, Arthur Rochfort. When a judgment was handed down in favor of the Earl, Arthur fled to escape paying £20,000 damages. The enraged Earl imprisoned his wife in an old family house at Gaulstown, county Westmeath, until his death in 1774. Mary died in Dublin a few years later. Kevin Sullivan gives a much fuller discussion of this episode, showing that these incidents have no connection with the site of Belvedere College, Dublin, and discussing changes Joyce made in the *Little Review* version of this passage on the basis of information received in correspondence in 1921 (*Joyce Among the Jesuits*, pp. 60–64).

223.31/220.25 EIACULATIO SEMINIS INTER VAS NATURALE MULIERIS   "Ejaculation of semen within the natural female organ"—this phrase is used on pp. 736.8/720.36 and 736.14/721.3. As the context here indicates, Father Conmee is thinking of the definition in canon law of a consummated or "perfect" act of intercourse. The precise wording of the definition varies, and it usually, though not always, occurs in regard to adultery. In Joyce's notes to *Exiles*, speaking of Bertha's relationship to Robert, he says, ". . . for her the supreme concession is what the fathers of the church call *emissio seminis inter vas naturale*" (p. 173).

224.4/220.39 BREADTHS OF CABBAGES, CURTSEYING TO HIM WITH AMPLE
UNDERLEAVES   Fritz Senn suggests that this recalls "some phrase
of popular usage" in which "to be 'found under a cabbage leaf'
connotes exemption from the taint of sexualism or any knowledge
about it" (*JJQ*, II, 137–38). He finds a humorous irony in this, in
light of Father Conmee's superficial dismissal of the problem of sex.

224.19/221.12 PATER AND AVE   Joyce has just told us that Conmee
is reading his hours for Nones; the reading for Nones, every day
of the week, begins with the Lord's Prayer and the Ave. See *The
Roman Breviary . . . A New Edition for Use in England* (Edinburgh and London, 1908), III (the third volume is devoted to
Summer), p. 66. The rest of Father Conmee's section of this episode contains successive allusions to his reading the Nones.

224.20/221.13 DEUS IN ADIUTORIUM   In the reading for Nones in
the *Breviary*, after the Pater and Ave have been said, then is said
aloud the beginning of Psalm 70 (Psalm 69 in the Vulgate): "Deus,
in adiutorium meum intende; Domine, ad adiuvandum me festina"
("Make haste, O God, to deliver me; make haste to help me, O
Lord").

224.22/221.15 RES IN BEATI IMMACULATI . . .   Father Conmee is
reading from Psalm 119 (Vulgate 118), which is subdivided by
the letters of the Hebrew alphabet. The reading for Nones begins
with section *Phe*, so Father Conmee has now read through *Phe*,
Sade, and *Coph*, and, as Joyce tells us, is reading in *Res*: the quotation is from Psalms 119:160: "Thy word is true from the beginning: and every one of thy righteous judgments endureth for ever."
("Res in Beati immaculati" means "the *Res* section of Psalm 119,"
since the Psalm begins "Beati immaculati in via, quia ambulant in
lege Domini"—"Blessed are the undefiled in the way, who walk
in the law of the Lord.")

224.31/221.24 SIN: PRINCIPES PERSECUTI SUNT ME GRATIS . . .   Continuing his reading for Nones, Father Conmee is now in the section
of Psalm 119 (Vulgate 118) which is named for the Hebrew letter
Sin: "Princes have persecuted me without cause: but my heart
standeth in awe of thy word" (verse 161).

225.19/222.13 FOR ENGLAND . . . HOME AND BEAUTY   As Hodgart
and Worthington point out, this alludes to the English song "The
Death of Nelson" ("For England, Home, and Beauty") by S. J.
Arnold and John Braham. The song depicts the death of Nelson,
and says in part, " 'England expects that every man this day will
do his duty, This day will do his duty.' At last the fatal wound,
which spread dismay around, The hero's breast received, 'Heav'n

fights upon our side! The day's our own,' he cried! 'Now long
enough I've liv'd! In honour's cause my life was pass'd, In honour's
cause I fall at last, For England, home, and beauty, For England,
home, and beauty.' " For words and music, see Hatton and Faning,
Songs of England, I, 216–19.

227.3/223.36 OUR FATHER WHO ART NOT IN HEAVEN   An obvious
parody of the Pater Noster, which is alluded to frequently in
Ulysses.

227.6/223.39 ELIJAH IS COMING   See entry 151.15.

228.14/225.9 GOLDSMITH'S KNOBBY POLL   This refers to the statue
of Irish-born writer Oliver Goldsmith (1730–74) which stands on
the grounds of Trinity College, facing College Green. Goldsmith
attended Trinity.

228.29/225.23 THE STERN STONE HAND OF GRATTAN   On Grattan, see
entry 139.3. A statue of Grattan, with hand uplifted, stands in the
middle of College Green.

229.10/226.3 THE WOMAN IN WHITE   Wilkie Collins' novel *The
Woman in White* (1860) is full of secrets, intrigue, and characters
whose identity is long withheld. Marian—not Marion—whom Miss
Dunne mentions on p. 229.14/226.7, is Marian Halcombe, one of
the main characters in the novel.

229.14/226.7 MARY CECIL HAYE   Mary Cecil Hay (1840?–86) was
a popular English author. Her best-known novel is *Old Myddle-
ton's Money* (1874), but she wrote several more that were widely
read. The *DNB* has a short note on her, but a fuller account can
be found in Allibone's *Dictionary of Authors* (Supplement, vol.
II).

229.20/226.13 WOLFE TONE'S STATUE WAS NOT   Theobald Wolfe
Tone (1763–98) was one of Ireland's greatest patriots and most
popular heroes. He was a founder of the United Irishmen in 1791.
After the arrest of some members of the group in 1794, Tone went
to America and from there to France, hoping to gather French
aid for the Irish rebels. French General Hoche was sympathetic,
but after his death in 1797 Tone's dealings with Napoleon were
unsatisfactory. When the rebellion broke out in 1798, all that
Tone could get from the French were several small squadrons.
Tone was captured with one of these near Lough Swilly in October, 1798. He was tried and found guilty of treason. On being refused his request for a soldier's execution before a firing squad, he
was sentenced to be hanged. He was imprisoned at Arbour Hill,
Dublin. On November 11, 1798, he cut his throat with a pen-
knife and, on November 19, he died of the wound. Cosgrave and

Strangways *Dictionary of Dublin* mentions that "in 1898 the foundation stone of a monument to Wolfe Tone and the United Irishmen was laid in S. Stephen's-green facing Grafton-street" (p. 200). The statue was never completed.

229.23/226.15 MARIE KENDALL, CHARMING SOUBRETTE   Marie Kendall was apparently a music hall performer of the day. Both the *Freeman's Journal* and the *Evening Telegraph* of the day advertised "The Great Marie Kendall" as being at the Empire Palace Theatre of Gaities. She is also mentioned briefly in W. J. Mac-Queen-Pope's *The Melodies Linger On*, pp. 338, 431.

230.15/227.9 WHERE SILKEN THOMAS PROCLAIMED HIMSELF A REBEL   On "Silken Thomas," Lord Thomas Fitzgerald, tenth earl of Kildare, see entry 45.26. It was at St. Mary's Abbey, Dublin, that Thomas summoned the Council on June 11, 1534, and proclaimed himself no longer loyal to Henry VIII.

230.19/227.13 THE ORIGINAL JEWS TEMPLE WAS HERE TOO   Though it was not the "original" (i.e., first) Jewish place of worship in Dublin, St. Mary's Abbey did serve as the Jewish meeting house during the nineteenth century. Bernard Shillman's *A Short History of the Jews in Ireland* (Dublin, 1945) has a chapter entitled "Mary's Abbey Synagogue," which begins, "In the issue of the London *Sunday Times*, dated 18th October, 1835, the following interesting item appears: 'The Jews residing in Dublin have purchased a chapel formerly the property of a Presbyterian seceding congregation and converted it into a synagogue. This is the only one in Ireland.' The reference is to the Synagogue at Mary's Abbey, Dublin, which was used by the Dublin Jewish Community as a place of worship from 1836 to 1892" (p. 77). In 1892, the Jewish congregation moved into the Adelaide Road synagogue, which was consecrated on December 4, 1892 (Shillman, p. 99).

231.14/228.1 THE FITZGERALDS   The Fitzgeralds comprise a famous family in Irish history. The family is descended from Gerald, son or grandson of Walter Fitzother (who is in Domesday Book). Gerald married a Welsh princess, Nesta (see Curtis, *A History of Ireland*, p. 48), and from this marriage was born Maurice Fitzgerald (d. 1176), the first of many members of the family who are in the *DNB*.

231.18/228.5 A NEW GUNPOWDER PLOT   The Gunpowder Plot was a plot by English Catholics to blow up the House of Parliament on November 5, 1605, while Parliament and King James were assembled there. Among the main perpetrators were Robert Catesby and Guy Fawkes; Henry Garnett, the provincial of the English

Jesuits, also knew of the plot. The plot was betrayed and the principals were executed. Cf. entry 205.4.

231.21/228.8   THE EARL OF KILDARE AFTER HE SET FIRE TO CASHEL CATHE-
DRAL . . .   Gerald, the eighth earl of Kildare (d. 1513) was called
"Mor" (the Great), or "The Great Earl," or "Garret More." The
story of his burning the cathedral is recounted in Donough Bryan's
Gerald Fitzgerald, the Great Earl of Kildare (1456–1513) (Dublin:
Talbot Press, 1933). Bryan says, "His [the Great Earl's] audacity
is still more clearly shown in the story of the burning of Cashel
Cathedral:—'Being charged before Henrie the seventh, for burning the Church of Cashell and manie witnesses prepared to adouch
against him the truth of that article, he suddenlie confessed the
fact to the great wondering and detestation of the councell. When
it was looked into how he wold iustifie the matter: "By Jesus,"
(quoth he) "I would never have doone it, had it not beene told
me that the archbishop was within." And bicause the same archbishop was one of his busiest accusers there present, the king
merilie laughed at the plainesse of the noble man, to see him alledge
that thing for excuse which most of all did aggruate his offense.'
What was the cause of the enmity between the Great Earl and
the Archbishop is not stated. Ware says that according to tradition the Earl was later on touched with remorse of conscience and
laid out money for the repair of the cathedral" (pp. 203–4). In
footnotes Bryan explains that the archbishop was David Creagh,
and cites as the source of his quote *Holinshed's Chronicles*, I, 83;
Ware is Sir James Ware's *Annals of Ireland*.

231.25/228.12   THAT WAS THE GREAT EARL, THE FITZGERALD MOR . . .
THE GERALDINES   On the Great Earl, see entry 231.21; on the
Geraldines (the Fitzgeralds), see entry 231.14.

232.37/229.25   MARIE KENDALL   See entry 229.23.

233.31/230.16   THE BLOOM IS ON THE RYE   This alludes to the song
"When the Bloom Is on the Rye," words by Edward Fitzball,
music by Sir Henry Bishop. The song begins "My pretty Jane!
My pretty Jane!/ Ah! never, never look so shy,/ But meet me,
meet me in the evening,/ While the bloom is on the rye." The song
is sometimes titled "My Pretty Jane." For words and music, see
H. F. Reddall, *Songs That Never Die*, pp. 278–79.

234.28/231.15   LO, THE EARLY BEAM OF MORNING   "Lo, the early
beam of morning" is a quartet which occurs just before the finale
of act I of Edward Fitzball and Michael William Balfe's opera
The Siege of Rochelle (1835). It begins, "Lo! the early beam of
morning softly chides our longer stay; hark! the matin bells are

chiming, Daughter, we must hence away." The quartet is sung by
Father Azino, Clara, the servant Michel, and his wife Marcella,
and it expresses Clara's need to flee from Rochelle if she is to remain
safe and undetected. The opera was first done at Drury Lane Theatre, London, October 29, 1835.

235.18/232.3 THE AWFUL DISCLOSURES OF MARIA MONK   Maria
Monk (*ca.* 1817–50) wrote *Awful Disclosures of Maria Monk as
Exhibited in a narrative of her . . . residence of five years as a novice,
and two years as a black nun, in the Hotel Dieu Nunnery at Mon-
treal* (New York, 1836). Though she was finally shown to be an
imposter and her stories were revealed to be untrue, the book was
estimated to have sold 200,000 to 250,000 copies in America and
England by 1851. See *Appleton's Cyclopaedia of American Biography.*

235.19/232.4 ARISTOTLE'S MASTERPIECE   This is the title of a semi-
pornographic work, falsely attributed to Aristotle, which has been
in circulation at least since the seventeenth century. The *Catalogue
of Printed Books* in the British Museum lists several editions of
Aristotle's Masterpiece, the earliest of which (London, 1694) carries a revealing subtitle: *or, the Secrets of Generation displayed in
all the parts thereof.*

235.25/232.10 TALES OF THE GHETTO BY LEOPOLD VON SACHER MASOCH
Austrian novelist Leopold von Sacher-Masoch (1835–95) is the
man from whom masochism takes its name. I have not located a
work bearing this English title in any of the catalogues I have
examined. Perhaps Joyce simply translated the title of *Scene del
Ghetto*, an Italian version of a Sacher-Masoch work that he had
in his own library (see R. Ellmann, *JJ*, p. 794). I have found this
Italian title listed elsewhere (it was published in Milan in 1909),
but I have not examined a copy of the work and cannot say what
German original it is a translation of, though Sacher-Masoch's
Polnische Ghetto-Geschichten (1886) seems most likely.

235.37/232.22 FAIR TYRANTS BY JAMES LOVEBIRCH   The pseudonym
Lovebirch occurs commonly in flagellation literature, and there
is a James Lovebirch listed in the *Catalogue* of the Bibliothèque
Nationale (vol. 100, cols. 1001–02) as the author of several works,
published between 1910 and 1925, which have obvious semi-
pornographic overtones. Apparently his most popular was *Les Cinq
fessées de Suzette* (1910?). But I have found no book entitled *Fair
Tyrants* in any of the catalogues I have used.

236.5/232.27 SWEETS OF SIN   A work by this title is mentioned and
quoted from several times in *Ulysses*, but, after having searched

through a variety of catalogues, indexes, etc., of ordinary and pornographic literature, I cannot confirm that such a book exists. It is unlike Joyce to fabricate something like this, however, and I suspect that there is such a work and that I simply have not found it. Probably the work is not pornography, but lower class erotica, which might make it even harder to find.

236.29/233.12 AN ELDERLY FEMALE . . .   R. M. Adams says (*SS*, p. 226), " . . . the description . . . of three lawsuits listened to by the elderly female in the Four Courts is taken word-for-word (at the occasional expense of intelligibility) from the legal calendar on p. 2 of the *Irish Independent*'s issue of June 16, 1904." But the account in the *Irish Independent* is no closer to that in *Ulysses* than is the *Freeman's Journal* account, June 16, p. 2, col. a, so it may as well have served as Joyce's source. And of course all of the trial proceedings reported in those papers on June 16 actually occurred on June 15. On the *Lady Cairns* versus the *Mona*, see entry 638.13.

238.33/235.16 LEAVE YOU ALL WHERE JESUS LEFT THE JEWS   Though this sounds like a popular catch phrase, I have not found it in any of the dictionaries or phrase books I have examined.

239.22/236.7 GENERAL SLOCUM EXPLOSION   The *General Slocum* disaster, which occurred in the East River in New York on June 15, 1904, was reported in New York, London, and Dublin papers on June 16. The *General Slocum* was loaded with members of an excursion party from St. Mark's German Lutheran Church in New York City. Most of those aboard were women and children. There was a fire, followed by an explosion, which in turn spread the fire. In all, more than eight hundred persons died, though early estimates ran as high as one thousand. The *Freeman's Journal* account mentions the fire-hose being decayed and the life boats not being used.

239.39/236.24 FATHER COWLEY   Stephen P. Ryan has suggested that Father Cowley's name is an allusion to the Anglican religious order, the Society of Saint John the Evangelist, more popularly known as the Cowley Fathers. This order was founded in 1866 by Richard Meux Benson and S. W. O'Neill and was the first Anglican religious order. Ryan feels that "through the character of Father Cowley, Joyce is asserting his refusal to accept the validity of Anglican orders," and that the indications that Cowley is himself an Anglican are "developed subtly and obliquely— through the associations attached to the name" (*Notes and Queries*, IX, 305–6).

240.12/236.36 THE CUP THAT CHEERS BUT NOT INEBRIATES   Probably

the best-known source of this now common saying is William
Cowper's poem *The Task* (1785), in Book IV of which Cowper
mentions "the cups/ That cheer but not inebriate" (ll. 39–40). But
the saying goes back to Bishop Berkeley's *Siris* (1744). In section
217 of that work Berkeley, describing his vaunted tar-water, says
it is "of a nature so mild and benign and proportioned to the human
constitution as to warm without heating, to cheer, but not inebriate."

240.16/236.40 ELIJAH IS COMING   See entry 151.15.

240.27/237.8 EMMET WAS HANGED, DRAWN AND QUARTERED   Apparently the tradition that Robert Emmet was drawn and quartered has no basis, though he was beheaded after he was hanged. See
entry 114.18. Perhaps there is some basis for the story of the dogs'
drinking his blood. Helen Landreth (*op. cit.*, entry 114.18) says
that, after the beheading, people went furtively to dip their hand-
kerchiefs in Emmet's blood and "an hour later, a woman who lived
nearby saw dogs lapping it up" (p. 352).

241.2/237.25 TIMES OF THE TROUBLES   Though Ireland has had many
"times of the troubles" (and for any modern-day Irishman this
would mean 1916–23, and especially 1921–22), this probably refers
to the period from 1791 to 1803, and particularly to 1798.

241.3/237.26 REMINISCENCES OF SIR JONAH BARRINGTON   H. Gorman
mentions Jonah Barrington's *Recollections of His Own Times* as
one of the few books making up John Joyce's "library" (*James
Joyce*, p. 16). Both Gorman and Bloom must be thinking of Sir
Jonah Barrington's *Personal Sketches of His Own Times* (3 vols.;
London, 1827–32). Perhaps Bloom's thought about gaming at
Daly's (p. 241.5/237.27) comes from an episode recounted in Barrington's book this is certainly the kind of episode the book
abounds in—but I have not found in it any reference to this specific event.

241.7/237.29 LORD EDWARD FITZGERALD ESCAPED FROM MAJOR SIRR.
STABLES BEHIND MOIRA HOUSE   Lord Edward Fitzgerald (1763–
98) is one of the heroes of the 1798 rebellion. He served in the
American Revolution and joined the United Irishmen in 1796. He
was the leader of the plan to have France collaborate in the rebellion. In March, 1798, several United Irishmen were arrested,
and Lord Edward went into hiding. A £1,000 reward was offered
for information leading to his arrest. On one occasion Major Henry
Charles Sirr (1764–1841), who became Town Major (i.e., Chief
of Police) of Dublin in 1798, did lay an ambush for Lord Edward
near Moira House, but Lord Edward eluded him. Lord Edward

was finally captured by Major Sirr on May 19, 1798, on information provided, supposedly, by Francis Higgins, and for which Higgins received £1,000 (see entry 126.26). Lord Edward was wounded while battling his captors and died in prison a few days later.

241.10/237.33   FINE DASHING YOUNG NOBLEMAN . . . THAT SHAM SQUIRE . . . GAVE HIM AWAY   The nobleman is Lord Edward Fitzgerald; the "sham squire" who supposedly turned him in is Francis Higgins. See entries 241.7 and 126.26.

241.12/237.35   THEY ROSE IN DARK AND EVIL DAYS. FINE POEM THAT IS: INGRAM   The poem alluded to is by Irish scholar and poet John Kells Ingram (1823–1907) and is entitled "The Memory of the Dead (1798)." It begins, "Who fears to speak of Ninety-Eight?/ Who blushes at the name?" Stanza five of the poem begins, "They rose in dark and evil days/ To right their native land." See Hoagland, pp. 505–6, and cf. entry 257.17.

241.16/237.38   AT THE SIEGE OF ROSS DID MY FATHER FALL   This is from "The Croppy Boy"; see entry 91.1.

241.27/238.7   WINEDARK STONES   This is a variation on the common Homeric epithet, "winedark sea." See entry 5.7.

241.29/238.9   EVIL LIGHTS SHINING IN THE DARKNESS   From John 1:5. See entries 28.16 and 48.18.

241.30/238.10   WHERE FALLEN ARCHANGELS FLUNG THE STARS OF THEIR BROWS   Stephen's remark may echo Revelation 12:1–4, where the fallen angels are described as stars, and the woman clothed with the sun is said to be wearing a crown of twelve stars. There is also a suggestion here of some tradition that the jewels of the earth were derived from the stars of the crowns of the fallen angels, but I have not located such a tradition.

242.4/238.22   ANTISTHENES   See entries 148.29 and 201.17.

242.5/238.22   ORIENT AND IMMORTAL WHEAT STANDING FROM EVERLASTING TO EVERLASTING   From Thomas Traherne's *Centuries of Meditations*. See entry 38.8.

242.13/238.30   THROB ALWAYS WITHOUT YOU AND THE THROB ALWAYS WITHIN   Mason and Ellmann call attention to the similarity of this phrase to a passage Joyce quoted from James Lane Allen's *The Mettle of the Pasture* (New York, 1903) when he reviewed that novel for the Dublin *Daily Express*, September 17, 1903: " . . . without us and within us moves one universe that saves us or ruins us only for its own purposes" (*CW*, p. 118). Probably one reason that this passage stuck in Joyce's mind is that, in Allen's novel, it occurs immediately after Rowan Meredith's mother has tried to get him to agree to marry Isabel Conyers. Allen describes

Rowan's reaction to his mother's imploring: " 'No, no, no!' he cried, choking with emotion. 'Ah, mother, mother!'—and he gently disengaged himself from her arms" (p. 124). Rowan leaves and Mrs. Meredith immediately realizes that her cherished wish that Rowan and Isabel should marry will never be fulfilled. Allen then says, "For her it was one of those moments when we are reminded that our lives are not in our keeping, and that whatsoever is to befall us originates in sources beyond our power. Our wills may indeed reach the length of our arms or as far as our voices can penetrate space; but without us and within moves one universe that saves us or ruins us only for its own purposes; and we are no more free amid its laws than the leaves of the forest are free to decide their own shapes and season of unfolding, to order the showers by which they are to be nourished and the storms which shall scatter them at last" (p. 125).

242.20/238.37 YOU SAY RIGHT, SIR. A MONDAY MORNING, 'TWAS SO, INDEED Hamlet, feigning conversation with Rosencrantz and Guildenstern as Polonius approaches, says, "You say right, sir. O' Monday morning, 'twas so indeed" (*Ham.*, II, ii, 406–7).

242.23/239.1 1860 PRINT OF HEENAN BOXING SAYERS Britisher Tom Sayers fought American John C. Heenan at Farnborough, England, on April 7, 1860. The fight went thirty-seven rounds and lasted more than two hours. After Sayers' right arm was injured, the crowd pressed into the ring and the bout was declared a draw. The *Encyclopaedia Britannica* (11th ed.) says this fight "is perhaps the most famous in the history of the English prize ring" (*s.v.* Sayers, Tom).

242.29/239.7 THE IRISH BEEKEEPER. LIFE AND MIRACLES OF THE CURÉ OF ARS. POCKET GUIDE TO KILLARNEY Though books on each of these three subjects are easy to find, none of the catalogues I have examined lists any one of these titles exactly as they are given in *Ulysses.* Bee-keeping was quite popular in Ireland at this time, and a book by the Reverend J. G. Digges entitled *The Irish Bee Guide* had appeared in June, 1904, and had been reviewed in the *Freeman's Journal* of June 3, 1904 (p. 2, col. b). Also, a periodical entitled *Bee-keeper of Ireland* had appeared for a few months in 1902 before the title was changed to *Bee-keeper.* But nowhere have I found the exact title Joyce cites. The Curé of Ars was the blessed Jean-Baptiste-Marie Vianney (1786–1859). He was very popular (see *Cath. Encyc.*, VIII, 326–27), and many books have been written about him, but none bearing this exact title. There are also several guidebooks to Killarney, probably the best known of Joyce's day being *Black's Guide to Killarney and the South of Ireland,* which first appeared in 1854 and went through many editions, into the twentieth century. But again, I have found no guidebook by this exact title. I am uncertain whether to conclude that the titles Joyce cites do actually exist and the books were highly ephemeral, or that Joyce was simply assembling from memory a series of popular titles, and the result was approximate.

242.35/239.13   EIGHTH AND NINTH BOOK OF MOSES . . .   Though I have examined many catalogues and indexes, both ordinary and esoteric, I have not located either the *Eighth and Ninth Book of Moses* or abbot Peter Salanka.

243.3/239.23   JOACHIM'S. DOWN, BALDYNOODLE, OR WE'LL WOOL YOUR WOOL   See entry 40.1.

243.9/239.29   A STUART FACE OF NONESUCH CHARLES   Perhaps Stephen sees Dilly as a Stuart because both are lost causes. Dilly is drowning in Dublin, and the Stuarts were beheaded (Charles I) and exiled (James II). On p. 330.13/324.19, John Wyse says, "We fought for the royal Stuarts that reneged us against the Williamites and they betrayed us." If Stephen's phrase involves any more precise allusion than this, I am not aware of it.

243.19/239.39   CHARDENAL'S FRENCH PRIMER   Among many French grammar books by C. A. Chardenal, the *Catalogue of the British Museum* lists *The Standard French Primer* (London and Glasgow, 1877).

243.27/240.5   AGENBITE . . . AGENBITE . . . AGENBITE OF INWIT   See entry 16.7.

245.10/241.27   ATTENDED BY GERALDINES   The Geraldines and the Fitzgeralds (on whom Love is writing a book—see p. 231.13/227.42) are the same. See entries 231.14 and 231.25.

245.10/241.27   TOWARDS THE THOLSEL BEYOND THE FORD OF HURDLES   Of the Tholsel, Constantia Maxwell says, "The original Dublin Tholsel (Toll-gatherer's stall), the Guildhall of the Corporation of Dublin, was built in the reign of Edward II [i.e., 1307–27]. It was rebuilt (in Skinner's Row [i.e., Christchurch Place]) in 1683 and 1783, and, being in a state of decay, was pulled down in 1809. A new Session House was built in Green Street in 1797, and meetings of the Corporation were transferred to William Street" (*Dublin Under the Georges,* p. 87). The Ford of Hurdles alludes to the Irish name for Dublin—Baile Atha Cliath, "The Town of the Hurdle Ford." In early times there was supposedly a ford of wicker hurdles across the river at this point.

245.16/241.33   A CROSS BETWEEN LOBENGULA AND LYNCHEHAUN   Lobengula (*ca.* 1833–94), king of the Matabele, 1870–94, was an important minor figure in Anglo-African history for two decades. At first an opponent of European settlement, he later permitted use of part of his domain, but the Europeans and Matabele soon clashed, and the latter were slaughtered in several battles. The most decisive was on October 23, 1893, about thirty miles from Lobengula's capital, Bulawayo. Lobengula died during his attempt to recoup. R. M. Adams briefly discusses Lobengula and points out a reference to him in the *Freeman's Journal* of January 20, 1894, p. 5 (*SS*, pp. 207–8). According to a long article in the *United Irishman,* September 26, 1903, p. 5, cols. b and c, James Lynchehaun was an Irish scoundrel who assaulted, beat severely, and left for dead his former employer, a Mrs. MacDonnell of Achill Island. Lynchehaun was tried and sentenced to penal servitude for life on July 17, 1895, but he later escaped and fled to America. Apparently it was an article in the *Boston Pilot* gloryifying Lynchehaun that prompted the article in *United Irishman,* the main purpose of which is to explain the true character of Lynchehaun and to explain that "there is no sympathy in Ireland whatever for Lynchehaun—not an iota." R. M Adams (*SS*, p. 208) explains that Lynchehaun was an alias of James Walshe.

245.35/242.10 BARABBAS   See entry 94.27.

245.36/242.11 WHERE JACKO PUT THE NUTS   This apparently refers to some scurrilous joke, and the common "up his ass" is probably the direction intended, but I have not come across this particular version.

246.12/242.26 TOUCH ME NOT   In John 20:17, the resurrected Christ says to Mary Magdalene, "Touch me not."

246.27/243.2 I'LL SAY THERE IS MUCH KINDNESS IN THE JEW   In *The Merchant of Venice,* Antonio says of Shylock's offer to Bassanio, "I'll seal to such a bond/ And say there is much kindness in the Jew" (I, iii, 153–54).

247.11/243.27 HENRY CLAY   Henry Clay (1777–1852) was an American statesman and orator, but this refers to the cigar that went by this name at least as early as 1884 (M. M. Mathews, *A Dictionary of Americanisms* [2 vols.; Chicago: University of Chicago Press, 1951]).

247.16/243.32 HELL OPEN TO CHRISTIANS   Richard M. Kain has drawn my attention to the allusion here to the tract entitled *Hell Opened to Christians, To Caution Them from Entering into It,* by seventeenth-century Jesuit Giovanni Pietro Pinamonti. This tract was Joyce's primary source in writing the hell-fire sermons in chapter three of *A Portrait of the Artist*. It was first published, in Italian, in 1688, and it had been through several popular English translations by Joyce's time. For discussions of Joyce's use of the tract, see James R. Thane, "Joyce's Sermon on Hell: Its Source and its Backgrounds," *Modern Philology*, LVII (Feb., 1960), 172–98; Elizabeth F. Boyd, "James Joyce's Hell-Fire Sermons," *MLN*, LXXV (Nov., 1960), 561–71; and James Doherty, "Joyce and *Hell Opened to Christians*: The Edition He Used for His 'Hell Sermons,' " *Modern Philology*, LXI (Nov., 1965), 110–19.

248.34/245.13 SHAKESPEARE IS THE HAPPY HUNTING GROUND OF ALL MINDS THAT HAVE LOST THEIR BALANCE   William S. Walsh explains (*Handy-Book of Literary Curiosities, s.v.* Happy hunting-grounds) that the Happy Hunting Grounds is "the Elysium or Paradise of the Indian, which he hopes to find in the next world, and which paints itself to his mind's eye as a prarie chock full of buffalo and other game," and Walsh goes on to point out that the term "has come into general use in American colloquial speech as a synonyme for Kingdom Come or other facetious name for Heaven." Haines's statement suggests that he may have read Justice Madden's book on Shakespeare, mentioned on p. 200.17/197.41. The book is fanciful in its presentation and might provoke a reaction like Haines's. And in his Preface, Madden explains that the germ of the idea for the book was certain hunting experiences in England. Madden says, "Again and again I revisited those happy hunting grounds, and in each succeeding autumn the thoroughly Shakespearean character of the sport and of its surroundings impressed me more and more" (p. v).

248.37/245.16 ENGLAND EXPECTS   This is from "England, Home and Beauty"; see entry 225.19 and cf. entry 15.32.

249.2/245.20 WANDERING AENGUS   See entry 214.33.

249.8/245.26 THE NOTE OF SWINBURNE   Mulligan has quoted Swinburne repeatedly, often in connection with his espousal of the Greek. See, e.g., entries 5.5 ff.

249.9/245.27 THE WHITE DEATH AND THE RUDDY BIRTH   The context here suggests an allusion to Swinburne. But, while the contrast of life and death and the association of white or paleness with death and of redness or rosiness with life are common in Swinburne, I have not found this specific phrase anywhere in his works. The word *ruddy* seems so untypical of Swinburne that it is probably Mulligan's own.

249.10/245.28 HE CAN NEVER BE A POET   This refers to Dryden's remark about Swift; see entry 40.19.

249.13/245.31 PROFESSOR POKORNY OF VIENNA   This undoubtedly refers to Julius Pokorny (b. 1887), but if so, the allusion involves an anachronism, for Pokorny was only seventeen years old in 1904 and was not "Professor Pokorny" until several years later. Pokorny did go to Vienna as Privatdozent (private lecturer) of Celtic Philology in 1914, and he remained there until 1921, when he became Professor of Celtic in the University of Berlin. I have not been able to confirm Haines's statement that Pokorny "can find no trace of hell in ancient Irish myth."

249.33/246.8 ELIJAH   See entry 151.15. Elijah is referred to again on p. 250.8/246.22.

251.5/247.20 MARIE KENDALL   See entry 229.23.

251.10/247.25 FITZSIMONS . . . JEM CORBETT . . .   Robert L. Fitzsimmons (1863–1918), British boxer, held at various times the middleweight, heavyweight, and lightheavyweight boxing crowns. He won the heavyweight title in 1897 by defeating American boxer James J. Corbett (1866–1933) at Carson City, Nevada. He lost the heavyweight crown to James J. Jeffries at Coney Island, New York, in 1899.

253.17/249.30 MARIE KENDALL   See entry 229.23.

253.31/250.1 KING BILLY'S HORSE   This refers to the equestrian statue of King William III which stood in College Green. D. A. Chart, in his *Story of Dublin*, devotes more than a page to describing various abuses of and assaults upon the statue, including one explosion in 1836 which blew King William from his horse (pp. 202–04).

254.1/250.14 MY GIRL'S A YORKSHIRE GIRL   This refers to the song "My Girl's a Yorkshire Girl," by C. W. Murphy and Dan Lipton. For words, see the Appendix.

254.37/251.8 MR EUGENE STRATTON   See entry 92.5.

255.4/251.15 THE HOUSE SAID TO HAVE BEEN ADMIRED BY THE LATE QUEEN . . .   This apparently refers to a house at the intersection of Northumberland and Landsdowne roads, but I have not been able to confirm that Queen Victoria praised a house in that vicinity. The Queen did visit Dublin in 1849, arriving in the city on August 6 and leaving on August 10, and the newspapers followed her movements closely. The *Freeman's Journal* of Tuesday, August 7, describes in great detail her entry into the city the preceding day, but the cortege apparently did not travel on Northumberland or Landsdowne roads. The *Freeman's Journal* account picks the procession up at Sandymount Avenue and traces its progress through Pembroke Road, Upper and Lower Baggot streets, around Merrion Square on the east and north sides, and up Clare and Nassau streets to Grafton Street and across the river towards the viceregal lodge. The account of her movements during the next few days does not seem to place the Queen in SE Dublin, and her exit to Kingstown was made by rail from the Westland Row station. Consequently, she seems to have had no opportunity to praise a house at the Landsdowne-Northumberland Road intersection.

256.6/252.6 BLUE BLOOM IS ON THE   This alludes to the song "When the Bloom Is on the Rye," by Fitzball and Bishop; see entry 233.31.

256.8/252.8 ROSE OF CASTILLE   See entry 134.19.

256.9/252.9 IDOLORES   This is the first of several allusions in this episode to a song that appeared in the light operetta *Florodora* (book by Owen Hall, lyrics by E. Boyd-Jones and Paul Rubens, music by Leslie Stuart). The opera was first done at the Lyric Theatre on November 11, 1899. The allusions in *Ulysses* are to the chorus of a song entitled "The Shade of the Palm" (sometimes called "O My Delores"), which is sung by Frank Abercoed in act I of the opera. The song begins, "There is a garden fair, Set in an Eastern sea," and the chorus says, "Oh, my Delores Queen of the Eastern sea! Fair one of Eden, Look to the West for me! My star will be shining, love, when you're in the moonlight calm, So be waiting for me by the Eastern sea, In the shade of the shelt'ring palm."

256.12/252.12 AND A CALL, PURE, LONG AND THROBBING. LONGINDYING CALL.   If this is an allusion, I have not been able to identify it.

Hodgart and Worthington take no note of this. Cf. entry 279.4.

256.13/252.13   THE BRIGHT STARS FADE . . . THE MORN IS BREAKING
This alludes to the song "Goodbye, Sweetheart, Goodbye," by
Williams and Hatton. The song begins, "The bright stars fade, the
morn is breaking, The dew-drops pearl each bud and leaf." The full
text of the song can be found in the Appendix; words and music
can be found in Chapple, *Heart Songs*, pp. 160–61. As Hodgart and
Worthington point out, the allusions to the song continue on pp.
256.17, 18, 19/252.17, 18, 19; but the allusion they see on p. 256.33/
252.33 seems unlikely to me.

256.21/252.21   WHEN LOVE ABSORBS. WAR! WAR   Hodgart and Worthington list this as an allusion to "Love and War" ("When Love
Absorbs My Ardent Soul"), by Cooke. The song is alluded to
several times in this chapter and is apparently a duet sung by a
man and a woman. But, though I have searched through a large
number of song books and indexes, I have not located the song
or any information about it.

256.24/252.24   LOST . . . ALL IS LOST NOW   This alludes to the aria
"Tutto è sciolto" ("All Is Lost"), from Vincenzo Bellini's (1801–
35) opera *La Sonnambula* (*The Sleepwalker*). The opera had its
première in Milan in 1831; it is usually done in two acts, though
some versions have three. The aria is sung by the young farmer,
Elvino, in act II, and it expresses his unhappiness over what he
falsely believes is the unfaithfulness of his fiancée, Amina, who has
got into a compromising situation through her sleepwalking. Bloom
recalls the circumstances of the opera on p. 272.42/268.31. There
are several English versions of the aria. *The Favorite Songster*
prints one beginning, "All is lost now,/ Oh! for me love's sun is
set for ever" (p. 276). Joyce later used the phrase "Tutto è
sciolto" as the title of one of his poems.

256.26/252.26   WHEN FIRST HE SAW   Hodgart and Worthington list
this as an allusion to the aria "M'Appari," from Flotow's opera
Martha (on which see entry 117.34). This well-known aria is sung
by Lionel in act III. There are many English translations of it,
but nowhere have I located a printed copy of the version sung in
Ulysses (cf. entry 273.30).

256.34/252.34   SO LONELY BLOOMING   This alludes to Thomas
Moore's song "The Last Rose of Summer." And since the song
figures prominently in Flotow's opera *Martha* (see entries 117.34
and 256.26), it may also be considered an allusion to that. In
Martha, the song is sung twice by Martha, and part of it is sung
by Lionel. Since most of the allusions are to the first of the song's
three stanzas, I quote that entire stanza: " 'T is the last rose of

summer/ Left blooming alone;/ All her lovely companions/ Are faded and gone;/ No flower of her kindred,/ No rose-bud is nigh,/ To reflect back her blushes,/ Or give sigh for sigh." The song is alluded to again on p. 257.15/253.15.

256.38/252.38 LISZT'S RHAPSODIES   Hungarian composer Franz Liszt (1811–86) composed a series of rhapsodies known as the *Hungarian Rhapsodies*, which are among his best-known works. Cf. p. 282.32/ 278.10.

257.1/253.1 WAIT WHILE YOU WAIT . . . WAIT WHILE YOU HEE   This probably alludes to line nine of "The Croppy Boy"; see entry 91.1 and the Appendix. The song is also alluded to on p. 257.4, 6, 12/ 253.4, 6, 12.

257.3/253.3 LOW IN THE DARK MIDDLE EARTH, EMBEDDED ORE   While I suspect that this alludes to some song and that the allusion is repeated on p. 283.14/278.34, I have not been able to identify it. Hodgart and Worthington do not list this.

257.4/253.4 NAMINEDAMINE. ALL GONE. ALL FALLEN   These words blend allusions to "The Croppy Boy" (see entry 91.1 and the Appendix) and "The Last Rose of Summer" (see entry 256.34).

257.15/253.15 LAST ROSE CASTILLE OF SUMMER   This blends allusions to *The Rose of Castille* (see entry 134.19) and "The Last Rose of Summer" (see entry 256.34).

257.17/253.17 TRUE MEN . . . LIKE YOU MEN. WILL LIFT YOUR TSCHINK WITH TSCHUNK   This blends allusions to Ingram's "The Memory of the Dead" (see entry 241.12) and Sullivan's "The Thirty-Two Counties" (see entry 257.18). The first stanza of Ingram's song ends, "But a true man, like you, man,/ Will fill your glass with us," and the penultimate line of each stanza has some variation on "true men, like you, men."

257.18/253.18 TSCHINK WITH TSCHUNK   This alludes to T. D. Sullivan's song "The Thirty-Two Counties" (sometimes "Ireland, or the Thirty-Two Counties"), a toasting song in which each of Ireland's thirty-two counties is named. The chorus says, "Then clink, glasses, clink—'tis a toast for all to drink,/ And let every voice come in at the chorus:/ For Ireland is our home, and wherever we may roam,/ We'll be true to the dear land that bore us." For words, see *Walton's Treasury of Irish Songs and Ballads*, p. 91.

257.23/253.23 THEN. NOT TILL THEN. MY EPPRIPFFTAPH. BE PFRWRITT   This is from Robert Emmet's speech, which is quoted later in this episode; see entry 290.34.

258.10/254.11 SWEETS OF SIN . . . FOR RAOUL   Bloom is remembering *Sweets of Sin*; see entry 236.5.

259.40/255.40 BLUEROBED, WHITE UNDER . . .   Bloom is looking at statues of the Virgin Mary in Bassi's window; the Virgin's colors are white and blue.

260.4/256.3 THE SWEETS OF SIN. SWEET ARE THE SWEETS   Bloom is still thinking of *Sweets of Sin* (see entry 236.5), but the second phrase probably alludes to Queen Gertrude's statement "Sweets to the sweet" (see entry 272.17). *Sweets of Sin* is thought of again on p. 260.42/256.39.

260.25/256.23 RINGING IN CHANGES   This may recall Tennyson's "Ring out the old, ring in the new" in *In Memoriam*, section CVI, stanza 2.

261.20/257.16 SIMPLE SIMON   This refers to the character in the well-known nursery rhyme "Simple Simon met a pieman." For the rhyme and some comments on the possible origin of *Simple Simon*, see *ODNR*, p. 385.

261.32/257.28 THE MOURNE MOUNTAINS   Hodgart and Worthington list this and p. 263.7/259.2 as an allusion to Percy French's song "The Mountains of Mourne." But in neither of these contexts is there any verbal echo of the song beyond the title, and the allusion seems doubtful to me.

261.39/257.35 O, IDOLORES, QUEEN OF THE EASTERN SEAS   See entry 256.9.

262.2/257.40 BLUE BLOOM IS ON THE RYE   See entry 233.31.

262.19/258.15 HE READ BY ROTE A SOLFA FABLE FOR HER . . . AH FOX MET AH STORK . . .   The Aesop fable alluded to here is not about the fox and the stork, but about the wolf and the crane. The wolf, having a bone lodged in his throat, offered to pay well anyone who would remove the bone. The crane agreed, and removed it, but when he asked for payment, the wolf replied that he had already had payment enough in being allowed to escape with his life. Aesop's fox and stork fable is about the fox's asking the stork to dinner and then serving the food in a vessel the stork could not eat from; in recompense the stork soon did the same to the fox.

262.40/258.35 THE LABOUR OF HIS MUSE   Thinking of praise for Desdemona, Iago says, "But my Muse labors,/ And thus she is delivered" (*Oth.*, II, i, 128–29).

263.3/258.40 THAT MINSTREL BOY OF THE WILD WET WEST   Hodgart and Worthington list this as blending allusions to Thomas Moore's song "The Minstrel Boy" and the anonymous song "The Men of the West." Moore's "The Minstrel Boy" begins, "The Minstrel-Boy to the war is gone,/ In the ranks of death you'll find him;/ His father's sword he has girded on,/ And his wild harp slung behind him." A copy of "The Men of the West," said to be by William Rooney, is to be found in the paperback *'98 Song Book* (Dublin: Irish Book Bureau, n.d.), pp. 8–9. I quote the entire chorus, which is closer to the line in *Ulysses* than anything else in the song: "I give you the gallant old West, boys,/ Where rallied our bravest and best/ When Ireland lay broken and bleeding;/ Hurrah for the men of the West!"

263.7/259.2 FARAWAY MOURNING MOUNTAIN EYE Hodgart and Worthington list this as another allusion to P. French's "The Mountains of Mourne," but this seems doubtful to me; see entry 261.32.

263.35/259.28 A PIN CUTS LO Bloom is remembering the proverb he thought of earlier; see entry 168.28.

263.40/259.33 FOR RAOUL Another echo of *Sweets of Sin*; see entry 236.5.

264.11/260.4 A CALL CAME, LONG IN DYING (The allusion is continued on p. 264.15/260.8.) See entry 256.12.

264.19/260.12 THE BRIGHT STARS FADE . . . THE MORN IS BREAKING . . . These lines allude to "Goodbye, Sweetheart, Goodbye"; see entry 256.13. The allusion is continued in the italicized lines on p. 264.26/260.19 and p. 265.3/260.37.

264.28/260.21 ROSE OF CASTILLE (The allusion is repeated on p. 264.30/260.23.) This alludes to *The Rose of Castille*; see entry 134.19.

264.39/260.32 SEE THE CONQUERING HERO COMES The song "See the Conquering Hero Comes" was written by English classical scholar Dr. Thomas Morell (1703–84). It was used in Handel's oratorios *Joshua* and *Judas Maccabeus*, and was introduced into later stage versions of Nathaniel Lee's tragedy *The Rival Queens* (1677). In Handel's *Joshua* it occurs in act III, scene 2, where it is sung by a Chorus of Youths. It begins, "See the conquering hero comes! Sound the trumpet, beat the drums."

265.39/261.30 IDOLORES. THE EASTERN SEAS See entry 256.9.

266.2/261.34 FAIR ONE OF EGYPT . . . LOOK TO THE WEST . . . FOR ME Though Hodgart and Worthington list part of this as an allusion to "The Men of the West" (see entry 263.3), this alludes, with some variation, to a line from the song "The Shade of the Palm," mentioned in the preceding entry: "Fair one of Eden, Look to the West for me." For more information and a fuller quotation, see entry 256.9.

266.10/261.42 BLOOM BY RYEBLOOM This alludes to "When the Bloom Is on the Rye"; see entry 233.31.

266.17/262.7 TO FLORA'S LIPS DID HIE   This alludes to "Goodbye, Sweetheart, Goodbye"; see entry 256.13. The allusion is continued in the italicized lines on p. 266.23/262.13 and p. 267.8/262.41.

267.22/263.13 WE'LL PUT A BARLEYSTRAW IN THAT JUDAS ISCARIOT'S EAR THIS TIME   There may be some allusion here to a variation on the common proverb "He will go to law for the wagging of a straw" (this is the form the *ODEP* gives). *Stevenson's Book of Quotations* (p. 1082, no. 7) gives "Thou knowest a barley straw/ Will make a parish parson go to law" (William Goddard, *Nest of Wasps* [1615], no. 16).

267.33/263.23 BEGONE, DULL CARE   "Begone! Dull Care" is the title of an anonymous seventeenth-century English song. It begins "Begone! dull Care, I prithee begone from me Begone! dull Care, You and I will never agree." For words and music, see Hatton and Faning, *Songs of England*, I, 40.

268.4/263.36 LOVE AND WAR   See entry 256.21.

268.28/264.17 THE LOST CHORD   "The Lost Chord" is a well-known song by Adelaide A. Proctor and Sir Arthur Sullivan. It begins "Seated one day at the organ, I was weary and ill at ease." For words and music, see Chapple, *Heart Songs*, pp. 294–97.

269.13/265.1 MET HIM PIKE HOSES   Metempsychosis; see entry 64.18.

269.13/265.1 PAUL DE KOCK   See entry 64.39.

269.20/265.8 DAUGHTER OF THE REGIMENT   Italian composer Gaetano Donizetti (1797–1848) wrote an opera entitled *La Figlia del Reggimento* ("The Daughter of the Regiment"). The Dublin newspapers of June 16, 1904, announced that this opera was to be done by the Elster-Grime Company at the Queen's Theatre on the following night, Friday, June 17.

269.26/265.14 MY IRISH MOLLY, O   Hodgart and Worthington list this as an allusion to "My Irish Molly, O," by Jerome and Schwartz. But S. Spaeth (*History of Pop. Music in Amer.*, p. 331) gives the date of the William Jerome and Jean Schwartz song as 1905, so the allusion here is probably to the anonymous Irish ballad "Irish Molly," which several times uses the phrase "my Irish Molly, O." Words may be found in *Irish Literature*, VIII, 3288–89.

269.31/265.19   IDOLORES, A QUEEN, DELORES   See entry 256.9.

270.5/265.35 WHEN LOVE ABSORBS MY ARDENT SOUL   Here and on p. 270.29/266.19 are lines from the song "Love and War," alluded to earlier, and Bloom thinks of the title on p. 270.31/266.21. See entry 256.21.

270.13/266.3 YOU'D BURST THE TYMPANUM OF HER EAR . . . WITH AN ORGAN LIKE YOURS   See entry 521.23.

271.20/267.10 THE HARP THAT ONCE   This alludes to Moore's "The Harp That Once Through Tara's Halls"; see entry 168.1.

271.25/267.15 M'APPARI   This alludes to Lionel's aria "M'Appari" in Flotow's opera *Martha*; see entry 256.26. The opening lines of the Italian version of the aria are quoted correctly on p. 271.33/ 267.23.

271.28/267.18 A LAST FAREWELL   Hodgart and Worthington list this as an allusion to "A Last Farewell (Epilog)," but this seems unlikely, especially since this refers to a print on the wall of the bar.

271.38/267.28 AH, SURE MY DANCING DAYS ARE DONE   The *ODEP* lists several instances of this proverbial phrase, including *Romeo and Juliet*, I, v, 35, and James Kelly's *Proverbs* (1721). It is also in Swift's *Polite Conversation*, first conversation, in which Lady Answerall says of Lady Dimple, "Her dancing Days are over" (p. 78).

272.9/267.41 SONNAMBULA   The tenor air Richie means is "Tutto è sciolto," from Bellini's *La Sonnambula*; see p. 272.32/268.21 and entry 256.24.

272.10/267.42 JOE MAAS . . . M'GUCKIN   Joseph Maas (1847–86) was a well-known English tenor. He began his career as a chorister at Rochester Cathedral and made his debut in London in 1871. He was principal tenor of the Carl Rosa Company for several years. Among his best parts was Raoul in Meyerbeer's *Les Huguenots*. Maas was popular for his fine voice, said to resemble Giuglini's, rather than for his dramatic power. Dublin born Barton M'Guckin (1852–1913) began his career as a chorister at Armagh Cathedral. He made his stage debut under Carl Rosa at Birmingham on September 10, 1880, and his Dublin debut on May 9, 1881. Joyce's father's recollections of M'Guckin may be found in Scholes and Kain, *The Workshop of Daedalus*, p. 121.

272.16/268.6 DOWN AMONG THE DEAD MEN   Hodgart and Worthington's reference here to " 'Down Among the Dead Men' (Here's a Health unto His Majesty) by Dyer and Savile" is confusing. Dyer and Saville did do a song entitled "Here's a Health unto His Majesty," but it is not the same as "Down Among the Dead Men," and it is not alluded to here. The allusion here is to the anonymous English drinking song "Down Among the Dead Men," which begins, "Here's a health to the King, and a lasting peace,/ To faction an end, to wealth increase." The chorus says, "Down among the dead men,/ Down among the dead men,/ Down, down, down, down,/ Down among the dead men let him lie" (the *him* being anyone who will not drink with the toasters). For words and music, see G. Bantock, *One Hundred Songs of England*, pp. 50–51.

272.17/268.7 SWEETS TO THE   This apparently alludes to Queen Gertrude's statement as she scatters flowers on the dead Ophelia, "Sweets to the sweet" (*Ham.*, V, i, 266).

272.32/268.21 ALL IS LOST NOW   This alludes to "Tutto è sciolto"; see entry 256.24. The allusion is repeated in Bloom's variations on the phrase "all is lost" in the following paragraphs.

272.38/268.27 ECHO. HOW SWEET THE ANSWER   This alludes to Thomas Moore's song "Echo," which begins, "How sweet the answer Echo makes."

272.42/268.31 IN SLEEP SHE WENT TO HIM   Bloom is thinking of the sleepwalking in Bellini's *La Sonnambula*. See entry 256.24.

273.7/268.38 STILL HARPING ON HIS DAUGHTER   During his conversation with Hamlet, Polonius says to himself, "Still harping on my daughter" (*Ham.*, II, ii, 188).

273.8/268.39 WISE CHILD THAT KNOWS HER FATHER   This misquotes a passage from *The Merchant of Venice*; Simon Dedalus said the same earlier—see entry 88.19.

273.24/269.13 A HEART BOWED DOWN   "The Heart Bowed Down" is from Irish composer William Balfe's (1803–70) opera *The Bohemian Girl*, the text of which was by English theatrical manager and verse writer Alfred Bunn. The opera had its première at Drury Lane, London, on November 27, 1843. This song is sung by Count Arnheim in act II and begins, "The heart bowed down by weight of woe,/ To weakest hopes will cling." For words and music, see Chapple, *Heart Songs*, pp. 190–91.

273.30/269.19 WHEN FIRST I SAW THAT FORM ENDEARING   This is from "M'Appari"; see entry 256.26. The allusions to this song are continued in the italicized lines on the following pages, down to p. 276.6/271.34.

274.6/269.37 LOVE'S OLD SWEET SONG   See entry 63.31.

274.13/270.2 MY HEAD IT SIMPLY . . . YOUR HEAD IT SIMPLY SWURLS   See entry 62.36.

274.19/270.8 HANDS FELT FOR THE OPULENT   Another echo of *Sweets of Sin*; see entry 236.5.

274.28/270.17 JENNY LIND SOUP   Jenny Lind (1820–87), "the Swedish nightingale," was one of the most famous sopranos of her day. None of the biographical sources about her which I have seen mentions "Jenny Lind soup," though Edward Wagenknecht, in his *Jenny Lind* (Boston: Houghton Mifflin Company, 1930), does briefly discuss her "complete indifference to the pleasures of the table" and her abstemiousness of diet (pp. 116–17).

274.36/270.24 TIPPING HER TEPPING HER TAPPING HER TOPPING HER Hodgart and Worthington list this as an allusion to the opening chorus of Gilbert and Sullivan's *Iolanthe* (1882), in which the Fairies sing "Tripping hither, tripping hither,/ Nobody knows why or whither;/ We must dance and we must sing/ Round about our fairy ring!" However, the allusion seems doubtful to me.

275.23/271.10 WAITING According to S. Spaeth (*History of Popular Music in America*, p. 166), "Waiting," by Ellen H. Flagg and Harrison Millard, was one of the popular songs of 1867. The only copy of a song by this title which I have found is in the paperback *Harding's Nightingale Song Book*. No information about author, composer, or date is included; the song has three four-line stanzas. It begins, "The stars shine on his pathway, the trees bend back their leaves/ To guide them to the meadow among the golden sheaves,/ Where stand I, longing, loving, and listening as I wait,/ To the nightingale's wild singing, singing, sweet singing to its mate." The third stanza says, "I hear his foot-fall's music, I feel his presence near,/ All my soul, responsive, answers and tells me he is here;/ O, stars, shine out your brightest, O, nightingale, sing sweet,/ To guide him to me, waiting, and speed his flying feet" (no. 12, p. 278).

275.27/271.14 IN OLD MADRID This refers to "In Old Madrid," a song by G. Clifton Bingham and Henry Trotere (real name Henry Trotter). The song begins, "Long years ago, in old Madrid, Where softly sighs of love the light guitar, Two sparkling eyes a lattice hid, Two eyes as darkly bright as love's own star!" Words and music can be found in Chapple, *Heart Songs*, pp. 306–9.

275.27/271.14 DOLORES SHEDOLORES See entry 256.9.

276.18/272.5 MONUMENTS OF SIR JOHN GRAY, HORATIO ONEHANDLED NELSON, REVEREND FATHER THEOBALD MATTHEW Each of these has been mentioned earlier in *Ulysses*: on Gray's statue, see entry 94.8; on Nelson and Nelson's Pillar, see entries 148.9 and 95.9; on Father Mathew's statue, see entry 95.39 (*Mathew* is the correct spelling of his name).

276.39/272.26 'TWAS RANK AND FAME This alludes to the ballad from Balfe's *The Rose of Castille* first alluded to on p. 130.28/ 129.19. There are several allusions in the following lines to the opening lines of the song—quoted in entry 130.28—and to its last two lines: "Yes, false one, we had better part,/ Since love lives not in thee."

277.9/272.36   WE NEVER SPEAK AS WE PASS BY   This alludes to Frank Egerton's song "We Never Speak As We Pass By" (1882). It is a sentimental song about infidelity—about a man whose wife was tempted away from him. The chorus says, "We never speak as we pass by, Although a tear bedims her eye; I know she thinks of her past life, When we were loving man and wife." For words and music, see S. Spaeth, *Read 'Em and Weep*, pp. 71–72.

277.10/272.36   RIFT IN THE LUTE   This alludes to the song "The Rift in the Lute," from Tennyson's "Merlin and Vivien." In that poem, Vivien sings the song to Merlin to encourage him to trust her. Singing of "unfaith" and its effects on love, she says, "It is the little rift within the lute,/ That by and by will make the music mute,/ And ever widening slowly silence all" (ll. 390–92).

277.17/273.2   BARRACLOUGH'S VOICE PRODUCTION   This refers to a Dublin voice teacher; Thom's *Dublin Directory* (1904) lists Arthur Barraclough, professor of singing, at 24 Pembroke Street, lower (p. 1803).

277.23/273.8   THOU LOST ONE   From "M'Appari"; see entry 256.26.

277.27/273.12   CORPUS PARADISUM   This seems to blend two bits of liturgical Latin Bloom has heard during the day; see pp. 80.34/ 79.31 and 104.25/103.13.

278.32/274.16   BLUMENLIED   As Hodgart and Worthington suggest, this probably refers to Heinrich Heine's well-known poem that begins "Du bist wie eine Blume." The poem has been frequently translated and set to music.

279.4/274.28   A MOONLIGHT NIGHTCALL   Hodgart and Worthington list this as an allusion to "Goodbye, Sweetheart, Goodbye" (on which see entry 256.13), but I find no line similar to this in that song. If there is any allusion here, it is to the same thing that is alluded to on p. 256.12/252.12. See entry 256.12.

279.19/275.1   ELIJAH IS COM   See entry 151.15.

279.23/275.4   O, MAIRY LOST THE PIN OF HER . . . TO KEEP IT UP   See entry 78.38.

279.31/275.12   SAUCE FOR THE GANDER   "What's sauce for the goose is sauce for the gander" is proverbial and is listed in the *ODEP*. It occurs in Swift's *Polite Conversation*, second conversation, when Neverout says, "What's Sawce for a Goose, is Sawce for a Gander." Partridge cites John Ray's *Proverbs* (1670) and quotes Ray as saying, "This is a woman's proverb" (p. 158).

279.38/275.20 THIS IS THE JINGLE THAT JOGGLED AND JINGLED   The rhythm here suggests an allusion to the nursery rhyme "The House That Jack Built," which is clearly alluded to twice later in *Ulysses*; see entry 391.36.

280.21/276.2 MATCHAM OFTEN THINKS OF THE LAUGHING WITCH   See entry 68.39.

280.23/276.4 MUSIC HATH CHARMS SHAKESPEARE SAID   Bloom is mistaken here. Apparently the earliest writer to use this now common phrase was William Congreve (1670–1729) in *The Mourning Bride* (1697), I, i, 1.

280.24/276.5 QUOTATIONS EVERY DAY IN THE YEAR   Of this, Wm. Schutte says (*JS*, p. 126), "The last half of the nineteenth century produced many such compilations. One wonders if perhaps Joyce had seen *The Shakespeare Calendar, or Wit and Wisdom for Every Day in the Year*, ed. William C. Richards, New York, Putnam, 1850."

280.25/276.5 TO BE OR NOT TO BE   From Hamlet's soliloquy, *Hamlet*, III, i, 56.

280.26/276.7 IN GERARD'S ROSERY OF FETTER LANE . . .   See entry 202.9.

280.27/276.8 DO. BUT DO   The context here recalls p. 202.9/199.32; see entry 202.9.

281.8/276.30 HOW WALTER BAPTY LOST HIS VOICE . . .   R. M. Adams (*SS*, p. 73) points out that Bapty (d. 1915) was an actual Dubliner— a professor of music and one of the main organizers of the first Feis Ceoil but Adams finds no basis in fact for the uncomplimentary story told about him here.

281.22/277.2 LOVELY SEASIDE GIRLS . . . YOUR HEAD IT SIMPLY   See entry 62.36.

281.27/277.7 YASHMAK   R. M. Adams (*SS*, p. 113) says this word was "doubtless brought to Joyce's attention as the title of an 1897 musical comedy." Allardyce Nicoll's *History of English Drama* lists *The Yashmak*, by Cecil Raleigh, written in collaboration with Sir S. Hicks, music by N. Lambelet, first done at the Shaftesbury Theatre, London, March 31, 1897 (V, 534).

281.30/277.10 WELL, IT'S A SEA. CORPUSCLE ISLANDS   R. M. Adams (*SS*, p. 150) points out that in the University of Buffalo MSS of this episode, this read "Blood is a sea, sea with purple islands," which makes an allusion to Phineas Fletcher more obvious. Phineas Fletcher's (1582–1650) chief work was an allegorical poem on the body, mind, virtues, and vices, entitled *The Purple Island* (1633).

281.34/277.13 WHAT ARE THE WILD WAVES SAYING   This alludes to the song "What Are the Wild Waves Saying" (1850), with words by J. E. Carpenter and music by Stephen Ralph Glover. It is a duet in which a brother and sister hear in the waves "the voice of the great Creator." For words and music, see Reddall, *Songs That Never Die*, pp. 60–61.

281.38/277.17 BOLD LARRY O'   See entry 58.7.

282.11/277.31 MINUET OF DON GIOVANNI   This refers to the minuet in the finale of act I of Mozart's opera. The scene is the ballroom in Don Giovanni's palace, and the Don hopes to win Zerlina during the dance. As W. Y. Tindall points out (*RG*, p. 187), this minuet "implies seduction, offstage."

282.22/278.1 QUIS EST HOMO: MERCADANTE   This suggests that Bloom mistakenly thinks of Mercadante as the composer of the *Stabat Mater*. See entries 82.15 and 82.16.

282.25/278.4 DANDY TAN SHOE OF DANDY   Hodgart and Worthington list this as an allusion to "Handy Spandy," a music hall song by Tabrar, but I have not located a copy of the song.

282.32/278.10 RHAPSODIES OF LISZT'S, HUNGARIAN   See entry 256.38.

282.36/278.14 PAUL DE KOCK   See entry 64.39.

282.39/278.17 QUI SDEGNO   "Qui sdegno," as Hodgart and Worthington point out, is the opening phrase of the Italian translation of Sarastro's aria "In diesen heiligen Hallen" in act II of Mozart's opera *Die Zauberflöte* (*The Magic Flute*).

282.40/278.18 THE CROPPY BOY   On "The Croppy Boy," see entry 91.1 and the Appendix. The next several pages of *Ulysses* are filled with allusions to the song, as comparison with the text of the song in the Appendix will show. The allusions occur on pp. 282.42/278.20; 283.18/278.38; 283.27/279.5; 283.31–34/279.9–12; 284.3–5/279.23–25; 284.13–17/279.33–36; 285.1–3/280.19–21; 285.7/280.24; 285.12/280.29; 285.15/280.32; 285.24–27/280.41–281.2; 286.1–3/281.17–19; 286.5/281.21; 286.10/281.26; 286.19/281.35; 286.27/281.42; 286.39/282.11; and 287.6–7/282.19–21.

283.14/278.34 IN A CAVE OF THE DARK MIDDLE EARTH. EMBEDDED ORE   See entry 257.3.

283.35/279.13 ANSWERS   The magazine *Answers* was one of the great successes of journalist Alfred Harmsworth (on whom see entry 139.5). He founded the weekly in 1888, and within five years it recorded net weekly sales of more than a million copies. *Willing's Press Guide . . . 1905* (for 1904) lists it as a weekly appearing on Tuesday (for Saturday) at a cost of 1*d*.

283.37/279.15 LAY OF THE LAST MINSTREL HE THOUGHT IT WAS   Sir Walter Scott wrote a poem entitled *The Lay of the Last Minstrel* (1805).

284.8/279.28 CORPUSNOMINE   While this is no doubt prompted by "The Croppy Boy," ll. 14–15, it also recalls Bloom's thoughts during Paddy Dignam's funeral, e.g., p. 103.27/102.15. A similar instance occurred on p. 277.27/273.12.

284.27/280.4 HOME SWEET HOME   The well-known "Home, Sweet Home" was written by John Howard Payne and set to an air adapted by Sir Henry Rowley Bishop. Words and music can be found in most collections of popular songs. See, for example, Helen K. Johnson, *Our Familiar Songs*, pp. 43–44.

284.32/280.9 MUSIC HATH JAWS   This is a parody of "music hath charms"; see entry 280.23.

284.36/280.13 TOLD HER WHAT SPINOZA SAYS IN THAT BOOK OF POOR PAPA'S   Baruch Spinoza (1632–77) was a Dutch Jewish philosopher, whose monistic thought was largely a product of his thorough knowledge of the Jewish scriptures. What Bloom told Molly is never explained (though she thinks of it on p. 769.15/754.18), but it probably came from the book on his bookshelf, *Thoughts from Spinoza* (p. 708.26/693.14).

284.40/280.17 GOD MADE THE COUNTRY MAN THE TUNE   This is Bloom's parody of the well-known "God made the country and man made the town," from William Cowper's *The Task* (1785), Book I, l. 749.

284.41/280.18 MET HIM PIKE HOSES   Metempsychosis; see entry 64.18.

285.2/280.20 WE ARE THE BOYS OF WEXFORD   "The Boys of Wexford," by R. D. Joyce; see entry 129.13.

285.9/280.26 BIG BEN HIS VOICE UNFOLDED   This probably alludes to the Ghost's words to Hamlet when he says, "lend thy serious hearing/ To what I shall unfold," and "I could a tale unfold" (*Ham.*, I, v, 5–6, 15).

285.13/280.30 WHO FEARS TO SPEAK OF NINETEEN FOUR   This is Bloom's variation on "Who fears to speak of Ninety-Eight," the opening line of Ingram's "The Memory of the Dead." See entry 241.12.

285.20/280.37 THOSE GIRLS, THOSE LOVELY   This is apparently from Boylan's song; see entry 62.36.

285.20/280.37 BY THE SAD SEA WAVES   This alludes to a song entitled "By the Sad Sea Waves," by J. Benedict. The song begins,

"By the sad sea waves I listen while they moan A lament o'er graves
of hope and pleasure gone." Words and music can be found in
Chapple, *Heart Songs*, pp. 490–91.

285.37/281.11 SONGS WITHOUT WORDS   German composer Felix
Mendelssohn (1809–47) did eight sets of "Songs Without Words"
(1832–45), which are among his best-known piano works.

285.39/281.13 UNDERSTAND ANIMALS TOO THAT WAY. SOLOMON DID
I know of no specific statement in the Bible that Solomon under-
stood animals well. Perhaps Bloom is basing this on the occasional
use of animal lore in the book of Proverbs, which is attributed to
Solomon. See, for example, Proverbs 6:6 and 30:24 ff.

286.11/281.27 HER HEAVING EMBON   An echo from *Sweets of Sin*;
see entry 236.5.

286.14/281.30 THE BRIGHT STARS FADE . . . THE MORN   From "Good-
bye, Sweetheart, Goodbye"; see entry 256.13.

286.14/281.30 O ROSE! CASTILLE   An allusion to *The Rose of Castille*; see entry 134.19.

286.31/282.4 WALK, WALK, WALK   Though it is doubtful, this may
allude to the same song Stephen alludes to through these words
later in *Ulysses*—"Shule Aroon." See entry 688.3.

286.34/282.6 O'ER RYE-HIGH BLUE. BLOOM   An allusion to "When
the Bloom Is on the Rye"; see entry 256.6.

286.40/282.12 DOLOR! O HE DOLORES   From "O My Delores"; see
entry 256.9.

287.17/282.30 LABLACHE   Luigi Lablache (1794–1858) was an Italian bass singer whose mother was Irish. His talent appeared at an
early age, and he was proclaimed all over Europe as a marvelous
basso cantante.

287.33/283.5 RIFT IN THE LUTE   See entry 277.10.

288.5/283.18 THE LAST ROSE OF SUMMER   (The allusion is repeated
on p. 288.8/283.21.) On "The Last Rose of Summer," see entry
256.34.

288.13/283.26 HER HAND THAT ROCKS THE CRADLE RULES THE . . . THAT
RULES THE WORLD   American lawyer and verse writer William
Ross Wallace (*ca.* 1819–81) is the author of "The Hand That Rocks
the Cradle is the Hand That Rules the World." Each of the poem's
four stanzas ends with the statement "For the hand that rocks the
cradle/ Is the hand that rules the world." For the poem, see Ralph
L. Woods, *A Treasury of the Familiar*, pp. 326–27.

288.17/283.30 LIONELLEOPOLD   This, a combination of Lionel and
Leopold, alludes to Flotow's *Martha*. Lionel is the tenor who sings
"M'Appari." See entries 117.34 and 256.26.

288.18/283.31   WITH SWEETS OF SIN WITH FRILLIES FOR RAOUL   From *Sweets of Sin;* see entry 236.5.

288.18/283.31   MET HIM PIKE HOSES   Metempsychosis; see entry 64.18.

288.23/283.35   THE WAY OF A MAN WITH A MAID   Kipling begins the fifth stanza of his poem "The Long Trail" with the lines, "There be triple ways to take, of the eagle or the snake,/ Or the way of a man with a maid." But apparently the original source for this now common phrase is Proverbs 30: 18–19: "There be three things which are too wonderful for me, yea, four which I know not: The way of an eagle in the air; the way of a serpent upon a rock; the way of a ship in the midst of the sea; and the way of a man with a maid."

288.31/284.1   SEATED ALL DAY AT THE ORGAN   From "The Lost Chord"; see entry 268.28.

288.32/284.2   MAUNDER ON FOR HOURS   Richard M. Kain has suggested to me that this alludes to John Henry Maunder (1858–1920), organist, choirmaster, and composer, of whose compositions the *Oxford Companion to Music* (ninth ed., London, 1955) says that they "still aid the devotions of undemanding congregations in less sophisticated areas" (p. 614, *s.v.* Maunder).

289.1/284.13   SIMONLIONEL   This alludes to Flotow's *Martha*, through Lionel, the tenor who sings "M'Appari." See entries 117.34 and 256.26, and cf. entry 288.17.

289.12/284.24   ONE LAST, ONE LONELY, LAST SARDINE OF SUMMER   This alludes to "The Last Rose of Summer." See entry 256.34.

289.26/284.37   YASHMAK   See entry 281.27.

289.37/285.7   ALL IS LOST NOW   This alludes to "Tutto è sciolto"; see entry 256.24.

289.38/285.8   LONG JOHN. WAKEN THE DEAD   This alludes to the anonymous old hunting song "John Peel." It begins "D' ye ken John Peel with his coat so gay, D' ye ken John Peel at the break o' the day?" The refrain says that Peel's early-morning cry to hunting "would awaken the dead." For words and music, see Hatton and Faning, *Songs of England*, III, 186–87.

289.39/285.9   POOR LITTLE NOMINEDOMINE   This alludes to "The Croppy Boy," which is also alluded to on p. 290.2–4/285.14–16. See entry 91.1 and the Appendix.

289.41/285.11   AS WE MARCH WE MARCH ALONG, MARCH ALONG   If this is a refrain from an actual song, I have not located it; the context suggests that Bloom is merely making up a rhythmic phrase. Hodgart and Worthington do not list this.

290.8/285.19 WHEN FIRST HE SAW THAT FORM ENDEARING   From "M'Appari"; see entry 256.26.

290.14/285.25 NEVER, WELL HARDLY EVER   In act I of Gilbert and Sullivan's *H.M.S. Pinafore* (1878), Captain Corcoran and the crew sing a song which says: *Capt.*: "I am never known to quail/ At the fury of a gale,/ And I'm never, never sick at sea!" *All*: "What, never?" *Capt.*: "No, never!" *All*: "What, *never*?" *Capt.*: "Hardly ever!" But more pertinent to the present context is the variation on this song which occurs late in act II, when the following exchange occurs: *Capt. Corcoran*: "I shall marry with a wife,/ In my humble rank of life!/ And you, my own, are she—/ I must wander to and fro;/ But wherever I may go,/ I shall never be untrue to thee!" *All*: "What, never?" *Capt.*: "No, never!" *All*: "What, *never*?" *Capt.*: "Hardly ever!"

290.15/285.26 HOME SWEET HOME   On "Home, Sweet Home," see entry 284.27.

290.18/285.29 LIONEL . . . HENRY LIONEL LEOPOLD   This alludes to Lionel, the tenor who sings "M'Appari" in Flotow's *Martha*. See entries 117.34 and 256.26, and cf. entry 288.17.

290.27/285.38 THEY CHINKED THEIR CLINKING GLASSES   This alludes to "The Thirty-Two Counties"; see entry 257.18.

290.29/285.40 LAST ROSE OF SUMMER   On "The Last Rose of Summer," see entry 256.34.

290.29/285.40 ROSE OF CASTILLE   On *The Rose of Castille*, see entry 134.19.

290.34/286.3 ROBERT EMMET'S LAST WORDS   On Emmet's death and burial, see entry 114.18. Helen Landreth (*op. cit.*, entry 114.18) points out that there are many versions of the speech Emmet delivered in the dock after the verdict had been found against him and before the death sentence was passed, September 19, 1803, though the "unforgettable last paragraph" is agreed upon. She gives the close of the speech as follows: "Let no man write my epitaph; for as no man who knows my motives now dares vindicate them, let not prejudice or ignorance asperse them. Let them rest in obscurity and peace. Let my memory be left in oblivion, and my tomb remain uninscribed, until other times and other men can do justice to my character. When my country takes her place among the nations of the earth, then, and not till then, let my epitaph be written. I have done" (Landreth, p. 338). Most of this final sentence was quoted in the September 19, 1903, *United Irishman*, in an article beginning, "On Sunday it will be exactly one hundred years since Robert Emmet was hanged and beheaded . . ." (p. 1,

col. a). The *United Irishman* followed in some detail the attempts
to determine Emmet's burial place, which were taking place in
1903–4. The allusions to Emmet's final speech are continued on
pp. 291.3, 8, 10, 12/286.14, 19, 21, 23.

290.34/286.3 SEVEN LAST WORDS. OF MEYERBEER THAT IS   Meyerbeer
was the author of *Les Huguenots* (see entry 168.20), but not of a
setting of *The Seven Last Words*. See entry 82.16 and cf. entry
661.8.

290.36/286.5 TRUE MEN LIKE YOU MEN   This alludes to Ingram's
"The Memory of the Dead"; see entries 257.17 and 241.12.

290.40/286.9 TSCHINK. TSCHUNK   This alludes to "The Thirty-Two
Counties"; see entry 257.18.

290.41/286.10 AN UNSEEN STRIPLING STOOD IN THE DOOR   This alludes
to "The Croppy Boy"; see entry 91.1 and the Appendix.

292.3/287.3 HE NEAR DROVE HIS GEAR INTO MY EYE This echoes Ulysses' blinding the Cyclops with a burning olive stake in book IX of the *Odyssey*.

292.23/287.21 A BIT OFF THE TOP This probably alludes to a music hall song of the day—Murray and Leigh's "A Little Bit Off the Top Will Do for Me," which was sung and made popular by Harry Bedford. Each verse of the song describes a different situation and provides a different meaning for the chorus, which begins, "Carve a little bit off the top for me, For me!" For words and music, see the *Song Dex Treasury of Humorous and Nostalgic Songs*, I, 115.

292.27/287.25 HOW ARE THE MIGHTY FALLEN In David's lament after hearing of the deaths of Saul and Jonathan, he twice says, "How are the mighty fallen" (II Samuel 1:19, 25).

293.38/288.36 IN INNISFAIL THE FAIR THERE LIES A LAND . . . Innisfail is one of the many poetic names for Ireland; it is usually explained as meaning "Isle of Destiny." Kiernan's pub was in St. Michan's parish. There is considerable internal evidence that this paragraph is based largely on James Clarence Mangan's translation of the poem "Prince Alfrid's Itinerary through Ireland." I quote the portions of the poem that seem to be used most directly, but the entire poem deserves comparison with this paragraph.

I found in Innisfail the fair,
In Ireland, while in exile there,
Women of worth, both grave and gay men,
Many clerics and many laymen.   (stanza one)

I travelled its fruitful provinces round,
And in every one of the five I found,
Alike in church and in palace hall,
Abundant apparel, and food for all.   (stanza two)

*   *   *

I also found in Armagh the splendid,
Meekness, wisdom, and prudence blended,
Fasting, as Christ hath recommended,
And noble councillors untranscended.   (stanza four)

I found in Munster unfettered of any,
Kings and queens, and poets a many . . . . (stanza seven)

*   *   *

I found in Connaught the just, redundance
Of riches, milk in lavish abundance;
Hospitality, vigor, fame,
In Cruachan's land of heroic name.   (stanza eight)
    [Mangan annotates "Cruachan, or
      Croghan, was the name of the royal
      palace of Connaught."]

*   *   *

I found in Leinster the smooth and sleek,
From Dublin to Slewmargy's peak,
Flourishing pastures, valor, health,
Long-living worthies, commerce, wealth. (stanza twelve)
      [Mangan annotates "Slewmargy, a mountain
        in Queen's County, near the river
        Barrow."]

The poem has fifteen four-line stanzas.
293.39/288.37   THERE SLEEP THE MIGHTY DEAD AS IN LIFE THEY SLEPT
This alludes to the fact that the corpses in St. Michan's crypt do

not deteriorate, but are somehow strangely preserved, perhaps by the atmosphere. This phenomenon is described in almost every handbook to Dublin, but one of the most vivid and detailed descriptions of the state of the corpses is in Mr. and Mrs. S. C. Hall's *Ireland: Its Scenery, Character, &c.* (London, 1842), II, 312.

294.4/289.3 THE WAFTY SYCAMORE, THE LEBANONIAN CEDAR, THE EXALTED PLANETREE   These three trees are all mentioned in the Bible, and the *Lebanonian Cedar* specifically suggests a biblical allusion. *Planetree*, however, does not occur in the King James version, but does in the Douay. If this line reflects any single passage in the Bible, it is probably Ecclesiasticus (Sirach) 24:13–22, where Wisdom describes herself metaphorically as various trees, including the cedar of Lebanon and the planetree. Ecclesiasticus 24:17–20 was quoted in Latin in *A Portrait of the Artist*, p. 105.

294.16/289.15 THE SONS OF KINGS   Cf. entry 31.30.

294.18/289.16 A SHINING PALACE WHOSE CRYSTAL GLITTERING ROOF Though this refers primarily to the Dublin Fish and Vegetable Market, the description is probably meant to recall the Crystal Palace, erected in Hyde Park, London, in 1851 for the Great Exhibition. This building, constructed of iron, glass, and laminated wood, was moved to Sydenham in 1854 and was still standing in 1904.

294.20/289.18 ALL HERDS AND FATLINGS AND FIRST FRUITS OF THAT LAND The Israelites were directed to sacrifice first fruits to God, and words similar to these are commonly used in the Bible to describe the sacrifices. See Exodus 23:19 and Leviticus 23:10, 17.

294.21/289.19 O'CONNELL FITZSIMON TAKES TOLL OF THEM   This refers not to an Irish chieftain, but to the superintendent of the Dublin Food Market. Thom's *Dublin Directory* (1904) lists O'Connell Fitzsimon as the "Superintendent of Food Market" (p. 1347).

295.13/290.11 GARRYOWEN   "Garryowen" is the title of an anonymous Irish ballad about the Limerick suburb, Garryowen. T. C. Croker, *Popular Songs of Ireland*, prints seven verses and a chorus, with footnotes and a discussion of the song's backgrounds. Hoagland, *1000 Years*, gives four verses and chorus. Sparling's *Irish Minstrelsy* prints a text substantially identical with Croker's. The first verse and chorus are: "Let Bacchus's sons be not dismayed,/ But join with me each jovial blade;/ Come boose and sing, and lend your aid/ To help me with the chorus." *Cho.* "Instead of Spa, we'll drink brown ale,/ And pay the reckoning on the nail,/ No man for debt shall go to gaol/ From Garryowen in Glory" (*Irish Minstrelsy*, p. 478). See also entry 352.23.

295.15/290.13 CRUISKEEN LAWN "Cruiskeen Lawn" ("Little Full Jug") is an anonymous Irish folksong that exists in several versions and is included in act I of Benedict's *The Lily of Killarney* (on which see entry 92.6). The song usually begins "Let the farmer praise his grounds, Let the sportsman praise his hounds. . . ." For words and music, see Moffatt, *Minstrelsy of Ireland*, 3rd ed., pp. 136–37.

295.27/290.25 DOING THE RAPPAREE Irish poet and journalist Sir Charles Gavan Duffy (1816–1903) wrote a song entitled "The Irish Rapparees." As Duffy himself explains in a footnote, the Rapparees were Irish soldiers who stayed in Ireland, harassing the English army, after the defeat of James II. The song mentions *Rory* several times. The second verse says, "O never fear for Ireland, for she has soldiers still;/ For Rory's boys are in the wood, and Remy's on the hill;/ And never had poor Ireland more loyal hearts than these—/ May God be kind and good to them, the faithful Rapparees!/ The fearless Rapparees!/ The jewel were you, Rory, with your Irish Rapparees!" For text, see Sparling, *Irish Minstrelsy*, pp. 71–73.

295.27/290.25 RORY OF THE HILL This alludes to the song "Rory of the Hill," by Fenian journalist and poet Charles Joseph Kickham (1825–82), which celebrates a peasant farmer called "Rory of the Hill" who fought for Ireland's freedom. For a text, see Hoagland, pp. 525–26. And E. C. Brewer explains (*Historic Note-Book*) that Captain Rory o' the Hill was a name used by the writer of threatening letters to landlords, tenants who paid rents, and those who took the farms of evicted tenants, under the authority of the Irish Land League (*s.v.* Rory o' the Hill).

296.7/291.5 A ROUND TOWER See entry 164.34.

296.10/291.8 HIS ROCKLIKE KNEES WERE COVERED . . . THE MOUNTAIN GORSE This probably owes something to the description of the Cyclops as being "like a wooded peak of the towering hills" in book IX of the *Odyssey* (Butcher and Lang translation, p. 128).

296.17/291.15 A TEAR AND A SMILE This alludes to Thomas Moore's song "Erin, the Tear and the Smile in Thine Eyes," which begins, "Erin, the tear and the smile in thine eyes/ Blend like the rainbow that hangs in the skies!"

296.35/291.32 CUCHULIN, CONN OF THE HUNDRED BATTLES Cuchulain, legendary hero of Ulster, is one of the greatest and best-known Irish heroes; he is chief hero of the Red Branch Cycle of Irish literature. Conn Ced-cathach (Conn of the hundred fights) ruled as King of Ireland *ca.* A.D. 200; E. Curtis (*Hist. of Ire.*) says of

him, "In Conn, from whom Connacht gets its name, we have the
first of the line of the High Kings of Ireland, the Dal Cuinn or
'Race of Conn,' who lasted until 1022 and gave Ireland a centre of
national unity" (p. 4).

296.36/291.32 NIALL OF NINE HOSTAGES, BRIAN OF KINCORA, THE ARDRI
MALACHI   Curtis (*Hist. of Ire.*) says, "In Niall of the Nine
Hostages, who ruled at Tara from 380 to 405, appears the greatest
ruler of the race of Conn" (p. 5); Niall was progenitor of a line
of High Kings who were known until 1022 as the Ui Neill or
"descendants of Niall." Brian of Kincora is Brian Boru (or Boroimhe), on whom see entry 99.25; James Clarence Mangan translated a poem entitled "Kinkora" which begins, "O where, Kinkora!
is Brian the Great . . . ?"; Mangan's note says it is a "lamentation
for the fallen condition of Kinkora, the palace of that Monarch,
consequent on his death." The Ardri Malachi is Malachi II, Ard
Ree or High King of Ireland, on whom see entry 45.12.

296.37/291.33 ART MACMURRAGH, SHANE O'NEILL, FATHER JOHN MURPHY
Art Oge MacMurrough (1357–1417), king of Leinster, 1377–1417,
is called by Curtis (*Hist. of Ire.*) "the greatest of Donal's descendants and of the medieval chiefs of Ireland the one who most
ruined the English colony" (p. 122); he warred against Richard
II. Shane O'Neill, "the Proud" (*ca.* 1530–67), was the son of Conn
O'Neill, first earl of Tyrone, and Curtis says (*Hist. of Ire.*) he was
"the most uncompromising opponent of English rule in Ireland that
had yet appeared" (pp. 184–85); he invaded the Pale and burned
Armagh. Father John Murphy (1753–98), incensed by the burning
of the chapel at Boleyvogue near Enniscorthy, led his parishioners
in one of the first parts of the 1798 revolt.

296.38/291.34 OWEN ROE, PATRICK SARSFIELD, RED HUGH O'DONNELL
Owen Roe O'Neill (*ca.* 1590–1649) was in the Spanish service for
thirty years, and was summoned from the continent in 1642; he
led the old Irish contingency in support of Charles II and routed
the Parliamentary army under General Monro in June, 1646. On
Sarsfield, see entry 330.16. Hugh Roe O'Donnell, lord of Tyrcon-
nell (*ca.* 1571–1602), who was imprisoned by Sir John Perrot in
1587, escaped in 1591 and became leader of his clan; he tried to get
aid from Philip III of Spain, with no success; he died of poisoning.

296.39/291.35 RED JIM MACDERMOTT, SOGGARTH EOGHAN O'GROWNEY,
MICHAEL DWYER   Though I have learned little about him, Red
Jim MacDermott was apparently an Irish traitor. In his essay
"Stephens, Devoy, Tom Clarke," Desmond Ryan describes Red
Jim MacDermott as "the infamous spy and evil genius of the Fenian
organization for many years" (in *The Shaping of Modern Ireland,*

ed. Conor Cruise O'Brien [University of Toronto Press, 1960], p. 36). Soggarth Eoghan O'Growney is Father Eugene O'Growney (d. 1903), author of *Simple Lessons in Irish* and Professor of Irish at Maynooth College, who was one of the prime movers in the founding of the Gaelic League in 1893. Michael Dwyer (1771–1826), who was a leader in the 1798 rebellion in county Wicklow, was loosely affiliated with Emmet's insurrection in 1803; sentenced to transportation, he became high constable of Sydney, Australia (see *DNB*).

296.40/291.36 FRANCY HIGGINS, HENRY JOY M'CRACKEN, GOLIATH, HORACE WHEATLEY Francy Higgins is probably Francis Higgins, the Sham Squire; see entry 126.26. M'Cracken (1767–98) was a United Irishman who led the Antrim group in a short-lived rebellion in June, 1798; he was captured, court-martialed, and executed. Goliath is the Philistine giant David slew, I Samuel 17. Horace Wheatley was a music hall performer of the day, but I have not been able to find any detailed information about him.

296.41/291.37 THOMAS CONNEFF, PEG WOFFINGTON, THE VILLAGE BLACKSMITH I have not been able to identify Thomas Conneff (nor could R. M. Adams, *SS*, p. 156). Margaret (Peg) Woffington (*ca.* 1714–60) was a Dublin-born actress who won acclaim in London; she had been born in poverty and sold fruit and vegetables on the street (see *DNB*). The Village Blacksmith is the pious, hardworking character of Henry Wadsworth Longfellow's poem "The Village Blacksmith." But this probably also refers to the heroic, patriotic blacksmith of R. D. Joyce's poem "The Blacksmith of Limerick"; see *Irish Literature*, V, 1741–43.

296.42/291.38 CAPTAIN MOONLIGHT, CAPTAIN BOYCOTT, DANTE ALIGHIERI E. C. Brewer explains (*Historic Note-Book*) that "Captain Moonlight" was the name assumed by some unknown Irish chief of the Land League and Fenians who wrote warning letters to those who refused to join the League, and followed the letters with mutilation of the person's cattle or himself, or even with murder; Brewer says that fear of a visitation by Captain Moonlight dominated Ireland for several years. Captain Charles Cunningham Boycott (1832–97) was the agent for the estates of the Earl of Erne in county Mayo who, in 1880, refused to accept rents at rates fixed by tenants and was as a result "boycotted" by his servants and workers. On Dante, see the comment on St. Fursa in the following entry.

297.1/291.39 CHRISTOPHER COLUMBUS, S. FURSA, S. BRENDAN, MARSHALL MACMAHON On Columbus, see the comment on St. Brendan in this entry. St. Fursa, or Fursey (d. *ca.* 648) was born near Lough Corrib and established monasteries in England and Gaul; Joyce

says he is "described in the hagiographic calendar of Ireland as
the precursor of Dante Alighieri" (*CW*, p. 236). S. Brendan,
abbot (Brendan the Voyager, d. 577 or 583), is one of the most
famous Irish saints, though the legends of his voyages are now admitted to be fictitious; Joyce mentions the legend that St. Brendan
sailed from the Aran Islands to Florida a thousand years before
Columbus (*CW*, pp. 235–36). Marshall MacMahon (1808–93),
president of France, was of Irish descent; a *Freeman's Journal* editorial on his death (Oct. 18, 1893, p. 4, cols. g–h) said that he loved
France and Ireland equally.

297.2/291.40 CHARLEMAGNE, THEOBALD WOLFE TONE, THE MOTHER OF
THE MACCABEES   On Wolfe Tone, see entry 229.20. The Holy
Maccabees are the only Old Testament saints to figure in the
general calendar of the Western Church; seven children and their
mother, Salome, were martyred under Antiochus IV (Epiphanes),
ca. 168 B.C., for refusal to apostatize from Judaism; shrines to the
children and to their mother have been established (Butler, *Lives
of the Saints*, III, 237).

297.3/291.41 THE LAST OF THE MOHICANS, THE ROSE OF CASTILLE   On
The Last of the Mohicans, see entry 660.5. On *The Rose of Castille*,
see entry 134.19.

297.4/291.42 THE MAN FOR GALWAY, THE MAN THAT BROKE THE BANK
AT MONTE CARLO   Charles Lever (1806–72) wrote a song entitled
"The Man for Galway"; the chorus says, "With debts galore, but
fun far more;/ Oh, that's 'the man for Galway' "; for text, see
Hoagland, pp. 441–42. "The Man That Broke the Bank at Monte
Carlo" was a popular music hall song written in 1892 by Fred
Gilbert; words can be found in R. Woods, *A Treasury of the
Familiar*, pp. 548–49.

297.5/292.1 THE MAN IN THE GAP, THE WOMAN WHO DIDN'T, BENJA-
MIN FRANKLIN   On "the Man in the Gap," see entry 614.42.
"The Woman Who Didn't" is a variation on the title of a popular
novel of the day: Grant Allen (pseudonym of Canadian novelist
Charles Grant Blairfindie Allen, 1848–99) wrote a novel entitled
The Woman Who Did (1895) about a woman who engaged in
free love.

297.6/292.2 NAPOLEON BONAPARTE, JOHN L. SULLIVAN, CLEOPATRA
American prizefighter John L. Sullivan (1858–1918) was the son
of Irish parents; he won the heavyweight title from Paddy Ryan in
1882 and lost it to James J. Corbett in 1892; Sullivan's paternal
grandfather was onetime shillelagh champion of Ireland.

297.7/292.3 SAVOURNEEN DEELISH, JULIUS CAESAR, PARACELSUS, SIR

THOMAS LIPTON   "Savourneen Deelish" is a song by George Colman, the younger (1762–1836); for words and music, see Herbert
Hughes, *Irish Country Songs*, III, 33–35. Paracelsus (1493?–1541)
was a Swiss physician and alchemist; disdainful of past authorities,
his thought often mixed the scientific and the occult; he was one
of the initiators of modern chemistry. Sir Thomas Lipton (1850–
1931) was a Scottish merchant millionaire and yachting enthusiast;
he began with a small grocery in Glasgow and became a multi-
millionaire; he is most famous for his tea; he was knighted in 1898,
created a baronet in 1902.

297.8/292.4 WILLIAM TELL, MICHELANGELO, HAYES, MUHAMMED   On
William Tell, see entry 626.19. There have been several people
named Hayes who have been prominent in Irish history; I cannot
say which specific one, if any, Joyce has in mind.

297.9/292.5 THE BRIDE OF LAMMERMOOR, PETER THE HERMIT, PETER
THE PACKER   *The Bride of Lammermoor* (1819) is a novel by
Sir Walter Scott, the basis of Donizetti's opera *Lucia di Lammer-
moor* (1835). Peter the Hermit (*ca.* 1050–1115) was a French
preacher, famous for his preaching and his leadership in the First
Crusade. Peter the Packer was Lord Peter O'Brien, Lord Chief
Justice of Ireland, so called "for his hostility to land leagues and
nationalists, who accused him of 'packing' the juries and nick-
named him, 'Peter the Packer'" (Crone, *Concise Dict. of Irish
Biog.*); see also entry 488.6.

297.10/292.6 DARK ROSALEEN, PATRICK W. SHAKESPEARE, BRIAN CON-
FUCIUS   "My Dark Rosaleen" is a sixteenth-century Gaelic song,
which has been translated by several modern poets; Joyce alludes
to James Clarence Mangan's version in *Letters*, pp. 338 and 392–93;
for three versions, including Mangan's, see Hoagland, pp. 142–48.
On Shakespeare's "Irish connections," see entry 198.27. I have
found no Brian Confucius; this name and the two following seem
to refer to nonexistent characters who share the name of some
world-renowned figure; Confucius (551–478 B.C.) was a great
Chinese philosopher.

297.11/292.7 MURTAGH GUTENBERG, PATRICIO VELASQUEZ, CAPTAIN NEMO
The first two names here continue the pattern set with Brian Confucius (see the preceding entry). Johann Gutenberg (*ca.* 1397–
1468) is famous as the first European to print from movable type
cast in molds. Diego Velásquez (1599–1660) was a famous Spanish
painter. Captain Nemo is the captain of the submarine *Nautilus* in
Jules Verne's novel *Twenty Thousand Leagues Under the Sea*
(1870).

297.12/292.8 TRISTAN AND ISOLDE, THE FIRST PRINCE OF WALES, THOMAS
COOK AND SON   The love story of Tristram and Isolde is Irish
in origin, Isolde is herself Irish, and part of the scene of the work
is laid in Ireland; there have been many tellings, but the best
known are those of Malory, in *Morte D'Arthur*, and Wagner, in
Tristan und Isolde (1865). I do not understand the reference to
the "first Prince of Wales"; the term *prince* was used to describe
Welsh rulers at least as far back as the well known Howel Dda
(Howel the Good, d. 950); it was first appropriated by the English
royal family in 1301, when Edward III created his eldest surviv-
ing son, Edward, the "Prince of Wales"; but there may be an
allusion here to Llywelyn ap Gruffydd (d. 1282), who in 1258
pointedly proclaimed himself Prince of Wales to show his independence of the English. Thomas Cook (1808–92) and his son John
Mason Cook (1834–99) were English pioneers in the travel and
tourist agency business.

297.13/292.9 THE BOLD SOLDIER BOY, ARRAH NA POGUE, DICK TURPIN
"The Bowld Sojer Boy" is a song by Samuel Lover; see entry
588.24. *Arrah-na-Pogue or, the Wicklow Wedding* (1864) is a
play by Irish playwright Dion Boucicault (1820?–90); the title
means "Arrah of the kiss." Richard Turpin (1706–39) was a famous
English highwayman and robber.

297.14/292.10 LUDWIG BEETHOVEN, THE COLLEEN BAWN, WADDLER HEALY
The Colleen Bawn or, The Brides of Garryowen (1860) is the
title of a play by Irish playwright Dion Boucicault; "The Colleen
Bawn" is also the title of a song sung in *The Lily of Killarney* (see
entry 92.6), which was based on Boucicault's play; for words to
the song, see *Walton's Treasury of Irish Songs and Ballads*, p. 142.
R. M. Adams says that "Waddler" Healy may be the Very Reverend John Healy, Archbishop of Tuam (1841–1918), and quotes
a passage from the *Life* of Healy which describes him as " 'inclined
to waddle in his gait' " (*SS*, p. 154). But it could also be Timothy
Michael Healy (1855–1931), who "waddled" in his politics, beginning as a Parnellite and becoming an anti-Parnellite.

297.15/292.11 ANGUS THE CULDEE, DOLLY MOUNT, SYDNEY PARADE, BEN
HOWTH   Angus the Culdee was an Irish poet who flourished
about A.D. 800; see D. Hyde's *Literary History of Ireland*, esp. pp.
412 ff. The last three items in this entry are not people, but places,
in or near Dublin. Dollymount is a section northeast of the city,
beyond Clontarf. Sydney Parade is in the southeast section of the
city and is the scene of the death of Mrs. Sinico in "A Painful
Case." Ben Howth refers to the Hill of Howth, northeast of the

city, *ben* deriving from the Gaelic *beann*, a peak or pinnacle.

297.16/292.12 VALENTINE GREATRAKES, ADAM AND EVE, ARTHUR WEL-
LESLEY   Valentine Greatrakes (1629–83) was an Irishman from
county Waterford who was known as "The Stroker," from his
claim to be able to cure scrofula by stroking with his hand; several
eminent men saw and attested his cures. "Adam and Eve" may refer
to Adam and Eve's tavern in Dublin, on which see entry 688.37. Arthur Wellesley was the Duke of Wellington; see entry 332.23.

297.17/292.13 BOSS CROKER, HERODOTUS, JACK THE GIANTKILLER, GAU-
TAMA BUDDHA   American politician Richard ("Boss") Croker
(1841–1922) was born in county Cork, Ireland; he was head of
Tammany Hall political machine in New York City from 1886
to 1902. Jack the Giant Killer is the hero of the well-known nursery
story; in the English version he was the son of a Cornwall farmer
in the days of King Arthur who rid his land of giants.

297.18/292.14 LADY GODIVA, THE LILY OF KILLARNEY, BALOR OF THE EVIL
EYE   On Lady Godiva, see entry 163.27. On *The Lily of Killarney*, see entry 92.6. Balor of the Evil Eye is a character from
Irish myth; he was a Fomorian king whose eye vanquished those it
fell upon; see D. Hyde, *Literary History of Ireland*, pp. 290–91.

297.19/292.15 THE QUEEN OF SHEBA, ACKY NAGLE, JOE NAGLE, ALLE-
SANDRO VOLTA   The Queen of Sheba is probably best known for
her visit to King Solomon, which is described in I Kings 10 and
in II Chronicles 9; she came to test his reputed wisdom and found
that it exceeded even the reports she had heard. Of Acky and Joe
Nagle, R. M. Adams explains, "The reference is evidently to two
of three brothers Nagle who ran a well-known public house at
25 Earl Street North. Their names were James Joseph, John Joachim, and Patrick Nagle; and the first two were the men referred
to as 'Joe' and 'Acky' (from Joachim) Nagle" (*SS*, p. 154). Adams
goes on to give some further information, but does not cite any
source. Allesandro Volta (1745–1827) was an Italian physicist,
famous for his discoveries in electricity.

297.20/292.16 JEREMIAH O'DONOVAN ROSSA, DON PHILIP O'SULLIVAN
BEARE   O'Donovan Rossa (1831–1915), Fenian patriot and writer, was an uncompromising opponent of British rule in Ireland; he
was found guilty on a charge of treason-felony in 1865 and sentenced to life imprisonment; later released, he went to the U.S.,
where he edited the *United Irishman* in New York. Philip O'Sullivan Beare (1590?–1660?) was a historian born in county Cork,
but sent to Spain as a boy; his best-known work is *Historiae Catholicae Iberniae Compendium* (Libson, 1621); the *Don* here is ap-

parently a Spanish title, but it may cast a side glance at another
O'Sullivan of Beare—Donall (or Donough) O'Sullivan Beare (1560–
1618), uncle of the historian.

297.37/292.32 COD'S EYE   W. Y. Tindall (*RG*, p. 191) says that this
implies Jesus. The fish was used as a symbol of Christ among the
early Christians. Cf. entry 162.18.

297.40/292.35 O'BLOOM, THE SON OF RORY   There are many famous
Rorys in Irish history, but this probably refers to Roderick (Rory)
O'Connor (1116?–98), last high king of Ireland, during whose
reign the English first invaded Ireland.

297.42/292.37 THE OLD WOMAN OF PRINCE'S STREET   The *Freeman's
Journal*; see entry 137.23.

298.1/292.38 THE PLEDGEBOUND PARTY ON THE FLOOR OF THE HOUSE
Mabel P. Worthington (*PMLA*, LXXI,334) sees in this a possible
allusion to a parody of T. D. Sullivan's "God Save Ireland" (on
which see entry 163.16), which contains the phrase "the party on
the floor." Worthington quotes several lines of the parody, but
cites no source.

298.3/292.40 THE IRISH INDEPENDENT . . . FOUNDED BY PARNELL TO BE
THE WORKINGMAN'S FRIEND   R. Barry O'Brien (*Life of Parnell*)
says that the *Freeman's Journal* withdrew its support of Parnell
after his marriage to Mrs. O'Shea, and "on the defection of the
'Freeman's Journal' he set immediately to work to found a new
morning paper—'The Irish Daily Independent' " (II, 340; see also
II, 349, 350, 351).

298.21/293.17 MARTIN MURPHY, THE BANTRY JOBBER   This refers
to Bantry-born William Martin Murphy (1844–1921), wealthy
M.P., businessman, and owner of the *Irish Independent*. Murphy
was a consistent opponent of Parnell in the Irish Party split of December, 1890.

298.23/293.19 THANKS BE TO GOD THEY HAD THE START OF US   Hodgart and Worthington list this as an allusion to " 'One More Drink
for the Four of Us' (Glorius!)," which they say is mentioned in
Joyce's *Letters*, p. 206 (but I can find no such). I have not been
able to locate a printed copy of the song.

299.31/294.26 THE NOBLE TWIN BROTHERS BUNGIVEAGH AND BUNGARDI-
LAUN   On these brothers (though they are not twins), see
entry 70.24.

299.33/294.28 THE SONS OF DEATHLESS LEDA   According to Greek
myth, the twins Castor and Pollux were the sons of Leda by the
Swan.

299.38/294.33 AS TO THE MANNER BORN   In reply to Horatio's question about whether the carousing of the court and firing of the can-

non is a custom, Hamlet replies "Aye, marry, is't./ But to my mind, though I am native here/ And to the manner born, it is a custom/ More honored in the breach than the observance" (*Ham.*, I, iv, 13–16).

300.5/294.41 VICTORIA . . .   Though Joyce might have gotten Victoria's formal title from many places, it was readily available to him in Thom's *Dublin Directory* (1904), where King Edward's title is almost exactly what Joyce gives: ". . . of the United Kingdom of Great Britain and Ireland, and of the British dominions beyond the seas, king, Defender of the Faith, and Emperor of India" (p. 103). That Joyce used some such source is suggested by the fact that "and of the British dominions beyond the seas" was not part of Victoria's title. According to Sir Sidney Lee's biography of Edward VII, this phrase was first used when Edward acceded to the throne (*King Edward VII: A Biography* [New York, 1927], II, 7).

300.10/295.4 FROM THE RISING OF THE SUN TO THE GOING DOWN THEREOF Psalms 50:1 says, "The Mighty God, even the Lord, hath spoken, and called the earth from the rising of the sun unto the going down thereof." A very similar phrase is used in Psalms 113:3 and Malachi 1:11.

301.5/295.39 DEAD! SAYS ALF. HE IS NO MORE DEAD THAN YOU ARE . . . This anecdote occurs in Swift's *Polite Conversation*, first conversation, when Col. Atwit says, "But is it certain that Sir *John Blunderbuz* is dead at last?" and Lord Sparkish replies, "Yes, or else he's sadly wrong'd; for they have bury'd him" (p. 74). Ellmann records Joyce's father using this same joke (*JJ*, p. 11).

301.13/296.5 IN THE DARKNESS SPIRIT HANDS . . .   This paragraph parodies a seance and uses a variety of theosophical terms. Specific annotation seems unnecessary; further information on the various technical terms from theosophy can be found in the sources cited in entry 185.29.

301.26/296.18 HE HAD SEEN AS IN A GLASS DARKLY   I Corinthians 13:12 says, "For now we see through a glass, darkly; but then face to face."

302.15/297.6 FLEET WAS HIS FOOT ON THE BRACKEN: PATRICK OF THE BEAMY BROW   Though this phrase sounds generally poetic and Irish, and may allude to some turn-of-the century Irish poet, I have not located it.

302.16/297.7 WAIL, BANBA WITH YOUR WIND . . .   Banba is traditionally said to have been one of the queens of the Tuatha De Danann, and her name has been used as a poetic name for Ireland. I have found no passage in Irish literature exactly like this one in *Ulysses*.

Mangan's "Lament for Banba" is generally similar, but lacks specific verbal parallels. Perhaps this phrase also echoes Hosea 8:7; see entry 125.14.

303.1/297.34   THE TEAR IS BLOODY NEAR YOUR EYE   This may allude to Moore's "Erin, the tear and the smile in thine eyes"; see entry 296.17.

303.23/298.14   I HANGED JOE GANN . . . PRIVATE ARTHUR CHACE . . . JESSE TILSIT . . . BILLINGTON . . . TOAD SMITH . . . H. RUMBOLD   As R. Ellmann explains (*JJ*, p. 472) Rumbold, Gann, and Smith are names Joyce used because members of the British Consul in Zurich by these names were involved in his unsuccessful lawsuit in 1918–19. R. M. Adams points out (*SS*, p. 228) an account in the *Weekly Freeman* for January 14, 1899, about an English executioner named Billington who had performed several executions in Ireland. I have found no evidence that any of these names represent actual murderers or victims. The Index to the *English and Empire Digest* lists no cases of the Crown against such people.

304.16/299.8   THEY LEAD TO EREBUS   Erebus, in Greek myth, is the impenetrable darkness under the earth which the dead pass through on their way to Hades.

304.17/299.9   FOR I WILL IN NOWISE SUFFER IT EVEN SO SAITH THE LORD   Though this has a distinctly biblical ring, I have found no direct source for it in either the King James or the Douay Bible.

304.30/299.22   IN KILMAINHAM WHEN THEY HANGED JOE BRADY, THE INVINCIBLE   Joe Brady was one of the principals in the Phoenix Park murders (on which see entry 81.26). He was hanged at Kilmainham Gaol on the morning of May 14, 1883. The London *Times* description of the execution is quite detailed and contains the following item that is interestingly similar to the claim of hangman Rumbold on p. 303.32/298.23: "Marwood [the hangman] then adjusted the rope in a peculiar manner of his own which need not be described, and in a few minutes his ghastly work was done" (May 1, 1883, p. 4, col. c). William J. Feeny suggests that the unverifiable detail Alf is so fascinated by "might have been occasioned by the fact that Brady was one of more than twenty children, and a man of uncommon stature and strength" (*JJQ*, I, 58).

305.11/300.2   THE INVINCIBLES AND THE OLD GUARD AND THE MEN OF SIXTY-SEVEN   These are the names of Irish revolutionary groups. On the Invincibles, see entry 81.26. "Sixty-seven" refers to 1867, when there was an abortive insurrection; see P. S. O'Hegarty, *Ireland Under the Union*, chaps. 36 and 37.

305.12/300.3   WHO FEARS TO SPEAK OF NINETYEIGHT   This alludes to

Ingram's "The Memory of the Dead"; see entry 241.12.

305.30/300.20 HE GOLLOPED IT DOWN LIKE OLD BOOTS The simile "like old boots" occurs commonly and in a wide variety of contexts. There seems to be no agreed-upon explanation for its origin. Redding Ware (*Passing English of the Victorian Era*, p. 186) cites "To fight like old boots" and says it refers to the first duke of Marlborough (1650–1722)—"the first English general to wear immense jack boots." But that explanation seems inappropriate here.

305.34/300.24 THE BROTHERS SHEARES Henry and John Sheares were United Irishmen, executed during the 1798 uprising. They went to death on the scaffold hand in hand. Lady Wilde (1826–96) wrote a popular song entitled "The Brothers: Henry and John Sheares," words of which may be found in *Walton's Treasury of Irish Songs and Ballads*, pp. 217–18.

305.34/300.24 WOLFE TONE BEYOND ON ARBOUR HILL On Wolfe Tone, see entry 229.20.

305.35/300.25 ROBERT EMMET AND DIE FOR YOUR COUNTRY On Emmet, see entries 114.18 and 290.34, and the entry following this one.

305.35/300.25 TOMMY MOORE TOUCH ABOUT SARA CURRAN AND SHE'S FAR FROM THE LAND Thomas Moore's song "She is far from the Land" (1803) was written about Robert Emmet's fiancée, Sarah Curran. The first stanza says, "She is far from the land where her young hero sleeps,/ And lovers are round her, sighing;/ But coldly she turns from their gaze, and weeps,/ For her heart in his grave is lying." On Emmet, see entry 114.18.

306.17/301.6 THE MEMORY OF THE DEAD On Ingram's "The Memory of the Dead," see entry 241.12.

306.22/301.10 SINN FEIN! . . . SINN FEIN AMHAIN Hodgart and Worthington list this as an allusion to a song entitled "Sinn Fein, Sinn Fein Amhain," by O'Higgins, but I have not located such a song. On the Sinn Fein movement, see entry 163.38.

306.22/301.10 THE FRIENDS WE LOVE ARE BY OUR SIDE AND THE FOES WE HATE BEFORE US This is from Thomas Moore's song "Where is the slave," which begins, "Oh, where's the slave so lowly," and contains the lines "The friends we've tried/ Are by our side,/ And the foe we hate before us."

306.39/301.27 THE MATCHLESS MELODY . . . SPERANZA'S PLAINTIVE MUSE "Speranza" was the pen name of Lady Wilde (1826–96), mother of Oscar Wilde. I am not certain which of her songs could be described in this way, but it may be the one which was mentioned in entry 305.34—"The Brothers: Henry and John Sheares." Certainly that song is appropriate to the present context.

307.3/301.32 THE NIGHT BEFORE LARRY WAS STRETCHED   "The Night before Larry Was Stretched" is a ballad of disputed authorship in late eighteenth century Dublin slang. It begins, "The Night before Larry was stretched,/ The boys they all paid him a visit." For words, see Hoagland, pp. 289–92.

307.18/302.4 FRIENDS OF THE EMERALD ISLE   Though there were many groups sympathetic to Ireland, especially among the Irish in America, I have not found a group by this title. The description in the following lines makes it unlikely that Joyce had any actual group in mind.

307.26/302.13 ALI BABA BACKSHEESH   This blends Ali Baba, the poor woodcutter in *The Arabian Nights* who learns the password "Open, Sesame," to the robbers' cave, and "Baa, baa, black sheep," the well-known nursery rhyme. For Ali Baba's story, usually called "Ali Baba and the Forty Thieves," see any *Arabian Nights* collection; for "Baa, baa black sheep," see *ODNR*, p. 88. Backsheesh, as William Walsh explains (*Handy-Book of Literary Curiosities*, s.v. Backsheesh), is "an Oriental term for a present of money, a gratuity, a *poirboire*."

307.30/302.16 PAN POLEAXE PADDYRISKY   Wm. Schutte (p. 190) lists this as an allusion to Horatio's description of King Hamlet, "So frowned he once when, in an angry parle,/ He smote the sledded pollax on the ice" (*Ham.*, I, v, 62–63). Pollax is the spelling of the first two Quartos and the First Folio; some editors give *Poleaxe*, others *Polacks*. There is also an allusion here to Polish pianist and composer Ignace Jan Paderewski (1860–1941).

307.34/302.20 KRIEGFRIED UEBERALLGEMEIN   This probably alludes to the German national song "Deutschland, Deutschland über Alles," written by A. H. Hoffman von Fallersleben in 1841 to a melody by Joseph Haydn.

307.40/302.26 THE CORRECT DATE OF THE BIRTH OF IRELAND'S PATRON SAINT   Ireland's patron saint, St. Patrick, has been so clouded by the passage of time that almost everything about him is a matter of controversy and dispute. His saint's day is March 17.

308.31/303.17 THE EUNUCH CATALANI   I can find no evidence of such a person in the history of music (nor can R. M. Adams, SS, pp. 72–73). The singer that the name *Catalani* suggests (and Joyce would certainly have known this) is the soprano Angelica Catalani (1780–1849), who was said to have had a magnificent soprano voice, of excellent range and purity.

308.37/303.22 THE REVOLUTION OF RIENZI   Cola de Rienzi (1313?–51), Roman popular leader, tried to establish a democratic state with Rome as its capital. In May, 1347, he gathered supporters and headed a procession to the capitol; some laws were passed by acclamation, and Rienzi was given unlimited authority and took the title of Tribune. During the rest of the year he became dictatorial and unpopular, and by December he had abdicated and fled, denounced by the Pope as a criminal, a pagan, and a heretic. After several ups and downs he tried again in 1354, but was unsuccessful and was killed. His revolution was partly a product of the study of the Roman classics and a desire to re-establish the Empire in all its glory.

309.34/304.19   SHEILA, MY OWN   Hodgart and Worthington list an allusion here to "Mona, my Own Love," a song by Weatherly and Adams. The only copy of this song which I have seen is in *Harding's Nightingale Song Book*, a paperback song book at the National Library of Ireland. The song begins, "O, swift goes my barque like a bird on the billow,/ The boat of my heart, my trim Ben-my-chree." The chorus varies slightly, but the first chorus is of most interest here; it says "Mona, my own love; Mona, my true love,/ Art thou not mine thro' the long years to be/ By the bright stars above thee, I love thee, I love thee,/ Live for thee, die for thee, only for thee,/ Oh, Mona, Mona, my own love,/ Art thou not mine thro' the long years to be" (no. 11, p. 244).

311.2/305.29   THE GAELIC LEAGUE AND THE ANTITREATING LEAGUE   On the Gaelic League, see entry 193.4. The Anti-Treating League is probably St. Patrick's Anti-Treating League, which was formed April 20, 1902. *The Irish Catholic Directory and Almanac for 1903* (Dublin, 1903) describes the origin and purpose of the League: "The latest development which the crusade against intemperance has assumed has been the formation of a body known as St. Patrick's Anti-Treating League. Though but a very brief period in existence, the League has met with a very encouraging measure of success. . . . Its primary object is to combat one special and very grave drinking abuse. Treating in publichouses is now justly held to be the chief cause of drunkenness in this country, and it follows our young countrymen like a curse into other lands. St. Patrick's League is a crusade against treating, with a view to promote sobriety in Ireland" (pp. 433–34).

311.7/305.34   SHE COULD GET UP ON A TRUSS OF HAY SHE COULD MY MAUREEN LAY   This alludes to "The Low-Backed Car," a song by Samuel Lover. The first verse says, "When first I saw sweet Peggy, 'Twas on a market day, A low-back'd car she drove, and sat Upon a truss of hay: But when that hay was blooming grass

And deck'd with flow'rs of spring, No flow'r was there that could compare With the blooming girl I sing—As she sat in her low-back'd car, The man at the turnpike bar Never ask'd for his toll, but just rubb'd his old poll, And look'd after the low-back'd car." For words and music, see Moffat, *Minstrelsy of Ireland*, 3rd ed., pp. 304–5. Vernon Hall has suggested that the song alluded to in *Ulysses* may be a bawdy version of Lover's song (*Explicator*, XII [Feb., 1954], item 25), but Mabel Worthington argues against it (*Explicator*, XIII [Dec., 1954], item 20).

311.9/305.36 BALLYHOOLY BLUE RIBBON BADGE   This alludes to the song "Ballyhooly" (or "The Ballyhooly Blue Ribbon Army"), which I have seen only in a book by Robert J. Martin entitled *Bits of Blarney* (London, 1899). Apparently everything in the book— including this song—is by Martin. The opening stanza of the song says, "There's a dashing sort of boy, who is called his mother's joy,/ For his ructions and his elements they charm me,/ He takes the chief command in a water-drinking band,/ Called the Ballyhooly Blue Ribbon Army./ The ladies all declare, he's the pride of every fair,/ And he bears the patriotic name of Dooley,/ When the Temperance Brigade they go out on parade,/ There's not a sober man in Ballyhooly" (p. 9; the complete text of the song is on pp. 9–11).

311.10/305.37 COLLEEN BAWNS   See entry 297.14/292.10.

311.13/305.39 IRELAND SOBER IS IRELAND FREE   Though this temperance slogan is probably the motto of some group such as St. Patrick's Anti-Treating League (see entry 311.2), I have not found it in print anywhere.

311.15/305.41 THE TUNE THE OLD COW DIED OF   John J. Marshall, *Popular Rhymes and Sayings of Ireland* (Dungannon, 1924) says, "Another expression common to both Ireland and England is 'The tune the old cow died of.'" Marshall quotes the following rhyme: "There was an old man who had an old cow,/ And he had no fodder to give her,/ So he took up his fiddle, and played her this tune,/ 'Consider, good cow, consider,/ This isn't the time for grass to grow,/ Consider, good cow, consider.'" Marshall then comments, "So that the cow died of having a tune played to her which was an inefficient substitute for fodder as a means of sustenance. Hence 'the tune the old cow died of' has become a proverbial or slang way of describing music that is insufferably bad" (p. 8). P. W. Joyce (*English As We Speak It*, p. 124) notes this phrase and says, "Very bad slow music is described as *the tune the old cow died of.*"

311.38/306.23 GARRYOWEN "Garryowen" is an anonymous Irish ballad; see entry 295.13.

312.7/306.33 THE GRACEFUL PSEUDONYM OF THE LITTLE SWEET BRANCH An Craoibhin Aoibhinn (Sweet Little Branch) was the pseudonym of Douglas Hyde, on whom see entry 186.25.

312.12/306.38 THE FAMOUS RAFTERY AND OF DONALD MACCONSIDINE Anthony Raftery (1784?–1835) was the blind poet of county Mayo whose work was discovered by Douglas Hyde and Lady Gregory. *Irish Literature*, X, has a brief biographical sketch and account of Hyde's role in bringing his poetry to light. I have not located Donald MacConsidine (nor has R. M. Adams, SS, p. 107). The only writer of a similar name I have found is James Considine (Seamus Mac Consaidn), who is mentioned by James Clarence Mangan in his *Poets and Poetry of Munster* (Dublin, 1849). Mangan says almost nothing about Considine except that he was a shepherd and flourished about the close of the eighteenth century; Mangan's collection includes one poem by him—"The Fair-Haired Child."

312.19/307.3 THE INTRICATE ALLITERATIVE AND ISOSYLLABIC RULES OF THE WELSH ENGLYN The englyn is a metrical form in Welsh verse which is characterized by demanding rules of syllable count, end rhyme, internal rhyme, and alliteration. The form had reached its full development by the fourteenth century and was considered suitable for the highest poetic subjects. For discussion and illustrations, see Gwyn Williams, *An Introduction to Welsh Poetry* (London, 1953), esp. pp. 91–92 and 232–36.

312.25/307.9 THE CURSE OF MY CURSES . . . Of this entire parody, Vivian Mercier says, "This parody has so many possible applications that one wavers between the original verse of Synge and the translations of Douglas Hyde, or between Yeats and Lady Gregory in certain phases, before finally deciding that the entire Anglo-Irish Literary Revival is their true victim" (*The Irish Comic Tradition* [Oxford, 1962], p. 212). As R. M. Adams suggests (SS, p. 107), "Lowry's lights" probably refers to Dan Lowry's Music Hall, the Empire Palace, which was mentioned on p. 232.37/229.25.

312.37/307.21 HE'S NOT AS GREEN AS HE'S CABBAGELOOKING This may allude to the popular saying "found under a cabbage leaf," discussed in entry 224.4.

313.1/307.26 COULD A SWIM DUCK P. W. Joyce (*English As We Speak It*, p. 13) says, "A person who is offered anything he is very willing to take, or asked to do anything he is anxious to do, often answers in this way:—'James, would you take a glass of punch?' or 'Tom, will you dance with my sister in the next round?' In either case the answer is, 'Would a duck swim?' "

313.11/307.35 SHYLOCK   This refers to the Jewish moneylender in *The Merchant of Venice.*

313.24/308.8 ROYAL HUNGARIAN PRIVILEGED LOTTERY   R. M. Adams explains that Joyce picked up the idea of Bloom's trouble about the lottery from an article in the *Irish Independent* of June 16, 1904, about an incident in London. Adams says, "The episode in question took place in London; a printer was summoned into court by the Treasury, on charges of having published announcements describing the 'Privileged Royal Hungarian Lottery' " (*SS*, pp. 100–1).

313.33/308.17 SHAKE HANDS, BROTHER, YOU'RE A ROGUE AND I'M ANOTHER   Though I have not found this recorded in print, I know it to be a fairly common Irish saying.

315.1/309.25 HAIRY IOPAS . . .   Near the end of book I of the *Aeneid*, Virgil tells us, "Then the long-haired Iopas,/ A pupil of Atlas, made the hall hum with his golden zither" (ll. 740–41, C. Day Lewis' translation). The bard Iopas is long-haired like his patron Apollo. Though it is doubtful, the last part of this phrase may allude to Byron's description of Thomas Moore in his dedication to *The Corsair* as "the poet of all circles, and the idol of his own."

315.11/309.35 TEACH YOUR GRANDMOTHER HOW TO MILK DUCKS   Swift uses a similar saying in his *Polite Conversation*, first conversation, when Miss Notable says to Neverout "Go teach your Grannum to suck Eggs" (p. 86). Partridge says, "with such variations as 'to spin' and 'to sup milk,' this proverb goes back to the early 16th century."

315.21/310.3 BLACK LIZ IS OUR HEN   I suspect that this alludes to some nursery rhyme, but I have not found one exactly like this. For "Hickety, pickety, my black hen," and for another hen rhyme which begins "Chook . . . ," see *ODNR*, pp. 201–2.

315.38/310.18 THE SLUAGH NA H-EIREANN   This means "The People of Ireland," and was the title of a chauvinistic group of the time. An article in the *Irish Daily Independent* of June 16, 1904, entitled "Games in Phoenix Park," says, "Mr. Nanetti will to-day ask the Chief Secretary whether he is aware that, while the game of polo is allowed to be played in that part of Phoenix Park known as the Nine Acres, the members of the Sluagh na h-Eireann are not allowed to play Gaelic games there; and if so, will he state under what authority the Commissioners of Police are under an obligation not to increase the enclosures or number of allotments in the Park; whether the Commissioners have authority to enforce prohibitive measures against the games played by most of the young men in Dublin, seeing that the history of the Phoenix Park clearly shows that the Park belongs to the citizens of Dublin" (p. 5, col i).

315.39/310.19 MR COWE CONACRE This seems to blend *conacre* and "three acres and a cow" (on the latter, see entry 489.23). E. C. Brewer (*Historic Note-Book, s.v.* Conacre System) explains the Conacre system as the practice of sub-subletting land so that it is finally broken into small patches on which the landlord and several middlemen have made a profit. P. W. Joyce (*English As We Speak It*, p. 238) also discusses this briefly.

316.16/310.38 DON'T HESITATE TO SHOOT See entry 187.31.

316.21/311.1 THE MAN THAT GOT AWAY JAMES STEPHENS See entry 68.26.

316.33/311.12 A NATION ONCE AGAIN This alludes to "A Nation Once Again," a song by Irish journalist, politician, and writer Thomas Osborne Davis (1814–45). The song begins, "When boyhood's fire was in my blood,/ I read of ancient freemen. . . ." For words, see *Irish Literature*, III, 827 (though that copy lacks a chorus which I have seen: "A Nation once again,/ A Nation once again,/ And Ireland, long a province, be/ A Nation once again"). K. Sullivan says that this song was sung by the students at Joyce's graduation from University College so as to drown out the speech of the stoutly conservative chancellor of the University, Lord Meath (*Joyce Among the Jesuits*, p. 223).

317.14/311.34 FINN MACCOOL Finn MacCool (or Fionn MacCumhail), the central figure of the Osiannic or Fenian cycle, was a third-century poet and leader of the early Irish army called the Fianna or Fenians.

317.21/311.41 THOMAS OSBORNE DAVIS' EVERGREEN VERSES . . . A NATION ONCE AGAIN See entry 316.33.

317.25/312.3 THE IRISH CARUSO-GARIBALDI Enrico Caruso (1873–1921) is the famous Italian operatic tenor. Italian patriot Garibaldi was alluded to earlier; see entry 163.41.

318.23/313.1 HEENAN AND SAYERS On the famous Heenan-Sayers bout, see entry 242.23.

319.25/314.3 MRS B. IS THE BRIGHT PARTICULAR STAR This alludes to Helena's statement about Bertram in *All's Well That Ends Well*: "There is no living, none,/ If Bertram be away. 'Twere all one/ That I should love a bright particular star/ And think to wed it, he is so above me" (I, i, 95–98).

319.28/314.6 SAYS I TO MYSELF, SAYS I   Hodgart and Worthington suggest that this alludes to the oft-repeated line "Said I to myself—said I" in the Lord Chancellor's song "When I went to the bar as a very young man" in act I of Gilbert and Sullivan's *Iolanthe* (1882).

319.28/314.6 THAT EXPLAINS THE MILK IN THE COCOANUT AND THE ABSENCE OF HAIR ON THE ANIMAL'S CHEST   Though these seem to be set phrases, and may be common Irish expressions, I have not located them in any of the dictionaries of quotations or proverbs which I have used.

319.30/314.8 THE TOOTLE ON THE FLUTE   This alludes to Percy French's song "Phil the Fluter's Ball." The only copy of this song I have found is in *Harding's Nightingale Song Book*, a paperback song book at the National Library of Ireland. The song begins, "Have you heard of Phil the Fluter, from the town of Ballymuck . . . ," and the chorus says, "With the toot of the flute, and the twiddle of the fiddle, O,/ Hopping in the middle like a herrin' on a griddle, O,/ Up, down, hands aroun', crossing to the wall,/ Oh, hadn't we the gaiety at Phil the Fluter's Ball" (no. 12, p. 283).

320.23/315.1 YE'LL COME HOME BY WEEPING CROSS ONE OF THESE DAYS   "He that goeth out with often loss, at last comes home by weeping cross" is proverbial and is listed in the *ODEP*, including instances from Montaigne and John Ray's *Proverbs* (1670).

321.11/315.29 A FELLOW THAT'S NEITHER FISH NOR FLESH. NOR GOOD RED HERRING   "Neither fish nor flesh (nor good red herring)" is proverbial and is listed in the *ODEP*. Among the seven instances the *ODEP* lists are John Heywood's *Proverbs* (1546) and Shakespeare's *I Henry IV*, III, iii, 144. Two of the quotations in the *ODEP* clearly suggest a sexual meaning for the phrase.

321.31/316.6 THE TEST CASE OF SADGROVE V. HOLE   This refers to an actual case, which did involve the points that O'Molloy mentions, but, strangely, he is mistaken about its outcome. The case was heard by the Court of Appeal on March 8, 1901, and was reported in the London *Times* of March 9 (p. 17, col. a). The case involved a possible libel through something written on a postcard, but the Appeal Court reversed the decision of the lower court and held that the postcard was not publication but privileged communication, and that there was no sufficient evidence of malice. For a fuller account than the *Times* gives, see *The Law Reports: King's Bench Division, 1901*, II, 2–6.

322.3/316.19 HOW DID THAT CANADA SWINDLE CASE GO OFF   There was such a case tried in Dublin on June 16, 1904, and reported in the newspapers, though Joyce changed some of the details. The

June 16 *Evening Telegraph* and the June 17 *Freeman's Journal* carried the same article on the case. It was brought by a man named Zaretsky against James Wrought, whose aliases included Sparks and Saphero. Wrought had sold Zaretsky and others tickets to Canada for only £ 1; they were, of course, bogus. The case was heard not by Sir Frederick Falkiner but by Mr. Swifte, in the Southern Divisional Police Court. The accused was remanded (from the *Evening Telegraph*, June 16, 1904, p. 3, col. b).

322.34/317.6 THE MONTH OF THE OXEYED GODDESS   This refers to Juno (and June), who is occasionally described by Homer as the "oxeyed goddess."

322.35/317.7 IN THE THIRD WEEK AFTER THE FEASTDAY OF THE HOLY AND UNDIVIDED TRINITY   In 1904, Easter was on April 3, Whit Sunday on May 22, and Trinity Sunday on May 29, so that Thursday, June 16, was in the third week after the feast day of the Trinity. But Willis E. McNelly, though finding the tabulation of the date correct, says, ". . . the Catholic Church never uses Trinity Sunday as a base from which to measure liturgical time. Pentecost is the base to be used in this instance," and McNelly says this should read "the third week after Pentecost" (*JJQ*, II, 293–94).

323.6/317.20 THE LAW OF THE BREHONS   The Brehon Law was the legal system of Old Ireland, administered by judges called "brehons." See P. W. Joyce, *Short History*, part I, chap. vi ("The Brehon Law").

323.9/317.22 THE HIGH SINHEDRIM OF THE TWELVE TRIBES OF IAR . . .   There were no such twelve tribes of Ireland. These tribes—also the twelve men of a jury—are based on the twelve tribes of Israel, described in Genesis 49. The sinhedrim (or sanhedrin) was a Jewish court of justice consisting of seventy-one members. Information about it is vague and contradictory; it is mentioned several times in the Bible (see Matt. 26:59, Mark 14:1, and Acts 4:5 ff.). The names given to these twelve tribes of Iar are so common in Irish history that some of them are impossible to identify specifically. I annotate those that may refer to some particular person, but the identifications must be conjectural. Patrick is doubtless St. Patrick, patron saint of Ireland. Conn is probably Conn Ced-cathach; see entry 296.35. The name Fergus is common in early Irish history; perhaps the best-known person of this name is Fergus mac Roigh, who was misled into leading Deirdre and the sons of Usnach to King Concobar, by whom they were treacherously destroyed; see chap. XXV of D. Hyde, *Literary History of Ireland*. Finn is Finn Mac-Cool; see entry 317.14. Dermot is probably Dermot MacMurrough, king of Leinster; see entry 34.42. Cormac is probably Cormac

MacArt, third-century king; see entries 169.23 and 666.38. Kevin is St. Kevin; see entry 339.26. Caolte is probably Caoilte, son of Ronan, an ancient who lived three hundred years and had a colloquy with St. Patrick; see G. Keating, *History of Ireland*, Irish Text Society edition, Book I, sec. 5. Ossian is the famous poet Ossian, son of Finn MacCool; see the index of D. Hyde's *Literary History of Ireland*.

323.15/317.28   TWELVE GOOD MEN AND TRUE   This reference to the jurymen seems to blend two phrases. One is Lord Brougham's (1778–1868) description of a jury as "twelve good men in a box," and the other is Dogberry's question of Verges and the watch in *Much Ado About Nothing*: "Are you good men and true?" (III, iii, 1).

323.16/317.30   BY HIM WHO DIED ON ROOD   The description of Christ as dying "on rood" (i.e., on the cross) is fairly common in Old and Middle English and persists into Modern English as an archaic phrase. The *OED* lists many instances of the phrase "On rood" without the definite article; see *OED*, s.v. *rood* 2.a and 2.b.

323.40/318.12   STRANGERS IN OUR HOUSE   See entry 184.40.

324.4/318.18   THE ADULTERESS AND HER PARAMOUR BROUGHT THE SAXON ROBBERS HERE   See entry 34.42, and cf. entries 34.41 and 35.2.

324.25/318.39   THERE'S HAIR   Hodgart and Worthington list this as an allusion to a music hall song entitled "There's Hair Like Wire Coming Out of the Empire." I have not been able to find any information about the song or to locate a printed text.

324.36/319.8   THE THOLSEL   See entry 245.10.

325.2/319.15   THE NELSON POLICY PUTTING YOUR BLIND EYE TO THE TELESCOPE   This refers to Nelson's famous refusal to obey the signal to withdraw during the Battle of Copenhagen in 1801. Southey's account says that, on being told by his men that the signal for withdrawal had been hoisted by the commander-in-chief, Nelson said, " 'I have only one eye—I have a right to be blind sometimes': —and then, putting the glass to his blind eye, in that mood of mind which sports with bitterness, he exclaimed, 'I really do not see the signal!' " (Robert Southey's *Life of Nelson*, chap. VII). Nelson did go on to win the battle.

325.19/319.31   FULL MANY A FLOWER IS BORN TO BLUSH UNSEEN   This is from stanza fourteen of Thomas Gray's "Elegy Written in a Country Churchyard," which says, "Full many a flower is born to blush unseen,/ And waste its sweetness on the desert air."

325.21/319.33   PERFIDE ALBION   This phrase, "Treacherous England," has long been a set phrase. Napoleon is supposed to have said it in 1815 on leaving England for St. Helena, though this attribution has never been confirmed. An earlier form, "Ah! la perfide Angleterre," has been attributed to Bossuet. If the preceding phrase, "Spit upon England!" is an allusion, I am unaware of it.

325.24/319.36 LAMH DEARG ABU P. W. Joyce (*English As We Speak It*, p. 179) says, "The war-cry of the great family of O'Neill of Tyrone was *Lauv-derg-aboo* (the Red Hand to Victory: the Red Hand being the cognisance of the O'Neills): and this cry the clansmen shouted when advancing to battle; and yet it is remembered in popular sayings to this day. In Tyrone when a fight is expected one man will say to another 'there will be *Dergaboos* today': not that the cry will be actually raised; but *Dergaboo* has come to be a sort of symbolic name for a fight." But, as R. M. Adams explains (*SS*, pp. 142–43), the phrase has another meaning as well: since the Allsop bottle carries a red hand on its label, this is a common drinking cry.

325.25/319.37 RULERS OF THE WAVES In view of a definite allusion to it later in this episode (p. 329.15/323.24), this probably alludes to the song "Rule, Britannia," by Thomson and Arne. The refrain is "Rule Britannia, Britannia rule the waves! Britons never, never, never will be slaves" (for words and music, see Chappell, *Popular Music of the Olden Time*, pp. 686–89).

325.40/320.10 FRAILTY, THY NAME IS SCEPTRE In his first soliloquy, thinking of his mother's hasty marriage, Hamlet says, "Frailty, thy name is woman!" (I, ii, 146).

326.1/320.13 OLD MOTHER HUBBARD WENT TO THE CUPBOARD The text of the well-known nursery rhyme "Old Mother Hubbard" can be found in *ODNR*, pp. 317–22.

326.8/320.20 THE MOTE IN OTHER'S EYES BUT THEY CAN'T SEE THE BEAM IN THEIR OWN In the Sermon on the Mount, Christ says, "And why beholdest thou the mote that is in thy brother's eye, but considerest not the beam that is in thine own eye?" (Matt. 7:3; Luke 6:41 is substantially the same).

326.10/320.22 THERE'S NO-ONE AS BLIND AS THE FELLOW THAT WON'T SEE This phrase, which has been proverbial at least since John Heywood's *Proverbs* (1546), occurs in Swift's *Polite Conversation*, third conversation, when Lady Smart says, "There's none so blind, as they that won't see" (p. 161). Partridge says "16th-20th centuries. Occasionally with addition: 'nor deaf as those who will not hear.'"

326.13/320.25 OUR LOST TRIBES The citizen is comparing the Irish loss of population from starvation, persecution, and emigration to the lost tribes of Israel. The ten lost tribes of Israel were those of the Northern Kingdom, who were exiled after the invasions by the Assyrians, 721–15 B.C. These lost tribes have been identified with segments of various peoples from the Japanese to the English. Cf. entry 323.9.

326.14/320.26   WOOL THAT WAS SOLD IN ROME IN THE TIME OF JUVENAL
Though most of the Citizen's statements about Irish history are correct, this one is almost certainly erroneous. D. A. Chart, in his *An Economic History of Ireland* (Dublin, 1920), does discuss this period of Ireland's history, but says nothing of such a trade. As a matter of fact, most of his statements cast doubt on it (see pp. 6–7); certainly if there was a wool trade with Rome at the time, it was very small.

326.18/320.30   JACQUARD DE LYON   Joseph Marie Jacquard of Lyons (1752–1834) was not, as the text implies, a developer of poplin in Ireland, but was the inventor of the Jacquard loom (1801); on poplin in Ireland, see entry 168.20. Of the Jacquard machine in Ireland, Mr. and Mrs. S. C. Hall (*Ireland: Its Scenery, Character, &c.* [London, 1842], II, 330) say it was "introduced a few years ago by some of the leading manufacturers, is now in general use, and gives great facility in producing a variety of patterns in poplins, or any other description of figured fabric."

326.24/320.36   READ TACITUS AND PTOLEMY, EVEN GIRALDUS CAMBRENSIS
Roman historian Tacitus (A.D. *ca.* 55– *ca.* 120) made only brief passing references to Ireland, in his *Agricola*, sec. 24. Tacitus' comment is reproduced by James F. Kenny in his *Sources for the Early History of Ireland*, pp. 131–32. Ptolemy (*fl.* A.D. 127–51), Greek geographer and astronomer, discussed Ireland in a section of his *Geography*. Kenny briefly discusses Ptolemy on Ireland and says that his account is "by far the most complete and detailed to be found among all Greek and Roman writers, and is the earliest source for Irish history of really first-rate importance" (*Sources*, pp. 132–34). Norman-Welsh historian Giraldus Cambrensis (*ca.* 1146–1223) wrote two works on Ireland as a result of a visit to that country. One, the *Topographia Hibernica*, is basically factual; the other, *Expugnatio Hibernica*, is a biased history of the conquest of Ireland.

326.27/320.39   KING PHILIP OF SPAIN OFFERING TO PAY CUSTOMS DUTIES FOR THE RIGHT TO FISH IN OUR WATERS   R. Bagwell says (*Ireland Under the Tudors*) that ". . . in 1553 Philip II agreed to pay £1,000 a year for twenty-one years to gain for his subjects the right to fish on the Irish coast" (III, 447).

326.41/321.10   ON THE FAIR HILLS OF EIRE, O   This alludes to "The

Fair Hills of Eire, O," translated by James Clarence Mangan from the Irish of Donogh Mac Con-Mara. It begins, "Take a blessing from my heart to the land of my birth,/ And the fair hills of Eire, O." Words may be found in *Irish Literature*, VI, 2378–79.

327.10/321.21 MISS BEE HONEYSUCKLE   This probably alludes to the popular song "The Honeysuckle and the Bee," by Albert H. Fitz and William H. Penn (1901). Words and music may be found in the *Song Dex Treasury of Humorous and Nostalgic Songs*, II, 166.

327.11/321.22 MISS O MIMOSA SAN   O Mimosa San is the chief Geisha in the opera *The Geisha*; see entry 96.40.

327.17/321.27 M'CONIFER OF THE GLANDS   This may allude to James MacDonnell (d. 1565), who was known as the "lord of the Glens" (or perhaps to the O'Donoghue of the Glens—see entry 599.2).

327.30/321.40 WOODMAN, SPARE THAT TREE   "Woodman, Spare that Tree" is a sentimental American song with words by George P. Morris and music by Henry Russell. It begins, "Woodman, spare that tree!/ Touch not a single bough;/ In youth it sheltered me,/ And I'll protect it now." For words and music, see Helen K. Johnson, *Our Familiar Songs*, pp. 25–28.

327.34/322.2 IVYTOD, HOLLYBERRIES   As Hodgart and Worthington suggest, this probably alludes to the English folk carol "The Holly and the Ivy." The song begins, "The holly and the ivy,/ When they are both full grown,/ Of all the trees that are in the wood,/ The holly bears the crown." Text may be found in any collection of English folk carols, such as *The Oxford Book of Carols*.

327.37/322.5 WE HAD OUR TRADE WITH SPAIN . . . SPANISH ALE IN GALWAY   In his essay on Galway, "The City of the Tribes" (1912), Joyce talks at some length about Galway as a trading center, says it was the second most important harbor in the United Kingdom in Cromwell's time, and specifically speaks of its vast wine trade: "Almost all the wine imported into the United Kingdom from Spain, Portugal, the Canary Islands, and Italy passed through this port, the annual import amounting to 1500 'tuns,' that is to say, almost two million litres" (*CW*, p. 230).

327.40/322.8 THE WINEDARK WATERWAY   *Winedark* is a common Homeric epithet; see entry 5.7.

328.2/322.12 QUEENSTOWN, KINSALE, GALWAY, BLACKSOD BAY, VENTRY . . . KILLYBEGS . . .   All of these are famous ports or bays in Ireland, and all were more important or prosperous in the past than they are now (on Galway, for example, see entry 327.37).

328.5/322.14 THE GALWAY LYNCHES AND THE CAVAN O'REILLY'S AND THE O'KENNEDY'S OF DUBLIN   In his "City of the Tribes" essay on

Galway, Joyce spends three paragraphs on the Lynches, whom he
calls the most famous of all the tribes (*CW*, pp. 231–32). Edmund
Curtis, in his *History of Medieval Ireland*, lists the Lynches among
the Galway tribes, but his chronological scope prevents his discussing them very fully. Curtis does discuss the O'Reilly's of county
Cavan (see his Index, and esp. p. 236), but Curtis does not discuss
any O'Kennedy's of Dublin, though he does deal with the O'Kennedy's of Ormond (see his Index).

328.6/322.16   WHEN THE EARL OF DESMOND COULD MAKE A TREATY WITH
THE EMPEROR CHARLES THE FIFTH HIMSELF   This refers to attempts by James Fitzmaurice Fitzgerald, tenth earl of Desmond
(d. 1529), to form a treaty with Emperor Charles the Fifth for
aid against the English. The dealings occurred in 1529, and Charles
did go so far as to send his chaplain, Gonzalo Fernandez, to Ireland
to view the situation, but nothing came of it. The episode is described in Brian Fitzgerald's *The Geraldines: An Experiment in
Irish Government, 1169–1601* (London: Staples Press, 1951), pp.
182–89.

328.9/322.19   NONE OF YOUR HENRY TUDOR'S HARPS   As an emblem of
his rule over Ireland, Henry VIII chose to place in the royal
standard a gold harp on a blue field. For an illustration of this, see
Gordon Campbell and I. O. Evans, *The Book of Flags* (2nd ed.,
1953), plates I and II and p. 8. See also W. J. Gordon, *Flags of the
World Past and Present* (London, 1915), where Gordon says, "The
golden harp on an escutcheon in the center of the Union has for
years been the flag of the Lord Lieutenant of Ireland" (p. 101);
the badge is depicted on plate xv, opposite p. 104.

328.10/322.19   THE OLDEST FLAG AFLOAT, THE FLAG OF THE PROVINCE OF
DESMOND AND THOMOND, THREE CROWNS ON A BLUE FIELD, THE THREE
SONS OF MILESIUS   The three sons of Milesius (or Mileadh) are
traditionally the progenitors of the Gaels; see Keating's *History of
Ireland*, Irish Text Society edition, Book I, secs. xxii and xxiii. Desmond and Thomond are names for two of the five provinces, according to its division by the Firbolgs, which Keating says is "the
division which is the most permanent that was ever made in Ireland" (Book I, sec. ii). Desmond is from the Gaelic for South
Munster (Deas Mhumha); Thomond for North Munster (Tuadh
Mhumha). The flag described—three crowns on a blue field—is
traditionally said to have been the flag of the Milesians. I have not
been able to find the flag depicted, but since the opening of the
Martello Tower as a Joyce museum in June, 1962, such a flag has
flown over the Tower.

328.14/322.23   COWS IN CONNACHT HAVE LONG HORNS   Thomas F. O'Rahilly's *A Miscellany of Irish Proverbs* (Dublin: Talbot Press, 1922) lists a proverb similar to this: "Mór-thaidhbhseach iad ad-harca na mbó tar lear" (" 'Far-off cows have long horns,' i.e. 'Distance lends enchantment to the view' "; proverb 117, p. 33).

328.17/322.26   MOLLY MAGUIRES   The "Molly Maguires" was an Irish society organized in county Monaghan to co-operate with the Ribbonmen (an anti-Orangemen society dating back to the end of the eighteenth century). The purpose of the Molly Maguires was to harass process servers and landlords' agents who were demanding rent and serving eviction notices. A group of the same name appeared among Irish Americans in the U.S. in 1854.

328.31/322.40   BLACK BEAST BURNED IN OMAHA, GA.   R. M. Adams (*SS*, pp. 204–5) says he can find no trace of any lynching in Omaha, Georgia, though one did occur in Lumpkin, Georgia(both are in Stewart County) in 1897 which Joyce may possibly have drawn on. Perhaps this owes something to a brief (*ca.* 150-word) description of a lynching in Springfield, Ohio, which appeared in the *Freeman's Journal*, Wednesday, March 9, 1904. According to the account, the Negro was hanged on a telegraph pole and riddled with bullets (p. 5, col. g). The paper of Thursday, March 10, had a brief follow-up on this which says that two thousand whites invaded the Negro section and set fire to it (p. 2, col. e).

328.32/322.40   DEADWOOD DICKS   Deadwood Dick was the hero of more than one hundred nineteenth-century American "dime novels," written by Edward L. Wheeler. See A. Johannsen, *The House of Beadle and Adams*, II, 293–98, 358–59.

328.39/323.6   THE REVELATIONS THAT'S GOING ON IN THE PAPERS ABOUT FLOGGING   R. M. Adams points out that flogging, which was not abolished until 1906, was a frequent newspaper topic of the day, and he cites an example in the *Freeman's Journal* of July 13, 1904 (*SS*, p. 227). Though I have found no letter signed "Disgusted One," there was an interesting exchange of letters on this topic in the London *Times* of June 13 and 14, 1904. The first is a long letter defending corporal punishment and quoting the regulations about it, signed "In Partibus Maris" (*Times*, June 13, p. 5, cols. e–f). The reply, attacking corporal punishment and "In Partibus Maris," is from George Bernard Shaw (*Times*, June 14, p. 11, col. f).

329.5/323.14   THAT OLD RUFFIAN SIR JOHN BERESFORD   This probably refers to Sir John Poo Beresford (1766–1844), admiral in the British navy. I have found no long biographical accounts of Beresford, but none of the brief articles I have seen supports the flogging charge.

329.9/323.18   'TIS A CUSTOM MORE HONOURED IN THE BREACH THAN IN THE OBSERVANCE   Concerning Claudius' revelry, Hamlet tells Horatio "it is a custom/ More honored in the breach than the observance" (*Ham.*, I, iv, 15–16). Cf. entry 299.38.

329.15/323.24   THE FELLOWS THAT NEVER WILL BE SLAVES   This alludes to "Rule, Brittania"; see entry 325.25.

329.20/323.29   ON WHICH THE SUN NEVER RISES   A variation of an old proverb; see entry 30.35.

329.22/323.31   YAHOOS   Though *yahoo* means *bumpkin*, this recalls the brutish race of human form ruled over by the Houyhnhnms in Part IV of Swift's *Gulliver's Travels*.

329.23/323.32   THEY BELIEVE IN ROD, THE SCOURGER ALMIGHTY . . . This is a parody in nautical terms of the Apostles' Creed.

329.37/324.1   OUR GREATER IRELAND BEYOND THE SEA   This is a set phrase often used to describe the United States, especially since the emigration to America following the Great Famine. For example, E. Curtis, describing this emigration, says, "Emigration to America set in with a vast and steady flow (in 1852 there were two hundred and twenty thousand emigrants) and continuing for the next sixty years kept the population at home in a state of decline and made a greater Ireland in America of millions to whom Ireland has been either a passionate memory or an ancestral poetry" (*Hist. of Ire.*, p. 370).

329.37/324.2   THEY WERE DRIVEN OUT OF HOUSE AND HOME IN THE BLACK 47   "The black forty-seven" is a traditional way of referring to the famine that increasingly struck Ireland during 1845, 1846, and 1847. During the period 1846–51, hundreds of thousands died in Ireland from starvation, and more than one million emigrated to America. See P. S. O'Hegarty, *Ireland Under the Union*, chap. XXV, "The Great Starvation."

329.40/324.4   THE TIMES RUBBED ITS HANDS AND TOLD THE WHITELIVERED SAXONS THERE WOULD SOON BE AS FEW IRISH IN IRELAND AS REDSKINS IN AMERICA   In the chapter entitled "The Great Famine" in his *Story of the Irish Race*, Seumas MacManus says, "*The London Times* . . . when the exodus was most pitiful, screamed with delight in one of its editorials, 'They are going! They are going! The Irish are going with a vengeance. Soon a Celt will be as rare in Ireland as a Red Indian on the shores of Manhattan'" (p. 610). I have not located the editorial in the *Times*.

329.42/324.7   THE GRAND TURK SENT US HIS PIASTRES   Though this may be fact, I have been unable to confirm it. Many countries did form Irish Relief Associations during the Famine, but I have not found definite evidence that the Ottoman Empire was among them.

330.3/324.10 THE PEASANTS . . . TWENTY THOUSAND OF THEM DIED IN THE COFFINSHIPS   "The coffin ships" is what the ships transporting Irish emigrants from Ireland to America came to be called. Scumas MacManus discusses these ships and the great numbers who died in transit or immediately after arrival (*Story of the Irish Race*, chap. LXX, "The Great Famine").

330.4/324.11 THOSE THAT CAME TO THE LAND OF THE FREE REMEMBER THE LAND OF BONDAGE   This probably alludes to the American national anthem, "The Star-Spangled Banner," by Francis Scott Key. The final line of each verse of the song describes the U.S. as "the land of the free and the home of the brave." This can be found in any collection of American songs. There is also a Hebraic parallel suggested here by the use of *bondage*, the word frequently used to describe the Hebrews in Egypt, as in Deuteronomy 5:6: "I am the Lord thy God, which brought thee out of the land of Egypt, from the house of bondage." See entry 122.22.

330.7/324.13 THE SONS OF GRANUAILE, THE CHAMPIONS OF KATHLEEN NI HOULIHAN   On Granuaile, or Grace O'Malley, see entry 628.12. Kathleen ni Houlihan is, of course, a poetic name for Ireland; cf. Mangan's poem "Kathaleen Ny Houlihan" and Yeats's play *Cathleen Ni Houlihan* (see entries 184.39 and 184.40).

330.11/324.17 THE POOR OLD WOMAN TOLD US THAT THE FRENCH WERE ON THE SEA   This alludes to "The Shan Van Vocht"; see entry 17.36.

330.12/324.18 LANDED AT KILLALA   Hodgart and Worthington list this as an allusion to "The Men of the West" (see entry 263.3), but if so it is an allusion only to the situation described in the song (i.e., the taking of Killala) and not to any phrase in it.

330.13/324.19 WE FOUGHT FOR THE ROYAL STUARTS   This refers to the Irish support of King James II when he was deposed as king of England in 1688. James, a Roman Catholic, found his only support in the Irish, many of whom supported him and opposed the kingship of William III. James went to Ireland but left for France when it became clear that William's forces would win. The war between the Irish supporters of the Stuarts and the English forces of William lasted from 1689 to 1691 and ended with the Treaty of Limerick, signed October 3, 1691. See the next entry.

330.15/324.21 LIMERICK AND THE BROKEN TREATYSTONE   (See the preceding entry.) The Treaty of Limerick was in effect broken by the drastic anti-Catholic modifications of the original Treaty in the British Parliament. See Curtis, *A History of Ireland*, pp.

272–77, 280–81. The stone on which the Treaty was signed is famous and has been placed as a monument beside Thomond Bridge in Limerick. For a picture of it, see *Irish Literature*, III, facing p. 956.

330.15/324.21   WE GAVE OUR BEST BLOOD TO FRANCE AND SPAIN, THE WILD GEESE   The "wild geese" were Irishmen who left Ireland after the defeat of James II. The loss to France, Spain, etc., is developed in the following sentences. See entry 41.17 and cf. entry 132.35.

330.16/324.22   FONTENOY . . . SARSFIELD AND O'DONNELL, DUKE OF TETUAN IN SPAIN, AND ULYSSES BROWNE OF CAMUS . . .   Fontenoy, in western Belgium, was the scene of a battle between French forces and the Anglo-Allied army (English, Dutch, Hanoverians, Austrians) in 1745. The allusion here is certainly to the renowned performance of the Irish Brigade, which fought on the side of the French. Thomas Osborne Davis has commemorated it in his poem "Fontenoy," for which see *Irish Literature*, III, 823. Sarsfield is Patrick Sarsfield, earl of Lucan (?–1693), Irish soldier and supporter of James II. Sarsfield fought at the Battle of the Boyne (1690) and was very important in arranging the Treaty of Limerick. After William III's victory, Sarsfield went to France. He died in the battle of Landen or Neerwinden. O'Donnell is Leopold O'Donnell, duke of Tetuan (1809–67), Spanish general and statesman. He was a descendant of the O'Donnells who left Ireland in 1690. Maximilian Ulysses Browne, Graf von Browne, Baron of Camus and Mountany (1705–57), was the son of Ulysses Freiherr von Browne, an Irish exile of 1690. Browne was an Austrian field marshall and one of Maria Theresa's most successful commanders.

330.22/324.28   AN ENTENTE CORDIALE NOW AT TAY PAY'S DINNERPARTY WITH PERFIDIOUS ALBION   The *Entente cordiale* referred to here is the diplomatic agreement between England and France which was concluded in April 8, 1904. On "Tay Pay" (T. P. O'Connor), see entry 137.27. On "perfidious Albion," see entry 325.21.

330.26/324.32   THE HANOVERIANS . . . FROM GEORGE THE ELECTOR DOWN TO THE GERMAN LAD   The House of Hanover, the German royal family, acceded to the English throne in the person of George I; the English changed the dynastic name to Windsor during World War I. George the Elector is George I (1660–1727; reigned 1714–27), who succeeded to his father's position as elector of Hanover when his father died in 1698. The German lad apparently refers to Prince Albert of Saxe-Coburg-Gotha (1819–57), whom Victoria ("the flatulent old bitch") married in 1840.

330.29/324.35 THE FLATULENT OLD BITCH THAT'S DEAD . . . Queen
Victoria, who died on January 22, 1901. The coachman alluded to
was John Brown, Victoria's coachman, body servant, and friend.
Lytton Strachey discusses Victoria's "affectionate friendship" for
the coachman at some length and says, ". . . and yet—such is the
world!—there were those who actually treated the relations between their Sovereign and her servant as a theme for ribald jests"
(*Queen Victoria* [New York, 1921], p. 374).

330.35/324.41 EHREN ON THE RHINE Hodgart and Worthington
list this as an allusion to "Ehren on the Rhine," by Cobb and Hutchinson. The only place I have found a printed copy of this song is
in the periodical *Ireland's Own*, October 30, 1912, where the song
is printed, but no reference is made to the author. The song has
three eight-line stanzas and two refrains of four lines that vary
slightly. It begins "A soldier stood in the village street,/ Bidding
his love adieu;/ His gun and knapsack at his side,/ His company
in view. . . ." The first refrain says, " 'My love, my love, be true,/
This heart is only thine;/ When the war is o'er/ We'll part no
more/ At Ehren on the Rhine.' " But the soldier dies.

330.35/324.41 COME WHERE THE BOOZE IS CHEAPER Hodgart and
Worthington list this as an allusion to George Dance's parody of
Stephen Foster's well-known "Come Where My Love Lies Dreaming." Dance's authorship of "Come Where the Booze Is Cheaper"
is mentioned by W. J. MacQueen-Pope (*The Melodies Linger On*,
p. 423), but I have not located a copy of the song.

330.37/325.1 EDWARD THE PEACEMAKER NOW According to the
DNB, the French called Edward VII "le roi pacificateur" after
the conclusion of the 1904 Entente (see entry 330.22).

330.39/325.3 EDWARD GUELPH-WETTIN The family name of the
Hanoverian line was Guelph, but when Victoria married Prince
Albert in 1840, the name Wettin supplanted Guelph as the family
name of the British royal family.

330.40/325.4 THE PRIESTS AND BISHOPS OF IRELAND DOING UP HIS ROOM
IN MAYNOOTH IN HIS SATANIC MAJESTY'S RACING COLORS . . . Perhaps this information comes from a letter from W. B. Yeats which
appeared in the August 1, 1903, issue of the *United Irishman*.
Yeats's letter begins, "Sir—I read in the English Times of July 25th
this description of the room prepared for the King's reception at
Maynooth: 'The King's room afforded a very pleasant instance
of the thoughtful courtesy of his hosts; for by a happy inspiration
hardly to have been expected in such a quarter, the walls were

draped in His Majesty's racing colours, and carried two admirable engravings of Ambush II. and Diamond Jubilee. When the King and Queen had taken their places in the refectory, Mgr. Molloy read the following address,' &c." Yeats goes on to comment ironically on how popular racing is becoming among the clergy (p. 6, col. d–p. 7 col. a). There is also another letter on the same subject immediately preceding Yeats's (p. 6, col. d), complaining about the Catholic hierarchy's kowtowing to the English crown. The insult to Ireland continued to be the subject of letters and editorials for several weeks.

331.1/325.7 THE EARL OF DUBLIN   On September 10, 1849, Queen Victoria, to show her satisfaction with her visit to Ireland (see entry 255.4), created Edward VII (then the Prince of Wales), Earl of Dublin (Sidney Lee, *Queen Victoria*, 1903, p. 202).

331.3/325.8 ALL THE WOMEN HE RODE HIMSELF   This alludes to Edward's VII's notorious immorality, a quality in him which the Irish always emphasized. Cf. entry 751.27.

331.11/325.16 MAY YOUR SHADOW NEVER GROW LESS   Though I know this to be a common Irish saying, I have not located it in print.

331.39/326.3 ANCIENT IRISH FACECLOTH   S. Gilbert says this description of the Citizen's handkerchief "brings to our mind Homer's detailed description of the golden baldric of Hercules (*Odyssey*, XI, 609–14), 'whereon wonderous things were wrought,' scenes of hunting and war" (*JJU*, p. 276).

331.40/326.4 SOLOMON OF DROMA AND MANUS TOMALTACH OG MAC-DONOGH, AUTHORS OF THE BOOK OF BALLYMOTE   In his Introduction to *The Book of Ballymote* (Dublin: Royal Irish Academy, 1887), Robert Atkinson briefly discusses the history of the manuscript and its scribes. Three scribes are mentioned, Solam (or Solomon) O'Droma, Magnus (or Manus) O'Duigenan, and Robert mac Sheehy. The manuscript does contain a note that Atkinson includes which mentions its being written "in the house of Tomaltoch mac Tadg . . . mac Donogh . . . mac Dermod, from whom are the mac Dermods of Ballymote" (p. 1; the ellipses are in the original).

332.3/326.8 EACH OF THE FOUR EVANGELISTS IN TURN PRESENTING TO EACH OF THE FOUR MASTERS IN TURN HIS EVANGELICAL SYMBOL . . . The symbols of Matthew, Mark, Luke, and John are, respectively, an angel (or winged man) carrying a lance, a lion (often winged), an ox (often winged), and a flying eagle. These symbols derive from Revelation 4:7. The four masters are the four compilers of one of the most important Irish historical documents, *The Annals of the Four Masters*, a work done in 1632–36 at the Franciscan monastery of Donegal by Michael O'Clery, Conaire O'Clery, Cucogry (or Peregrine) O'Clery, and Ferfeasa O'Mulconry.

332.12/326.17 LONG LONG AGO IN THE TIME OF THE BARMECIDES   This alludes to James Clarence Mangan's poem "The Time of the Barmecides." The first stanza ends, "To the old, old time, long, long ago,/ The time of the Barmecides!/ To the old, old time, long, long ago,/ The time of the Barmecides!" The phrase "long, long ago,/ In the time of the Barmecides" occurs many times in the poem. For the text, see *Irish Literature*, VI, 2367. The Barmecides (or Barmakids) were a Persian noble family of the eighth century.

332.13/326.18 GLENDALOUGH . . .   The places in this list are actual places in Ireland, and most of them are considered "sights worth seeing." Only those which seem to have some allusive element are separately noted.

332.17/326.22 THE VALE OF OVOCA   This is the vale celebrated in Thomas Moore's song "The Meeting of the Waters" (Ovoca is a variant spelling of Avoca), see entry 162.30.

332.18/326.24 THE GLEN OF AHERLOW   Hodgart and Worthington list this as an allusion to "The Glen of Aherlow," by Kickham. But Charles Joseph Kickham's song is probably better known as "Patrick Sheehan." The song begins, "My name is Patrick Sheehan,/ My years are thirty-four," and most of the song's seven stanzas end with some variation on the phrase "in the Glen of Aherlow." See *Irish Literature*, V, 1831.

332.23/326.28 THE THREE BIRTH PLACES OF THE FIRST DUKE OF WELLING-
TON   Arthur Wellesley, first duke of Wellington (1769–1852), was born in Dublin, but there is some uncertainty about the exact house in which he was born. D. A. Chart mentions the dispute and says that no. 24 Merrion Street is the most probable house (*Story of Dublin*, p. 255).

332.39/327.1 SOLD BY AUCTION OFF IN MOROCCO . . .   Though I cannot confirm their sale as slaves, the Jews in Morocco were at this time (1904) subject to constant and detailed restriction and abuse. Only with the Franco-Spanish occupation in 1907–8 did Moslem persecution of the Jews begin to be ameliorated. According to the *Universal Jewish Encyclopedia*, it was not until 1907 that compulsory service of Jews to Moslems and the bastinado as punishment were abolished.

332.40/327.3 THE NEW JERUSALEM   The New Jerusalem is the
Christian heavenly city described by St. John in Revelation 21
and 22.

333.20/327.22 A NEW APOSTLE TO THE GENTILES   Paul was the
"apostle to the Gentiles." In Romans 11:13 we read, "For I speak
to you Gentiles, inasmuch as I am the apostle of the Gentiles." See
also Acts 9:15. This is vaguely similar to an earlier remark of
Stephen's; see entry 29.27.

333.22/327.24 LOVE YOUR NEIGHBORS   Jesus several times said "Love
thy neighbor"; see, for example, Matthew 19:19 and 22:39.

333.24/327.26 BEGGAR MY NEIGHBOR IS HIS MOTTO   "Beggar-my-
neighbor" is the name of a simple card game for children. Bloom
mentions this game on p. 686.3/670.8.

334.3/328.5 SANCTIMONIUS CROMWELL . . .   Cromwell's assault on
Drogheda, in which the entire garrison of at least three thousand
were killed, is probably the most notorious episode of his bloody
career in Ireland. No account I have seen mentions the literal use of
a motto around the cannonmouth, and the Citizen may be hyper-
bolically referring to Cromwell's gross sanctimoniousness. Cromwell did say, "I am persuaded, that this is a righteous judgment of
God upon those barbarous wretches, who have imbrued their
hands in so much innocent blood" (quoted in Maurice Ashley's
Oliver Cromwell: The Conservative Dictator [London, 1937],
p. 165).

334.6/328.8 DID YOU READ THAT SKIT IN THE UNITED IRISHMAN TODAY
ABOUT THAT ZULU CHIEF THAT'S VISITING ENGLAND   No such
sketch appeared in the *United Irishman*, though similar sketches
did occasionally appear. This probably derives from the *Freeman's
Journal* of June 2, 1904, which carried a brief article beginning,
"The Alake of Abeokuta was the principal guest of our patriotic
countrywoman, Mrs. J. R. Green, wife of the great historian, on
Tuesday, at Mrs. Green's home in Westminster" (p. 4, col. h).
The article goes on to list the eminent persons whom the poten-
tate met there. R. M. Adams (*SS*, p. 202) points out that an article
in the *Irish Independent* of Tuesday, May 31, 1904, mentions a
Bible given to the Alake by Queen Victoria (p. 6).

334.18/328.20 ANANIAS PRAISEGOD BAREBONES   Praise-God Barebone
(Barebon) (1596?–1679) was an English lay preacher and a member of the so-called "Barebone's Parliament" assembled by Cromwell in 1653. Ananias may refer to the biblical liar of that name;
see entry 686.31.

334.38/328.39 IS THAT BY GRIFFITH? . . .   Arthur Griffith was editor of the *United Irishman*, and, according to R. M. Adams (*SS*, p. 202), he did do skits and sketches under the pseudonym "Shanganagh." No such sketch, however, appeared in either the June 11 or June 18, 1904, issue of the paper, so the sketch in *Ulysses* is presumably original with Joyce. B. Benstock has suggested that P is said to be a very good initial in allusion to Parnell (*JJQ*, III [Winter, 1966], 161).

335.4/329.4 DID YOU READ THAT REPORT BY . . . CASEMENT   Sir Roger Casement (1864–1916), who was born in Dun Laoghaire, published a report in February, 1904, on his investigations into the methods of white traders in the Belgian Congo. The report led to a Belgian commission that supported his findings and brought about a change in Congo government. Casement was executed for treason by the British during World War I after his plan to get German help for Irish independence fell through.

335.39/329.39 BLOOM GAVE THE IDEA FOR SINN FEIN TO GRIFFITH   See entry 163.38.

336.2/330.1 ROBBING PETER TO PAY PAUL   "To rob Peter to pay Paul" is proverbial and is listed in the *ODEP*.

336.4/330.3 GOD SAVE IRELAND   This alludes to the song by T. D. Sullivan; see entry 163.16.

336.6/330.5 OLD METHUSALEM BLOOM   This refers to Methuselah, who lived longer than any other man—969 years, according to Genesis 5:27. But it also seems to identify Bloom's father with the "old" Jerusalem in contrast to the new Jerusalem mentioned on p. 332.41/327.3

337.18/331.16 BLOOM AND THE SINN FEIN   This repeats the idea expressed on p. 335.39/329.39; see entry 163.38.

337.31/331.27 WHO IS JUNIUS   "Junius" was the pen name of the writer of a series of letters which appeared in the London *Public Advertiser* from January, 1769, to January, 1772, criticizing and satirizing George III and his ministers. The true identity of Junius is not definitely known even today. One of those most frequently suggested to have been Junius is Dublin-born Sir Philip Francis (1740–1818), though in recent years evidence has appeared which points in another direction. For a brief discussion of the question, which reflects the opinion of that day, see the sketch of Sir Philip Francis in *Irish Literature*, III, 1226–28.

337.33/331.29 HE DREW UP ALL THE PLANS ACCORDING TO THE HUNGARIAN SYSTEM   This suggests that Bloom was behind Arthur Griffith's idea that Ireland should use Hungary as its example in its attempts to gain independence from England. Griffith's *The Resurrection of Hungary* began appearing serially in his paper *The United Irishman* on January 2, 1904, and ran until June 25, 1904. The purpose of the work, as Griffith explained, was to tell the story of how the resurrection of Hungary developed and to propose the adoption of a similar plan for Ireland. The work appeared in book form later in 1904. For a discussion of the backgrounds of this allusion, with emphasis on Bloom's Hungarian qualities and on Joyce's use of Griffith's book, see Robert Tracy, "Leopold Bloom Fourfold: A Hungarian-Hebraic-Hellenic-Hibernian Hero," *Massachusetts Review*, VI (Spring–Summer, 1965), 523–38.

337.39/331.35   ISLAND OF SAINTS AND SAGES   See entry 40.19.

338.15/332.11   THERE'S MANY A TRUE WORD SPOKEN IN JEST   This proverbial saying which is listed in the *ODEP*, occurs in Swift's *Polite Conversation*, first conversation, when Miss Notable says, "for they say, many a true Word spoken in jest" (p. 118).

338.26/332.21   A WOLF IN SHEEP'S CLOTHING   The *ODEP* lists several instances of this proverbial saying, including two in Shakespeare. The phrase goes back to Aesop's fable "The Wolf in Sheep's Clothing," but in that story, the wolf's disguise destroys him, for he is killed by the hungry shepherd who mistook him for a sheep.

338.27/332.22   AHASUERUS   Ahasuerus is one of the names by which the legendary Wandering Jew is known; see entry 217.35 and the source cited there. An obviously less relevant instance is Ahasuerus (identified with Xerxes), king of Persia and husband of Esther in the book of Esther.

338.32/332.26   SAINT PATRICK WOULD WANT TO LAND AGAIN AT BALLY-KINLAR AND CONVERT US   As everything else about St. Patrick, the place of his landing in Ireland is disputed, but none of the authorities I have consulted gives Ballykinlar as the site.

339.1/332.36   MONKS OF BENEDICT OF SPOLETO, CARTHUSIANS AND CAMAL-DOLESI   St. Benedict of Nursia (d. *ca.* 547) is the founder of the Benedictines and the father of western monasticism (Nursia is a small town near Spoleto, Italy). The Carthusian order was founded by St. Bruno in 1084 at La Grande Chartreuse, near Grenoble, France. The Camaldolese order was founded by St. Romauld at Camaldoli, Italy, *ca.* 1012.

339.2/332.37   CISTERCIANS AND OLIVETANS, ORATORIANS AND VALLOM-BROSANS   The Cistercians, or Order of Citeaux, was a Benedictine reform, established at Citeaux, Burgundy, in 1098 by St.

Robert, Abbot of Molesme, to restore literal observance of the rule of St. Benedict. The Olivetans are a branch of the white monks of the Benedictine order, founded in 1319. The Oratorians, or Oratory of St. Philip Neri, is an order founded by St. Philip Neri at Rome in 1575 and promoted by Gregory III. The Vallombrosan order was founded by St. John Gualbert, *ca.* 1056; it takes its name from the mother-house at Vallombrosa, near Florence.

339.3/332.38 THE FRIARS OF AUGUSTINE, BRIGITTINES, PREMONSTRATE-SIANS The Augustinians or Hermits of St. Augustine is a religious order formed by the union of several monastic societies following the rule of St. Augustine; the union occurred in 1256 through the efforts of Pope Alexander VI. The Brigittines or Order of St. Saviour is an order for monks and nuns founded by St. Briget of Sweden at Vadstena in 1346. The Premonstratensians or Order of Canons Regular of Prémontré was founded by St. Norbert at Prémontré, France, in 1120.

339.4/332.39 SERVI, TRINITARIANS, AND THE CHILDREN OF PETER NOLASCO The Servi (or Servites) or Order of Servants of Mary was founded by seven noble youths of Florence in 1233. The Trinitarians or Order of the Most Holy Trinity was founded in the twelfth century by St. John of Matha and St. Felix of Valois, for the ransom of captives. The Children of Peter Nolasco refers to the Mercedarians, or Order of Our Lady of Mercy for the Ransom of Captives, a congregation founded by St. Peter Nolasco in 1218 and especially devoted to the ransom of captives from the Moors.

339.5/332.40 FROM CARMEL MOUNT THE CHILDREN OF ELIJAH PROPHET LED BY ALBERT BISHOP AND BY TERESA OF AVILA, CALCED AND OTHER This refers to the Carmelites or Order of Our Lady of Mount Carmel, which traces its origin back to the prophet Elijah, whom the Carmelites claim as their founder. Albert bishop refers to St. Albert, patriarch of Jerusalem, who, in 1206, gave the Rule which the Order now observes to the Hermits of Mount Carmel in Palestine. St. Teresa of Jesus, the virgin of Avila, introduced (along with St. John of the Cross) a great reformation into the Order in the sixteenth century. Since then, the Order has been divided into two branches, that of the Calced Carmelites, who observe a rule modified by Eugenius IV, and the Discalced Carmelites, who keep the primitive rule of St. Albert without any mitigation. *Discalced* refers to going barefoot or wearing sandals, as a form of austerity.

339.7/332.42 FRIARS BROWN AND GREY, SONS OF POOR FRANCIS, CAPUCHINS Friars brown probably alludes to the Dominicans or "black friars," mentioned a few lines later. Friars grey and Sons of St. Francis both refer to the Franciscan Order, founded by St. Francis of Assisi in 1209; there may also be an allusion here to the song "I Am a Friar of Orders Grey," by O'Keefe and Reeve, words and music of which can be found in Hatton and Faning, *Songs of England*, I, 44–46.

339.8/333.1 CORDELIERS, MINIMES AND OBSERVANTS AND THE DAUGHTERS OF CLARA   A cordelier is a Franciscan friar of the strict rule, so called from the knotted cords the friars wear around their waists. The minimes are friars belonging to the mendicant Order of Minims (Ordo Minimorum Eremitarum), founded by St. Francis of Paula in 1454. The observants is a name given to the Friars Minor of the Regular Observance, a branch of the Franciscan Order, incorporated in the Order of Friars Minor by Leo XIII. The daughters of Clara must refer to the Poor Clares (or Poor Ladies, or Sisters of St. Clare), an order founded by St. Francis of Assisi and by St. Clare of Assisi in 1212.

339.9/333.2 THE SONS OF DOMINIC, THE FRIARS PREACHERS, AND THE SONS OF VINCENT   The sons of Dominic are the Dominicans, or Dominican Order, founded by St. Dominic in 1215. The friars preachers, or Order of Preachers, is the principal part of the Order of St. Dominic. The Sons of Vincent are the Vincentians, or Congregation of the Mission of St. Vincent de Paul, founded by St. Vincent de Paul in 1625 (cf. entry 339.18).

339.10/333.3 THE MONKS OF S. WOLSTAN: AND IGNATIUS HIS CHILDREN St. Wolstan (*ca.* 1008–95) was a Benedictine monk and a bishop, but he did not, as the phrase implies, found an order. Ignatius his children probably refers to the Society of Jesus (Jesuits), founded by St. Ignatius Loyola in 1534.

339.11/333.4 THE CONFRATERNITY OF THE CHRISTIAN BROTHERS LED BY THE REVEREND BROTHER EDMUND IGNATIUS RICE   Edmund Ignatius Rice (1762–1844), who was born in Callan, Ireland, was the founder of the Institute of Brothers of the Christian School, commonly known as the Irish Christian Brothers.

339.13/333.7 [LIST OF SAINTS]   While most of the names in the following list refer to actual saints, some do not. For names that indicate actual saints, I have given brief information and a reference to *Butler's Lives of the Saints* (1962 ed.) as a source of further information.

339.13/333.7 S. CYR AND S. ISIDORE ARATOR   St. Cyr probably refers to St. Cyricus, or Quiricus, martyr, who was killed while he was still a young child; he is commonly called St. Cyr in France (d.

304?; Butler, II, 552; June 16). St. Isidore the Husbandman (d. 1130) is the patron of Madrid (Butler, II, 323; May 15).

339.14/333.7 S. JAMES THE LESS AND S. PHOCAS OF SINOPE AND S. JULIAN HOSPITATOR   St. James the Less was an apostle, called the Less to distinguish him from another apostle, James the son of Zebedee; he became bishop of Jerusalem (Butler, II, 203; May 1). St. Phocas is probably St. Phocas, gardener (date unknown), who dwelt near the gate of Sinope, a city in Paphlagonia; he allowed a group that was searching for him in order to kill him to spend the night with him; during the night he prepared himself for death and the next morning revealed his identity; his executioners were impressed, but killed him anyway (Butler, III, 617, Sept. 22). St. Julian the Hospitaller (date unknown) is said to have slain his parents in bed, having mistaken them for his wife and an adulterous lover; in penance he built a hospice near a river (Butler, I, 314; Feb. 12).

339.15/333.8 S. FELIX DE CANTALICE AND S. SIMON STYLITES   St. Felix of Cantalice (1513–87) was born at Cantalice in Apulia; his vocation was shown to him via a miraculous escape from an accident, in which the bullocks and plow with which he was plowing passed over him (Butler, II, 344; May 18). St. Simeon Stylites (d. 459) is among the most famous of the saints who lived on pillars; he spent thirty-seven years on his pillar on Mount Telanissae (Butler, I, 34; Jan. 5).

339.16/333.9 S. STEPHEN PROTOMARTYR AND S. JOHN OF GOD AND S. FERREOL   St. Stephen Protomartyr was the first martyr of the Christian church; his death by stoning is described in Acts 6 and 7 (Butler, IV, 616; Dec. 26). St. John of God (1495–1550), born in Portugal, was the founder of the Order of the Brothers Hospitallers, and is the patron of hospitals and of the sick (Butler, I, 517; March 8). There is more than one St. Ferreolus, but this St. Ferreol is probably St. Ferreolus, martyr (third century?), of whom little is known; he was put to death near Vienne on the Rhone river (Butler, III, 591; Sept. 18).

339.17/333.10 S. LEUGARDE AND S. THEODOTUS AND S. VULMAR   St. Leugarde is probably St. Molua (or Lughaidh, or Lugaid), abbot, an Irish saint who died in 608 (Butler, III, 264; August 4). St. Theodotus, martyr (d. 304?), is said to have been tortured and beheaded for having given Christian burial to the bodies of some Christian maidens (Butler, II, 341; May 18). St. Vulmar (or Wulmar), abbot (d. ca. 700), was born in Picardy and founded a monastery there (Butler, III, 154; July 20).

339.18/333.11 S. RICHARD AND S. VINCENT DE PAUL AND S. MARTIN OF

TODI   St. Richard is probably the St. Richard (d. 720) who is called "St. Richard, King of England," although there is no historical basis for the appellation; he was the father of several saints (Butler, I, 270, Feb. 7). St. Vincent de Paul (*ca.* 1580–1660), the son of a farmer in Gascony, founded the Congregation of the Mission and the Sisters of Charity and is especially associated with relief of the destitute (Butler, III, 141; July 19—see also entry 339.9). I have located no St. Martin of Todi; since the next several names refer in part to characters in *Ulysses*, this may be pointed at Martin Cunningham and may suggest that he "toadys" to the forces at Dublin Castle.

339.19/333.12   S. MARTIN OF TOURS AND S. ALFRED AND S. JOSEPH AND S. DENIS   St. Martin of Tours (d. 397) was the son of a pagan Roman officer; he conscientiously objected to fighting in war and lived as a recluse; he was made bishop of Tours against his will (*ca.* 371); he was the pioneer of monasticism in Gaul and thereby considerably influenced the Celtic church (Butler, IV, 310; Nov. 11). St. Alfred is probably St. Alfred the Great of England, though no such saint is listed in Butler; Baring-Gould lists St. Alfred and criticizes his not having been authoritatively inscribed in the calendars of the church (Baring-Gould, *Lives*, XVI [Appendix], 285). St. Joseph is probably the St. Joseph who is husband of the Blessed Virgin Mary (Butler, I, 631; March 19). St. Denis is probably St. Dionysius, bishop of Paris, on whom see entry 357.8.

339.20/333.13   S. CORNELIUS AND S. LEOPOLD AND S. BERNARD AND S. TERRENCE   St. Cornelius (d. 253) was a pope who was killed in the persecution of Gallus; he is named in the Canon of the Mass (Butler, III, 560; Sept. 16). St. Leopold of Austria (1073–1136), known as Leopold the Good, reigned as Margrave of Austria for forty years; he also founded several monastic institutions (Butler, IV, 350; Nov. 15). St. Bernard (d. 1153) was one of the Doctors of the Church (Butler, III, 360; Aug. 20; see entry 356.31). Though *Butler's Lives* does not include any St. Terence, there have been several saints by that name; all are minor, but the best known may be St. Terence, bishop and martyr (first century), who is briefly noted in *The Book of Saints*, 5th edition (N.Y.: T. Y. Crowell Company, 1966), p. 666.

339.21/333.14   S. EDWARD AND S. OWEN CANICULUS AND S. ANONYMOUS . . . S. SYNONYMOUS   St. Edward is probably St. Edward the Confessor (1004–66), King of England from 1042 through 1066, known in his lifetime for his holiness and gentility. There is no St. Owen Caniculus; this refers to the dog, Garryowen. The last several items in this list have named characters in *Ulysses* (most of them in this episode) as well as saints, and Garryowen culminates this movement. The next six names in the list—Anonymous through Synonymous—do not, of course, represent actual saints.

339.23/333.17   S. LAURENCE O'TOOLE AND S. JAMES OF DINGLE AND COMPOSTELLA AND S. COLUMCILLE   St. Laurence O'Toole (1128–80) is one of the better-known Irish saints; he was archbishop of Dublin for many years (Butler, IV, 341; Nov. 14). St. James of Compostella is St. James the Greater, Apostle, whose relics are said to be at Compostella (Butler, III, 182; July 25), but I do not know why he is said to be "of Dingle" (Dingle Bay is in county Kerry). St. Columcille (or Columba), Abbot of Iona (d. 597), is among the most famous of the Celtic saints; he is especially noted for the many monastery schools he founded in Ireland and Scotland (Butler, II, 506; June 9).

339.25/333.18   S. COLUMBA AND S. CELESTINE AND S. COLMAN   Columba is simply another name for Columcille; see the preceding entry. Both Pope Celestine I and Pope Celestine V are saints, but this probably alludes to the latter, since he was the pope who sent St. Patrick to Ireland (Butler, II, 40; July 27—and see entry 666.38). There have been several Irish saints named Colman, and it is impossible to know which, if any specific one, is intended here; perhaps the best known is St. Colman of Cloyne (sixth century), first bishop of Cloyne; little is known of him, but he was supposedly a poet at the court of Cashel and was a heathen until middle age (Butler, IV, 419; Nov. 24).

339.26/333.19   S. KEVIN AND S. BRENDAN AND S. FRIGIDIAN AND S. SENAN   St. Kevin (d. 618) is among the best-known Irish saints; he founded the famous monastery at Glendalough and is one of the principal patrons of Dublin (Butler, II, 463; June 3). On St. Brendan, see entry 297.1. St. Frigidian (d. 558?), bishop of Lucca, was an Irishman who went on a pilgrimage to Italy and became a hermit there on Mount Pisano (Butler, I, 626; March 18). There are some twenty-two Irish saints named Senan; the best known is St. Senan (d. *ca.* 560), who founded a monastery on what is now called Scattery Island in the Shannon estuary; he was apparently consecrated a bishop at some time (Butler, I, 522; March 8).

339.27/333.20   S. FACHTNA AND S. COLUMBANUS AND S. GALL AND S. FURSEY   St. Fachtna (or Fachanan) was a sixth-century Irish saint who founded the important monastic school of Ross in county Cork (Butler, III, 329; Aug. 14). St. Columbanus (or Columban; d. 615) was among the most important of the Irish saints who went to the continent; he established several important abbeys and monasteries in France and Italy (Butler, IV, 409; Nov. 23–see also entry 27.38). St. Gall (d. *ca.* 635), Irish saint, is the best known of the twelve monks who left Ireland with St. Columban (Butler, IV, 126; Oct. 16). On St. Fursa (or Fursey), see entry 297.1.

339.28/333.21   S. FINTAN AND S. FIACRE AND S. JOHN NEPOMUC AND S. THOMAS AQUINAS   There are several Irish saints Fintan, but this is probably St. Fintan of Cloneenagh (d. 603), a saint who lived so austere a life that monks of neighboring monasteries protested (Butler, I, 356; Feb. 17). St. Fiacre (d. 670?) is another of the famous Irish saints who went to the continent; he is known for his miracles of healing, and his shrine is still resorted to (Butler, III, 460; Sept. 1—see also entry 42.8). St. John Nepomuc, martyr (*ca.* 1345–93), was born in Nepomuk, Bohemia; there is a controversy over the details of his murder by King Wenceslaus IV of Bohemia, but one version holds that St. John was killed because he would not reveal the confessional secrets of Sophia, the king's wife, whom he suspected of adultery (Butler, II, 332; May 16). St. Thomas Aquinas needs no identification (Butler, I, 509; March 7).

339.29/333.22   S. IVES OF BRITTANY AND S. MICHAN   St. Ives of Brittany is probably St. Ivo of Kermartin (d. 1303); his name was Yves Hélory, and he was born near Tréguier in Brittany; he became an ecclesiastical and civil lawyer, built a hospital with his legal fees, and is the patron of lawyers (Butler, II, 351; May 19). St. Michan (tenth or eleventh century?) although well-known to Dubliners as patron of St. Michan's parish and church, is a rather obscure Irish or Danish saint. He is not listed in Butler. There is an account in John O'Hanlon's *Lives of the Irish Saints* (Dublin: James Duffy and Sons, n.d.), VIII, 365–78 (Aug. 25), but most of the article deals with the parish and the church rather than with the saint. O'Hanlon says he is listed in the Calendar prefixed to the Martyrology of Christ Church, Dublin, under August 25, as "*S. Michee Confessoris*" (p. 366).

339.30/333.22   S. HERMAN-JOSEPH AND THE THREE PATRONS OF HOLY YOUTH . . .   This must refer to the German mystic, the Blessed Herman Joseph (d. 1241), though he has never been canonized (Butler, II, 48; April 7). The next three saints were all Jesuits, and all three died quite young. On St. Aloysius Gonzaga, see entry 685.35. St. Stanislaus Kostka (1550–68) overcame family opposition to join the Jesuits; he was distinguished for his innocence (Butler, IV, 335; Nov. 13—on the Joyce family's use of this saint's name, see Ellmann, *JJ*, p. 12). St. John Berchmans (1599–1621) was not canonized until 1888 (Butler, IV, 429; Nov. 26).

339.32/333.25 SAINTS GERVASIUS, SERVASIUS, AND BONIFACIUS St. Gervasius (usually paired with St. Protasius, both martyrs) was an early martyr of unknown date; the relics of these two martyrs found by St. Ambrose are now held to be valid, but the stories told about them have no basis (Butler, II, 583; June 19). St. Servatius (d. 384) was an early bishop of Tongres who had a considerable cultus during the middle ages (Butler, II, 297; May 13). The best known of the many Saints Boniface is St. Boniface, bishop and martyr, who was born probably in Devonshire, *ca.* 680, and became the Apostle of Germany; he was murdered by heathens at Dokkum in 754 (Butler, II, 477; June 5).

339.33/333.25 S. BRIDE AND S. KIERAN AND S. CANICE OF KILKENNY AND S. JARLATH OF TUAM St. Bride is a variant name of St. Brigid (*ca.* 450–*ca.* 525), one of the most venerated of Irish saints; her founding the monastery at Kildare made her the spiritual mother of Irish nuns for many centuries; she is called "the Mary of the Gael" (Butler, I, 225; Feb. 1). St. Kieran of Ossory, bishop (d. *ca.* 530), is another Irish saint; he was probably one of the twelve consecrated by St. Patrick and is venerated as the first bishop of Ossory and the founder of the monastery at Saighir (Butler, I, 487; March 5). St. Canice, abbot (d. *ca.* 599), was born in Derry and founded monasteries at Aghaboe and Kilkenny; he was a zealous missionary to Scotland under St. Columba (Butler, IV, 86; Oct. 11—see also entry 44.4). Little is known of St. Jarlath, bishop (d. *ca.* 550), but he is venerated as the founder of the see at Tuam in Galway, and his feast is kept throughout Ireland (Butler, II, 489; June 6).

339.34/333.27 S. FINBARR AND S. PAPPIN OF BALLYMUN St. Finbarr, bishop (d. *ca.* 633), is venerated as the founder of the city and see of Cork; his monastery in the river Lee had a strong influence over all the south of Ireland (Butler, III, 634; Sept. 25). I have found no St. Pappin in any of the sources I consulted, though there may well be such a saint.

339.35/333.27 BROTHER ALOYSIUS PACIFICUS AND BROTHER LOUIS BELLICOSUS St. Francis of Assisi had a Brother Pacificus who is the best-known person of that name (see *Cath. Encyc.*, XI, 382). I have found no Brother Bellicosus, and the neat pairing of the names suggests that he is fictional.

339.36/333.28 SAINTS ROSE OF LIMA AND OF VITERBO AND S. MARTHA OF BETHANY There are saints Rose of Lima and Viterbo, both

virgins. The former (1586–1617) was born of Spanish parents in
Lima, Peru, and was the first canonized saint of the New World
(Butler, III, 444: Aug. 30). St. Rose of Viterbo (d. *ca.* 1252?)
preached in the streets of Viterbo, in the Romagna, against the
emperor Frederick II and the Ghibelline garrison (Butler, III, 487;
Sept. 4). St. Martha of Bethany is the sister of Lazarus, whose
resurrection is described in John II (Butler, III, 205; July 29).

339.37/333.29   S. MARY OF EGYPT AND S. LUCY AND S. BRIGID   St. Mary
of Egypt (fifth century?) was supposedly an actress and courtesan
who fled into the desert beyond the Jordan to expiate her sins, and
was found dead (Butler, II, 14; April 2). St. Lucy, virgin and
martyr, suffered at Syracuse, *ca.* 304, but little else is known of
her; a legend says that a disappointed suitor denounced her as a
Christian and she was exposed in a brothel, though no harm resulted; her eyes were put out, either by a tyrant or by herself,
but were miraculously restored more beautiful than before (Butler, IV, 548; Dec. 13). On St. Brigid, see St. Bride, in entry 339.33.

339.38/333.30   S. ATTRACTA AND S. DYMPNA AND S. ITA AND S. MARION
CALPENSIS   St. Attracta (or Araght), virgin, was an Irish saint
of the sixth (?) century; she was a solitary, first at Killaraght, on
Lough Gara, and then at Drum, near Boyle (Butler, III, 304; Aug.
11). St. Dympna (d. *ca.* 650?) was a virgin whose relics were
found at Gheel near Antwerp, in the thirteenth century and produced so many miracles of curing insanity that she is venerated
as a patroness of lunatics; her feast is kept in Ireland because of
the popular story that she was an Irish princess (Butler, II,
320; May 15). St. Ita (or Ida, or Mida; d. *ca.* 750) is the most popular female Irish saint after St. Brigid; she had a community of
maidens and a school for small boys southwest of Limerick (Butler, I, 96; Jan. 15). There is no St. Marion Calpensis; this refers to
Molly, who was described earlier as the "pride of Calpe's rocky
mount" (p. 319.37/314.14). Calpe is an ancient name for Gibraltar.

339.39/333.31   THE BLESSED SISTER TERESA OF THE CHILD JESUS AND S.
BARBARA   Blessed Sister Teresa-of-the-Child-Jesus is now St.
Teresa of Lisieux, having been canonized in 1925 (and Willis E.
McNeely says that "Blessed" here is an anachronism, since St.
Teresa was not beatified until 1923 [*JJQ*, II, 294]); St. Teresa
(1873–97) was a young Carmelite nun who became known for her
simplicity and perfection in doing the small parts of her daily
duties (Butler, IV, 12; Oct. 3). St. Barbara, virgin and martyr (date
unknown), was one of the most popular saints of the middle ages,
though there is now some doubt whether she ever existed; legend

says she was imprisoned and finally killed by her father for being a Christian; she is invoked against lightning and fire, and by gunners (Butler, IV, 487; Dec. 4).

339.40/333.32 S. SCHOLASTICA AND S. URSULA . . . St. Scholastica, virgin (d. 543), was the sister of St. Benedict and ruled a convent at Plombariola, near Monte Cassino, under his direction (Butler, I, 292; Feb. 10). On St. Ursula (Butler, IV, 165; Oct. 21), see entry 6.33.

340.1/333.35 THE BLESSED SYMBOLS OF THEIR EFFICACIES . . . These saints' symbols are impossible to annotate precisely, since most of the emblems represent, or are associated with, more than one saint (sometimes with a dozen or more). Anyone interested in finding out which saints these emblems can refer to should consult a book on saints and their symbols which has an index of symbols. One of the best of these is F. C. Husenbeth, *Emblems of Saints: By Which They Are Distinguished in Works of Art* (London, 1850). Almost every item in this list can be found in Husenbeth, provided that some of them are translated into the ordinary language of saints' symbolism. For "cruse," see "earthen vessel" or "pot" in Husenbeth, for "babes in a bathtub," see *s.v.* "children" in Husenbeth; by "buckshot" Joyce may be referring to "balls"; "soupladles" probably should be read "spoons"; boxes of vaseline" probably means "box of ointment"; for "crutches," see "staffs"; for "forceps," see "tongs" or "pinchers"; I am not sure what Joyce means by "watertight boots," unless it is a reference to those many saints who are depicted as walking on water (see "river," "sea," "water," and "sacrament" in Husenbeth). The rest of these terms can be found without difficulty in Husenbeth or similar dictionaries.

340.9/334.1 THE INTROIT IN EPIPHANIA DOMINI WHICH BEGINNETH SURGE, ILLUMINARE What this means is that the Introit for the Mass for the Epiphany of our Lord (Jan. 6) is being chanted, but the phrase quoted is not from the Introit, but from the Epistle of that day. The Epistle is from Isaiah 60:1–6, and begins, "Surge, illuminare, Ierusalem, quia venit lumen tuum, et gloria Domini super te orta est" ("Arise, shine; for thy light is come, and the glory of the Lord is risen upon thee"). See the following entry.

340.11/334.3 THE GRADUAL OMNES WHICH SAITH DE SABA This does refer correctly to the Gradual of the Mass for the Epiphany of our Lord (cf. the preceding entry). The Gradual for this day says, "Omnes de Saba venient, aurum et thus deferentes, Et laudem Domino annuntiantes" ("all they from Sheba shall come: they shall bring gold and incense; and they shall show forth the praises of the Lord"—Isaiah 60:6).

340.12/334.4 DIVERS WONDERS SUCH AS CASTING OUT DEVILS . . .   Most of these are miracles of Christ. For his casting out devils, see Matthew 9:32–34, Mark 5:1–20, and Luke 8:26–39; for raising the dead, see the story of the widow's son (Luke 7:11–17), the story of Jairus' daughter (Matt. 9:18–26, Mark 5:21–43, and Luke 8:40–56), and the story of Lazarus (John 11:1–44); for multiplying fishes, see Matthew 14:13–21 and 15:32–38, Mark 6:34–44 and 8:1–9, Luke 9:12–17, and John 6:1–14. Jesus often healed the halt and blind; for some instances see Matthew 9:1–18, 9:27–31, 15:30, and 20:29–34.

340.17/334.9 FATHER O'FLYNN   This alludes to the song "Father O'Flynn"; see entry 170.30.

340.31/334.24 ADIUTORIUM NOSTRUM IN NOMINE DOMINI . . .   These four lines are a common formula before prayers. They say "Our help is in the name of the Lord," "Who made heaven and earth," "The Lord be with you," "And with your spirit." These lines are said before the "Benedictio ad Omnia," which follows on p. 340.37/334.30.

340.37/334.30 DEUS, CUIUS VERBO . . .   This is the "Benedictio ad omnia" ("Blessing for all things"), about which the *Ritual* says, "This formula of blessing may be used by any priest for all things for which a special blessing is not given in the Roman Ritual." The prayer says, "O God, by whose word all things are made holy, pour down your blessing on these which you created. Grant that whoever, giving thanks to you, uses them in accordance with your law and your will, may by calling on your holy name receive through your aid health of body and protection of soul, through Christ our Lord." (In most *Rituals* this blessing can be found in Tit. VIII, cap. 8.) But Willis E. McNeely points out the strangeness of using this blessing here whereas two special blessings, the *Benedictio Domorum*, and the *Benedictio Panis, Vini, Aquae et Fructum* might well have been used instead (*JJQ*, II, 295–96).

342.1/335.36 CURSING THE CURSE OF CROMWELL ON HIM   P. W. Joyce (*English As We Speak It*, p. 166) says, "When one desires to give another a particularly evil wish he says, 'The curse of Cromwell on you!' So that Cromwell's atrocities are stored up in the people's memories to this day, in the form of a proverb." The *ODEP* lists this, but gives no explanation.

342.2/335.37 BELL, BOOK, AND CANDLE   Frederick George Lee, in

A Glossary of Liturgical and Ecclesiastical Terms (London, 1877), says that to anathematize by bell, book, and candle "was to pronounce the greater excommunication against a person who had been regularly and formally convicted of any of the heaviest crimes; done only after the most careful inquiry, and by the highest ecclesiastical authority" (p. 50). He then briefly describes the use of bell, book, and candle in the ceremony. The phrase has now become proverbial and is listed in the *ODEP*. It occurs once in Shakespeare's works, in *King John*, when Philip, the bastard, says, "Bell, book, and candle shall not drive me back/ When gold and silver becks me to come on" (III, iii, 12–13).

342.20/336.13   IF THE MAN IN THE MOON WAS A JEW, JEW, JEW Hodgart and Worthington list this as an allusion to "If the Man in the Moon Were a Coon," by Fisher. But if Fred Fisher did create the song, there is a slight anachronism here, for S. Spaeth dates Fisher's song in 1905 (*Hist. of Pop. Music in Amer.*, p. 349); however, it is possible that there was an earlier music hall song by this title. I have not located a copy of the song.

342.24/336.17   MENDELSSOHN WAS A JEW AND KARL MARX AND MERCADANTE AND SPINOZA   As R. M Adams has pointed out (*SS*, pp. 197–98), this is a strange list, for one of these was not a Jew at all, and the others were either apostates or unorthodox. The Mendelssohn referred to here is probably composer Felix Mendelssohn-Bartholdy (1809–47), whose father added Bartholdy to the family name when he rejected Jewry. Karl Marx (1818–83) was a German Jew, but his parents abandoned Judaism before he was born and had him baptized at the age of six. The *Standard Jewish Encyclopedia* says of Marx, "His attitude toward the Jews was characterized by antipathy and contempt, and he described Judaism and the Jews in terms similar to those used by many anti-semites" (*s.v.* Marx). I can find no evidence that Saverio Mercadante was a Jew; Bloom is simply mistaken here. Philosopher Baruch Spinoza (1632–77) was a Dutch Jew, but his unorthodox religious views led to his formal excommunication by the Sephardi community in 1656.

343.11/337.4   COME BACK TO ERIN   This alludes to "Come Back to Erin," a song by "Claribel" (Mrs. Charlotte Alington Barnard, 1830–69). It begins, "Come back to Erin, Mavourneen, Mavourneen,/ Come back Aroon, to the land of thy birth." Words and music may be found in H. F. Reddall, *Songs That Never Die*, pp. 126–27.

343.12/337.4 RAKOCZY'S MARCH   This refers to the "Rakoczi March," composed by Miklos Scholl in 1809. Words and music may be found in *Songs of Many Wars* (New York, 1943), pp. 84–89.

343.15/337.7 THE MOUNTAINS OF MOURNE   Hodgart and Worthington list this as an allusion to Percy French's song "The Mountains of Mourne"; see entry 261.32.

343.27/337.19 VISSZONTLATASRA, KEDVES BARATON! VISSZONTLATASRA This is Hungarian and means "Goodbye, my dear fellow! Goodbye!" If this involves any allusion, I am not aware of it.

343.27/337.20 GONE BUT NOT FORGOTTEN   Hodgart and Worthington list this as an allusion to "Dixie," by Daniel Decatur Emmet; presumably the allusion is to the second line of the song: "Old times dar am not forgotten," but this seems unlikely to me. (For words and music, see Chapple, *Heart Songs*, pp. 166–67.) This phrase is often used as a statement of remembrance about the dead.

343.35/337.27 I'LL BE IN FOR THE LAST GOSPEL   I presume that the allusion here is not to the fourth and last gospel, the gospel of John, but rather to The Last Gospel which is read at the conclusion of the Mass (which is John 1:1–14).

344.7/337.40 THE EARTHQUAKE OF 1534, THE YEAR OF THE REBELLION OF SILKEN THOMAS   This probably derives from the "Dublin Annals" section of Thom's *Dublin Directory* (1904), for the entry under 1534 in those "Annals" mentions the rebellion of Silken Thomas and then concludes, "An earthquake felt in Dublin" (p. 2093). On Thomas and his rebellion, see entries 45.26 and 230.15.

345.23/339.15 THEY BEHELD THE CHARIOT WHEREIN HE STOOD ASCEND TO HEAVEN   This paragraph blends several passages from the Bible. Important among them is the description of Elijah's ascent to heaven, described in II Kings 2:11: "And it came to pass, as they went on, and talked, that, behold, there appeared a chariot of fire, and horses of fire, and parted them both [Elijah and Elisha] asunder; and Elijah went up by a whirlwind into heaven." Also present is the description of the transfigured Christ in Matthew 17:2: "And his face did shine as the sun, and his raiment was white as the light," blended with Song of Solomon 6:10: "Who is she that looketh forth as the morning, fair as the moon, clear as the sun, and terrible as an army with banners?" And the voice out of heaven recalls the statement "While he yet spake, behold, a bright cloud overshadowed them: and behold a voice out of the cloud, which said, This is my beloved Son, in whom I am well pleased; hear ye him" (Matt.

17:5; similar passages occur in Mark 9:1–7 and Luke 9:28–35). Also, *Abba* recalls Christ's prayer in Gethsemane: "And he said Abba, Father, all things are possible unto thee; take this cup away from me; nevertheless not what I will, but what thou wilt" (Mark 14:36). S. Gilbert says, "Abba! Adonai!" is "a substitute for the divine name, the 'ineffable tetragrammaton' " (*JJU*, p. 272).

346.9/340.9 MARY, STAR OF THE SEA   Though not so called in the Litany of our Lady of Loreto, Mary is often addressed in Catholic prayers and liturgy as "Maris stella," "star of the sea," as, for example, in the hymn sung at Vespers of our Lady, which begins "Ave, maris stella." The Star of the Sea is also the name of the nearby church, as Richard M. Kain has pointed out.

346.13/340.12 MANY A TIME AND OFT   In *The Merchant of Venice*, Shylock says to Antonio, "Signior Antonio, many a time and oft/ In the Rialto you have rated me/ About my moneys and my usances" (I, iii, 107–9).

346.41/340.40 NONE OF YOUR SPOILT BEAUTIES, FLORA MACFLIMSY SORT   American lawyer and verse writer William Allen Butler (1825–1902) wrote a poem entitled "Nothing to Wear," which begins, "Miss Flora McFlimsey, of Madison Square,/ Has made three separate journeys to Paris." It goes on to describe Flora's extended shopping sprees and ends, "This same Miss McFlimsey, of Madison Square,/ The last time we met was in utter despair/ Because she had nothing whatever to wear!" The poem, which first appeared in 1857, was an immediate success in America, England, and on the continent. For text and comment, see Burton Stevenson, *Famous Single Poems* (New York, 1935), pp. 193–222.

347.2/341.1 CHERRYRIPE RED LIPS   The description of lips as ripe cherries is common in poetry. Thomas Campion and Robert Herrick both wrote light lyrics entitled "Cherry Ripe" built around this image. And in *A Midsummer Night's Dream*, Demetrius says, "Oh, how ripe in show/ Thy lips, those kissing cherries, tempting grow!" (III, ii, 139–40).

347.7/341.6 THE APPLE OF DISCORD   This refers to the apple that Eris or Discord threw among the guests at the wedding of Peleus and Thetis, labeled "For the fairest." Juno, Venus, and Minerva all claimed the apple, and Paris was called upon to make the decision. (The parallel suggested between that event and this episode in *Ulysses* is maintained by several situational similarities.) "Apple of discord" has become proverbial and is listed in the *ODEP*.

347.12/341.11 EVERY LITTLE IRISHMAN'S HOUSE IS HIS CASTLE   This is a variation on the proverbial "A man's house is his castle," which is listed in the *ODEP*.

347.36/341.32 WHAT'S YOUR NAME? BUTTER AND CREAM   The *ODNR* lists several rhymes that begin, "What's your name?," but none have "butter and cream"; see pp. 156–58.

349.4/342.41 MADAME VERA VERITY DIRECTRESS OF THE WOMAN BEAUTIFUL PAGE OF THE PRINCESS NOVELETTE   *Willing's Press Guide . . . 1905* (for 1904) lists *Princess Novelette* as a weekly magazine, founded in 1886, and appearing each Monday at a price of one pence. But I have not examined any copies of this magazine and cannot confirm that Madame Vera Verity edited the Woman Beautiful page.

349.15/343.10 THURSDAY FOR WEALTH   This alludes to an old proverb or rhyme that supposedly tells what days of the week are good for marrying. The attributes of the days are widely different in various versions; I have seen versions that say "Monday for wealth" or "Tuesday for wealth," but none saying "Thursday for wealth," though such probably exists. The rhyme usually begins "Monday for . . . ." An example can be found in *The Annotated Mother Goose*, ed. William S. and Ceil Baring-Gould [New York, 1962], p. 218.

349.28/343.22 SOMEBODY'S NOSE WAS OUT OF JOINT   This is proverbial. The *ODEP* lists "Nose out of joint, To put (or thrust) one's," and says it means "to displace or supplant someone; to disconcert."

349.41/343.35   EVERY INCH A GENTLEMAN   This is a variation of the phrase "A man every inch of him," which is listed in the *ODEP*. It also may echo Lear's "every inch a king," in *King Lear*, IV, vi, 108–9.

350.10/344.4   THE LADY'S PICTORIAL   According to *Willing's Press Guide . . . 1905* (for 1904), the *Lady's Pictorial*, which began in 1880, was a weekly paper. In an advertisement in the *Press Guide*, the *Lady's Pictorial* describes itself as "An Illustrated Society Journal. A First-class Medium for all Advertisers" (p. 452).

350.24/344.17   SMILING AT THE LOVELY REFLECTION WHICH THE MIRROR GAVE BACK TO HER   In light of p. 351.17/345.10, this probably alludes to the story "Snowwhite"; see entry 351.17.

351.17/345.10   THE MIRROR. YOU ARE LOVELY, GERTY, IT SAID   This alludes to the fairy story "Snowwhite and the Seven Dwarfs" (sometimes "Snowdrop"), in which Snowwhite's stepmother-queen asks the mirror who is the loveliest, in some phrase such as "Mirror, mirror, on the wall,/ Who is the fairest of them all?" to which the mirror replies that the stepmother is. When Snowwhite grew to beauty, however, the mirror truthfully told the stepmother that Snowwhite was fairer, and Snowwhite's troubles began.

351.35/345.28   BUT WAITING, ALWAYS WAITING   This probably alludes to the song "Waiting"; see entry 275.23.

351.37/345.30   PRINCE CHARMING   Prince Charming is the name of the traditional hero of several fairy stories, among them "Snowwhite," alluded to on p. 351.17/345.10.

352.4/345.38   FOR RICHES FOR POOR, IN SICKNESS IN HEALTH . . .   Gerty is thinking of the marriage service. In the Roman Catholic Church, both the bride and the groom say, "I, ——, take you, ——, for my lawful wife [husband], to have and to hold, from this day forward, for better, for worse, for richer, for poorer, in sickness and in health, until death do us part."

352.23/346.15   GRANDPAPA GILTRAP'S LOVELY DOG GARRYOWEN   Richard M. Kain has called my attention to a brief letter in the London *Times* Literary Supplement of January 9, 1964, which says that Garryowen was the name of a "famous Irish setter" owned by J. J. Giltrap of Dublin. The letter says the dog was whelped in 1876 (*Times* Literary Supplement, Jan. 9, 1964, p. 27, col. d). On the ballad "Garryowen," see entry 295.13.

352.42/346.33   WIGS ON THE GREEN   The *ODEP* lists "There will be wigs on the green" (*s.v.* wigs), and says, "a colloq. expression (orig. Irish) for coming to blows or sharp altercation."

353.13/347.5   HERE'S THE LORD MAYOR . .   This alludes to the nursery rhyme and children's game "Here sits the lord mayor"; see *ODNR*, p. 279.

354.3/347.37 BENEDICTION OF THE MOST BLESSED SACRAMENT   This service is overheard several times in this episode. Though the rite varies in detail from place to place, it usually contains a litany (often the Litany of Our Lady of Loreto—see the following entry), the "Tantum Ergo," and Psalm 117 (Vulgate 116). See entries 354.8, 360.6, 362.11, and 365.8.

354.8/347.42 THE LITANY OF OUR LADY OF LORETO . . .   This well-known Litany is being said as a part of the Benediction of the Most Blessed Sacrament (see entry 354.3). This Litany, which in part addresses Mary as "Holy Mary, Holy Mother of God, Holy Virgin of virgins," can be found in any missal.

354.12/348.4 PEARSON'S WEEKLY   *Pearson's Weekly*, founded in 1890, is listed in *Willing's Press Guide . . . 1905* (for 1904) as appearing every Thursday at a price of one pence.

354.15/348.7 IN A BROWN STUDY   This proverbial phrase, which is listed in the *ODEP*, occurs in Swift's *Polite Conversation*, first conversation, when Neverout says to Miss Notable, "Why Miss, you are in a brown Study" (p. 69). Partridge says it means "gloomily, or concentratedly, thoughtful. Probably suggested by the now obsolete *brown* = gloomy."

354.26/348.18 VIRGIN MOST POWERFUL, VIRGIN MOST MERCIFUL   These phrases are used in the Litany of Our Lady of Loreto to describe Mary. See entry 354.8.

354.34/348.26 A PALPABLE CASE OF DOCTOR FELL   This alludes to an incident in which seventeenth-century satirist Thomas Browne (1663–1704) was threatened with expulsion from Christ Church College, Oxford, by the dean, Dr. John Fell, who promised forgiveness if Browne would paraphrase impromptu Martial's thirty-second epigram, which Brown cleverly did as follows: "I do not love thee, Doctor Fell,/ The reason why I cannot tell;/ But this I know, and know full well:/ I do not love thee, Doctor Fell."

354.36/348.28 WITH ALL HIS FAULTS SHE LOVED HIM STILL   Though this is a common phrase, and it has been specifically applied to England by eighteenth-century poets, this probably alludes to Monroe H. Rosenfeld's sentimental ballad "With All Her Faults I Love Her Still," which was one of the most popular songs of 1888. The song begins, "With all her faults I love her still, And even though the world should scorn; No love like hers, my heart can thrill, Although she's made that heart forlorn!" For words and music, see Boni, *Songs of the Gilded Age*, pp. 53–54.

354.37/348.29 TELL ME, MARY, HOW TO WOO THEE   This refers to

"Tell me, Mary, How to Woo Thee," a song by G. A. Hodson. The song begins, "Tell me, Mary, how to woo thee, Teach my bosom to reveal All its sorrows sweet unto thee, All the love my heart can feel." For words and music, see Hatton and Faning, *Songs of England*, I, 222–24.

354.37/348.29 MY LOVE AND COTTAGE NEAR ROCHELLE   This refers to "My Love and Cottage near Rochelle," an aria sung by Michel in act II of Fitzball and Balfe's *The Siege of Rochelle* (on which see entry 234.28). The song begins, "When I beheld the anchor weighed, and with the shore thine image fade, I deemed each wave a boundless sea that bore me still from love and thee." The refrain of the song proclaims "my love and cottage near Rochelle."

354.40/348.31 THE MOON HATH RAISED   This alludes to "The Moon Hath Raised Her Lamp Above," a song in *The Lily of Killarney* (on which see entry 92.6). This song is first sung by Danny Mann and Hardress in act I, and later in the same act Hardress sings a part of it. It begins "The moon hath raised her lamp above, to light the way to thee my love."

355.11/349.4 A MINISTERING ANGEL   In *Hamlet*, Laertes tells the priest who has refused full Christian burial for Ophelia, "I tell thee, churlish priest,/ A ministering angel shall my sister be/ When thou liest howling" (V, i, 263–65).

355.12/349.4 WORTH ITS WEIGHT IN GOLD   "He is worth his weight in gold" is proverbial and is listed in the *ODEP* (*s.v.* worth).

355.21/349.14 HALCYON DAYS   In *I Henry VI*, Joan la Pucelle (Joan of Arc) says, "Expect Saint Martin's summer, halcyon days,/ Since I have entered into these wars" (I, ii, 131–32). The allusion is to the tradition explained by Pliny in his *Natural History* that for a week before and after midwinter's day, the sea remains calm so that the halcyon (kingfisher) may hatch her eggs. Cf. entry 355.31.

355.31/349.24 WALKER'S PRONOUNCING DICTIONARY . . . HALCYON DAYS This must refer to John Walker's *A Critical Pronouncing Dictionary and Expositor of the English Language* (there were many editions; the one I examined was the third edition, from the last London edition, New York, 1807). *Walker's Dictionary* lists *halcyon* as both noun and adjective: the noun form is defined as "A bird that is said to breed in the sea, and that there is always a calm during her incubation"; the adjective is defined as "Placid, quiet, still." See also entry 355.21.

356.9/350.1 IF YOU FAIL TRY AGAIN   Apparently this is Edy's version of English educational writer William E. Hickson's (1803–70) advice in his poem "Try and Try Again": "If at first you don't succeed,/ Try, try, try again."

356.25/350.17 SPIRITUAL VESSEL, PRAY FOR US . . .   This is from the Litany of Our Lady of Loreto; see entry 354.8.

356.28/350.19 TOILERS FOR THEIR DAILY BREAD   This echoes the Pater Noster or Lord's Prayer: "Give us this day our daily bread."

356.31/350.22 WHAT THE GREAT SAINT BERNARD SAID IN HIS FAMOUS PRAYER OF MARY . . .   This alludes to the prayer called "The Memorare" (from its opening words), popularly, but inaccurately, attributed to St. Bernard (see *A Dictionary of Mary*, by D. Attwater [New York, 1956], *s.v.* Memorare). The prayer can be found in most missals. It says, "Remember, O most loving Virgin Mary, that it is a thing unheard of that anyone ever had recourse to thy protection, implored thy help, or sought thy intercession, and was left forsaken. Filled, therefore, with confidence in thy goodness, I fly to thee, O Mother, Virgin of virgins: to thee I come, before thee I stand a sorrowful sinner. Despise not my poor words, O mother of the Word of God, but graciously hear and grant my prayer. Amen."

357.8/350.42 HOLY SAINT DENIS   Though this is a mild oath rather than an allusion, the reference here is to St. Dionysius, Bishop of Paris (d. 258), who is commonly known as St. Denis and popularly regarded as the patron saint of France. For fuller information, see Butler, *The Lives of the Saints*, IV, 67–68 (Oct. 9). I can see no relationship between the saint and the present context, unless Joyce found a humorous connection between St. Denis' body being thrown into the Seine after he was beheaded, and baby Boardman's being "posing wet."

357.33/351.25 MARTIN HARVEY, THE MATINÉE IDOL   This refers to Sir John Martin-Harvey (1863–1944), English actor-manager who, after having acted minor parts for some years, sprang into prominence with his production of *The Only Way* (see entry 767.8) at the Lyceum in 1899, in which Martin-Harvey played Sydney Carton and his wife played Mimi.

357.36/351.27 WANTED THEY TWO TO ALWAYS DRESS THE SAME ON ACCOUNT OF A PLAY   This may allude to the popular comedy *Two Roses* by James Albery (1838–89), which first appeared in 1870. In the play the two sisters Lotty and Ida (the "Two Roses" of the title) do dress alike. The stage direction describing their entrance says *"They are both dressed in light summer costume, almost exactly alike, nothing costly, but everything made with great taste and daintily trimmed."*

358.10/351.42 MORE SINNED AGAINST THAN SINNING   During the storm on the heath, Lear says of himself, "I am a man/ More sinned against than sinning" (*King Lear*, III, ii, 59–60).

358.18/352.8 THE MEMORY OF THE PAST   This may allude to the song "There is a flower that bloometh" in W. V. Wallace's *Maritana* (on which see entry 86.22). It is sung by Don Caesar, usually in act II, and in it Don Caesar says of the flower, "O! pluck it ere it wither, 'Tis the memory of the past."

358.22/352.12 REFUGE OF SINNERS. COMFORTRESS OF THE AFFLICTED. ORA PRO NOBIS   This is from the Litany of Our Lady of Loreto (see entry 354.8), which says in part, "Refuge of sinners, Comfortress of the afflicted . . . Pray for us."

358.25/352.15 THE SEVEN DOLOURS WHICH TRANSPIERCED HER OWN HEART   This alludes to the dolors or sorrows in the life of the Virgin Mary, now generally enumerated as seven. The seven sorrows are commemorated in feasts and devotions, and in art Our Lady of Sorrows is depicted with her heart pierced by seven swords. For more detail, including a list of the seven sorrows, see the *Catholic Encyclopedia*, XIV, 151–52.

358.34/352.24 THE NOVENA OF SAINT DOMINIC   Gerty probably thinks of St. Dominic and the Dominicans because of this saint's great devotion to the Virgin. It was St. Dominic who popularized the Rosary as a devotion "as an antidote to heresy and sin" (*Cath. Encyc.*, XIII, 184).

358.41/352.30 OUR BLESSED LADY HERSELF SAID TO THE ARCHANGEL GABRIEL LET IT BE DONE UNTO ME ACCORDING TO THY WORD   Luke 1:38 says that Mary said to Gabriel, "Behold the handmaid of the Lord; be it unto me according to thy word."

359.6/352.38 THE FORTY HOURS' ADORATION   This refers to the Forty Hours' Devotion (or Adoration, or Prayer) in which the Blessed Sacrament is exposed for forty consecutive hours, during which continuous prayers take place. The forty hours is approximately the time Christ lay in the tomb. Some attempt is made to have this devotion begin at one church when it is ending at another, so that the devotion is continually going on (see *Cath. Encyc.*, VI, 151–53).

359.37/353.25 QUEEN OF ANGELS . . .   This is from the Litany of Our Lady of Loreto (see entry 354.8). The Litany says in part, "Queen of angels, Queen of Patriarchs, Queen of prophets . . . Queen of all saints . . . Queen of the most holy rosary."

360.6/353.35 TANTUM ERGO   The hymn "Tantum Ergo" (actually the last two stanzas of St. Thomas' famous hymn "Pange, lingua") is commonly sung at Benediction ceremonies, following the Litany (see entry 354.3). On p. 360.7/353.37 Gerty swings her foot to the opening line, "Tantum ergo sacramentum" ("Down in adoration falling").

360.29/354.17   HE WAS EYEING HER AS A SNAKE EYES ITS PREY . . . SHE HAD RAISED THE DEVIL IN HIM   The language here clearly suggests Eve and the serpent, in chapter three of Genesis.

360.40/354.27   A PENNY FOR YOUR THOUGHTS   This proverbial statement is listed in the *ODEP* and occurs in Swift's *Polite Conversation*, both in Swift's Introduction (p. 36) and in the first conversation, when Neverout says to Miss Notable, "Come, a Penny for your Thought" (p. 58).

361.27/355.14   TANTUM ERGO   See entry 360.6.

362.11/355.40   PANEM DE COELO PROESTITISTI EIS   In the Benediction service (see entry 354.3), following the "Tantum ergo," the celebrant says, "Panem de caelo praestitisti eis" ("You have given them bread from Heaven").

363.11/356.39   BILLY WINKS WAS COMING   Billy Winks is probably a nursery rhyme character, similar to the Sandman or Wee Willie Winkie, but I have not located him.

363.17/357.3   O MY! PUDDENY PIE! . . .   Hodgart and Worthington list this as an allusion to the nursery rhyme "Georgie Porgie." Though there is no very precise verbal similarity, the allusion seems likely. The rhyme, which begins "Georgie Porgie, pudding and pie,/ Kissed the girls and made them cry," may be found in *ODNR*, pp. 185–86.

363.30/357.16   THE LAST GLIMPSE OF ERIN   Hodgart and Worthington point this out as an allusion to Thomas Moore's song that begins, "Though the last glimpse of Erin with sorrow I see,/ Yet wherever thou art shall be Erin to me."

363.31/357.17   THOSE EVENING BELLS   This alludes to Thomas Moore's song "Those Evening Bells," which begins "Those evening bells! Those evening bells!/ How many a tale their music tells."

363.40/357.26   THE LAMPLIGHTER BY MISS CUMMINS, AUTHOR OF MABEL VAUGHAN   Maria Susanna Cummins (1827–66) was an American novelist. According to the *DAB*, *The Lamplighter* (1854) was her one striking success. It was immediately very popular, was published in England, and was translated and published in France and Germany. The *DAB* says "The novel is the story of a child lost in infancy, rescued from a cruel woman by an old lamplighter, adopted by a blind woman, and later discovered by her well-to-do father. A double love story slightly enlivens the plot, which is worked out at great length. The style is tediously detailed and the point of view is one of extreme piety. Later books of Miss Cummins did not win so much public approval, though *Mabel Vaughan* (1857) was considered by some critics to be better."

S. Sultan (*The Argument of Ulysses*, chap. VIII) feels that *The Lamplighter* is the specific object of Joyce's parody and satire in this episode, and he points out that one of the main characters in the book is named Gerty.

364.14/357.41 ART THOU REAL, MY IDEAL . . . LOUIS J. WALSH, MAGHERA-FELT . . .   Walsh (1880–1942) was an actual person; Ellmann identifies him as follows: "District Justice in Donegal from 1923 till his death. Known in youth as 'the boy orator,' he wrote several books of no consequence" (*MBK*, p. 165). Joyce quoted this same stanza more fully in *Stephen Hero*: "Art thou real, my Ideal?/ Wilt thou ever come to me/ In the soft and gentle twilight/ With your baby on your knee?" (p. 87).

364.23/358.8 LOVE LAUGHS AT LOCKSMITHS   George Colman the younger (1762–1836) wrote a play entitled *Love Laughs at Locksmiths* (1803). This is also similar to a passage in *Venus and Adonis*: "Were beauty under twenty locks kept fast,/ Yet love breaks through and picks them all at last" (ll. 575–76). The phrase is now proverbial and is listed in the *ODEP*.

364.28/358.13 SOME TRAGEDY LIKE THE NOBLEMAN WITH THE FOREIGN NAME FROM THE LAND OF SONG HAD TO HAVE HER PUT INTO A MAD-HOUSE   Though this probably alludes to some nineteenth-century melodrama about an Italian nobleman, I have not located the work alluded to.

364.30/358.15 CRUEL ONLY TO BE KIND   When Hamlet is confronting his mother in her chamber, he says, "I must be cruel only to be kind" (*Ham.*, III, iv, 178).

364.40/358.25 FROM THE DAYS BEYOND RECALL   This is from "Love's Old Sweet Song"; see entry 63.31. S. Sultan says (*The Argument of Ulysses*, chap. VIII) that this song is "one of the two principal allusive elements in this chapter" (p. 272).

364.42/358.27 THE OLD LOVE WAS WAITING, WAITING   Though this is uncertain, there may be an allusion here to the song "Waiting"; see entry 275.23.

365.2/358.29 SHE WOULD FOLLOW HER DREAM OF LOVE   This may allude to Thomas Moore's song "Love's Young Dream." The first stanza begins, "Oh! the days are gone, when Beauty bright/ My heart's charm wove;/ When my dream of life, from morn to night,/ Was love, still love." The stanza ends, "No, there's nothing half so sweet in life/ As love's young dream."

365.8/358.35 LAUDATE DOMINUM OMNES GENTES   This is another allusion to Benediction service (see entry 354.3). *Laudate Dominum omnes gentes* ("Praise the Lord, all ye nations") is the opening line of Psalms 117 (Vulgate 116), a short Psalm which is said at the conclusion of the Benediction service.

368.25/362.8 ALIVE, O This is from the refrain of the anonymous Irish ballad "Cockles and Mussels" (or "Sweet Molly Malone"), which says that sweet Molly Malone went through the streets "Crying, 'Cockles and mussels, alive, alive, oh.'" For words, see Hoagland, p. 256.

368.27/362.11 PEEPING TOM See entry 163.27.

368.29/362.12 FELT FOR THE CURVES INSIDE HER DESHABILLÉ From *Sweets of Sin*; see entry 236.5.

368.35/362.18 HE WORE A PAIR OF GAITERS THE NIGHT THAT FIRST WE MET . . . This alludes to "She Wore a Wreath of Roses the Night When First We Met," a popular song by Thomas Haynes Bayly and Joseph Philip Knight. The song begins, "She wore a wreath of roses The first time that we met; Her lovely face was smiling Beneath her curls of jet." For words and music, see H. F. Reddall, *Songs That Never Die*, p. 239. M. Disher says of the song that it "was easily first favorite among parodists, proper and improper" (*Victorian Song*, p. 90), but if Bloom is thinking of some specific parody, I have not discovered it.

368.36/362.19 HIS LOVELY SHIRT WAS SHINING BENEATH HIS WHAT? OF JET Hodgart and Worthington list this as an allusion to the music hall song "Her Golden Hair Was Hanging Down Her Back," but an examination of that song reveals no allusion; this is simply a continuation of the allusion in the preceding line.

368.38/362.21 O MAIRY LOST THE PIN OF HER See entry 78.38.

368.40/362.23 ON THE TRACK OF THE SECRET . . . Bloom's bookshelf contains a book entitled *On the Track of the Sun*, which seems to be the source of some of his thoughts about the East. See entry 57.33.

368.41/362.23 MARY, MARTHA See entry 79.6.

369.7/362.32 BARBED WIRE Bloom is remembering his earlier notion that a nun invented barbed wire; see entry 155.15.

369.35/363.17 BEAUTY AND THE BEAST This alludes to the well-known fairy story "Beauty and the Beast," which goes back at least as far as the sixteenth century.

370.16/363.41 NELL GWYNN, MRS BRACEGIRDLE, MAUD BRANSCOMBE On actress Nell Gwynn, see entry 204.9. Anne Bracegirdle (1663–1748) was a famous actress who contributed greatly to the popularity of Congreve's comedies. Maud Branscombe was a minor actress contemporary with Bloom. One of the Queen's Royal Theatre programs in the National Library of Ireland lists "Miss

Maude Branscombe and her London Comedy and Burlesque Company" in a performance on November 5, 1883. But I have not been able to get any further information about her.

370.22/364.5 LACAUS ESANT TARATARA   This allusion is less esoteric than it has appeared to some commentators. Bloom is thinking of "La Causa è santa" and of the "Rataplan chorus." See entry 168.20.

371.22/365.3 THE WAYS OF THE WORLD   Though this phrase is very common, it may echo the title of William Congreve's comedy *The Way of the World* (1700).

371.27/365.8 SAY PRUNES AND PRISMS FORTY TIMES EVERY MORNING . . . This may owe something to Mrs. General's advice to Amy in Dickens' *Little Dorrit*: "Papa, potatoes, poultry, prunes, and prism, are all very good words for the lips: especially prunes and prism. You will find it serviceable, in the formation of a demeanour, if you sometimes say to yourself in company—on entering a room, for instance—Papa, potatoes, poultry, prunes and prism, prunes and prism" (Book II, chap. V).

371.32/365.13 THOSE GIRLS, THOSE GIRLS, THOSE LOVELY SEASIDE GIRLS See entry 62.36.

372.16/365.38 WAYS OF THE WORLD   See entry 371.22.

372.21/366.2 BEEF TO THE HEEL   See entry 66.8.

372.30/366.10 FOR THIS RELIEF MUCH THANKS. IN HAMLET THAT IS Francisco says, "For this relief much thanks" to Bernardo in *Hamlet*, I, i, 8.

372.32/366.12 YOUR HEAD IT SIMPLY SWIRLS   See entry 62.36.

372.38/366.18 HER MAIDEN NAME WAS JEMIMA BROWN . . . Apparently Bloom is thinking of some Dublin ballad, but I have not identified it.

373.1/366.22 EVERY BULLET HAS ITS BILLET   This phrase is proverbial and is listed in the *ODEP*. But, as Hodgart and Worthington point out, it is also the title of a song by Charles Dibdin and Sir Henry R. Bishop. The song begins, "I'm a tough, true-hearted sailor. . . ," and the chorus begins, "Ev'ry bullet has its billet; Man the boat, boys, Yo, heave ho. . . ." For words and music, see Alfred H. Miles, *Our National Songs*, p. 26.

373.4/366.25 AND PAPA'S PANTS WILL SOON FIT WILLY   Hodgart and Worthington list this as an allusion to the American nonsense song "Looking Through the Keyhole" ("Papa's pants will soon fit Willie"). I have not located a copy of the song in print.

373.24/367.4 HANDS FELT FOR THE OPULENT   From *Sweets of Sin*; see entry 236.5.

373.32/367.12 AS GOD MADE THEM HE MATCHED THEM   Though

this statement seems to me proverbial, it is not listed in the *ODEP* or in Apperson. Compare Mrs. Poyser's statement in George Eliot's *Adam Bede*, "I'm not denyin' the women are foolish: God Almighty made 'em to match the men" (chap. LIII).

373.35/367.14 MARRY IN MAY AND REPENT IN DECEMBER   This statement, or some close variant on it, has been proverbial for centuries and is listed in the *ODEP*. Swift's *Polite Conversation*, first conversation, contains a similar proverb in Lady Smart's statement "marry in haste, and repent at leisure" (p. 116).

373.42/367.22 CAT'S AWAY THE MICE WILL PLAY   This statement, which has been proverbial at least since Ray's *Proverbs* (1670), is listed in the *ODEP*. It occurs once in Shakespeare, in *Henry V*, when Westmoreland, speaking of the danger of Scottish attack while England is engaged against France, speaks of their "playing the mouse in absence of the cat" (I, ii, 172).

374.18/367.40 HOW GIUGLINI BEGAN   This must refer to Italian tenor Antonio Giuglini (1827–65), who first appeared in London in 1857. I have not been able to confirm Bloom's idea that he began as a house painter.

374.26/368.5 I LEAVE YOU THIS TO THINK OF ME WHEN I'M FAR AWAY ON THE PILLOW   Though this sounds like a phrase from a popular poem or song (perhaps with *billow* for *pillow*), I have not located it.

374.31/368.10 DANCE OF THE HOURS   See entry 69.28.

375.21/368.41 THE TREE OF FORBIDDEN PRIEST   This is Bloom's variation on the tree of forbidden fruit, the Tree of Knowledge, of Genesis 2:17 and 3:3, used here to describe the temptation presented to a woman by a priest's chastity.

376.2/369.22 SEE OURSELVES AS OTHERS SEE US   See entries 6.28 and 169.22.

376.5/369.24 PRIZE TITBIT STORY . . .   Bloom is thinking of his morning's reading; see entry 68.39.

376.10/369.30 MOTHER SHIPTON'S PROPHECY . . . Mother Shipton, the English prophetess (*ca.* 1487–*ca.* 1561) did not prophesy about anything so mundane as the weather. Her most famous prophecies concerned Cardinal Wolsey, the Duke of Suffolk, Lord Percy, and others of the court of Henry VIII. She is also said to have prophesied the Great Fire of 1666, and many English people stood in awe of her prophecies in the late nineteenth century (see *Encyc. Brit.*, 11th ed., XXIV, *s.v.* Shipton, Mother). Probably Bloom is remembering here that one of Mother Shipton's prophecies was that ships should go without sails. But if Bloom is thinking of an actual weather verse from the *Royal Reader*, I have not located it. Cf. entry 376.15.

376.15/369.35 GRACE DARLING   Grace Darling (1815–42) was the daughter of a lighthouse keeper on the Farne Islands. She became an English heroine overnight after aiding her father in the rescue of five passengers from the shipwrecked steamer *Forfarshire* on September 7, 1838. Wordsworth wrote a poem entitled "Grace Darling" which was in the *Royal Reader*, No. V (London, 1876), pp. 41–44 (Bloom has just thought of the *Royal Reader*; see entry 376.10).

376.24/370.1 A STAR I SEE . . . TWO, WHEN THREE IT'S NIGHT   J. Prescott (*MLQ*, XIII, 156) says this "recalls an old Jewish ecclesiastical principle for distinguishing night from day," and quotes a passage from the *New Edition of the Babylonian Talmud* which makes the same distinction between day and night that Bloom makes.

376.27/370.4 LAND OF THE SETTING SUN THIS   Though this sounds like a set phrase, and Ireland's position to the west of Europe might suggest its description in this way, I have not found this phrase used to describe Ireland.

376.27/370.5 HOMERULE SUN SETTING IN THE SOUTHEAST   This is the logical complement of Bloom's earlier "Homerule sun rising up in the northwest." See entry 57.35.

376.28/370.5 MY NATIVE LAND, GOODNIGHT   This is a line from a lyric in Byron's *Childe Harold's Pilgrimage*, canto I, following stanza thirteen. It is Childe Harold's farewell to his native country as he sails away from it. The lyric begins, "Adieu, adieu! my native shore," and its first and last stanzas end with the line "My native Land—Good Night!"

377.1/370.21 YE CRAGS AND PEAKS I'M WITH YOU ONCE AGAIN   This alludes to a line in Anglo-Irish dramatist James Sheridan Knowles' tragedy *William Tell* (1825; I have seen some editions of this play which have this line in modified form, but others give it exactly as Bloom has it). William Tell opens scene two of the first act with an apostrophe that begins, "Ye crags and peaks, I'm with you once again!"

377.14/370.33 NOTHING NEW UNDER THE SUN   Ecclesiastes 1:9 says, "The thing that hath been, it is that which shall be; and that which is done is that which shall be done: and there is no new thing under the sun."

377.23/370.42 RIP VAN WINKLE . . .   This alludes to Washington Irving's story "Rip Van Winkle." Bloom correctly remembers the

detail of the rusty gun, but he is mistaken about the setting of the
story. Rip's home town is never named; Sleepy Hollow—though
it sounds appropriate enough to the story—is the setting of the
story of Ichabod Crane and the Headless Horseman, "The Legend
of Sleepy Hollow." For fuller comment to show the relevance
of the story to Bloom's situation, see entry 542.3.

377.30/371.7 METEMPSYCHOSIS. THEY BELIEVED YOU COULD BE CHANGED
INTO A TREE FROM GRIEF   On metempsychosis, see entry 64.18.
Stories of characters' being changed into trees are common in myth.
One of the best known is that of Daphne, who, in her flight from
Apollo, was metamorphosed into a laurel (see Ovid's *Metamorphoses*, I, 452 ff.). Another well-known such story, which more specifically involves grief, is that of Phaeton's sisters, who had yoked
the horses to his chariot, and who, after Phaeton's death, died
of grief and were transformed into trees, and their tears into
amber (see *Metamorphoses*, I–II).

377.35/371.12 PRAY FOR US. AND PRAY FOR US. AND PRAY FOR US
Bloom is thinking of the refrain of litanies such as that of Our
Lady of Loreto. See entry 354.8.

378.2/371.20 THE BIRD IN DROUTH GOT WATER OUT OF THE END OF A
JAR BY THROWING IN PEBBLES   Bloom is thinking of Aesop's
fable "The Crow and the Pitcher," in which a crow saves himself
from perishing by raising the water level in a jar through dropping
pebbles into the water.

378.6/371.24 STARE THE SUN FOR EXAMPLE LIKE THE EAGLE   One of
the old traditions about the eagle is that it can stare directly into
the sun without being dazzled. This notion goes back at least as
far as Pliny, who says that this power to stare into the sun is so
important to the eagle that the mother bird throws out of the
nest any of its young that lack the power.

378.12/371.31 GLASS FLASHING . . . BURNING GLASS . . . ARCHIMEDES. I
HAVE IT   Bloom seems to be blending two stories about Archimedes. He is said to have exclaimed "Eureka!" after figuring out
how to measure the gold in Hiero's crown (on which see entry
213.28). But Archimedes is also said to have set Roman ships on
fire by concentrating the sun's rays through the use of large con-
cave mirrors (see Sir Thomas Heath, *A History of Greek Mathematics* [Oxford, 1921], II, 18–19).

378.26/372.2 FAUGH A BALLAGH   Hodgart and Worthington list this
as an allusion to a Thomas Moore song, "To ladies' eyes around
(Clear the way) (Faugh a Ballagh)," but that seems unlikely since
"Faugh a ballagh" (which means "clear the way") is simply the

name of the air to which the Moore song is sung. More likely, it is an allusion to a song by Charles Gavan Duffy, entitled "Faugh a Ballagh" (or "Fag an Bealach"). The only copies of this song which I have seen have been in paperback song books in the National Library of Ireland. In the version given in the *Favorite Songster*, each verse begins, "Faugh-a-ballagh—clear the way, boys!" and the chorus says, "Faugh-a-ballagh—clear the way boys!/ On amid the thrilling fray,/ Fourth Dragoon Guards, charge to glory,/ As ye did at Llerena" (p. 376).

378.29/372.4 WHEN THE STORMY WINDS DO BLOW   Hodgart and Worthington list this as an allusion to a sea chanty, "The Mermaid," by Parker. Words and music for the song can be found in Chapple, *Heart Songs*, pp. 360–61 (although nothing is said there about the author of the song). It begins, " 'Twas Friday morn when we set sail," and the chorus says, "O, the ocean waves may roll, And the stormy winds may blow, While we poor sailors go skipping to the tops, And the land-lubbers lie down below."

378.32/372.7   TILL JOHNNY COMES MARCHING HOME   This alludes to "When Johnny Comes Marching Home Again," an American Civil War song written by the bandmaster of the Union army, Patrick Sarsfield Gilmore (1829–92), and based on a much older Irish song and air. For words and music, see Olin Downes, *Treasury of American Song* (2nd ed.; New York, 1943), pp. 188–89.

378.35/372.10 THE ANCHOR'S WEIGHED   This alludes to "The Anchor's Weighed," a song by Arnold and Braham. It begins "The tear fell gently from her eye When last we parted on the shore"; later in the song, the departing tar tells his lamenting sweetheart, "The anchor's weigh'd, the anchor's weigh'd, farewell! farewell! remember me:" For words and music, see Hatton and Faning, *Songs of England*, I, 210–12.

378.36/372.11 AND THE TEPHILIM NO WHAT'S THIS THEY CALL IT POOR PAPA'S FATHER HAD ON HIS DOOR TO TOUCH   Bloom thinks of the tephillin (or tefillin) when trying to think of the mezuzah. The tephillin are phylacteries (i.e., black leather boxes on leather straps) containing four parts of the Pentateuch. They are worn (or "laid") on the arm or head (see *Jewish Encyc.*, X, 21–28). The mezuzah (Hebrew "doorpost") is a rectangular piece of parchment inscribed with Deuteronomy 6:4–9 and 11:13–21, written in twenty-two lines. The parchment is rolled up and put into a wooden or metal case that is affixed to the right side of the door of the Jewish home. The pious touch or kiss it as they pass through. The *Jewish Encyclopedia* says the mezuzah "is obligatory for every building used as a residence" (VIII, 531–33).

378.38/372.12 THAT BROUGHT US OUT OF THE LAND OF EGYPT AND INTO THE HOUSE OF BONDAGE   See entry 122.22.

379.4/372.20 DAVY JONES' LOCKER   The use of this phrase to describe "the watery deep" is now proverbial and too common to specify a single source. The *ODEP* explains it as meaning "the deep, a watery grave."

379.11/372.27 THE GLOWWORM'S LAMP . . . GLEAMING   This is from T. Moore's song "The Young May Moon"; see entry 167.21.

379.35/373.9 BABES IN THE WOOD   "The Babes in the Wood" is a well-known English nursery tale. And, though Bloom may not be aware of it, the phrase was also used to describe "insurrectionary hordes that infested the mountains of Wicklow and the woods of Enniscorthy towards the close of the 18th century" (Brewer, *Dictionary of Phrase and Fable, s.v.* Babes in the Wood).

380.20/373.35 LEAH, LILY OF KILLARNEY   Bloom is thinking of entertainments playing in Dublin. See entries 76.23 and 92.6.

380.32/374.5 THE SISTER OF THE WIFE OF THE WILD MAN OF BORNEO HAS JUST COME TO TOWN   Hodgart and Worthington point out the allusion here to the song "The Wild Man from Borneo Has Just Come to Town," by Schaum. Though I know such a song exists, I have not located a printed copy.

380.34/374.7 EVERYONE TO HIS TASTE AS MORRIS SAID WHEN HE KISSED THE COW   This is proverbial. Swift's *Polite Conversation*, first conversation, gives a more usual form, when Col. Atwit says, "Why; every one as they like; as the good Woman said, when she kiss'd her Cow" (p. 55).

380.41/374.14 HER WIDOW'S MITE   This alludes to the widow whom Christ saw throw two mites into the offertory. He praised her for having given more than the wealthy, "For all they did cast in of their abundance; but she of her want did cast in all that she had, even all her living" (Mark 12:44; the story is also told in Luke 21:1–4).

381.7/374.21 LOVE, LIE, AND BE HANDSOME FOR TOMORROW WE DIE   Bloom is here playing on a phrase he used earlier. See entry 172.4.

381.24/374.38 BREAD CAST ON THE WATERS   Ecclesiastes 11:1 says, "Cast thy bread upon the waters: for thou shalt find it after many days."

381.28/374.42 MUST COME BACK. MURDERERS DO   This alludes to the well-known superstition that the murderer always returns to the scene of the crime.

382.1/375.14 ROUND THE KISH IN EIGHTY DAYS   This alludes to the English title of Jules Verne's popular novel *Around* [or *Round* in some translations] *the World in Eighty Days* (1873). The Kish is a floating lightship, moored at the northern end of Kish Bank, SE of Dublin. Bloom saw the light from the lightship on p. 379.23/ 372.39.

382.13/375.26 BRACEGIRDLE   Bloom is remembering the actress, Mrs. Bracegirdle. See entry 370.16.

382.14/375.27 GRACE DARLING   On Grace Darling, see entry 376.15.

382.15/375.28 MET HIM PIKE HOSES   Metempsychosis; see entry 64.18.

382.15/375.28 FOR RAOUL . . . HEAVE UNDER EMBON   From *Sweets of Sin*; see entry 236.5.

382.18/375.31 NEXT YEAR . . . RETURN NEXT . . .   Bloom is probably remembering part of the Passover ritual he thought of earlier. See entry 122.21.

382.23/375.36 CUCKOO . . .   This recalls Spring's song in *Love's Labor's Lost*, which Mulligan alluded to earlier. See entry 212.36.

OXEN OF THE SUN

This episode poses unique problems for an allusion study, since its style echoes and recapitulates various English styles from Anglo-Saxon literature to modern slang and evangelical oratory, and since Joyce apparently used certain books on English style and literary history as sources for some of the material in the episode. Thus the line between an allusion to a specific work and a parody of a period style is difficult to trace, as is the difference between an allusion to a certain work and Joyce's use of a source that may have included that work. As a result, the limits of inclusion for this chapter of the list are probably less satisfactory than for any other chapter. My policy has been to exclude a "style" as an allusion, except when Joyce seems to have some specific work in mind. I have also chosen to avoid the study of Joyce's sources and keep the list for this chapter (as for others) focused on allusions present in the final text. I have done this because of the realization that a study of Joyce's sources for this episode is a sizable task in itself, and because that task has been undertaken by Robert Janusko of Ashland College, Ashland, Ohio.

383.3/377.3 SEND US, BRIGHT ONE, LIGHT ONE, HORHORN, QUICKENING
AND WOMBFRUIT   S. Gilbert (*JJU*, p. 296) says of this that it is
"an invocation to the Sun, Helios, personified by Sir Andrew
Horne, the head of the Lying-in Hospital, the 'House of Horne.' "
He also says that this thrice-repeated invocation is "in the manner
of the *Fratres Arvales*." The Fratres Arvales (Arval Brothers)
were an ancient Roman college or priesthood consisting of twelve
members whose chief duty was to offer an annual public sacrifice
for the fertility of the fields. Theodor Mommsen, in his *History
of Rome*, quotes the ancient incantation of the Brothers, and points
out that most of it was repeated three times. (1887 ed., I, 294).

383.35/377.35 THAT EVANGEL SIMULTANEOUSLY COMMAND AND PROM-
ISE . . .   This apparently alludes to God's statement to Adam and
Eve in Genesis 1:28–30. In Genesis 1:28 we are told, "And God
blessed them, and God said unto them, Be fruitful, and multiply,
and replenish the earth, and subdue it."

383.42/377.41 THE ART OF MEDICINE SHALL HAVE BEEN HIGHLY HON-
OURED . . . THEIR GREATEST DOCTORS, THE O'SHIELS, THE O'HICKEYS,
THE O'LEES . . .   In a pamphlet entitled *Three Centuries of
Irish Chemists*, edited by Deasmumhan Ó Raghallaigh (Cork: Cork
University Press, 1941), the following lines occur: "A long and
great tradition attaches to Irish medicine, the profession of which
was hereditary for centuries. The O'Hickey's were hereditary
physicians to the O'Briens of Thomond, and the O'Shiels to the
Mahoneys of Oriel. . . . After a visit to Ireland in 1640, Van Hel-
mont, the great Dutch Chemist, rated the skill and chemical knowledge of Irish physicians at a high level and he placed their medical
ability above that of the Italians" (pp. 1–2). And John Fleetwood,
in his *History of Medicine in Ireland* (Dublin: Browne and Nolan,
Limited, 1951), mentions the O'Shiels, the O'Hickeys, and the
O'Lees in his chapter on "The Renaissance Period" (pp. 25–40).

384.12/378.11 MATERNITY WAS SO FAR FROM ALL ACCIDENT POSSIBILITY
REMOVED . . .   In D. A. Chart's *The Story of Dublin*, speaking
of the period of Grattan's Parliament, the author says, "Dublin
began to be honorably distinguished for the number of its founda-
tions for the advancement of science and the mitigation of pain
and suffering. . . . Hospitals rose all over the city" (p. 110). Among
the most famous of Dublin's hospitals was the Rotunda Hospital,
a maternity hospital built between 1751 and 1757, the first maternity hospital in the British Isles. It was built at great personal expense
and effort by Dr. Bartholomew Mosse, who had opened a lying-in
house in George's Lane in 1745, which soon proved inadequate

to the need (see C. Maxwell, *Dublin Under the Georges*, p. 63, and Cosgrave and Strangeway's *Dictionary of Dublin*, pp. 182–83).

385.3/378.41   SOME MAN THAT WAYFARING . . .   This recalls the Old English poem "The Wanderer," whose protagonist resembles Bloom in some important respects. The Wanderer, whose lord, kinsmen, and friends have been slain, knows the loneliness of a lordless man, can find no one to whom he can express his heart, and knows the value of guarding one's tongue and speaking temperately.

385.9/379.5   SO GOD'S ANGEL TO MARY QUOTH   This suggests the annunciation of the angel Gabriel to Mary in Luke 1:26–38, though none of the phrases in this sentence is very closely paralleled in the Bible.

385.17/379.12   GOD THE WREAKER ALL MANKIND WOULD FORDO WITH WATER FOR HIS EVIL SINS   This recalls the flood described in Genesis 6–8.

385.24/379.19   NINE YEAR HAD LONG OUTWANDERED   This recalls Ulysses' ten years' wandering after the Trojan War.

386.5/379.41   THEREFORE, EVERYMAN, LOOK TO THAT LAST END THAT IS THY DEATH   This alludes to the fifteenth-century morality play *Everyman*. It may allude specifically to the Messenger's prologue to the play, in which he says, "Man, in the beginning,/ Look well, and take good heed to the ending,/ Be you never so gay./ You think sin in the beginning full sweet,/ Which in the end causeth the soul to weep,/ When the body lieth in clay."

386.6/379.42   EVERY MAN THAT IS BORN OF WOMAN   Though this is a common phrase, it may allude to Job 14:1: "Man that is born of a woman is of few days, and full of trouble." Cf. the next entry.

386.7/380.1   AS HE CAME NAKED FORTH FROM HIS MOTHER'S WOMB . . .   Both Job 1:21 and Ecclesiastes 5:15 contain phrases very similar to this. Job 1:21 says "Naked came I out of my mother's womb, and naked shall I return thither."

387.9/381.1   MAGIC OF MAHOUND   Mahound, or Mahoun, are contemptuous names for Mohammed or for any Moslem, and the names occur commonly in romances of the Crusades. The name is also sometimes used to mean the Devil.

387.20/381.11   WHEAT KIDNEYS   This alludes to Deuteronomy 32:14; see entry 40.7.

387.28/381.19   AND CHILDE LEOPOLD DID UP HIS BEAVER   This may allude to Horatio's answer to Hamlet's question about whether the Ghost's face was visible: "Oh yes, my lord, he wore his beaver up" (*Ham.*, I, ii, 229). Cf. entry 197.12.

389.1/382.34 IN THE BEGINNING THEY SAID THE WOMAN SHOULD BRING FORTH IN PAIN   This blends Genesis 1:1 and 3:16.

389.17/383.8 SAINT ULTAN OF ARBRACCAN   St. Ultan of Ardbraccan (d. 657) is an Irish saint. He is supposed to have shown particular care for children, especially orphans and those sick. For further information, see Butler, *The Lives of the Saints*, III, 485–86 (Sept. 4).

389.22/383.12 THE ONE IN LIMBO GLOOM, THE OTHER IN PURGE FIRE   Stephen seems to have in mind the two main divisions of Limbo, one of which he alluded to earlier. See entry 188.10.

389.33/383.22 THAT BEAST THE UNICORN HOW ONCE IN THE MILLENIUM HE COMETH BY HIS HORN   The context and phrasing render this phrase ambiguous and potentially bawdy. But, though I have consulted several sources on the unicorn, I have found no tradition about the unicorn's horn and the passing of one thousand years, and I presume this to be without basis in unicorn lore.

389.36/383.26 SAINT FOUTINUS   I have located no such saint, and I suspect that none exists. The name probably derives from the indecent French verb *foutre*, meaning "to have intercourse with."

390.1/383.33 LILITH, PATRON OF ABORTIONS   Lilith (according to popular etymology, the "demon of the night") is the Hebrew word for "night hag." She is a female demon, apparently of Babylonian origin. The Hebrew word occurs only once in the Bible, in Isaiah 34:14, where it is variously translated "screech owl," "night hag," or "lamia." This demon was said to haunt wildernesses in stormy weather and to be particularly dangerous to children and to pregnant women, though she is more often associated with the slaughter of newborn infants than with abortion. According to one legend, she was Adam's first wife, and Eve was created after she had left Adam and refused to return. Another version says she forced Adam to cohabit with her after the Fall, and in kabbalistic literature she is the symbol of sensual lust and sexual temptation. Lilith, or the Lamiae, appears briefly during the "Walpurgis Night" section of act II of Goethe's *Faust*. She is mentioned again on p. 497.12/487.9.

390.2/383.33 OF BIGNESS WROUGHT BY WIND OF SEEDS OF BRIGHTNESS . . . The rest of this sentence lists several superstitions about means of becoming pregnant. Though I have not located specific instances of each of these beliefs, I suspect that all of them do represent opinions actually held at one time or another. The most helpful source I have found on these matters is E. S. Hartland's *Primitive Paternity*, especially the first chapter. Arthur William Meyer's

The Rise of Embryology has also been helpful (again, especially the first chapter). The idea that pregnancy can be caused by wind is common in primitive cultures and is found in myth and folklore (see Hartland, I, 22). "Seeds of brightness" may blend the ideas that pregnancy is caused by some kinds of seeds and that it can be caused by the sun or by the stars; Paracelsus specifically said that sperm falls from the stars, and Lao Tse, the Chinese religious leader, is said to have been conceived when his mother saw a falling star. I have found nothing in vampire lore about women becoming pregnant by vampires; perhaps this refers to the incubus, a male demon said to impregnate women while they sleep (there is also an allusion here to Hyde's poem cited earlier—see entry 48.3). The allusion to Virgil is to the third book of his *Georgics*, where he describes mares being impregnated by the west wind, and going toward the west to seek the wind. Though I have not found anything specifically on the moonflower, the idea of conceiving by smelling a flower is a motif in folklore (see Stith Thompson, *Motif-Index of Folk-Literature*, Motif T532.1.1.1, and see Hartland, I, 17). I have not found anything on the *effectu secuto*. Hartland records that "In the twelfth century the Moorish philosopher Averrhoes of Cordova related, as having actually occurred, a case of a woman who became pregnant in a bath by attracting the semen of a man bathing near" (I, 24). I have not, however, confirmed that Moses Maimonides held a similar opinion.

390.8/383.39 AT THE END OF THE SECOND MONTH A HUMAN SOUL WAS INFUSED Though modern Roman Catholic theologians generally hold that the soul is present from the moment of conception, St. Thomas followed Aristotle in believing that the embryo first had a vegetative soul, which was then replaced by a sensitive soul, which was finally replaced by a rational soul. But nowhere in St. Thomas' account of this matter have I found a specific reference to the second month. See Joseph Needham, *A History of Embryology* (New York: Abelard-Schuman, 1959), pp. 93–94, and the *Summa Theologica*, Part I, question cxviii, arts. 1 and 2.

390.12/384.1 HE THAT HOLDETH THE FISHERMAN'S SEAL, EVEN THAT BLESSED PETER ON WHICH ROCK WAS HOLY CHURCH FOR ALL AGES FOUNDED "The fisherman's seal" alludes to the papal seal, usually called the "fisherman's ring." Actually, the first mention of the fisherman's ring was in 1265, but St. Peter is, by extension, the first wearer (see *Cath. Encyc.*, XIII, 60–61). In Matthew 16:18 Christ says, ". . . thou art Peter, and upon this rock I will build my church," and in John 1:42 he says, "Thou art Simon the son of

Jona: thou shalt be called Cephas, which is by interpretation, A
stone." Both of these passages involve a play on the Aramaic word
kephas (rock), which becomes *petros* in Greek.

390.24/384.13 HE WHO STEALETH FROM THE POOR LENDETH TO THE
    LORD   See entry 23.7.

391.2/384.30 MURDERED HIS GOODS WITH WHORES   In light of the
    several other allusions in *Ulysses* to the story of the Prodigal Son,
    this probably alludes to the phrase the older brother uses in de-
    scribing the Prodigal. He tells his father that his younger brother
    "hath devoured thy living with harlots" (Luke 15:30).

391.8/384.37 VICAR OF BRAY   This alludes to a song entitled "The
    Vicar of Bray" about a clergyman who, in order to keep his po-
    sition, changed his theology to suit whatever ruler was on the
    throne. The chorus says, "And this is law that I'll maintain Until
    my dying day, Sir, That whatsoever King shall reign, Still I'll be
    the Vicar of Bray, Sir." For words, music, and commentary, see
    Chappell, *Popular Music of the Olden Time*, pp. 652–54.

391.8/384.37 NOW DRINK WE, QUOD HE, OF THIS MAZER . . .   This
    depicts the Last Supper, described in Matthew 26, Mark 14, and
    Luke 22.

391.11/384.39   THEM THAT LIVE BY BREAD ALONE   In Matthew
    4:4, Christ, quoting Deuteronomy 8:3, says, "It is written, Man
    shall not live by bread alone, but by every word that proceedeth
    out of the mouth of God."

391.11/384.40 BE NOT AFEARD   "Be not afraid" and "Fear not, be
    not dismayed" are common in the Bible, as a check of any concor-
    dance will show.

391.18/385.4 TIME'S RUINS BUILD ETERNITY'S MANSIONS   This al-
    ludes to a statement William Blake made in a letter to William
    Hayley, May 6, 1800: "Every mortal loss is an immortal gain. The
    ruins of Time build mansions in Eternity" (1957 Keynes ed. of
    Blake's *Complete Writings*, p. 797). Stephen may have come across
    the phrase in Yeats's "Preface" to Lady Gregory's *Cuchulain of
    Muirthemne* (London, 1902), which was alluded to earlier on p.
    216.27/213.39. In that "Preface," Yeats says, "He [the Irish story-
    teller] understands as well as Blake that the ruins of time build
    mansions in eternity . . ." (p. xiii). See also the following entries.

391.19/385.5 DESIRE'S WIND BLASTS THE THORNTREE BUT AFTER IT
    BECOMES FROM A BRAMBLEBUSH TO BE A ROSE UPON THE ROOD OF TIME
    The last portion of this phrase alludes to Yeats's poem "To the
    Rose upon the Rood of Time." Morton D. Paley says (*JJM III*,
    pp. 179–81) that Stephen weaves meanings of several of Blake's

poems into a single statement. The poems he specifies are a Note-book lyric which begins, "I fear'd the fury of my wind/ Would blight all blossoms fair & true" (1957 Keynes ed., p. 166), and two poems from *Songs of Experience*, "The Sick Rose" and "My Pretty Rose Tree" (1957 Keynes ed., pp. 213 and 215). But this passage also owes something to Dante's tercet in canto XIII of "Paradiso": "For I have seen/ The thorn frown rudely all the winter long/ And after bear the rose upon its top" (ll. 127–30; Cary's translation).

391.21/385.7 IN WOMAN'S WOMB WORD IS MADE FLESH BUT IN THE SPIRIT OF THE MAKER ALL FLESH THAT PASSES BECOMES THE WORD THAT SHALL NOT PASS AWAY   Morton D. Paley (*op. cit.*, entry 391.19, pp. 180–81) says that Blake treats a similar theme in "Ah! Sunflower" in *Songs of Experience*. Paley quotes the second (final) stanza of the poem: ". . . the Youth pined away with desire,/ And the virgin shrouded in snow/ Arise from their graves and aspire/ Where my Sun-flower wishes to go" (1957 Keynes ed., p. 215). The similarity of theme here is not clear to me.

391.23/385.10 OMNIS CARO AD TE VENIET   See entry 48.1.

391.24/385.11 WHO AVENTRIED THE DEAR CORSE OF OUR AGENBUYER   The sense of this phrase is "who took into her womb the body of our Redeemer." Though the word *agenbuyer* is fairly common for Christ in Middle English (see the *Middle English Dictionary*, s.v. *agenbuyer*), I have not found the word *aventried* in any of the English dictionaries I have consulted. Other words in this sentence suggest that this word may derive from the French. Godefroy's *Dictionnaire de L'Ancienne Langue Française* lists no *aventrer*, but it does list *enventrer* (to put within the womb), and cites a use referring to Mary's conception of Christ.

391.25/385.12 OUR MIGHTY MOTHER   See entry 5.13.

391.26/385.12 MOTHER MOST VENERABLE   In the well-known litany of Our Lady of Loreto, the blessed Virgin is addressed under a dozen aspects of her motherhood and then is called "Virgo prudentissima,/ Virgo veneranda" ("Virgin most prudent,/ Virgin most venerable"). Though Mary is both mother and virgin, there is some irony in Stephen's using one of her attributes as a virgin as an attribute of motherhood.

391.26/385.13 BERNARDUS SAITH APTLY THAT SHE HATH AN OMNIPOTEN-TIAM DEIPARAE SUPPLICEM . . .   St. Bernard of Clairvaux (1090–1153) is well known for his devotion to the Virgin Mary. But while the idea that Mary has the "almightiness of petition of the mother of God" is typical of St. Bernard's thought, nowhere have

I found his use of this exact phrase. The prayer "Memorare," usually attributed to St. Bernard, expresses this idea; see entry 356.31.

391.28/385.15 SHE IS THE SECOND EVE AND SHE WON US, SAITH AUGUS-
TINE   The notion of Mary as second Eve is very common, and goes back in Christian tradition far beyond St. Augustine. The *Book of Catholic Quotations* has a section on comparisons of Mary with Eve, which includes three quotations from St. Iranaeus (second century) and one from St. Augustine.

391.30/385.16 OUR GRANDAM . . . SOLD US ALL . . . FOR A PENNY PIPPIN
This alludes to Eve's fall through eating the apple.

391.34/385.20 VERGINE MADRE FIGLIA DI TUO FIGLIO   This is the opening line of the last canto of the *Divine Comedy*. There, St. Bernard, calling on Mary, addresses her as "Vergine Madre, figlia del tuo Figlio" ("Virgin Mother, daughter of thy Son"). This entire paragraph in *Ulysses* seems to owe something to the "Paradiso," and especially to the concluding cantos. St. Bernard appears in these cantos and praises Mary in terms similar to those in the prayer Stephen cites. Also, in canto xxxii, Mary and Eve are paired and Mary is said to have closed and anointed the wounds which Eve opened.

391.34/385.20 OR SHE KNEW HIM NOT AND THEN STANDS SHE IN THE
ONE DENIAL OR IGNORANCY WITH PETER PISCATOR   With a play on the word *know*, this blends allusions to the Holy Spirit's "knowing" the Virgin Mary in the conception of Christ, and to Peter's denying Christ, described in Matthew 26:69–75, Mark 14:66–72, Luke 22:56–62, and John 18:15–27. In one instance Peter says of Christ, "I do not know the man." *Piscator* refers to Peter's having been a fisherman.

391.36/385.22 WHO LIVES IN THE HOUSE THAT JACK BUILT   In addition to alluding to the common nursery rhyme "The House that Jack Built" (on which see *ODNR*, pp. 229–32), this also alludes to the church that Christ built. Cf. entry 394.29.

391.37/385.23 JOSEPH THE JOINER   See entry 19.29.

391.38/385.24 M. LÉO TAXIL . . .   See entries 41.14 and 41.21.

392.1/385.29 A BODY WITHOUT BLEMISH, A BELLY WITHOUT BIGNESS
See entries 38.3 and 38.7.

392.5/385.33 STABOO STABELLA . . . Hodgart and Worthington list this as an allusion to "Staboo, Stabella," a "bawdy catch" with many variants. R. M. Adams (*SS*, p. 209) says this song is of Gogarty's making, and R. Ellmann (*JJ*, p. 122) refers to a song by Gogarty untitled "Landlord, landlord, bring us some wine, saboo, saboo" which Joyce used in *Ulysses*. I have not found the song in Gogarty's published works or in his correspondence with Joyce.

392.30/386.15 OBEDIENCE IN THE WOMB, CHASTITY IN THE TOMB BUT INVOLUNTARY POVERTY ALL HIS DAYS This parodies the three vows of religious profession, those of poverty, chastity, and obedience.

392.39/386.23 HIS CURIOUS RITE OF WEDLOCK FOR THE DISROBING AND DEFLOWERING OF SPOUSES, AS THE PRIESTS USE IN MADAGASCAR ISLAND Though this seems to allude to some finding of contemporary anthropology, I have not been able to confirm what the allusion suggests, or to locate a possible source for it. Madagascar was a frequent topic of anthropological discussion at the time, but what evidence I have seen on sexual practices in that country tends to contradict rather than confirm what is said in *Ulysses*.

393.1/386.27 KYRIES This refers to musical settings of the "Kyrie eleison," ("Lord have mercy") the short petition that occurs early in the Mass and in many Roman Catholic hymns and prayers.

393.1/386.28 THE ANTHEM UT NOVETUR SEXUS OMNIS CORPORIS MYSTERIUM The title of this supposed anthem may be translated "That the whole mystery of physical sexuality may be known." I have located no such song, and am skeptical that one exists. There may be a parodic side-glance at the "Tantum ergo sacramentum," on which see entry 360.6.

393.2/386.29 A MUCH ADMIRABLE HYMEN MINIM BY THOSE DELICATE POETS MASTER JOHN FLETCHER AND MASTER FRANCIS BEAUMONT . . . TO BED, TO BED This alludes to the "Third Song" in act I, scene ii, of *The Maid's Tragedy* (in the masque in that scene). It is sung by Neptune and begins, "To bed, to bed! Come, Hymen, lead the bride,/ And lay her by her husband's side."

393.14/386.41 THEY HAD BUT ONE DOXY BETWEEN THEM This alludes to a statement by John Aubrey in his brief sketch of Beaumont and Fletcher: "They lived together on the Banke side, not far from the Play-house, both bachelors; lay together; had one Wench in the house between them, which they did so admire; the same cloathes and cloake, &c.; betwcene them" (Aubrey's *Brief Lives*, ed. Oliver Lawson Dick [Univ. of Michigan Press, 1957], p. 21).

393.16/387.1 LIFE RAN VERY HIGH IN THOSE DAYS This remark was earlier attributed to Dowden about Shakespeare (on p. 204.20/202.3; cf. entry 204.19).

393.17/387.2 GREATER LOVE THAN THIS, HE SAID, NO MAN HATH THAT A MAN LAY DOWN HIS WIFE FOR HIS FRIEND. GO THOU AND DO LIKEWISE This parodies John 15:13, which says, " 'Greater love hath no man

than this, that a man lay down his life for his friends,' " and also
alludes to Luke 10:37 in which Christ concludes the parable of the
Good Samaritan by saying, " 'Go, and do thou likewise.' "

393.19/387.4   THUS . . . SAID ZARATHUSTRA   See entry 23.7.

393.24/387.8   THE SECONDBEST BED   From Shakespeare's will. See entry 203.22.

393.24/387.8   ORATE, FRATES, PRO MEMETIPSO   This is based on the
Mass. At the end of the Offeratory, the priest turns to the people
and says, "Orate, frates, ut meum ac vestrum sacrificium acceptabile
fiat apud Deum Patrem omnipotentem" ("Brothers and sisters,
pray that my sacrifice and yours may be acceptable to God the
almighty Father"). Stephen's adaptation says, "Pray, brothers,
for I myself."

393.25/387.9   REMEMBER, ERIN, THE GENERATIONS AND THY DAYS OF OLD
. . .   The opening phrase of this passage alludes to Moore's
song "Let Erin Remember the Days of Old," on which see entry
45.12. This and the next several sentences consist of such a pastiche
of common biblical phrases that it would be pointless to list them
all. Anyone who wishes to locate every instance of these various
phrases can do so with an exhaustive concordance. I shall list only
the less common phrases or those passages that seem specifically
alluded to. The opening phrase that I have cited alludes to Deuteronomy 32:7: "Remember the days of old, consider the years
of many generations" (Psalms 143:5 is quite similar, but the Jeshurum allusion a few lines later makes Deuteronomy the more likely
source). S. Gilbert (*JJU*, pp. 300–1) suggests that the structure
and theme of this passage recall the *Improperia* of the Catholic
liturgy for Holy Week, and he quotes from it at some length.
The Improperia ("The Reproaches") is a part of the service for
Good Friday and can be found in most missals.

393.27/387.11   A STRANGER TO MY GATES   References to a "stranger
within my gates" occur several times in the Old Testament, usually
in connection with some prohibition that extends to such strangers,
as in Exodus 20:10: "But the seventh day is the sabbath of the Lord
thy God: in it thou shalt not do any work, thou, nor thy son, nor
thy daughter, thy manservant, nor thy maidservant, nor thy cattle, nor thy stranger that is within thy gates." See also Deuteronomy 5:14 and 14:21.

393.28/387.12   TO WAX FAT AND KICK LIKE JESHURUM   This alludes
to Deuteronomy 32:15, which says, "But Jeshurum waxed fat, and
kicked." Jeshurum means "upright one," and is usually used poetically as an honorable title for Israel, though in this verse it is used
in reproach.

393.30/387.14   THE SLAVE OF SERVANTS   Perhaps this alludes to Genesis 9:25: "Cursed be Canaan, a servant of servants shall he be unto
his brethren." See entry 11.23.

393.30/387.14   RETURN, RETURN, CLAN MILLY: FORGET ME NOT, O
MILESIAN   This probably alludes specifically to Psalms 137:5:
"If I forget thee, O Jerusalem, let my right hand forget her cunning," but there are other similar phrases in the Bible. Milesian
alludes to the idea that the present Irish race is descended from
Milesius (see entry 328.10). *Clan Milly* is probably a semi-phonetic
spelling of "Clan Mileadh"—clan of the Milesians.

393.33/387.17   DIDST DENY ME TO THE ROMAN   This alludes to Peter's
denial of Christ, which is described in each of the four gospels.
See entry 391.34.

393.36/387.19   HOREB . . . NEBO . . . PISGAH . . . A LAND FLOWING WITH
MILK AND HONEY   Horeb, Nebo, and Pisgah are mountains mentioned frequently in the Old Testament. The final phrase parodies
the "land flowing with milk and honey" mentioned several times
in the Old Testament. It was the land God promised to lead the
Israelites into out of the land of Egypt. See e.g., Exodus 3:8, 17;
13:5; and 33:3.

394.1/387.26   THE SEPTUAGINT   The Septuagint is an old Greek version of the Old Testament made in Alexandria in the third or second
century B.C. It was the version of the Old Testament used by
Hellenistic Jews and Greek-speaking Christians.

394.3/387.28   ASSUEFACTION MINORATES ATROCITIES (AS TULLY SAITH OF
HIS DARLING STOICS)   The first part of this phrase means that
habitual contact with any atrocity lessens its impact. These words
are so uncommon that this almost certainly derives from a passage
in Sir Thomas Browne's *Christian Morals* where two of these
words appear: "Forget not how assuefaction unto any thing minorates the passion from it, how constant Objects loose their hints, and
steal an inadvertisement upon us" (Part III, sec. 10). But Browne
says nothing of Tully or the Stoics in this section. Tully (Marcus
Tully Cicero, 106–43 B.C.) was a Stoic, and many of his works
embody Stoic principles. Stephen may be thinking specifically of
his *Tusculan Disputations*, III, xiv, where Cicero develops the idea
that the "anticipation . . . of the future mitigates the approach of
evils whose coming one has long foreseen."

394.4/387.30   HAMLET HIS FATHER SHOWETH THE PRINCE NO BLISTER OF
COMBUSTION   Taken literally, this seems to allude to act I,
scene v, of *Hamlet* and to say that, though in that scene the Ghost
speaks of the fires of purgatory and threatens to tell secrets of his
prison house which would terrify Prince Hamlet, he does not

show him any blisters from the combustion. Perhaps there is also an oblique allusion to Hamlet's later speaking to his mother of such an act that "takes off the rose/ From the fair forehead of an innocent love,/ And sets a blister there" (*Ham.*, III, iv, 42–44).

394.6/387.31 AN EGYPT'S PLAGUE   The plagues visited by God on Egypt are described in Exodus 7–11.

394.13/387.38 THE AGED SISTERS   Most directly, this refers to the midwives, but it also refers to the Fates of Greek myth.

394.15/387.40 FIRST SAVED FROM WATER OF OLD NILE, AMONG BULRUSHES . . .   This alludes to Moses' being hidden among the bulrushes, described in Exodus 2. Cf. entry 45.7.

394.20/388.3 TO TOPHET OR TO EDENVILLE   These refer to heaven and hell. Tophet was a place in the valley of Hinnom, south of Jerusalem, where refuse and carcasses were burnt, and, at times, human beings, especially infants, were sacrificed to Moloch. The name means "place of burning." For Stephen's earlier use of Edenville, see entry 38.4.

394.25/388.8 WISDOM HATH BUILT HERSELF A HOUSE   This alludes to Proverbs 9:1: "Wisdom hath builded her house, she hath hewn out her seven pillars."

394.26/388.9 THE CRYSTAL PALACE   See entry 294.18.

394.27/388.10 A PENNY FOR HIM WHO FINDS THE PEA   Though I do not understand this phrase in its context, it perhaps alludes to the old swindle called the shell game in which a confidence man tricks people into betting money that they can say under which of several shells a pea is hidden.

394.29/388.11 BEHOLD THE MANSION REARED BY DEDAL JACK . . . This is a parody of the nursery rhyme "The House That Jack Built," which was alluded to on p. 391.36/385.22. But the parody is not original with Joyce, for in their discussion of this rhyme in the *ODNR*, the Opies have a section entitled "Parodies, poetic," where they say "The best known, beginning 'Behold the mansion reared by Daedal Jack' is sometimes attributed to Pope. It first appeared, however, c. 1870, and is merely an improvement of 'Behold the mansion swift upreared for Jack!' by E. L. Blanchard, 1861" (*ODNR*, p. 232).

394.33/388.15 LOUD ON LEFT THOR THUNDERED . . . THE HAMMERHURLER   Thor, son of Woden, is the second god in the ancient Scandinavian pantheon. One of his principal possessions in his hammer that typifies lightning and thunder and has the miraculous power of returning to him after he has hurled it.

395.4/388.17 AN OLD NOBODADDY   See entry 205.41.

395.16/388.39 BOASTHARD'S FEAR . . . CALMER'S WORDS   Though no characters by these names appear in that work, this clearly alludes to John Bunyan's extensive use of personification in his allegory *The Pilgrim's Progress* (1678–79).

395.36/389.17 THERE IS NO DEATH AND NO BIRTH NEITHER WIVING NOR MOTHERING   This probably derives in part from Christ's description of the situation after the resurrection. In Mark 12:25 he says, "For when they shall rise from the dead, they neither marry, nor are given in marriage . . ." (Luke 20:35 is very similar). There may also be an echo here of Hamlet's statement to Ophelia, "I say we will have no more marriages" (*Ham.*, III, i, 154).

396.38/390.17 THE BIG WIND OF LAST FEBRUARY A YEAR . . .   This refers to the gale of February 26–27, 1903. Though winds had been high all that week, on Thursday night and Friday morning, February 26 and 27, the whole United Kingdom, but especially Scotland and Ireland, was swept by a destructive gale. The London *Times* of Saturday, February 28 contains an account of damage and deaths resulting from the winds in various cities in the United Kingdom (p. 9, cols. a–b). The *Times* of Monday, March 2, contains a more detailed account of damage to Dublin. It calls the gale "a storm more violent than any which the oldest inhabitants can remember," and says the streets of Dublin Friday morning looked "as if they had just suffered a siege or an earthquake" (p. 7, col. a). Yeats refers to this gale in a note to his *In the Seven Woods* (1903): "I made some of these poems walking about among the Seven Woods, before the big wind of nineteen hundred and three blew down so many trees, and troubled the wild creatures, and changed the look of things . . ." (for this note, see the *Variorum Poems*, p. 814). Cf. entry 138.3.

397.20/390.42 BEEF TO THE HEEL   See entry 66.8.

398.3/391.24 AND AFTER WIND AND WATER FIRE SHALL COME   Wind, water, and fire are all common agents of destruction in the Bible, and the second coming of Christ is to be accompanied by fire (see entry 428.10), but nowhere in the Bible have I found this exact phrase.

398.5/391.25 MR RUSSELL HAS DONE A PROPHETICAL CHARM OF THE SAME GIST OUT OF THE HINDUSTANISH   This refers to A. E.'s weekly agricultural paper *The Irish Homestead* (see entry 191.29), but an examination of all issues of the paper for April, May, June, July, and August of 1904 revealed nothing like this in it. Probably *Hindustanish* simply refers the Dublin theosophical group's interest in Indian writings (see entry 13.6).

398.31/392.10 KERRY COWS   Though the allusion is unlikely, there is an Irish song entitled "The Kerry Cow," words and music of which are in Alfred Perceval Graves's *Irish Folk Songs* (London: Boosey & Co., 1897), pp. 10–13. The song has four four-line stanzas, and it begins, " 'Oh what are you seeking, my pretty colleen,/ So sadly, tell me now?' "

398.37/392.16 MORT AUX VACHES   This clearly recalls the killing of the oxen of the sun in book XII of the *Odyssey*.

399.2/392.22 HE TOOK THE BIT BETWEEN HIS TEETH   "To take the bit in one's teeth" is proverbial and is listed in the *ODEP*.

399.26/393.5 TAKE THE BULL BY THE HORNS   This too is proverbial; see entry 33.16.

399.31/393.9 AN IRISH BULL IN AN ENGLISH CHINASHOP   "A bull in a china shop" is proverbial and is listed in the *ODEP*. P. W. Joyce also cites the phrase in his *English As We Speak It*, p. 137. An "Irish bull" is an illogical statement that does make some kind of sense, as, for example, Disraeli's "It is curious to observe the various substitutes for paper before its invention." For a discussion of Irish bulls, with many examples, see Walsh's *Handy-Book of Literary Curiosities*, pp. 124–32. See also the next entry.

399.31/393.9 I CONCEIVE YOU   This may allude to a statement attributed to Irish professor Robert Yelverton Tyrrell (1844–1914), professor of classical languages and ancient history at Trinity College, Dublin. In his *Recreations of an Anthologist* (New York: Dodd, Mead & Co., 1904) Brander Matthews says, " . . . it was Professor Tyrrel [*sic*] who neatly explained that the Irish bull differed from the bull of all other islands in that 'it was always pregnant' " (pp. 19–20).

399.32/393.10 THAT SAME BULL THAT WAS SENT TO OUR ISLAND BY FARMER NICHOLAS . . .   The rest of this long paragraph describes in bovine terms the relationships between the papacy, the English sovereigns, and Ireland. The point of departure is the papal "bull," "Laudibiliter," by which Pope Adrian IV (pope from 1154–59), who was born an Englishman named Nicholas Breakspear, granted Ireland to English King Henry II (reigned 1154–89) as a papal fief. Later in this paragraph the "Harry" is Henry VIII, and the subject is his break with the Roman Catholic Church and his establishment of the Church of England. S. Gilbert (*JJU*, p. 304) suggests that this may also owe something to the passage in section IV of Swift's *Tale of a Tub* which describes Peter's fondness for his bulls.

399.33/393.11 WITH AN EMERALD RING   This probably alludes to the golden ring set with an emerald which Pope Adrian IV is said to have sent to Henry II. In his *Metalogicon*, John of Salisbury (*ca.* 1115–80) says "By me [Pope] Adrian dispatched a golden ring, set with a magnificent emerald, whereby he invested [our] Henry II with the authority to rule Ireland" (Book IV, chap. 42; see the edition by Daniel D. McGarry [Univ. of California Press, 1955], pp. 274–75; the brackets in the quotation are in McGarry's text).

400.5/393.25 HE TAUGHT HIM A TRICK WORTH TWO OF THE OTHER The *ODEP* lists "A trick worth two of that" and gives three instances of the phrase, including one from Shakespeare's *1 Henry IV*. In that play, the first carrier says of Gadshill's request to lend him a lantern, "Nay, by God, soft, I know a trick worth two of that, i' faith" (II, i, 40).

400.10/393.29 THE FOUR FIELDS OF ALL IRELAND   See entry 184.40.

400.17/393.36 THE FATHER OF THE FAITHFUL   The context suggests that this is a title of the Pope, but nowhere have I found it used as such.

400.35/394.12 THE LORD HARRY CALLED FARMER NICHOLAS ALL THE OLD NICKS IN THE WORLD AND AN OLD WHOREMASTER THAT KEPT SEVEN TRULLS IN HIS HOUSE   This alludes to Henry VIII's break with the Roman Catholic Church; see entry 399.32 (though Adrian IV was of course no longer pope; during Henry's break the popes were Clement VII and Paul III). Both Old Harry (or Lord Harry) and Old Nick are popular names for the devil. The final clause probably alludes to the Anglican penchant for describing the Roman Catholic Church in terms of the imagery of the book of Revelation; see especially Revelation 17.

400.40/394.17 CLEANING HIS ROYAL PELT   This alludes to a song by blind Irish balladeer Michael Moran (b. *ca.* 1794), who called himself "Zozimus." Colm O'Lochlainn briefly discusses Zozimus and this ballad, entitled "The Finding of Moses," and prints part of one version of it in his *Irish Street Ballads*. The version O'Lochlainn gives begins, "In Agypts land, contaygious to the Nile,/ Old Pharo's daughter went to bathe in style,/ She tuk her dip and came unto the land,/ And for to dry her royal pelt she ran along the strand . . ." (p. 230). The song is also printed in two versions in an article entitled "The Name is Zozimus: The Last Gleeman of the Coombe," which appeared in *Ireland of the Welcomes*, Jan.–Feb., 1962 (X, no. 5, 17–21). And, as J. Prescott has pointed out (*PMLA*, LXVIII, 1226–27; reprinted in *Exploring James Joyce*), Yeats discusses this poet and poem in his *The Celtic Twilight* (1893).

401.25/395.1 LET THE BULLGINE RUN   This alludes to a sea chantey entitled "Let the bullgine run," which begins, "We'll run from night till morning. O run, let the bullgine run." Words and music can be found in Cecil J. Sharp, *English Folk-Chanteys*, p. 16. In a note Sharp says " 'Bullgine' is, I believe, nigger slang for 'engine' " (p. 68). This phrase occurs occasionally in other chanteys.

401.29/395.5 POPE PETER'S BUT A PISSABED./ A MAN'S A MAN FOR A' THAT   This alludes to Robert Burns's song "For A' That.and A' That" (or "Is there for honest poverty"), which contains the line "A man's a man for a' that." But I have yet to locate the first line of this parody in print.

402.4/395.21 SIR FOPLING POPINJAY AND SIR MILKSOP QUIDNUNC   If these are specific characters in literature I have not discovered them. The names Popinjay and Quidnunc are often used to designate characters who are fops or busybodies.

402.8/395.25 'TIS AS CHEAP SITTING AS STANDING   The *ODEP* lists "It is as cheap sitting as standing," and cites three instances, one of which is Swift's *Polite Conversation*. In the first conversation of that work, Lady Answerall says to Col. Atwit, "Well, but sit while you stay; 'tis as cheap sitting, as standing" (p. 58). Partridge says the proverb is "17th–20th centuries."

402.19/395.35 WHO HIDE THEIR FLAMBEAU UNDER A BUSHEL   In the sermon on the mount, Christ says "Neither do men light a candle and put it under a bushel, but on a candlestick" (Matt. 5:15; Mark 4:21 and Luke 11:33 are very similar).

402.28/396.3 LAMBAY ISLAND . . . LORD TALBOT DE MALAHIDE   Lambay Island is a small island in the Irish Sea, northeast of Dublin. Though the de Malahide family did own the island during the nineteenth century, acquiring it about 1814 and selling it in 1888, they did not own it at the time *Ulysses* is set. See Lawrence Weaver's *Houses and Gardens by E. L. Luytens* (London, 1913), pp. 213–14.

402.31/396.6 OMPHALOS   See entries 7.33, 17.37, and 38.3.

403.12/396.29 CARRY COALS TO NEWCASTLE   This familiar phrase, which is included in the *ODEP*, has been proverbial at least since the sixteenth century.

403.16/396.32 TALIS AC TANTA DEPRAVATIO HUJUS SECULI . . .   Though this claims to be from the classics, and though the style is Ciceronian, I do not think this alludes to or parodies any specific passage in Cicero. The statement may be translated, "Such and so great is the depravity of our age, O citizens, that our women greatly prefer the lascivious titillations of lustful half-men to the ponderous testes and the grand erection of the Roman centurion." This last phrase probably alludes to the idea that Christ was fathered by a Roman centurion; see entry 521.21.

403.31/397.6 LOAVES AND FISHES   It was with loaves and fishes that Christ fed the multitude. See Matthew 14:17 ff. (or Mark 6:38, Luke 9:13, or John 6:9).

404.1/397.17 A WOLF IN THE STOMACH   This apparently alludes to the proverbial "A growing youth has a wolf in his belly," which is listed in the *ODEP*. Dr. Austin Meldon was a distinguished Dublin surgeon of the day, but I do not know why Joyce chose him here.

404.4/397.20 MOTHER GROGAN   See entry 12.33.

404.5/397.21 'TIS PITY SHE'S A TROLLOP   This echoes the title of John Ford's tragedy *'Tis Pity She's a Whore* (1633).

405.29/399.2 ARK OF SALVATION   The context indicates an allusion to Noah's ark, described in Genesis 6–8.

406.34/400.4 A CLOUD OF WITNESSES   Hebrews 12:1 says, "Wherefore seeing we also are compassed about with so great a cloud of speaks of "my misshaped trunk"; and in V, v, 35, Prince Edward easily beset us, and let us run with patience the race that is set before us,"

407.11/400.22 HONOUR THY FATHER AND THY MOTHER   An allusion to the fifth commandment: "Honor thy father and thy mother" (Exod. 20:12; also Deut. 5:16).

407.26/400.36 A CROPEARED CREATURE OF A MISSHAPEN GIBBOSITY   Though not always allusions to specific lines, many of these words and phrases seem to echo the descriptions of Richard, Duke of Gloucester, in *III Henry VI*. For example, three of the six uses of *misshaped* or *misshapen* in Shakespeare's plays occur in descriptions of Richard in this play: in II, ii, 136, Queen Margaret describes Richard as "Like a foul misshapen stigmatic"; in III, ii, 170, Richard witnesses, let us lay aside every weight, and the sin which doth so refers to Richard as "thou misshapen Dick." Though *gibbosity* does not occur in Shakespeare, the *OED* definition of *gibbous* as "of persons and animals: Hunch-backed; having a hump" is certainly appropriate to Richard. See also entry 407.27. Interestingly, *cropeared* occurs only once in Shakespeare, and that in another play frequently alluded to in this episode—*I Henry IV*. In that play Hotspur describes a horse as "A roan, a crop-ear, is it not?" (II, iii, 72).

407.27/400.37 THRUST LIKE A CROOKBACK TEETHED AND FEET FIRST INTO THE WORLD   As Wm. Schutte has pointed out (*JS*, p. 188), this alludes to Richard's description of himself in *III Henry VI*, V, vi, 70 ff. See also entry 407.26.

407.30/400.40   THAT MISSING LINK . . .   This refers to the search by evolutionist Charles Darwin (1809–82) and others for information about a link between man and the anthropoid apes.

408.6/401.15   FOR EATING OF THE TREE FORBID   An allusion to the forbidden tree of Genesis 2:17 ff.

408.22/401.31   EPHESIAN MATRON   This alludes to the well-known story of the matron of Ephesus who bewailed and mourned her husband's death to an uncommon degree, but was soon persuaded out of grief, and into love, by a handsome young soldier. Though not original with Petronius, the story is told in his *Satyricon*, and most later retellings derive from that source.

408.29/401.37   'SLIFE, I'LL BE ROUND WITH YOU   A. Heine (*Shakespeare Association Bulletin*, XXIV, 56–70) lists this as an allusion to Malvolio's words in *Twelfth-Night*: "Sir Toby, I must be round with you" (II, iii, 102), but the allusion is doubtful, because very similar phrases occur in *Timon of Athens*, II, ii, 8, and in *Hamlet*, III, i, 191, and III, iv, 5. And this was a fairly common Elizabethan turn of speech. Schutte does not include this allusion in his list in *JS*.

408.33/401.41   THE MAN IN THE GAP   See entry 614.42.

408.36/402.3   METEMPSYCHOSIS   See entry 64.18.

409.2/402.10   BIRDS OF A FEATHER LAUGH TOGETHER   This is a variation on the proverbial "Birds of a feather flock together," which is listed in the *ODEP*.

409.24/402.31   A VERY PELICAN IN HIS PIETY   Traditionally, it was thought that young pelicans fed on the blood of the breast of the parent bird. Apparently this idea arose from the pelican's feeding its young on partially masticated food directly from its own bill sac, held flat against the breast so the young may eat. The phrase "pelican in its piety" is the correct heraldic term for a parent bird depicted in performing this act. In early church tradition and in the medieval bestiary, the pelican was an emblem of Christ, both for the reason just explained and because the female was supposed to revive the young slain by the male bird through pouring her blood over them and sitting on the dead birds for three days.

409.28/402.36   HAGAR, THE EGYPTIAN   Hagar, an Egyptian, was the handmaid of Abraham's wife Sarai (later Sarah). When Sarai bore him no children, Abraham "went in unto Hagar, and she conceived" (Gen. 16:4).

409.36/403.1   BALM OF GILEAD   Jeremiah 8:22 says, "Is there no balm in Gilead; Is there no physician there? Why then is not the health of the daughter of my people recovered?" Another juxta-position of balm and Gilead occurs in Jeremiah 46:11.

410.8/403.14 THE SUBLIME PORTE "The Sublime Porte" is the official title of the central office of the Ottoman Empire under the sultans. In Arabic it is "Bab-i-ali"; perhaps "Sublime Porte" comes from the Italian translation "La Porte Sublima."

410.26/403.32 THE FRATRICIDAL CASE KNOWN AS THE CHILDS MURDER . . . See entry 100.2.

410.33/403.38 CHINLESS CHINAMEN From *The Geisha*; see entry 215.31.

411.6/404.11 ARISTOTLE HAS CLASSIFIED IN HIS MASTERPIECE On this spurious work, see entry 235.19.

411.19/404.23 THE CASE OF MADAME GRISSEL STEEVENS As R. M. Adams explains (*SS*, pp. 56–57), Grissel Steevens (1653–1746) was the sister of Richard Steevens, Dublin physician and founder of Steevens' Hospital. Her generosity made construction of the hospital possible much sooner than her brother's will had provided. She was said to bear pig's features, but this has no basis in fact. In his biography of Sir William Wilde, T. G. Wilson discusses the Steevens and conjectures that the myth about Miss Steevens "prob-ably arose because she was usually veiled when she went among the poor" (*Victorian Doctor* [New York, 1946], p. 17).

411.28/404.33 THE MINOTAUR . . . ELEGANT LATIN POET . . . METAMORPHOSES In Greek myth, the Minotaur was a monster with a man's body and the head of a bull. Born of Queen Pasiphae, wife of King Minos of Crete, and of a white bull, it was kept in a labyrinth built by Daedalus. Ovid tells the story in book VIII of his *Metamorphoses*. Joyce's epigraph for *A Portrait of the Artist* comes from this book of the *Metamorphoses*, immediately after the story of the Minotaur. See also entries 207.40 and 569.8.

412.1/405.5 IN OBEDIENCE TO AN INWARD VOICE This perhaps alludes to the "inward light" of the Quakers. See entry 193.15.

412.3/405.7 THE ECCLESIASTICAL ORDINANCE FORBIDDING MAN TO PUT ASUNDER WHAT GOD HAD JOINED In Matthew 19:6 Christ says, "What therefore God hath joined together, let not man put as-under." This part of the gospel is read during the Wedding Mass.

412.13/405.17 I AM THE MURDERER OF SAMUEL CHILDS Childs was mentioned on p. 410.26/403.32 and is mentioned again on p. 412.33/405.36. See entry 100.2.

412.23/405.27 THE BLACK PANTHER See entry 412.33.

412.29/405.32 MANANAAN Mananaan is the Irish god of the sea. See entries 38.24 and 510.7.

412.29/405.32 LEX TALIONIS See entry 139.31.

412.29/405.33 THE SENTIMENTALIST IS HE WHO . . .   From Meredith's *Richard Feverel*; see entry 199.21.

412.32/405.35 HAINES WAS THE THIRD BROTHER   On the third brother motive, see entry 210.40.

412.33/405.36 THE BLACK PANTHER WAS HIMSELF THE GHOST OF HIS OWN
FATHER   In early tradition and in the medieval bestiary, the panther was thought to be friendly and was often used as an emblem
of Christ, though this tradition died when the true nature of the
animal was learned. For an essay developing the symbology of
the panther, see the essay cited in entry 4.23. The final part of this
entry repeats what Mulligan earlier said of Stephen's Shakespeare
theory on p. 18.11/19.33.

412.35/405.38 FOR THIS RELIEF MUCH THANKS   This is from *Hamlet*; see entry 372.30.

412.35/405.38 THE LONELY HOUSE BY THE GRAVEYARD   This probably alludes to Irish writer Joseph Sheridan LeFanu's (1814–73)
novel *The House by the Churchyard* (1863). In his *Books at the
Wake*, J. S. Atherton points out that this was one of four books
listed by Gorman as "Joyce's father's library," and Atherton discusses the importance of the book to *Finnegans Wake* (p. 110).

413.20/406.22 WITH JACOB'S PIPE   Though I suspect that this alludes to some well-known brand of smoking pipe of the day, I
have not been able to confirm this.

413.27/406.28 THE WISE FATHER KNOWS HIS OWN CHILD   This is
from *The Merchant of Venice*; see entry 88.19. Another allusion
to a closely adjacent line of this play follows on p. 414.13/407.13.

413.35/406.36 IN AN INSTANT (FIAT!) LIGHT SHALL FLOOD THE WORLD
This recalls God's creation of light in Genesis 1:14: "Let there
be lights in the firmament of the heaven" ("Fiant luminaria in firma-
mento caeli").

414.13/407.13 SCREECHOWLS   This probably alludes to Lilith, mentioned earlier in this episode on p. 390.1/383.33. *Lilith* is translated
screech owl in the King James version of Isaiah 34:14.

414.13/407.13 SANDBLIND   Especially in light of the allusion on p.
413.27/406.28, this seems to recall the use of *sandblind* twice in
The Merchant of Venice, II, ii, 37 and 77. These are the only instances of the word in Shakespeare's works. On the upupa, see
T. H. White, *The Bestiary*, p. 150, where the bird's filthy habits
are described, but nothing is said of its vision.

414.17/407.16 THE LANCINATING LIGHTNINGS OF WHOSE BROW ARE
SCORPIONS   Though the allusion is uncertain this may owe
something to the description of scorpions as a means of torment in
Revelation 9.

414.18/407.17 THE BULLS OF BASHAN AND OF BABYLON   Various kinds of cattle "of Bashan," but not of Babylon, are mentioned in the Old Testament. Psalms 22:12 says, "Many bulls have compassed me: strong bulls of Bashan have set me round."

414.20/407.20 THEY MOAN . . . MURDERERS OF THE SUN   As S. Gilbert has pointed out (*JJU*, p. 308), this recalls the account of the killing of the oxen of the sun in book XII of the *Odyssey*. We are told that after Ulysses' men had killed the cattle, "The skins were creeping, and the flesh bellowing upon the spits, both the roast and the raw, and there was a sound as the voice of kine" (Butcher and Lang trans., p. 188).

414.29/407.29 THE HOUSE OF VIRGO   S. Gilbert points out (*JJU*, p. 308) that the constellation Virgo governs the womb, the organ of the body to which this episode is related.

414.29/407.29 METEMPSYCHOSIS   See entry 64.18.

414.30/407.30 THE EVERLASTING BRIDE, HARBINGER OF THE DAYSTAR, THE BRIDE, EVER VIRGIN   Each of these phrases is very close to phrases applied to the Virgin Mary. In the Litany of Our Lady of Loreto, for example, she is referred to as Virgin, as Mother, and as the Morning Star. She is also regarded as the Bride of the Holy Ghost. See Donald Attwater, *A Dictionary of Mary*.

414.31/407.31 MARTHA, THOU LOST ONE   From Flotow's *Martha*, on which see entry 117.34.

414.38/407.37 SIMPLY SWIRLING   From Boylan's song; see entry 62.36.

415.2/407.42 GLAUCON, ALCIBIADES, PISISTRATUS   Alcibiades and Pisistratus are well known to Greek history: Pisistratus (*ca.* 605–527 B.C.) was tyrant of Athens; Alcibiades (*ca.* 450–404 B.C.) was a politician and general. Glaucon is less well known, and it is uncertain which person of this name is alluded to; most likely it is the Glaucon who was a brother of Plato and who is one of the speakers in *The Republic* (a person of the same name speaks in other Platonic dialogues, but his identity is uncertain). And this may also allude to Walter Savage Landor's *Imaginary Conversations*, for two of them are entitled "Solon and Pisistratus" and "Alcibiades and Xenophon."

415.4/408.3 IF I CALL THEM INTO LIFE ACROSS THE WATERS OF LETHE . . . This recalls Ulysses' summoning the ghosts of the dead during his visit to Hades, described in book XI of the *Odyssey*.

415.6/408.5 BOUS STEPHANOUMENOS   See entry 210.19.

415.23/408.22 PHYLLIS   Phyllis is a traditional name for a maiden in pastoral poetry; this is the first of several such names in this paragraph. Cf. entry 415.40.

415.27/408.25 ALL WAS LOST NOW   See entry 256.24.

415.40/408.38 LALAGE WERE SCARCE FAIR BESIDE HER   Lalage is one
of the many traditional names for beautiful women. S. T. Coleridge's poem "Names" is a catalog of such names; it begins, "I
ask'd my fair one happy day,/ What I should call her in my lay;/
By what sweet name from Rome or Greece;/ Lalage, Neaera,
Chloris,/ Sappho, Lesbia, or Doris/ Arethusa or Lucrece." Lalage
goes back at least as far as Horace's *Odes*, Book II, V, line 15.

416.13/409.10 GLYCERA OR CHLOE   Glycera is the name of several
notorious Greek courtesans, most notably a mistress of Menander
and a favorite of Horace. Chloe is the traditional name for a country maiden or shepherdess, as in Sidney's *Arcadia* and the Greek
pastoral romance *Daphnis and Chloe*. Cf. entries 415.23 and 415.40.

416.15/409.12 A SLIGHT DISORDER IN HER DRESS   This is from Robert
Herrick's "Delight in Disorder," which begins, "A sweet disorder
in the dress/ Kindles in clothes a wantonness."

416.28/409.24 THEOSOPHOS TOLD ME SO . . .   This and the following
sentence parody theosophical writings; see entry 185.29 and the
works cited there.

418.7/411.2 THE INSPIRED PENCIL OF LAFAYETTE HAS LIMNED FOR AGES
YET TO COME   Lafayette was not an artist, but a Dublin photographer. Thom's *Dublin Directory* (1904) lists "Lafayette, James,
photographer, 30 Westmoreland st." (p. 1925). See p. 652.34/
636.39.

418.19/411.14 THE VIEW OF EMPEDOCLES OF TRINACRIA . . .   Empedocles of Trinacria (*ca.* 495–*ca.* 435 B.C.) is also known as Empedocles of Acragas, since he was born in Acragas, Sicily (Trinacria is
an old name for Sicily). Though better known for his theory that
everything is composed of four elements, he did believe that the
sex of a child was determined by which side of the ovary it developed on and that males came from the right side. See Arthur
William Meyer, *The Rise of Embryology*, p. 23.

418.24/411.18 CULPEPPER, SPALLANZANI, BLUMENBACH, LUSK, HERTWIG,
LEOPOLD, AND VALENTI   R. M. Adams discusses these men briefly
(*SS*, p. 157). One of the many books by Nicholas Culpeper
(1616–54) is *A Directory for Midwives; or, A Guide for Women,
in their Conception, Bearing and Suckling their Children* . . . (London, 1651); there is a *DNB* article on Culpeper. Italian naturalist
Abbe Lazarro Spallanzani (1729–99) did some important work in
embryology toward disproving the theory of spontaneous generation. Johann Friedrich Blumenbach (1752–1840) was primarily
an anthropologist, but he did significant work in embryology

toward developing the idea of a *nisus formativus*, which was his term for a directing morphogenic force peculiar to living bodies. Lusk must refer to American physiologist and nutritionist Graham Lusk (1866–1932), though his contributions to embryology have proved negligible. Oscar Hertwig (1849–1922) was an embryologist; he is credited with establishing the fact that fertilization consists of the union of the nuclei of a male and a female sex cell. That Christian Gerhard Leopold (d. 1911) was an embryologist is obvious from the list of his books in the *Catalogue* of the British Museum, but I have learned no more about him. The fullest account I have found of Italian physician Giulio (or Julio) Valenti (b. 1860) is a brief note in the Spanish *Enciclopedia Universal Ilustrada*, LXVI, 671; some of the works listed there show an embryological interest.

418.27/411.21 NISUS FORMATIVUS   On the *nisus formativus*, see under Blumenbach in the preceding entry.

419.3/411.39 THE CLASSICAL STATUES SUCH AS VENUS AND APOLLO There are many statues of both of these figures. For more specific references to statues of Venus, see pp. 201.11/198.35, 425.40/418.26, and 490.15/480.25.

419.31/412.24 MUST CERTAINLY, IN THE POET'S WORDS, GIVE US PAUSE Hamlet, in the "To be or not to be" soliloquy, says that "in that sleep of death what dreams may come/ When we have shuffled off this mortal coil/ Must give us pause" (III, i, 66–68).

419.42/412.34 THE SURVIVAL OF THE FITTEST   This alludes to the well known principle of Darwinism set forth by Charles Darwin in his *Origin of Species* (1859) and elaborated in his *The Descent of Man* (1871).

420.23/413.15 LET THE CAT INTO THE BAG   This is a pointed variation on the proverbial phrase "To let the cat out of the bag," which the *ODEP* lists and explains as meaning "to disclose a guarded secret."

420.34/413.26 SHE HAD FOUGHT THE GOOD FIGHT   This echoes passages from I and II Timothy. I Timothy 6:12 says, "Fight the good fight of faith"; II Timothy 4:7 says, "I have fought a good fight, I have finished my course, I have kept the faith." This is alluded to again on p. 421.26/414.17.

420.41/413.33 THE UNIVERSAL HUSBAND   This probably involves a gibe at the theosophists, for the phrase "Universal ———" is very common in theosophical lore (see the index to Mme Blavatsky's *Key to Theosophy*, cited in entry 185.29), though I have never seen this exact phrase.

420.42/413.34 HER DEAR DOADY   This alludes to Dickens' novel *David Copperfield* (1849–50), in which Dora, David's child-wife, frequently addresses David by the pet name "Doady." The name is repeated on pp. 421.6/413.40 and 421.21/414.12.

421.4/413.38 THE WHIRLIGIG OF YEARS   In *Twelfth Night*, Feste, the clown, says, "And thus the whirligig of time brings in his revenges" (V, i, 385).

421.7/413.41 THAT FAROFF TIME OF THE ROSES   This may allude to Thomas Hood's "Ballad," which begins, "It was not in the winter/ Our loving lot was cast;/ It was the time of roses,/ We plucked them as we passed!" But in view of Joyce's familiarity with James Clarence Mangan's works, this may well allude to his poem "The Time of the Roses," which laments the rapid passage of the time of the roses.

421.13/414.5 OUR FAMOUS HERO OF THE SOUTH AFRICAN WAR, LORD BOBS OF WATERFORD AND CANDAHAR   "Lord Bobs" was the nickname of Frederick Sleigh Roberts, first earl Roberts of Kandahar, Pretoria, and Waterford (1832–1914). After an impressive military career in India, Lord Roberts, in 1899, was appointed commander in chief of British forces in the South African War. He made many changes and improvements in the forces, and was returned to England in 1900, where he was awarded an earldom and made commander in chief of the British army.

421.19/414.11 FATHER CRONION   Father Time. Cronus or Cronion in Greek myth came to be a personification of Time through confusion with the Greek word *chronos*. Cronus was the son of Uranus, whom he attacked and mutilated; he was later overthrown by his own son, Zeus.

421.26/414.17 YOU TOO HAVE FOUGHT THE GOOD FIGHT   See entries 420.34 and 421.27.

421.27/414.19 WELL DONE, THOU GOOD AND FAITHFUL SERVANT   This is what the master says to the servant in Christ's parable of the talents: "Well done, good and faithful servant" (Matt. 25:23). Interestingly, in Milton's *Paradise Lost*, God's congratulation of the faithful angel Abdiel also blends the two biblical allusions here in *Ulysses*: "Servant of God, well done, well hast thou fought/ The better fight" (*Paradise Lost*, VI, 29–30).

422.33/415.23 THE VIGILANT WATCH OF SHEPHERDS . . .   This recalls the description of Christ's birth in Luke 2:1–20.

423.14/416.4 DOCTOR DIET AND DOCTOR QUIET   It is proverbially said that these are the best doctors. In Swift's *Polite Conversation*, second conversation, Lord Smart says, "And the best Doctors in the

World, are Doctor *Diet*, Doctor *Quiet*, and Doctor *Merryman*." Partridge says this "occurs in Bulleyn's *Government of Health*, 1558, with 'physicians' for 'doctors,' and the prescription is still recommended" (p. 142).

423.30/416.19 MALTHUSIASTS   Malthusiasts are those enthusiastic for Malthus (with an echo of Latin *malus*). English political economist Thomas Robert Malthus (1766–1834) said that population tends to outrun means of support and will be held in check by disaster if not controlled by sexual restraint. There may also be specific allusion here to the Malthusian League, founded in 1877 to further knowledge of contraceptives and to encourage birth control.

423.34/416.22 GATHER THY HOMER OF RIPE WHEAT   The homer is a biblical measure, equal to about eleven bushels. Though this passage obviously has biblical overtones, I can find no passage very similar to this in the Bible.

423.34/416.23 THY FLEECE IS DRENCHED   A dew-dampened fleece was the sign by which Gideon knew that God would use him to save Israel from the Midianites. Judges 6:37–38 says, "Behold, I will put a fleece of wool in the floor; and if the dew be on the fleece only, and it be dry upon all the earth beside, then shall I know that thou wilt save Israel by mine hand, as thou hast said. And it was so: for he rose up early on the morrow, and thrust the fleece together, and wringed the dew out of the fleece, a bowl full of water."

423.35/416.23 DARBY DULLMAN THERE WITH HIS JOAN   This alludes to a song by F. E. Weatherly and J. L. Molloy, entitled "Darby and Joan." It is a sentimental song about a couple "old and gray" who have been together, thick and thin, for fifty years. It begins "Darby dear, we are old and gray, Fifty years since our wedding day," and the chorus says, "Always the same, Darby my own, Always the same to your old wife Joan." For words and music, see Chapple, *Heart Songs*, pp. 124–25. The song does tell of their losing a child, but no mention is made of a bird or dog.

423.39/416.27 HEROD'S SLAUGHTER OF THE INNOCENTS   In an attempt to destroy the new Messiah, Herod had slaughtered all children in and near Bethlehem who were two years old or younger. See entry 172.3.

424.3/416.33 A TRUCE TO THRENES AND TRENTALS AND JEREMIES AND ALL SUCH CONGENITAL DEFUNCTIVE MUSIC   Part of this alludes to Shakespeare's "The Phoenix and the Turtle." "Defunctive music" (i.e., music about death) is mentioned in line 14 of that poem, and "whereupon it made this threne/ To the phoenix and the dove" occurs in lines 49–50. *Threne* is from the Greek *threnos*, a dirge. *Trental*, which the OED says means a set of thirty requiem masses, and by extension an elegy or dirge, is used in two poems by Herrick, but Shakespeare never used the word. Skeat mentions a poem by St. Gregory entitled "Trental." Jeremies, obviously derived from Jeremiah and also meaning a lamentation, is not in the *OED* or in Skeat.

424.7/416.37 HOW SAITH ZARATHUSTRA   See entry 23.7.

424.8/416.38 DEINE KUH TRÜBSAL MELKEST DU. NUN TRINKST DU DIE SÜSSE MILCH DES EUTERS   This German says, "You are milking your cow, Adversity. Now you are drinking the sweet milk of her udders." Though this is similar to the phrase "Adversity's sweet milk, philosophy," from *Romeo and Juliet*, III, iii, 55, there is probably no allusion involved. Nor does this seem to allude to a German proverb or set phrase.

424.13/417.1 MILK OF MADNESS   The phrase "milk of kindness" or "milk of human kindness" (deriving from Lady Macbeth's words in *Mac.*, I, v, 18) is so common that this may be regarded as a variation on it.

424.14/417.1 THE HONEYMILK OF CANAAN'S LAND   See entry 393.36.

424.17/417.4 PER DEAM PARTULAM ET PERTUNDAM NUNC EST BIBENDUM "By the goddess Partula and Pertunda, now must we drink." Partula is the goddess who presides over birth; Pertunda the goddess who presides over the loss of virginity or over coition. "Nunc est bibendum" are the well-known opening words of Horace's Ode xxxvii (Book I), "Now must we drink."

424.25/417.12 BENEDICAT VOS OMNIPOTENS DEUS, PATER ET FILIUS This is from the Dismissal portion of the Mass. Just before the Last Gospel, the priest says, "Benedicat vos omnipotens Deus, Pater et Filius, et Spiritus Sanctus" ("May almighty God, the Father, and the Son, and the Holy Spirit, bless you").

424.26/417.13 THE DENZILLE LANE BOYS   In his article on this portion of this episode, Daniel Weiss cites T. W. Pugh of Dublin as saying that this refers to " 'the Revolutionary Society named "the Invincibles"—many of whose members lived in Denzille Street, adjoining Denzille Lane' " (*Analyst*, IX, 4). On the Invincibles, see entry 81.26; but I have never come across any connection between the Invincibles and a Denzille Lane group.

424.30/417.17 THENCE THEY ADVANCED FIVE PARASANGS   Daniel Weiss (*op. cit.*, entry 424.26) points out that the parasang is a Persian unit of length, and that this alludes to Xenophon's *Anabasis*. The parasang is thought to have been approximately three

to three-and-one-half English miles. Many English translations
of Xenophon retain this term, and phrases similar to the one in
Ulysses occur frequently. For example, "From Issi, he marched a
single stage—five parasangs—to the gates of Cilicia and Syria"
(from Book I, chap. 4 of H. G. Dakyns' translation [London,
1901], p. 14).

424.31/417.18 SLATTERY'S MOUNTED FOOT   This alludes to the comic
song "Shlathery's Mounted Fut," by Irishman Percy French. The
song, appropriately, is about a brigade of drinkers who come down
from the mountains. Some lines from the second stanza seem most
appropriate to the present context; we are told that upon arriving
at one pub, "there we saw a notice which the brightest heart un-
nerved—/ 'All liquor must be settled for before the dhrink is
served.'/ So on we marched, but soon again each warrior's heart
grew pale,/ For risin' high in front o' us we saw the County Jail"
(*Prose, Poems and Parodies of Percy French*, p. 136).

424.32/417.19 APOSTATE'S CREED   A parody of "Apostle's Creed,"
which was parodied in detail on p. 329.23/323.32.

424.35/417.21 BRITISH BEATITUDES   These "beatitudes," which are
apparently the things the British hold blessed, are specified on
p. 424.41/417.28 as "Beer, beef, business, bibles, bulldogs, battle-
ships, buggery and bishops." Christ's beatitudes are given in Matthew 5:2–12; cf. entry 509.8.

424.35/417.22 RETAMPLAN DIGIDI BOUM BOUM   Daniel Weiss suggests (*op. cit.*, entry 424.26) that this represents the sound of
drums. This is probably correct, and the word *Retamplan* suggests
the Rataplan songs in various operas, such as Donizetti's *The
Daughter of the Regiment* (on which see entry 269.20).

424.36/417.22 TO BE PRINTED AND BOUND AT THE DRUIDDRUM PRESS BY
TWO DESIGNING FEMALES   This alludes to the press of the Dun
Emer guild at Dundrum, county Dublin, and to Yeats's sisters'
work at the guild. See entry 13.1.

424.38/417.25 MOST BEAUTIFUL BOOK COME OUT OF IRELAND MY TIME
This alludes to Yeats's comment on a book by Lady Gregory. See
entry 216.27.

424.41/417.27 TRAMP, TRAMP THE BOYS ARE . . . PARCHING   This alludes to a song by George F. Root entitled "Tramp! Tramp!
Tramp!" which was a marching song of the Union armies during
the American Civil War. The chorus begins, "Tramp, tramp,
tramp! the boys are marching." Words and music may be found
in Chapple, *Heart Songs*, p. 449. See also the following entry.

425.1/417.29 WHETHER ON THE SCAFFOLD HIGH . . . WHEN FOR IRELAN-

DEAR . . . WE FALL   This alludes to T. D. Sullivan's song "God Save Ireland," on which see entry 163.16. This song is sung to the same tune as "Tramp! Tramp! Tramp!" which was alluded to just previously.

425.9/417.37 THE UBERMENSCH   See entry 22.27.

425.11/417.40 STOPPED SHORT NEVER TO GO AGAIN WHEN THE OLD   This alludes to a song by American song writer Henry C. Work, entitled "My Grandfather's Clock" (or "Grandfather's Clock"), which appeared in 1876. The refrain says that the clock "stopped short—never to go again—/ When the old man died." Words may be found in Ralph L. Woods, *Treasury of the Familiar*, pp. 384–85.

425.15/418.2 GOT BET BE A BOOMBLEBEE WHENEVER HE WAS SETTIN SLEEPIN IN HES BIT GARTEN   Though this obviously refers to Bloom's being stung by a bee, "sleepin" suggests an allusion to the murder of King Hamlet while he was "sleeping within [the] orchard" (*Ham.*, I, v, 59).

425.19/418.6 PULL DOWN THE BLIND, LOVE   Hodgart and Worthington list this as an allusion to "O my Love, Won't You Please Pull Down the Curtain?," by McCarthy and Monaco. I have located a song by a Charles McCarthy, specifically entitled "Pull Down the Blind," which may be the same song Hodgart and Worthington have in mind, though I cannot confirm this. The chorus of the song I have found says, "Pull down the blind, Pull down the blind; Pull down the blind, love, come don't be unkind." For words and music, see Reddall, *Songs That Never Die*, pp. 380–81.

425.23/418.9 YOUR STARVING EYES AND ALLBEPLASTERED NECK YOU STOLE MY HEART   Though I have not located it, I suspect this alludes to a song that involves a line about "your starry eyes and alabaster neck," and says, "You stole my heart." Hodgart and Worthington take no note of this.

425.27/418.13 YOUR COPOROSITY SAGACIATING O K   This probably alludes to Joel Chandler Harris' Uncle Remus stories, in which the word *sagaciate* occasionally occurs. The best-known instance is in the well-known "Wonderful Tar-Baby Story," when Brer Rabbit asks the tar-baby, "How duz yo' sym'tums seem ter segashuate?" This is certainly the best known of Harris' stories, and is the one Joyce would have known if he had known no other. For another probable allusion to this same story, see entry 508.26.

425.29/418.15 THERE'S HAIR   Hodgart and Worthington list this as an allusion to the music hall song "There's Hair like Wire Coming out of the Empire." See entry 324.25.

425.29/418.15   THE WHITE DEATH AND THE RUDDY BIRTH   See entry
249.9.

425.31/418.17   MUMMER'S WIRE. CRIBBED OUT OF MEREDITH   This
refers to the wire or telegram that Stephen ("loveliest mummer of
them all," p. 5.27/7.23) sent to Buck Mulligan earlier in the day:
"The sentimentalist is he who would enjoy without incurring the
immense debtorship for a thing done." The message alludes to
Meredith's *The Ordeal of Richard Feveral*; see entry 199.21.

425.35/418.21   HERE, JOCK BRAW HIELENTMAN'S YOUR BARLEYBREE
Hodgart and Worthington list this as an allusion to Robert Burns's
song "Willie Brewed a Peck o' Maut," and this is probably correct,
though there is a much clearer allusion here to "A Highland Lad
My Love Was Born," from Burns's *The Jolly Beggars*. The chorus
to that song goes "Sing hey my braw John Highlandman! Sing ho
my braw John Highlandman!/ There's not a lad in a' the lan'/
Was match for my John Highlandman!" The chorus to "Willie
Brewed a Peck o' Maut" says, "We are na fou, we're no that fou,/
But just a drappie in our e'e;/ The cock may craw, the day may
daw,/ And ay we'll taste the barley bree" (*fou* means *drunk*, *bree*
means *brew*).

425.39/418.25   EVERY COVE TO HIS GENTRY MORT   See entry 47.13.

425.40/418.26   VENUS PANDEMOS   Venus (or Aphrodite) Pandemos
(meaning "of all the people") is Venus as the representation of
sensual or earthly love. Fourth-century B.C. Greek sculptor Scopas
did a statue of Venus Pandemos, riding on a goat. For more information, see *Encyclopaedia Britannica*, 11th ed., II, 167–68, and IX,
279.

425.42/418.28   ON THE ROAD TO MALAHIDE   Hodgart and Worthing
ton list this as an allusion to both "The Bridal of Malahide" by
Griffin and to "On the Road to Mandalay" by Kipling. On the
Griffin song, see entry 43.26. Kipling's poem "Mandalay" (or "On
the Road to Mandalay") has been set to music by several people;
Oley Speaks's setting, which is probably the most popular, was
done in 1907. Patrick Henchy has suggested that this may recall
the Percy French song "On the Road to Castlebar" (*Analyst*, X
[March, 1956], 16).

426.1/418.28   IF SHE WHO SEDUCED ME HAD LEFT BUT THE NAME   This
alludes to Thomas Moore's song "When He Who Adores Thee,"
which begins, "When he who adores thee, has left but the name/
Of his fault and his sorrows behind,/ Oh! say wilt thou weep,
when they darken the fame/ Of a life that for thee was resign'd?"

426.2/418.30   MACHREE, MACRUISKEEN   This alludes to "The Cruiskeen Lawn"; see entry 295.15.

426.3/418.31   AND A PULL TOGETHER   This apparently alludes to the
refrain of the "Eton Boating Song," by Johnson and Drummond
(also called "Boating Song," or "All Pull Together"). In some
versions the refrain says, "All pull together, With your backs between your knees." Sears's *Song Index* lists several collections which
include the song. Alfred MacLochlainn has said of this, "See the
'Eton boat song' and various bawdy parodies on it, e.g., 'We'll all
pull together with our —— between our knees' " (*Analyst*, X
[March, 1956], 16).

426.5/418.33   UNDERCONSTUMBLE   Mackie Jarrell suggests (*PMLA*,
LXXII, 550) that this is a portmanteau of two phrases in Swift's
Polite Conversation, first conversation. When Miss Notable says,
"I understumble you, Gentlemen," Neverout replies, "Madam, your
humblecumdumble." Partridge says of *understumble*, "a mid-
16th–20th century pun on *understand*. Compare the dialectal *under-
cumstand* and the mid 19th–20th century slang *undercumstumble*"
(p. 115).

426.11/418.39   WE ARE NAE FOU. WE'RE NAE THA FOU   This is another allusion to Burns's "Willie Brewed a Peck o' Maut"; see
entry 425.35.

426.14/418.42   MOWSING NOWT BUT CLARETWINE   This alludes to
the anonymous Irish song "The Rakes of Mallow," which begins,
"Beauing, belleing, dancing, drinking,/ Breaking windows, swearing, sinking,/ Ever raking, never thinking,/ Live the rakes of
Mallow." The second verse begins, "One time naught but claret
drinking." For words and music, see A. Moffat's *Minstrelsy of
Ireland*, 3rd ed., p. 21.

426.17/419.3   ROSE OF CASTILLE   See entry 134.19.

426.19/419.5   THE COLLEEN BAWN, MY COLLEEN BAWN   See entry
297.14.

426.21/419.7   THE RUFFIN CLY THE NAB OF STEPHEN   In his article
cited in entry 424.26, Daniel Weiss drew on Joyce's own notes to
Georg Goyert, the German translator of *Ulysses*, to explain that
this refers to Stephen Dedalus, who steamed open a telegram (cf.
entry 426.24) bearing a tip on the Gold Cup race, followed the tip
to bet on the race, and lost some money. Weiss's interpretation
brought a reply from Ellsworth Mason in the next number of the
Analyst which denied that Stephen had bet on the race, and said
he did not open a telegram, "since such an act is not in Stephen's
character" (*Analyst*, X [March, 1956], 17). The editors replied

that "Mr. Weiss's reading of this passage is explicitly supported in Joyce's unpublished note to his German translator." But examination of Joyce's notes to Goyert (now in the library of Southern Illinois University) and correction of a misprint in *Ulysses* bring a new perspective to light which vindicates Mason's faith in Stephen (as well as introducing another minor character into *Ulysses*). In his notes on this passage, Joyce consistently refers to "S. H.," which seems to be a mistake for "S. D." until Joyce himself clarifies it. Joyce says, "S. H. met a telegram boy who was bringing a private racing telegram from the stable of the celebrated English brewer Bass to the police depot in Dublin to a friend there to back B's horse *Sceptre* for the Cup. S. H. gives the boy 4 pence, opens the telegram over steam (grahamising), recloses it and sends the boy on with it, backs *Sceptre* to win and loses. (This really happened and his name was Stephen Hand though it was not the Gold Cup)." The Stephen who opens the telegram and does the betting, then, is not Stephen Dedalus, but Stephen Hand (who apparently does not appear elsewhere in *Ulysses*). This probably would have been clear to Weiss and the editors of the *Analyst* except for the fact that an inadvertent period has crept into the text of *Ulysses* at this point, so that all current editions read "The ruffin cly the nab of Stephen. Hand as give me the jady copaleen," instead of the correct reading, which omits the mid-sentence period and reads, " . . . Stephen Hand. . . ." (These notes from Joyce to Goyert have recently been printed, edited, and with annotations by Alan M. Cohn, see *JJQ*, IV [Spring, 1967], 194–201.) William Schutte has also pointed out that the phrase "the ruffin cly the nab of Stephen" alludes to a song printed in Richard Head's *The Canting Academy* (see entry 47.13). This song, entitled "The Beggars Curse," begins, "The Ruffin cly the nab of Harmanbeck," which Head translates, "The Devil take the Constables head" (p. 14). The allusion is continued in the phrase "Land him in chokeechokee if the harman beck copped the game" (p. 426.26/419.12).

426.24/419.10 GRAHAMISE   During his term as Home Secretary, Sir John Graham (1792–1861) opened correspondence while it was passing through the post, and this word has come to refer to any such action. See the *OED*, s.v. grahamize, and the *DNB*, VIII, 331, s.v. Graham.

426.28/419.14 O, LUST, OUR REFUGE AND OUR STRENGTH   As Joyce explained in the notes to Goyert (cf. entry 426.21), this parodies the prayer after low Mass, to be said in the language of the country, which was written by Pope Leo XIII. Since the prayer is alluded to several times in the following lines, I quote the whole of it here: "O God, our refuge and our strength, look down in mercy on thy people who cry to thee; and by the intercession of the glorious and immaculate virgin Mary, Mother of God, of Saint Joseph her spouse, of thy blessed apostles Peter and Paul, and of all the saints, in mercy and goodness hear our prayers for the conversion of sinners, and for the liberty and exaltation of our holy mother the Church: through the same Christ our Lord. Amen." Cf. p. 82.37/ 81.29, where the priest begins this prayer.

426.33/419.18 OF JOHN THOMAS, HER SPOUSE   This continues the parody of the prayer quoted in entry 426.28. "John Thomas" is common British slang for the phallus.

426.36/419.22 THROUGH YERD OUR LORD, AMEN   This continues the parody of the prayer quoted in entry 426.28. "Yerd" has the same meaning as "John Thomas" in the preceding entry.

426.42/419.27 LANDLORD, LANDLORD, HAVE YOU GOOD WINE   Hodgart and Worthington list this as an allusion to "Staboo, Stabella," which they describe as "a 'bawdy catch' with many variants," and they say that this is the same song as was alluded to on p. 392.5/385.33. See entry 392.5.

427.1/419.28 HOOTS, MON, WEE DRAP TO PREE   This alludes to Burns's "Willie Brewed a Peck o' Maut," which begins, "Willie brewed a peck o' maut,/ and Rob and Allen came to see." Though "see" is the correct reading, there is an unauthorized reading "pree" which Joyce knew. In his notes to Georg Goyert (cf. entry 426.21), Joyce quotes the opening lines of the poem and explains *pree* as "Scotch for: examine and taste whisky." See entry 425.35.

427.2/419.29 RIGHT BONIFACE   This parody on the military command "Right face" involves a play on the name of one of the popes or saints named Boniface, but which specific one, if any, is intended, is impossible to say.

427.2/419.29 NOS OMNES BIBERIMUS VIRIDUM TOXICUM DIABOLUS CAPIAT POSTERIORIA NOSTRIA   As Daniel Weiss says (*op. cit.*, entry 424.26), this may be translated, "We'll drink the green poison and the devil take the hindmost." The green poison is absinthe, but if there is an allusion here, I am unaware of it.

427.6/419.33 BONSOIR LA COMPAGNIE   Hodgart and Worthington list this as an allusion to the song "Bonsoir la Compagnie," by Maud. I have not been able to locate a copy of the song.

427.6/419.33 SNARES OF THE POXFIEND   This parodies another prayer that is commonly said after low Mass, not the same prayer as that quoted in entry 426.28. The text of this prayer is given in *Ulysses*,

p. 83.22/82.13, and the phrase specifically parodied here is "be our safeguard against the wickedness and snares of the devil."

427.7/419.34 NAMBY AMBY   This may allude to Namby Pamby, which was a nickname given to eighteenth-century poet Ambrose Phillips by Harry Carey and Alexander Pope.

427.14/419.41 THRUST SYPHILIS DOWN TO HELL AND WITH HIM THOSE OTHER LICENSED SPIRITS . . .   This continues the parody of the prayer after low Mass which was referred to in entry 427.6, and the text of which can be found on p. 83.22/82.13. This parodies the statement "thrust Satan down to hell and with him those other wicked spirits who wander through the world for the ruin of souls."

427.15/420.1 WHO WANDER THROUGH THE WORLD   Hodgart and Worthington list this as an allusion to the Irish song "Garryowen" (see entry 295.13), but none of the versions I have seen has such a line. This is clearly a continuation of the allusion in entry 427.14.

427.17/420.3 DUSTY RHODES   A note in the *Analyst* of March, 1956, says of Dusty Rhodes, "Mr. B. W. Huebsch, of the Viking Press, writes that he has an impression (which other persons have since confirmed) that 'Dusty Rhodes' was an American cartoon character belonging to the period around 1900. He seems to have been an indomitable tramp, like Happy Hooligan or Panhandle Pete, but he has not been further identified" (X, 18).

427.19/420.4 JUBILEE MUTTON   Daniel Weiss quotes T. W. Pugh as explaining, " 'During Queen Victoria's Jubilee in 1897 mutton was distributed among some of the poor of Dublin in order I suppose to make them more kindly to English rule. When she visited Dublin later the crowds used to chant, "Here she is! What has she got? Jubilee mutton [i.e. not much]" ' " (*Analyst*, IX, 13; the words in brackets in the quote were in the original and apparently supplied by Weiss).

427.19/420.5 D'YE KEN BARE SOCKS   As Hodgart and Worthington suggest, this probably alludes to the song "John Peel," which begins "D' ye ken John Peel with his coat so gay?" See entry 289.38.

427.23/420.8 MAN ALL TATTERED AND TORN THAT MARRIED A MAIDEN ALL FORLORN   This alludes to the nursery rhyme "The House That Jack Built"; see entry 391.36.

427.33/420.18 LAY YOU TWO TO ONE JENATZY LICKS HIM   Jenatzy was one of the drivers in the Gordon Bennett auto race (see entry 97.14). The *Freeman's Journal* of June 16, 1904, says, "Mr. Jenatzy, the German who won the race in Ireland, is said to have been over the course in his Mercedes car over fifty times. He is, perhaps, the favorite" (p. 5, col. g). Jenatzy, who was actually a Belgian driv-

ing for Germany, had won the race in 1903 when it was held in
Ireland, but in 1904 he finished second, the race being won by
Thery of France.

427.34/420.19   JAPPIES . . . ROOSHIAN   This is a rather general allusion
to the Russo-Japanese War (on which see entry 58.11), which was
being reported by "War Specials" in the newspapers.

427.37/420.22   MAY ALLAH, THE EXCELLENT ONE, YOUR SOUL THIS NIGHT
EVER TREMENDOUSLY CONSERVE   This appears to be a Moslem
prayer, but I have not located this specific formula in any of the
works on Moslem scripture or prayer which I have seen.

427.39/420.24   WE'RE NAE THA FOU   This is another allusion to
Burns's "Willie Brewed a Peck o' Maut"; see entry 425.35.

427.39/420.24   THE LEITH POLICE DISMISSETH US   Joyce explains in
his notes to Goyert (see entry 426.21) that this is "a phrase which
the police sergeant asks drunkards to repeat in order to test their
state of sobriety." As Robert Janusko has pointed out to me, a
tongue twisting rhyme that begins, "The Leith police dismisseth
us" can be found in *The Annotated Mother Goose*, ed. William
S. Baring-Gould and Ceil Baring-Gould (New York, 1962), p.
284.

427.41/420.26   MONA, MY THRUE LOVE . . . MONA, MY OWN LOVE
This alludes to the song "Mona, My Own Love"; see entry 309.34.

428.6/420.32   WE TWO, SHE SAID, WILL SEEK THE KIPS WHERE SHADY
MARY IS   Robert Janusko has called my attention to the allusion
here to Dante Gabriel Rosetti's poem "The Blessed Damosel,"
where the following lines occur: " 'We two,' she said, 'will seek
the groves/Where the lady Mary is . . .' " (ll. 103–4).

428.7/420.33   LAETABUNTUR IN CUBILIBUS SUIS   "Let them sing
aloud upon their beds." This alludes to Psalms 149:5: "Let the
saints be joyful in glory: let them sing aloud upon their beds"
(Vulgate: *"Exsultabunt sancti in gloria, Laetabuntur in cubilibus
suis"*).

428.10/420.35   EVEN NOW THAT DAY IS AT HAND WHEN HE SHALL COME
TO JUDGE THE WORLD BY FIRE   The Day of Judgment is traditionally described in terms of fire and burning. See II Thessalon-
ians 1:7–8 and the whole of the book of Revelation, but especially
chapters 8 and 9. The well-known hymn "Dies Irae" also describes
the Day of Judgment as a day of burning.

428.11/420.37   UT IMPLERENTUR SCRIPTURAE   "That the scriptures
might be fulfilled." This is probably an intentional variation on
Matthew 26:54: *"Quomodo ergo implebuntur Scripturae, quia sic*

oportet fieri?" ("But how then shall the scriptures be fulfilled, that thus it must be?").

428.12/420.38 THEN OUTSPAKE MEDICAL DICK TO HIS COMRADE MEDICAL
DAVY   This alludes to Gogarty's song "Medical Dick and Medical Davy"; see entry 209.18.

428.14/420.40 ELIJAH IS COMING   See entry 151.15.

428.14/420.40 WASHED IN THE BLOOD OF THE LAMB   See entry 151.11.

428.19/421.2 ALEXANDER J. CHRIST DOWIE   See entry 151.15.

In the Introduction the problem posed by parallels between *Ulysses* and other works which remain situational and do not emerge in specific words and phrases was briefly discussed. That problem is present throughout *Ulysses*, but it is particularly clear in this episode. Two works deserve special mention as sources and parallels to this chapter, Goethe's *Faust*, epecially the "Walpurgis Night" section, and Flaubert's *The Temptation of St. Anthony*. There are definite allusions to both of these works in this episode, but the technical and situational similarities between the works and "Circe" go far beyond that which the meager number of allusions suggests.

429.3/422.3 WILL-O'-THE-WISPS   This recalls the Will-o'-the-Wisp that leads Faust and Mephistopheles at the opening of the "Walpurgis Night" section of Goethe's *Faust*.

430.17/423.16 I GAVE IT TO MOLLY . . .   (continued on pp. 430.29/ 423.28 and 431.7/424.7). I have not located any original for the bawdy verse Cissy sings.

431.15/424.15 VIDI AQUAM EGREDIENTEM DE TEMPLO A LATERE DEXTRO.
ALLELUIA   As Willis E. McNelly has pointed out (*JJQ*, II,
293), what Stephen chants is not the Introit for Paschaltide, but
the Antiphon that is used with the Asperges during Paschaltide
(i.e., from Easter Sunday to Whit Sunday). Stephen goes on to
chant more of this same Antiphon on pp. 431.22/424.22 and 432.10/
425.10. The entire passage he chants may be translated, "I saw a
stream of water welling forth from the right of the temple, Alleluia: bringing salvation to all those who stood in its course." Cf.
Ezekiel 47:1.

432.18/425.17   GESTURE, NOT MUSIC, NOT ODOURS, WOULD BE A UNIVERSAL
LANGUAGE   The idea that gesture constitutes a universal language is very common and quite ancient; most books on mime or
pantomime begin with a discussion of the idea. Stephen's statement seems too general to suggest any specific source.

432.19/425.18   THE GIFT OF TONGUES   This recalls the several references to "speaking with tongues" which occur in the New Testament. Speaking with tongues was a sign of the Holy Spirit. In Acts
2:4 we read, "And they were all filled with the Holy Ghost, and
began to speak with other tongues, as the Spirit gave them utterance." Another similar instance occurs in Acts 19:6, and Paul talks
in some detail about speaking in tongues in I Corinthians 14.

432.20/425.19   THE FIRST ENTELECHY   Stephen has earlier referred
to "entelechy, form of forms" on p. 189.39/187.34. I am not sure
whether he means anything more specific by "first entelechy,"
unless perhaps it is the "entelechy of entelechies," i.e., the under-
lying one which makes the rest possible. See entry 189.39.

432.25/425.24   SHREWRIDDEN SHAKESPEARE AND HENPECKED SOCRATES
The idea that Anne Hathaway dominated Shakespeare runs
throughout Stephen's theory of Shakespeare in "Scylla and Charybdis." On henpecked Socrates, see entries 190.27 and 202.26.

432.26/425.25   EVEN THE ALLWISEST STAGYRITE WAS BITTED, BRIDLED
AND MOUNTED BY A LIGHT OF LOVE   The "allwisest Stagyrite" is
Aristotle; see entries 204.5 and 37.8. This statement about him
probably refers to Aristotle's mistress, Herpyllis, rather than his
wife, Pythias. Stephen is probably presuming a great deal from the
generous provisions for Herpyllis in Aristotle's will. See entry
204.6. On the phrase "light of love," see entry 191.4.

433.3/426.1   THE LOAF AND JUG OF BREAD AND WINE IN OMAR   Though
containing a veiled allusion to the Eucharist, this refers to the well-
known stanza of Edward Fitzgerald's translation of "The Rubaiyat

of Omar Khayyam": "A Book of Verses underneath the Bough,/ A Jug of Wine, a Loaf of Bread—and Thou/Beside me singing in the Wilderness—/ Oh, Wilderness were Paradise enow!"

433.8/426.6 LA BELLE DAME SANS MERCI   This is probably an allusion to John Keats's poem "La Belle Dame sans Merci," though Keats did not himself originate the phrase, and the idea of such a woman is common in myth and folklore.

433.9/426.7 AD DEAM QUI LAETIFICAT JUVENTUTEM MEAM   At the beginning of the Mass, the priest says, "Introibo ad altare Dei" ("I will go up to God's altar"), and the server replies, "Ad Deum qui laetificat juventutem meam" ("To God who gives joy to my youth"). Stephen's pointed change of gender from *Deum* to *deam* makes his statement read "to the goddess who gives joy to my youth." This text comes from Psalms 43:4. Cf. entry 3.5.

433.16/426.14 TAKE YOUR CRUTCH AND WALK   In John 5:8 Christ says to a lame man, "Rise, take up thy bed, and walk" (the phrase is repeated in John 5:11 and 5:12; Matt. 9:6, Mark 2:9, and Luke 5:24 are similar).

433.32/426.30 NELSON'S IMAGE . . . GLADSTONE . . . WELLINGTON   Each of these men is alluded to elsewhere in *Ulysses*. On Nelson, see entry 148.9; on Gladstone, see entry 80.7; on Wellington, see entry 332.23. For a full list of cross references, consult the Index.

434.4/426.35 JOLLYPOLDY THE RIXDIX DOLDY   In *The Lore and Language of Schoolchildren* the Opies quote four similar rhymes on various names. For example, they give "Joan the roan/ The rix stix stoan,/ The iron-nosed,/ The copper-nosed,/ The bandy-legged Joan" (p. 158) and "George, Porge, the rix-tix Torge, The rhibo, the rhambo, The cocktail'd George" (p. 159). Apparently these nonsense verses vary with the name and personality of the person. Other similar rhymes are given for Maggy and Jenny, but none for Leopold or Poldy. In *Stephen Hero*, Stephen remembers such verses on his name and the name of his dead sister, Isabel: "Stephen, the Reephen, the Rix-Dix Deephen" and "Isabel, the Risabel, the Rix-Dix Disabel" (p. 170).

434.29/427.23 LONDON'S BURNING, LONDON'S BURNING   This is an adaptation of the round "Scotland's Burning." Since it is brief, I quote the entire round: "Scotland's burning! Scotland's burning! Look out! Look out! Fire! fire! fire! fire! Pour on water! Pour on water!" (from *The David Bispham Song Book* [Philadelphia, 1920], p. 242).

435.20/428.18 ARE YOU DOING THE HATTRICK   W. Y. Tindall explains this as "a dirty Irish trick: an Irishman covers a turd on a curb with his hat. Telling a policeman it is a bird, the Irishman goes off for help, asking the policeman to stand guard" (*RG*, p. 209).

435.25/428.23 SANDOW'S EXERCISES   On Sandow and his exercises, see entry 61.25.

435.26/428.24 THE PROVIDENTIAL   The context here, and the name itself, suggests that Bloom is thinking of an insurance firm, but Thom's *Dublin Directory* (1904), in its list of "Insurance Companies and Agents," lists none by this exact title, though it lists several with *Provident* in the title, as, for example, the Irish Provident Assurance Co.

435.29/428.27 THIRD TIME IS THE CHARM   This notion is proverbial. The *ODEP* lists several similar sayings, such as "The third time's lucky" and "The third is a charm." P. W. Joyce, in his *English As We Speak It*, has the following: "First and second go alike:/ The third throw takes the bite," said, according to Joyce, by "a person who is about to make a third and determined attempt at anything" (p. 119).

436.4/428.31 TRUE WORD SPOKEN IN JEST   On this proverbial saying, see entry 338.15.

436.6/429.2 MARK OF THE BEAST   The "mark of the beast" is mentioned several times in the book of Revelation, most fully in chapter thirteen, where the beast is described, and we are told, "And he [the beast] causeth all, both small and great, rich and poor, free and bond, to receive a mark in their right hand, or in their foreheads. And that no man might buy or sell, save he that had the mark, or the name of the beast, or the number of his name" (Rev. 13:16–17). See also Revelation 16:2, 19:20, and 20:4.

436.19/429.13 GAELIC LEAGUE   See entry 193.4.

436.29/429.24 IN DARKEST STEPASIDE   Bloom's letter may have had its title suggested by Sir Henry Morton Stanley's *In Darkest Africa* (1890), or, more appropriately, by General William Booth's work of social protest, *In Darkest England, And the Way Out*, which appeared later in 1890 and took its title from Stanley's book. Stepaside is a town in the southern part of county Dublin.

436.29/429.24 KEEP, KEEP, KEEP TO THE RIGHT   Though it is doubtful, there may be an echo here of the anonymous Irish song "Shule Aroon." See entry 688.3.

436.31/429.26 WASH OFF HIS SINS OF THE WORLD   Bloom is probably thinking here of the "Lamb of God, which taketh away the sins of the world," which is the description of Christ given by John the Baptist in John 1:29, and which is common in Catholic prayers and liturgy (the Latin is "Agnus Dei, qui tollis peccata mundi"). Note that when Bloom's mother appears on p. 438.29/431.26, she has an Agnus Dei. See entries 560.14 and 560.16.

437.7/430.3 SWEETS OF SIN   On *Sweets of Sin*, see entry 236.5.

437.26/430.22 ARE YOU NOT MY DEAR SON LEOPOLD WHO LEFT THE HOUSE OF HIS FATHER . . .   As the reference to Mosenthal (p. 437.30/430.26) shows, Bloom is remembering a passage he earlier thought of from Mosenthal's *Deborah*. See entries 76.29 and 76.30.

438.23/431.20 WIDOW TWANKEY'S BLOUSE   As R. M. Adams explains (*SS*, p. 204), "Widow Twankey is by tradition Aladdin's mother in the pantomime." Pantomimes on some fairy tale or folk tale subject were staged at the theaters in Dublin every Christmas, and Aladdin was one of the favorite subjects.

439.9/432.4 OPULENT CURVES   This is from *Sweets of Sin*; see entry 236.5.

440.2/432.27 NEBRAKADA! FEMINIMUM   This is part of a phrase that earlier was said to be one of the charms of the blessed abbot Peter Salanka, but I have located no such. Cf. entry 242.35.

440.23/433.16 WE'RE A CAPITAL COUPLE ARE BLOOM AND I;/HE BRIGHTENS THE EARTH, I POLISH THE SKY   I have been told that this alludes to a contemporary advertisement slogan, perhaps for Sunshine Soap. But I have not yet located a copy of the advertisement in any of the newspapers or magazines of the day.

441.8/434.2 TI TREMA UN POCO IL CUORE   This question, "Does your heart tremble a little?" adapts a line from the duet in *Don Giovanni* which was first alluded to on p. 63.31/63.24. In that duet Zerlina says to Don Giovanni, "Mi trema un poco il cor" ("My heart trembles a little"). See entry 63.31.

441.12/434.6 ARE YOU SURE ABOUT THAT VOGLIO   This also alludes to the *Don Giovanni* duet alluded to a few lines earlier. See entries 77.15 and 63.31.

442.4/434.24 SIXTYSEVEN   Norman Silverstein analyzes the Bawd's statement in detail and explains it, and the specific use of "sixty-seven," as deriving from Giordano Bruno's *Ars memoriae;* see "Bruno's Particles of Reminiscence," *JJQ*, II (Summer, 1965), 271–80.

442.9/434.28 WITH ALL MY WORLDLY GOODS I THEE AND THOU   Here, as on p. 352.4/345.38, Gerty thinks vaguely of the words of the marriage service. Though the Irish Catholic service at this point has since been modified, in Gerty's day the groom said, "With this ring I thee wed: this gold and silver I thee give: and with all my worldly goods I thee endow."

443.6/435.25 WALLS HAVE HEARS   See entry 83.6.

443.18/436.6 OTHELLO BLACK BRUTE. EUGENE STRATTON. . . . LIVERMORE
CHRISTIES. BOHEE BROTHERS   Bloom's thought of Negro servants
leads him to think of Othello, the Moor, and then to think of
blackface entertainers. On Stratton, see entry 92.5. The "Livermore Brothers' World Renowned Court Minstrels" was a minstrel
group of the day. In a *Freeman's Journal* advertisement of February
3, 1894 (p. 4, col. a), which announces their performance at the
Rotunda, the Livermore Brothers are called "The Acme of Refined
Minstrelsy," and are said to have fifty star artistes. The Bohee
Brothers were also well-known minstrels. Edward B. Marks says,
"There were the Bohee Brothers, featured in colored minstrel
shows. They were, so far as I know, the first team to play banjos
while dancing. . . . At any rate they were great song and dance
men, and eventually went to London, where they were a sensa-
tion" (*They All Sang: From Tony Pastor to Rudy Vallee* [New
York, 1934], p. 92). As R. M. Adams points out (*SS*, p. 74), "The
Bohee Brothers' Operatic Minstrels," including thirty principal
artistes, performed at Leinster Hall, Dublin, in August of 1894.
Their performance was reviewed in the *Irish Independent* of Tuesday, Aug. 28, 1894 (p. 5, col. g).

443.29/436.17 THERE'S SOMEONE IN THE HOUSE WITH DINA . . .   This
is from the popular American song "I've Been Working on the
Railroad." The origin of the song is obscure, but it was popular
across the U.S. by 1881. The usual form of the portion of the song
alluded to in *Ulysses* is "Someone's in the kitchen with Dinah,/
Someone's in the kitchen I know;/ Someone's in the kitchen with
Dinah,/ Strummin' on the old banjo." For words and music, see
Theodore Raph, *The Songs We Sang* (New York, 1964), pp.
195–200.

444.14/437.2 THE DEAR GAZELLE   This alludes to a passage from
Thomas Moore's poem *Lalla Rookh*. The passage is alluded to more
fully later; see entry 477.2.

444.24/437.12 THE IRVING BISHOP GAME . . .   Since the game involves
mind reading or mental telepathy, this probably refers to Washington Irving Bishop, a reputed mind reader, who, in January,
1885, in London, was sentenced to pay £10,000 damages to a Mr.
Maskelyne for having libeled him in *Truth* in July, 1883. Bishop
died May 13, 1889, in New York, at the age of forty-two, of unknown causes. See Charles E. Little, *Cyclopedia of Classified
Dates* [New York, 1900], *s.v.* Bishop, in the Index.

445.5/437.22 IRELAND, HOME AND BEAUTY   This variation on "For

England, Home, and Beauty" alludes to the song "The Death of Nelson." See entry 225.19.

445.7/437.24   THE DEAR DEAD DAYS BEYOND RECALL. LOVE'S OLD SWEET SONG   On "Love's Old Sweet Song" see entry 63.31.

445.13/437.30   LONDON'S TEAPOT   Apparently the parlor game being played involves substituting one word for another. The word *teapot* seems to be substituted for the word *burning*. See entry 434.29, on "London's burning." I do not understand Tindall's statement " 'Teapot' is a parlor guessing game. 'Lemon' is the answer" (*RG*, p. 209). It seems more likely to me that Mrs. Breen's statement "The answer is a lemon" (p. 446.21/439.3) refers to the earlier question "What is in this snuffbox?" (p. 444.25/437.13).

445.16/438.2   TWO IS COMPANY   "Two is company, but three is none" (or "Two is company, but three is a crowd") is proverbial and is listed in the *ODEP*.

445.21/438.6   THE WITCHING HOUR OF NIGHT   This alludes to a passage in *Hamlet* which Bloom has already thought of earlier in the day. See entry 108.5.

445.23/438.8   LA CI DAREM LA MANO   This is from the duet in *Don Giovanni*. The allusion is continued in the "*Voglio e non*" of p. 445.29/438.13. See entries 63.31 and 64.4.

446.2/438.16   BEAUTY AND THE BEAST   Bloom thought of this fairy story earlier; see entry 369.35.

446.14/438.28   HIGH JINKS BELOW STAIRS   "High Jinks" is a parlor game in which someone is chosen by lot to perform a ridiculous task. This phrase probably echoes the title of James Townley's (1714–78) farce *High Life Below Stairs* (1759).

446.25/439.6   LEAH. MRS BANDMAN PALMER . . .   See both of the entries for p. 76.23/75.19.

447.9/439.21   HEE HEE HEE   Though this is clearly an echo of Pat's laugh in the "Sirens" episode, it probably owes something, as Mackie Jarrell has suggested (*PMLA*, LXXII, 548), to the recurrent "he he he" in Swift's *Polite Conversation*, usually following some foolish remark. See, for example, pp. 59, 60 (Partridge's edition).

447.18/440.1   I AM NOT ON PLEASURE BENT. I AM IN A GRAVE PREDICAMENT   Though this sounds like an allusion, perhaps to a contemporary musical or operetta, I have not located its source.

447.21/440.4   COCK AND BULL STORY   This expression is proverbial and is listed in the *ODEP*, which explains it as "a rambling, idle story," though to me the expression means a fanciful and exaggerated story.

450.13/442.22 SIZE AND LIME OF THEIR LODGES   The word *lodge* here indicates an allusion to Freemasonry, but the allusion seems to be quite general. I have not found the specific terms *size* or *lime* listed as technical terms in any dictionary of Freemasonry I have consulted.

451.17/443.26 WE ARE THE BOYS. OF WEXFORD   (the allusion is continued on p. 451.24/444.5)   This alludes to "The Boys of Wexford"; see entry 129.13.

452.5/444.10 WILDGOOSE CHASE   "To run the wild goose chase" is proverbial and is listed in the *ODEP*, where it is explained as meaning "a foolish, fruitless, or hopeless quest." For a special Irish meaning of "wild goose," see entry 41.17.

452.14/444.19 SOON GOT, SOON GONE   The *ODEP* and Apperson list "Soon gotten, soon spent."

452.16/444.21 JUGGERNAUT   Juggernaut, or Jagannatha ("Lord of the World"), is a Hindu deity. It is the name under which the god Vishnu is worshipped at Puri. The god is best known for the famous Car Festival, at which the image of the god is drawn for a distance on a high platform or car. For many years stories came out of India about devotees sacrificing themselves by throwing themselves under the wheels of the car, but such stories have been largely discredited.

452.30/444.35 SWEET ARE THE SWEETS   Here, as on p. 260.4/256.3, Bloom is probably alluding to Queen Gertrude's remark about Ophelia. See entry 260.4.

452.30/444.35 SWEETS OF SIN   See entry 236.5.

453.3/445.7 CHACUN SON GOÛT   This is one of the most familiar forms of the proverbial "Everyone to his own taste." Cf. entry 380.34.

453.5/445.9 GARRYOWEN   This recalls earlier allusions to the anonymous Irish ballad "Garryowen." See entry 295.13.

454.16/446.17 SIGNOR MAFFEI   Signor Maffei and Ruby (p. 454.31/446.31) are characters from *Ruby: the Pride of the Ring*. See entry 64.25.

455.26/447.25 YOU KNOW THAT OLD JOKE, ROSE OF CASTILLE   See entry 134.19.

456.2/447.31 YOU DO GET YOUR WATERLOO   Waterloo, Belgium, was the scene of Napoleon's final defeat by Wellington and Blucher, June 18, 1815. It has come to represent any final, decisive defeat.

456.13/448.10 LIONEL, THOU LOST ONE   This alludes to Flotow's *Martha*. See entries 117.34 and 256.26, and consult the Index for a full list of cross references.

456.18/448.14 PLUCKING AT HIS HEART AND LIFTING HIS RIGHT FOREARM
. . .   Bloom is giving a Masonic sign. Fellow-Craft is the Second
Degree of Freemasonry. For further detail, see any dictionary of
Freemasonry, *s.v.* Fellow-Craft.

456.20/448.16 LIGHT OF LOVE   Stephen used this phrase earlier in
this episode, on p. 432.27/425.26. See entry 191.4.

456.21/448.17 THE LYONS MAIL. LESURQUES AND DUBOSC   This alludes to one of the most famous cases of mistaken identity. Joseph
Lesurques (1763–96) was identified by several women as the man
who held up the Lyons mail and killed the courier on April 27,
1796. Lesurques was executed for the crime on October 30, 1796.
Several years later it was learned that the criminal was really one
Duboscq, who bore an amazing resemblance to Lesurques. This
incident was the subject of plays by several authors.

456.22/448.18 THE CHILDS FRATRICIDE CASE   See entry 100.2.

456.24/448.19 BETTER ONE GUILTY ESCAPE THAN NINETY-NINE WRONG-
FULLY CONDEMNED   Bloom confusedly remembers Mr. Cunningham's earlier observation about the Childs case. See entry
100.8.

457.3/448.27 THE PAST OF EPHRAIM. SHITBROLEETH   In the conflict
between the Ephraimites and the Gideonites recounted in Judges
12, the Gideonites, who were led by Jephthah, asked all those
who attempted to cross the fords of the Jordan and who were
suspected of being Ephraimites to say "Shibboleth." The Ephraimites could not say it, but said "Sibboleth" instead. All who could
not pronounce "Shibboleth" were slain.

457.8/449.2 A PURE MARE'S NEST   "To find a mare's nest" is listed
in the *ODEP* and explained as "an illusory discovery." The phrase
occurs in Swift's *Polite Conversation*, first conversation, when
Neverout says, " . . . you have found a Mare's Nest and laugh at
the Eggs" (p. 83).

457.15/449.9 THE HEROIC DEFENSE OF RORKE'S DRIFT   Rorke's Drift
was the scene of a heroic defense by the British garrison against an
attacking Zulu army in January of 1879, during the Zulu War. The
British numbered about eighty men (plus thirty or forty in hospital) and successfully repulsed a Zulu force of about 4,000, of whom
350 were killed.

457.19/449.13 THE SALT OF THE EARTH   In the Sermon on the Mount,
Christ said, "Ye are the salt of the earth: but if the salt have lost
his savour, wherewith shall it be salted? It is thenceforth good for
nothing, but to be cast out, and to be trodden under foot of men"

(Matt. 5:13; similar passages occur in Mark 9:49–50 and Luke 14: 34–35).

457.26/449.20 UP THE BOERS   See entry 163.10.

457.26/449.20 WHO BOOED JOE CHAMBERLAIN   See entry 162.40.

457.30/449.24 THE ABSENTMINDED WAR   This alludes to Kipling's poem "The Absent-Minded Beggar," and refers to the Boer War. See entry 187.22.

457.31/449.25 GENERAL GOUGH IN THE PARK   This refers to Hugh Gough, first Viscount Gough (1779–1869), whose statue stood in Phoenix Park, Dublin. The statue was unveiled on February 21, 1880, and the inscription on the pedestal said, "In Honour of/ Field-Marshall Viscount Gough, K.P.,/ G.C.B., K.G.,/ An Illustrious Irishman,/ whose achievements in the Peninsular War,/ in China and India,/ have added to the lustre of the/ Military Glory of the Country, which he faithfully/ served for 75 years. . . ." The statue is no longer there.

458.1/449.25 SPION KOP AND BLOEMFONTEIN   Spion Kop, a mountain in Natal, was the scene of a battle in the Boer War, January 24, 1900, in which the British were defeated by the Boers, with a loss to the British of seventeen hundred men. Bloemfontein, capital of the Orange Free State, was captured by British forces under Lord Frederick Roberts on March 13, 1900.

458.2/449.27 JIM BLUDSO. HOLD HER NOZZLE AGAIN THE BANK   This alludes to a ballad by American author and statesman John Hay (1838–1905), entitled "Jim Bludso." The ballad tells of a Mississippi riverboat engineer named Jim Bludso who died while holding his boat against the bank to permit passengers to escape from the burning boat. The poem is one of Hay's "Pike County Ballads" and can be found in any collection of his work.

458.21/450.13 MR PHILIP BEAUFOY   Earlier in the day Bloom read a story by Mr. Philip Beaufoy, from which he quotes on p. 459.6/ 450.31. See entry 68.39.

459.15/451.6 JACKDAW OF RHEIMS   "The Jackdaw of Rheims" is a brief verse story in *The Ingoldsby Legends* which tells of the theft of the ring of the cardinal archbishop of Rheims by a jackdaw. The bird finally reveals his theft and is canonized on his death by the name of Jem Crow. *The Ingoldsby Legends* were by Richard Harris Barham (1788–1845), who used the pseudonym Thomas Ingoldsby.

459.23/451.14 THE HALLMARK OF THE BEAST   Bloom thought of the mark of the beast earlier in this episode. See entry 436.6.

459.25/451.16 MOSES, MOSES, KING OF THE JEWS . . . Hodgart and Worthington list this as an allusion to a song entitled "Moses, Moses, King of the Jews," but they have a question mark by it, indicating that they have not identified it. I have not located this, or anything it might parody, in print.

460.1/451.23 STREET ANGEL AND HOUSE DEVIL   This proverbial phrase refers to one who presents one face to the world and another to his family. *Racial Proverbs*, ed. Selwyn Gurney Champion, lists "House devil; street angel" as a German proverb (p. 169).

461.28/453.20 THE MEMORY OF THE PAST   This alludes to the song "There Is a Flower That Bloometh" in W. V. Wallace's *Maritana*. On the song, see entry 358.18; on the opera, see entry 86.32.

462.12/453.33 SCENES TRULY RURAL   This perhaps owes something to a description of the Dublin pantomime *Little Red Riding Hood* which appeared in the *Freeman's Journal* of December 27, 1893, and which Joyce apparently used in writing a passage later in *Ulysses*. In the *Freeman's Journal* review, one of the scenes (stage settings) singled out for particular praise is "the opening 'Village of Truly Rural' by Mr. George A. Jackson, the Gaiety artist" (Speilberg, Buffalo Catalogue, item IX.A.4., p. 12). See entry 678.32.

462.36/454.21 TITBITS   On *Titbits*, the magazine in which Bloom read Beaufoy's story, see entry 67.39.

463.9/454.30 AN INFANT . . . WHO STARTED SCRATCH AS A STOWAWAY The context suggests an allusion here to Moses' having been hidden by his mother in an ark of bulrushes, which is described in Exodus 2.

463.14/455.1 THE LAND OF THE PHARAOH   Though this is clearly a biblical allusion, this precise phrase does not occur in the Bible; the set phrase is "the land of Egypt," which occurs more than fifty times.

463.20/455.7 HE COULD A TALE UNFOLD   This alludes to the Ghost's words to Hamlet; see entry 162.36.

463.33/455.19 LI LI POO LIL CHILE . . .   Hodgart and Worthington list this as an allusion to "Pov' Lil Lolo," or "Pov' Piti Lolotte," a Creole song which is alluded to only this once in *Ulysses*, but the dialect here is clearly Chinese, not Creole, and the allusion seems unlikely.

464.4/455.26 MOSAIC CODE   This recalls O'Molloy's statements about Seymour Bushe's defense in the Childs case. See entry 139.31, and cf. entry 464.15.

464.11/455.33 THE HIDDEN HAND   See entry 163.38.

464.15/455.37 TO CAST A STONE AT A GIRL WHO TOOK THE WRONG TURNING   A few lines earlier, O'Molloy spoke of the Mosaic code replacing the law of the jungle. This recalls the story of the woman taken in adultery, about whom Christ said, "Now Moses in the law commanded us, that such should be stoned: but what sayest thou? . . . He that is without sin among you, let him first cast a stone at her" (John 8:5–7).

464.25/456.10 THE LAKE OF KINNERETH   See entry 59.16.

465.5/456.27 SEYMOUR BUSHE   See entry 100.4.

465.17/457.5 SIR ROBERT AND LADY BALL   Sir Robert Ball, Irish astronomer, was alluded to earlier. See entry 154.5.

465.19/457.7 MRS YELVERTON BARRY   This name reverses that of a prominent eighteenth-century Irishman, Barry Yelverton, first Viscount Avonmore (1736–1805). Born in county Cork and educated at Trinity College, Dublin, he became chief baron of the exchequer in 1783. He was an eloquent speaker, and he helped to found the Dublin Historical Association. See the *DNB* article on him.

465.25/457.13 JAMES LOVEBIRCH   Lovebirch was mentioned earlier as the author of *Fair Tyrants*; see entry 235.37.

465.27/457.15 LA CIGALE   *La Cigale et la Fourmi* ("The Grasshopper and the Ant") is an opera by Henri Chivot, Alfred Duru, and Edmond Audran, based on La Fontaine's well-known fable. It was first done in Paris in 1886, and first done in London, in an English adaptation, in 1890. The Theatre Royal is presumably the one in Dublin, which was on Hawkins Street.

465.31/457.19 A WORK OF FICTION BY MONSIEUR PAUL DE KOCK, ENTITLED THE GIRL WITH THE THREE PAIRS OF STAYS   On de Kock and this book, see entry 64.39.

465.33/457.21 MRS BELLINGHAM   R. M. Adams points out that Sir Daniel Bellingham was the first Lord Mayor of Dublin in 1665 and says that Joyce's use of the name here was probably suggested "by the circumstance that on June 11, 1904, Charlotte Elizabeth, daughter of Alfred Payne and widow of Frederick Gough, was married to Sir Edward Henry Charles Patrick Bellingham, fifth Baronet, second creation, former Lieutenant-Colonel in the Royal Dublin Fusiliers" (*SS*, p. 218).

466.15/458.2 BLUEBEARD   In the fairy story "Bluebeard," Bluebeard is the villain who slays several wives. The story goes back at least as far as Charles Perrault's *Histoires ou Contes du Tems Passé* (1697).

466.21/458.8 A VENUS IN FURS   This alludes to the title of a novel by Austrian writer Leopold von Sacher-Masoch (1835–95), *Venus im Pelz* ("Venus in Furs"). On the importance of the novel for *Ulysses*, see R. Ellmann, *JJ*, p. 380, and S. Sultan, *The Argument of Ulysses*, pp. 315 ff.

467.10/458.28 DON JUAN   Don Juan is the traditional "great lover"; this recalls the many allusions to *Don Giovanni* in *Ulysses*. See entry 63.31 and the Index.

467.16/458.35 TO DO LIKEWISE   Bloom may be remembering an earlier statement of Stephen's which blends two biblical allusions. See entry 393.17.

468.2/459.17 I'LL MAKE YOU DANCE JACK LATTEN FOR THAT   P. W. Joyce records and explains this phrase in his *English As We Speak It*, pp. 172–73. He says it is a "threat of chastisement," and explains that "John Lattin of Morristown House county Kildare (near Naas) wagered that he'd dance home to Morristown from Dublin—more than twenty miles—changing his dance-steps every furlong: and won the wager. 'I'll make you dance' is a common threat heard everywhere: but 'I'll make you dance Jack Lattin' is ten times worse—'I'll make you dance excessively.' "

468.26/460.13 HE OFFERS THE OTHER CHEEK   This alludes to Christ's admonishment in the Sermon on the Mount: "Whosoever shall smite thee on thy right cheek, turn to him the other also" (Matt. 5:39; Luke 6:29 is very similar).

469.23/461.8 CUCKOO . . .   This recalls the conclusion of the "Nausicaa" episode, and alludes to a song in *Love's Labor's Lost;* see entries 382.23 and 212.36.

470.5/461.20 THE NAMELESS ONE   James Clarence Mangan wrote a poem entitled "The Nameless One," which is about his own hidden self or soul. One stanza says, "Tell how this Nameless, condemned for years long/ To herd with demons from hell beneath,/ Saw things that made him, with groans and tears, long/ For even death."

470.15/462.2 ANOTHER GIRL'S PLAIT CUT   There seems to be some allusion here, but I am uncertain about its object. There is a motif in European folk literature which involves a girl's cutting off her plait to escape from an undesired lover (see Stith Thompson, *Motif-Index of Folk-Literature*, Motif T327.7). Or perhaps this alludes to the tradition that the cutting of the plait is offensive and degrading to an oriental.

470.15/462.2 JACK THE RIPPER   This was a famous London murderer who brutally murdered several lower-class women in the Whitechapel district of London during the autumn and winter of 1888. Seven victims may be attributed to the killer, all of them prostitutes and most of them killed while plying their trade on the streets. In each case the throat was cut, and in most the bodies were mutilated, apparently by someone with a knowledge of anatomy. The crimes were never solved.

470.26/462.13 FROM HIS FOREHEAD ARISE STARKLY THE MOSAIC RAMS-HORNS This alludes to Michelangelo's famous statue of Moses (cf. entry 139.31). In that work Michelangelo follows an old tradition that Moses, coming down from Mount Sinai, was "horned." This is an error which resulted from the Vulgate translation in which a Hebrew word that could mean either that Moses "sent forth *beams*" or "sent forth *horns*" was translated in the latter fashion (see Exodus 34:29–30). See the article in Walsh's *Handy-Book of Literary Curiosities*, s.v. Horns.

471.10/462.24 SMOKING A PUNGENT HENRY CLAY See entry 247.11.

471.13/462.27 WHO'LL HANG JUDAS ISCARIOT Matthew 27:5 says that after receiving his payoff, Judas, feeling remorse, "went and hanged himself." There may also be an echo here of the nursery rhyme "Who Killed Cock Robin," on which see entry 103.23.

471.22/463.3 NECK OR NOTHING In Swift's *Polite Conversation*, first conversation, when the footman falls down the stairs, Lady Answerall says, "Neck, or nothing. Come down, or I'll Fetch you down: Well, but I hope the poor Fellow has not saved the Hangman a Labour" (p. 112).

473.2/464.10 BLOOM, I AM PADDY DIGNAM'S SPIRIT. LIST, LIST, O LIST Both of these phrases allude to *Hamlet*: on the first, see entry 188.35; on the second, see entry 188.3.

473.4/464.12 THE VOICE IS THE VOICE OF ESAU This recalls Bloom's earlier thoughts of Mosenthal's play, *Deborah*. See entry 76.30 and cf. entry 437.26.

473.10/464.18 METEMPSYCHOSIS See entry 64.18.

473.27/465.6 NAMINE. JACOBS VOBISCUITS. AMEN Bloom is thinking of the service he heard Father Coffey read earlier in the day and blending the service with the name of a well-known Dublin biscuit maker, Jacobs and Jacobs. On *namine*, see entry 103.27. Jacobs vobiscuits is *Dominus vobiscum* ("the Lord be with you"). Hodgart and Worthington list this as an allusion to "The Croppy Boy" (see entry 91.1), but in the present context that seems unlikely.

474.5/465.12 WITH PRICKED UP EARS . . . MY MASTER'S VOICE W. Powell Jones says of this passage, "Paddy wriggles forward, places an ear to the ground like the dog in the old Victor phonograph advertisements, and then says, 'My master's voice!' (Incidentally, the reference here to the phonograph humorously mentioned in the

'Hades' episode is even clearer when it is remembered that in England and on the continent 'His Master's Voice' was not only the legal name for Victrola but a household synonym for all phonographs.)" (*James Joyce and the Common Reader* [Norman, Okla., 1955], p. 123). But in all the examples of the Victor dog I have seen, he is sitting up, with his head tilted and one ear cocked.

474.17/465.24 DIGNAM'S VOICE, MUFFLED, IS HEARD BAYING UNDER GROUND   In light of his recently speaking the Ghost's words (entry 473.2), this probably alludes to the Ghost's speaking from under the stage in *Hamlet*, I, v.

474.18/465.24 DIGNAM'S DEAD AND GONE BELOW   Hodgart and Worthington list this as an allusion to " 'Old Roger is dead and gone to his grave,' a singing game." A. B. Gomme's *Traditional Games* . . . lists this game and many variants of the song sung to it, though none of the variants has a line precisely like this one in *Ulysses*. The closest is the version from Bath, beginning "Old Roger is dead and gone to his grave." The game and the song tell of old Roger's being laid away, but rising up to give a knock to an old woman who picks up apples around his grave (Gomme, *Traditional Games*, II, 16–24).

474.24/465.31 FOLLOW ME UP TO CARLOW   Mabel Worthington identifies this as an allusion to the patriotic song "Follow Me up to Carlow," by P. J. McCall (*PMLA*, LXXI, 337). She quotes the entire chorus, which ends, "Follow me up to Carlow," and cites *Songs of Ireland* (New York: Irish Industries Depot, 1924), p. 15 as a source.

475.18/466.23 YOU MIGHT GO FARTHER AND FARE WORSE   "Go farther and fare worse" is proverbial and is listed in the *ODEP*. It also occurs in Swift's *Polite Conversation*, second conversation, when Lady Answerall says, "Come, Sir *John*, you may go further, and fare worse" (p. 128). Partridge says the proverb is "16th–20th centuries." P. W. Joyce also cites a use of this phrase in witty repartee (*English As We Speak It*, p. 64).

475.19/466.24 MOTHER SLIPPERSLAPPER   See entry 87.18.

477.2/468.2 I NEVER LOVED A DEAR GAZELLE . . .   This alludes to a passage in Thomas Moore's poem *Lalla Rookh* (1817). In the third section of that long narrative poem (the section is entitled "The Fire-Worshippers"), the maiden Hinda says to her young lover, "I never nursed a dear gazelle,/ To glad me with its soft black eye,/ But when it came to know me well,/ And love me, it was sure to die" (ll. 283–86). Dickens parodies these lines in *The Old Curiosity Shop* when he has Dick Swiveller say, "I never nursed a dear Gazelle, to glad me with its soft black eye, but when it came to know me well and love me, it was sure to marry a market-gardener" (chap. 56).

477.14/468.14   SCHORACH ANI WENOWACH, BENOITH HIERUSHALOIM
This is the Hebrew version of the Song of Songs 1:5: "I am black, but comely, O ye daughters of Jerusalem." The transliteration of the Hebrew is so inaccurate here that it raises the question of whether Joyce may be intentionally varying the phrase (see entry 479.30). But it seems more likely that this is simply inaccurate Hebrew.

477.18/468.18   AND YOU KNOW WHAT THOUGHT DID   Bloom's statement and Zoe's reply have their parallel in Swift's *Polite Conversation*, first conversation, when Lady Answerall says to Miss Notable, "I thought you did [lie] just now," to which Lord Sparkish replies, "Pray, Madam, what did thought do?" (p. 105). Partridge says this is a catch phrase which is still current in the form "You know what thought did," and says the polite version of the answer is "kissed another man's wife." Mackie Jarrell says (*PMLA*, LXXII, 547) that the answer recorded by John Ray's *Collection of English Proverbs* is that "Thought lay a bed and besh —— himself."

478.9/469.7   SIR WALTER RALEIGH BROUGHT FROM THE NEW WORLD THAT POTATO AND THAT WEED . . .   Traditionally, Raleigh is said to have brought the potato and tobacco from the New World to the British Isles. Probably there is something to the claim for tobacco, for, though it was taken to Europe by the Spanish, the first to reach England probably did come from Virginia. But few authorities today still believe that he introduced the potato (see Roger McKay's Introduction to *An Anthology of the Potato* [Dublin, 1961], p. 9). Perhaps Bloom got his information from the *Royal Reader*, No. III (London, 1876), which has an illustrated reading that begins "In the reign of Queen Elizabeth, two plants were brought to England, for the first time, by Sir Walter Raleigh, both of which are now very much used—the tobacco-plant and the potato" (p. 177; on the *Royal Readers*, cf. entries 376.10 and 376.15). But Thom's *Dublin Directory* (1904), in its "Dublin Annals," says, *s.v.* 1565, "John Hawkins, from Santa Fe, New Spain, introduced potatoes into Ireland" (p. 2093).

478.18/469.16   TURN AGAIN, LEOPOLD! LORD MAYOR OF DUBLIN   This alludes to the nursery story "Dick Whittington and His Cat," in which Dick heard the bells of Bow Church say "Turn again, Whittington,/ Thrice Lord Mayor of London."

478.23/469.21   CUI BONO   This proverbial Latin phrase means "Who profits by it?" (though it is often popularly translated "What good is it?").

478.24/469.22   VANDERDECKENS IN THEIR PHANTOM SHIP   This alludes to the legend of the Flying Dutchman, in most versions of which the captain of the phantom ship was named Vanderdecken. There is more than one version of the legend, but the most popular casts Vanderdecken as a Wandering Jew of the ocean. The Dutch captain tried to round the Cape of Good Hope in a gale and encountered difficulty, whereupon he vowed he would round the Cape if he had to sail forever. The devil heard his oath and condemned him to sail until Judgment Day, unless he could find a woman who would love him faithfully until death. Once every seven years he is permitted to go ashore in search of this woman. Richard Wagner wrote an opera called *The Flying Dutchman* (1843), and there is a song by this title, by Richard Ryan and John Parry, Jr., words and music of which can be found in Hatton and Faning, *Songs of England*, III, 212–15.

479.19/470.13   THESE FLYING DUTCHMEN   See entry 478.24.

479.27/470.21   BUT THEIR REIGN IS ROVER FOR REVER AND EVER AND EV   In Revelation 11:15, great voices in heaven say, "The kingdoms of this world are become the kingdoms of our Lord, and of his Christ; and he shall reign for ever and ever." Handel used this verse as part of the basis of the "Hallelujah Chorus" in *The Messiah* (on which see entry 183.7).

479.30/470.24   CEAD MILLE FAILTE AND MAH TTOB MELEK ISRAEL   "Cead Mile Failte" is a traditional Irish greeting that means "A Hundred Thousand Welcomes." It is also the title of a song by Gerald Griffin, words of which can be found in the *Dublin Book of Irish Verse*, pp. 123–24. Mah Ttob Melek Israel, which means "How beautiful is thy king, O Israel," is apparently a variation on the phrase "May Tovu Oholeko Yaäcov" ("How goodly are thy tents, O Jacob"), which occurs in Numbers 24:5.

480.4/470.32   THE PILLAR OF THE CLOUD APPEARS   See entry 143.11.

480.6/470.34   KOL NIDRE   The "Kol Nidre" is a Jewish prayer or chant that begins with the words "Kol Nidre" ("All vows"). It is the formula for the annulment of vows, recited on the eve of the Day of Atonement.

480.7/470.34   IMPERIAL EAGLES   The imperial eagle refers to the most important of the *signa militaria* of the Roman Empire, the *aquila* or eagle. Since Roman times the eagle has been the emblem of many countries, including France, Prussia, and the United States.

480.40/471.30   SAINT STEPHEN'S IRON CROWN . . .   Most of the items in these sentences are identifiable as elements of a coronation processional. Robert Tracy contends that this description derives in part from Arthur Griffith's description of Franz Josef's coronation in his *The Resurrection of Hungary*; and Tracy says that the "iron crown of St. Stephen" directly reproduces an error Griffith makes, "for this crown has no existence outside Griffith's pages" (*op. cit.*, entry 337.33, pp. 531–32). But such a crown does exist, and Richard M. Kain has called my attention to a newspaper article describing it and its recent history in some detail. The New York *Times* of August 16, 1965, carried an illustrated article on the crown, which explained that it was originally presented to Hungarian king Stephen I (975–1038—first king of Hungary and patron saint of that country) by Pope Sylvester II, and pointed out that the crown has been a cherished symbol of Hungarian sovereignty for many years. For the past twenty years the crown has been in American hands, in spite of several attempts by the Communist Hungarian government to regain it. The U.S. State Department will not reveal the exact location of the crown and says that it is being " 'held in trust as property of the Hungarian nation.' " Further details may be found in the New York *Times*, August 16, 1965, p. 1, cols. c–d, and p. 2, cols. c–e.

481.12/472.2 THE WREN, THE WREN ... In their *Lore and Language of Schoolchildren*, the Opies give three slightly different versions of this song, and a discussion of the custom of "Hunting the Wren." On St. Stephen's Day the children go from house to house with a piece of holly or gorse with a wren hanging in it and demand money for his burial (pp. 288–89, *s.v.* St. Stephen's Day: 26 December). Moffat's *Minstrelsy of Ireland*, 3rd ed., pp. 252–53, gives words and music for this rann.

481.17/472.7 FOR THE HONOUR OF GOD This may owe something to the Jesuit motto "Ad Majorem Dei Gloriam" ("For the greater glory of God").

481.17/472.7 HE SCARCELY LOOKS THIRTYONE This is probably intended to allude to Christ's age at the beginning of his ministry, though traditions about this vary. Luke 3:23 says, "And Jesus himself began to be about thirty years of age." *A Catholic Commentary on Holy Scripture* (London, 1953) says this falls in with "traditional Jewish ideas according to which it was unfitting that a man should come forward as a religious master before the age of thirty" (p. 945).

482.3/472.21 A SUNBURST APPEARS IN THE NORTHWEST See entry 57.35.

482.18/473.9 PLACING HIS RIGHT HAND ON HIS TESTICLES, SWEARS Zoe has just mentioned Bloom's testicles (p. 476.2/467.6), but this probably alludes to a form of oath-taking which occurs in the Old Testament. In Genesis 24:2, Abraham tells the oldest and most responsible servant in his house to "Put, I pray thee, thy hand under my thigh" as they prepare to swear an oath. *The Oxford Annotated Bible* explains, "Putting the hand under the thigh, an old form of oath taking ([Gen.] 47:29), reflected the view that the fountain of reproductivity was sacred to the deity."

482.21/473.12 GAUDIUM MAGNUM ANNUNTIO VOBIS. HABEMUS CARNEFICEM   This parodies the formula used by the senior cardinal deacon as he announces the election of a new pope from the balcony of St. Peter's to the people assembled in the piazza below: *Annuntio vobis gaudium magnum: habemus papam* ("I announce to you a great joy: we have a pope"). The parody in *Ulysses* says, "we have an executioner."

482.27/473.18 JOYBELLS RING IN . . . GAY MALAHIDE   This alludes to the opening lines of Gerald Griffin's song "The Bridal of Malahide": "The Joybells are ringing/ In gay Malahide." See entries 43.26 and 223.16.

483.4/473.24 THE KOH-I-NOOR DIAMOND   This famous diamond became part of the crown jewels of England when it was acquired by Queen Victoria in 1849. At that time it weighed 191 carats, but it was cut in 1852 and reduced to 108 carats. The name means "mountain of light."

483.9/473.29 COPULA FELIX   This alludes to the "felix culpa," or "fortunate fall." Though generally attributed to St. Augustine, this phrase does not appear in his works, and the idea is fairly common among the church fathers. Father William T. Noon has suggested to me that the source of the phrase is the "Exsultet" of the service for Holy Saturday, which Stephen alluded to on p. 50.24/51.13. During that part of the service, the deacon praises God for his love in sending Christ and says, "O certe necessarium Adae peccatum, quod Christi morte deletum est! O felix culpa, quae talem ac tantum meruit habere redemptorem!" ("Needful indeed was Adam's sin for the death of Christ was its atoning! Happy that fault that won so great and glorious a redeemer!"). Though this "Exsultet" is sometimes said to be by St. Augustine, there is apparently no sound basis for the tradition.

483.12/473.32 THE PRINCESS SELENE, THE SPLENDOUR OF NIGHT   Selene was a primitive goddess of the moon among the Greeks, later identified with Artemis, the Diana of the Romans.

484.2/474.17 ON THIS DAY TWENTY YEARS AGO WE OVERCAME THE HEREDITARY ENEMY AT LADYSMITH   J. Prescott (*MLQ*, XIII, 157) has pointed out Bloom's chronological and geographical confusion in this paragraph. Ladysmith, a town in Natal, was the location of a British garrison which was besieged by the Boers from October 29, 1899, until it was relieved by British troops under General Buller on February 28, 1900.

484.4/474.19 HALF A LEAGUE ONWARD   This is from Tennyson's poem "The Charge of the Light Brigade," commemorating the heroic but disastrous charge of the Light Brigade at Balaclava, in the Crimea, on September 26, 1854 (during the Crimean War).

484.5/474.20 ALL IS LOST NOW   This alludes to "Tutto è sciolto," from Bellini's *La Sonnambula*. See entry 256.24.

484.7/474.22 THE HEIGHTS OF PLEVNA   On Plevna, which was besieged in 1877 during the Russo-Turkish War, see entry 56.32.

484.8/474.22 BONAFIDE SABAOTH   This phrase blends the ordinary meaning of *bona fide* with the Hebrew word *Sabaoth*, which means "armies," or "hosts." The word occurs untranslated in two places in the King James Bible, Romans 9:29 and James 5:4 (the Douay version retains it in Jeremiah 11:20 as well). The word each time occurs in the phrase "Lord of Sabaoth," which Old Testament passages translate "Lord of Hosts."

484.12/474.27 THE MAN THAT GOT AWAY JAMES STEPHENS   See entries 43.25 and 68.26.

484.21/475.7 VERILY IT IS EVEN NOW AT HAND   On several occasions Christ made a statement similar to this. Matthew 4:17 says, "Jesus began to preach, and to say, Repent: for the kingdom of heaven is at hand." Similar statements occur in Matthew 3:2 and 10:7, Mark 1:15, and Luke 21:31. "Verily I say unto you" is also common in Christ's speech, occurring at least thirty times in the Gospels.

484.22/475.8 THE GOLDEN CITY . . . THE NEW BLOOMUSALEM   The New Jerusalem, which was alluded to earlier on p. 332.40/327.3, is the Christian heavenly city described by St. John in Revelation 21 and 22. Hodgart and Worthington also list this as alluding to three songs, "The Holy City," "Jerusalem the Golden," and "Kafoozalem." On the first of these, see entry 504.30. For words and music of "Jerusalem the Golden," by Bernard of Cluny, see Reddall, *Songs That Never Die*, pp. 474, 499. The allusion to the popular American song "Kafoozalem" seems less likely. The Kafoozalem of the song was a Moslem girl whose father killed her and her lover Sam (not a Moslem) with a bowstring greased with goozalem. The song appeared about 1866 and was probably written by F. Blume. For words and music, see Spaeth, *Read 'Em and Weep*, pp. 148–49.

484.24/475.10 THIRTYTWO WORKMEN . . . FROM ALL THE COUNTIES OF

IRELAND   Robert Tracy suggests that this derives from Arthur Griffith's description of the acclaim of Franz Josef in his book *The Resurrection of Hungary*. Tracy quotes a passage from Griffith's book which says that Franz Josef is hailed by "fifty-two working men from all the counties of Hungary" (see entry 337.33 and see p. 532 of Tracy's essay cited there).

484.26/475.12   A COLOSSAL EDIFICE, WITH CRYSTAL ROOF . . .   This is probably meant to remind us of the Crystal Palace; see entry 294.18.

485.7/475.22   MORITURI TE SALUTANT   "Those who are dying salute you." This was the statement of the Roman gladiators to Caesar as they went by him into the arena: "Ave, Imperator, morituri te salutant." The phrase is sometimes given "Morituri salutamus," which Longfellow used as the title of a poem.

485.12/475.27   HIGGINS   This probably refers to Francis Higgins, the Sham Squire. See entry 126.26.

485.14/475.29   SO MUCH FOR M'INTOSH   This alludes to a melodramatic line in Colley Cibber's adaptation of Shakespeare's *Richard III*: "Off with his head. So much for Buckingham" (IV, iv, 188; see Christopher Spencer, *Five Restoration Adaptations of Shakespeare* [Urbana, Ill., 1965], p. 331).

485.20/476.3   LOAVES AND FISHES . . . HENRY CLAY CIGARS   Both of these have been mentioned earlier. On the first, see entry 403.31; on the second, see entry 247.11.

485.29/476.11   CHEAP REPRINTS OF THE WORLD'S TWELVE WORST BOOKS . . . While some of these titles are clearly facetious, others are plausible enough that such books might exist, but a search of standard bibliographical sources has not turned any of them up. But many of these, if they do exist, would probably have been printed in ephemeral editions or privately printed and consequently might not show up in something like the *English Catalogue of Books*. Perhaps in the future someone will come across a dealer's catalogue from which Joyce took some of these, but I am skeptical of it.

486.2/476.19   WOMEN PRESS FORWARD TO TOUCH THE HEM OF BLOOM'S ROBE   In Matthew 9:20, a woman who had been diseased with an issue of blood for twelve years came up to Christ "and touched the hem of his garment," saying that if she could only do so, she would be whole. Similar passages are found in Mark 5:27 and 6:56 and in Luke 8:44.

486.6/476.23   BABES AND SUCKLINGS   In Matthew 21:16 Jesus chides the priests and scribes, "Yea; have ye never read, Out of the mouth of babes and sucklings thou hast perfected praise?" Jesus is citing Psalms 8:2.

486.11/476.28 CLAP CLAP HANDS TILL POLDY COMES HOME . . . This alludes to the nursery rhyme and children's amusement that begins, "Clap hands, clap hands,/ Till father comes home." One of the variants given in the *ODNR* mentions "With his pockets full of plums,/ And a cake for Johnny" (pp. 196–97).

486.20/477.2 PUSSY FOURCORNERS This is probably the same as "Puss in the Corner," a children's game described in Gomme's *Traditional Games*, although this variant name is not given there. Four children at four corners swap places while a fifth in the middle tries to catch one vacant and force someone else into the middle position (*Traditional Games*, II, 88–89).

486.21/477.3 PEEP! BOPEEP This seems to allude not to the well-known nursery rhyme "Little Bo Peep," but to a baby's game consisting solely of the statement "Bo-peep, Little Bo-peep,/ Now's the time for hide and seek" (*ODNR*, p. 93). Mackie Jarrell (*PMLA*, LXXII, 551) sees this as a possible allusion to Swift's "A Cantata," which ends with "Bo peep, bo peep . . . peep, bo bo peep" (see *Poems of Swift*, ed. Harold Williams [Oxford, 1937], pp. 955–61, esp. p. 961).

486.22/477.4 TICKTACKTWO WOULDYOUSEETASHOE? This seems to allude to some children's game or nursery rhyme, but none of the books I have consulted has anything very similar to this. The closest is a rhyme listed in the *ODNR* which begins, "Tit, tat, toc" (variant "Tick, tack, toe"), but the rest of the rhyme is not similar. Hodgart and Worthington do not include this.

486.25/477.7 ABSENCE MAKES THE HEART GROW YOUNGER This is a variation on the now proverbial "Absence makes the heart grow fonder," which occurs in "Isle of Beauty," a poem by English poet Thomas Haynes Bayly (1797–1839): "Absence makes the heart grow fonder,/ Isle of Beauty, Fare thee well." But the phrase goes back beyond that to an anonymous poem that appeared in Francis Davison's *Poetical Rhapsody* (1602).

487.4/477.21 THE RAMS' HORNS SOUND FOR SILENCE. THE STANDARD OF ZION IS HOISTED J. Prescott (*MLQ*, XIII, 157) says, "The association between rams' horns and the standard of Zion is as old as the Bible, shofars having been used as battle trumpets by the Hebrews. (Cf. Joshua 6:4.) And Bloom might well be aware that rams' horns are still used in the synagogues of the children of Zion upon sacred festivals, as on Yom Kippur . . . and the New Year, i.e., 'Roschaschana.' " Joshua 6:4 says, "And seven priests shall bear before the ark seven trumpets of rams' horns."

487.8/477.25 ALEPH BETH GHIMEL DALETH . . . The first four of these are the first four letters of the Hebrew alphabet. On Hagadah, see entries 122.15 ff. On Tephilim, see entry 378.36. Kosher refers to the regulations determining the Jewish dietary laws. On Yom Kippur, see entry 152.1. Hanukah (Hanukkah) is the eight-day celebration commemorating the victory of Judah the Maccabee over Antiochus Epiphanes and the subsequent rededication of the Temple and the altar. Roschaschana (Rosh Hashana) is the two-day holiday at the beginning of the month Tishri. The name literally means "head of the year," but the Bible refers to it as the first day of the seventh month; the shophar (ram's horn) is blown on this occasion. Beni Brith (B'nai B'rith) is the oldest, largest, and most active of Jewish fraternal orders, created in 1843. Bar Mitzvah is the ceremony marking the initiation of a boy at age thirteen into the Jewish religious community. Mazzoth is the un-leavened bread. Askenazim refers to the German Jews and their descendants. Meshuggah is a Hebrew word meaning crazy. A Talith is a prayer shawl, worn by adult males during certain prayers. Further information on these can be found in any encyclo-pedia of Judaism.

488.6/478.14   A DANIEL DID I SAY? NAY! A PETER O'BRIEN   This Daniel is the wise young man in the apocryphal book of Susanna who questioned separately the two elders who had falsely accused Susanna of adultery. Daniel found that their testimonies differed, and they were put to death. But this probably alludes primarily to the disguised Portia's being called a "Daniel" by both Shylock and Gratiano in *The Merchant of Venice*, IV, i, 223, 333, and 340. Peter O'Brien, Baron O'Brien of Kilfenora (1842–1914), was Lord Chief Justice of Ireland. The *DNB* has a highly complimentary article on him ("penetrating to essentials, dispelling irrelevancies, he chiselled argument with common sense to sound decision"). But most Irishmen would take a different view: see entry 297.9.

488.23/479.6   WHEN MY PROGENITOR OF SAINTED MEMORY WORE THE UNIFORM OF THE AUSTRIAN DESPOT IN A DANK PRISON WHERE WAS YOURS   This allusion is not clear to me, but it seems most likely that this refers to the abortive Hungarian revolt against Austria in 1848–49, and that the Austrian despot referred to is Franz Joseph (1830–1916). Perhaps Bloom's progenitor was, though Hungarian, a member of the Austrian army and was imprisoned during the revolt.

489.21/480.4   THE PLAIN TEN COMMANDMENTS   The ten command-ments are given in Exodus 20 and Deuteronomy 5.

489.23/480.6   THREE ACRES AND A COW   Though this perhaps goes back to John Stuart Mill's description of peasant farming in Flanders (in *Principles of Political Economy*, II, chap. VI, sec. 5), it certainly refers to the use of this exact phrase by Jesse Collings (1831–1920), a member of Parliament who, in 1886, carried the "small holdings amendment" against Lord Salisbury's government. According to the *DNB* article on Collings, "three acres and a cow" was for many years the war-cry of the land reformers.

490.15/480.25 VENUS CALLIPYGE, VENUS PANDEMOS, VENUS METEMPSYCHOSIS   On the first of these, see entry 201.11; on the second, see entry 425.40; the third is Bloom's own creation, but on metempsychosis, see entry 64.18.

490.17/480.27 NEW NINE MUSES   The original nine muses and their subjects were Clio, history; Euterpe, lyric poetry; Thalia, comedy and pastoral poetry; Melpomene, tragedy; Terpsichore, dancing; Erato, erotic poetry; Polyhymnia, sacred song; Calliope, epic poetry; and Urania, astronomy.

490.23/481.2 AN ANYTHINGARIAN   In Swift's *Polite Conversation*, first conversation, Lady Smart asks of someone, "What Religion is he of?" to which Lord Sparkish replies, "Why; he is an Anythingarian" (p. 89).

490.27/481.6 MOTHER GROGAN   See entry 12.33.

491.2/481.10 ONE OF THE OLD SWEET SONGS   This alludes to "Love's Old Sweet Song"; see entry 63.31.

491.5/481.13 I VOWED THAT I NEVER WOULD LEAVE HER   Apparently this is the same song Bloom thinks of Corny's singing on p. 71.16/70.16; see entry 71.16.

491.13/481.21 THE ROWS OF CASTEELE   See entry 134.19.

492.6/482.11 NELSON'S PILLAR   On Nelson's Pillar, see entry 95.9.

492.11/482.15 ALEXANDER J. DOWIE   On fanatical American evangelist Dowie, see entry 151.15.

492.14/482.18 THIS STINKING GOAT OF MENDES   Mendes was a city in the Nile delta. The Mendesian goat in Egyptian mythology was one of the three most sacred animals, the others being the bulls Apis and Mnevis. This goat was called the Ram, and was held to be an incarnation of Osiris. When it died there was ritual mourning. Plutarch says that the most beautiful women were offered in coitus to this divine goat.

492.16/482.20 THE CITIES OF THE PLAIN   See entry 61.12.

492.17/482.21 THE WHITE BULL MENTIONED IN THE APOCALYPSE   I can find no mention of a bull, white or other, in Revelation. The only white animal mentioned is a white horse, in Revelation 6:2 and 19:11.

492.18/482.22 THE SCARLET WOMAN   This probably refers to the woman described in Revelation 17:4–5: "And the woman was arrayed in purple and scarlet color, and decked with gold and precious stones and pearls, having a golden cup in her hand full of abominations and filthiness of her fornication: and upon her forehead was a name written, MYSTERY, BABYLON THE GREAT, THE MOTHER OF HARLOTS AND ABOMINATIONS OF THE EARTH."

492.20/482.24 CALIBAN   Caliban is the "creature of earth" in *The Tempest.*

492.22/482.26 HE'S AS BAD AS PARNELL WAS. MR FOX   On Parnell, see entry 35.2 and the Index. Mr. Fox was one of the aliases Parnell used, and this fact came out at the divorce trial. See F. S. L. Lyons, *The Fall of Parnell*, pp. 275, 290.

492.23/482.27 MOTHER GROGAN   See entry 12.33.

492.29/482.33 THIS IS MIDSUMMER MADNESS   In *Twelfth Night*, Olivia says of Malvolio's puzzling quotations from what he thinks is Olivia's letter, "Why, this is very midsummer madness" (III, iv, 61).

492.30/483.1 I AM GUILTLESS AS THE UNSUNNED SNOW   In his soliloquy in *Cymbeline*, II, v, Posthumus says of Imogen, "I thought her/ As chaste as unsunned snow" (12–13). Stephen earlier alluded to a later line of this same soliloquy; see entry 201.37.

492.32/483.3 SLANDER, THE VIPER, HAS WRONGFULLY ACCUSED ME   Though the characterization of slander as a viper is common, and though there is no line in *Cymbeline* exactly like this, the allusion on p. 492.30/483.1 suggests that this refers to Pisanio's description of slander as a viper while he observes Imogen reading the letter from Posthumus commanding her death (*Cym.*, III, iv, 35–41).

492.33/483.4 SGENL INN BAN BATA COISDE GAN CAPALL   Vivian Mercier has suggested to me that this consists of two phrases, both having the same point, and both expressing Bloom's view that the charges against him are false and baseless. According to Mr. Mercier, the first phrase is "sgéul i mbarr bata" ("a story at the top of a stick"—metaphorically used to mean an unreliable rumor); and the second is "cóiste gan capall" ("a coach without a horse"), which it seems to me can carry the same connotation as the first. G. J. Visser (*English Studies*, XXIV, 45–56, 79–90) comes to essentially the same conclusion, for he says the first three words appear mangled, and suggests, "sgeul i mbárr bata cóiste gan capall"; but, apparently not recognizing the metaphorical meaning of the opening phrase, he translates it "a telegram is a coach without horses," or literally, "a story in top of a stick (is) a coach without horses" (p. 80).

493.13/483.17 I BELIEVE HIM TO BE MORE SINNED AGAINST THAN SIN-NING   From *King Lear*; see entry 358.10.

494.30/484.31 NASODORO, GOLDFINGER, CHRYSOSTOMOS . . .   Of these names playing on precious metals (and parts of the body) in various languages, only one seems to be allusive; on Chrysostomos, see entry 3.28.

495.2/485.2 BLOOM, ARE YOU THE MESSIAH BEN JOSEPH OR BEN DAVID Traditionally, the Messiah of the Jewish people is to be a scion of the house of David. The Messiah ben Joseph is a messianic figure in rabbinical apocalyptic literature. Traditions about him vary, but "he has an established place in the apocalypses of later centuries" (*Jewish Encyc.*, VIII, 511, *s.v.* Messiah). The traditions hold that the Messiah ben Joseph will precede the Messiah ben David; he will gather Israel around him, march to Jerusalem and establish his dominion, and then be slain by hostile hosts. For more detail, see the source cited.

495.10/485.10 NELSON'S PILLAR   See entry 95.9.

495.14/485.14 LORD BEACONSFIELD, LORD BYRON, WAT TYLER, MOSES OF EGYPT   Lord Beaconsfield is Benjamin Disraeli (1804–81), English statesman and writer. Wat Tyler (d. 1381) was an English rebel, leader of the peasant rebellion of 1381.

495.15/485.15 MOSES MAIMONIDES, MOSES MENDELSSOHN, HENRY IRVING, RIP VAN WINKLE   On Moses Maimonides, see entry 28.14. Moses Mendelssohn (1729–86) was a German Jewish philosopher. Sir Henry Irving (1838–1905) was an English actor and theater manager. On Rip van Winkle, see entries 377.23 and 542.3.

495.16/485.16 KOSSUTH, JEAN JACQUES ROUSSEAU, BARON LEOPOLD ROTHS-CHILD   Kossuth is Louis Kossuth (1802–94), Hungarian revolutionary leader and one of the principals of the Hungarian Revolution of March, 1848. Lionel Nathan de Rothschild (1808–79) was the first Jewish member of the English Parliament.

495.17/485.17 ROBINSON CRUSOE, SHERLOCK HOLMES, PASTEUR   Louis Pasteur (1822–95) was a French scientist who disproved the theory of spontaneous generation, and developed pasteurization.

495.19/485.18 BIDS THE TIDE TURN BACK   There are stories of a hero who fights with the sea or bids the tide not to rise in the mythologies of most countries, but perhaps the one most relevant here is the story of Canute (or Cnut, 995?–1035), King of England. According to a story in Holinshed, King Canute sat down on the shore near Southampton and bade the tide rise no more. When it came on and wetted him, he told his courtiers that though they called him king he could not control even this small portion of water.

495.19/485.19 ECLIPSES THE SUN BY EXTENDING HIS LITTLE FINGER See entry 166.36.

495.24/485.24 LEOPOLDI AUTEM GENERATIO . . . ET VOCABITUR NOMEN EIUS EMMANUEL   Leopold's genealogy is patterned on those of the Bible; see Genesis 5, 10, and 11, and especially the genealogy of Christ given in Matthew 1 and Luke 3. The opening phrase is based on Matthew 1:18: "Christi autem generatio sic erat" ("Now the birth of Christ was on this wise"). The concluding Latin phrase is from Isaiah's prophecy in Isaiah 7:14: "Ecce virgo concipiet, et pariet filium, et vocabitur nomen eius Emmanuel" ("Behold, a virgin shall conceive, and bear a son, and shall call his name Emmanuel"). Many of the names in the genealogy are facetious or impossible of specific identification. I annotate those that seem to have some identifiable allusive element. Moses and Noah are the biblical characters, and Eunuch is probably Enoch, of whom there are two in the Bible: first, Enoch, son of Cain and father of Irad (Gen. 4: 17–18); second, Enoch, son of Jared and father of Methuselah (Gen. 5:18–24); it was the second Enoch who "walked with God," and was "translated" by faith (Heb. 11:5). On Jeshurum, see entry 393.28. Ichabudonosor seems to blend Ichabod, son of King Phineas in I Samuel 4:21, with Nabuchodonsor, King of Babylon, referred to in II Kings 24:1, Daniel 1:1, and many other places (cf. entry 496.9). O'Donnell Magnus probably means "the Great O'Donnell," and perhaps alludes to Red Hugh (or Hugh Roe) O'Donnell (b. 1572), best known and most glorious of the O'Donnell clan. Ben Maimon may refer to Moses Ben Maimon, Maimonides, on whom see entry 28.14. On Dusty Rhodes, see entry 427.17.

496.9/486.7 A DEADHAND WRITES ON THE WALL   This alludes to the handwriting on the wall of Belshazzar's palace in Daniel 5. Daniel 5:5 says, "In the same hour came forth fingers of a man's hand, and wrote over against the candlestick upon the plaister of the wall of the king's palace." Belshazzar was the son of Nebuchadnezzar.

496.16/486.14 A HOLLYBUSH   This probably alludes to the riddle Stephen recited earlier. See entry 26.33.

496.17/486.15 AND IN THE DEVIL'S GLEN?   Hodgart and Worthington list this as an allusion to "Pretty Molly Branigan." The first stanza of that song contains the lines "The place where my heart was you'd aisy roll a turnip in,/ 'Tis as large as all Dublin, and from Dublin to the Divil's Glen." For words and music, see P. Colum, *Treasury of Irish Folklore*, pp. 594–95.

496.24/486.22 ASSES' EARS   This probably alludes to the story of King Midas' being given asses' ears by Apollo because Midas was so ignorant as to prefer Pan's music to Apollo's. See Ovid's *Metamorphoses*, book XI.

496.25/486.23 DON GIOVANNI A CENAR TECO   See entry 179.35 and related entries.

497.2/486.28 YOU HIG, YOU HOG, YOU DIRTY DOG . . .   Though this seems to be a song, or a parody on a song, Hodgart and Worthington do not list it, and I have not been able to identify it.

497.5/487.2 IF YOU SEE KAY . . .   Understandably, I have not found this pornographic rhyme in print, and if it is a parody or take-off on any song, I am unaware of it. Perhaps it owes something to the musical comedy *The Girl from Kay's* (book by Owen Hall, lyrics by Adrian Ross and Claude Aveling, music by Ivan Caryll), which was first performed in Dublin on Easter Monday, 1904. But I have not been able to get a copy of the musical and cannot confirm this.

497.10/487.7 EPHOD   This is a Jewish priestly vestment, described in Exodus 28:4 ff.

497.10/487.7 AND HE SHALL CARRY THE SINS OF THE PEOPLE TO AZAZEL, THE SPIRIT WHICH IS IN THE WILDERNESS   In Leviticus 16 is described the sending of a goat bearing the sins of the people out into the desert "for Azazel." This is of course the scapegoat. The Hebrew word *Azazel* appears in the Vulgate and Catholic versions, but not in the King James, where it is translated "the scapegoat." See especially Leviticus 16:8, 10, 26,

497.12/487.9 LILITH, THE NIGHTHAG   On Lilith, see entry 390.1.

497.12/487.9 AND THEY SHALL STONE HIM AND DEFILE HIM . . .   Although this may allude to the biblical style generally rather than to any specific passage, it does have elements in common with Leviticus 20:2, where God tells Moses, "Whosoever he be of the children of Israel, or of the strangers that sojourn in Israel, that giveth any of his seed unto Moloch; he shall surely be put to death: the people of the land shall stone him with stones."

497.20/487.17 BELIAL! LAEMLEIN OF ISTRIA! THE FALSE MESSIAH! ABULAFIA   Belial is sometimes identified with Satan, but in the Bible, the phrase "sons of Belial" is used to designate those who would lead the people to worship false gods; see Deuteronomy 13:13 and Judges 19:22, and consult the *Jewish Encyclopedia*, II, 658–59, *s.v.* Belial. Asher Lemmlein appeared in Istria (near Venice) in 1502 and proclaimed himself a forerunner of the Messiah. He gained wide credence for his claim that the Messiah was imminent, but he suddenly disappeared, and the agitation ended. Abraham Ben Samuel Abulafia (1240–post 1291) was a pseudo-Messiah who went to Rome to try to convert Pope Nicholas III to Judaism and was saved from death at the stake only by the Pope's sudden death.

497.27/487.24 BLACKBEARDED ISCARIOT, BAD SHEPHERD   In John 10:14, Christ says, "I am the good shepherd."

498.10/488.5 FORGIVE HIM HIS TRESPASSES   This alludes to the Pater Noster or Lord's Prayer. See Matthew 6:12 and Luke 11:4.

498.16/488.11 IN A SEAMLESS GARMENT MARKED I.H.S.   John 19:23 says of Christ's coat, ". . . now the coat was without seam, woven from the top throughout." On I.H.S., see entry 81.20.

498.16/488.11 AMID PHOENIX FLAMES   The fabulous phoenix was said to live more than five hundred years, after which it gathered material for its own funeral pyre and then set fire to itself. Nine days later it arose again from its own ashes. The bird was seen as an image of Christ, and its death and rebirth symbolized resurrection. See T. H. White, *The Bestiary*, s.v. Phoenix.

498.17/488.12 WEEP NOT FOR ME, O DAUGHTERS OF ERIN   As Christ was carrying his cross to Calvary, he said to the women who were weeping and lamenting, "Daughters of Jerusalem, weep not for me, but weep for yourselves, and for your children" (Luke 23:28).

498.23/488.17 KIDNEY OF BLOOM, PRAY FOR US . . .   This list, which is a summary of Bloom's episodes up to this point, parodies litanies in which the object of the litany is addressed under its various aspects, with the repeated plea "pray for us," as in the Litany of the Sacred Heart or the Litany of Our Lady of Loreto (on the latter, see entry 354.8).

498.29/488.23 SWEETS OF SIN   See entry 236.5.

498.30/488.24 MUSIC WITHOUT WORDS   See entry 285.37.

499.5/488.30 THE ALLELUIA CHORUS   This chorus is from *The Messiah* by Handel. See entries 183.7 and 479. 27.

499.11/489.2 IN CAUBEEN WITH CLAY PIPE STUCK IN THE BAND . . .   This is probably a general parody of the Abbey Theatre movement and the "stage Irishman" rather than a parody of any specific play. The black pig may allude to the black pig that occurs commonly in Irish tales and folklore; see for example the "Lay of the Enchanted Pigs" in Hoagland, pp. 132–33. The smile in his eye (followed by a tear on p. 499.16/489.6) alludes to Thomas Moore's song "Erin, the Tear and the Smile in Thine Eyes"; see entry 296.17.

499.17/489.8 TO BE OR NOT TO BE   This repeats Bloom's earlier allusion to Hamlet's soliloquy; see entry 280.25.

499.24/489.15 GOT UP THE WRONG SIDE OF THE BED   "To rise on the wrong side of the bed" is proverbial and is listed in *ODEP* and Apperson.

499.25/489.16 O, I CAN READ YOUR THOUGHTS   In Swift's *Polite Conversation*, second conversation, Miss Notable says to Neverout, "No, indeed, you shan't drink after me; for you'll know my Thoughts," to which he replies, "I know them already; you are thinking of a good Husband" (pp. 146–47). A similar statement occurs in the third conversation, when Lady Smart says to Lady Answerall, "Madam, I fancy I know your Thoughts, as well, as if I were within you" (p. 162).

500.5/489.26 HOG'S NORTON WHERE THE PIGS PLAY THE ORGANS   In Swift's *Polite Conversation*, second conversation, Neverout says of Sir John Linger, "Faith, I believe he was bred at *Hogsnorton*, where the Pigs play upon the Organs" (p. 156). Partridge says that Hogsnorton was usually written Hogs Norton, and points out, citing Apperson, that Hogs Norton was mentioned as early as *ca.* 1554, and the full statement made in 1593 by Nashe.

500.7/489.28 TOMMY TITTLEMOUSE   This alludes to the well-known nursery rhyme "Little Tommy Tittlemouse/ Lived in a little house;/ He caught fishes/ In other men's ditches" (*ODNR*, p. 416).

500.19/490.9 THE GREENEYED MONSTER   In *Othello*, Iago says to Othello, "Oh, beware, my lord, of jealousy./ It is the green-eyed monster which doth mock/ The meat it feeds on" (III, iii, 165–67). Cf. entry 43.20.

500.22/490.12 WHAT THE EYE CAN'T SEE THE HEART CAN'T GRIEVE FOR   This phrase is proverbial and goes back at least as far as John Heywood's *Proverbs* (1546).

500.25/490.15 LAUGHING WITCH   This is from Beaufoy's story, mentioned earlier on p. 459.6/450.31. See entry 68.39.

500.25/490.15 THE HAND THAT ROCKS THE CRADLE   See entry 288.13.

501.7/490.24 LOVE ME. LOVE ME NOT. LOVE ME   This alludes to a game children play to determine whether someone loves them. They point to a series of objects (or perhaps pull petals from a flower) saying alternately "She loves me," "She loves me not." The truth is indicated by whichever phrase happens to be said with the final object. The Opies list several such games in their *Lore and Language of Schoolchildren*, pp. 334 ff., but they do not list this one.

501.9/490.26 SILENT MEANS CONSENT   "Silence gives consent" is a proverbial saying. The *ODEP* lists several instances of the expression, including James Kelly's *Proverbs* (1721).

501.11/490.28 HOT HANDS COLD GIZZARD   This is probably a variation on the proverbial "Cold hands, warm heart"; the *ODEP* lists "A cold hand and a warm heart."

501.29/491.15 THE JUST MAN FALLS SEVEN TIMES   Proverbs 24:16 says, "For a just man falleth seven times, and riseth up again: but the wicked shall fall into mischief."

501.30/491.16 AFTER YOU IS GOOD MANNERS   In Swift's *Polite Conversation*, second conversation, Lady Answerall says to Lady Smart, "O, Madam, after you is good Manners" (p. 133). Partridge says this is "17th–19th century" and that James Kelly (1721) notes that it is "spoken when our betters offer to serve us first."

503.29/493.12 BENEDETTO MARCELLO   Marcello (1686–1739) was an Italian composer, best known for his musical setting of fifty of the Psalms (1724–27), an English edition of which was brought out in London in 1757.

503.30/493.13 IT MAY BE AN OLD HYMN TO DEMETER OR ALSO ILLUSTRATE CAELA ENARRANT GLORIAM DOMINI   Demeter (Ceres in the Roman pantheon) was goddess of all grains and fruits, of sowing and reaping, and of agriculture generally. Stephen is probably thinking specifically of the ancient Greek "Hymn to Demeter," ascribed to Homer, "a composition of great ritualistic value, probably of the 7th century B.C." (*Encyc. Brit.*, 11th ed., XIX, 118; the article goes on to describe the hymn in some detail). Stephen's Latin phrase slightly modifies the Vulgate version of Psalms 18:1 (King James 19): "Caeli enarrant gloriam Dei" ("The heavens declare the glory of God"—Stephen's says "of the Lord").

504.3/493.16 HYPERPHRYGIAN AND MIXOLYDIAN   These terms refer to "modes" or "keys" of ancient Greek music. It was thought that the various modes were associated with and expressed particular emotions. Stephen's statement may derive from discussions of this idea by Plato and Aristotle. In Book III of *The Republic*, Plato characterizes the Phrygian harmonies as expressive of religious feeling and of temperance, while the Lydian harmonies are said to be expressive of sorrow and to be soft and relaxed (Book III, secs. 398–400). Aristotle also contrasts the mixed Lydian and the Phrygian modes, saying the former produces "a mood of comparative melancholy and restraint," and that by the latter "we are excited to enthusiasm" (*Politics*, Book V, chap. v). For a general discussion of this subject, see D. B. Monro, *The Modes of Ancient Greek Music* (Oxford, 1894).

504.4/493.17 DAVID'S THAT IS CIRCE'S OR WHAT AM I SAYING CERES' ALTAR Ceres is another name for Demeter. Stephen is still thinking about his comparison between the "Hymn to Demeter" and David's Psalms. Cf. entry 503.30. "Circe's" is an inebriated, but thoroughly appropriate, interpolation.

504.5/493.18 DAVID'S TIP FROM THE STABLE TO HIS CHIEF BASOONIST "Tip from the stable" is probably equivalent to "tip straight from the horse's mouth"; cf. entry 146.33. Stephen seems to be thinking of the titles or superscriptions that preface many of the Psalms. While none refer specifically to a basoonist, several do say "To the chief musician," and among these is the Psalm Stephen alluded to in entry 503.30. (See, for example, Psalms 11, 14, 19, 31.) The meaning of these superscriptions has long been a puzzle; see *A Catholic Commentary on Holy Scripture* (London, 1953), pp. 443–44.

504.7/493.20 JETEZ LA GOURME "Sow the wild oats"; see entry 192.28.

504.16/493.29 WHETSTONE See entry 211.21.

504.31/494.12 THE HOLY CITY "The Holy City" is a song by Frederick Edward Weatherly and Stephen Adams (pseudonym of Michael Maybrick), written in 1892. The chorus says, "Jerusalem, Jerusalem, Lift up your gates and sing, Hosanna in the highest, Hosanna to your king." I have never seen or heard a version of the song with exactly the words given on p. 507.5/496.15. For words and music, see the *Song Dex Treasury of Humorous and Nostalgic Songs*, I, 483.

505.2/494.14 WHAT WENT FORTH TO THE ENDS OF THE WORLD . . . SELF WHICH IT ITSELF WAS INELUCTABLY PRECONDITIONED TO BECOME This echoes Stephen's earlier thoughts about a passage from Maeterlinck. See p. 217.24/214.33 and entry 213.14. R. Ellmann also finds in this paragraph what seems to him an echo of Benedetto Croce's précis of Vico in his chapter on Vico in his *Aesthetic* (*JJ*, p. 351).

505.3/494.15 GOD, THE SUN, SHAKESPEARE See entry 212.40.

505.5/494.17 NOISE IN THE STREET See entry 34.33.

505.22/495.6 ANTICHRIST The Antichrist is conceived of as a figure of great evil whose coming will precede the Second Coming and the Day of Judgment. He is mentioned several times in I and II John. In I John 2:18 we read, "Little children, it is the last time: and as ye have heard that antichrist shall come, even now are there many antichrists; whereby we know that it is the last time." I John

2:22 defines the antichrist as he "that denieth the Father and the Son."

506.6/495.15 A TIME, TIMES AND HALF A TIME   This formula is used several times in the Bible to indicate the span of time that must pass before the Day of Judgment. Revelation 12:14 says, "And to the woman were given two wings of a great eagle, that she might fly into the wilderness, into her place, where she is nourished for a time, and times, and half a time, from the face of the serpent." See also Daniel 7:25 and 12:7.

506.7/495.16 REUBEN J. ANTICHRIST, WANDERING JEW   This blends Reuben J. Dodd, an actual person who was first mentioned on p. 94.16/93.9, and Antichrist, on which see entry 505.22. On the Wandering Jew, see entry 217.35.

506.8/495.17 ACROSS HIS LOINS IS SLUNG . . .   In light of entry 506.12, this probably alludes to and parodies the procedure for mourning for an only son, described in Jeremiah 6:26 and Amos 8:10. See entry 506.12.

506.12/495.20 HIS ONLY SON   Though this clearly echoes Christ's frequently being called God's "only begotten son" (see John 1:18 and 3:16 for example), the context suggests an allusion to Old Testament passages that describe mourning for an only son (cf. entry 506.8). Amos 8:10 says, "And I will turn your feasts into mourning, and all your songs into lamentation; and I will bring up sackcloth upon all loins, and baldness upon every head; and I will make it as the mourning of an only son, and the end thereof as a bitter day." The metaphorical application of these mourning procedures for an only son to the end of Israel is appropriate to this apocalyptic section of *Ulysses*.

506.15/495.24 ALLY SLOPER NOSE   J. Redding Ware explains Ally Sloper as "A dissipated-looking old man with a red and swollen nose. Invented by Mr. Charles Ross, who ran him in print for a score of years" (*Passing English of the Victorian Era*, p. 6).

506.23/496.1 L'HOMME QUI RIT   This alludes to the title of a novel by Victor Hugo, *L'Homme Qui Rit* (1869). The title means "The Man Who Laughs"; Gwynplaine, the title character of the novel, was mutilated as a child, and one result of the mutilation is that his mouth stretches from ear to ear in the semblance of a perpetual laugh.

507.5/496.15 JERUSALEM . . .   From "The Holy City"; see entry 504.31.

507.10/496.19 SECOND COMING OF ELIJAH   The second coming of

Elijah is to precede "the great and dreadful day of the Lord" (Mal. 4:5). See entry 151.15.

507.11/496.21 THE END OF THE WORLD, A TWOHEADED OCTOPUS . . . The context here is similar to that on p. 165.25/163.11; see entry 165.25.

507.14/496.23 THE THREE LEGS OF MAN   This alludes to the triskellion, a device depicting three human legs radiating from a single center. The symbol, which was probably originally a solar emblem, is ancient, going back at least as far as the coinage of fifth century B.C. Lycia. It is also the heraldic device of the Isle of Man, on which see entry 120.30.

507.16/496.26 WHA'LL DANCE THE KEEL ROW . . .   This alludes to an old Scottish song, "Weel May the Keel Row," or "Smiling Polly." The girl singing the song says, "O weel may the keel row, the keel row, the keel row, O weel may the keel row, that my laddie's in." For words and music, see Chapple, *Old English Popular Music*, II, 185–86.

507.21/496.31 OLD GLORY   Old Glory is a popular name for the American flag. American poet James Whitcomb Riley (1849–1916) wrote a poem entitled "The Name of Old Glory."

507.27/497.3 TELL MOTHER YOU'LL BE THERE   *Variety Cavalcade* lists "Tell Mother I'll Be There" as the title of a hymn written by Charles M. Fillmore, copyrighted in 1890. The *Judson Concordance to Hymns* lists the song and says that it begins, "When I was but a little child."

507.30/497.5 JUST ONE WORD MORE.   Robert Browning wrote a poem to his wife entitled "One Word More," but allusion to it here seems unlikely.

507.31/497.9 BE ON THE SIDE OF THE ANGELS   This alludes to Benjamin Disraeli's well-known comment in his speech at the Oxford Diocesan Conference, 1864: "The question is this: Is man an ape or an angel? I, my lord, am on the side of the angels." Cf. the following entry.

508.1/497.10 BE A PRISM   Since this immediately follows Disraeli's comment about being on the side of the angels (preceding entry), it suggests an allusion to the occasionally quoted statement Disraeli made in a speech before the House of Commons on February 15, 1849: "A man, always studying one subject, will view the general affairs of the world through the colored prism of his own atmosphere."

508.1/497.11 THE HIGHER SELF   This term is common in theosophical lore, but since the context here is American, Joyce may be alluding in part to Transcendentalism. For the use of "Higher Self" in theosophy, see Mme Blavatsky's *Key to Theosophy*, esp. pp. 153 ff. (see entry 185.29).

508.2/497.11   A JESUS, A GAUTAMA, AN INGERSOLL   Siddhartha Gautama was the name of the Buddha. American orator, lawyer, and writer Robert G. Ingersoll (1833–99) was known as "the great agnostic."

508.9/497.18   A. J. CHRIST DOWIE   On fanatical American evangelist Alexander J. Dowie, see entry 151.15.

508.14/497.23   JERU . . . WHORUSALAMINYOURHIGHHOHHHH   From "The Holy City"; see entry 504.31.

508.23/497.33   CERTAINLY, I SORT OF BELIEVE STRONG IN YOU . . .   H. K. Russell has pointed out to me that this portion of *Ulysses* owes something to Gertrude Stein's "Melanctha," though this involves an anachronism since that work was not published until after 1904. The passage in "Melanctha" which this section of *Ulysses* seems to echo most closely is a conversation between Melanctha and Dr. Campbell, in which Melanctha says, "It don't seem to me Dr. Campbell that I admire that way to do things very much. It certainly ain't really to me being very good. It certainly ain't any more to me Dr. Campbell, but that you certainly are awful scared about really feeling things way down in you, and that's certainly the only way Dr. Campbell I can see that you can mean, by what it is that you are always saying to me" (*Three Lives*, Vintage Books, p. 123).

508.26/497.36   I DON'T NEVER SEE NO WUSSER SCARED FEMALE . . . AND HE AIN'T SAYING NOTHING   Words and phrases here suggest an allusion to Joel Chandler Harris' Uncle Remus stories. Probably Joyce is interested mainly in bringing this kind of American speech into the passage, and there may be no allusion to a specific story. But "and he ain't saying nothing" is very close to the refrain describing the tar-baby in "The Wonderful Tar-Baby Story"—which is the best known of all the stories. Several times we are told that Brer Rabbit tries to get the tar-baby to speak, "but Tar-Baby ain't sayin' nothin." Also, "done seed" for "saw" or "have seen" is typical of Uncle Remus, but too common in the stories to specify a single source. The only other allusion to these stories in *Ulysses* occurs in a similar context near the end of the "Oxen of the Sun" episode. See entry 425.27.

508.34/498.8   A MONTMORENCY   The Montmorency family is an old, distinguished French family. The name derives from Montmorency,

NNW of Paris, and dates back to the tenth century. The family has included many constables, marshalls, cardinals, and grandmasters of knightly orders, etc., and was declared by Henry IV to be, after the Bourbons, the first house in Europe.

509.8/498.17 IN THE BEGINNING WAS THE WORD, IN THE END THE WORLD WITHOUT END. BLESSED BE THE EIGHT BEATITUDES   "In the beginning was the Word" is John 1:1. "World without end" is from the Gloria Patri; see entry 29.24. The beatitudes occur in Matthew 5:2–12, but there are more than eight. On the eight British beatitudes, see entry 424.35.

509.15/498.24 BARNUM   This may allude to the American showman P. T. Barnum (1810–91), founder of the circus called "The Greatest Show on Earth."

509.19/498.28 SEEK THOU THE LIGHT   This probably derives from Christ's statement "I am the light of the world: he that followeth me shall not walk in darkness, but shall have the light of life" (John 8:12; John 9:5 is similar). But Lyster is doubtless also referring to the "inward light"; see entry 193.15.

509.21/498.30 HE CORANTOS BY   This probably alludes to Twelfth Night; see entry 184.14.

509.28/499.6 A THING OF BEAUTY . . .   Keats's Endymion begins, "A thing of beauty is a joy forever." Molly later thinks of this line on p. 771.6/756.8.

510.5/499.11 TANDERAGEE   Tanderagee is a town in county Armagh, in the north of Ireland. But I have not been able to learn whether there is any sound basis for Joyce's associating Eglinton with this town (see entry 206.37).

510.7/499.14 MANANAAN MACLIR   Mananaan MacLir is the Irish god of the sea; see entry 38.24. But there may also be an allusion here to A.E.'s play Dierdre, for in his As I Was Going Down Sackville Street, Oliver St. John Gogarty says that A.E. appeared in this play as the head of Mananaan (New York, 1937, p. 292). In every printed copy of the play I have seen, Mananaan does not appear, but is simply invoked by the druid, Cathvah. But it would be an easy matter to alter the play in production so as to allow Mananaan to appear briefly, and Gogarty's description is probably correct.

510.14/499.21 AUM! HEK! WAL! AK! LUB! MOR! MA! . . .   This entire paragraph involves esoteric and theosophical lore, and the sources cited in entry 185.29 should be consulted. For a discussion of the mysterious monosyllable AUM, see Mme Blavatsky's Isis Unveiled, II, 31 ff. Many of these exclamations are discussed by A.E. in his *The Candle of Vision* (London, 1931), esp. pp. 116–34. Hermes Trismegistus is the name given by Neo-Platonists to the Egyptian god Thoth (cf. entry 193.38); various esoteric writings were attributed to him. Shiva and Shakti are a man-and-wife pair of Hindu deities. Shiva is known as "The Destroyer," while Shakti represents the female principal or creative power.

510.22/499.29   I AM THE LIGHT OF THE HOMESTEAD   This blends Christ's statement "I am the light of the world" (see entry 509.19) and the *Irish Homestead*, a magazine edited by A.E. See entries 191.29, 185.32, and 510.23.

510.23/499.30   I AM THE DREAMERY CREAMERY BUTTER   This combines A.E.'s theosophical and dairying interests. See the preceding entry and entry 185.32.

510.24/499.31   A SKELETON JUDASHAND STRANGLES THE LIGHT   I can find no specific allusion here beyond that to Judas as traitor and the light as representative of Christ (cf. entry 509.19).

511.14/500.18   MAKES SHEEP'S EYES   This familiar expression occurs in Swift's *Polite Conversation*, first conversation, when Lady Smart says to Miss Notable, "Pray, Miss, how do you like Mr. *Spruce*, I swear I have seen him often cast a Sheep's Eye out of a Calve's Head at you, deny it if you can" (p. 71). Partridge says "Earliest and usually *cast a sheep's eye*: 16th–20th centuries. A sheep has a large, soft, liquid eye."

511.21/500.25   LIPOTI VIRAG   F. Budgen points out the similarity of Virag to Hilarion, the pupil of St. Anthony who repeatedly appears to the saint in Flaubert's *The Temptation of St. Anthony* (*JJMU*, p. 239).

512.7/501.10   OUR TRIBAL ELIXIR OF GOPHERWOOD   Gopherwood is mentioned only once in the Bible, as the wood of which Noah's ark was built (Gen. 6:14). The term occurs in the King James, but not in the Douay Bible.

512.12/501.15   HIPPOGRIFF   The hippogriff is a fabulous beast with the wings, head, and claws of a griffin and the hindquarters of a horse.

512.21/501.24   NEVER PUT ON YOU TOMORROW WHAT YOU CAN WEAR TODAY   This plays on the proverbial "Never put off till tomorrow what you can do today." The *ODEP* lists many instances.

512.30/501.33   LILY OF THE ALLEY   This derives originally from the statement in Song of Solomon 2:1: "I am the rose of Sharon, and the lily of the valleys," now often applied to Christ. Hodgart and Worthington also list this as an allusion to two songs, "The Lily of the Valley," by Gilbert and Friedland, and "Sally in Our

Alley," by Carey. But allusion to L. Wolfe Gilbert and Anatole Friedland's "Lily of the Valley," while possible, is unlikely, since the song was not copyrighted until 1917 (see Spaeth, *Hist. of Pop. Music in Amer.*, p. 404, or *Variety Cavalcade*, p. 353).

512.31/501.33 BACHELOR'S BUTTON DISCOVERED BY RUALDUS COLUMBUS As R. M. Adams has explained (*SS*, p. 140), anatomist Rualdus (or Realdus) Columbus (1516–59) is said to have discovered the clitoris. But though Rualdus himself thought that he had discovered the organ, its existence had already been pointed out by earlier anatomists.

512.31/502.1 TUMBLE HER This probably alludes to Ophelia's song, which Stephen alluded to earlier. See entries 191.17 and 191.13.

513.3/502.5 WHAT HO, SHE BUMPS As Hodgart and Worthington point out, this alludes to a music hall song, "What Ho, She Bumps." The song was apparently written by Harry Castling and A. J. Mills and sung by Charles Bignall.

513.4/502.5 UGLY DUCKLING This alludes to Hans Christian Andersen's nursery story which tells of an ungainly duckling who was derided by his fellow ducklings for his ugliness but who finally put them to shame by turning out to be a beautiful swan.

513.7/502.8 WHEN YOU COME OUT WITHOUT YOUR GUN The context and the word "regretfully" suggest an allusion to the proverb that says, "What things we see when we don't have a gun!" The only place I have found this saying listed is in the "Proverbs" section of *Stevenson's Book of Quotations*, which says that the origin of the proverb is unknown (p. 1644).

513.9/502.10 PAY YOUR MONEY, TAKE YOUR CHOICE This alludes to the proverbial "You pays your money and you takes your choice," listed in the *Oxford Dictionary of Quotations* and the *ODEP*.

513.10/502.11 HOW HAPPY COULD YOU BE WITH EITHER This alludes to a song sung by Macheath in act II of John Gay's *The Beggar's Opera* (1728). The song begins, "How happy I could be with either,/ Were t'other dear charmer away."

513.28/502.28 FLESHHOTPOTS OF EGYPT TO HANKER AFTER This alludes to a passage in Exodus which has been alluded to earlier in *Ulysses*. See entry 41.32.

513.28/502.29 LYCOPODIUM Though this appears to be an allusion, it is not, for, as R. M. Adams has explained (*SS*, p. 140), a lycopodium is a type of club moss, of the genus *Lycopodium*. It is known as "vegetable brimstone" because of its inflammability, and it is used in theaters in the production of stage lighting.

513.29/502.30 SLAPBANG! THERE HE GOES AGAIN Hodgart and Worthington list this as an allusion to a music hall song entitled "Slap Bang! Here We Are Again," by Sheridan. Christopher Pulling, in his *They Were Singing*, briefly mentions the song and quotes the chorus: "Slap bang! Here we are again;/ Here we are again; here we are again./ Slap bang! Here we are again./ What jolly dogs are we!" (p. 123). Words to a similar song entitled "Bang Slap, What Jolly Dogs" can be found in the paperback *Favorite Songster* (Dublin, n.d.), p. 79.

514.4/503.2   IN THE CONSULSHIP OF DIPLODOCUS AND ICHTHYOSAURUS These are not allusions to persons in Greek or Roman history. Both of these are extinct reptiles. *Argumentam ad feminam* is a variation of the logical fallacy called *argumentam ad hominem*, which involves identifying the truth of a thesis with the character of the person supporting the thesis.

514.5/503.2   FOR THE REST EVE'S SOVERIGN REMEDY   Though the context suggests that the "soverign remedy" is sex, I do not understand the basis of the allusion, unless Eve is used generally to represent all women.

514.6/503.3   HUGUENOT   See entry 168.20.

514.9/503.6   WHEATENMEAL WITH HONEY AND NUTMEG   The context suggests that this is a traditional remedy for warts, but though I have read of many strange cures, I have not come across this one. Many such cures are listed in E. and M. A. Radford, *Encyclopaedia of Superstitions*, *s.v.* Warts.

514.18/503.16   LA CAUSA È SANTA. TARA. TARA   See entry 168.20.

514.22/503.20   TOUCH OF A DEADHAND CURES   This refers to an old superstition. In his book *The Old Bailey and Newgate* (New York and London, n.d.), Charles Gordon devotes several paragraphs (and an illustration) to discussing and quoting accounts of peoples' allowing the executioner to rub a newly hanged man's hand on them as a reputed cure for wens and marks (pp. 226–28).

514.31/503.29   BULGAR AND THE BASQUE   I do not understand what Virag means here; if this phrase involves an allusion, it eludes me. "Bulgar" means Bulgarian, and the Basques live in the Pyrenees.

515.2/503.34   FROM THE SUBLIME TO THE RIDICULOUS IS BUT A STEP This phrase is proverbial (the *ODEP* lists "There is but one step from the sublime to the ridiculous"), but its origin is unknown. It is usually attributed to Napoleon or to Thomas Paine.

515.11/504.7   BUT TOMORROW IS A NEW DAY WILL BE   "Tomorrow is a new day" is proverbial and is listed in the *ODEP*. It also occurs in Swift's *Polite Conversation*, first conversation, when Miss Notable says, "Well, well, To morrow's a new Day" (p. 77). Partridge says it is a "16th-20th century proverb, with an Ancient Greek prototype."

515.19/504.14 THEY HAD A PROVERB IN THE CARPATHIANS ...   Mackie Jarrell says of this, "This inflated version of 'Honey draws more flies than vinegar' is probably modeled on one, or two, of Swift's favorite devices: the 'ancient' proverbs of his own manufacture, as in 'the old Sclavonian proverb' in *A Tale of a Tub*, and his frequent distortion of proverbs and other familiar sayings" (*PMLA*, LXXII, 551).

516.5/505.1 OPEN SESAME   This is from the *Arabian Nights* story "Ali Baba and the Forty Thieves." See entry 307.26. The allusion is repeated on p. 516.16/505.12.

516.13/505.9 WITH MY EYEGLASS IN MY OCULAR   This alludes to a duet by Bunthorne and Jane in act II of Gilbert and Sullivan's *Patience* (1881). Bunthorne says of his rival, the "Idyllic Poet," Grosvenor, "I'll tell him that unless he will consent to be more jocular—/ To cut his curly hair, and stick an eyeglass in his ocular—/ ... He'd better clear away with all convenient rapidity."

516.18/505.14 YET EVE AND THE SERPENT CONTRADICT   Bloom is thinking of Eve's lack of fear of the serpent in the story of the temptation in Genesis 3.

516.22/505.18 ELEPHANTULIASIS   As R. M. Adams points out (*SS*, p. 140), this is a nonsense word. Apparently it is based on elephantiasis, a disease of the lymphatic system.

516.35/505.32 O, I MUCH FEAR HE SHALL BE MOST BADLY BURNED   There may be an echo here of Stephen's statement to Father Artifoni about Giordano Bruno, as recorded in *Stephen Hero*. When Father Artifoni refers to Bruno as a "terrible heretic," Stephen replies, "Yes ... and he was most terribly burned" (p. 175). Bruno (*ca.* 1548–1600), Italian philosopher and monk, was constantly in trouble with the Church for his unorthodox ideas. He was finally excommunicated and burned at the stake in 1600.

517.6/506.3 I'M A TINY TINY THING ...   This seems to be a nursery rhyme, and Hodgart and Worthington list it as one, but I have not been able to find it in any of the collections or indexes of children's rhymes or nursery rhymes which I have consulted.

517.18/506.15 JACOB'S PIPE   See entry 413.20.

517.22/506.19 THE TENOR MARIO, PRINCE OF CANDIA   On Mario, who did come from a noble family and had the title Cavaliere de Candia, see entry 117.30.

517.28/506.23 THERE IS A FLOWER THAT BLOOMETH   This is from W. V. Wallace's *Maritana*. See entry 461.28.

517.33/506.29   FILLING MY BELLY WITH HUSKS OF SWINE . . . I WILL ARISE
AND GO TO MY   Both of these phrases allude to the Parable of the
Prodigal Son. Luke 15:16 says, "And he would fain have filled his
belly with the husks that the swine did eat: and no man gave unto
him," and in Luke 15:18 the Prodigal says, "I will arise and go to
my father, and I will say unto him, Father, I have sinned against
heaven, and before thee."

517.35/506.31   THOU ART IN A PARLOUS WAY   In *As You Like It*,
Touchstone says to Corin, "Thou art in a parlous state, shepherd"
(III, ii, 45).

518.11/507.6   LOVE'S OLD SWEET SONG   On "Love's Old Sweet Song,"
see entry 63.31.

518.16/507.11   THE BIRD THAT CAN SING AND WON'T SING   This alludes
to the proverbial "The bird that can sing and won't sing must be
made to sing." The *ODEP* lists this proverb, *s.v.* "Little birds,"
and cites several instances, including two early proverb collections.

518.17/507.12   PHILIP DRUNK AND PHILIP SOBER   "To appeal from
Philip drunk to Philip sober" is proverbial. It goes back to the story
of a woman who was given an unjust sentence by Philip of Macedon while he was drunk. She said she would appeal, and when
asked "To whom?" said "From Philip drunk to Philip sober." The
story says that Philip allowed the appeal and, when sober, reversed
his judgment.

518.19/507.14   MATTHEW ARNOLD'S FACE   See entry 7.30.

518.23/507.18   IF YOUTH BUT KNEW   Stephen alluded to this same
proverb earlier; see entry 30.24.

519.1/507.25   ZOE MOU SAS AGAPO   This is the Greek line that ends
each stanza of Byron's poem "Maid of Athens, ere We Part." It
says "My life, I love you."

519.4/507.27   SWINBURNE   A. C. Swinburne is alluded to several
times in *Ulysses*; see the Index.

519.8/508.2   SPIRIT IS WILLING BUT THE FLESH IS WEAK   When Christ
found Peter and the two sons of Zebedee asleep while he was pray-
ing in Gethsemane, he said, "The spirit indeed is willing, but the
flesh is weak" (Matt. 26:41; Mark 14:38 is similar).

519.23/508.17   FALL OF MAN   The Fall of Man is described in Genesis
3. Cf. entry 516.18.

519.24/508.18   NOTHING NEW UNDER THE SUN   This alludes to Ecclesiastes 1:9, "and there is no new thing under the sun."

519.26/508.20   WHY I LEFT THE CHURCH OF ROME. READ THE PRIEST, THE
WOMAN AND THE CONFESSIONAL   On *Why I Left the Church of
Rome*, see entry 189.26.

519.27/508.21   FLIPPERTY JIPPERT   "The foul fiend Flibbertigibbet" is one of the fiends mentioned by Mad Tom (Edgar) in *King Lear*, III, iv, 120. Shakespeare got the names of most of these fiends from a book by Samuel Harsnett entitled *A Declaration of Egregious Popish Impostures* . . . (1602–3). Cf. entry 519.26.

519.29/508.23 OFFERS HER ALLMOIST YONI TO MAN'S LINGAM   *Lingam* and *yoni* are Sanskrit words for the male and female sexual organs, respectively. The terms occur commonly in Hindu writings, especially in the *Kama Sutra*, the famous Hindu work on love.

520.20/509.12 MOONCALF   In *The Tempest*, II, ii, Stephano several times refers to Caliban as a "mooncalf."

520.22/509.14 HE HAD TWO LEFT FEET   As J. S. Atherton points out (*Books at the Wake*, p. 65), this alludes to a depiction of Christ in the *Book of Kells*. In Sir Edward Sullivan's edition (2nd ed.; London, 1920) of the book it appears in Plate II, "The Virgin and the Child." In this depiction both of the child's feet are left feet, and both of the Virgin's are right feet.

520.22/509.14 HE WAS JUDAS IACCHIAS   This sentence offers various attempts to explain who Christ was and is based on a similar passage in Flaubert's *The Temptation of St. Anthony*. Since Iacchias (or Iacchus) was the name given to Bacchus in certain of the Eleusinian mysteries, and Judas was the betrayer of Christ, the name suggests that Christ was a Dionysiac who betrayed his cult. If the other two phrases in this sentence involve specific allusions, I am not aware of it.

520.25/509.17 A SON OF A WHORE, APOCALYPSE   Apocalypse is the name of the book of Revelation in the Douay Bible. I can find nothing precisely like this in Revelation. Probably this is related to the earlier charge that Bloom is a worshiper of the Scarlet Woman; see entry 492.18.

521.2/509.25 QUI VOUS A MIS DANS CETTE FICHUE POSITION   This alludes to Léo Taxil's book mentioned earlier. See entry 41.14.

521.10/510.4 METCHNIKOFF   Elie Metchnikoff (1845–1916) was a Russian bacteriologist and Nobel prize winner (1908). In 1904 he showed that higher apes can be inoculated with syphilis.

521.17/510.11 THREE WISE VIRGINS   See entry 145.18.

521.21/510.15 PANTHER, THE ROMAN CENTURION, POLLUTED HER WITH HIS GENITORIES   The story that Mary's child was by a soldier named Panthera apparently goes back to the second-century Roman philosopher Celsus, an avid anti Christian. He wrote a tract called *The True Discourse*, which has not survived, but much of it is given in Origen's detailed reply *Contra Celsus* (see Wm. Schutte, *JS*, p. 101). This story about Panther is mentioned in a section of Flaubert's *Temptation of St. Anthony*, similar to the present one in *Ulysses*, in which a variety of explanations of Christ's birth are offered.

521.23/510.17 HE BURST HER TYMPANUM   This alludes to the idea, quite common in the Middle Ages, that the Virgin Mary conceived Christ through her ear, by the agency of the Word of God. E. S. Hartland, in his *Primitive Paternity*, briefly discusses the idea, quotes examples of it from St. Augustine and from a hymn by St. Bonaventura, and cites further material on it (I, 20).

521.25/510.19 HIK! HEK! HAK! HOK! HUK! KOK! KUK!   Cf. entry 510.14.

522.3/510.26 WHEN LOVE ABSORBS MY ARDENT SOUL   This is from "Love and War"; see entry 256.21.

522.15/511.7 WHEN FIRST I SAW   This is from "M'Appari," from Flotow's *Martha*. See entry 256.26.

522.21/511.13 FAREWELL. FARE THEE WELL   In light of the recent Byron allusion (p. 519.1/507.25), this may allude to Byron's poem to his wife which begins, "Fare thee well! and if for ever,/ Still for ever fare *thee well*."

522.25/511.16 HIS WILD HARP SLUNG BEHIND HIM   This alludes to Thomas Moore's song "The Minstrel Boy." See entry 263.3.

523.4/511.23 ALL IS LOST NOW   From "Tutto è Sciolto." See entry 256.24.

523.11/511.30 THE FIGHTING PARSON WHO FOUNDED THE PROTESTANT ERROR   This refers to Martin Luther (1483–1546), German leader of the Protestant Reformation.

523.12/512.1 BUT BEWARE ANTISTHENES, THE DOG SAGE   See entry 148.29.

523.13/512.2 THE LAST END OF ARIUS HERESIARCHIUS. THE AGONY IN THE CLOSET   On Arius, see entry 21.8; on his death, see entry 38.18.

523.18/512.7 SOVERIGN LORD OF ALL THINGS   Though this sounds biblical, it is not. The word *sovereign* does not occur in the King James Bible, and while "sovereign Lord" is used several times in the Douay Bible, Stephen's exact phrase is not used.

523.24/512.13 MONKS OF THE SCREW   The Monks of the Screw, or the Order of St. Patrick, was an eighteenth-century Irish convivial society. During meetings they wore monkish habits. Irish lawyer and orator John Philpott Curran, who was a member of the group, wrote a song entitled "The Monks of the Screw." The third stanza begins, "My brethren, be chaste, till you're tempted;/ While sober, be grave and discreet;/ And humble your bodies with fasting,/ As oft as you've nothing to eat." For the words of the song and a description of the society, see *Irish Literature*, II, 797–98.

524.10/512.24 CONSERVIO LIES CAPTURED . . . In his "Alphabetical Notebook," Joyce has the following: "The verses he [i.e., his father, John Joyce] quotes most are: *Conservio lies captured! He lies in the lowest dungeons/ With manacles and chains around his limbs/ Weighing upwards of three tons*" (*s.v.* Pappie). Conservio is probably a character from a pantomime or popular entertainment of some sort, but I have not identified him.

524.18/513.1 O, THE POOR LITTLE FELLOW . . . Mabel Worthington has pointed out the allusion here to the anonymous Irish ballad "Nell Flaherty's Drake" (*PMLA*, LXXI, 338). She also prints the second stanza of the ballad, of which this passage in *Ulysses* is an adaptation. For complete words to the song, see Hoagland, p. 289.

525.3/513.19 SHALL CARRY MY HEART TO THEE . . . Hodgart and Worthington consider this a part of the song "Winds That Blow from the South," which was alluded to earlier on p. 156.8/154.3. I have not located the song.

525.25/514.6 FINGERS WAS MADE BEFORE FORKS This proverbial saying occurs in Swift's *Polite Conversation*, second conversation, when Colonel Atwit says to Miss Notable, "Here, Miss, they say, Fingers were made before Forks, and Hands before Knives" (p. 132). Partridge says that this proverb "goes back to *ca.* 1550. In the 19th–20th centuries, the latter half has usually been omitted."

525.28/514.9 HAVE IT NOW OR WAIT TILL YOU GET IT? This, too, occurs in Swift's *Polite Conversation*, first conversation. Miss Notable says to Neverout, "Will you have it now, or stay till you get it?" (p. 61). Partridge says this is a 17th to 20th century catch-phrase, "the 19th–20th form being '. . . wait . . .'."

526.9/514.22 IN SVENGALI'S FUR OVERCOAT Svengali is the scheming hypnotist in British writer George Du Maurier's (1834–96) popular novel *Trilby* (1894). The novel was also adapted for the stage by several writers and was a popular melodrama.

526.9/514.22 WITH FOLDED ARMS AND NAPOLEONIC FORELOCK This refers to a traditional stance of Napoleon.

526.12/514.25 GIVES THE SIGN OF PAST MASTER . . . Here, as earlier on p. 456.18/448.14, Bloom gives a Masonic sign. The degree of Past Master is an honorary degree conferred on the Master of a lodge at his installation into office. See any dictionary of Freemasonry for further details.

526.27/515.8 EAT AND BE MERRY FOR TOMORROW See entry 172.4.

526.29/515.10 BETTER LATE THAN NEVER This common proverbial phrase is listed in the *ODEP*.

527.4/515.15 MINNIE HAUCK IN CARMEN Minnie Hauck (or Hauk)

(1852–1929) was an American mezzo-soprano, best known for the performance as Carmen in Bizet's opera *Carmen*. She studied assiduously for the role and made a great hit in it in London, and hers was the first American performance of the work, October 23, 1878. She sang the role some five hundred times in French, English, German, and Italian.

527.20/515.31 PETTICOAT GOVERNMENT   "Petticoat government," though now a common phrase, apparently originated with Washington Irving, who used it in *Knickerbocker's History of New York*, chap. IV, and in "Rip Van Winkle." For allusions to "Rip Van Winkle" in *Ulysses*, see entries 377.23 and 542.3 and the Index.

528.22/516.29 KING DAVID AND THE SUNAMITE   Abishag the Shunammite was a maiden David took to himself in his old age as a nurse, but "he knew her not." The decision had been made to get a young maiden for David because he was cold and she was to lie in his bosom and keep him warm. See I Kings 1, esp. verses 1–5.

528.26/517.2 MOCKING IS CATCH   The proverbial saying alluded to here occurs in Swift's *Polite Conversation*, first conversation, when Lady Answerall says, "they say mocking is catching" (p. 96). Partridge says this is a sixteenth- to twentieth-century proverb.

528.29/517.5 ALL THINGS END   This, too, has its counterpart in Swift's *Polite Conversation*, first conversation, in Mr. Neverout's "Well, all Things have an End, and a Pudden has two" (p. 103). Partridge says this proverb is "mid-16th-mid-19th century."

529.23/517.27 MY LOVE'S YOUNG DREAM   This alludes to Thomas Moore's song "Love's Young Dream." See entry 365.2.

530.4/518.8 HANDY ANDY   Andy Rooney, known as "Handy Andy," is a character in Irish writer Samuel Lover's novel *Handy Andy* (1842). Known for his faculty of doing everything wrong, he is finally discovered to be an Irish peer, Lord Scatterbrain.

530.17/518.21 WITH A HARD BASILISK STARE   On the basilisk, see entry 194.21.

531.10/519.13 WITH A PIERCING EPILEPTIC CRY SHE SINKS ON ALL FOURS   Bloom's falling down before Bella as a pig is one of the clearest echoes in this episode of the Circe story in the *Odyssey*, book X, where Circe transforms the men into beasts.

532.23/520.26 THE NUBIAN SLAVE OF OLD   The idea of a Nubian as a slave is so common that one meaning the *OED* gives for *Nubian* is "a Nubian slave." If this phrase involves any specific allusion, I have not discovered it.

532.29/521.3 LICENSED VICTUALLER'S GAZETTE   In the Cornell "Alphabetical Notebook," *s.v.* Pappie, Joyce records of his father, "He reads the *Licensed Victuallers' Gazette.*" According to *Willing's Press Guide* . . . 1905 (for 1904), the *Licensed Victuallers' Gazette* was a weekly appearing on Friday, which sold for 2*d.* This magazine has an advertisement on p. 443 of *Willing's* which is interesting: "Attention is called to the fact that in all the principal hotels, taverns, and other licensed houses throughout England, Scotland, Ireland, and Wales, is the *Licensed Victuallers' Gazette* taken in, because its well known literary features form an attraction to the proprietors' customers themselves. . . . The ordinary business advertiser may be sure of his announcements being read by multitudes of the general public, as the *Licensed Victuallers' Gazette* lies about all the week in the licensed houses throughout the kingdom."

534.20/522.24 A COCKHORSE TO BANBURY CROSS   This alludes to the well-known nursery rhyme "Ride a cock-horse to Banbury Cross,/ To see a fine lady upon a white horse." For text and comment, see *ODNR*, pp. 65–66. Part of the comment says, " 'To ride a cockhorse' is usually taken to refer to straddling a toy horse (or grown-up's knee) and is found in this sense since 1540."

534.24/522.28 THE LADY GOES A PACE A PACE . . .   This alludes to the nursery rhyme and children's game "This is the way the ladies ride." The *ODNR* prints several variants, but none exactly like this. The Opies point out that there are many more variants of the rhyme than they print. Cf. entry 50.8.

535.7/523.10 BY JINGO   Though the phrase is of long standing, "By Jingo" took on new meaning in 1877 when it was used in a music hall song entitled "We Don't Want to Fight," by G. W. Hunt, the chorus of which said "We don't want to fight, but by Jingo if we do,/ We've got the ships, we've got the men, and got the money, too./ We've fought the Bear before, and while we're Britons true,/ The Russians shall not have Constantinople" (Disher, *Victorian Song*, p. 165). Walsh's *Handy-Book of Literary Curiosities, s.v.* Jingo—Jingoism, has a similar but fuller account.

535.12/523.15 NO MORE BLOW HOT AND COLD   See entry 125.21.

535.22/523.25 AS THEY ARE NOW, SO WILL YOU BE   This alludes to the tombstone inscription that Bloom thought of earlier in the "Hades" episode; see entry 113.42.

535.31/524.2 MARTHA AND MARY   See entry 79.6.

536.25/524.27 SIGNOR LACI DAREMO   This alludes to the duet "La ci darem" in *Don Giovanni*; see entry 63.31.

536.26/524.28 HENRY FLEURY OF GORDON BENNETT FAME   On the Gordon Bennett race, see entry 97.14. But no one by this name was associated with the race in 1904, or with the one run in 1903, in Ireland. In the accounts I have seen, the only name vaguely similar to "Henry Fleury" is that of Henri Fournier, whom Joyce interviewed in April, 1903; see *CW*, pp. 106–8.

536.27/524.29 SHERIDAN, THE QUADROON CROESUS   Croesus was a king of Lydia who flourished in the sixth century B.C., and who was noted for his great wealth. This phrase implies that there was a wealthy quadroon named Sheridan, but I have not located any such person.

536.29/524.31 BOBS, DOWAGER DUCHESS OF MANORHAMILTON   Manorhamilton is a small town in county Leitrim. But I have not located any dowager duchess named Bobs who is associated with the town.

536.34/525.2 VICE VERSA   *Vice Versa* (1882) was a farce by F. Anstey (pseudonym of Thomas Anstey Guthrie, 1856–1934). Joyce played a part in this play when he was a student at Belvedere, but apparently it was a different role from the one Bloom plays (see K. Sullivan, *Joyce Among the Jesuits*, p. 89).

537.15/525.17 BY THE ASS OF THE DORANS   This may allude to the anonymous Irish ballad "Doran's Ass," which tells of Paddy Doyle's getting so drunk that he mistook Doran's ass for his sweetheart, Betty Toole. Words of the song may be found in Hoagland, pp. 260–262.

538.6/526.6 POLDY KOCK   Paul de Kock; see entry 64.39.

538.21/526.21 HOLD YOUR TONGUE! SPEAK WHEN YOU'RE SPOKEN TO Both of these are proverbial and are listed in the *ODEP*. "Hold your tongue" occurs three times in Swift's *Polite Conversation* (pp. 136, 173, 175).

539.2/526.31 WITH THIS RING I THEE OWN   This parodies the marriage service; see entry 442.9.

539.12/527.8 MISS RUBY   This probably alludes to *Ruby: The Pride of the Ring*. See entry 64.25.

540.19/528.14 THE CALIPH HAROUN AL RASCHID   See entry 47.5.

540.26/528.21 FOUR INCH LOUIS XV HEELS   This refers to the extravagant, rococo style of dress during the reign of Louis XV (1715–74).

540.26/528.22 THE GRECIAN BEND   "The Grecian bend" was a set phrase and the title of a song. J. Redding Ware dates the phrase 1865–70 and explains that it was "a satirical description of a stoop forward noticed amongst the women of extreme fashion during the last years of the Second French Empire, and which was due to the use of enormously high-heeled French boots. The fashion fell with the Empire" (*Passing English of the Victorian Era*, p. 147, *s.v.* Grecian Bend). The only copy of the song "The Grecian Bend" which I have found is in the cheap paperback *Favorite Songster* (Dublin, n.d.). It says nothing about the author of the song, but S. Spaeth says its was by William Horace Lingard, and dates it 1868 (*Hist. of Pop. Music in Amer.*, pp. 167–68). The chorus of the version given in the *Favorite Songster* says, "The Grecian bend, now go to it ladies,/ Shake yourselves, and set us crazy;/ Double up, and show the men,/ The style is now the Grecian bend" (p. 316).

540.29/528.24 PANDER TO THEIR GOMORRAHAN VICES   Gomorrah was one of the sinful cities of the plain in Genesis. See entry 61.12. Gomorrah is also used several times later in the Bible as the epitome of sin; see, e.g., Matthew 10:15. *Pander* may also be considered an allusion to the character in Chaucer's *Troilus and Criseyde*, since according to the *OED*, the word came into the language with Chaucer. And in Shakespeare's *Troilus and Cressida*, Pandarus says, ". . . let all pitiful goers-between be called to the world's end after my name—call them all Pandars" (III, ii, 209–10).

541.6/528.33 SING, BIRDY, SING   This probably alludes to the proverb quoted earlier: "The bird that can sing and won't sing must be made to sing." See entry 518.16.

541.13/529.7 THE TABLES ARE TURNED   "To turn the tables" on someone (i.e., to unexpectedly reverse the situation) is semi-proverbial. See Stevenson's *Home Book of Proverbs*, p. 2267.2.

542.3/529.28 SINCE YOU SLEPT HORIZONTAL IN SLEEPY HOLLOW YOUR NIGHT OF TWENTY YEARS   Here, as on p. 377.23/370.42, Sleepy Hollow is brought in, though Washington Irving's story is not set there; see entry 377.23. "Rip Van Winkle" is particularly appropriate to the present context since Irving stresses how henpecked Rip was; he calls Dame Van Winkle a "virago." The story makes it clear that Rip's sleep of twenty years, which passed as a single night, was largely to escape his wife. The allusion is continued in the rusty fowlingpiece mentioned on p. 542.9/530.2. Irving says that when Rip awoke and looked for his gun, " . . . in place of the clean well-oiled fowling piece, he found an old firelock lying by him, the barrel incrusted with rust, the lock falling off, and the stock wormeaten."

542.18/530.11 SIMPLY SWIRLING   From Boylan's song; see entry 62.36.

542.26/530.19 THE CUCKOO'S REST   This is Bella's name for the house where Bloom and others like him have retired. Cuckoo suggests cuckold; see entry 212.36.

542.29/530.22 SAUCE FOR THE GOOSE, MY GANDER, O   This proverb was alluded to earlier; see entry 279.31.

543.7/530.29 ART FOR ART'S SAKE   This phrase became common in nineteenth century French criticism and in *fin de siècle* English writing, and by 1904 was too common to specify a single source, though it was probably associated in the popular mind more with Oscar Wilde than any other single writer. The phrase goes back at least as far as Victor Cousin's Lecture XXII at the Sorbonne in 1818.

543.16/531.5 SWEAR   This recalls that in *Hamlet*, the voice of the Ghost says "Swear" three times to Hamlet from beneath the stage (*Ham.*, I, v, 149, 155, 182).

543.20/531.9 YOU HAVE MADE YOUR SECONDBEST BED AND OTHERS MUST LIE IN IT   Though this echoes the semi-proverbial "You have made your bed and must lie in it," it also alludes to Shakespeare's provision in his will leaving his wife his second best bed. See entry 203.22.

543.21/531.10 YOUR EPITAPH IS WRITTEN   This alludes to Robert Emmet's last words. See entry 290.34.

543.29/531.18 I CAN GIVE YOU A RARE OLD WINE THAT'LL SEND YOU SKIPPING TO HELL AND BACK   This specifically recalls Circe's advice to Odysseus about how to go to Hades and return. Her instructions include the use of a sweet wine as a libation (*Odyssey*, book X).

544.11/531.29 I HAVE SINNED! I HAVE SUFF . . .   Bloom is remembering his speculations about I.H.S. See entry 81.20.

544.15/532.2 CROCODILE TEARS   This phrase is proverbial and is listed in the *ODEP* (including three instances from Shakespeare).

544.18/532.5 THE CIRCUMCISED, IN SACKCLOTH AND ASHES, STAND BY THE WAILING WALL   Circumcision, required of all male Jews, and sackcloth and ashes, the traditional signs of mourning, are too common in the Bible to specify a single source. The wailing wall, which is not mentioned in the Bible, is part of a wall in Jerusalem surrounding the Temple Mount and is the last remnant of the Jewish sanctuary. It is a place of prayer, mourning, and meditation for Jews. See *Universal Jewish Encyclopedia*, X, 441–42, *s.v.* Wailing Wall.

544.26/532.13 SHEMA ISRAEL ADONAI ELOHENU ADONAI ECHAD   This is Hebrew for "Hear, O Israel: the Lord our God is one Lord" (Deut. 6:4). This is Judaism's confession of faith, proclaiming the absolute unity of God. This saying is also uttered by or in behalf of a dying Jew, and many Jewish martyrs have met death proclaiming these words.

544.31/532.18 THE SUTTEE PYRE   Bloom earlier thought of the Hindu custom of *suttee*, though he did not call it by name. See entry 102.11.

545.14/533.2 LA AURORA AND KARINI, MUSICAL ACT, THE HIT OF THE CENTURY   This seems to refer to some music hall or circus act, but I have not been able to identify it. Nothing like this is listed in the index of the *Circus and Allied Arts Bibliography*.

546.2/533.19 PHOTO BITS   See entry 65.12.

546.10/533.27 A THING OF BEAUTY   See entry 509.28.

546.21/534.6 FRAILTY, THY NAME IS MARRIAGE   This varies a quotation from *Hamlet* alluded to earlier; see entry 325.40.

548.14/535.25 THERE WERE SUNSPOTS THAT SUMMER   Since Bloom was born in 1866, this would seem to refer to some time from about 1879 to 1885. But, even though an earlier reference by Bloom to sunspot activity was quite accurate (see entry 166.39), this one does not seem to be. Sunspot activity in 1879 was very low, and was generally low during the entire next decade. See the chart in *Encyclopaedia Britannica*, 11th ed., II, 931, *s.v.* Aurora Polaris.

548.17/535.26 HALCYON DAYS   See entries 355.21 and 355.31.

548.23/535.33 MACKEREL   See entry 162.18.

548.26/536.2 HOBBLEDEHOY . . . I FEEL SIXTEEN   This may derive from a statement in Swift's *Polite Conversation*, first conversation, in which Lord Sparkish says, "Why, he's a meer Hobbledehoy, neither Man nor Boy" (p. 99). The *OED* defines hobbledehoy as "a youth at the age between boyhood and manhood, a stripling; *esp.* a clumsy or awkward youth."

549.3/536.10 HAMADRYADS   Hamadryads are wood nymphs. They are said to come into being and die with the birth and death of a particular tree, and they suffer and rejoice with the tree.

549.16/536.23 THE FAUNS   The fauns, followers of the Roman deity Faunus (who came to be identified with the Greek Pan), were mischievous, sportive creatures like the Greek satyrs. (But Norman Silverstein draws on the Rosenbach MS of this episode to argue that "fauns" here is a misprint for "fauna.")

549.17/536.24 THE FLOWERS THAT BLOOM IN THE SPRING   This alludes to the duet "The Flowers That Bloom in the Spring," sung by Nanki-Poo and Ko-Ko in act II of Gilbert and Sullivan's *The Mikado* (1885).

550.10/537.14 CIRCUMSTANCES ALTER CASES   This is proverbial; the *ODEP* lists this exact phrase.

550.12/537.16 ELIJAH   Elijah is alluded to frequently in *Ulysses*; see entry 151.15 and Index.

550.24/537.27 WHEN MY COUNTRY TAKES HER PLACE AMONG THE

NATIONS OF THE EARTH . . .   This is from Emmet's final speech, which was alluded to on p. 543.21/531.10. See entry 290.34.

551.16/538.16 PECCAVI   "I have sinned." Though this phrase occurs in a variety of contexts in the Bible, this is probably an allusion to the Confiteor portion of the Mass, in which is said, "Confiteor . . . quia peccavi nimis cogitatione, verbo, et opere . . ." ("I confess . . . that I have sinned exceedingly in thought, word, and deed . . .").

551.18/538.18 THE HAND THAT RULES   Bloom is probably thinking of "The hand that rocks the cradle rules the world," alluded to earlier. See entry 288.13.

551.28/538.28 PIPING HOT. . . . CAME FROM A HOT PLACE   This probably derives from the similar exchange in Swift's *Polite Conversation*, first conversation, when Lord Sparkish says, "This Tea's very hot?" and Lady Answerall replies, "Why, it came from a hot Place my Lord" (p. 82). Partridge says that this catch-phrase is still current, though less common since *ca.* 1940.

552.6/539.4 SITTING BULL   Sitting Bull (*ca.* 1831–90) was the famous Indian chief, leader of the Sioux in the battle of Little Bighorn (1876) in which General Custer and many of his soldiers were killed. Later, Sitting Bull appeared with Buffalo Bill's Wild West Show.

552.21/539.19 MOUNT CARMEL, THE APPARITIONS OF KNOCK AND LOURDES   On the Feast of Our Lady of Mount Carmel, see entry 155.9. On Knock and Lourdes, see entries 81.12 and 81.12.

553.2/539.28 O LEOPOLD LOST THE PIN OF HIS DRAWERS . . . This is a variation on the earlier "Mary" song. See entry 78.38.

553.21/540.16 NEBRAKADA   This was earlier given as part of a charm of the blessed abbot Peter Salanka, though I have not located anything like this; see entry 242.35.

553.21/540.16 CAT OF NINE LIVES   "A cat has nine lives" is proverbial and is listed in the *ODEP*. "Cat o' nine tails" is, of course, a common name for a nine-thonged whip.

553.22/540.17 THE FOX AND THE GRAPES   This alludes to Aesop's well-known fable "The Fox and the Grapes," which tells of a fox who finally disdained grapes he found it impossible to reach.

553.23/540.18 YOUR BARBED WIRE   Bloom is again remembering his earlier idea that a nun invented barbed wire. See entry 155.15.

553.25/540.20 THE SPOUTLESS STATUE OF THE WATERCARRIER   The watercarrier refers to the zodiacal sign of Aquarius, who is depicted as a man pouring water. Cf. entry 671.27.

553.26/540.21 GOOD MOTHER ALPHONSUS, EH REYNARD   Reynard presumably alludes to Reynard the Fox, the central character of the medieval beast-epic *Reynard the Fox.* The reference to Mother Alphonsus seems tied in with the Reynard allusion, but I have located no such character. Professor Alfred Engstrom has suggested to me that Joyce may be alluding to Mother Alphonsa, who was Rose Hawthorne, daughter of Nathaniel Hawthorne. Rose Hawthorne (1851–1926) and her husband, George Parsons Lathrop, were converted to the Roman Catholic faith in 1891, and she later founded a religious sisterhood known as Servants of Relief for Incurable Cancer and took the name Sister Alphonsa as a member of the Community. See the *DAB, s.v.* Alphonsa, Mother.

555.2/541.22 THE DEAD MARCH FROM SAUL See entry 97.21.

555.8/541.28 WHAT'S YOURS IS MINE AND WHAT'S MINE IS MY OWN This statement occurs in identical form in Swift's *Polite Conversation,* second conversation, when Neverout says to Miss Notable, "What's yours is mine, and what's mine is my own" (p. 159).

555.19/542.8 GIVE A THING AND TAKE IT BACK . . . The Opies, in *Lore and Language of Schoolchildren,* list this as a swapping or giving rhyme used between children. Among the examples of such rhymes they give is this from Laurencetown, county Galway: "Give a thing, take it back,/ God will ask you, Where is that?/ You say you don't know,/ Then God will send you down below" (p. 133).

555.26/542.15 TO HAVE OR NOT TO HAVE, THAT IS THE QUESTION This alludes to Hamlet's soliloquy (III, i, 56), which has been alluded to several times earlier in *Ulysses.* Cf. entry 280.25.

556.3/542.18 THOSE THAT HIDES KNOWS WHERE TO FIND This is proverbial; the *ODEP* lists "He that hides can find" and cites several instances, including an early proverb collection.

556.11/543.26 THIS SILKEN PURSE I MADE OUT OF THE SOW'S EAR OF THE PUBLIC This proverbial statement occurs in Swift's *Polite Conversation,* second conversation, when Neverout says, "You can't make a Silk Purse out of a Sow's Ear" (p. 156). Partridge says the proverb goes back to the sixteenth century.

556.14/543.1 DAN CE BORDEL OÙ TENONS NOSTRE ÉTAT In *The Great Testament* of Françoise Villon (1431–63?) occurs, between stanzas 140 and 141, the "Ballade of Villon and Fat Margot." Each of the four stanzas of this ballade ends with the line "En ce bordeau où tenons nostre état" ("In this brothel where we keep our state").

558.2/544.14 THE FOX CREW, THE COCKS FLEW . . . See entry 26.33.

558.15/544.26 DEEP AS A DRAWWELL Though this phrase is not listed in the *ODEP,* it certainly is very common. Probably its best-known occurrence is in *Romeo and Juliet,* where Mercutio says of his death wound, " 'tis not so deep as a well nor so wide as a church door, but 'tis enough, 'twill serve" (III, i, 99–100).

558.21/545.4   ABSENTMINDED BEGGAR   This alludes to Kipling's poem "The Absent-Minded Beggar." See entry 187.22. *Le distrait* was the title given *Hamlet* on p. 187.15/185.12.

558.27/545.10   LUCIFER   Though *lucifer* was at this time a fairly common name for a friction match, this also alludes to the fall of Lucifer. See entry 50.24.

559.5/545.15   BE JUST BEFORE YOU ARE GENEROUS   This statement is proverbial and is listed in the *OEDP*; one of the instances cited there is Sheridan's *School for Scandal* (1777), IV, i.

559.10/545.20   MOMENT BEFORE THE NEXT LESSING SAYS   Lessing is Gotthold Ephraim Lessing (1729–81), German aesthetician and dramatist. The allusion here, as Fritz Senn has pointed out, is to his *Laokoon* (1766), also alluded to earlier (see entry 37.14 and source cited there). Senn says, " 'Moment before the next' recalls *Laokoon* where Lessing discusses the significance of the *Augenblick* (moment) in both poetry and the plastic arts" (*op. cit.*, p. 136).

559.11/545.21   THIRSTY FOX . . . BURYING HIS GRANDMOTHER   Stephen is again remembering the riddle he thought of on p. 558.2/544.14. See entry 26.33.

560.5/546.17   INELUCTABLE MODALITY OF THE VISIBLE   See entry 37.1.

560.6/546.18   SPHINX   Bloom thought of the sphinx earlier; see entry 77.25.

560.6/546.18   THE BEAST THAT HAS TWO BACKS AT MIDNIGHT   This alludes to Iago's statement in *Othello*; see entry 139.28.

560.14/546.26   LAMB OF LONDON, WHO TAKEST AWAY THE SINS OF OUR WORLD   This varies the well-known phrase from the Bible and the Mass. See the following entry and entry 436.31.

560.16/546.28   DONA NOBIS PACEM   This phrase, "Grant us thy peace," occurs commonly in prayers, litanies, and liturgy. During the Rites of Communion in the Mass, the priest says, "Agnus Dei, qui tollis peccata mundi, miserere nobis. Agnus dei, qui tolla peccata mundi, miserere nobis. Agnus Dei, qui tollis peccata mundi, dona nobis pacem" ("Lamb of God, who takest away the sins of the world, have mercy on us. Lamb of God, who takest away the sins of the world, have mercy on us. Lamb of God, who takest away the sins of the world, grant us thy peace"). See also entry 436.31.

560.26/547.7   THE AIR OF THE BLOODOATH IN THE DUSK OF THE GODS . . .   The air of the blood oath alludes to the scene in act I of Wagner's *Dusk of the Gods* in which Siegfried and Gunther swear an oath of blood brotherhood. Stephen's lines derive in part (as R. Ellmann has pointed out, *JJ*, p. 474) from a passage in *The Valkyrie* (act I, scene ii) in which Siegmund addresses Sieglinde as "Fragende Frau" ("questioning wife"). Stephen's whole phrase may be translated "Unfulfilled longing, a questioning wife, ruin us everyone."

561.2/547.13 HAMLET, I AM THY FATHER'S GIMLET   A parody of the Ghost's words in *Hamlet*, I, v, 9; see entry 152.39.

561.4/547.15 NO WIT, NO WRINKLES   This may echo an exchange in Swift's *Polite Conversation*, first conversation, in which Miss Notable says, "I never heard that," to which Neverout says, "Why then, Miss, you have one wrinkle—more than ever you had before," and Miss Notable replies, "Well; live and learn" (p. 96).

561.4/547.15 TWO, THREE, MARS, THAT'S COURAGE   The allusions to palmistry on this and the following pages seem accurate, but they are too vague (and palmistry interpretations vary from text to text) to permit scrutiny. For instance, there are two Mounts of Mars, one on the inner margin of the hand, the other on the outer. While both denote courage, the former denotes active courage, the latter passive courage. See any complete handbook of palmistry, such as *Cheiro's Guide to the Hand* (Chicago: Rand, McNally and Co., 1900).

561.7/547.18 THE YOUTH WHO COULD NOT SHIVER AND SHAKE   This alludes to the Grimm's fairy tale "The Boy Who Could Not Shiver and Shake" (sometimes "The Tale of a Youth Who Set Out to Learn What Fear Was"). The boy could not shiver, no matter how harrowing an experience he faced, but he finally shuddered when his wife threw a bowl of goldfish on him.

562.2/548.9 I NEVER COULD READ HIS HANDWRITING EXCEPT HIS CRIMINAL THUMBPRINT ON THE HADDOCK   As R. M. Adams explains (*SS*, pp. 202–3) this alludes to the popular superstition that the haddock bears the fingerprints of St. Peter, since it is the fish in whose mouth Peter found the tribute money (cf. Matt. 17:24–27). This superstition is briefly discussed in E. and M. A. Radford's *Encyclopaedia of Superstition*, pp. 138–39, s.v. haddock.

562.10/548.17 THURSDAY'S CHILD HAS FAR TO GO   This is a line from a nursery rhyme that begins "Monday's child is fair of face." For text and discussion, see *ODNR*, pp. 309–10.

563.6/549.12 BLACK LIZ   See entry 315.21.

563.15/549.21 I SEE, SAYS THE BLIND MAN   This common proverbial expression has two parallels in Swift's *Polite Conversation*. In the first conversation, Miss Notable replies to an extravagant statement by Neverout by saying, "Would I could see it, quoth blind Hugh"

(p. 77). And earlier in the same dialogue, Colonel Atwit has said, "A blind Man would be glad to see that" (p. 61). Partridge says that the first of these, a sixteenth- to eighteenth-century proverb, is the older, and the second probably derives from the "blind Hugh" proverb.

563.15/549.21 TELL US NEWS   This too probably derives from Swift's *Polite Conversation*, first conversation. There Neverout says to Miss Notable, "Indeed, Miss, you are very handsome," to which she replies, "Poh, I know that already, tell me News" (p. 93). Partridge says the phrase was current from the seventeenth to the mid-nineteenth century; since then, "Tell me something new."

563.17/549.23 MOVES TO ONE GREAT GOAL   See entry 34.27.

563.17/549.23 SIXTEEN YEARS AGO I TWENTY-TWO TUMBLED   Hodgart and Worthington, and Schutte, list this as an allusion to Ophelia's song in *Hamlet*, IV, v; see entries 191.13 and 191.17.

565.21/551.20 RAOUL   Raoul is from *Sweets of Sin*. See entry 236.5.

565.21/551.20 I'M IN MY PELT   This alludes to Sacher-Masoch's *Venus im Pelz*; see entry 466.21. Hodgart and Worthington also list it as an allusion to Michael Moran's song about Moses; see entry 400.40.

566.3/552.1 BARTHOLOMONA, THE BEARDED WOMAN   Though there were many bearded women making the rounds with various circuses at this time, I have not located a bearded woman by this name in any of the sources I have examined (including the *Circus and Allied Arts Bibliography*).

566.26/552.24 RIDE A COCK HORSE   From the nursery rhyme; see entry 534.20.

567.2/552.27 HEE HEE HEE   This probably derives from Swift's *Polite Conversation*. See entry 447.9.

567.15/553.10 THE MIRROR UP TO NATURE   In Hamlet's statement to the players, he says, "For anything so overdone is from the purpose of playing, whose end, both at the first and now, was and is to hold as 'twere the mirror up to Nature" (*Ham.*, III, ii, 22–24).

567.22/553.17 'TIS THE LOUD LAUGH BESPEAKS THE VACANT MIND   This is from Oliver Goldsmith's *The Deserted Village*, where he speaks of "the loud laugh that spoke the vacant mind" (l. 122), but in Goldsmith's context the phrase is used in praise, not criticism: *vacant* there means idle and contented, and Goldsmith is praising it. Jarrell (*PMLA*, LXXII, 548) sees a similarity between this phrase in *Ulysses* and Swift's stage direction, "*Here a loud laugh, often repeated,*" in *Polite Conversation* (see, for example, pp. 73, 130, 170).

567.25/553.20 IAGOGO! HOW MY OLDFELLOW CHOKIT HIS THURSDAY-
MOMUN. IAGOGOGO   This refers to Iago, and to Othello's choking
Desdemona.

568.4/553.25 BEFORE YOU'RE TWICE MARRIED AND ONCE A WIDOWER
Though this sounds like a proverb or set phrase, I have not located
it in any of the dictionaries I have used; and if it is an allusion, I
am unaware of it.

568.6/553.27 EVEN THE GREAT NAPOLEON . . .   There is some factual
basis for Bloom's suggestion about Napoleon. After his death
an autopsy was performed, and detailed measurements of his
body were taken. The English physician in attendance, Dr. Arch-
ibald Arnott, is said to have remarked the resemblance of Napoleon's body to that of a woman, and to have specifically called attention to the unusually marked development of his breasts.

568.25/554.16 WEDA SECA WHOKILLA FARST   This is the player
queen's statement in *Hamlet*: "None weds the second but who
killed the first." See entry 203.1.

569.3/554.24 AND THEY CALL ME THE JEWEL OF ASIA   This is from
The Geisha; see entry 96.40.

569.8/554.29 ET EXALTABUNTUR CORNUA IUSTI   This is from Psalms
75:10: " . . . the horns of the righteous shall be exalted" (Vulgate
74:11).

569.8/554.29 QUEENS LAY WITH PRIZE BULLS . . .   This alludes to
Daedalus' (the "grandoldgrossfather") making for Queen Pasiphae
a wooden cow so that she could gratify her lust for the white bull
which Poseidon had granted King Minos. As a punishment for
Minos' failure to follow his instructions and sacrifice the bull,
Poseidon caused Pasiphae to conceive a passion for the animal, and
she lured him by hiding herself in the wooden cow Daedalus had
made for her. The product of this union was the minotaur. Cf.
entries 207.40 and 411.28.

569.10/554.31 MADAME GRISSEL STEEVENS NOR THE SUINE SCIONS OF THE
HOUSE OF LAMBERT   On Madame Grissel Steevens, see entry
411.19. R. M. Adams has correctly said (*SS*, p. 204) that the Lambert allusion is ambiguous, for it may refer either to the well-
known English fat man Daniel Lambert (1770–1809) or to a family
named Lambert whose men were born for several generations with
spines all over their bodies. Both of these are briefly described in
George M. Gould and Walter L. Pyle, *Anomalies and Curiosities
of Medicine* (1896; reprinted 1956), and Daniel Lambert is mentioned frequently in the *Circus and Allied Arts Bibliography* (see
the Index).

569.11/554.32 AND NOAH WAS DRUNK WITH WINE. AND HIS ARK WAS
OPEN   This alludes to Genesis 9:21: "And he [Noah] drank of
the wine and was drunken; and he was uncovered within his tent."
Noah was seen in this state by his son Ham. The second sentence
in this allusion has no biblical basis. In this context it suggests that
Noah fornicated with the animals of his ark, which also has no
biblical basis.

571.3/556.20 DOUBLE ENTENTE CORDIALE   This blends *double entente* (or *double entendre*) and *entente cordiale*. See entry 330.22.

571.4/556.21 WATERLOO   See entry 456.2.

571.20/557.5 BEELZEBUB   Beelzebub is mentioned occasionally in
the Bible, where he is usually characterized as "the prince of the
devils" (see Matt. 12:24, Mark 3:22, and Luke 11:15). In Milton's
Paradise Lost, Beelzebub is second in command to Satan in Hell.

572.2/557.10 I FLEW . . . PATER   Stephen is recalling his earlier allusion to Icarus. See entry 210.35.

572.2/557.10   AND EVER SHALL BE. WORLD WITHOUT END   From
the Gloria Patri. See entry 29.24.

572.8/577.16 HOLA! HILLYHO   This and the "Ho, boy!" of p. 572.14/
557.22 allude to the exchange between Hamlet and Marcellus
in *Hamlet*, I, v, in which they call to one another as the fal-
coner calls to his bird: Marcellus says "Illo, ho, ho, my lord," and
Hamlet replies, "Hillo, ho, ho, boy! Come, bird, come" (ll. 115–
16).

572.21/557.29 A STOUT FOX DRAWN FROM COVERT . . .   This alludes
to "The Cock Crew"; see entry 26.33.

573.11/558.21 A DARK HORSE, RIDERLESS, BOLTS LIKE A PHANTOM PAST
THE WINNINGPOST, HIS MANE MOONFOAMING, HIS EYEBALLS STARS
This echoes an earlier allusion to Swift. See entry 39.38.

573.14/558.24 THE DUKE OF WESTMINSTER'S SHOTOVER, REPULSE, THE
DUKE OF BEAUFORT'S CEYLON, PRIX DE PARIS   See entry 32.15.

573.18/558.28 COCK OF THE NORTH   R. M. Adams (*SS*, p. 24) says
of Deasy's appearing on the "Cock of the North" that it "makes
multiple reference to his Ulster origins, his sexual inadequacies,
and George, the fifth Lord Gordon, who commanded the Gordon
Highlanders when they put down the 1798 rebellion in county
Wexford (a tune by this name is the regimental march)." The *DNB*
has a complimentary article on George Gordon, fifth Duke of
Gordon (1770–1836).

573.21/558.31 JOGS ALONG THE ROCKY ROAD   This alludes to the
song "The Rocky Road to Dublin." See entry 31.35.

573.30/559.3 PER VIAS RDOTAS   See entry 31.29

574.2/559.8 SIR JOHN   Sir John Blackwood. See entry 31.29.

574.6/559.12 NOISE IN THE STREET   Earlier Stephen described God as "a shout in the street." See entry 34.33.

574.10/559.16 YET I'VE A SORT A/ YORKSHIRE RELISH FOR . . .   This is from "My Girl's a Yorkshire Girl"; see entry 254.1 and the Appendix.

574.21/559.27 AUGUR'S ROD   See entry 48.19.

575.11/560.15 MY GIRL'S A YORKSHIRE GIRL   See entry 254.1 and the Appendix.

575.29/560.33 MADAM LEGGET BYRNE'S OR LEVINSTONE'S   This alludes, with some inaccuracy in the spelling of the names, to two contemporary Dublin teachers of dancing and piano, Madame T. Leggett Byrne and Mrs. K. Levenston, both of whom are listed in Thom's *Dublin Directory* for 1904.

575.30/560.34 DEPORTMENT   See entry 220.24.

575.30/560.34 KATTY LANNER   Katti Lanner (1829–1915) was a Vienna-born ballet mistress and choreographer. She made her first appearance in 1843 and retired in 1877.

576.2/561.6 TWO YOUNG FELLOWS WERE TALKING ABOUT THEIR GIRLS . . .   From "My Girl's a Yorkshire Girl"; see entry 254.1 and the Appendix. The allusion is continued on p. 576.26/561.29.

576.4/561.8 FROM A CORNER THE MORNING HOURS RUN OUT . . .   This and the other appearances of the hours on this and the next page allude to the "Dance of the Hours" in Ponchielli's *La Gioconda*. See entry 69.28.

576.18/561.21 YOU MAY TOUCH MY . . . MAY I TOUCH YOUR . . .   Though this seems to be an allusion, I have not located its source. The "Dance of the Hours" section of Ponchielli's *La Gioconda* has no words.

577.14/562.18 SIMPLY SWIRLING   See entry 62.36.

577.28/563.2 BEST, BEST OF ALL   From "My Girl's a Yorkshire Girl"; see entry 254.1 and Appendix. The allusions to this song are continued on pp. 578.9/563.12; 578.11/563.14; and 578.26/563.29; and throughout the stage direction beginning on p. 579.7/564.7.

579.6/564.6 DANCE OF DEATH   The Dance of Death (*danse macabre*) apparently began as a fourteenth-century morality poem, and its earliest development was mainly in France. But it is now best known as a series of depictions of people of all classes being pulled away from their occupations by Death. The woodcuts of Hans Holbein the younger (*ca.* 1497–1543) are probably best known. Several writers have taken this as their theme, including Goethe (*Der Totentanz*) and Strindberg (*Totentanz*).

579.8/564.8   LAME CRUTCH AND LEG SAILOR   Hodgart and Worthington list this and the "blind coddoubled bicyclers" of p. 579.15/564.14 as allusions to the anonymous Irish ballad "Johnny I Hardly Knew Ye," but this seems unlikely to me. See entry 86.19.

579.11/564.11   GADARENE SWINE   In the Bible we are told that Christ cast the demons out of two demoniacs in the country of the Gadarenes into a herd of swine which was passing by. This caused the whole herd to run into the sea and perish. The story is told in Matthew 8:28–34, Mark 5:1–20, and Luke 8:26–39.

579.11/564.11   ONEHANDLED NELSON   See entry 148.9.

580.2/564.33   LILIATIA RUTILANTIUM . . .   See entry 10.23.

580.15/565.12   LEMUR   The lemures of the Roman religion were the ghosts of the dead who arose out of their graves at night and frightened people, especially children. Wm. Schutte suggests that Stephen may have recalled Milton's line "The Lars and Lemurs moan with midnight plaint" ("On the Morning of Christ's Nativity," l. 191). This also probably owes something to the lemurs that appear in the "Burial" scene of Goethe's *Faust*, Part II, act V.

580.20/565.17   OUR GREAT SWEET MOTHER! EPI OINOPA PONTON   On the first phrase, see entry 5.5; on the second, see entry 5.7.

580.24/565.21   MORE WOMEN THAN MEN IN THE WORLD   See entry 102.9.

581.2/565.28   A GREEN RILL OF BILE   J. Prescott (*MLQ*, XIII [June, 1952], 159) points out the similarity of this to a passage in Flaubert's *Madame Bovary*, describing Emma Bovary's corpse: "Then they leaned over the bed in order to arrange her wreath. In order to do this, it was necessary to raise her head slightly, and as they did so a flood of black liquid came from her mouth, as though she were vomiting" (Gerard Hopkins' translation [New York: Oxford University Press, 1949], p. 382).

581.3/565.29   LOVE'S BITTER MYSTERY   This is from Yeats's poem "Who Goes with Fergus?" See entry 9.22.

581.5/566.2   TELL ME THE WORD, MOTHER . . .   Stephen's request of his mother's ghost is one of the more obvious echoes in this scene of Ulysses' discourse with his mother's spectre in Hades in book XI of the *Odyssey*. Ulysses questions his mother about what caused her death, and asks other information of her.

581.14/566.11   HYENA   Wm. Schutte (*JS*, p. 114) quotes a passage about the hyena from Brunetto Latini's *Il Tesoro*, II, 253 (Stephen alluded to Latini earlier; see entry 194.21). The passage Schutte cites says, "The hyena is a beast that at one time is male and at another female; it lives wherever it can near a cemetery of dead men, and it digs out the bodies of the men, and eats them."

581.17/566.14 YEARS AND YEARS I LOVED YOU, O MY SON, MY FIRSTBORN, WHEN YOU LAY IN MY WOMB   The language here sounds biblical, but I have not found any clear source for this in the Bible. Perhaps this owes something to Isaiah 49:15: "Can a woman forget her sucking child, that she should not have compassion on the son of her womb?"

581.28/566.25 RAW HEAD AND BLOODY BONES   Wm. S. Walsh, in his *Handy-Book of Literary Curiosities* lists "Rawhead-and-bloody-bones" (p. 949) and explains it as "a former spectre of the nursery, inspiring as much awe among the nurses as among their charges." Walsh quotes John Locke as saying, "Servants awe children, and keep them in subjection, by telling them of Rawhead-and-bloody-bones." And he quotes Washington Irving, in his "Spectre Bride-groom," as saying someone was "as effective in frightening little children into obedience and hysterics as the redoubtable Rawhead-and-bloody-bones himself."

582.5/567.2 GOD'S HAND   The Hand of God (sometimes called the *Manus Dei*) has long been a traditional symbol of God the Father. Clara E. Clement, *Handbook of Christian Symbols*, pp. 9–10, describes the symbol in some detail.

582.5/567.2 A GREEN CRAB WITH MALIGNANT RED EYES . . .   Wm. Schutte (*JS*, p. 114) suggests that this may owe something to the definition of cancer in Skeat's *Etymological Dictionary*. Skeat says, "CANCER, a crab, a corroding tumor. The tumor was named from the notion that the swollen veins round it were like a crab's limbs."

582.14/567.11 NON SERVIAM   "I will not serve!" In *A Portrait of the Artist*, Stephen says, in his conversation with Cranly, "I will not serve" (p. 239), and earlier, in the retreat sermon, he had heard the priest say of Lucifer that his sin "was the sin of pride, the sinful thought conceived in an instant: *non serviam: I will not serve*" (p. 117). Apparently this comes from the Douay Version of Jeremiah 2:20, where God is chastising Israel: "Of old time thou hast broken my yoke, thou hast burst my bands, and thou saidst: I will not serve" (Vulgate: "non serviam"; this is the only instance of the phrase in the Vulgate).

582.18/567.15 O SACRED HEART OF JESUS, HAVE MERCY ON HIM . . .   Though the phrasing is not precisely the same, this may owe something to the Litany of the Sacred Heart, the refrain of which is "have mercy on us."

582.27/567.24 MOUNT CALVARY   Mount Calvary (from Latin *cal-varia*, skull,) was the place of Christ's crucifixion. In the King James version, the word is used only in Luke 23:33, whereas the Aramaic equivalent, Golgotha, is used in Matthew 27:33, Mark 15:22, and John 19:17. The Douay Bible uses *Calvary* in all four places.

583.2/567.26 NOTHUNG   Nothung is the sword of Siegfried in Wagner's *The Ring of the Nibelung*. It first appears in *The Valkyrie*, when Siegmund, the father of Siegfried, draws the sword from the ash tree and names it (apparently this is the scene Joyce has most in mind). Later in this same opera, Wotan intervenes in Siegmund's battle with Hunding to break the sword and give the victory to Hunding. In *Siegfried*, Siegfried himself reforges the sword and slays the dragon Fafner with it. And in *The Dusk of the Gods*, Siegfried sees the sword as the guardian of his trust in his oath (made while under a spell) with Gunther.

583.5/568.1 RUIN OF ALL SPACE, SHATTERED GLASS AND TOPPLING MASONRY   See entry 24.9.

586.5/570.30 INCOG HAROUN AL RASCHID   Haroun al Raschid (on whom see entry 47.5) is said to have gone incognito through the streets of Bagdad on occasion.

586.16/571.7 WOMAN'S SLIPPERSLAPPERS   This alludes to "Old Mother Slipperslopper." See entry 87.18.

586.17/571.9 FOLLOW MY LEADER   "Follow My Leader" is a boys' game, described in Gomme, *Traditional Games*, I, 131–32. The leader performs gymnastic and athletic feats across fields, ditches, etc., and the others follow as best they can. In the list that follows, most of the persons are characters in *Ulysses*; I annotate only those that seem to have some allusive element.

586.21/571.12 THE NAMELESS ONE   See entry 470.5.

586.22/571.13 GARRYOWEN   See entry 295.13.

586.29/571.21 MAN IN THE STREET   The phrase "the man in the street" is proverbial and is listed in the *ODEP*.

586.38/571.29 SWEETS OF SIN   See entry 236.5.

587.13/572.6 BY VIRTUE OF THE FIFTH OF GEORGE AND SEVENTH OF EDWARD   Though George Frederick Ernest Albert (1865–1936) was heir apparent in 1904, he did not become George V until 1910. Edward VII (1841–1910) reigned from 1901 to 1910.

587.14/572.7 FABLED BY MOTHERS OF MEMORY   See entry 24.7.

587.16/572.9 PRIVATE CARR   Several critics have suggested that the episode between Stephen and Private Carr may owe something to

William Blake's troubles with a Private Scholfield. For the fullest development of this idea, see Morton D. Paley, *JJM III*, pp. 181–85. Joyce's choice of the name Carr goes back to his own trouble with Henry Carr of the Zurich consulate in 1918; see Ellmann, *JJ*, pp. 439 ff.

587.30/572.23 HAIL, SISYPHUS   Sisyphus, legendary king of Corinth, was condemned eternally to push a rock uphill, only to have it roll back down when he neared the summit. He is among those Odysseus sees in Hades in the *Odyssey*, book XI.

588.13/573.9 THEIR'S NOT TO REASON WHY   Tennyson's poem "The Charge of the Light Brigade" (on which see entry 484.4) includes the lines "Theirs not to make reply,/ Theirs not to reason why,/ Theirs but to do and die:/ Into the valley of Death/ Rode the six hundred."

588.18/573.14 DOCTOR SWIFT SAYS ONE MAN IN ARMOUR WILL BEAT TEN MEN IN THEIR SHIRTS   Mackie Jarrell (*PMLA*, LXXII, 551) says this is "a garbled version of Swift's 'But in Fact, Eleven Men well armed will certainly subdue one Single Man in his Shirt.' " She cites *The Drapier's Letters*, ed. Herbert Davis (Oxford, 1935), p. 79.

588.24/573.19 THE BOLD SOLDIER BOY   This alludes to Samuel Lover's song "The Bowld Sojer Boy," which celebrates the pleasures of a soldier's life. The song has three stanzas of twenty lines each, and begins, "Oh! there's not a trade that's going,/ Worth showing,/ Or knowing,/ Like that from glory growing/ For a bowld sojer boy." Complete words can be found in Lover's *Poetical Works* (London: George Routledge & Sons, 1868), pp. 138–40.

589.4/573.27 ENFIN, CE SONT VOS OIGNONS   Though this seems to be a quotation or set phrase, I have not identified it. The closest I have come is a French proverb about the children of Israel looking back from the wilderness on their situation in Egypt: "Regretter les oignons d'Egypte" ("To regret the onions of Egypt"—from Stevenson's *Home Book of Proverbs*, p. 674.1). This should be compared with Stephen's and Bloom's earlier thoughts of the fleshpots of Egypt: see pp. 41.32/42.30 and 86.15/85.2.

589.6/574.1 DOLLY GRAY   This alludes to a Boer War song by Will D. Cobb and Paul Barnes, entitled "Goodbye, Dolly Gray." For the refrain and some discussion of the song, see C. Pulling, *They Were Singing*, p. 79. The allusion is continued on p. 589.8/574.3.

589.7/574.2 THE SIGN OF THE HEROINE OF JERICHO. RAHAB   According to chapters 2 and 6 of the book of Joshua, Rahab was a harlot who, convinced of the power of the Israelites' God, aided the

Jewish spies into her city and was promised that, in return, her house would be spared when the city was besieged. Her signal to the Israelites was a scarlet thread hung out her window.

589.8/574.3 COOK'S SON, GOODBYE   From Kipling's "The Absent-Minded Beggar." See entry 187.22.

589.9/574.4 DREAM OF THE GIRL YOU LEFT BEHIND   This alludes to the song "The Girl I Left Behind me." See entry 191.1.

589.28/574.23 HE TAPS HIS BROW. BUT IN HERE IT IS I MUST KILL THE PRIEST AND THE KING   Morton D. Paley (*JJM III*, p. 187) says of this "Blake's political philosophy in a nutshell, as well as an echo of such lines as: '. . . gone to praise God & his Priest & King/ Who make up a heaven of our misery.'—'The Chimney Sweeper,' p. 212. Also see Blake's letter to George Cumberland, April 12, 1827, where he speaks of 'The Mind, in which every one is King & Priest in his own House' (p. 879)." But there seems to me to be an even more concrete source in a quatrain by Blake quoted by Stanislaus Joyce (*MBK*, p. 154): "The harvest shall flourish in wintry weather/ When two virginites meet together:/ The King & the Priest must be tied in a tether/ Before two virgins can meet together." This is item no. 36 of the "Poems and Fragments from the Note-Book written about 1793," entitled "Merlin's Prophecy" (p. 177—all page references here are to the 1957 Keynes edition).

590.15/575.10 EDWARD THE SEVENTH   Edward VII is alluded to several times in *Ulysses*. See entry 587.13 and the Index.

590.17/575.12 GARTER AND THISTLE, GOLDEN FLEECE . . .   The first three of these are well-known knightly orders and can be found discussed in the *Encyclopaedia Britannica* (11th ed.) article on Knighthood and Chivalry (XV, 851 ff.). Skinner's Horse was a regiment of irregular horse raised in India by British military adventurer James Skinner (1778–1841). Probyn's Horse (Eleventh King Edward's Own Lancers) was probably named after General Sir Dighton Macnaghton Probyn (d. 1924), who is listed in *Who Was Who, 1916–1928* (London, 1929). A Bencher is a senior member of one of the Inns of Court. There was an Ancient and Honorable Artillery Company of Massachusetts, formed in the seventeenth century, but I have learned little about it. Some information can be found in the *Records of the Governor and Company of the Massachusetts Bay in New England* (Boston, 1854), V, 151.

590.22/575.17 MADE IN GERMANY   This alludes to the Germanic origins of the British royal house. See entries 330.26 and 330.39.

590.26/575.21 PEACE, PERFECT PEACE "Peace, Perfect Peace" is the title of several hymns, the best known being that written by Bishop Edward Henry Bickersteth in 1875. It begins "Peace, perfect peace, in this dark world of sin? The blood of Jesus whispers peace within." The hymn can be found in most hymnals. Edward speaks these words because he is "the Peacemaker"; see entry 330.37.

590.30/575.24 MAHAK MAKAR A BACK In view of the context, I suspect that this phrase alludes to some formula of Freemasonry, but I have been unable to confirm this.

591.18/576.9 MY METHODS ARE NEW AND ARE CAUSING SURPRISE . . . This is a continuation of "The Ballad of Joking Jesus." See entry 19.3.

591.21/576.12 KINGS AND UNICORNS Since the unicorn has long been a traditional symbol of Scotland, there may be some suggestion here of conflict between England and Scotland. The nursery rhyme "The Lion and the Unicorn" has been interpreted as expressing this struggle (see *ODNR*, p. 269). The unicorn was alluded to earlier on p. 389.33/383.22.

591.28/576.18 ABSINTHE, THE GREEN EYED MONSTER Stephen earlier called absinthe "green fairy" (pp. 42.37/43.35 and 43.7/44.4). This statement parodies a line from *Othello*; see entry 500.19.

592.9/576.29 GREEN RAG TO A BULL This statement combines the traditional association of green with Ireland and red with England and the traditional description of England as "John Bull," with the common notion that a bull is disturbed by a red rag. Cf. entry 593.4.

592.11/577.2 PEEP-O'-DAY BOY'S HAT See entry 43.24.

592.13/577.4 THE VIEILLE OGRESSE WITH THE DENTS JAUNES See entry 43.13.

592.18/577.9 DON EMILE PATRIZIO FRANZ RUPERT POPE HENNESSY The first four parts of this name, and the title *Don*, probably allude not to specific persons, but to the "wild geese" generally. See entries 132.35, 330.15, and 330.16. The last two parts of the name seem to allude to Sir John Pope Hennessy (1834–91), lawyer, M.P., and British colonial governor. In December of 1890 he won a seat as M.P. from Kilkenny over the strong opposition of the then deposed Charles Stewart Parnell, who was supporting Vincent Scully.

592.19/577.10 WILD GEESE See entry 41.17 and cf. entries 330.15 ff.

593.4/577.21 GREEN ABOVE THE RED This alludes to a song by Thomas Osborne Davis entitled "The Green Above the Red."

I have located the words of the song only in paperback collections, such as *Harding's Dublin Songster* (n.p., n.d.). The song has eight four-line stanzas, the first of which says, "Full often when our fathers saw the Red above the Green,/ They rose in rude but fierce array, with sabre, pike, and sgian./ And over many a noble town, and many a field of dead,/ They proudly set the Irish Green above the English Red" (p. 367).

593.4/577.21 WOLFE TONE   See entry 229.20.

593.7/577.24 KING EDWARD   See entry 587.13 and the Index.

593.9/577.26 HANDS UP TO DE WET   De Wet was a Boer general; see entry 163.10.

593.12/578.3 MAY THE GOD ABOVE/ SEND DOWN A DOVE . . . (*cove* here should read *dove*)   Though this seems to be an Irish song or poem, I have not been able to identify it. Hodgart and Worthington do not list it.

593.18/578.9 THE CROPPY BOY   On "The Croppy Boy," see entry 91.1 and the Appendix; p. 594.5/578.26, "Horhot ho hray ho rhother's hest" mangles a line from the song: "Forgot to pray for my mother's rest."

593.26/578.17 MRS PEARCY TO SLAY MOGG . . . VOISIN . . . MISS BARROW . . . SEDDON   I have found no record of the murder of Mogg by Mrs. Pearcy. The other two cases are included in Colin Wilson's *Encyclopedia of Murder* (New York, 1962) but both are anachronistic to *Ulysses*. Louis Voisin's murder-dismemberment of his countrywoman Émilienne Gérard occurred on October 31, 1917. Part of the body was found in a meat sack and sheet in Regent Square, Bloomsbury, London, and the rest was found a few days later in Voisin's basement. He was a butcher and had used a butcher's knife. Voisin was hanged for the crime (*Encyc. of Murder*, pp. 532–33). Frederick Seddon poisoned a moderately wealthy lodger named Miss Barrow in September, 1912. At first she was thought to have died of epidemic diarrhea, and the poisoning was not discovered until the body was exhumed and found to contain a large amount of arsenic. Both Mr. and Mrs. Seddon were charged, but only Mr. Seddon was executed (*Encyc. of Murder*, pp. 483–84).

594.8/578.29 MRS BELLINGHAM, MRS YELVERTON BARRY   See entries 465.33 and 465.19.

594.21/579.8 ON CORONATION DAY . . .   See entry 11.10. On King Edward, see entry 587.13 and the Index.

594.28/579.15 WANT MUST BE HIS MASTER   This proverbial statement, which is listed in the *ODEP*, occurs in Swift's *Polite Conver-*

sation, first conversation, when Neverout says to Miss Notable, "Miss, I want that Diamond Ring of Yours," and Miss Notable replies, "Why then, Want's like to be your Master" (p. 88). Partridge says "Want's like to be your master" is eighteenth century only; "Want will be your master" is nineteenth- and twentieth-century.

595.6/579.23 BY SAINT PATRICK   This may allude to Hamlet's swearing by St. Patrick. See entry 198.27.

595.7/579.24 OLD GUMMY GRANNY   Old Gummy Granny is apparently a parody of the "Poor Old Woman," of the song "The Shan Van Vocht." See entries 14.2 and 17.36.

595.11/579.28 HAMLET, REVENGE   This probably alludes to the Ghost's command to Hamlet: "If thou didst ever thy dear father love . . . Revenge his foul and most unnatural murder" (*Ham.*, I, v, 23, 25). *OR ALLUS. TO UR-HAM. FROM TS.LODGE —*

595.14/579.31 THE KING OF SPAIN'S DAUGHTER   This alludes to the nursery rhyme "I had a little nut tree," which says, in part, "The King of Spain's daughter/ Came to visit me,/ And all for the sake/ Of my little nut tree." For full text and discussion, see *ODNR*, pp. 330–31.

595.15/580.1 STRANGERS IN MY HOUSE   See entry 184.40.

595.16/580.2 SILK OF THE KINE! . . . YOU MET WITH POOR OLD IRELAND AND HOW DOES SHE STAND   "Silk of the kine" is a name for Ireland; see entry 14.2. The second phrase alludes to a line from "The Wearin' of the Green": "I met with Napper Tandy, and he took me by the hand,/ And he said, "How's poor old Ireland, and how does she stand?" See entry 44.5.

595.20/580.6 THE HAT TRICK   See entry 435.20.

595.21/580.7 SOGGARTH AROON   "Soggarth Aroon" ("Priest Dear") is the title of a song by Irish writer John Banim (1798–1844). It begins, "Am I the slave they say,/ *Soggarth aroon*?/ Since you did show the way,/ *Soggarth aroon*. . . ." For words, see *Irish Literature*, I, 56–57.

595.21/580.7 THE REVEREND CARRION CROW   The Carrion Crow occurs occasionally as a character in nursery rhymes and folk ballads. One such rhyme begins, "A carrion crow sat on an oak . . . ," and goes on to tell how a tailor shot at the crow, but missed and killed his sow. Part of the refrain goes "Sing heigh-ho, the carrion crow." The rhyme is not in *ODNR*, but can be found in many Mother Goose collections. J. Prescott (*MLQ*, XIII, 159) suggests that this may owe something to a statement in Flaubert's *Madame Bovary*, in which, shortly before Emma's death, we are told "Homais, in deference to his principles, compared all priests to carrion-crows attracted by the smell of death" (Gerard Hopkins' translation [New York: Oxford University Press, 1949], p. 373).

596.5/580.20 ERIN GO BRAGH   "Erin go Bragh" ("Ireland Forever") is a common Irish expression and the title of an apparently anonymous Irish song which I have found only in cheap paperback collections such as *The Favorite Songster* (Dublin, n.d.). The copy I found there has three four-line stanzas and a four-line chorus. It begins, "Go to Munster, to Leinster, to Connaught, or Kerry,/ An Irishman, sure you will always find merry," and the chorus says, "Oh, then his shillelah he flourishes gaily,/ With rattle 'em, battle 'em, crack and see-saw,/ Och, liberty cheers him, each foe, too, it fears him,/ While he roars out the chorus of Erin-go-Bragh" (p. 224).

596.14/580.29 WE FOUGHT FOR YOU IN SOUTH AFRICA. . .   There were several Irish units fighting for the British in the Boer War, including the First and Second Royal Dublin Fusiliers. See *The Times History of the War in South Africa 1899–1902* (London, 1909), Index. See also entries 163.10 an'd 749.17.

596.21/581.7 MOUSTACHED LIKE TURKO THE TERRIBLE   See entries 10.2 and 57.22.

596.24/581.10 GIVES THE PILGRIM WARRIOR'S SIGN OF THE KNIGHTS TEMPLARS   The Knights Templars was a military order founded in the twelfth century; see *Encyclopaedia Britannica*, 11th ed., XXVI, 591 ff. But there is a more direct allusion here to Freemasonry, for the Freemasons trace a connection between themselves and the original Knights Templars. See any dictionary of Freemasonry, *s.v.* Knights Templars and Pilgrim Warrior.

596.27/581.13 RORKE'S DRIFT   See entry 457.15.

596.27/581.13 UP, GUARDS, AND AT THEM   These words are traditionally supposed to have been said by the Duke of Wellington at Waterloo, though the Duke himself disclaimed them, saying that he might have said "Stand up, Guards," and then given the order to attack. See Wm. S. Walsh, *Handy-Book of Literary Curiosities, s.v.* Guards. Up, Guards, and at them!

596.28/581.13 MAHAL SHALAL HASHBAZ   "Maher-shalal-hash-baz" ("speeding for booty," or "hastening to the spoil") is the phrase God commanded Isaiah to write on a great scroll, and Isaiah then symbolically named his son this, to suggest how quickly destruction would come from the Assyrians. See Isaiah 8: 1–4.

597.6/581.20 GARRYOWEN AND GOD SAVE THE KING   On the Irish song "Garryowen," see entry 295.13. On "God Save the King," see entry

151.4. In his "Ireland, Island of Saints and Sages," Joyce, illustrating the moral separation between England and Ireland, says, "I do not remember ever having heard the English hymn 'God Save the King' sung in public without a storm of hisses, shouts, and shushes that made the solemn and majestic music absolutely inaudible" (*CW*, p. 163).

597.10/581.24 THE BRAVE AND THE FAIR   John Dryden's "Alexander's Feast" contains the line "None but the brave deserves the fair," both in the first stanza and in the chorus. "Alexander's Feast" has been given many musical settings, probably the best known being that of Handel.

597.15/581.29 SAINT GEORGE   St. George (d. 303) is the patron saint of England. See *Butler's Lives of the Saints*, II, 148 (April 23).

597.17/582.2 THE HARLOT'S CRY FROM STREET TO STREET . . .   This is a variation on two lines from William Blake's "Auguries of Innocence": "The Harlot's cry from Street to Street/ Shall weave Old England's winding Sheet" (ll. 115–16; p. 433 of the 1957 Keynes ed.).

598.6/582.16 WHITE THY FAMBLES . . .   See entry 47.23.

598.11/582.21 DUBLIN'S BURNING! DUBLIN'S BURNING! . . .   This is a variation on the old round "Scotland's Burning." See entry 434.29.

598.13/582.23 PANDEMONIUM   The context here recalls that the word *Pandemonium* came into the language as the name of the devil's palace in Milton's *Paradise Lost*, I, 756.

598.29/583.8 FACTORY LASSES WITH FANCY CLOTHES . . .   This alludes to "My Girl's a Yorkshire Girl." See entry 254.1 and the Appendix.

598.32/583.10 LAUGHING WITCHES IN RED CUTTY SARKS   "Laughing witches" recalls the story by Beaufoy which Bloom read earlier; see entry 68.39. But the whole sentence alludes to Burns's "Tam o' Shanter." In that poem Tam breaks up the witches' conclave he has been watching by exclaiming over one in a "cutty sark," i.e., a "short shirt." On hearing him, they pursue him, and the witch in the cutty sark misses him but gets his mare's tail. The poem, with its "Walpurgis Night" elements—a witches' dance, abused altar, etc.—has much in common with this episode of *Ulysses*.

598.33/583.12 IT RAINS DRAGON'S TEETH. ARMED HEROES SPRING UP FROM THE FURROWS   Cadmus, in Greek myth, sowed the teeth of a dragon he had slain, and they produced armed men; he threw a stone in their midst, causing civil warfare among them, and the five who survived helped Cadmus in the founding of Thebes (see also entry 26.2). But this also alludes to the apostrophe of the Irish orator Walter Hussey de Burgh (1742–83) in November,

1779: "Talk not to me of peace. Ireland is not at peace. It is smoth-
ered war. England has sown her laws as dragon's teeth, and they
have sprung up as armed men" (see *DNB*, III, 330, *s.v.* Burgh).

599.1/583.13   THE PASS OF KNIGHTS OF THE RED CROSS   This alludes
to Freemasonry; the Knight of the Red Cross is a Masonic degree.
For further detail, see any dictionary of Freemasonry, *s.v.* Knight
of the Red Cross.

599.2/583.15   WOLFE TONE . . .   Most of the persons named in this
list have been referred to earlier in *Ulysses*; some are fictitious. On
Wolfe Tone, see entry 229.30. On Henry Grattan, see entry 139.3.
On Smith O'Brien, see entry 68.27. On Daniel O'Connell, see entry
31.18. On Michael Davitt, see entry 657.7. On Isaac Butt, see entry
138.11. Justin McCarthy (1830–1912), Irish novelist and politician,
was a Member of Parliament and led the majority of the Irish
Party in splitting off from Parnell, though in spite of this he and
Parnell were later friendly; see R. Barry O'Brien, *Life of Parnell*.
On Parnell, see entry 35.2 and the Index. On Arthur Griffith, see
entry 43.8 and the Index. John Redmond (1856–1918) was leader
of the Home Rule Party, a supporter of Parnell through his dif-
ficulties, and was elected leader of the re-united Party in 1900; he
lost his position through support of England in World War I. John
O'Leary (1830–1907) was a Fenian and the editor of the Fenian
organ *The Irish People*; he was arrested, tried, and sentenced to
prison (later commuted to exile), but later returned to Ireland; he
wrote *Recollections of Fenians and Fenianism* (1896). On Lord
Edward Fitzgerald, see entry 241.7. There was a branch of the
O'Donoghue family known as the O'Donoghue of the Glen; see
D. Hyde, *Literary History of Ireland*, p. 62.

599.9/583.21   THE FIELD ALTAR OF SAINT BARBARA   Of St. Barbara,
R. M. Adams says (*SS*, p. 29), " . . . she is appropriate here because
she is, evidently, mythical in origin; because she protects against
lightning, sudden death, and impenitence; and because she is the
special patroness of firework-makers, artillery-men, architects, and
grave-diggers—with all of whom Joyce, in this section, has an af-
finity."

599.14/583.26   FATHER MALACHI O'FLYNN   This probably alludes to
"Father O'Flynn," on which see entry 170.30. R. M. Adams dis-
cusses Father Malachi O'Flynn and the Reverend Mr. Hugh C.
Haines Love at some length; see *SS*, pp. 29–35.

599.15/583.27   TWO LEFT FEET BACK TO THE FRONT   This may repeat
the earlier allusion to the depiction of Christ with two left feet in
the *Book of Kells*. See entry 520.22.

599.21/583.33 INTROIBO AD ALTARE DIABOLI   In keeping with the "Black Mass" that is being celebrated, this perverts the opening "Introibo ad altare Dei" ("I will go unto the altar of God") to "I will go unto the altar of the Devil." Cf. entry 3.5.

599.23/583.35 TO THE DEVIL WHICH HATH MADE GLAD MY YOUNG DAYS This, too, parodies the opening of the Mass. See entry 433.9.

599.26/583.38 CORPUS MEUM   In the Consecration of the Host in the Mass, the priest says, "Hoc est enim corpus meum" ("For this is my body"). The allusion is continued on p. 599.29/584.3.

599.32/584.6 HTENGIER TNETOPINMO DOG DROL EHT ROF, AIULELLA Again in keeping with the "Black Mass," this reverses a formula of praise for God, said correctly by the Blessed on p. 600.4/584.11. This is from Revelation 19:6 and is used in the "Hallelujah Chorus" in Handel's *Messiah* (on which see entry 183.7).

600.9/584.16 KICK THE POPE AND DAILY, DAILY SING TO MARY   "Kick the Pope" is a song mentioned by title in the well-known Orange song "The Old Orange Flute." "The Old Orange Flute" can be found in O'Lochlainn, *Irish Street Ballads*, pp. 100–1, but I have not located a copy of "Kick the Pope." "Daily, Daily Sing to Mary" is a well-known Catholic hymn. It is also called St. Casimir's hymn, after a fifteenth-century Polish saint, though it existed long before his time. The Latin title is "Omni die dic Mariae," and it has been variously translated. See Julian, *Dictionary of Hymnology*.

600.15/584.22 OLD GUMMY GRANNY   See entry 595.7.

600.17/584.24 IRELAND WILL BE FREE   This alludes to "The Shan Van Vocht," which includes the lines "And will Ireland then be free?/ Says the Shan Van Vocht;/ Will Ireland then be free?/ Says the Shan Van Vocht;/ Yes Ireland shall be free/ From the centre to the sea/ Then hurrah for Liberty!/ Says the Shan Van Vocht." See entry 17.36.

600.26/585.6 EXIT JUDAS. ET LAQUEO SE SUSPENDIT   This is the Vulgate version of Matthew 27:5, which says of Judas that, after Christ was delivered to Pilate, "et abiens laqueo se suspendit" ("and departing, he went and hanged himself").

601.5/585.11 THIS FEAST OF PURE REASON   This probably alludes to a line by Alexander Pope. In his "Imitations of Horace: Satires. Book II, Satire I," he says, "There St. John mingles with my friendly bowl/ The feast of reason and the flow of soul" (ll. 127–28).

604.22/588.24 COME WIPE YOUR NAME OFF THE SLATE   Though this phrase is common and though allusion seems unlikely, there is a passage in Kipling's poem "The Absent-Minded Beggar" which is similar: "He's an absent-minded beggar, and his weaknesses are great—/ But we and Paul must take him as we find him—/ He is out on active service, wiping something off a slate—/ And he's left a lot of little things behind him!" Cf. entry 187.22.

604.23/588.25   TOORALOOM TOORALOOM . . .   See entry 71.16.

605.9/589.11   JUST A LITTLE WILD OATS   See entry 192.28.

606.21/590.21   HE, HE, HE   See entry 447.9.

608.8/592.4   TOORALOOM . . . TOORALOOM   See entry 71.16.

608.23/592.19   BLACK PANTHER VAMPIRE   See entries 4.23 and 412.33.

608.26/592.21   WHO . . . DRIVE . . . FERGUS NOW . . .   From Yeats's "Who Goes with Fergus"; see entry 9.22. The allusion is continued on p. 609.3/592.32, and in Bloom's misconstructions on p. 609.11/593.6.

609.13/593.8   SWEAR THAT I WILL ALWAYS HAIL, EVER CONCEAL . . . Bloom is reciting a form of the oath of secrecy of the Freemasons.

609.15/593.10   IN THE ROUGH SANDS OF THE SEA . . .   Though these words sound like an allusion, perhaps to a sailor's song, I have not located their source. Hodgart and Worthington do not list this as an allusion to a song.

609.20/593.14   A FAIRY BOY OF ELEVEN, A CHANGELING   In Irish fairy lore, it is thought that the fairies sometimes steal a healthy human child and leave a shrivelled fairy in its place. Stories involving such changelings can be found in *Irish Literature*, II, 731–34 and V, 1877–84.

613.3/597.3 IN ORTHODOX SAMARITAN FASHION   In Luke 10:25–37
Christ tells the parable of the Good Samaritan who helped a man
attacked by robbers, when no one else would help him.

613.12/597.12 HOW TO GET THERE WAS THE RUB   In Hamlet's "To
be or not to be" soliloquy, he says, "Aye, there's the rub" (*Ham.*,
III, i, 65).

613.23/597.23 DONE YEOMAN SERVICE   Though this phrase is quite
common, in light of the recent Hamlet allusion (p. 613.12/597.12)
this may echo Hamlet's use of the phrase in *Hamlet*, V, ii, 36: "It
[the ability to write fair] did me yeoman's service." This is the
only use of the phrase in Shakespeare's works.

613.30/597.29 A JEHU   Jehu, now meaning simply a coachman or
a driver, derives from II Kings 9:20, where King Joram's watchman
reports about the people approaching, " . . . the driving is like
the driving of Jehu the son of Nimshi; for he driveth furiously."

614.1/598.1 GONE THE WAY OF ALL BUTTONS   The "timehonoured
adage" being varied here is the proverbial "To go the way of all
flesh," which is listed in the *ODEP*. This exact phrase does not

[429]

occur in the King James Bible, though Joshua 23:14 and I Kings 2:2 are quite close. In the Douay version, the words of the dying King David are, "I am going the way of all flesh" (III Kings 2:2).

614.5/598.5 VISITATION OF JUPITER PLUVIUS   Jupiter, Roman equivalent of Zeus, was god of the sky and of light and was also controller of the weather. Pluvius, meaning "rain giver," was one of the epithets commonly applied to him.

614.20/598.19 THINK OF IBSEN, ASSOCIATED WITH BAIRD'S   In *A Portrait of the Artist*, Joyce says of Stephen, " . . . as he went by Baird's stonecutting works in Talbot Place the spirit of Ibsen would blow through him like a keen wind, a spirit of wayward boyish beauty" (p. 176). A metaphor that Joyce used concerning Ibsen in his "Alphabetical Notebook" may give some clue to the association with a stone-cutter. Joyce says of Ibsen, "He seems witty often because his discoveries at such startling angles to applauded beliefs" [*sic*] (*s.v.* Ibsen).

614.22/598.22 FIDUS ACHATES   On *fidus Achates*, see entry 88.15.

614.25/598.25 OUR DAILY BREAD   From the Pater Noster or Lord's Prayer, alluded to often in *Ulysses*. See entry 6.33.

614.27/598.26 BREAD, THE STAFF OF LIFE, EARN YOUR BREAD   The idea that bread is the staff of life is common and proverbial; the *ODEP* lists the phrase. It occurs in section IV of Swift's *Tale of a Tub*, when Peter says, "Bread . . . Dear Brothers, is the Staff of Life. . . ." The common phrase "earn your bread" may allude to God's curse on Adam in Genesis 3:19: "In the sweat of thy face shalt thou eat bread, till thou return unto the ground."

614.27/598.27 O TELL ME WHERE IS FANCY BREAD? AT ROURKE'S THE BAKER'S, IT IS SAID   This alludes to Portia's song in *The Merchant of Venice*, III, ii, 63–64: "Tell me where is fancy bred,/ Or in the heart or in the head?"

614.42/598.42 THAT MAN IN THE GAP   P. W. Joyce (*English As We Speak It*, p. 182) lists this phrase and explains that in earlier days in Ireland, a king would post a good man at the most dangerous ford or pass when an invasion was expected. He says this able defender is remembered in the phrase "the man in the gap" applied to any "man who courageously and successfully defends any cause or any position," and Joyce quotes lines from Thomas Davis about the old Irish chiefs: "Their hearts were as soft as the child in the lap,/ Yet they were the men in the gap."

615.33/599.33 AND THAT ONE WAS JUDAS   This repeats Stephen's earlier characterization of Lynch as Judas; see entry 600.26.

616.22/600.23 TO POINT A MORAL   Though the phrase is now quite common, this recalls Samuel Johnson's closing couplet about Charles XII of Sweden in "The Vanity of Human Wishes": "He left a name at which the world grew pale,/ To point a moral, or adorn a tale" (ll. 221–22).

616.34/600.34 THE LORDS TALBOT DE MALAHIDE   This family has been alluded to previously in *Ulysses*. See entries 223.16 and 402.28.

617.27/601.26 THE BRAZEN HEAD OVER IN WINETAVERN STREET . . . FRIAR BACON   This alludes to Robert Greene's play *The Honorable Historie of Friar Bacon and Friar Bungay* (1594), in which the main characters make a head of brass which the devil endows with the power of speech. However, they lose all their labor when it speaks while they are asleep and they fail to hear it, after which the head falls down and breaks. Wm. Schutte (*JS*, p. 12) notes this allusion and says that the words of the Brazen Head in the play are, "Time is! . . . Time was! . . . Time is past!" which Schutte says are recalled twice in *A Portrait of the Artist* (on pp. 113, 124).

617.35/601.34 HAUD IGNARUS MALORUM MISERIS SUCCURRERE DISCO . . . This alludes to the passage in Virgil's *Aeneid* in which Dido tells Aeneas "Non ignara mali miseris succurrere disco" ("myself not ignorant of adversity, I have learned to befriend the unhappy"; book I, l. 630).

618.19/602.19 THE BLEEDING HORSE IN CAMDEN STREET   R. M. Adams points out (*SS*, pp. 205–6) that this pub, which is quite low on the social scale, occupies "a position of some importance in Le Fanu's novel, *The Cock and Anchor*, where it serves as a center of low scheming." Joseph Sheridan Le Fanu (1814–73) was an Irish writer; the novel appeared anonymously in 1845.

618.23/602.23 THE CARL ROSA   Carl Rosa (originally Rose, 1842–89) was a German violinist and impressario who, in 1873, founded the Carl Rosa Opera Company, for the production of opera in English. The company's main work has always been in the provinces, though it has given many London seasons.

619.6/603.7 IN EVERY DEEP . . . A DEEPER DEPTH   Though this saying is common, it apparently is not proverbial, and the best-known source is Milton's *Paradise Lost*, Book IV, in which Satan, thinking of his inescapable predicament, says, "Which way I fly is Hell; myself is Hell;/ And in the lowest deep a lower deep/ Still threat-'ning to devour me opens wide,/ To which the Hell I suffer seems a Heav'n" (ll. 75–78).

619.7/603.8 THE MAN IN THE STREET   This is proverbial; see entry 586.29.

619.24/603.23 THE FARFAMED NAME OF EBLANA   Eblana was the

name used by Ptolemy for a town somewhere near the north of
county Dublin, though the town, and the section it is in, Eblani,
"appear to be unknown to Irish tradition" (T. F. O'Rahilly, *Early
Irish History and Mythology*, p. 7). Eblana is occasionally seen in
imprints, where it means Dublin.

619.35/603.35 EVERYONE ACCORDING TO HIS NEEDS AND EVERYONE
ACCORDING TO HIS DEEDS   Though he gets it confused so as to
include the essence of both socialism and capitalism, Bloom has in
mind here Marx's dictim "From each according to his ability, to
each according to his needs." (This is Marx's third note to the
Programme of the German Workers' Party.)

619.42/603.42 WHY DID YOU LEAVE YOUR FATHER'S HOUSE   The idea
of leaving one's father's house is common in the Old Testament, as
a check of a concordance will show. But Bloom probably has
Mosenthal's play, *Deborah*, in the back of his mind; see entry 76.30.

620.27/604.28 IN ACCORDANCE WITH THE THIRD PRECEPT OF THE CHURCH
TO FAST AND ABSTAIN ON THE DAYS COMMANDED . . .   The third
of the (usually) five Precepts of the Church (also called Commandments of the Church) is "to observe the fasts on the days
during the seasons appointed" (*Cath. Encyc.*, IV, 155). Ember days
(from the Latin *Quator Tempora*, four times) "are the days at the
beginning of the seasons ordered by the Church as days of fast and
abstinence" (*Cath. Encyc.*, V, 399). They are the Wednesday,
Friday, and Saturday after December 13, after Ash Wednesday,
after Whitsunday, and after September 14. If the information in
this paragraph can be taken seriously, Joyce is dating Stephen's
last visit with his family. In 1904, Easter was on April 3 and Whitsunday was on May 22. Putting the dates of Ember Days together
with Stephen's statement about the "Friday herrings" suggests
Friday, May 27, 1904, as the last time Stephen was with his family.

620.34/604.35 HE KNOWS WHICH SIDE HIS BREAD IS BUTTERED ON   "To
know which side one's bread is buttered on" is proverbial and is
listed in the *ODEP*.

621.37/605.39 THE ONCE FAMOUS SKIN-THE-GOAT, FITZHARRIS, THE IN-
VINCIBLE   On Skin-the-Goat, see entries 136.11 and 137.5. On
the Invincibles, see entry 81.26.

622.16/606.19 VOGLIO   Bloom is remembering his misquotation of
the Don Giovanni–Zerlina duet in *Don Giovanni*; see entry 64.4.
The allusion is repeated on p. 622.22/606.25.

622.41/607.2 CICERO, PODMORE, NAPOLEON, MR GOODBODY, JESUS, MR
DOYLE   R. M. Adams (*SS*, p. 223) says of this, "A muzzy but
deliberate name-puzzle set by Stephen on p. 607 can be worked

out fairly easily. Cicero as a name comes from Latin *cicera*, chick-pea, and might well be something like Podmore in English; Napo-leon = Buonaparte = Goodbody; and Jesus = Christ = Anointed = oiled = Doyle." S. Sultan suggests that Podmore may owe something to Frank Podmore (1865–1910), a contemporary spir-itualist (*Argument of Ulysses*, p. 393).

622.43/607.4 WHAT'S IN A NAME   This alludes to Juliet's words in the balcony scene: "What's in a name" (*Rom. and Jul.*, II, ii, 43). Cf. entry 209.10.

623.21/607.25 ALL TOO IRISH   See entry 119.11.

624.1/608.6 BUFFALO BILL SHOOTS TO KILL,/ NEVER MISSED NOR HE EVER WILL   Buffalo Bill was William Frederick Cody (1846–1917), American plainsman. He got his popular name from his supplying of buffalo meat to the companies building railroads in the American West. He later founded Buffalo Bill's Wild West Show, which toured all over the U.S. and to Europe. I have not located this verse, and Hodgart and Worthington take no note of it. It may have been a popular entertainment slogan.

624.4/608.9 A MARKSMANSHIP COMPETITION LIKE THE BISLEY   This refers to the annual contests of the English National Rifle Asso-ciation, which began to be held at Bisley, in Surrey, SW of London, in 1890.

624.11/608.16 HENGLER'S ROYAL CIRCUS   See entry 64.29.

624.20/608.25 FOR ENGLAND, HOME AND BEAUTY   This alludes to "The Death of Nelson"; see entry 225.19.

624.25/608.30 DAVY JONES   See entry 379.4.

624.27/608.32 THAT PARTICULAR ALICE BEN BOLT TOPIC . . .   All of these stories involve long periods of separation. "Ben Bolt" is a popular English song, words by Thomas Dunn English, music by Nelson Kneass. It tells of Ben Bolt, a sailor who has been away so long that everything has changed; the closing lines specifically mention twenty years. The song begins, "Don't you remember sweet Alice, Ben Bolt," and it ends, "Twelve months twenty have past, Ben Bolt,/ Since first we were friends—yet I hail/ Your presence a blessing, your friendship a truth,/ Ben Bolt of the salt-sea gale." For words, see Ralph L. Woods, *A Treasury of the Familiar*, pp. 473–74. In Tennyson's poem "Enoch Arden," Enoch is shipwrecked and away from home for more than ten years. On his return he finds his wife happily married to a childhood friend. He resolves not to reveal himself, and his return is unknown until after his death. Washington Irving's Rip Van Winkle, in the story "Rip Van Winkle," fell asleep for twenty years and found all changed on his return; see entries 377.23 and 542.3. "Does anybody here remember Caoc O'Leary" alludes to a line from the poem "Caoch the Piper," by Irish writer John Keegan (1809–49). The piper Caoch O'Leary sings once for a boy and then disappears for twenty years before returning with his pipes and his same dog, Pinch. On his return, after twenty years' absence, he calls out, "Does anybody hereabouts/ Remember Caoch the Piper?" For the full text of this sentimental, melancholy poem, see *Irish Literature*, V, 1762–64.

624.30/608.35   JOHN CASEY   Perhaps confused by the similarity of the names, Bloom thinks that John Casey wrote "Caoch O'Leary," whereas it was really John Keegan (see preceding entry). John Keegan Casey (1846–70) was a Fenian and a poet of some skill. Casey's sad early death in 1870, said to have been caused by his sufferings in prison, attracted to his funeral some fifty thousand mourners, according to tradition. For a brief biographical sketch and three of his poems, see *Irish Literature*, II, 572–75.

624.37/609.1   ROCKED IN THE CRADLE OF THE DEEP   "Rocked in the Cradle of the Deep" (1839) is a song by Emma Willard and Joseph Philip Knight. It tells of a person who falls into calm and peaceful sleep, rocked in the cradle of the deep, secure in the power of the Lord to save. For words and music, see Chapple, *Heart Songs*, pp. 196–97.

624.42/609.6   WITH A HIGH RO! AND A RANDY RO! AND MY GALLOPING TEARING TANDY O   This is almost certainly a refrain from some sailors' song, but I have not identified it. Hodgart and Worthington do not list it.

625.1/609.7   GRIN AND BEAR IT   The *ODEP* lists four instances of this proverbial expression. The first is interesting because it says the proverb has a nautical origin. It is W. Hickey's *Memoirs* (before 1775), I, 196: "'I recommend you to grin and bear it' (an expression used by sailors after a long continuance of bad weather.)"

625.26/609.32   CAPTAIN DALTON THE BEST BLOODY MAN THAT EVER SCUTTLED A SHIP   If there was such a ship's captain, I have not located him, and I am skeptical that this alludes to an actual person.

625.27/609.33   GOSPODI POMILOOY   This is Russian for "God have mercy on us." The words are too common in prayers and liturgy to specify a single source.

625.35/609.41   MANEATERS IN PERU THAT EATS CORPSES   Presumably this refers to cannibalism, but whatever cannibalism there may have been among the natives of Peru must be an inconsiderable part of their culture, for none of the sources I have seen on that country makes any reference to it.

626.19/610.27 WILLIAM TELL   William Tell, legendary thirteenth-fourteenth century Swiss patriot of the liberation of Switzerland from Austria, is famous for being punished by having to shoot an apple off his son's head with a bow and arrow, and succeeding. His story has been the basis of several works, the best known being a drama by Schiller (1804) and an opera by Rossini (1829). James Sheridan Knowles's drama *William Tell* was alluded to on p. 377.1/370.21.

626.19/610.27 THE LAZARILLO–DON CESAR DE BAZAN INCIDENT DEPICTED IN MARITANA   In act III of W. V. Wallace's *Maritana* (on which see entry 86.32), Lazarillo, acting under orders from the scheming Don Jose, fires on Don Caesar and barely misses him. As Don Caesar comes in, he is, according to the stage direction, "*shaking a bullet from his hat.*"

627.2/611.11 OUR MODERN BABYLON   On Babylon as symbolic of sinfulness, see entry 193.22.

627.18/611.26 ELSTER GRIMES AND MOODY-MANNERS   On the Elster-Grime Grand Opera Company, see entry 92.7. Charles Manners (real name Southcote Mansergh, 1857–1935) was an Irish bass singer and operatic impresario. In 1890 he married the soprano Fanny Moody, and in 1897 they formed the Moody-Manners Opera Company and played in London and the provinces. The company consisted of 115 members and had a repertory of 30 operas. Note the precise similarity between Moody-Manners and Tweedy-Flower, both using the wife's maiden name and an assumed name for the husband.

627.27/611.30 THAT WAS THE RUB   See entry 613.12.

627.33/611.41 THE MAN IN THE STREET   This proverbial expression was used on p. 619.7/603.8. See entry 586.29.

628.4/612.13 FARTHER AWAY FROM THE MADDING CROWD   In his "Elegy Written in a Country Churchyard," Thomas Gray says of the people he is praising, "Far from the madding crowd's ignoble strife,/ Their sober wishes never learned to stray" (ll. 73–74). Thomas Hardy's novel *Far from the Madding Crowd* appeared in 1874.

628.12/612.21 SILKEN THOMAS   Silken Thomas was Thomas Fitzgerald, tenth earl of Kildare, on whom see entries 45.26 and 230.15. Probably he is associated with Howth because during his rebellion, he captured Lord Howth, and for several weeks his forces were camped around the Hill of Howth in an attempt to prevent the landing of English troops. See R. Bagwell, *Ireland Under the Tudors*, I, 169.

628.12/612.21 GRACE O'MALLEY   Grace O'Malley, or "Granua Waile" (*ca.* 1530–*ca.* 1600), was a famous female Irish sea-captain who is celebrated in Irish song and legend. She was known for her independence and rebelliousness. Lord Henry Sydney, then Lord Deputy, described her as "famous for her stoutness of courage, of person, and for sundry exploits done by her by sea," and another observer, in 1593, called her the "nurse of all rebellions in Connaught for the last forty years." The story is told of her that on her return from a visit to Queen Elizabeth, she put in at Howth Castle and sought admission at the dinner hour, only to find all doors closed. She thereupon kidnapped the young heir from the grounds and held him until the Lord of Howth agreed to keep his door open during dinner. See Archbishop Healy's lecture "Grace O'Malley, Irish Sea Queen," in P. Colum's *Treasury of Irish Folklore*, pp. 152–58.

628.12/612.21 GEORGE IV   George IV was King of England, 1820–30. This probably refers to his landing at Howth on August 12, 1821, on the first visit of an English king to Ireland since the time of William III. Thom's *Dublin Directory* (1904) records his landing at Howth prior to his public entry into Dublin (p. 2098).

628.15/612.23 IN THE SPRING WHEN YOUNG MEN'S FANCY   In "Locksley Hall" Tennyson says, "In the spring a young man's fancy lightly turns to thoughts of love" (l. 20). The expression is now quite common.

629.8/613.17 THAT WAS WHY THEY THOUGHT THE PARK MURDERS OF THE INVINCIBLES WAS DONE BY FOREIGNERS ON ACCOUNT OF THEM USING KNIVES   The Phoenix Park murders are alluded to frequently in *Ulysses*; see entry 81.26 and the Index. An examination of the London *Times* for the days following the murder yields several statements similar to this one in *Ulysses*. The *Times* of May 8, 1882, says that speculation was busy concerning the identity of the killers and that ". . . there is a universal feeling that the assassins were not members of any political organization in Ireland—that the crime was, in fact, an exotic one" (p. 8, col. d). Doubt as to the Irish nationality of the killers was also expressed in an article on p. 8, col. e, and a letter on p. 8, cols. e–f, of the same issue, though none of these specifically mentions the use of knives as the source of their speculation. But the *Times* of May 12, 1882, says that the police "believe that the murderers belong to and are still in Dublin. No credit is attached to the theory that the [murderers] were Irish-Americans imported for the purpose. [The police] have ascertained that a butcher's knife, having a strong handle and a blade eight inches long, sharpened for about three inches, was bought on Saturday shortly after 1 o'clock. In the hands of a strong man it would be quite capable of inflicting any of the wounds which were found upon the victims" (p. 10, col. c). Wm. J. Feeny says that "the use of knives led police to theorize that the killers were Irish-Americans, or hired assassins from the Continent" (*JJQ*, I, 56), but he cites no contemporary evidence for the statement. Skin-the-Goat, mentioned on p. 629.15/ 613.24, was mentioned on 621.37/605.39; see entries 136.11 and 137.5.

629.11/613.20 WHERE IGNORANCE IS BLISS   Thomas Gray's "Ode on a Distant Prospect of Eton College" ends, "Where ignorance is bliss,/ 'Tis folly to be wise."

629.17/613.26 BEGGARING DESCRIPTION   This may allude to Enobarbus' statement in *Antony and Cleopatra*; after describing her barge, Enobarbus says of Cleopatra herself, "For her own person,/ It beggared all description" (II, ii, 202–3).

629.28/613.37 EIGHTYONE TO BE CORRECT   The Phoenix Park murders actually occurred on May 6, 1882; Myles Crawford earlier made this same mistake on p. 136.3/134.17. R. M. Adams (*SS*, pp. 161–62) says the error may have been Joyce's own, but I doubt this.

630.11/614.20 RULE THE WAVES   This alludes to "Rule, Britannia"; see entry 329.15.

630.15/614.24 DREAMING OF FRESH WOODS AND PASTURES NEW   Milton's "Lycidas" ends, "At last he rose, and twitched his mantle blue:/ To-morrow to fresh woods, and pastures new."

630.35/615.2 IRELAND EXPECTS THAT EVERY MAN   See entry 15.32.

631.12/615.22 THE SKIBBEREEN FATHER   This alludes to the Irish ballad of the 1848 famine, "Skibbereen" (sometimes "Old Skibbereen"), in which a father tells his inquiring son why they left "old Skibbereen." For words and music, see H. Hughes, *Irish Country Songs*, II, 76–84.

632.10/616.21 AS BAD AS OLD ANTONIO . . .   See entry 97.20.

632.15/616.25 GRIST TO HER MILL   This proverbial expression occurred earlier; see entry 204.39.

632.31/616.41 LOVE ME, LOVE MY DIRTY SHIRT   This is a variation of the proverbial "Love me, love my dog," which goes back to medieval times. The *ODEP* lists six instances of this, including John Heywood's *Proverbs* (1546).

633.11/617.21   FEAR NOT THEM THAT SELL THE BODY BUT HAVE NOT THE
POWER TO BUY THE SOUL   This is a variation on Christ's words in
Matthew 10:28: "And fear not them which kill the body, but
are not able to kill the soul: but rather fear him which is able to
destroy both soul and body in hell."

633.35/618.3   IT IS A SIMPLE SUBSTANCE AND THEREFORE INCORRUPTIBLE
. . . CORRUPTIO PER SE AND CORRUPTIO PER ACCIDENS   In *Summa
Theologica*, Part I, question LXXV, art. 6 ("Whether the Human
Soul is Corruptible"), St. Thomas points out that human souls
"have an incorruptible substantial life." In his discussion he specifies
two ways a thing may be corrupted, *per se* and *per accidens*, and
then proceeds to show that neither of these is possible in the case
of the human soul.

634.7/618.16   TO INVENT THOSE RAYS RÖNTGEN DID, OR THE TELESCOPE
LIKE EDISON . . . GALILEO   German physicist Wilhelm Conrad
Röntgen (1843–1923) discovered the X-ray in 1895. Though the
telescope was probably invented by Dutch optician Hans Lipper-
shey (*ca.* 1608), it was Galileo who constructed the first complete
astronomical telescope in 1609. Bloom probably thought of American inventor Thomas A. Edison (1847–1931) because of his work
on the telegraph.

634.11/618.20   IT'S A HORSE OF QUITE ANOTHER COLOUR   This phrase is
proverbial and is listed in *ODEP* and Apperson. In an earlier form
it appears in *Twelfth Night*, where Maria replies to Sir Toby's
comment on her plan to gull Malvolio by saying, "My purpose
is indeed a horse of that color" (II, iii, 181).

634.26/618.34   THE BIG QUESTION OF OUR NATIONAL POET OVER AGAIN . . .
LIKE HAMLET AND BACON   This alludes to the authorship controversy—the idea that Francis Bacon, or any one of several other
candidates, wrote Shakespeare's plays. Cf. entries 208.12 and 210.4.

635.25/619.32   THAT KNIFE . . . IT REMINDS ME OF ROMAN HISTORY
Stephen is recalling his earlier thought of Caesar's being knifed to
death. See entry 25.14.

635.32/619.38   OUR MUTUAL FRIEND'S STORIES   Though this is a common phrase, it may allude to Charles Dickens' novel *Our Mutual
Friend* (1864–65), which involves a situation of return from a
voyage and assumed identity to test a fiancé.

635.35/619.41   LIE LIKE OLD BOOTS   On "old boots," see entry 305.30.

636.1/620.7   SHERLOCKHOLMESING   This alludes to Sherlock Holmes,
the main character of many of Arthur Conan Doyle's (1859–1930)
detective stories.

636.10/620.16   IN DURANCE VILE   This semi-proverbial phrase goes back at least as far as William Kendrick's (d. 1777) play *Falstaff's Wedding* (1766), I, ii. A more recent instance is Robert Burns's "Epistle from Esopus to Maria," line 57.

636.10/620.16 THE ANTONIO PERSONAGE . . . There are several Antonios in Shakespeare, but the best known, and probably the one alluded to here, is that in *The Merchant of Venice*.

636.16/620.22 TEMPT ANY ANCIENT MARINER . . . TO DRAW THE LONG BOW This alludes to Coleridge's "The Rime of the Ancient Mariner," and specifically recalls the mariner's shooting the albatross with his crossbow. "To draw the long bow" is proverbial for "to lie." The *ODEP* lists several instances, including John Ray's *Proverbs* (1678).

636.17/620.23 SAILED THE OCEAN SEAS . . . THE SCHOONER HESPERUS This alludes to Longfellow's poem "The Wreck of the Hesperus," which begins, "It was the schooner Hesperus,/ That sailed the wintry sea."

636.19/620.25 COULDN'T PROBABLY HOLD A PROVERBIAL CANDLE TO "Not able to hold a candle to" is proverbial and is listed in the *ODEP*. P. W. Joyce includes "couldn't hold a candle to" in his *English As We Speak It*, pp. 230–31.

636.24/620.30 GIANTS . . . YOU SEE ONCE IN A WAY If there is any specific allusion here, it is probably to some of the giants Ulysses encountered in his voyages, such as the Cyclops or the Lestrygonians.

636.25/620.31 MARCELLA, THE MIDGET QUEEN I have not identified Marcella. Perhaps she was a part of some circus, but the index of the *Circus and Allied Arts Bibliography* does not list her, nor do any of the other circus books I examined.

636.26/620.32 AZTECS . . . SITTING DOWLEGGED . . . The Aztecs did worship their kings as gods, but none of the accounts I have seen mention that they debilitated themselves by sitting too long in a single posture.

636.33/620.39 SINBAD Sindbad the Sailor is the main character in a series of the Arabian Nights tales. While on his voyage he has several marvelous adventures, including an encounter with the Old Man of the Sea. Sindbad was also the subject of a very popular Dublin pantomime. See entries 678.32 and 737.17.

636.34/620.40 LUDWIG, ALIAS LEDWIDGE . . . THE GAIETY WHEN MICHAEL GUNN . . . IN THE FLYING DUTCHMAN . . . Michael Gunn (d. 1901) was one of the original proprietors of the Gaiety Theatre, Dublin, when it opened on November 27, 1871, and he continued to be proprietor for at least twenty-five years. William Ludwig (actually Ledwidge, 1847–1923) was a Dublin-born baritone with the Carl Rosa Company who came into prominence through singing the Dutchman in Wagner's *The Flying Dutchman* in 1877. It was during this season that the Carl Rosa Company performed the opera at the Gaiety, and a *Souvenir of the Twenty-Fifth Anniversary of the Opening of the Gaiety Theatre* (Dublin, [1896]), says of the 1877 performance "Ludwig was also in the Company, and the season was made memorable by his extraordinary and unsurpassed performance of 'Vanderdecken' in the 'Flying Dutchman,' with which his name has since become so inseparably identified" (p. 20).

637.9/621.16 IMPETUOUS AS OLD NICK   Old Nick is the Devil, although the basis and origin of the name is obscure. The *OED* lists an instance as early as 1643.

637.10/621.17 GIVE YOU YOUR QUIETUS DOUBLE QUICK   This alludes to Hamlet's phrase in his "To be or not to be" soliloquy, asking who would bear the pains of life "When he himself might his quietus make/ With a bare bodkin" (*Ham.*, III, i, 75–76).

637.25/621.31 DANTE AND THE ISOSCELES TRIANGLE, MISS PORTINARI, HE FELL IN LOVE WITH   Dante's Beatrice, the object of his idealistic love, is generally believed to have been Beatrice Portinari (1266–90), wife of a banker Simone de' Bardi. Probably Stephen is alluding ironically to the idealism and restraint of Dante's love. In *A Portrait of the Artist*, when Stephen begins to feel affection, he says, "Turned off that valve at once and opened the spiritual-heroic refrigerating apparatus, invented and patented in all countries by Dante Aligheri" (p. 252).

637.26/621.32 LEONARDO AND SAN TOMMASO MASTINO   Leonardo is Leonardo da Vinci (1452–1519), Italian artist, sculptor, engineer. San Tommaso Mastino is St. Thomas Aquinas (1225–74), who was also an Italian; cf. entry 208.9.

637.27/621.33 ALL ARE WASHED IN THE BLOOD OF THE SUN   This, even to the appropriateness of the sun/son pun, recalls the earlier allusions to the hymn "Washed in the Blood of the Lamb." See entry 151.11.

638.4/622.11 THE WRECK OF DAUNT'S ROCK, WRECK OF THAT ILLFATED NORWEGIAN BARQUE . . . PALME, ON BOOTERSTOWN STRAND . . . This account of the wreck is sketchy, inaccurate, and misleading. The *Palme* was one of several ships that had serious trouble off the east coast of Ireland during a storm on Christmas Eve, 1895. The *Palme* was out of Marieham, Finland, and was commanded by a Captain Weren. On Christmas Eve, it went aground opposite

Blackrock, south of Dublin. Two lifeboats manned by local men set out to rescue the crew; one of the lifeboats capsized with its crew of fifteen, the other returned, unsuccessful. The *Palme* remained stranded over Christmas and the crew was safely removed on December 26 by the steamer *Tearaght*, of the Irish Lights Board. The fifteen Irishmen manning the rescue boat were the only ones lost. One account does describe the crowds watching the rescue from the shore, but says that only those with glasses could make out anything. See *Freeman's Journal*, December 26, p. 5, cols. c–f; and December 27, p. 4, cols. d–e, and p. 5, cols. a–f.

638.9/622.15   ALBERT WILLIAM QUILL WROTE A FINE PIECE OF ORIGINAL VERSE . . . FOR THE IRISH TIMES   Albert W. Quill, who was a contemporary Dublin barrister, wrote a poem entitled "The Storm of Christmas Eve, 1895," which appeared under the heading "An Antispastic Dithyramb" in the *Irish Times* of January 16, 1896, p. 5, col. d. The poem had ten four-line stanzas, of which I quote the first two: "Is it Christmas Eve? Is it Christmas, when the world is in harmony,/ When the Child, the Prince of Peace, smiles from the manger in Bethlehem?/ But hark to the dirge of the waters and the winds in their agony,/ As the voice that was heard in Ramah by the seer of Jerusalem!// Awake! to the sea! to the sea! raging, and surging, and eddying,/ The billows gape in twain, yawning and fain for the sacrifice!/ The crested dragon glares hitherward, hungry and ravening,/ Befleck'd with the froth and the foam back from the mouth of the fortalice." The poem goes on in this manner for another eight stanzas, describing the wreck of the *Palme* and the loss of the fifteen Irish boatmen.

638.13/622.20   THE O. 3. LADY CAIRNS OF SWANSEA, RUN INTO BY THE MONA . . .   The collision between the German barque *Mona* and the English barque *Lady Cairns* took place off Kish Bank on Sunday, March 20, 1904. The weather was very hazy and visibility poor. The ships were on opposite tacks, and the German ship, which was running with the wind, struck the starboard side of the *Lady Cairns* and cut clean into her. The *Lady Cairns* at once began to fill, and "within two minutes turned over and disappeared" (*Freeman's Journal*, Mar. 22, p. 5, col. d). All hands on the *Lady Cairns* were lost. The *Mona* itself was severely damaged and was unable to render aid. It was finally towed in by another ship. (Accounts of the accident can be found in the *Freeman's Journal*, Mar. 21, 1904, p. 8, col. j, and Mar. 22, p. 5, col. d). The legal case that resulted from this collision was still being tried on June 16, 1904 (cf. p. 236.32/233.15), and the final judgment is described in the

Freeman's Journal of June 27, 1904. The court found the crew of
the *Lady Cairns* at fault for having made no sufficient lookout.
It also said that in view of the roughness of the sea and the fact
that the *Mona* had suffered injuries, the captain of that ship was
not criminally negligent for failing to put out all his life boats
(p. 2, col. b).

639.11/623.18 IN THE ARMS OF MORPHEUS   In Greek and Roman
mythology Morpheus was the god of dreams, and the son of Som-
nus, god of sleep. The phrase "in the arms of Morpheus" is common.

639.16/623.22 TO MAKE GENERAL DUCKS AND DRAKES OF   This phrase
is proverbial and is listed in the *ODEP*. P. W. Joyce lists it in his
English As We Speak It (p. 108) and explains that it describes what
a spendthrift son does to his father's property.

639.17/623.24 PAINTED THE TOWN TOLERABLY PINK   This is a witty
variation on the semi-proverbial phrase "to paint the town red."
Stevenson's *Home Book of Proverbs* contains instances of the
phrase (p. 2356.1).

639.31/623.37 THE GALWAY HARBOUR SCHEME . . . CAPTAIN JOHN LEVER
The Galway Harbor scheme, mentioned by Deasy on p. 33.3/
33.41, was a plan to make Galway an important transatlantic port.
Such a plan has been tried several times during the past century,
but it has never been successful. One such attempt was going on
when Joyce wrote "The Mirage of the Fisherman of Aran" (1912),
and he mentions "the place where the new transatlantic port is,
perhaps, destined to rise" (*CW*, p. 235). The incident alluded to
in *Ulysses* is, as is typical for this episode, complicated and mis-
leadingly alluded to, and information about it is hard to come by.
R. M. Adams' account of it (*SS*, pp. 23–24) is erroneous in some
particulars. The event referred to in *Ulysses* occurred on June 16,
1858, when the *Indian Empire*, one of the ships of a newly formed
company to run ships between Galway and Halifax, ran upon the
Santa Marguerita rock as it was going into Galway harbor. Since
the night was clear and the channel wide—it was pointed out that
this was the only rock in a channel nine miles wide—speculation
was rampant that the accident was in reality an attempt to sabotage
the new company. But the *Indian Empire* was not seriously damaged by the rock, and it departed from Galway on June 19—only
to break a piston rod in mid-ocean and consequently arrive at Halifax several days late. This was the beginning of a series of accidents
which happened to the ships of this line as it struggled through
the next several years, and each of the successive accidents brought

charges of sabotage. The company did not finally cease to exist until 1864. John Orell Lever, while not a captain, was a Manchester man who owned the ships and was founder of the new company. I can find no reference to any Worthington involved in the 1858–64 Galway harbor attempt. I suspect that this is an anachronistic reference to Mr. Robert Worthington, a Dublin promoter, who was among the chief supporters of the idea of Galway as a trans-atlantic port when it was revived in 1912. (Most of the above comes from the *Freeman's Journal* of June 18, 1858, p. 2, cols. f–g and p. 3, col. a, and June 19, p. 2, cols. e–g, p. 3, cols. a–b; see also Ernest B. Anderson, *Sailing Ships of Ireland* . . . , Dublin: Morris and Company, [1951?], pp. 207–11.)

640.6/624.13 THE BISCUITS WAS AS HARD AS BRASS . . . Hodgart and Worthington list this as an allusion to a sea chantey entitled "Leave Her, Johnny, Leave Her." Cecil J. Sharp, in his *English Folk-Chanteys*, prints a chantey entitled "Leave Her Johnny," which is clearly the one alluded to, though *Ulysses* presents a livelier version. Verse two of Sharp's chantey says simply, "The bread is hard and the beef is salt" (p. 3).

640.6/624.33 COLONEL EVERARD DOWN THERE IN CAVAN GROWING TOBACCO This information probably came from the *Irish Home-stead* of July 9, 1904, where there is an article entitled "Tobacco Growing in Meath," which is reprinted from the *Irish Peasant*. It tells of extensive experiments in tobacco growing by Colonel N. T. Everard of Randlestown, county Meath. At the time of the interview, Colonel Everard had twenty acres of tobacco under cultivation. I cannot explain the substitution of Cavan for Meath; at one point in the interview, Colonel Everard, when asked whether tobacco is grown in any other district in Ireland, replied that " 'it is only in co. Meath that its cultivation is organized on a considerable scale' " (p. 568; the article is on pp. 568–69). The following remark in *Ulysses*—about the quality of Irish bacon—is much like a statement in a letter on the Irish bacon industry which appeared in the June 4, 1904, issue of the *Irish Homestead*, from M. J. Hickey of Enniscorthy. In his letter Hickey says, "Irish bacon is the best in the world. The Danes produce good bacon, so do the Germans and the Americans, but their experts admit that it has not the same flavour as ours" (p. 465).

640.33/624.40 THE BOERS WERE THE BEGINNING OF THE END This simply means that the Boer War, 1899–1902, was the beginning of the end of British world domination. The war is alluded to often in *Ulysses*.

640.35/625.1 HER ACHILLES HEEL . . .   The following lines sketch the well-known story. Achilles' mother, Thetis, tried to make him immortal by dipping him in the river Styx, but he remained vulnerable in the heel by which she held him. He was killed at Troy when Paris inflicted a fatal wound in the heel.

640.41/625.6 IRELAND, PARNELL SAID, COULD NOT SPARE A SINGLE ONE OF HER SONS   I have not been able to verify the phrase here attributed to Parnell, though it is quite possible, even likely, that he said it.

641.24/625.31 PENDING THAT CONSUMMATION DEVOUTLY TO BE OR NOT TO BE WISHED FOR   This mixes two lines from Hamlet's soliloquy in *Hamlet*, III, i: "To be or not to be" (l. 56), and " 'Tis a consummation/ Devoutly to be wished" (ll. 63–64).

641.30/625.37 SISTER ISLAND   Hodgart and Worthington list this as an allusion to "Harp or Lion," an Irish song by Sullivan. The only copy of T. D. Sullivan's "Harp or Lion?" which I have seen is in the paperback *Irish National Comic Song Book* (Dublin: Irish Book Bureau, n.d.), pp. 1–2. The song has five stanzas and a brief refrain. It begins, "Neighbors! list and hear from me/ The wondrous news I've read to-day. . . ." I quote the entire third stanza: "Only think of Hugh O'Neill/ Thundering down in furious style,/ To assail, with lead and steel,/ The reivers from our SISTER isle!/ Chiefs and clans from all directions,/ With their far and near connections;/ Warriors bold and swift uprisers,/ Rushing on their 'civilisers'!/ Ha-ha-ha! Ha-ha-ha!/ On their gracious 'civilisers'!/ Ha-ha-ha!"

641.41/626.5 FITZHARRIS, THE FAMOUS INVINCIBLE   On Fitzharris, who is mentioned again later in this paragraph and has already been mentioned several times in this chapter, see entries 136.11 and 137.5.

642.8/626.15 A DANNYMAN COMING FORWARD AND TURNING QUEEN'S EVIDENCE . . . LIKE DENIS OR PETER CAREY   On James Carey, see entry 81.26. Dannyman presumably alludes to Danny Mann, a character in Dion Boucicault's play *The Coleen Bawn* (1860) and in *The Lily of Killarney* (see entry 92.6), which was based on that play. Danny Mann is the subservient, hunchbacked servant of Hardress Cregan, who attempts to murder Eily O'Connor, the Coleen Bawn, wife of Cregan, because he feels she is standing in Cregan's way.

642.24/626.31 FITZ, NICKNAMED SKIN-THE-GOAT, MERELY DROVE THE CAR . . .   See entries 136.11 and 137.5.

642.31/626.38 OR ON THE SCAFFOLD HIGH   This alludes to "God Save Ireland"; see entry 163.16.

642.33/626.40 GENEROUS TO A FAULT   This phrase is semi-proverbial. See Stevenson's *Home Book of Proverbs*, p. 939.2, for several instances of it.

642.34/626.41 ALWAYS SNAPPING AT THE BONE FOR THE SHADOW   This alludes to Aesop's fable "The Dog and His Shadow," which tells of a dog who, crossing a bridge over a stream with a piece of meat in his mouth, saw his reflection in the water and took it to be another dog with a larger piece of meat. Greedily snapping at his reflection, the dog dropped his own meat and lost it in the stream.

642.36/627.1 MR JOHNNY LEVER   See entry 639.31.

642.38/627.3 COME BACK TO ERIN   This alludes to "Come Back to Erin"; see entry 343.11.

643.4/627.12 A SOFT ANSWER TURNS AWAY WRATH   Proverbs 15:1 says, "A soft answer turneth away wrath: but grievous words stir up anger."

643.11/627.19 EX QUIBUS . . . CHRISTUS . . . SECUNDUM CARNEM   This comes from Romans 9, where Paul is grieving over the Jews. In his desire to save them Paul says, "For I could wish that I myself were accursed and cut off from Christ for the sake of my brethren, my kinsmen by race. They are Israelites, and to them belong the sonship, the glory, the covenants, the giving of the law, the worship, and the promises; to them belong the patriarchs, *and of their race, according to the flesh, is the Christ*" (Romans 9:3–5; I have used the Revised Standard Version here because the King James is obscure). In the Vulgate, the portion of verse five which I have italicized reads, "*et ex quibus est Christus secundum carnem.*"

643.17/627.25 EVERY COUNTRY, THEY SAY . . . HAS THE GOVERNMENT IT DESERVES   French writer Joseph Marie, Comte de Maistre (1753–1821) said, "Every country has the government it deserves."

643.17/627.25 COUNTRY . . . OUR OWN DISTRESSFUL   This alludes to a line in "The Wearin' of the Green" (on which see entry 44.5) which says of "poor old Ireland" that "She's the most distressful country that ever yet was seen,/ They are hanging men and women for the wearing of the green."

643.26/627.34 MEMORABLE BLOODY BRIDGE BATTLE AND SEVEN MINUTES, WAR . . . BETWEEN SKINNER'S ALLEY AND ORMOND MARKET   R. M. Adams (*SS*, p. 199) says this refers to a battle that took place "during the eighteenth century," but he cites no source, and I have not been able to learn of such a battle at Bloody Bridge during the eighteenth century. J. T. Gilbert's *History of the City of Dublin* (1861) has a long section on Skinner's Row, but says nothing of it. Perhaps this refers to the battle from which Bloody Bridge took its name, which occurred in 1670 (or 1671 according to some authorities). Of this, Gilbert says, "In 1670 a wooden bridge, at some distance westward of the old one, was built across the Liffey, but being found to interfere with the interest in a ferry which had previously plied in the same location, a number of apprentices assembled riotously for the purpose of destroying the new erection; twenty of them were, however, seized and committed to the Castle; 'but afterwards, as a guard of soldiers were conveying them to Bridewell, they were rescued, and four of them killed in the fray, from which accident it took the name of Bloody Bridge.' After the erection of the Barracks an unsuccessful attempt was made to change this name to 'Barrack Bridge,' but the structure, over which vehicles are not now permitted to pass, still retains the appellation of the 'Bloody Bridge' " (I, 388). But I suspect that Stephen is blending allusions to this battle and the one mentioned by Adams, and that is the source of vagueness here.

644.3/628.12   SPAIN DECAYED WHEN THE INQUISITION HOUNDED THE JEWS OUT   The Catholic expulsion of the Jews from Spain, an attempt to gain religious unity, took place in 1492. The *Columbia Encyclopedia* says, "The expulsion of the Jews deprived Spain of part of its most useful and active population" (3rd ed., p. 2009).

644.4/628.13   ENGLAND PROSPERED WHEN CROMWELL . . . IMPORTED THEM   Oliver Cromwell did favor readmission of the Jews to England (they had been expelled in 1290), and his reasons were primarily economic, though he tried to give them a religious coloring. He could not get governmental sanction for his policy, but his attitude was so conciliatory that, under his aegis in 1656, some Jewish families that had been posing as Spanish Roman Catholics threw off their disguise and were not expelled (*Jewish Encyclopedia, s.v.* Cromwell).

644.10/628.18   THE PRIEST SPELLS POVERTY. SPAIN AGAIN, YOU SAW IN THE WAR, COMPARED WITH GOAHEAD AMERICA   This refers to the short and one-sided Spanish-American War (April–August, 1898), in which the U.S. stripped Spain of her overseas holdings, including Cuba and the Philippines.

644.11/628.20   TURKS, ITS IN THE DOGMA   Though there is a definite idea of rewards and punishments for good and evil actions in Mohammedan theology, I can find no basis for the idea that economic competition is a part of the doctrine. As a matter of fact, some of their ethical principles work counter to this, such as the obligation to give to the poor. See Dwight M. Donaldson, *Studies in Muslim Ethics* (London, 1963), esp chap 7

644.13/628.22 THAT'S THE JUGGLE ON WHICH THE P.P.'S RAISE THE WIND
ON FALSE PRETENCES   This probably alludes to anti-Semitic incidents that had occurred in Limerick earlier in 1904. The fire of
discord was fanned, if not set, by a sermon by the local parish
priest, Father Creagh ("p.p." in this entry stands for "parish
priest"). See M. Magalaner, "The Anti-Semitic Limerick Incidents
and Joyce's 'Bloomsday,' " *PMLA*, LXVIII (Dec., 1953), 1219–23.
Magalaner quotes from editorials and letters in the *All Ireland
Review* about the incident, some of which may be the germ of
certain passages about the Jews in *Ulysses*.

644.23/628.31 UBI PATRIA ... VITA BENE ...   Bloom is probably
trying to think of "Ubi bene, ibi patria" ("Where I am well off,
there is my country"), but there may also be overtones of the
similar "Patria est ubicunque est bene" ("My country is wherever
I find happiness").

645.6/629.15 FAUBORG SAINT PATRICE CALLED IRELAND FOR SHORT
Stephen's designation of Ireland as "St. Patrick's suburb" probably alludes to its being, in his opinion, a subordinate province of
the Roman Catholic Church.

645.35/630.1 THE CASE OF O'CALLAGHAN ... THE HALF CRAZY FADDIST ...
I have not been able to identify this faddist named O'Callaghan, if
such really existed. R. M. Adams mentions him briefly, but does
not identify him (*SS*, p. 239).

645.43/630.9 A BLIND HORSE   Hodgart and Worthington list this as
an allusion to a nursery rhyme entitled "Old Dolly Dinkins," but
I have not been able to locate the rhyme in any of the collections
or indexes I have used.

646.2/630.10 SECTION TWO OF THE CRIMINAL LAW AMENDMENT ACT
W. Y. Tindall's statement (*RG*, p. 219) that this is the act and
section under which Oscar Wilde was convicted is mistaken, but
understandably so, and it points up the potential confusion here.
Wilde was actually convicted under section eleven, not section
two, of the Criminal Law Amendment Act, 1885, but some type
fonts, more common in British typography, make it impossible to
distinguish between the numerals for roman numeral two and
arabic numeral eleven. See, for example, *Finnegans Wake*, p. 61.9,
where this same Act is mentioned, but the numeral that is used
makes it impossible to tell whether section two (roman) or section
eleven (arabic) is referred to. The possibilities are complicated by
several factors: If Oscar Wilde is being alluded to, then section
eleven is the one intended, but if not, section two might be appropriate, for, while section eleven deals with homosexuality, sec-

tion two deals with attempts to draw any woman or girl into un-
lawful carnal connection, or attempts to procure women for sexual
purposes. In the Act itself, the sections are designated by arabic
numerals, but Joyce may not have known this. And there is the
possibility that Joyce himself saw the sections of the act referred
to in numerals and mistook an arabic eleven for a roman two. For
the text of the Act, see *The Statutes* (3rd revised ed.; London,
1950), XI, 129–35.

646.7/630.15 ANTONIO   Hodgart and Worthington list this as an
allusion to "Kelly from the Isle of Man" (see entries 97.20 and
97.21), but this more probably echoes the reference to Antonio on
p. 636.10/620.16 (see entry 636.10).

646.9/630.17 EARLY IN LIFE THE OCCUPANT OF THE THRONE, THEN HEIR
APPARENT . . .   This alludes to the moral looseness of Edward
VII; see entries 331.3 and 751.27, and compare the statements about
King Edward in Joyce's "Ivy Day in the Committee Room." I
have not identified the Cornwall case alluded to a few lines later.

646.15/630.23 GOOD MRS GRUNDY   Mrs. Grundy, the symbol of the
British idea of propriety, originated in the play *Speed the Plough*
(1798), by Thomas Morton (1764?–1838). Mrs. Grundy never appears in the play, but Dame Ashfield constantly wonders what
her neighbor Mrs. Grundy will think and say about whatever
happens.

647.2/631.9 TO IMPROVE THE SHINING HOUR   The first stanza of
English hymn writer Isaac Watts's (1674–1748) "Against Idleness"
(perhaps better known as "How Doth the Little Busy Bee") reads
"How doth the little busy bee/ Improve each shining hour,/ And
gather honey all the day/ From every opening flower!"

647.3/631.11 MR PHILIP BEAUFOY   See entry 68.39.

647.15/631.22 GIVE US THIS DAY OUR DAILY PRESS   A parody on
"Give us this day our daily bread," from the Pater Noster or Lord's
Prayer, which is alluded to often in *Ulysses*. See entry 6.33.

647.18/631.24 GREAT BATTLE TOKIO . . .   On this series of items re-
putedly being read about in the *Evening Telegraph* of June 16,
1904 (some of which were actually in the paper, others not), see
R. M. Kain, *FV*, pp. 56 ff. I annotate only those that have some
allusive element. On the Gordon Bennett race, see entry 97.14. On
the emigration swindle, see entry 322.3. No item about the victory
of Throwaway in the Ascot recalling the Derby of 1892 appeared
in the newspaper, but there was such a horse as Sir Hugo; about this,
R. M. Adams says (*SS*, p. 165), " . . . though Sir Hugo did win the

Derby in '92 at 40 to 1 . . . , he was owned by Lord Bradford, not Captain Marshall, and Jeddah, which won at 100 to 1 in 1898, was an even longer shot." On the New York disaster, see entry 239.22.

648.7/632.14 IS THAT FIRST EPISTLE TO THE HEBREWS . . . IN? TEXT: OPEN THY MOUTH AND PUT THY FOOT IN IT   There is, of course, only one Hebrews in the Bible. "You never open your mouth but you put your foot in it," is proverbial and is listed in the *ODEP*, though the only instance it lists is P. W. Joyce's *English As We Speak It*. Joyce explains of the phrase that it is said to one "who habitually uses unfortunate blundering expréssions" (p. 128).

648.43/633.7 RETURN OF PARNELL . . .   This paragraph and the ones following contain many references to Parnell. Some of these are accurate, some inaccurate, some reflect popular opinions and traditions concerning Parnell. In compiling the notes concerning Parnell in the following pages, I have relied primarily on books by Katherine O'Shea, Barry O'Brien, St. John Ervine, Joan Haslip, Conor Cruise O'Brien, and F. S. L. Lyons (see the bibliography for a fuller citation of these). Further information on most of the points dealt with can be found in these books. Concerning the traditions mentioned in the present paragraph of *Ulysses*, St. John Ervine says, "Legend, indeed, became very busy with him then. [i.e., with Parnell after his death] Many said and believed to the end of their days that he was alive. The present writer remembers in his boyhood being told in Belfast, during the Boer War, that General De Wet was really Mr. Parnell. The cause of this belief was, first, the singular shape of the coffin in which he was carried to his grave; it was of medieval shape, without shoulders, and was the sort that he had often said he desired; second, the fact that his coffin was closed down very soon after his death, and no one was permitted to see his body, not even his sister, Mrs. Dickinson" (*Parnell*, pp. 313–14). F. S. L. Lyons briefly mentions the rumor that no one was allowed to see the dead Parnell and says it was not true (*Fall of Parnell*, p. 307).

649.18/633.25 HE PETERED OUT TOO TAMELY OF ACUTE PNEUMONIA . . . The immediate cause of Parnell's death is not certain. His strength had been failing for some time, and on September 27, 1891, Parnell spoke in the rain and had to wear wet clothes for several hours. He had also been suffering from rheumatism, and the doctor who attended him said he died of rheumatic fever, and that he had a weak heart. Parnell had refused his wife's request to call a doctor. See F. S. L. Lyons, *The Fall of Parnell*, pp. 304–7.

649.29/633.35 ALICE, WHERE ART THOU   This alludes to the popular
sentimental song "Alice, Where Art Thou?" by Wellington
Guernsey and Joseph Ascher. The speaker of the song is Alice's
sweetheart; apparently Alice has been gone for nearly a year, and
he asks, "Alice, where art thou?" For words and music, see Chapple, *Heart Songs*, pp. 462–63.

649.30/633.36 SEVERAL ALIASES SUCH AS FOX AND STEWART   During
his affair with Katherine O'Shea, Parnell assumed various aliases,
including Fox and Stewart. Most of the biographers make some
mention of this; see Ervine, *Parnell*, p. 167.

649.38/634.2 THE IDOL WITH FEET OF CLAY   In Oscar Wilde's *Dorian
Gray*, chap. 15, Lord Henry Wotton says to Dorian, "It is the feet
of clay that makes the gold of the image precious." This well-
known phrase apparently goes back to the biblical book of Daniel,
where, in describing the image in Nebuchadnezzar's dream, Daniel
says, "This image's head was of fine gold, his breast and his arms
of silver, his belly and his thighs of brass, His legs of iron, his feet
part of iron and part of clay" (Dan. 2:32–33; see also 2:41–42).

649.39/634.3 SEVENTYTWO OF HIS TRUSTY HENCHMEN ROUNDING ON HIM
This is an inaccurate description of the vote when Parnell was
ousted as head of the Irish Party. Probably the number seventy-two
comes from the fact that seventy-two of the eighty-five members
of the Irish Party were present at the Committee Room Fifteen
meetings, and the total number who voted was seventy-two, though
it was forty-five against and twenty-seven for Parnell. See F. S. L.
Lyons, *The Fall of Parnell*, chap. V, esp. pp. 121 and 149.

649.40/634.4 AND THE IDENTICAL SAME WITH MURDERERS. YOU HAD TO
COME BACK. See entry 381.28.

649.43/634.7 WHEN THEY BROKE UP THE TYPE IN THE INSUPPRESSIBLE
OR WAS IT UNITED IRELAND   In December, 1890, Parnell returned
to Dublin from London after having been removed from his position as head of the Irish Party. One of his first acts was to take
over the *United Ireland*, a paper which had begun in 1881 as a
vehicle for Parnell's opinions. He and several of his supporters
went to the offices of the paper, followed by a crowd, and deposed
the acting editor, Matthew Bodkin. Later that same day, anti-
Parnellites retook the offices of the *United Ireland*. On the following day, Parnell and a sizeable crowd went again to the offices and
Parnell forced entry by beating the door open with a crowbar.
Barry O'Brien quotes a fine account by an eyewitness, which includes the detail that when Parnell appeared at a second-story

window, "his hat was off now, his hair dishevelled" (*Life of Parnell*, II, 296). The *Insuppressible* was an anti-Parnellite journal that sprang up after Parnell "suppressed" the *United Ireland*. It ran from December, 1890, to January, 1891. Cf entry 654.29.

650.5/634.12 THE LITTLE MISADVENTURE MENTIONED BETWEEN THE CUP AND THE LIP   "Many things fall between the cup and the lip" (or "Many a slip . . .") is proverbial and is listed in the *ODEP*. It has classical antecedents.

650.6/634.13 WHAT'S BRED IN THE BONE   The *ODEP* lists "What is bred in the bone will not out of the flesh" and cites many instances. The phrase was also used in Mulligan's "Ballad of Joking Jesus"; see entry 19.3.

650.11/634.18 THE TICHBORNE CASE . . .   This alludes to a famous case of assumed identity in which Arthur Orton (1834–98) pretended to be Roger Charles Tichborne (1829–54), long lost son of the dowager Lady Tichborne. The son had actually been lost at sea when the *Bella* went down in 1854. Lady Tichborne believed Orton's claims in spite of clear evidence of his fraud. After her death, Orton went to court, supported by those who had a financial interest in his claim, to regain the baronetcy and estate which had passed to a younger brother in 1862. There were two lengthy trials, and Orton was finally sentenced for perjury. There was, as the text indicates, a Lord Bellew involved in the case, who claimed to have tattooed initials on Tichborne. See the complete and well-indexed book by Douglas Woodruff, *The Tichborne Claimant: A Victorian Mystery* (New York, 1957).

650.23/634.29 THAT BITCH, THAT ENGLISH WHORE . . .   This refers to Kitty O'Shea, whom Parnell committed adultery with and married. She was English, being the daughter of Reverend Sir John Page Wood, Bart., of Rivenhall place, Essex. Her husband, who is mentioned in the following paragraphs, was Captain William Henry O'Shea, who was as p. 651.27/635.33 says, a member of the Eighteenth hussars.

650.36/634.42 THE USUAL AFFECTIONATE LETTERS THAT PASSED BETWEEN THEM . . .   In her book *Charles Stewart Parnell: His Love Story and Political Life*, Katherine O'Shea included some of Parnell's early letters to her. Some of this early correspondence came out at the divorce trial (cf. entry 654.6).

651.3/635.10 PROCLAIM IT . . . FROM THE HOUSETOPS   To "Tell it from the housetops" is now a common saying. It goes back to Christ's statement when warning the disciples against hypocrisy:

"Therefore whatsoever ye have spoken in darkness shall be heard in the light; and that which ye have spoken in the ear in closets shall be proclaimed upon the house tops" (Luke 12:3).

651.17/635.22   FALLING A VICTIM TO HER SIREN CHARMS AND FORGETTING HOME TIES   This is an explicit echo of the situation in the *Odyssey*, in which the Sirens use their bewitching song to entice sailors to their death on the rocks.

651.26/635.32   FAREWELL, MY GALLANT CAPTAIN   In the finale of W. V. Wallace's *Maritana* (on which see entry 86.32), Don Caesar sings to the Captain of the Guard, whom he has just challenged, "Farewell, my gallant captain! I told you how 'twould be. . . . You'll not forget the lesson due to me."

651.34/635.39   DONE YEOMAN SERVICE   See entry 613.23.

651.37/635.42   COOKED HIS MATRIMONIAL GOOSE   "To cook one's goose" is proverbial for to "do for," or ruin a person. The phrase is listed in the *ODEP*.

651.37/635.42   HEAPING COALS OF FIRE ON HIS HEAD   In Romans 12:20, Paul says, "Therefore if thine enemy hunger, feed him; if he thirst, give him drink: for in so doing thou shalt heap coals of fire on his head."

651.38/636.1   THE FABLED ASS'S KICK   This may allude to Aesop's fable "The Ass and the Wolf." In it the ass tells the wolf that he has a sharp thorn in his hoof, and the wolf devotes his whole attention to removing the thorn. The ass then kicks him full in the teeth and gallops away, leaving the wolf to lament trying to be a physician when his natural trade is that of a butcher.

652.4/636.10   UPSETTING THE APPLECART   "To upset the apple cart" is proverbial and is listed in *ODEP* and Apperson.

652.12/636.17   THE KING OF SPAIN'S DAUGHTER   This alludes to the nursery rhyme "I Had a Little Nut Tree." See entry 595.14.

652.18/636.13   FAREWELL AND ADIEU TO YOU SPANISH ONIONS ...   This alludes to the anonymous sea ballad "Spanish Ladies" (or "Farewell to You, Ye Fine Spanish Ladies"). Wm. Chappell prints words and music in his *Popular Music of the Olden Time*, pp. 736–37. Stephen apparently alludes to several lines in the song. It begins, "Farewell and adieu to you, Spanish ladies"; the second stanza Chappell gives ends, "From Ushant to Scilly is thirty-five leagues"; and the fourth stanza begins, "The first land we made, it is called the Deadman,/ Next Ram Head, off Plymouth, Start, Portland, and Wight."

652.19/636.24   SWEETS OF   On *Sweets of Sin*, see entry 236.5.

652.32/636.36 IN OLD MADRID   On the song "In Old Madrid," see entry 275.27.

653.1/637.7 YEARS NUMBERED BARELY SWEET SIXTEEN   This probably alludes to James Thornton's popular song of 1898, "When You Were Sweet Sixteen"; for words and music, see the *Song Dex Treasury of Humorous and Nostalgic Songs*, II, 67. And though allusion to it seems unlikely in this context, this is also similar to a line in Ben Jonson's "Epitaph on Salomon Pavy," which says, "Years he number'd scarce thirteen/ When Fates turn'd cruel."

653.6/637.12 OPULENT CURVES   Here and on p. 653.26/637.32 Bloom is remembering *Sweets of Sin*. See entry 236.5.

653.15/637.21 THE SPIRIT MOVING HIM   Though the phrase is now common enough, the only closely similar statement I can find in the Bible is in Judges 13:25, where we are told of Samuel, "And the Spirit of the Lord began to move him at times."

653.35/637.41 THE BOOK ABOUT RUBY   On *Ruby: the Pride of the Ring*, see entry 64.25.

653.36/637.41 MET HIM PIKE HOSES   Metempsychosis; see entry 64.18.

653.38/638.2 LINDLEY MURRAY   Lindley Murray (1745–1826) was an Anglo-American grammarian who wrote several books on grammar and usage, and whose *Grammar* was a standard textbook in England and America for fifty years.

654.6/638.13 HOW THEY WERE FATED TO MEET . . .   At some indeterminate point in this paragraph, Bloom's daydream about adultery becomes a reverie on the love affair of Charles Stewart Parnell and Katherine O'Shea (see entry 648.43). Most of the details of the reverie are relevant to Parnell's love affair and trial. For instance, love letters did come out at the trial, and the result was a decree *nisi* in Captain O'Shea's favor. See F. S. L. Lyons, *The Fall of Parnell*, chap. II, "The O'Shea Affair."

654.20/638.26 ERIN'S UNCROWNED KING . . . THE FALLEN LEADER'S   These terms were applied to Parnell; but the first may have some tradition behind it: E. Curtis, in his *History of Medieval Ireland*, refers to the eighth earl of Kildare as "the first 'Uncrowned King of Ireland' " (p. 338).

654.25/638.31 PENETRATED INTO THE PRINTINGWORKS OF THE INSUPPRESSIBLE . . .   See entry 649.43.

654.29/638.35 THE FACILE PENS OF THE O'BRIENITE SCRIBES   This refers to William O'Brien (1852–1928), Irish journalist and politician. He was a friend of Parnell and had been editor of the *United*

Ireland since its founding (see entry 649.43), but when Gladstone came out in opposition to Parnell's continuing as leader of the Irish Party, O'Brien decided that Parnell must go, and he sided against Parnell at the split. The O'Brienite scribe is Matthew Bodkin, whom O'Brien appointed editor of the *United Ireland* in 1890. During the crisis of the O'Shea divorce suit and Gladstone's withdrawal of support, the paper first supported Parnell, but later went strongly to the anti-Parnell side.

654.35/638.41 THEIR IDOL HAD FEET OF CLAY   See entry 649.38.

655.6/639.13 WHAT'S BRED IN THE BONE   See entry 650.6.

655.13/639.20 AFTER THE BURIAL . . . LEFT HIM ALONE IN HIS GLORY
This alludes to "The Burial of Sir John Moore," by Irish clergyman and poet Charles Wolfe (1791–1823). The final stanza of the ode says, "slowly and sadly we laid him down,/ From the field of his fame, fresh and gory;/ We carved not a line, we raised not a stone—/ But we left him alone in his glory" (see Hoagland, pp. 388–89). Sir John Moore (1761–1809) was a British general who died fighting against the French at Coruña in 1809.

655.24/639.29 THE USUAL BOY JONES   Though there was a famous "boy Jones" who, in the early 1840's, sneaked in and out of Buckingham Palace at will, the context here shows that the allusion is not to him, but to a young man who was a student at Trinity College, Dublin, contemporary with Robert Emmet, and who later informed on Emmet and others. Helen Landreth repeatedly refers to this person as "the young Trinity boy 'Jones,'" and she says of him, "Since he was ostensibly an international courier for the United Irishmen and travelled much between Ireland, England, and France, he kept the governments of Ireland and England supplied with information about disaffected Irishmen at home and abroad. His secret service name was 'Jones.' At the time of Emmet's rising he wrote many long reports for the Castle about all the prominent men who had been acting with Emmet" (*The Pursuit of Robert Emmet*, pp. 61–62; see also Landreth's index, *s.v.* Jones).

656.11/640.18 MISS FERGUSON   This is an indirect allusion to W. B. Yeats's "Who Goes with Fergus?" via Bloom's misunderstanding of Stephen's words on p. 609.11/593.6.

656.25/640.31 HUMPTY DUMPTY   "Humpty Dumpty" is a well-known nursery rhyme. Though Lewis Carroll's *Through the Looking-Glass* (1872) is its best-known occurrence, it goes back much further and has analogues in many languages. See *ODNR*, pp. 213–16.

656.39/641.3 BUCKSHOT FOSTER William Edward ("Buckshot") Forster (1818–86) was Irish Chief Secretary from 1880 until May, 1882 (i.e., just prior to Lord Frederick Cavendish, who was killed in the Phoenix Park murders). He introduced a new Coercion Bill in Parliament in January, 1881, declaring it a "painful duty." He was nicknamed "Buckshot" by the press after reports that he had authorized police to use buckshot in dispersing a crowd.

656.42/641.6 THE EVICTED TENANTS' QUESTION During the years 1849–82 hundreds of thousands of Irish tenants were evicted from the land they were farming for their inability or refusal to pay rent. The evictions were most numerous during 1849–52 and 1879–82, periods of poor harvest and famine in Ireland. Bloom's statement suggests that he is referring to the days of the founding of the Land League. See entry 657.7.

657.7/641.14 MICHAEL DAVITT . . . Michael Davitt (1846–1906) was an Irish revolutionary best known for his work toward land reform. He joined the Fenian movement in 1865, and he and Parnell were leaders in forming the National Land League in 1879, though they later divided on the question of land nationalization. The objects of the National Land League were: "First, to bring about a reduction of rackrents; second, to facilitate the obtaining of the ownership of the soil by the occupiers" (O'Hegarty, *Ireland Under the Union*, p. 489). I have not come across the term "backtothelander," but it obviously refers to one sympathetic with the land reform movement.

658.5/642.11 MERRY OLD SOUL This may allude to the nursery rhyme "Old King Cole": see entry 162.4.

658.19/642.25 BLOOD AND OUNS CHAMPION On the phrase "blood and ouns," see entry 3.12.

658.22/642.27 A BITE FROM A SHEEP This may allude to the proverbial "A black sheep is a biting beast," which is listed in *ODEP* and Apperson.

658.22/642.27 THE MOST VULNERABLE POINT TOO OF TENDER ACHILLES See entry 640.35.

658.35/642.40 THAT BRAZEN HEAD See entry 617.27.

658.39/643.2 PRIZE TITBITS See entries 67.39 and 68.39.

658.43/643.6 TO TELL THE WORLD AND HIS WIFE FROM THE HOUSETOPS On "tell it from the housetops," see entry 651.3. "All the world and his wife" is proverbial and is listed in the *ODEP*. It also occurs in Swift's *Polite Conversation*, third conversation, where Miss Notable asks what company was present on a given occasion, and

Lady Smart replies, "Why; there was all the World, and his Wife" (p. 162). Partridge says that this proverbial expression was apparently first recorded by Swift.

659.2/643.8   HE HAD HIS FATHER'S VOICE   See entries 43.10 and 38.11.

659.7/643.12   THE FORMER VICEROY, EARL CADOGAN ...   R. M. Adams explains that "The meeting of the Cabdriver's Benevolent Association, in London, at which the former Viceroy, Earl Cadogan, presided, did not take place till the night of Monday, June 27. As for the note about Sir Anthony MacDonnell having left Euston yesterday for the under-secretary's lodge in Phoenix Park, it seems to have been copied from the London *Times* of Friday, June 17, p. 6; it did not appear in the *Telegraph* or any of the other Dublin papers" (*SS*, pp. 230–31). Adams sees the cabby's reading about events that have not yet happened as intentional on Joyce's part; W. B. Murphy, in contrast, reads only about actual events (p. 659.30/643.35 ff.).

659.15/643.20   THE ANCIENT MARINER   This alludes to Coleridge's poem, which was alluded to earlier in this episode; see entry 636.16.

659.28/643.32   THE ARABIAN NIGHTS' ENTERTAINMENT   This famous medieval collection of tales in Arabic was first translated into English in 1840 by Edward William Lane (with some omissions), and then in complete, unexpurgated form by Sir Richard Burton in 1885–88. Cf. entry 215.4.

659.29/643.33   RED AS A ROSE IS SHE   *Red As a Rose Is She* (1870) is a sentimental novel by English novelist Rhoda Broughton (1840–1920). Miss Broughton is listed in the *DNB*, and the novel is briefly described in E. Baker's *Guide to the Best Fiction.*

659.31/643.36   FOUND DROWNED ...   See entry 50.5. R. M. Adams says that when Murphy picks up the paper, "*he* can find only real things to read about" (cf. entry 659.7), and Adams mentions "the finding of the drowned man" as one of these (*SS*, p. 231). But I can find no account of the finding of a drowned man in the *Evening Telegraph*. I think what the text means at this point is that the old sailor simply looked for the "found drowned" headline, since drownings would be of great interest to him. And, though the paper did report the results of a cricket game between Nottinghamshire and Kent, in which Iremonger scored 155, the account makes no mention of "King Willow."

660.5/644.11   THE LAST OF THE MOHICANS   American novelist James Fenimore Cooper (1789–1851) wrote a novel entitled *The Last of the Mohicans* (1826), which forms part of his series, *The Leatherstocking Tales.*

660.6/644.12 FOR ALL WHO RAN TO READ   In Habakkuk 2:2, the Lord
tells Habakkuk, "Write the vision, and make it plain upon tables,
that he may run that readeth it."

660.26/644.32 HIS TENDER ACHILLES   See entry 640.35.

660.38/645.2 WRAPPED IN THE ARMS OF MURPHY   A variation on
"the arms of Morpheus"; see entry 639.11.

660.39/645.3 DREAMING OF FRESH FIELDS AND PASTURES NEW   From
Milton's "Lycidas"; see entry 630.15.

660.40/645.4 COFFIN OF STONES . . . STONING TO DEATH ON THE PART OF
SEVENTYTWO . . .   Bloom is here recalling some of the traditions
about Parnell which were mentioned earlier. See entry 648.43.
Perhaps the phrase "stoning to death" recalls the stoning to death
of St. Stephen, the first Christian martyr, which is described in
Acts 7:54–60.

661.5/645.11 WAGNERIAN MUSIC   Several of Wagner's works are
alluded to in *Ulysses*; see the Index.

661.8/645.14 MERCADANTE'S HUGUENOTS   On Meyerbeer's—not Mercadante's—opera *Les Huguenots*, see entry 168.20.

661.8/645.14 MEYERBEER'S SEVEN LAST WORDS ON THE CROSS   This
repeats a mistake Bloom has made earlier; Meyerbeer wrote no
Seven Last Words. See entry 290.34.

661.9/645.15 MOZART'S TWELFTH MASS . . .   The work Bloom is
referring to is spurious; see entry 82.17.

661.14/645.20 MOODY AND SANKEY HYMNS OR BID ME TO LIVE . . .
American evangelists Dwight L. Moody (1837–99) and Ira David
Sankey (1840–1908) compiled a famous hymn collection entitled
Sacred Songs and Solos. Though the hymns in the collection are
often referred to as "Moody and Sankey hymns," Moody wrote
none and Sankey composed very few of the hymns. "Bid Me to
Live" is not a hymn, but a poem by Robert Herrick, entitled "To
Anthea, Why May Command him Anything," which begins with
the words Bloom quotes.

661.16/645.22 ROSSINI'S STABAT MATER   See entry 82.9.

661.27/645.32 DON GIOVANNI   Mozart's *Don Giovanni* is alluded to
frequently in *Ulysses*; see entry 63.31 and the Index.

661.27/645.33 MARTHA   On Flotow's *Martha*, see entry 117.34; on
Lionel's aria, which is mentioned on p. 661.31/645.36, see entry
256.26.

661.29/645.34 THE SEVERE CLASSICAL SCHOOL SUCH AS MENDELSSOHN
On Felix Mendelssohn, who was of the Romantic, not the "severe
classical" school of composers, see entries 342.24 and 285.37.

661.37/645.42 SHAKESPEARE'S SONGS   Several of Shakespeare's songs are alluded to in *Ulysses*; see, for example, entries 191.13, 191.24, and 212.36.

661.38/646.1   THE LUTENIST DOWLAND WHO LIVED IN FETTER LANE NEAR GERARD THE HERBALIST, WHO ANNO LUDENDO HAUSI, DOULANDUS   On Gerard the herbalist, see entry 202.9. John Dowland (1563?–1626?) was an English composer and lutenist. His *Songs or Ayres* (1597–1603) showed him to be the foremost composer of songs of his day. R. M. Adams discusses this Latin phrase and says, ". . . the Latin anagram does not make much sense as given, because it was based on the Latin form of Dowland's name which Joyce does not give in full, Iohannes Doulandus, and he has misquoted it from '*Annos ludendo hausi*.' It is attributed to Ralph Sadler and Henry Peacham, and a rough translation would be, 'I used up my years in playing' " (*SS*, p. 95). Adams says that Dowland was living in Fetter Lane in 1603 and 1606, but cites no source. The *DNB* article on Dowland mentions his living in Fetter Lane in 1609, but suggests that he lived in Denmark from about 1600 to 1609.

662.1/646.6   FARNABY AND SON WITH THEIR DUX AND COMES CONCEITS   Giles Farnaby (*ca.* 1565?–1640) and his son Richard Farnaby (*ca.* 1590– ?) were English composers. Giles published a set of *Canzonets to Fowre Voyces* (1598) which contained twenty pieces for four voices and one for eight voices. Little is known about the son, Richard, but he apparently composed in the same vein as his father. *Dux* and *comes* refers to the *subject* and *answer* development so common in part singing at this time.

662.2/646.7   BYRD (WILLIAM), WHO PLAYED THE VIRGINALS . . . IN THE QUEEN'S CHAPEL   William Byrd (or Byrde, 1543–1623) was a composer and organist; though a Roman Catholic, he did compose English anthems and services and was one of the organists at the Chapel Royal.

662.4/646.9   TOMKINS WHO MADE TOYS OR AIRS   Tomkins was the name of a family of talented musicians and composers during the sixteenth and seventeenth centuries. The best known of these, and probably the one Stephen is referring to, is Thomas Tomkins (1572–1656), organist and composer of many songs and madrigals. To compound the potential confusion in Stephen's esoteric references, this Thomas Tomkins was both the son and the brother of other "Thomas Tomkinses."

662.4/646.9   JOHN BULL   Dr. John Bull (1563?–1628) was composer, singer, organist, and professor of music. A galliard of his composition may have been the origin of the melody of the English national anthem, "God Save the King."

662.10/646.16 JOHN BULL THE POLITICAL CELEBRITY   John Bull, the
popular representation of British government and the British tem-
perament, derives from a character in a series of satirical pamphlets
by Dr. John Arbuthnot, entitled *The History of John Bull* (1712).

662.22/646.28 PUTTING HIS HIND FOOT FOREMOST   This is another
of the "witty variations" on a common saying or proverb which
are so common in this chapter. This varies the proverbial "To put
one's best foot foremost (or forward)," which is listed in the
ODEP.

662.22/646.28 THE LORD OF HIS CREATION   Though this phrase sounds
biblical, it is also quite ordinary, and allusion of any sort is doubtful. There is no such phrase in the King James Bible, and the
closest in the Douay is Judith 9:17: "O God of the Heavens, creator of the waters, and Lord of the whole creation. . . ."

662.37/646.42 BRUTES OF THE FIELD   Especially in view of the
many variations on common phrases in this episode, this is probably
a variation on the common biblical phrase "beasts of the field." This
phrase occurs many times in the King James and the Douay Bibles,
but "brutes of the field" does not occur in either.

662.42/647.5 IN MEDIAS RES   Beginning *in medias res* ("in the middle of things") is one of the characteristics of the classical epic.

663.12/647.16 YOUTH HERE HAS END BY JANS PIETER SWEELINCK . . .
This alludes to a song entitled "Mein junges Leben hat ein End,"
by Dutch composer Jans Pieter Sweelinck (1562–1621). S. Sultan
points out that Stephen's approximate translation of the title obscures the fact that the song is sung by a dying youth (*Argument
of Ulysses*, pp. 380–81).

663.19/647.18 AN OLD GERMAN SONG OF JOHANNES JEEP . . .   Johann
Jeep (1582?–ca. 1650) was a German composer; he composed a
book of psalms and several books of secular songs, some appearing
in many editions. Richard K. Bass has identified this as a song
entitled "Dulcia dum loquitur cogitat insidias," which appeared in
Jeep's collection *Studentengärtlein*, Pt. II, no. 3 (*Explicator*, XXIV
[Feb., 1966], item 55). Bass assumes that Stephen sings the whole
song, and quotes the words of stanza three to show the relevance
of the song to the theme of "wrecked lives" in the "Eumaeus" episode.

663.26/647.30 BARRACLOUGH   Barraclough was a contemporary
Dubliner; see entry 277.17.

664.20/648.23 IVAN ST AUSTELL AND HILTON ST JUST   Of these two,
R. M. Adams says, "Both these splendidly titled gentlemen (their
names seem to come from Cornish towns) sang during the 1890's

with the Arthur Rouseby Opera Company. Mr. St. Austell's real name was W. H. Stephens, and Mr. St. Just no doubt concealed an equally plebian title under his superb stage pseudonym" (*SS*, p. 73). The names of both appear occasionally in accounts of operas performed by the Rouseby company in the Dublin daily papers.

664.40/649.1 FOOLS STEP IN WHERE ANGELS   The well-known "For fools rush in where angels fear to tread" is from Alexander Pope's *Essay on Criticism*, III, 66.

665.11/649.14 HIS SCYTHED CAR   This alludes to the practice of attaching scythes to the wheels of chariots and using them as weapons of war. *Harper's Dictionary of Classical Literature and Antiquities* says this was done by the Assyrians, the Persians, the Medes, and the Syrians in Asia, and by the Gauls and Britons in Europe. P. W. Joyce, in his *Short History*, says that the ancient Irish used chariots and "the war chariots are sometimes described as furnished with sharp spikes and scythe-blades like those of the old Britons" (p. 117).

665.17/649.20 UND ALLE SCHIFFE BRÜCKEN   This is from the song of Johann Jeep alluded to earler; see entry 663.14.

665.19/649.22 AS HE SAT ON HIS LOW BACKED CAR   This, and the italicized phrases on pp. 665.21/649.24 and 665.29/649.32, allude to "The Low-Backed Car"; see entry 311.7.

665.23/649.26 SIRENS, ENEMIES OF MAN'S REASON   The Sirens were alluded to earlier in this episode; see entry 651.17.

666.38/650.37 THE CONVERSION OF THE IRISH NATION TO CHRISTIANITY FROM DRUIDISM . . . On the death of King Cormac, see entry 169.23. Estimates of the date of his death vary. The *Annals of the Four Masters* gives A.D. 266 as the date and ascribes his death to choking on a salmon bone, which was caused by a spirit of the druid priests, who were incensed at his having turned from them to God. The anachronism that Stephen is referring to is that Cormac is often described as the last pagan king of Ireland, though he lived two centuries before Patrick's arrival. Though the annalists do not mention it, Cormac was, according to Keating, buried at Rossnaree (*History of Ireland*, Book I, sec. XLVI; Keating spells it Ros na Riogh). St. Patrick came to Ireland in 432, sent by Pope Celestine I. The Four Masters say this was in the fourth year of King Leary. The genealogy Stephen gives is based on one such as that given in the *Annals*. Patrick's father was named Calpornius; Potitus and Odyssus are probably based on "Fotaide" and "Deisse," Patrick's grandfather and great-grandfather according to the *Annals, s.v.* 432.

667.8/651.8 CLOUD . . . AT FIRST NO BIGGER THAN A WOMAN'S HAND
This alludes, with some variation, to the description of a cloud
given by Elijah's servant in I Kings. Elijah sends his servant to see
whether any cloud has appeared on the horizon, and the seventh
time he returns, the servant says, "Behold, there ariseth a little
cloud out of the sea, like a man's hand" (I Kings 18:44). Elijah
recognizes this as the cloud which will break the drought he himself had brought about (see I Kings 17:1, 18:43–45).

668.18/652.18 TO ENTER OR NOT TO ENTER . . .   This parodies Hamlet's "To be or not to be," in his soliloquy in *Hamlet*, III, i; this soliloquy has been alluded to several times earlier in *Ulysses*.

668.33/652.33 THE LAST FEAST OF THE ASCENSION, TO WIT, THE TWELFTH
OF MAY   The Feast of the Ascension is celebrated on the for-
tieth day after Easter—the Thursday after the fifth Sunday after
Easter—which in 1904 fell on Thursday, May 12.

668.35/652.35 JEWISH ERA FIVE THOUSAND SIX HUNDRED AND SIXTYFOUR
. . .   Joyce probably got this list of datings in terms of various
systems and calendars from Thom's *Dublin Directory* (1904), p. 1.
It explains there that 1904 is "Bissextile, or Leap Year," and says,
"The year 5665 of the Jewish era commences on September 10,
1904. . . . The year 1322 of the Mohametan Era commences on
March 18, 1904," and also contains the other information in this
paragraph.

670.17/654.17 THE FEAST OF SAINT FRANCIS-XAVIER 1898   St. Francis
Xavier (1506–62) was a Jesuit missionary who was called the
Apostle to the Indies. His feast day is December 3.

671.2/655.2 FROM ROUNDWOOD RESERVOIR IN COUNTY WICKLOW . . .
R. M. Adams says (*SS*, p. 226) that "the whole latter half of the
description of the Dublin waterworks . . . comes from a letter to
the *Irish Independent* written by Ignatius J. Rice, and published
in the issue of June 15, 1904." But this is misleading, for the letter
from Rice (who was a Law Agent for the Dublin Corporation)
deals solely with current litigation between the Dublin Corporation and the South Dublin Guardians (described in the last seven
lines of this paragraph in *Ulysses*), and has no description of the
waterworks system at all. The description given here derives in
large part, though not entirely, from Thom's *Dublin Directory*
(1904), where, in the "Dublin Annals," *s.v.* 1868 (the year of their
completion) the waterworks are described in similar terms and
details.

671.16/655.16 RECOURSE BEING HAD TO THE IMPOTABLE WATER OF THE

GRAND AND ROYAL CANALS AS IN 1893   The "Dublin Annals" section of Thom's *Dublin Directory* (1904), s.v. 1893, says "Unprecedented drought. Scarcity of water at Roundwood Reservoir. Grand Canal supply resorted to (Oct. 16)" (p. 2105). More detail can be found in F. E. Dixon's "Weather in Old Dublin," *Dublin Historical Record*, XIII (1952–53), 99, though Dixon mentions the use of water from only the Grand Canal, not the Royal. But contemporary newspaper accounts confirm that both canals were drawn upon.

671.26/655.25   DRAWER OF WATER   A "drawer of water" is mentioned several times in the Bible, and in each case the phrase refers to a menial servant or a slave. See Deuteronomy 29:11 and Joshua 9:21, 23, 27.

671.27/655.26   WATERCARRIER   This is the common name for the zodiacal sign of Aquarius, the eleventh sign of the zodiac. Bloom mentions the zodiac on p. 683.16/667.18.

671.30/655.29   MERCATOR'S PROJECTION   Gerardus Mercator (Gerhard Kremer, 1512–94) was a Flemish geographer, mathematician, and cartographer. The first map using his projection appeared in 1568. Since his projection increases the apparent area of the higher latitude and polar areas of the globe, it does make the ocean appear even more vast than it actually is.

674.38/659.1   THE END JUSTIFIED THE MEANS   "The end justifies the means" is proverbial and is listed in the *ODEP*. It is usually traced back to a book entitled *Medulla Theologiae*, by German Jesuit and casuist Hermann Busenbaum (1600–68).

675.35/659.35   TRUTH STRANGER THAN FICTION   Apparently this now proverbial phrase (it is listed in *ODEP* and Apperson) goes back to Byron's *Don Juan*, canto XIV, stanza 101, which begins, " 'Tis strange,—but true; for truth is always strange;/ Stranger than fiction."

676.7/660.7   ELIJAH, RESTORER OF THE CHURCH IN ZION   See entry 151.15.

676.15/660.15   THE LIGHT OF INSPIRATION SHINING IN HIS COUNTENANCE . . .   This is the description of Moses which was given in the speech by John F. Taylor, quoted earlier on pp. 142/140 ff. (see esp. p. 143.14/141.23).

676.30/660.30   LIGHT TO THE GENTILES   Stephen earlier referred to preaching to the Gentiles, and Bloom was sarcastically called "A new apostle to the Gentiles." See entries 29.27 and 333.20.

678.2/662.2   THE SHAMROCK, A WEEKLY NEWSPAPER   *Willing's Press*

Guide . . . 1905 (for 1904) lists the *Shamrock* as a weekly, published at 32 Lower Abbey St., Dublin, which began in 1866 and sells for one pence.

678.28/662.28 IF BRIAN BORU . . .   On Brian Boru, see entry 99.25.

678.32/662.31 THE GRAND ANNUAL CHRISTMAS PANTOMIME SINBAD
THE SAILOR . . .   R. M. Adams has shown (*SS*, pp. 76–82) that the information in this paragraph about *Sindbad the Sailor* derives from advertisements in the *Freeman's Journal* of December 24 and 26, 1892. In his detailed discussion Adams points out that Joyce uses many names directly from the advertisements, deletes many, and alters some. Peter Spielberg's catalogue of the Joyce collection at Buffalo lists several items which confirm this, under entry IX.A.4. Miscellaneous MSS: Notes. This includes reviews of *Sindbad the Sailor* from the *Freeman's Journal* of January 31, 1893 and from the *Irish Times* of January 30, 1893. It also includes what Spielberg calls "untitled, incomplete review," which is even more to our purpose, for examination of the contemporary newspapers shows that the unidentified pages 4–7 contain all but the first ten lines of a long review of this same pantomime from the *Freeman's Journal* of December 27, 1892. And this makes it very likely that the missing pages 1–3 contained copies of the advertisements from the issue of December 24 and 26 which Adams draws on.

678.40/663.1 DIAMOND JUBILEE OF QUEEN VICTORIA . . . THE NEW
MUNICIPAL FISHMARKET   The new Dublin Fish Market opened on May 11, 1897, and Queen Victoria's Diamond Jubilee was celebrated on June 22, 1897. Perhaps Joyce got the idea for placing these two events together from Thom's *Dublin Directory* (1904), which, in its "Dublin Annals" section, *s.v.* 1897, juxtaposes and specifically dates these two events. It also tells, under the same entry, of the arrival of "Their Royal Highnesses the Duke and Duchess of York" on August 18, 1897 (p. 2105).

679.5/663.6 HIS MAJESTY KING BRIAN BORU   Brian Boru was mentioned on p. 678.28/662.28; see entry 99.25.

679.7/663.8 THE RECENT ERECTIONS OF THE GRAND LYRIC HALL . . .
Thom's *Dublin Directory* (1904), in its "Dublin Annals," *s.v.* 1897, records that on November 26, "The Grand Lyric Hall on Burgh-quay, formerly the Conciliation Hall, opened," and on December 13, "The Theatre Royal, standing on the site of the old Theatre, and lately the Leinster Hall, opened" (p. 2105–the site was Hawkins Street).

679.16/663.16 EVERYBODY'S BOOK OF JOKES   Though this title seems ordinary enough, and there was a series of *Everybody's . . .* books

published about 1890, I have not found a book by this exact title.
I examined *Everybody's Book of Irish Wit and Humour*, ed. W. H.
Howe (London, 1890), but could find no evidence of Joyce's hav-
ing used it.

679.35/663.36 THE MAXIMUM ANTEDILUVIAN AGE, THAT OF METHUSA-
LAH, 969 YEARS   Genesis 5:27 records that Methuselah lived to
be 969 years old. Methuselah was also alluded to earlier on p. 336.6/
330.5.

681.17/665.20 CHARLES STEWART PARNELL AND FOR MICHAEL DAVITT
Parnell and Davitt were co-leaders in forming the National Land
League; see entry 657.7.

681.23/665.26 EUGEN SANDOW'S PHYSICAL STRENGTH AND HOW TO OBTAIN
IT   See entry 61.25.

682.9/666.11 TRANSUBSTANTIAL HEIR . . . CONSUBSTANTIAL HEIR
Though these words most directly evoke the theological arguments
about the nature of the sacrament of the Eucharist (i.e., whether
it is a sacrifice, whether the bread and wine are transformed into
the body and blood, or joined with it, or merely symbolize it), the
word *heir* suggests the various heresies about the relationship between the Father and the Son which have been alluded to in *Ulysses*.
See entries 21.8 ff.

683.16/667.18 THE TWELVE CONSTELLATIONS OF THE ZODIAC FROM ARIES
TO PISCES   In the normal ordering of the twelve signs of the
Zodiac, Aries, the Ram, is first, and Pisces, the Fish, last, since the
point from which the positions are located is the vernal equinox.

685.17/669.22 A PISGAH SIGHT OF PALESTINE   See entry 149.25.

685.21/669.26 MY FAVOURITE HERO   As Herbert Gorman points out
(*James Joyce*, p. 45), Joyce himself wrote an essay about Ulysses
while he was at Belvedere College and entitled it "My Favourite
Hero."

685.21/669.26 PROCRASTINATION IS THE THIEF OF TIME   This title
is, of course, proverbial. The *ODEP* lists this phrase.

685.28/669.33 PHILIP BEAUFOY OR DOCTOR DICK OR HEBLON'S STUDIES IN
BLUE   On Philip Beaufoy, see entry 68.39. I have not fully identified Doctor Dick, but it was the pseudonym of a Dublin writer
who "localized" pantomimes around the turn of the century. Several pantomime advertisements I have seen list him as the writer of
the "Local Verses and References," or the "Locals." He did this, for
example, for the pantomime *Jack and the Beanstalk* that played
at the Gaiety during the Christmas season of 1902–3. Heblon was
the pseudonym of Dublin lawyer Joseph K. O'Connor (b. 1878),
who attended Clongowes Wood College. *Studies in Blue* (Dublin,

1900) is described by Stephen J. Brown as "Sketches, true to life, and cleverly told, of the most disreputable side of Dublin slum-life, as seen, chiefly, in the Police Courts. Amusing, but at times verging on vulgarity" (*Ireland in Fiction*).

685.35/670.1   S. ALOYSIUS GONZAGA   St. Aloysius Gonzaga (1568–91), whose feast day is June 21, was a high-born boy who could not be dissuaded from joining the Jesuits. He died from nursing the plague-stricken, and he is a patron of youth (see Butler's *The Lives of the Saints*, II, 603). On Joyce's taking Aloysius as his saint's name at confirmation, see Ellmann, JJ, pp. 29–30.

686.31/670.36   METEMPSYCHOSIS . . .   As Bloom says on p. 154.7/ 152.4, "met him pike hoses" is Molly's version of "metempsychosis," on which see entry 64.18. And apparently *alias* makes her think of Ananias, the liar of Acts 5:1–11, whose name has become proverbial for a liar.

687.21/671.28   MOSES OF EGYPT, MOSES MAIMONIDES . . .   Maimonides has been mentioned several times earlier in *Ulysses*; see entry 28.14. He did write an important work entitled *Moreh Nebukim* ("Guide for the Perplexed") in which he explains esoteric points in the Bible, develops proofs of God's existence, and discusses many difficult philosophical and religious problems. The work reveals his great knowledge of Aristotle and has been influential on Jewish and Christian thinkers. Moses Mendelssohn (1729–86) was a German Jewish philosopher and theologian.

687.27/671.34   . . . ARISTOTLE . . .   The idea that Aristotle was influenced by Jewish thought and perhaps by a Jewish teacher is common in Jewish legend about Aristotle. Most such ideas are of relatively recent origin and are based on spurious works. See "Aristotle in Jewish Legend" in the *Jewish Encyclopedia*, II, 98–99.

687.31/672.3   SONS OF THE LAW AND CHILDREN OF A SELECTED OR REJECTED RACE   These phrases allude to the idea of the Jews as the "chosen people," though I have not found these exact phrases used to describe them. To the Jews, their being the chosen or selected race is closely tied up with their observation of the Law.

687.33/672.5   FELIX BARTHOLDY MENDELSSOHN . . .   On Mendelssohn, see entry 342.24 and the Index. On Spinoza, see entry 284.36. Daniel Mendoza (1763–1836) was an English Jewish pugilist. Nicknamed "Star of Israel," he was champion of England from 1792 to 1795. He is said to have done much to introduce science and skill into boxing. In 1791 Mendoza went on tour, and on August 2, 1791, he defeated an Irish amateur, "Squire Fitzgerald," who had on pressed a wish to meet him. Ferdinand Lassalle (1825–64), son of a Jewish merchant, was a well-known German lawyer. A disciple of Hegel, Lassalle was a Socialist who contributed importantly to forming the first workers' political party in Germany, a party which later developed into the Social Democratic Party. Lassalle was killed in a duel over a love affair. He is the basis of the hero, Alvan, of Meredith's novel *The Tragic Comedians* (1880).

688.3/672.11 SUIL, SUIL, SUIL ARUN . . .   This is the beginning of the chorus of a song usually called "Shule Aroon." The verses of the song are in English. It is the lament of an Irish girl whose sweetheart has gone to France to fight. Stephen's translation is not precisely accurate: the words he quotes say, "Walk, walk, walk, my darling, walk with safety, walk with care." For words and music, see Moffat's *Minstrelsy of Ireland*, 3rd ed., pp. 104–5.

688.6/672.14 KIFELOCH, HARIMON RAKATEJCH M'BAAD L'ZAMATEJCH . . . The Song of Solomon 4:3 says, ". . . thy temples are like a piece of a pomegranate within thy locks", and verse 6:7 is almost identical.

688.11/672.19 SWEETS OF SIN   See entry 236.5.

688.15/672.23 THE HEBREW CHARACTERS . . . THEIR ARITHMETICAL VALUES . . .   Bloom's Hebrew characters are written to parallel Stephen's Irish ones. Ghimel, third letter of the Hebrew alphabet, has a numerical value of 3; Aleph, first letter, has a value of 1; Daleth, fourth letter, has a value of 4; Mem (which Bloom apparently cannot remember) is the thirteenth letter and has a value of 40; Goph (more commonly Koph) is the nineteenth letter and has a value of one hundred.

688.27/672.35 BOTH HAVING BEEN TAUGHT ON THE PLAIN OF SHINAR . . . R. M. Adams has pointed out (*SS*, pp. 136–37) that this probably derives from G. Keating's *History of Ireland*, Book I, sec. XV, where Keating describes the founding of a language school in the Plain of Seanair by Fenius Farsaidh and dates the school 242 years after the deluge. Keating traces Farsaidh back to Magog (said in Gen. 10:2 to be the grandson of Noah), and says he was the ancestor of the children of Milcadh, which include Eibhear and Eireamhon. As a preparation for the story of the tower of Babel in Genesis 11, we are told, "And the whole earth was of one language, and of one speech. And it came to pass, as they journeyed from the east, that they found a plain in the land of Shinar; and they dwelt there" (11:1–2).

688.33/673.4 TORAH, TALMUD (MISCHNA AND GHEMARA) MASSOR, PENTATEUCH   In its narrow meaning, the Torah is synonymous with the Pentateuch, the books Genesis, Exodus, Leviticus, Numbers, and Deuteronomy, all of which are traditionally said to have been written by Moses. In its broader sense, the Torah includes the Written Law (Pentateuch), the Oral Law, and the entire talmudic literature and commentaries. The Talmud is the name given to each of two great compilations of records of academic discussion and judicial administration of the Jewish law, the Babylonian Talmud and the Palestinian Talmud. Each consists of a Mischna (codification of the core of the Oral Law) and a Gemara (commentary and supplement to the Mischna). The Masorah is a body of critical notes and traditions concerning the correct spelling, writing, and reading of the Hebrew scriptures.

688.34/673.5 BOOK OF THE DUN COW, BOOK OF BALLYMOTE, GARLAND OF HOWTH, BOOK OF KELLS   *The Book of the Dun Cow* (*Leabhar na h-Uidhre*) is a twelfth-century manuscript, compiled at the monastery of Clonmacnois in county Offaly. It is the oldest of the manuscripts which contain the old romances of Ireland. *The Book of Ballymote* (*Leabhar Baile an Mhota*) is another miscellaneous collection of tales and history, compiled about the beginning of the fifteenth century. I have located no "Garland of Howth"; the context suggests that the *Book of Howth* is meant. D. Hyde describes this book as "a small vellum folio of the sixteenth century, written in thirteen different hands" (*Lit. Hist. of Ireland*, p. 210). The *Book of Howth* has been published in the Calendar of State Papers; see *Calendar of the Carew Manuscripts Preserved in the Archiepiscopal Library at Lambeth* (London, 1871). The *Book of Kells* is a magnificent illuminated manuscript of the Latin gospels, prepared probably in the eighth century and now in the library of Trinity College, Dublin.

688.37/673.8 IN GHETTO (S. MARY'S ABBEY) AND MASSHOUSE (ADAM AND EVE'S TAVERN)   St. Mary's Abbey was for some time the Jewish synagogue in Dublin; see entry 230.19. The Church of St. Francis of Assisi on Merchant's Quay in Dublin is popularly known as "Adam and Eve's Church." The guidebook *Catholic Dublin* explains that even through the Tudor persecution of the Roman Catholic Church, the Franciscans managed to remain secretly in Dublin, and goes on to say that about 1618, the Franciscans "set up a church at Rosemary Lane (beside the present edifice). In this secluded thoroughfare there was, at this time, a tavern, known as *Adam and Eve's*; the sign board in connection with which, swinging at each end of the lane, proved a convenient 'cover' for the penalized Catholics stealing into the Franciscan Church to Mass.

The ancient tavern-name has remained, even though the little
Church which it served as subterfuge has passed away. Today
'Adam and Eve's' is among Dubliners the most familiar mode of
reference to the Church" (p. 61).

688.38/673.9 PROSCRIPTION OF THEIR NATIONAL COSTUMES   Both the
Irish and the Jews have at various times had certain traditional
items of dress outlawed. The well-known Irish song "The Wearin'
of the Green" says, in part, "No more Saint Patrick's day we'll
keep, his color can't be seen,/ For there's a cruel law agin the
wearin' o' the Green!" (cf. entry 44.5). On proscriptions concerning Jewish dress, see the article "Costume" in the *Jewish Encyclopedia*, which mentions several such laws in various countries.

688.39/673.10 THE RESTORATION IN CHANAN DAVID OF ZION   I have
found no modern-day Zionist by this name. Perhaps this alludes to
Anan ben David, who lived in the second half of the eighth century
and founded the Karaites, an austere Jewish sect. See the *Jewish
Encyclopedia* for information on Anan ben David and the Karaites.

689.5/673.15 KOLOD BALEJWAW PNIMAH . . .   These are the opening
lines of Austrian Hebrew poet Naphtali Herz Imber's (1856–1909)
"Ha Tikvah," which is now the Jewish national anthem and the
anthem of the State of Israel. Words, music, and a free translation
can be found in *National Anthems of the World*, ed. Martin Shaw
and Henry Coleman (London, 1963), pp. 185–86.

689.29/674.7 DEPICTED BY JOHANNES DAMASCENUS, LENTULUS ROMANUS
AND EPIPHANIUS MONACHUS AS LEUCODERMIC, SESQUIPEDALIAN WITH
WINEDARK HAIR   R. M. Adams says that all of these were historical figures who did deal with the personal appearance of Christ,
though they did not describe him in the terms Stephen uses (*SS*,
pp. 138–39). I have not satisfactorily identified Epiphanius Monachus, though I assume him to be St. Epiphanius of Salamis (d. 403),
since he was involved in a controversary over the depiction of Christ
and since St. John Damascene edited some of his works. St. John
Damascene (d. *ca.* 749) did write on Christ's personal appearance
and described him as "tall" and of "a pale complexion, olive-tinted,
and of the color of wheat" (see James Hastings, *Dictionary of
Christ and the Gospels* [New York, 1917], I, 315). Lentulus Romanus (or Publius Lentulus) is a fictitious person, said to have been
governor of Judea before Pontius Pilate, and to have written a
letter describing the personal appearance of Christ, which says that
he was "a man of tall stature" and that his hair was "somewhat
wine-coloured" (see Hastings, *Dictionary*, I, 315). Stephen's use
of "sesquipedalian" is puzzling and needs comment. Literally it

means "measuring a foot and a half," and figuratively it is used to mean "extremely long," as in "sesquipedalian words." I have found no meaning of the word which could be used to describe a person's height, unless in a loose, figurative sense that might mean "quite tall." But I suspect, without any very firm basis for it, that Stephen is referring to the old tradition that Christ was the only man exactly six feet tall. In *Stephen Hero*, Stephen and his mother argue about matters of tradition and belief, and Stephen, in two successive statements, specifically denies belief that Jesus was the only man who ever had pure auburn hair and that he was the only man who was exactly six feet tall (*Stephen Hero*, p. 139). On the Homeric epithet "wine-dark," see entry 5.7.

690.5/674.16   DR. ALEXANDER J. DOWIE . . . SEYMOUR BUSHE . . . RUFUS ISAACS . . . CHARLES WYNDHAM . . . OSMOND TEARLE   On Dowie, see entry 151.15. On Bushe, see entry 100.4. Rufus Daniel Isaacs, first marquess of Reading (1860–1935) was a Jewish English lawyer and statesman. He entered Parliament as a liberal in August of 1904; the *DNB* has a long article on him. Sir Charles Wyndham (born Charles Culverwell, 1837–1919) was an English actor and theater manager whose greatest success was in comedy and farce; the *DNB* has an article on him. George Osmond Tearle (1852–1901) made his debut as Guildenstern in 1869, and in 1871 he first played Hamlet, a role he played some eight hundred times. In 1888 he formed a Shakespearean touring company, and he conducted Stratford on Avon Shakespeare festivals in 1889 and 1890; the *DNB* also includes an article on him.

690.17/674.28   LITTLE HARRY HUGHES AND HIS SCHOOLFELLOWS ALL . . . Though Child gives no version exactly like this one, this is obviously a variant of Child's ballad no. 155, "Sir Hugh, or, the Jew's Daughter."

692.14/676.24   RITUAL MURDER   See entry 108.30.

693.3/677.19   PADNEY SOCKS . . .   Though this sounds as if it might allude to some nursery or children's rhyme, I have not been able to locate any such rhyme. Hodgart and Worthington do not list this.

695.15/679.34   A SCHOOLFELLOW AND A JEW'S DAUGHTER   Though this refers to Stephen and Milly, it also alludes to the ballad "Little Harry Hughes"; see entry 690.17.

696.20/680.37   ALBERT HENGLER'S CIRCUS   See entry 64.29.

697.34/682.15   THE EXODUS FROM THE HOUSE OF BONDAGE   This is a variation on a biblical phrase Bloom has thought of several times earlier; see entry 122.22.

698.7/682.23 THE 113TH, MODUS PEREGRINUS: IN EXITU ISRÄEL DE
    EGYPTO: DOMUS JACOB DE POPULO BARBARO   The Vulgate version
    of the 113th Psalm (114th in the King James numbering) begins,
    "In exitu Israel de Aegypto, Domus Iacob de populo barbaro"
    ("When Israel went out of Egypt, the house of Jacob from a peo-
    ple of strange language"). As W. Y. Tindall has pointed out (RG,
    p. 225), Dante chose the opening words of this psalm to illustrate
    the four levels of meaning (literal, allegorical, moral, anagogical)
    when discussing the matter in his letter to Can Grande Della Scala.
    See The Comedy of Dante Alighieri, III (Paradise), trans. by
    Dorothy L. Sayers (New York: Basic Books, 1962), pp. 45–46.
698.32/683.17 NOVA IN 1901   A nova is a variable star. This must al-
    lude to Nova Persei, which was discovered by T. D. Anderson on
    February 21–22, 1901. It soon grew to be the brightest star in the
    northern heavens and then decreased.
700.12/684.36 TO VANITIES, TO VANITIES OF VANITIES AND ALL THAT IS
    VANITY   This alludes to Ecclesiastes 1:2, which says, "Vanity
    of vanities, saith the Preacher, vanity of vanities; all is vanity."
700.25/685.10 GALILEO, SIMON MARIUS, PIAZZI, LE VERRIER, HERSCHEL,
    GALLE   R. M. Adams has commented on the strange combination
    of the accurate and misleading and puzzling in this list of astrono-
    mers (SS, pp. 157–58). The context implies that all of these men,
    or certain pairs of them, made simultaneous but independent dis-
    coveries in astronomy, but, while this is true of some of them, it
    is not true of all. German astronomer Simon Marius (1573–1624)
    was one of several who were working with rudimentary telescopes
    in 1609 when Galileo "discovered" the instrument, and both of
    them independently observed the four satellites of Jupiter. Italian
    priest and astronomer Guiseppe Piazzi (1746–1826) and French
    astronomer Urbain Jean Joseph Leverrier (1811–77) were not
    contemporaneous enough to make simultaneous discoveries, and
    Laverrier's relationship with German astronomer Johann Gott-
    fried Galle (1812–1910) suggests that they are to be paired off.
    These two jointly discovered the planet Neptune in 1846, Leverrier
    doing the calculations and Galle the observation. But this is not
    an "independent synochronous" discovery, though, strangely
    enough, the discovery of Neptune does provide one. English as-
    tronomer John Couch Adams (1819–92) predicted the existence
    of the then unknown Neptune simultaneously with and indepen-
    dently of Leverrier, but a delay in England in making a telescopic
    search caused Leverrier to be given credit for the discovery. The
    remaining two in the list, Piazzi and English astronomer Sir Wil-

liam Herschel (1738–1822), do pair off since they were close contemporaries and their fields of interest were very similar. Both did
important work with large telescopes and were interested in cat-
aloguing the stars (one of Herschel's main interests was double
stars, just mentioned). However, these two did not, to my knowledge, make simultaneous discoveries. As R. M. Adams points out,
passages such as these are puzzling since we do not know how much
Joyce knew. But my feeling is that in this instance, Joyce was in
control. Bloom's list contains the names of actual astronomers,
some rather recondite. One pair did actually make a disputed simultaneous discovery, another pair was involved in a simultaneous
discovery with another astronomer, and the third pair worked in
very similar fields. There seems to be enough order and control
here that we can attribute the ignorance and approximation to
Bloom rather than to Joyce.

700.26/685.11   THE SYSTEMATISATIONS ATTEMPTED BY BODE AND KEPLER
Bloom's statement correctly describes the third of Johannes Kepler's (1571–1630) three laws of planetary motion, i.e., that the
square of a planet's periodic time (time of complete orbit around
the sun) is proportional to the cube of its mean distance from the
sun. German astronomer Johann Elert Bode (1747–1826) gave
currency to an empirical rule concerning the relative distances of
the planets from the sun, though the rule was actually announced
by Johann Daniel Titus of Wittenberg in 1766. For a description
of Bode's complicated equation, see the *Encyclopaedia Britannica*,
s.v. Planet.

700.30/685.15   THE LIBYAN FLOODS ON MARS . . .   This seems to refer
to some phenomenon on the planet Mars about 1882. Mars was
being closely observed by G. V. Schiaparelli and others at this
time, and there is a section of the planet which is designated "Lib-
ya," but I do not know specifically what is referred to here.

700.33/685.18   FEAST OF S. LAWRENCE (MARTYR, 10 AUGUST)   St.
Lawrence (d. 258), Roman deacon and martyr, is said to have been
burned to death on a gridiron. He is highly venerated and is mentioned in the Canon of the Mass. His day is, as indicated, August the
tenth.

700.34/685.19   THE NEW MOON WITH THE OLD MOON IN HER ARMS   In
the ballad "Sir Patrick Spens," one of the seamen warns his captain
against the voyage by saying, "I saw the new moon late yestreen/
Wi' the auld moon in her arm;/ And if we gang to sea, master,/
I fear we'll come to harm."

700.36/685.20 THE APPEARANCE OF A STAR ... ABOUT THE PERIOD OF THE BIRTH OF WILLIAM SHAKESPEARE ...   See entry 210.7.

703.15/688.1 PROBLEM OF THE SACERDOTAL INTEGRITY OF JESUS CIRCUMCISED ...   Perhaps there has at some time been a theological debate concerning the effect of the circumcision on the "sacerdotal integrity" of Jesus, and concerning the exact type and degree of reverence due the divine prepuce, but I have found no such. The only information about the divine prepuce which I have found is in the *Acta Sanctorum*, I, 4–6, *s.v.* Jan. 1. There it says that during the sixteenth century a soldier removed the divine prepuce from the Laterean Basilica, was captured and taken to Calcata (a place a few miles from Rome) and was imprisoned in a cellar, where he buried the relic. On his deathbed he told of the act, and the prepuce was unsuccessfully sought. Finally in 1557, it was found and installed with honor in the church of Sts. Cornelius and Cyprian in Calcata.

704.10/688.32 LILIATIA RUTILANTIUM ...   See entry 10.23.

705.11/689.32 HIS GAZE TURNED IN THE DIRECTION OF MIZRACH, THE EAST Mizrah, or Mizrach, is a Hebrew word, meaning the east, or the rising of the sun; see Psalms 50:1. *The Jewish Encyclopedia, s.v.* Mizrah, says, "The custom of turning toward the east while at prayer, observed by Jews living west of Palestine, is of great antiquity."

706.26/691.11 LOVE'S OLD SWEET SONG ...   See entry 63.31.

708.4/692.27 BROTHERS AND SISTERS HAD HE NONE,/ YET THAT MAN'S FATHER WAS HIS GRANDFATHER'S SON   This is an example of a "genealogical riddle." Vernam Hull and Archer Taylor give several examples of this class of riddle in their *A Collection of Irish Riddles*. The most similar one says, "Who is that in the picture?/ I myself never had a brother or a sister,/ But my own father's son is father to that one.—It was a picture of his own son" (p. 79). The version I have always heard in my own experience is "Brothers and sisters have I none, but that man's father is my father's son.— The man is the speaker's own son." Perhaps Joyce slightly modified the riddle to fit the situation of the image in the mirror. In any event, the riddle in *Ulysses* is very loose, for the answer could be "himself" or "a male first cousin."

708.15/693.3 CATALOGUE THESE BOOKS ...   This catalogue of Bloom's books is puzzling, for some of the entries represent actual books, correctly cited, while others do not seem to. In the instance of items that I have not located (almost always those for which Joyce gives no author), I have frequently found books with very similar titles. It is, of course, possible that there are actual books by these titles which I have not yet discovered. But if not, two explanations suggest themselves: either Joyce is making up some of these titles, but patterning them on common titles, or he is drawing on a book dealer's catalogue, or perhaps on binders' titles observed and noted in a book store, so that the title citations are abbreviated or incomplete. I am inclined to the former explanation, but know of no way to prove it.

708.16/693.4   THOM'S DUBLIN POST OFFICE DIRECTORY, 1886   Apparently Joyce is here referring to the annual publication of Hely Thom, Ltd., Dublin, called the *Post Office Dublin Directory and Calendar*; I have found no work by the exact title given here. See the preceding entry.

708.17/693.5   DENIS FLORENCE M'CARTHY'S POETICAL WORKS   Denis Florence McCarthy (1817–82) was an Irish poet and translator. He wrote several volumes of poetry, including one entitled *Poems* (Dublin, 1882, 1884), but I can find none with the exact title given here.

708.20/693.8   THE USEFUL READY RECKONER   The British Museum *Catalogue of Printed Books* lists many books with *Ready Reckoner* in the title (see vol. 199, cols. 529–30), but lists no book with this exact title. See the note in entry 708.15.

708.21/693.9   THE SECRET HISTORY OF THE COURT OF CHARLES II   The British Museum *Catalogue* lists several books on Charles II which begin *Secret History* (see vol. 37, cols. 189, 193), but none bears this exact title. The closest is *The Secret History of the Court and Reign of Charles the Second* . . . (London, 1792), but this is two volumes. See entry 708.15.

708.23/693.11   THE CHILD'S GUIDE   I have found several books with titles such as *The Child's Guide to* ——, but none with this exact title (see the British Museum *Catalogue*, vol. 38, cols. 337–38). See entry 708.15.

708.24/693.12   WHEN WE WERE BOYS BY WILLIAM O'BRIEN M.P.   William O'Brien (on whom see entry 654.29) wrote a novel entitled *When We Were Boys* (1890), which went through several printings. Of it Stephen J. Brown says, "One of the most remarkable of Irish novels. A tale of Ireland in Fenian times. Scene: Glengariff, Co. Cork. A very brilliant book, sparkling with epigram and metaphor. . . . The central interest, perhaps, is the romantic excitement, enthusiasm, and exaltation of an impending rising" (*Ireland in Fiction*).

708.26/693.14 THOUGHTS FROM SPINOZA   Though the title *Thoughts from* — is quite common, and though selections from Spinoza's works have been published, I have located no book with this title. See entry 708.15.

708.27/693.15 THE STORY OF THE HEAVENS BY SIR ROBERT BALL   Sir Robert Ball did write a book by this title; see entry 154.5.

708.28/693.16 ELLIS'S THREE TRIPS TO MADAGASCAR   The *Catalogue* of the British Museum does list a book by William Ellis, missionary, entitled *Three Visits to Madagascar during the years 1853–1854–1856 . . .* Illustrated by woodcuts from photographs, etc., London, 1858. Ellis (1794–1872) is in the *DNB*, where his work in Madagascar is described.

708.30/693.18 THE STARK-MUNRO LETTERS BY A. CONAN DOYLE   Sir Arthur Conan Doyle (1859–1930) wrote a semi-autobiographical novel in the epistolary form entitled *The Stark Munro Letters: being a series of sixteen letters written by J. Stark Munro, M.B., to his friend and former fellow-student, Herbert Swanborough, of Lowell, Massachusetts, during the years 1881–1884* (London, 1895).

708.35/693.23 VOYAGES IN CHINA BY 'VIATOR'   See entry 114.24.

708.37/693.25 PHILOSOPHY OF THE TALMUD   English extracts from and commentaries on the Talmud are fairly common, but I have found no work with this exact title. See entry 708.15.

708.38/693.26 LOCKHART'S LIFE OF NAPOLEON   John Gibson Lockhart's (1794–1854) *Life of Napoleon Buonaparte* (1885 and later) was revised and abridged from his *The History of Napoleon Buonaparte* (1829). Lockhart, who is best known as the son-in-law and biographer of Sir Walter Scott, is included in the *DNB*.

709.3/693.29 SOLL UND HABEN BY GUSTAV FREYTAG   German novelist Gustav Freytag (1816–95) wrote a novel entitled *Soll und Haben* (1855) which has been translated under the title *Debit and Credit*. The novel depicts the rise of the middle class in Germany about 1848 and has anti-Semitic elements. E. Baker describes the book briefly in his *Guide to the Best Fiction* and says, ". . . it reached its hundredth edition in five years, and long came next to the Bible as a best-seller" (p. 187).

709.5/693.31 HOZIER'S HISTORY OF THE RUSSO-TURKISH WAR   Colonel Sir Henry Montague Hozier (d. 1907) wrote *The Russo-Turkish War; including an account of the rise and decline of the Ottoman Power, and the history of the Eastern Question*, published in two quarto volumes, London, 1877–79.

709.8/693.34 LAURENCE BLOOMFIELD IN IRELAND BY WILLIAM ALLINGHAM   William Allingham (1824–89) was an Irish poet whose most ambitious poem was *Laurence Bloomfield in Ireland. A Modern Poem* (London, 1864; new edition, 1890).

709.11/693.37   A HANDBOOK OF ASTRONOMY   As common as this title sounds, I have found no such book. The closest is George Frederick Chambers, *A Handbook of Descriptive Astronomy* (3rd. ed., 1877). See entry 708.15.

709.15/693.41   THE HIDDEN LIFE OF CHRIST   Here again, the title is quite ordinary sounding, but I have found no such book. The closest is *Hidden Life of Jesus a Lesson and Model to Christians* (1869).

709.16/694.1   IN THE TRACK OF THE SUN   See entry 57.33.

709.18/694.3   PHYSICAL STRENGTH AND HOW TO OBTAIN IT BY EUGENE SANDOW   See entry 61.25.

709.20/694.5   SHORT BUT YET PLAIN ELEMENTS OF GEOMETRY . . . The *Catalogue* of the British Museum does list, *s.v.* Pardies, Ignance Gaston, a book entitled *Short but yet plain Elements of Geometry and Plain Trigometry* [sic] . . . Rendered into English from the fourth . . . edition, by J. Harris. . . . With many additions. London, 1701. The *Catalogue* also lists a third edition in 1705 and a sixth in 1725, but contains no 1710 edition, but there very likely was one.

709.34/694.19   A PLACE FOR EVERYTHING AND EVERYTHING IN ITS PLACE This proverbial phrase is listed in the *ODEP* and Apperson.

709.41/694.26   HOZIER'S HISTORY OF THE RUSSO–TURKISH WAR   See entry 709.5.

710.11/694.37   PLEVNA   On Plevna, which is discussed in Hozier's book, see entry 56.32.

710.14/695.3   AN IMAGE OF NARCISSUS   Narcissus, in Greek myth, was the beautiful youth who was unresponsive to love, though wooed by many. The nymph Echo pined away to nothing but a voice because of her unrequited love for him. While drinking from a pool he saw his own image, fell in love with it, and languished and died for its failure to return his love. The flower, narcissus, sprang from the spot where he died.

712.24/697.14   RUS IN URBE OR QUI SI SANA   *Rus in urbe* is a fairly common classical phrase that means "the country in town," or refers to a house that blends the advantages of town living and country living. *Qui si sana* is incomplete or highly elliptical; it seems to mean something like "Who would be whole . . . ," and needs some added phrase to complete its sense.

715.32/700.21   SEMPER PARATUS   *Semper paratus* ("Always ready") is a Latin proverbial phrase that is too common to specify a single source.

716.13/701.1 THE LETTER OF THE LAW   The letter of the law is referred to several times in the Bible, most often in Romans. Romans
7:6 says, "But now we are delivered from the law, that being dead
wherein we were held; that we should serve in newness of spirit,
and not in the oldness of the letter."

716.33/701.21 THE EVOLUTIONARY THEORIES OF CHARLES DARWIN, EX-
POUNDED IN THE DESCENT OF MAN AND THE ORIGIN OF SPECIES
Darwin's *Origin of Species* appeared in 1859; *The Descent of Man*
came out in 1871.

716.37/701.24 JAMES FINTAN LALOR, JOHN FISHER MURRAY . . .   Lalor
(1807–49) was an Irish farmer and writer. In 1847 he wrote a
series of letters for the *Nation*, advocating land nationalization and
physical force. The *DNB* has a brief article on him. Murray (1811–
65) was an Irish writer, a member of Young Ireland and the Irish
Confederation, and a contributor to the *Nation* and the *United
Irishman*; the *DNB* has a brief article on him. John Mitchel (1815–
75) was an Irish revolutionary and journalist, who founded the
United Irishman in 1848. He was later tried for treason and sentenced to transportation; he came to America, but returned to
Ireland in 1872, and became an M.P. for Tipperary in 1875. James
Frances Xavier O'Brien (1828–1905), who was a Fenian, was arrested at a Fenian rising at Cork in 1867, and tried and sentenced
to death, though the sentence was later commuted to penal servitude. He was an M.P. for the last twenty years of his life. On
Davitt, see entry 657.7. On Parnell, who was an M.P. for Cork,
see the Index. On Gladstone, who was an M.P. for Midlothian, see
the Index.

717.3/701.32 A DEMONSTRATIVE TORCHLIGHT PROCESSION . . . THE MAR
QUESS OF RIPON AND JOHN MORLEY   George Samuel Frederick
Robinson, first Marquess of Ripon (1827–1909) and John Morley,
Viscount Morley of Blackburn (1838–1923), were given a torchlight reception into Dublin on February 1 (not 2), 1888. According
to a pamphlet entitled *Proceedings in Connection with the Visit
to Dublin of the Marquess of Ripon, K.G. and the Right Hon.
John Morley, M.P. 1st to 3rd February, 1888* (Dublin: Browne and
Nolan, 1888), ". . . some one hundred and twenty different bodies
took part, not less than 20,000 were in line, with over 2,000 torches"
(p. 31). Though, according to this pamphlet, the procession did not
go along Northumberland Road, the London *Times* account of the
event mentions Northumberland Road as the location where the
fire brigade took up a position (Feb. 2, p. 6, col. a).

717.34/702.23 VALUABLE ADHESIVE OR IMPRESSED POSTAGE STAMPS . . .

These references to stamps are puzzling, since the details of their description are accurate enough to show that Joyce was not simply making them up, but they are not always precisely accurate. And why Joyce chose these stamps is also puzzling, when others so similar are of much greater value. Hamburg did not print such a stamp as is described in 1866, but did print a very similar stamp in 1859—a 7-schilling, orange, imperforate, presently valued at $25.00 uncanceled or $20.00 canceled. But other stamps printed by Hamburg in this same year are much more valuable (see *Scott's Standard Postage Stamp Catalogue,* 1967, II, 471, col. c). Great Britain did print a 4*d.* stamp on bluish paper in 1855, worth $200.00 uncanceled, but a 4*d.* rose on whitish paper printed the same year is worth $775.00 uncanceled (*Scott's,* I, 98, col. c). Luxembourg did print an official stamp in 1878 of one franc denomination, rouletted, bistre in color, valued at $135.00 uncanceled and $65.00 canceled (*Scott's,* II, 718, col. c).

719.31/704.20   ROTHSCHILD, GUGGENHEIM, HIRSCH, MONTEFIORE, MORGAN, ROCKEFELLER   The Rothschild family was a prominent, wealthy family of international bankers. Amschel Mayer Rothschild (1773–1855) built, through himself and his five sons, one of the nineteenth century's chief financial powers. The family is strongly, traditionally Jewish, and has given generously to various philanthropies. The Guggenheim family, a wealthy American Jewish family, has developed around Meyer Guggenheim (1828–1905) and his seven sons. Maurice baron de Hirsch (1831–96) was a wealthy Jewish philanthropist who gave large sums of money for projects to improve the lot of the Jews. Sir Moses Haim Montefiore (1784–1885) was a Jewish British philanthropist who worked in many ways for political and civil emancipation of the Jews in England, Europe, and the Near East. The Morgan family is a wealthy American family, descended from Junius Spencer Morgan (1813–90), and most famous is John Pierpont Morgan (1837–1913). The money came mainly from mercantile trade and international banking enterprise, and the philanthropies have been mainly to art and to libraries. The Rockefeller family, descended from John D. Rockefeller (1839–1937), made most of its money in oil. It has been active in many philanthropies, including the Rockefeller Foundation and the Rockefeller Institute.

720.25/705.15   A VERE FOSTER'S HANDWRITING COPYBOOK   Irishman Vere Henry Lewis Foster (1819–1900) was the author of a series of drawing and copybooks, including *Vere Foster's Copy-Books,*

Bold Writing or Civil Service Series, in editions for all levels. The *Catalogue* of the British Museum lists many of these.

720.30/705.19 QUEEN ALEXANDRA OF ENGLAND AND OF MAUD BRANS-COMBE, ACTRESS AND PROFESSIONAL BEAUTY   Alexandra (1844–1925), daughter of Christian IX of Denmark, was queen consort of Edward VII, whom she married in 1863. On Maud Branscombe, see entry 370.16.

720.32/705.22 MIZPAH   *Mizpah* is a Hebrew word meaning "watchtower" or "place for watching." In Genesis 31, Laban and Jacob, unable to trust one another, erect a pillar and name it Mizpah, saying "The Lord watch between me and thee when we are absent one from another" (Gen. 31:49). But the biblical context is now commonly ignored, and either the word *Mizpah* or the phrase just cited is used as a prayer or blessing.

721.3/705.32 WILLIAM EWART GLADSTONE'S HOME RULE BILL OF 1886   On February 1, 1886, W. E. Gladstone became Prime Minister of England for the third time. During this ministry he did propose a Home Rule Bill for Ireland in 1886, though several of his colleagues, including some cabinet members, were opposed to the bill. It failed to pass and brought about the collapse of Gladstone's ministry, which ran only from February 1 to June 26, 1886. This bill is called Gladstone's first Home Rule Bill; he proposed a second in 1892 which passed the House of Commons but was thrown out by the House of Lords.

721.17/706.5 AN ENGLISH WEEKLY PERIODICAL MODERN SOCIETY   *Willing's Press Guide . . . 1905* (for 1904) lists *Modern Society* as a weekly published in Brighton, which appears on Wednesday (for Saturday) and sells for one pence; the magazine began publication in 1880.

721.33/706.21 THE REIGN OF QUEEN VICTORIA   Victoria, who is alluded to frequently in *Ulysses,* reigned from 1837 until 1901.

721.33/706.21 A CHART OF MEASUREMENTS . . .   Eugen Sandow's *Strength and How to Obtain It* (see entry 61.25) contains pages that are to be filled in by the student with his dimensions. It also describes a "Developer" invented by Sandow and costing "12 *s.* 6 *d.* complete." There is also a page listing Sandow's own measurements.

722.15/707.3 ABSENTMINDED BEGGAR   This alludes to Kipling's poem "The Absent-Minded Beggar," written about the men gone to the Boer War; see entry 187.22. This War is the "South African Campaign" alluded to on p. 722.19/707.8.

723.28/708.16 HAGADAH BOOK . . . PESSACH   See entries 122.15 ff.

724.12/709.2   THE PROHIBITION OF THE USE OF FLESHMEAT AND MILK AT
ONE MEAL . . .   The prohibition against eating milk and meat
together is an important part of the Jewish dietary laws; see *Jewish
Encyclopedia*, *s.v.* Dietary laws (IV, 596) and Milk (VIII, 590).
The traditional rite of circumcision goes back to the covenant
between God and Abraham, in which Abraham is told to circumcise all male infants as a token of his covenant with God (see
Gen. 17:9–14). The Tetragrammaton, from the Greek word for
"word of four letters," refers to the ineffable Hebrew word for
God, generally transliterated JHVH or YHWH. Usually spoken
as Jehovah or Yahweh, the pronunciation of the original word
was kept secret for fear of blasphemy.

724.27/709.17   MARIA THERESA, EMPRESS OF AUSTRIA, QUEEN OF HUNGARY
Maria Theresa (1717–80), consort of Emperor Francis I, was Empress of Austria and Queen of Bohemia and of Hungary.

724.28/709.18   HAVING TAKEN CARE OF PENCE, THE POUNDS HAVING TAKEN
CARE OF THEMSELVES   "Take care of the pence, and the pounds
will take care of themselves" is proverbial and is listed in the
ODEP.

726.27/711.18   THE CLIFFS OF MOHER . . .   All of these are actual
places in Ireland and can be found in an encyclopedia or guidebook to Ireland. I annotate only those that have some allusive element or that might be difficult to locate. Lough Neagh is a large
lake in Northern Ireland; tradition says that its waters cover whole
villages (see *Irish Lit.*, VI, 2277). Forts Camden and Carlisle guard
the entrance to Cork Harbor, on the west and east sides respectively. Brigid's elm in Kildare is puzzling, for the tree usually associated with St. Brigid (on whom see entry 339.33) is an oak;
she is said to have founded a church beside an ancient oak, and
the name *Kildare* means "Church of the Oak Tree" (see D. Hyde,
Lit. Hist. of Ireland, pp. 156 ff.). Ireland has many Salmon Leaps,
but this probably refers to the one at Leixlip (which itself means
Salmon Leap), just west of Dublin.

726.36/711.27   JERUSALEM, THE HOLY CITY . . .   There may be an
allusion here to the song "The Holy City"; see entry 504.31. The
Dome of the Rock (sometimes called the Mosque of Omar) is a
Moslem mosque in Jerusalem, which was built in the sixth century
on the location of the ancient Jewish temple; the site is thus sacred
to Jews, Christians, and Moslems. The Damascus gate is the principal gate to the old walled city of Jerusalem.

727.3/711.30   THE PARTHENON   The Parthenon, a temple sacred to

Athena, located on the Acropolis near Athens, is one of the architectural masterpieces of ancient Greece.

727.4/711.31 THE WALL STREET MONEY MARKET This refers to Wall Street, in New York City, which is the location of the New York Stock Exchange.

727.5/711.32 THE PLAZA DE TOROS AT LA LINEA, SPAIN (WHERE O'HARA OF THE CAMERONS HAD SLAIN THE BULL) Philip B. Sullivan (*A Wake Newslitter*, No. 11 [March, 1963], 3–4) identifies this as a British soldier named John O'Hara who became an accomplished bull-fighter, but Sullivan points out that O'Hara was a member of the Royal Welsh Fusiliers, not the Cameroons.

727.9/711.36 THE BAY OF NAPLES (TO SEE WHICH WAS TO DIE) This alludes to the Italian proverb "Vedi Napoli, e poi muori" ("See Naples and die") the English version of which is listed in the *ODEP*.

727.20/712.10 A PILLAR OF THE CLOUD BY DAY See entry 143.11.

727.31/712.21 EVERYMAN OR NOMAN On Everyman, see entry 386.5. "Noman" recalls Ulysses' ruse with the cyclops, Polyphemus, in which he told Polyphemus that his name was "Noman." After his eye was put out, Polyphemus appealed to his friends for help, declaring that Noman was slaying him by guile. They refused, saying that if no man caused his trouble, then it must be sent from the gods (*Odyssey*, book IX).

727.33/712.23 A NYMPH IMMORTAL . . . BRIDE OF NOMAN On Ulysses as Noman, see entry 727.31. On nymphs, including the nymph Calypso, see entry 65.15.

728.10/712.37 ROTHSCHILD OR OF THE SILVER KING On the Rothschilds, see entry 719.31. *The Silver King* (1882) was the title of a melodrama by English playwright Henry Arthur Jones (1851–1929). It was quite popular at the time and is generally said to be one of the best examples of melodrama. For text and comment, see J. O. Bailey, *British Plays of the Nineteenth Century* (New York, 1966).

728.23/713.13 STATUE OF NARCISSUS, SOUND WITHOUT ECHO On Narcissus and Echo, see entry 710.14.

728.35/713.25 THE PREPARATION OF BREAKFAST (BURNT OFFERING) . . . Each of these describes some event of the day in terms of a religious parallel (usually biblical) that applies to it in some sense. "Burnt offering" is one of several types of sacrifice in the Old Testament; it occurs far too frequently to list (see any concordance); rules for this type of sacrifice are found in Leviticus 1:1–2:3 and 6:8–13. The Holy of Holies was the innermost part of the tabernacle, separated from the rest of the interior (which was called the "holy place") by a veil and entered only by the high priest once a year on the Day of Atonement. The rite of John refers to baptism; see Matthew 3. The rite of Samuel probably refers to the death of Samuel, of which we are told "Now Samuel was dead, and all Israel had lamented him, and buried him in Ramah, even in his own city" (I Sam. 28:3). Urim and Thummin refer to the two essential parts of the sacred oracle by which the priest sought to learn the will of God; two objects thus named were worn in the breastplate of judgment of the priest (see Exod. 28:29–30). The words are usually translated "Light and Perfection" or "Fire and Truth." Their meaning is obscure, but they apparently served as a means of getting a "yea" or a "nay" to a question asked of God. For more information, see James Hasting's *Dictionary of the Bible* (rev. ed.; New York, 1963), *s.v.* Urim and Thummin. The king-priest Melchizedek is used in Hebrews 5 as an example of the ideal priest and the type of Christ; the allusion here is probably to Gen. 14:18, which says, "And Melchizedek king of Salem brought forth bread and wine: and he was the priest of the most high God." The holy place was the outer part of the interior of the tabernacle (see above in this entry). Simchath Torah (or Simḥat Torah—Hebrew for "rejoicing of the Law"), is a comparatively modern name for the holiday marking the annual completion of the synagogue reading of the Pentateuch (see *Jewish Encyc.*, XI, 364–65). Shira Shirim (Shir Ha-Shirim) is Hebrew for Song of Songs. Holocaust is another name for burnt offering (see above in this entry), from the Hebrew "ôlâ," though the word *holocaust* does not occur in either the King James or the Douay Bible. Various wildernesses are referred to in the Bible; this probably alludes to the desert of Arabia, in which the Israelites wandered for forty years after their exodus from Egypt. Rite of Onan refers to Onan's spilling his seed on the ground, for which the Lord slew him (Gen. 38:9–10). Heave offering is a type of offering mentioned frequently in the Pentateuch (see any concordance) in which the priest heaved or elevated the offering during the rite (see Exod. 29:27). Armageddon is the name of the place where the final battle between good and evil will be fought (Rev. 16:16). Atonement refers to the reconciliation of God and man through Christ (Romans 5:11 contains a clear use of the term).

729.28/714.17   WHERE WAS MOSES WHEN THE CANDLE WENT OUT   In *Weep Some More* (pp. 206–7), S. Spaeth prints words and music

of a song entitled "Where Was Moses When the Light Went Out?"
The chorus goes, "Where was Moses when the light went out?
Where was Moses? What was he about? Now my little man, tell
me if you can, Where was Moses when the light went out?"
Though Spaeth does not name an author or composer, he does
say, "One answer was 'Down the cellar, eating sauerkraut,' and
another implied that Moses had suffered the inferior extremity of
his shirt to escape from its confinement." The answer that Bloom
suddenly comprehends is "In the dark."

729.37/714.26 LEAH BY MRS BANDMAN PALMER   See entries 76.23
and 76.23.

733.32/718.22 TWO WRONGS DID NOT MAKE ONE RIGHT   "Two wrongs
don't make a right" is proverbial and is listed by both the *ODEP*
and Apperson.

734.5/718.34 THE PRESUPPOSED INTANGIBILITY OF THE THING IN ITSELF
This recalls the *Ding an sich* of Immanuel Kant's philosophy. Kant
uses the term ("Thing in itself") to designate the thing as it exists
independently of and apart from all knowledge of it. It represents
the noumenal reality that can never be fully known.

734.27/719.16 THE LAND OF THE MIDNIGHT SUN, THE ISLANDS OF THE
BLESSED, THE ISLES OF GREECE, THE LAND OF PROMISE   The arctic
and antarctic regions are sometimes described as the land of the
midnight sun, because the sun is visible at midnight in midsummer
in these areas. The islands of the blessed (or Fortunate Isles) occur
in classical and Celtic myth; they are islands in the western sea
where the souls of favored mortals dwell. The isles of Greece alludes to Byron's well known apostrophe in *Don Juan*, "The isles of
Greece, the isles of Greece!" This occurs as a poem interposed
between stanzas 86 and 87 of canto III of *Don Juan*. The land of
promise (or Promised Land) occurs generally in many cultures;
the biblical Promised Land immediately comes to mind (cf. entry
734.29) but there are others.

734.29/719.18 MILK AND HONEY   The "land flowing with milk and
honey" is the Promised Land in the Bible. See entry 393.36.

735.18/720.9 MRS BANDMAN PALMER OF LEAH   Mentioned earlier on
p. 729.37/714.26. See entries 76.23 and 76.23.

735.22/720.13 SWEETS OF SIN ...   On *Sweets of Sin*, see entry 236.5.

736.8/720.36 WITH EJACULATION OF SEMEN WITHIN THE NATURAL
FEMALE ORGAN   (The phrase is repeated on p. 736.14/721.3)
See entry 223.31.

737.8/721.36 GEA-TELLUS   Gaea, Gea, or Ge (called by the Romans

Tellus or Terra Mater) is Earth, mother of all creatures. She is usually depicted clothed in a long gown, reclining, and fondling two infants, with the fruits of earth nearby.

737.17/722.8   SINBAD THE SAILOR AND TINBAD THE TAILOR . . .   Sindbad the Sailor is a character in the *Arabian Nights* stories. For Joyce's use of material about a Dublin pantomime about Sindbad, see entry 678.32. R. M. Adams points out (*SS*, p. 80) that the pantomime had characters named Tinbad and Whinbad, which may be the germ of this list. Among Sindbad's adventures, many of which closely parallel those of Ulysses, is an encounter with the giant bird called the Roc, alluded to on p. 737.25/722.16.

738.35/723.34 TO NEVER SEE THY FACE AGAIN   This is almost certainly a refrain from a popular song, though I have not located any song with this exact phrase. Two songs by American song writer William (Billy) Jerome come quite close. "He Never Came Back" (1891) contains the words "He never came back, he never came back,/ His dear form she never saw more,/ But how happy she'll be, when his sweet face she'll see,/ When they meet on that beautiful shore." "His Sweet Face She Never Saw More" (1892) says, "His sweet face she never saw more; Each day as she strolls by the sea/ She cries in despair as she offers this pray'r, Oh, send back my darling to me." S. Spaeth briefly discusses Jerome and these songs and says, " . . . they were meant to be funny" (*Hist. of Pop. Music in Amer.*, p. 332).

739.5/724.5 POOLE'S MYRIORAMA   Poole's Myriorama was a popular Dublin entertainment. Most of what I have learned of it is contained in an article by Delia Moore entitled "Dublin in the 'Nineties: Forerunners of the Movies," published in the Dublin *Evening Herald*, Friday, January 3, 1941. I quote all the article says about the Myriorama: "Let me now recall some of the entertainments. The earliest I can remember was what was known as Poole's Myriorama. It used to come about once a year, and was both entertaining and instructive. It was, I should think, the beginning of the movies. The pictures were the full size of the stage of the theatre in which they were shown. Painted in natural colours, they embraced views of most countries in the world—and a sort of travel guide would stand at the corner of the stage and explain the various objects of interest" (p. 4, col. e; this article is cited by R. M. Adams, *SS*, p. 74).

739.20/724.20 NO FOOL LIKE AN OLD FOOL   This expression, which is listed in the *ODEP*, has been proverbial at least since John Heywood's *Proverbs* (1546).

740.10/725.9 IN MY HAND THERE STEALS ANOTHER   I suspect this of being an allusion to a popular song of the day, but I have not identified it, and Hodgart and Worthington take no note of it.

740.12/725.11 THE YOUNG MAY MOON SHES BEAMING LOVE   From Moore's "The Young May Moon"; see entry 167.21.

742.27/727.26 JESUSJACK THE CHILD IS A BLACK   Molly's exclamation sounds like a set phrase, and it may be an allusion, but if so I have not identified it.

742.42/727.40 OUR LORD BEING A CARPENTER   In Mark 6:3 Christ is specifically referred to as a carpenter: the people of his own country, astonished at his teachings, say "Is not this the carpenter, the son of Mary. . . ?"

743.11/728.10 LORD BYRONS POEMS   Lord Byron and his poetry are alluded to several times in *Ulysses*; see the Index.

743.40/728.38 TRYING TO LOOK LIKE LORD BYRON . . .   The handsomeness of Lord Byron is well known. Molly thought of his poetry on p. 743.11/728.10.

744.14/729.12 WHEN THE MAGGOT TAKES HIM   "When the maggot bites" is proverbial for "when the fancy seizes," and is listed in both the *ODEP* and Apperson. Swift, in his *A Discourse Concerning the Mechanical Operation of the Spirit*, apparently anatomizes this idea in his discussion of "the Opinion of Choice *Virtuosi*, that the Brain is only a Crowd of little Animals, but with Teeth and Claws extremely sharp," though he does not specifically mention maggots. See H. Davis, *The Prose Works* (Oxford, 1939), I, 181–82.

744.21/729.20 O SWEETHEART MAY   Hodgart and Worthington list this as an allusion to "Sweetheart May" by Stuart. Leslie Stuart (real name Thomas Augustine Barrett, b. 1864) did write a music hall song by this title, but I have not located a printed copy of it.

744.28/729.26 MRS MAYBRICK THAT POISONED HER HUSBAND   Mrs. Florence Maybrick poisoned her husband, James Maybrick, who died on May 11, 1889. The Maybricks had been married in 1881, and early in 1889 Mrs. Maybrick took a lover, a Mr. Brierly, and this affair led to her poisoning her husband. Though she was found guilty, there were some curious circumstances (Mr. Maybrick had long been taking drugs and patent medicines, including arsenic and strychnine), and her sentence was later commuted to life imprisonment. She was released in 1904 and later wrote a book entitled *My Fifteen Lost Years* (C. Wilson, *Encyclopedia of Murder*, pp. 383–85).

745.26/730.24 KATTY LANNER   On Katti Lanner, see entry 575.30.

745.33/730.31 GOUNODS AVE MARIA   The Ave Maria (Hail Mary), sometimes called the Angelical Salutation and based partly on the words of Gabriel and Elizabeth to Mary in Luke 1:28 and 42, is one of the most common Catholic prayers; Molly referred to it on p. 741.37/726.36. The prayer has been set to music by many composers, and the setting of Charles François Gounod (1818–93) is one of the most popular.

745.33/730.31 WHAT ARE WE WAITING FOR O MY HEART . . .   This is a direct quotation from the popular song "Good-Bye!" words by G. J. Whyte-Melville, music by F. Paolo Tosti. In the copy I examined, the line Molly is quoting goes, "What are we waiting for? Oh! my heart! Kiss me straight on the brows! and part!" For words and music, see *Everybody's Favorite Selected Songs* (N.Y.: Amsco Music Publishing Co., 1941), pp. 18–21.

746.15/731.13 STANDING AT THE CORNER OF THE HAROLDS CROSS ROAD   Hodgart and Worthington list this as an allusion to the music hall song "Standing on the Corner of the Street," by Formby *père*, but the context here makes any such allusion unlikely.

747.35/732.32 FOR ENGLAND HOME AND BEAUTY   From "The Death of Nelson"; see entry 225.19.

747.36/732.33 THERE IS A CHARMING GIRL I LOVE   This alludes to an air entitled "It is a charming girl I love" which is sung in act I of *The Lily of Killarney* (on which see entry 92.6) by Myles na Coppaleen. It begins, "It is a charming girl I love, she comes from Garryowen."

748.14/733.12 THEYD HAVE TAKEN US ON TO CORK   Hodgart and Worthington list this as an allusion to a music hall song by Le Brunn, entitled "O Mister Porter, Whatever Shall I Do?" Though the context in *Ulysses* makes the allusion less than certain, Molly may have in mind some Irish variation on the well-known song which was written by George Le Brunn and made popular by Marie Lloyd. The song tells of a young lady's meeting an old gentleman on the train and accepting the proposal for marriage which he makes. The only copy of the song which I have found is in the paperback *Harding's Nightingale Song Book*. It beings, "Lately I just spent a week with my old aunt Brown. . . ," and the chorus says, "Oh, Mr. Porter, what shall I do,/ I want to go to Birmingham and they're taking me on to Crewe,/ Send me back to London as quickly as you can,/ Oh, Mr. Porter, what a silly girl I am" (no. 11, p. 246).

748.29/733.26 THE ABSENTMINDED BEGGAR   This alludes to Kipling's poem "The Absent-Minded Beggar," which was set to music by Sir Arthur Sullivan; see entry 187.22.

748.30/733.27 LORD ROBERTS   See entry 421.13.

748.33/733.30 STABAT MATER   Bloom earlier thought of Rossini's *Stabat Mater*; see entry 82.9.

748.34/733.31 LEAD KINDLY LIGHT   This alludes to John Henry Newman's well-known hymn "Lead, Kindly Light," which begins, "Lead, kindly Light, amid the encircling gloom,/ Lead Thou me on!" Molly thinks of the second line on p. 748.36/733.33.

748.40/733.37 GRIFFITH   This alludes to Arthur Griffith, who was of small stature and had a short neck. See entry 57.35.

748.43/733.39 PRETORIA AND LADYSMITH AND BLOEMFONTEIN   All three of these were important sites in the Boer War. Pretoria, the administrative capital of the Union of South Africa, was evacuated by Kruger in May, 1900, and taken by Lord Roberts (mentioned on p. 748.30/733.27) without resistance on June 5, 1900. On Ladysmith, see entry 484.2, and on Bloemfontein, see entry 458.1.

749.8/734.5 OLD OOM PAUL AND THE REST OF THE OLD KRUGERS   Stephanus Johannes Paulus Kruger (1825–1904), South African statesman, was usually known as Paul Kruger or Oom Paul. He was for many years president of Transvaal and was a persistent opponent of the British in South Africa. He fought in the early stages of the Boer War, but in 1900 he went to Europe in an unsuccessful attempt to get aid for his country. He died on July 14, 1904, an exile in Switzerland.

749.17/734.15 THE DUBLINS THAT WON TUGELA   This alludes to the Battle of Colenso in the Boer War, which was fought at the Tugela River in December of 1899. Irish units in the British army—including the Royal Dublin Fusiliers—figured importantly, and suffered heavy losses, in the attempt to dislodge the Boer forces. See chap.

XXII of M. Davitt's *The Boer Fight for Freedom,* or Arthur Conan Doyle's account of the battle in his *The Great Boer War* (rev. ed., 1902). Cf. entries 163.10 and 596.14.

750.28/735.25   THE GENTLEWOMAN   *Willing's Press Guide . . . 1905* (for 1904) lists a magazine entitled *The Gentlewoman* as appearing on Thursday for Saturday at a price of six pence. An advertisement on p. 229 of *Willing's* describes it as "The Illustrated Weekly Journal for Gentlewomen," and says, "The 'Gentlewoman' is bought by women, read by women, and as women spend nine-tenths of what men earn, the moral is obvious."

751.24/736.21   KITTY OSHEA   R. M. Adams explains that this is not the Kitty O'Shea of Parnell fame. He says, "Kitty O'Shea in Grantham Street (p. 736) is only the namesake of Parnell's lady; living at #3 . . . according to *Thom's Directory* for 1882, was Miss O'Shea" (*SS,* p. 239).

751.27/736.24   MRS LANGTRY THE JERSEY LILY THE PRINCE OF WALES WAS IN LOVE WITH   Lillie Langtry (1852–1929) was an English actress known as the Jersey Lily. Though not very successful as an actress, she was known for her great beauty and for her liason with Edward VII.

751.36/736.32   THE WORKS OF MASTER FRANÇOIS SOMEBODY . . .   Molly is thinking of François Rabelais (*ca.* 1490–1553), author of *Gargantua,* who was a monk. She is thinking specifically of the birth of Gargantua, described in chap. VII of *Gargantua,* where we are told that as a result of eating too much tripe, Gargamelle's fundament or bum-gut fell out, and "The effect of this was that the cotyledons of matrix were all loosened above, through which the child sprung up and leaped, and so entering into the *Vena Cava,* did climb by the *Diaphragm* even above her shoulders (where that vein divides itself in two) and, from thence taking his way toward the left side, issued forth at her left ear."

751.41/736.37   RUBY AND FAIR TYRANTS   These novels were alluded to earlier. On *Ruby,* see entry 64.25; on *Fair Tyrants,* see entry 235.37. Molly goes on to think about an episode from *Fair Tyrants.*

752.3/736.42   AFTER THE BALL WAS OVER   This alludes to the very popular song "After the Ball" (1892), written and composed by Charles K. Harris. The chorus begins, "After the ball is over, after the break of morn." For words and music, see Boni, *Fireside Book of Favorite American Songs,* pp. 35–40.

752.3/736.42   THE INFANT JESUS IN THE CRIB AT INCHICORE . . .   The guidebook *Catholic Dublin* discusses the Christmas crib at Inchicore at some length (pp. 33, 35). It is housed in a building on the grounds of the Church of the Oblates of Mary Immaculate, at Inchicore. The book calls the depiction "the largest and most realistic representation of the Nativity of Our Saviour in Ireland, or Great Britain" (p. 33). Stanislaus Joyce mentions Dante's taking the Joyce children to see the manger scene at Inchicore (*MBK*, pp. 9–10).

752.8/737.5   H. R. H. HE WAS IN GIBRALTAR THE YEAR I WAS BORN   This clearly refers to the Prince of Wales, later Edward VII, but all the evidence I have found indicates that he took no trip to Gibraltar in 1870. For example, Sidney Lee's *King Edward VII, A Biography* mentions visits to Gibraltar in 1859 and 1876, but none in between.

753.25/738.21   THE NYMPHS   Bloom earlier thought of nymphs; see entry 65.15.

753.35/738.31   7 WONDERS OF THE WORLD   The Seven Wonders were seven structures regarded as the most remarkable monuments of the ancient world. Molly's specific knowledge of them is doubtful; she is using the phrase simply to mean something spectacular.

753.38/738.35   93 THE CANAL WAS FROZEN   I have been unable to confirm this and am skeptical of its being correct. In his article "Weather in Old Dublin" (*Dublin Historical Record*, XIII, 94–107), F. E. Dixon discusses frosts—and specifically discusses those in the 1890's—but says nothing of 1893. He says, "The first three months of 1881 were all cold, and there were some severe frosts in the 1890's, especially the winter 1890–91 and the beginning of 1895. . . . Mr. Mason remembers skating on the Liffey near Islandbridge in 1895 for a few days. Sir John Moore recorded that in February 1895 even the rushing waters of the Powerscourt waterfall were frozen almost solid" (101).

754.1/738.40   MET SOMETHING WITH HOSES IN IT   Metempsychosis; see entry 64.18.

754.17/739.14   SOMEBODY OUGHT TO PUT HIM IN THE BUDGET   I have not found this saying in any of the sources I have consulted, and the *OED* casts no light on this use of *budget*. I suspect that the saying originally referred to some humorous periodical whose title included *Budget*, as several of the old ones did (see entry 139.6).

754.40/739.36   LOVES OLD SWEET SONNNNG   On "Love's Old Sweet Song" see entry 63.31.

755.1/739.40   PHOTO BITS   On *Photo Bits*, see entry 65.12.

755.14/740.11   FADED ALL THAT LOVELY   This alludes to Moore's "The Last Rose of Summer," on which see entry 256.34.

755.15/740.12 MRS STANHOPE   R. M. Adams points out that Molly's friend Hester Stanhope is the "namesake of Lady Hester Stanhope, the great Victorian eccentric who retired to a monastery in the Middle East" (*SS*, p. 240). Adams has no explanation of Joyce's purpose in using this name, nor have I. For further information on Lady Hester, see the *Encyclopaedia Britannica*, 11th ed., *s.v.* Stanhope.

755.21/740.17 IN OLD MADRID OR WAITING   Both of these songs were alluded to earlier in *Ulysses*: on "In Old Madrid," see entry 275.27, and on "Waiting," see entry 275.23.

755.31/740.28 THE BULLFIGHT AT LA LINEA WHEN THAT MATADOR GOMEZ WAS GIVEN THE BULLS EAR   On the basis of Molly's age and the dates involved, Philip B. Sullivan identifies this bullfighter as "the famous Fernando Gomez (Gallio)," saying that "he was one of Spain's really great matadors" (*A Wake Newslitter*, no. 11 [March, 1963], 4).

756.18/741.15 THE MOONSTONE . . . WILKIE COLLINS   *The Moonstone* (1868), by English novelist Wilkie Collins, is a novel of mystery and intrigue, centering around the fortunes of the moonstone, an enormous diamond that once adorned the head of an Indian moon-god, and was brought to England by a British officer.

756.19/741.16 EAST LYNNE . . . THE SHADOW OF ASHLYDYAT MRS HENRY WOOD   *East Lynne* (1861) is a dramatic, sensational romance by English novelist Mrs. Henry Wood (1814–87). E. Baker says of *East Lynne*, "The main situation is one of harrowing pathos, a divorced wife re-entering her husband's house disguised as a governess, nursing her own child and dying there, tardily forgiven" (*Guide to the Best Fiction*). The novel also involves a murder, trial, cross-examination, etc. It was dramatized and became a stock piece for years. Mrs. Wood's *The Shadow of Ashlydyat* (1863) went into its 150,000th copy in 1899. Baker describes it as "Typical of a numerous class of Mrs. Wood's novels, in which the interest lies in the working out of a plot containing romantic and supernatural elements and a good deal of family history" (*Guide to the Best Fiction*).

756.20/741.17 HENRY DUNBAR . . .   *Henry Dunbar* (1864) is a novel by Miss Mary Elizabeth Braddon (Mrs. Maxwell; 1837–1915) which is a mystery involving a man's impersonation of a murdered millionaire; the solution to the mystery is revealed to the reader by degrees.

756.22/741.19 LORD LYTTON EUGENE ARAM   *Eugene Aram* (1832) is a novel by English novelist Edward Bulwer-Lytton about a sensitive, capable man who, because of dire poverty, becomes accomplice to a murder and is tried and convicted for it.

756.23/741.20 MOLLY BAWN . . . BY MRS HUNGERFORD   Mrs. Margaret Hungerford (nee Hamilton; 1855–97) wrote several dozen novels, most appearing anonymously. Her best known is *Molly Bawn* (1878), "A love-tale of a tender, frivolous, and petulant Irish girl, who flirts and arouses her lover's jealousy and offends against the conventions in all innocence. A gay and witty story, spiced with slang and touched with pathos" (E. Baker, *Guide to the Best Fiction*).

756.25/741.22 THE ONE FROM FLANDERS A WHORE   Molly is thinking of Defoe's novel *Moll Flanders* (1722). Moll is both whore and thief.

757.6/742.3 WAITING ALWAYS WAITING TO GUIIIIDE HIM TOOOO ME . . . This alludes to the song "Waiting," which was alluded to earlier in this episode on p. 755.21/740.18. See entry 275.23.

757.10/742.7 GENERAL ULYSSES GRANT . . .   R. M. Adams briefly discusses this allusion (*SS*, p. 233), saying that General Grant's visit to Gibraltar took place in 1877 and that he arrived at Gibraltar by train from Madrid, not by boat as Joyce says. But Adams cites no source, and all the evidence I have found says that Grant's visit was in 1878 and that he did arrive by boat. According to *The Life of General U. S. Grant . . . together with his Tour around the World*, by L. T. Remlap (New York: Loomis National Library Associations, 1888; the author's name is clearly a pseudonym), General Grant and his party left Cadiz by boat for Gibraltar on November 17, 1878, and the account specifically mentions the American Consul, Mr. Sprague, as greeting the General (pp. 340–41). Earlier in the book the author mentions the good-natured jokes that arose out of the much-traveled General's name being Ulysses (p. 249).

757.20/742.17 RORKES DRIFT AND PLEVNA AND SIR GARNET WOLSELEY AND GORDON AT KHARTOUM   On Rorke's Drift, see entry 457.15; on Plevna, see entry 56.32. Sir Garnet Joseph Wolseley, first Viscount Wolseley (1833–1913) was a British general (born in Ireland) who fought in many campaigns. Among them was his unsuccessful attempt to relieve General Charles George Gordon (1933–85) at Khartoum in the Sudan in 1885. Gordon was besieged by the Madhi (Moslem religious leader Mohammed Ahmed, 1844–85) for ten months. The relief expedition finally sent from England reached Khartoum two days after it had been stormed by the Moslems, who killed Gordon.

758.32/743.30 IN OLD MADRID . . . LOVE IS SIGHING I AM DYING   From "In Old Madrid," on which see entry 275.27.

759.13/744.12 4 DRUNKEN ENGLISH SAILORS TOOK ALL THE ROCK FROM THEM   Molly seems to be alluding to the British capture and occupation of Gibraltar. The Cape was taken by British and Dutch forces on July 24, 1704, as a part of the War of the Spanish Succession. It was insufficiently garrisoned and was taken after a siege of only three days.

759.28/744.26 SHALL I WEAR A WHITE ROSE   Hodgart and Worthington list this as an allusion to the English song "Shall I Wear a White Rose," by Clark and Farmer. I have not located a copy of the song.

759.30/744.29 MY SWEETHEART WHEN A BOY   Hodgart and Worthington list this as an allusion to a song entitled "My Sweetheart When a Boy," by "Enoch; Morgan." Though I have not found such a song by these authors, I did find a song by this title in the paperback *Erin's Call Song Book*, said to be by Irish song writer James Lyman Molloy. The version given there has three eight-line stanzas, and no chorus. I quote the entire first stanza: "Tho' many gentle hearts I've known,/ And many a pretty face,/ Where love sat gaily on his throne,/ In beauty and in grace,/ But never was my heart enthralled/ By such enchanting joy,/ As by the darling whom I called/ My sweetheart when a boy" (p. 4).

759.36/744.35 THERES MANY A TRUE WORD SPOKEN IN JEST   This proverbial phrase occurred earlier in *Ulysses*; see entry 338.15.

759.37/744.35 THERE IS A FLOWER THAT BLOOMETH   From Wallace's *Maritana*; see entry 358.18.

760.1/744.42 MAY WHEN THE INFANT KING OF SPAIN WAS BORN   As R. M. Adams points out (*SS*, p. 189), this refers to Alfonso XIII (1886–1941), posthumous son and successor to the throne of his father Alfonso XII (d. 1885). Born into the kingship on May 17, 1886, the child reigned with his mother, Maria Christina (1858–1929), as regent until 1902.

761.2/746.1 MOLLY DARLING   This alludes to the song "Molly Darling" (1871), one of the most popular songs of Will S. Hays. For words and music, see *Good Old Songs*, II, 112.

761.29/746.28 GOD SEND HIM SENSE AND ME MORE MONEY   This proverbial saying occurs in Swift's *Polite Conversation*, third conversation, when Lady Answerall says, "Well, God send him more Wit, and me more Money." Partridge calls this "a conversational shaping of the proverbial 'God send you more wit, and me more money,' current since *c*. 1600" (p. 164).

762.12/747.12   MOLLY DARLING   See entry 761.2.

762.20/747.20   SOUTH AFRICA WHERE THOSE BOERS KILLED HIM WITH THEIR WAR   This refers to the Boer War or South African War (1899–1902), which is alluded to frequently in *Ulysses*.

762.25/747.25   ONCE IN THE DEAR DEAEAD DAYS BEYOND RECALL . . . The following lines contain several allusions to "Love's Old Sweet Song," on which see entry 63.31.

763.9/748.10   COMES LOOOOVES OLD   Here again, as on p. 762.25/747.25, the following lines contain several allusions to "Love's Old Sweet Song," on which see entry 63.31.

763.10/748.11   MY LADY'S BOWER . . .   This alludes to the song "My Lady's Bower," words by F. E. Weatherly, music by H. Temple. I have not found a copy of the song.

763.12/748.13   WINDS THAT BLOW FROM THE SOUTH   See entry 156.8.

764.33/749.35   I HATE THOSE RUCK OF MARY ANN COALBOXES   Hodgart and Worthington list this as an allusion to "McGilligan's Daughter Mary Ann" (on which see entry 13.20), which is possible, though this still leaves the phrase unexplained.

765.10/750.12   SWEETS OF SIN . . . MR DE KOCK   On *Sweets of Sin*, see entry 236.5. Molly is wrong about de Kock being a nickname; see entry 64.39.

765.18/750.20   OLD LUIGI NEAR A HUNDRED THEY SAID CAME FROM GENOA   R. M. Adams says that the details about Luigi suggest that Joyce took them from the *Gilbraltar Directory and Guide Book*, which mentions that Catalan Bay is inhabited by descendants of Genoese fishermen, and that their chief catch is bream and sardines (*SS*, p. 232).

767.4/752.6   THE PAN CALLING THE KETTLE BLACKBOTTOM   "The pot (or pan) calling the kettle black" is a common proverbial expression; the *ODEP* lists several instances of the phrase, two of which involve the variation "burnt-arse" and "black A——."

767.8/752.10   ONLY WAY   *The Only Way* (1899) was a dramatic adaptation of Charles Dickens' *A Tale of Two Cities*, written by two Irish clergymen, Freeman Crofts Wills and Frederick Langbridge. It was in this simple and frankly sentimental play that Martin-Harvey, whom Molly thinks of on p. 767.29/752.30, sprang into prominence when he starred in it at the Lyceum in London in 1899.

767.13/752.15   BEERBOHM TREE IN TRILBY   Sir Herbert Beerbohm Tree (1853–1917) was an English actor-manager. *Trilby* (1894) was a popular novel by George Du Maurier which was written into dramatic form by several authors. According to play bills at the

National Library of Ireland, Beerbohm Tree did direct and play
Svengali in *Trilby* at the Gaiety Theatre in Dublin on October
10 and 11, 1895. Svengali was mentioned earlier on p. 526.9/514.22.

767.29/752.30 MARTIN HARVEY   On Sir John Martin-Harvey, see
entries 767.8 and 357.33.

767.30/752.32 IT MUST BE REAL LOVE IF A MAN GIVES UP HIS LIFE FOR
HER THAT WAY FOR NOTHING   This alludes to an incident in *The
Only Way* (see entry 767.8). In the play, as in Dickens' novel,
Sidney Carton (played by Martin-Harvey) assumes the identity
of the Marquis St. Evrémonde and dies at the guillotine in his
place so that Evrémonde may be with his wife Lucie, whom Carton
had always loved.

769.11/754.14 MRS. KENDAL AND HER HUSBAND   This refers to Mr.
and Mrs. William Hunter Kendal, a well-known acting pair of
this period. The way Molly remembers them suggests what was
true, that Kendal was "overshadowed by his more brilliant wife"
(*DNB*). Kendal (b. William Hunter Grimston, 1843–1917) married his wife Margaret (Madge) Robertson in 1869, and during
the next several decades they played together in London, the
English provinces, and the United States.

769.15/754.18 SPINOZA   Bloom has several times earlier mentioned
the Dutch Jewish philosopher Baruch Spinoza; see entry 284.36.

769.18/754.21 WIFE OF SCARLI   *The Wife of Scarli* (1897) was a
three act play (apparently anonymous) adapted from the *Tristi
Amori* of Guiseppe Giacosa. According to A. Nicoll's *History of
English Drama*, the play was first done at the Prince of Wales
Theatre in Birmingham on September 9, 1897. Playbills at the National Library of Ireland describe the first Dublin performance as
having been at the Gaiety Theatre on October 22, 1897.

769.32/754.34 SWEETS OF SIN   See entry 236.5.

770.6/755.8 I HOPE THEYRE BUBBLES ON IT   J. Prescott says of this,
"F. B. Dresslar, *Superstition and Education* (Berkeley, 1907), p.
14, lists three superstitions concerning bubbles on liquids as a sign
of money. Molly, on the chamber pot, seems to extend the scope
of the belief, for Dresslar mentions only tea and coffee" (*MLQ*,
XIII, 162).

770.12/755.14 THE JERSEY LILY   See entry 751.27.

770.12/755.15 O HOW THE WATERS COME DOWN AT LAHORE   This
seems to be Molly's variation on a line from Robert Southey's
poem "The Cataract at Lodore." The poem begins, " 'How does
the water/ Come down at Lodore?' " and describes the descent of
the water onomatopoetically for 120 lines (e.g., "And sounding

and bounding and rounding,/ And bubbling and troubling and doubling"). The last line says, "And this is the way the Water comes down at Lodore." The Lodore waterfall is in Cumberland county in northern England; Lahore is a city in West Pakistan. I do not know why Molly substitutes Lahore for Lodore, unless Lahore is simply a more familiar name (and, of course, the "la whore" echo is also apt).

771.6/756.8   A THING OF BEAUTY AND OF JOY FOR EVER   Keats's *Endymion* begins, "A thing of beauty is a joy forever. . . ." This line was alluded to earlier on p. 509.28/499.6.

771.18/756.20   HOME RULE AND THE LAND LEAGUE   Molly is probably referring to the same political interests Bloom spoke of on p. 656.42/641.6 ff.

771.19/756.21   A SONG OUT OF THE HUGUENOTS . . . O BEAU PAYS DE LA TOURAINE   On Meyerbeer's *Huguenots*, see entry 168.20. "O beau pays de la Touraine" is sung by Queen Marguerite de Valois at the beginning of act II. She praises the beauty of the country and feels in it a freedom from care.

771.34/756.36   BREATHING WITH HIS HAND ON HIS NOSE LIKE THAT INDIAN GOD . . .   Molly is probably thinking of the same statue of Buddha that Bloom referred to on p. 80.10/79.7. See entry 80.10.

772.7/757.10   LORD NAPIER   British general Robert Cornelis Napier, first Baron Napier of Magdala (1810–90) was governor of Gibraltar from 1876 to 1883. The *DNB* has an article on him.

772.12/757.15   HUGUENOTS OR THE FROGS MARCH   "Huguenots" probably refers to Meyerbeer's opera by that name, on which see entry 168.20. I do not know what Molly means by "frogs march," for I know of no such in opera or popular song. The phrase "frogmarch" or "frog's march" is slang for a method of carrying a drunken or refractory prisoner face down between four men, each carrying a limb (see the *OED*).

772.14/757.17   WORSE AND WORSE SAYS WARDEN DALY   I have not located this expression in any source I have consulted, nor have I identified Warden Daly.

772.23/757.26   SINNER FEIN   Molly is thinking of Sinn Fein. See entry 163.38.

772.24/757.27   THE LITTLE MAN . . . BY COADYS LANE   Though I suspect that Molly is thinking of Arthur Griffith (she thought of him earlier on p. 748.40/733.37 and has just thought of Sinn Fein), I can find no basis for her associating him with Coady's Lane.

772.37/757.39   THE ARISTOCRATS MASTERPIECE   Molly is probably thinking of *Aristotle's Masterpiece*, which has been mentioned earlier in *Ulysses*. See entry 235.19.

773.4/758.7   HE SLEPT ON THE FLOOR HALF THE NIGHT NAKED THE WAY THE JEWS USED WHEN SOMEBODY DIES   Though I have not found this exact custom described, Molly is probably correct. Traditionally Jews do "sit low," i.e., on the floor or on boxes, during the period immediately following burial of a loved one. This part of the mourning period is known as *shib'ah* or *shivah*.

773.19/758.22   SHEEPS EYES   This phrase, which occurs in Swift's *Polite Conversation*, was used earlier in *Ulysses*; see entry 511.14.

774.5/759.8   BILL BAILEY WON'T YOU PLEASE COME HOME   This alludes to the popular American song "Bill Bailey, Won't you Please Come Home" (1902), written by Hughie Cannon. The chorus begins, "Won't you come home, Bill Bailey, won't you come home?" For words and music, see Theodore Raph, *The Songs We Sang* (London and New York, 1964), pp. 271–75.

774.15/759.18   THE OLD LOVE IS THE NEW   Hodgart and Worthington suggest that this may allude either to "Don't Give Up the Old Love for the New," by Thornton, or to "The Old Love and the New," by Cowen. James Thornton's "Don't Give Up the Old Love for the New" appeared in 1896; Cowen is presumably Sir Frederic Hyman Cowen (1852–1935), but I have not located copies of these songs.

774.16/759.19   SO SWEETLY SANG THE MAIDEN ON THE HAWTHORN BOUGH   Bloom earlier referred to Simon Dedalus's waggish habit of singing the wrong words to a song (see p. 274.24/270.13), and this is doubtless an instance of it. But I have not been able to identify the song that Simon is parodying (perhaps it is one of those referred to in the preceding entry).

774.17/759.20   MARITANA   As the phrase "O Maritana wildwood flower" on p. 774.22/759.25 shows, this alludes to a duet entitled "O Maritana! Wildwood Flower," sung by Don Caesar de Bazan and Maritana in act III of W. V. Wallace's opera *Maritana* (on which see entry 86.32).

774.19/759.22   PHOEBE DEAREST   Hodgart and Worthington list this as an allusion to "Phoebe Dearest, Tell O Tell Me." by Bellamy and Hatton (presumably Claxon Bellamy and J. L. Hatton). I have seen the words of this song, without any indication of author or composer, in paperback Irish song books. *The Favorite Songster* prints a version that has three eight-line stanzas, the first of which begins, "Phoebe, dearest, tell, oh tell me,/ May I hope that you'll be mine?/ Oh, let no cold frown repel me,/ Leave me not with grief to pine" (p. 2).

774.19/759.22 GOODBYE SWEETHEART   This alludes to "Goodbye, Sweetheart, Goodbye," on which see entry 256.13.

775.11/760.14 A POET LIKE BYRON   Molly is probably thinking of Byron's appearance and personality rather than his poetry; cf. entry 743.40.

775.23/760.27 WHERE SOFTLY SIGHS OF LOVE THE LIGHT GUITAR   Here and in the following lines are several allusions to "In Old Madrid," on which see entry 275.27.

775.41/761.2 THAT LOVELY LITTLE STATUE   Bloom's statue is of Narcissus; see entry 728.23.

776.7/761.11 PIGS OF MEN   This recalls Circe's transformation of some of Ulysses' men into swine in the *Odyssey*, book X.

776.28/761.32 THOSE OLD HYPOCRITES IN THE TIME OF JULIUS CAESAR   I do not understand what Molly means here. Her thoughts move from Boylan in his shirt, to a priest, to a butcher, to the hypocrites in the time of Caesar. She seems to be thinking of the Roman toga, and of the male sexual parts, but I do not understand why she thinks of the men as hypocrites.

776.38/761.42 MY UNCLE JOHN HAS A THING LONG . . .   This is obviously a pseudo-bawdy children's riddle, but I have not found it in any of the sources such as the Opies' *Lore and Language of School-children*.

777.11/762.15 FAIR TYRANTS   On *Fair Tyrants*, see entry 235.37.

777.23/762.27 DIDNT HE KISS OUR HALL DOOR   If Bloom did kiss the hall door, it was probably in memory of the Jewish custom of touching or kissing the mezuzah; see entry 378.36.

778.5/763.10 THE WINDS THAT WAFT MY SIGHS TO THEE   This alludes to a song by W. V. Wallace entitled "The Winds That Waft My Sighs to Thee." A copy of this song, with music by Challis, can be found in *Good Old Songs* II, 124–26.

779.20/764.25 THAT NOVEL . . . BY VALERA   Molly is probably thinking of Juan Valera (1824–1905), Spanish writer and diplomat, author of several novels. His best-known novel is probably *Pepita Jiménez* (1874; English translation, 1886), a conventional story of a conflict between love and a religious vocation.

780.18/765.23 MI FA PIETÀ MASETTO   This and the "presto non son più forte" of p. 780.19/765.24 are allusions to the duet between Zerlina and Don Giovanni in Mozart's *Don Giovanni* (see entries 63.31 and 64.4 and the sources cited there). In the duet Zerlina says,

"Mi fa pietà Masetto" ("I am sorry for Masetto") and then "Presto non son più forte" ("All at once I am no longer strong").

780.31/765.35 THIS VALE OF TEARS   This now common phrase is used in the Douay version of Psalm 83: "Blessed is the man whose help is from thee; in his heart he hath disposed to ascend by steps, in the vale of tears, in the place which he hath set" (6–7: this is Psalms 84:5–6 in the King James version).

780.37/765.41 MY BROWN PART   Molly earlier used this phrase for "my brow and part" while thinking of Tosti's "Good-Bye"; see entry 745.33.

781.32/766.36 SHALL I WEAR A WHITE ROSE   From "Shall I Wear a White Rose or Shall I Wear a Red"; see entry 759.28.

782.27/767.30 THE SAILORS PLAYING ALL BIRDS FLY AND I SAY STOOP These phrases seem to refer to some games, but I have not identified them.

782.41/768.2 GLANCING EYES A LATTICE HID   From "In Old Madrid"; see entry 275.27.

783.8/768.12 OR SHALL I WEAR A RED   From "Shall I Wear a White Rose or Shall I Wear a Red"; see entry 759.28.

APPENDIX

The texts of the following songs are printed here for convenience, since these songs are alluded to in great detail at some points in the novel.

"The Croppy Boy"
by William B. McBurney (Carroll Malone)

"Good men and true! in this house who dwell,
To a stranger bouchal I pray you tell
Is the priest at home? or may he be seen?
I would speak a word with Father Green."

"The Priest's at home, boy, and may be seen:
'Tis easy speaking with Father Green;
But you must wait, till I go and see
If the holy father alone may be."

The youth has entered an empty hall—
What a lonely sound has his light foot-fall!   10
And the gloomy chamber's still and bare,
With a vested Priest in a lonely chair.

The youth has knelt to tell his sins;
"Nomine Dei," the youth begins:
At "mea culpa" he beats his breast,
And in broken murmurs he speaks the rest.

"At the siege of Ross did my father fall,
And at Gorey my loving brothers all,
I alone am left of my name and race,
I will go to Wexford and take their place.   20

"I cursed three times since last Easter day—
At mass-time once I went to play;
I passed the churchyard one day in haste,
And forgot to pray for my mother's rest.

"I bear no grudge against living thing;
But I love my country above the king.
Now, Father! bless me, and let me go
To die, if God has ordained it so."

The Priest said nought, but a rustling noise
Made the youth look above in wild surpise;   30
The robes were off, and in scarlet there
Sat a yeoman captain with fiery glare.

With fiery glare and with fury hoarse,
Instead of blessing, he breathed a curse:—
" 'Twas a good thought, boy, to come here and shrive,
For one short hour is your time to live.

"Upon yon river three tenders float,
The Priest's in one, if he isn't shot—
We hold his house for our Lord the King,
And Amen! say I, may all traitors swing!"   40

At Geneva Barrack that young man died,
And at Passage they have his body laid.
Good people who live in peace and joy,
Breathe a prayer and a tear for the Croppy Boy.

"Goodbye, Sweetheart, Goodbye"
by J. L. Hatton

The bright stars fade, the morn is breaking,
The dew-drops pearl each bud and leaf,
And I from thee my leave am taking,
With bliss too brief, with bliss, with bliss too brief.
How sinks my heart with fond alarms,
The tear is hiding in mine eye,
For time doth tear me from thine arms
Good-bye, sweetheart, good-bye, Good-bye sweetheart, good-bye
For time doth tear me from thine arms,
Good-bye, sweetheart, good-bye.

The sun is up, the lark is soaring,
Loud swells the song of chanticleer,
The lev'ret bounds o'er earth's soft flow'ring,
Yet I am here, yet I, yet I am here.
For since night's gems from heav'n do fade,
And morn to floral lips doth hie,
I could not leave thee though I said
Good-bye sweetheart, good-bye, Good-bye, sweetheart, good-bye,
I could not leave thee though I said
Good-bye, sweetheart, good-bye.

"My Girl's a Yorkshire Girl"
by C. W. Murphy and Dan Lipton

Two young fellows were talking about their girls, girls, girls,
Sweethearts they left behind—sweethearts for whom they pined;
One said, "My little shy little lass has a waist so trim and small,
Grey are her eyes so bright, but best, best of all

> Chorus:
> "My girl's a Yorkshire girl, Yorkshire through and through;
> My girl's a Yorkshire girl, Eh, by gum, she's a champion!
> Though she's a factory lass, and wears no fancy clothes,
> I've a sort of Yorkshire relish for my little Yorkshire Rose."

When they first finished singing in praise of Rose, Rose, Rose,
Poor Number Two looked vexed, saying in tones perplexed,
"*My* little lass works in a factory, too, and has *also* eyes of grey;
Her name is Rose as well, and strange, strange to say
                                                        Chorus.

To a cottage in Yorkshire they hied to Rose, Rose, Rose,
Meaning to make it clear which was the boy most dear.
Rose, their Rose, didn't answer the bell, but her husband did instead;
Loudly he sang to them as off, off they fled
                                                        Chorus.

BIBLIOGRAPHY

This Bibliography contains only those works that are not fully cited in the body of the list. It does not contain every work consulted, nor every work cited in the list. In general, books and articles which are mentioned only once or twice in the entire list are cited fully in the pertinent entries. Most standard works (e.g., those of Milton or Dickens) are cited by section, chapter, book, and line, or by act, scene, and line, so that no bibliographical information is needed for these.

Adams, Robert M. *Surface and Symbol: The Consistency of James Joyce's* ULYSSES. New York: Oxford University Press, 1962. This work is abbreviated *SS* in the list.

Adams, W. Davenport. *A Dictionary of Drama.* . . . London: Chatto & Windus, 1904. Apparently only vol. I (A–G) of this work appeared.

A. E. See Russell, George W.

Albert, Leonard. "*Ulysses,* Cannibals and Freemasons," *A.D.*, II (Autumn, 1951), 264–83.

Allen, James Lane. *The Mettle of the Pasture*. New York: The Macmillan Company, 1903.

Allibone, S. Austin. *A Critical Dictionary of English Literature and British and American Authors*. . . . 3 vols., plus supplements. Philadelphia: J. B. Lippincott Co., 1899.

Annals of the Kingdom of Ireland by the Four Masters from the Earliest Period to the Year 1171, ed. and trans. by John O'Donovan. 7 vols. Dublin: no publisher, 1849.

Annuaire de la Presse Française et Étrangère et du Monde Politique: Edition de 1905. Paris [1905].

Apperson, G. L. *English Proverbs and Proverbial Phrases: A Historical Dictionary*. London: J. M. Dent and Sons Ltd., 1929. This work is cited in the list as Apperson.

Appleton's Cyclopaedia of American Biography, ed. James Grant Wilson, John Fiske, and others. 6 vols., plus supplements. New York: D. Appleton and Co., 1888–1924.

Atherton, James S. *The Books at the Wake: A Study of Literary Allusions in James Joyce's* FINNEGANS WAKE. New York: The Viking Press, 1960.

Attwater, Donald. *A Dictionary of Mary*. New York: P. J. Kenedy & Sons, 1956.

Bagwell, Richard. *Ireland Under the Stuarts and During the Interregnum*. 3 vols. London: Longmans, Green, 1909–16.

——. *Ireland Under the Tudors with a Succinct Account of the Earlier History*. 3 vols. London: The Holland Press, 1963. First printed in 1885–90.

Baker, Ernest A., and James Packman. *A Guide to the Best Fiction English and American including Translations from Foreign Languages*. New and enlarged ed. London: George Routledge & Sons, Ltd., 1932.

Bantock, Granville, ed. *One Hundred Songs of England*. Boston: Oliver Ditson Company, 1914.

Baring-Gould, S. *The Lives of The Saints*. New and revised ed. 16 vols. Edinburgh: John Grant, 1914.

Benstock, Bernard. [Review of Frances M. Boldereff's *A Blakean Translation of Joyce's "Circe"*] *James Joyce Quarterly*, III (Winter, 1966), 160–62.

Blake, William. *The Complete Writings of William Blake*, ed. Geoffrey Keynes. London: The Nonesuch Press, 1957.

Blavatsky, Mme H. P. *The Key to Theosophy*. New York: Theosophical Publishing Company, 1896.

——. *Isis Unveiled: A Master Key to the Mysteries of Ancient and Modern Science and Theology.* 2 vols. New York: J. W. Bouton, 1886. First published *ca.* 1877.

Boni, Margaret Bradford, ed. *The Fireside Book of Favorite American Songs.* New York: Simon and Schuster, 1952.

——, ed. *Songs of the Gilded Age.* New York: Golden Press, Inc., 1960.

Book of Catholic Quotations. . . , ed. John Chapin. New York: Farrar, Straus and Cudahy, 1956.

Booth, John Bennian. *Old Pink 'un Days.* New York: Dodd, Mead, 1925.

Boucicault, Dion. *The Dolmen Boucicault,* ed. David Krause. Dublin: The Dolmen Press, 1964.

Boyd, Ernest A. *Ireland's Literary Renaissance.* Dublin: Maunsel & Company, Ltd., 1916.

Brandes, George. *William Shakespeare: A Critical Study.* New York: Macmillan, 1899. This work is referred to in the list as Brandes.

Brewer, E. C. *A Dictionary of Phrase and Fable.* New edition. Philadelphia: J. B. Lippincott Company, [1923].

——. *Historic Note-Book: With an Appendix of Battles.* Philadelphia: J. B. Lippincott Company, 1891.

British Museum. *General Catalogue of Printed Books.* 263 vols. London: Trustees of the British Museum, 1965–66.

British Union-Catalogue of Periodicals. . . , ed. James D. Stewart *et al.* 4 vols., plus Index. London: Butterworths Scientific Publications, 1955–58.

Brown, Stephen J., S.J. *Ireland in Fiction: A Guide to Irish Novels, Tales, Romances, and Folk-Lore.* New ed. Dublin: Maunsel and Company, Ltd., 1919.

Browne, Sir Thomas. *The Works of Sir Thomas Browne,* ed. Geoffrey Keynes. 4 vols. Chicago: The University of Chicago Press, 1964.

Budgen, Frank. *James Joyce and the Making of* ULYSSES. Bloomington, Ind.: Indiana University Press, 1960. First published in 1934. This work is abbreviated *JJMU* in the list.

Burke, Sir Bernard. *Burke's Genealogical and Heraldric History of the Landed Gentry of Ireland,* ed. L. G. Pine. 4th ed. London: Burke's Peerage, 1958.

Butler, Alban. *Butler's Lives of the Saints.* Complete edition, edited, revised and supplemented by Herbert Thurston, S.J., and Donald Attwater. 4 vols. New York: P. J. Kenedy & Sons, 1962. In one or two instances, an earlier edition of this work is cited, but this is always duly noted in the appropriate entries; when no statement is made, the 1962 edition is referred to.

The Cabinet of Irish Literature. . . , ed. Charles A. Read and T. P. O'Connor. 4 vols. London: Blackie & Son, Ltd. 1892.

Campbell, Gordon, and I. O. Evans. *The Book of Flags.* 2nd ed. Oxford: Oxford University Press, 1953.

A Catholic Commentary on Holy Scripture, ed. Don Bernard Orchard *et al.* London: Thomas Nelson and Sons Ltd., 1953.

Catholic Dublin: A Guide to All the Principal Churches and Places of Interest in and Around Dublin. Dublin: The Trinity Press, Ltd., n.d. [*ca.* 1932].

The Catholic Encyclopedia. 15 vols. New York: Robert Appleton Company, 1907–12. Vol. XVI (Index). New York: The Encyclopedia Press, Inc., 1914.

Chambers, E. K. *William Shakespeare: A Study of Facts and Problems.* 2 vols. Oxford: Clarendon Press, 1930. This work is referred to in the list as Chambers.

Chappell, William. *Old English Popular Music.* 2 vols. A new edition, revised by H. Ellis Wooldridge. New York: Jack Brussel, 1961. Originally published *ca.* 1838–40.

———. *Popular Music of the Olden Time.* . . . 2 vols., paged consecutively. London: Cramer, Beale, & Chappell, n.d. [*ca.* 1855–59].

Chapple, Joe Mitchell, ed. *Heart Songs Dear to the American People.* Cleveland: World Publishing Company, 1950.

Chart, D. A. *The Story of Dublin.* London: J. M. Dent & Co., 1907. In the Medieval Town Series.

The Christy Minstrel Song Books. . . . In one volume. London: Boosey & Co., n.d.

Circus and Allied Arts: A World Bibliography, 1500–1957, ed. R. Toole Stott. 3 vols. Derby, England: Harpur & Sons (Derby) Ltd., 1958–62. Vol. 2 is titled . . . *1500–1959;* vol. 3 is titled . . . *1500–1962.*

Clement, Clara Erskine. *A Handbook of Christian Symbols and Stories of the Saints as Illustrated in Art.* Boston: Houghton Mifflin Company, 1871.

Cokayne, George Edward. *The Complete Peerage of England, Scotland, Ireland, Great Britain, and the United Kingdom.* New ed., revised and much enlarged by The Hon. Vicary Gibbs, H. A. Doubleday, and others. 13 vols. in 14. London: The St. Catherine Press Ltd., 1910–40.

Colum, Mary, and Padraic Colum. *Our Friend James Joyce.* Garden City, N.Y.: Doubleday & Co., 1958.

Colum, Padraic. *Ourselves Alone! The Story of Arthur Griffith and the Origin of the Irish Free State.* New York: Crown Publishers, Inc., 1959.

———. *The Road Round Ireland.* New York: The Macmillan Co., 1926.

———, ed. *A Treasury of Irish Folklore.* New York: Crown Publishers, Inc., 1954.

The Columbia Encyclopedia, ed. William Bridgwater and Seymour Kurtz. 3rd ed. New York: Columbia University Press, 1963.

Complete Baronetage, ed. G. E. C. [George Edward Cockayne] 5 vols. Exeter: William Pollard & Co. Ltd., 1900–6.

Cosgrave, E. MacDowel, and Leonard R. Strangways. *The Dictionary of Dublin.* . . . Dublin: Sealy, Bryers & Walker, 1907.

Croker, T. Crofton, ed. *The Historical Songs of Ireland: Illustrative of the Revolutionary Struggle between James II and William III.* London: The Percy Society, 1841. In volume one of the Percy Society Publications in Early English Poetry, Ballads, and Popular Literature of the Middle Ages.

———, ed. *The Popular Songs of Ireland.* London: Henry Colburn, 1839.

Crone, John S. *A Concise Dictionary of Irish Biography.* New York: Longmans, Green and Co., 1928.

Curtis, Edmund. *A History of Ireland.* London: Methuen & Co., Ltd., 1936.

———. *A History of Medieval Ireland from 1086–1513.* Revised ed. London: Methuen & Co. Ltd., 1938.

Daiches, David, ed. An annotated edition of the "Proteus" and "Lestrygonians" episodes of *Ulysses* in *The Norton Anthology of English Literature.* New York: W. W. Norton & Co., 1962.

Davitt, Michael. *The Boer Fight for Freedom.* New York: Funk & Wagnalls Company, 1902.

Denson, Alan. *Printed Writings by George W. Russell (AE): A Bibliography* Evanston, Ill.: Northwestern University Press, 1961.

Dictionary of American Biography, ed. Allen Johnson *et al.* 20 vols. plus index and supplements. New York: Charles Scribner's Sons, 1928——. This work is abbreviated *DAB* in the list.

The Dictionary of National Biography, ed. Sir Leslie Stephen, Sir Sidney Lee *et al.* 22 vols. plus supplements. London: Oxford University Press, 1917——. This work is abbreviated *DNB* in the list.

Diogenes Laertius. *The Lives and Opinions of Eminent Philosophers,* trans. C. D. Yonge. London: Henry G. Bohn, 1853.

Disher, M. Willson. *Melodrama: Plots That Thrilled.* London: Salisbury Square, 1954.

———. *Victorian Song from Dive to Drawing Room.* London: Phoenix House Ltd., 1955.

Dublin and Cork. A book of photographs by R. S. Magowan. London: Spring Books, 1961.

The Dublin Book of Irish Verse, 1728–1909, ed. John Cooke. Dublin: Hodges, Figgis & Co., Ltd., 1915.

Dumas, Alexandre *(père)*. *Théatre Complet*. Nouvelle édition. 25 vols. Paris: Ancienne Maison Michel Levy Frères, 1883–89.

Duncan, Joseph E. "The Modality of the Audible in Joyce's *Ulysses*," *PMLA*, LXXII (March, 1957), 286–95.

Eglinton, John [W. K. Magee]. *Pebbles from a Brook*. Kilkenny and Dublin: Standish O' Grady, 1901.

Ellmann, Richard. *James Joyce*. New York: Oxford University Press, 1959. This work is abbreviated *JJ* in the list.

Enciclopedia Universal Ilustrada Europeo-Americana. 70 vols. plus appendices and supplements. Barcelona: Hijos de J. Espasa, n.d.

Encyclopaedia Britannica. 11th ed. 29 vols. Cambridge, Eng.: The University Press, 1910–11.

——. 24 vols. Chicago: Encyclopaedia Britannica, Inc., 1964.

The English Catalogue of Books. . . . London: Publishers' Circular, Ltd., 1914——. This series, which lists books printed in Great Britain from 1801 on, is still in progress.

Epstein, Edmund L. "Cruxes in *Ulysses*: Notes Toward an Edition and Annotation," *James Joyce Review*, I (September, 1957), 25–36.

——. [untitled review of William M. Schutte's *Joyce and Shakespeare*], *James Joyce Review*, I (June 16, 1957), 42–48.

Erin's Call Song Book. Dublin: Nugent and Co., n.d. In the National Library of Ireland collection of paperback song books.

Ervine, St. John. *Parnell*. Boston: Little, Brown, and Company, 1925.

Farmer, John S., and W. E. Henley, eds. *Slang and Its Analogues Past and Present*. . . . 7 vols. N.p., 1890–1904.

The Favorite Songster Being a Collection of the Most Popular Love, Sea, War, Nigger, Comic, Sentimental, National and Patriotic Songs. Dublin: P. Ward, n.d. In the National Library of Ireland collection of paperback song books.

Feeney, William J. "*Ulysses* and the Phoenix Park Murder," *James Joyce Quarterly*, I (Summer, 1964), 56–58.

French, Percy. *Prose, Poems and Parodies of Percy French*, ed. Mrs. de Burgh Daly. Dublin: Talbot Press, 1929.

Gilbert, Stuart. *James Joyce's* ULYSSES, 2nd ed., revised. New York: Vintage Books, 1952. First printed in 1930. This work is abbreviated *JJU* in the list.

Glasheen, Adaline. "Another Face for Proteus," *James Joyce Review*, I (June 16, 1957), 3–8.

Godefroy, Frederic. *Dictionnaire de l'Ancienne Langue Française*. . . .

10 vols. New York: Kraus Reprint Corporation, 1961. First printed in 1880–1902.

Goethe, Johann Wolfgang von. *Faust, Parts One and Two*, trans. by George Madison Priest. New York: Alfred A. Knopf, 1941.

Gogarty, Oliver St. John. *As I Was Going Down Sackville Street*. New York: Reynal & Hitchcock, 1937.

——. *The Collected Poems of Oliver St. John Gogarty*. New York: The Devin-Adair Company, 1954.

——. *Selected Poems*. New York: The Macmillan Company, 1933.

Gomme, Alice Bertha. *The Traditional Games of England, Scotland, and Ireland*. 2 vols. London: David Nutt, 1894–98. The volumes comprise Part I of *A Dictionary of British Folk-Lore*.

The Good Old Songs We Used to Sing. 2 vols. Boston: Oliver Ditson Company, 1895. I have used only the second volume of this work.

Gordon, W. J. *Flags of the World, Past and Present*. London: Frederick Warne & Co., 1915.

Gorman, Herbert. *James Joyce*. New York: Farrar and Rinehart, Inc., 1939.

Greene, Robert. *Groats-Worth of Witte. . .*, ed. G. B. Harrison. The Bodley Head Quartos. London: John Lane, The Bodley Head, Ltd., 1923.

Hall, Mr. and Mrs. S. C. *Ireland: Its Scenery, Character, &c.* 3 vols. London: How and Parsons, 1841–43.

Harding's Nightingale Song Book. Dublin: N. Harding, n.d. The National Library of Ireland has vols. 2–12 of this paperback set bound together and indexed in the Index prepared by J. Toomey.

Harper's Dictionary of Classical Literature and Antiquities, ed. Harry Thurston Peck. New York: American Book Company, 1896.

Harris, Frank. *The Man Shakespeare and His Tragic Life-Story*. New York: Mitchell Kennerley, 1909. This work is referred to in the list as Harris.

Harris, Walter. *The History and Antiquities of the City of Dublin, from the Earliest Accounts. . . .* London: John Knox, 1766.

Harrison, Henry. *Parnell Vindicated: The Lifting of the Veil*. London: Constable & Co., Ltd., 1931.

Harrison, Wilmot. *Memorable Dublin Houses: A Handy Guide*. Dublin: W. Leckie & Co., 1890.

Hartland, Edwin Sidney. *Primitive Paternity: The Myth of Supernatural Birth in Relation to the History of the Family*. 2 vols. London: David Nutt, 1909–10. These are vols. LXV and LXVII of the Publications of the Folk-Lore Society.

Haslip, Joan. *Parnell: A Biography*. New York: Frederick A. Stokes Company, 1937.

Hastings, James. *Dictionary of the Bible*. Revised ed. by Frederick C. Grant and H. H. Rowley. New York: Charles Scribner's Sons, 1963.

Hatton, J. L., and Eaton Faning, eds. *The Songs of England. A Collection of 274 English Melodies.* . . . 3 vols. (new edition). London: Boosey & Co., n.d.

Hatton, J. L., and J. L. Molloy. *The Songs of Ireland* (new and enlarged edition). London: Boosey & Co., n.d.

Heine, Arthur. "Shakespeare in James Joyce," *Shakespeare Association Bulletin*, XXIV (January, 1949), 56–70.

Hoagland, Kathleen. *1000 Years of Irish Poetry*. New York: The Devin-Adair Company, 1947. This work is referred to in the list as Hoagland.

Hodgart, Matthew J. C., and Mabel Worthington. *Song in the Works of James Joyce*. New York: Columbia University Press, 1959. This work is referred to in the list as Hodgart and Worthington.

The Home Book of Proverbs, Maxims and Familiar Phrases, ed. Burton Stevenson. New York: The Macmillan Company, 1948.

Homer. *The Odyssey*, trans. by S. H. Butcher and Andrew Lang. New York: The Macmillan Company, 1941.

Howarth, Herbert. "The Joycean Comedy: Wilde, Jonson, and Others," in *A James Joyce Miscellany, Second Series*, pp. 179–94. The *Miscellany* is separately listed in this Bibliography.

Howe, George, and G. A. Harrer. *A Handbook of Classical Mythology*. New York: F. S. Crofts & Co., 1947.

Hughes, Herbert, ed. *Irish Country Songs*. 4 vols. London: Boosey & Co., [*ca.* 1909–36].

Hull, Vernam, and Archer Taylor. *A Collection of Irish Riddles*. Berkeley, Calif.: University of California Press, 1955. University of California Publications, Folklore Studies: 6.

Husenbeth, F. C. *Emblems of Saints: By Which They Are Distinguished in Works of Art*. London: Burns and Lambert, 1850.

Hyde, Douglas. *A Literary History of Ireland from the Earliest Times to the Present Day*. London: T. Fisher Unwin Ltd., 1899.

——. *The Story of Early Gaelic Literature*. London: T. Fisher Unwin Ltd., 1895.

Irish Literature, ed. Justin McCarthy *et al.* 10 vols. Philadelphia: John D. Morris & Company, 1904.

A James Joyce Miscellany, Second Series, ed. Marvin Magalaner. Carbondale, Ill.: Southern Illinois University Press, 1959. This work is abbreviated *JJM II* in the list.

A James Joyce Miscellany, Third Series, ed. Marvin Magalaner. Carbondale, Ill.: Southern Illinois University Press, 1962. This work is abbreviated *JJM III* in the list.

Jarrell, Mackie L. "Joyce's Use of Swift's *Polite Conversation* in the 'Circe' Episode of *Ulysses*," *PMLA*, LXXII (June, 1957), 545–54.

The Jewish Encyclopedia. 12 vols. New York: Funk and Wagnalls Company, 1907.

Johannsen, Albert. *The House of Beadle and Adams and Its Dime and Nickel Novels: The Story of a Vanished Literature*. 3 vols. Norman, Okla.: University of Oklahoma Press, 1950–62.

Johnson, Helen Kendrick. *Our Familiar Songs and Those Who Made Them*. New York: Henry Holt and Company, 1881.

Joyce, James. "Alphabetical Notebook." This notebook, which Joyce kept *ca.* 1904–14, is now in the Cornell University Joyce collection and is described in Robert Scholes's catalogue of that collection (see the Scholes item in this Bibliography).

——. *The Critical Writings of James Joyce*, ed. Ellsworth Mason and Richard Ellmann. London: Faber and Faber, 1959. This work is abbreviated *CW* in the list.

——. "Daniel Defoe," ed. and trans. by Joseph Prescott, *Buffalo Studies*, I (December, 1964), 1–27.

——. *Exiles*, ed. Padraic Colum. London: Jonathan Cape, 1952.

——. "The First Version of 'A Portrait,' " in Scholes and Kain, *The Workshop of Daedalus*, pp. 56–74 (separately listed in this bibliography).

——. *Letters of James Joyce*, ed. by Stuart Gilbert. London: Faber and Faber, 1957.

——. *A Portrait of the Artist as a Young Man*. New York: Viking Press, 1964. The "definitive edition," by Chester G. Anderson and Richard Ellmann.

——. *Stephen Hero*, ed. by Theodore Spencer, added material by John J. Slocum and Herbert Cahoon. London: Jonathan Cape, 1956.

——. *Ulysses*. New York: Random House, 1934, 1961.

Joyce, Patrick Weston, ed. *Ancient Irish Music*. . . . London: Longmans, Green, & Co., 1910 (reissue).

——. *English As We Speak It in Ireland*. 2nd ed. London: Longmans, Green, & Co., 1910.

——. *A Short History of Ireland from the Earliest Times to 1608*. London: Longmans, Green, & Co., 1893.

Joyce, Stanislaus. *My Brother's Keeper*, ed. Richard Ellmann. New York: The Viking Press, 1958. Abbreviated in the list as *MBK*.

Judson Concordance to Hymns, comp. Thomas B. McDormand and Frederic S. Crossman. Valley Forge, Pa.: The Judson Press, 1965.

Julian, John, ed. *A Dictionary of Hymnology Setting Forth the Origin and History of Christian Hymns of All Ages and Nations.* Revised ed., with new supplement. London: John Murray, 1907.

Kain, Richard M. *Dublin in the Age of William Butler Yeats and James Joyce.* Norman, Okla.: University of Oklahoma Press, 1962.

——. *Fabulous Voyager: James Joyce's* ULYSSES. New York: The Viking Press, 1959. First published by the University of Chicago in 1947. This work is abbreviated *FV* in the list.

——. "James Joyce's Shakespeare Chronology," *The Massachusetts Review*, V (Winter, 1964), 342–55.

Keating, Geoffrey. *The History of Ireland*, trans. by David Comyn and Patrick S. Dineen. London: Irish Texts Society, 1902–14 (vols. 4, 8, 9, and 15 of the Irish Texts Society).

Kenny, James F. *The Sources for the Early History of Ireland: An Introduction and Guide.* New York: Columbia University Press, 1929. Although the title page says "in two volumes," and describes vol. I as "Ecclesiastical," the second volume never appeared.

Killham, John. " 'Ineluctable Modality' in Joyce's *Ulysses*," *University of Toronto Quarterly*, XXXIV (April, 1965), 269–89.

Klein, A. M. "The Black Panther: A Study in Technique," *Accent*, X (Summer, 1950), 139–55.

——. "Shout in the Street: An Analysis of the Second Chapter of Joyce's *Ulysses*," *New Directions 13*. Norfolk: New Directions Books, 1951. The essay is on pp. 327–45.

Kobbé, Gustave. *Kobbé's Complete Opera Book*, ed. and revised by the Earl of Harewood. London: Putnam, 1954. The original edition was first published in 1922.

Laforgue, Jules. *Oeuvres Complètes: Mélanges Posthumes.* Paris: Societe du Mercure de France, 1903.

Landreth, Helen. *The Pursuit of Robert Emmet.* New York: Whittlesey House, 1948.

Lee, Sidney. *A Life of William Shakespeare.* New York: Macmillan, 1898. This work is referred to in the list as Lee.

Liddell, Henry George, and Robert Scott. *A Greek-English Lexicon.* A new ed., revised and augmented by Sir Henry Stuart Jones. 2 vols. Oxford: Clarendon Press, [*ca.* 1940].

Litz, A. Walton. *The Art of James Joyce: Method and Design in*

ULYSSES *and* FINNEGANS WAKE. London: Oxford University Press, 1961. This work is abbreviated *AJJ* in the list.

Lubbock, Mark. *The Complete Book of Light Opera*. With an American section by David Ewen. New York: Appleton-Century-Crofts, 1962.

Lyons, F. S. L. *The Fall of Parnell, 1890–91*. Toronto: University of Toronto Press, 1962. Vol. I of Studies in Irish History, Second Series.

McAleer, Edward C. "The Ignorance of Mr. Bloom," in *Studies in Honor of John C. Hodges and Alwin Thaler*. Knoxville, Tenn.: University of Tennessee Press, 1961, pp. 121–29. *Tennessee Studies in Literature* Special Number.

McClintock, H. F. *Old Irish and Highland Dress and That of the Isle of Man*. 2nd and enlarged ed. Dundalk: Dundalgan Press Ltd., 1950.

MacManus, Seumas. *The Story of the Irish Race: A Popular History of Ireland*. New York: The Irish Publishing Co., 1921.

McNelly, Willis E. "Liturgical Deviations in *Ulysses*," *James Joyce Quarterly*, II (Summer, 1965), 291–98.

MacQueen-Pope, W. *Gaiety: Theatre of Enchantment*. London: Greenberg, in association with W. H. Allen, n.d. [1949?]

———. *The Melodies Linger On: The Story of the Music Hall*. London: W. H. Allen, n.d.

Magalaner, Marvin. *Time of Apprenticeship: The Fiction of the Young James Joyce*. New York: Abelard-Schuman, 1959.

Maxwell, Constantia. *Dublin Under the Georges, 1714–1830*. 2nd ed. London: Faber and Faber Ltd., 1956.

Meyer, Arthur William. *The Rise of Embryology*. Stanford, Calif.: Stanford University Press, 1939.

Middle English Dictionary, ed. Hans Kurath and Sherman M. Kuhn. Ann Arbor, Michigan: University of Michigan Press, 1956——. This work is in progress.

Miles, Alfred H., ed. *Our National Songs: A Collection of One Hundred and Eighty Songs of England, Ireland, Scotland, and Wales*. London: Hutchinson & Co., n.d.

Moffat, Alfred, ed. *The Minstrelsy of Ireland*. 3rd (enlarged) ed. London: Augener & Co., n.d. 1906.

Morse, J. Mitchell. "Another Goethe Allusion [in *Ulysses*]," *James Joyce Quarterly*, III (Winter, 1966), 163.

Needham, Joseph. *A History of Embryology*. 2nd ed., revised with the assistance of Arthur Hughes. New York: Abelard-Schuman, 1959.

Nicoll, Allardyce. *A History of English Drama, 1660–1900.* 2nd ed., 6 vols. Cambridge: Cambridge University Press, 1952–59.

Noon, William T., S.J. *Joyce and Aquinas.* New Haven: Yale University Press, 1957. This work is abbreviated *JA* in the list.

Nugent's Bohemian Songster. Dublin: Nugent & Co., n.d. In the National Library of Ireland collection of paperback song books.

O'Brien, Conor Cruise. *Parnell and His Party, 1880–90.* Oxford: The Clarendon Press, 1957.

O'Brien, R. Barry. *The Life of Charles Stewart Parnell, 1846–1891.* 2 vols. New York: Harper and Brothers, 1898.

O'Growney, Eugene. *Simple Lessons in Irish Giving the Pronunciation of Each Word.* In two parts (Part I, Dublin: Connradh na Gaedhilge, 1948; Part II, Dublin: The Gaelic League, 1936). This work was first published *ca.* 1894–95.

O'Hegarty, P. S. *A History of Ireland Under the Union, 1801 to 1922.* . . . London: Methuen & Co. Ltd., 1952.

O'Lochlainn, Colm. *Irish Street Ballads.* New York: Citadel Press, 1960.

Opie, Iona, and Peter Opie. *The Lore and Language of Schoolchildren.* Oxford: Clarendon Press, 1959.

O'Rahilly, Thomas F. *Early Irish History and Mythology.* Dublin: Dublin Institute for Advanced Studies, 1946.

O'Shea, Katherine (Mrs. Charles Stewart Parnell). *Charles Stewart Parnell: His Love Story and Political Life.* 2 vols. New York: George H. Doran Company, 1914.

O'Sullivan, Donal. *Songs of the Irish.* New York: Crown Publishers Inc., 1960.

The Oxford Annotated Bible with the Apocrypha, ed. Herbert G. May and Bruce M. Metzger. New York: Oxford University Press, 1965.

The Oxford Dictionary of English Proverbs. 2nd ed., revised throughout by Paul Harvey. Oxford: Clarendon Press, 1948. Abbreviated *ODEP* in the list.

The Oxford Dictionary of Nursery Rhymes, ed. Iona and Peter Opie. Oxford: Oxford University Press, 1952. Abbreviated *ODNR* in the list.

The Oxford Dictionary of Quotations. 2nd ed. London: Oxford University Press, 1953.

The Oxford English Dictionary. . . , ed. J. A. H. Murray *et al.* 13 vols. (including *Supplement and Bibliography*). Oxford: Clarendon Press, 1933. Abbreviated *OED* in the list.

Paley, Morton D. "Blake in Nighttown," in *A James Joyce Miscellany, Third Series,* pp. 175–187. The *Miscellany* is separately listed in this Bibliography.

Prescott, Joseph. *Exploring James Joyce*. Carbondale, Ill.: Southern Illinois University Press, 1964.

——. "Mosenthal's *Deborah* and Joyce's *Ulysses*," *Modern Language Notes*, LXVII (May, 1952), 334–36.

——. "Notes on Joyce's *Ulysses*," *Modern Language Quarterly*, XIII (June, 1952), 149–62.

Pulling, Christopher. *They Were Singing and What They Sang About*. London: G. G. Harrap, [1952].

Racial Proverbs: A Selection of the World's Proverbs arranged Linguistically, ed. Selwyn Gurney Champion. 2nd ed. New York: Barnes & Noble, Inc., 1950.

Radford, F., and M. A. Radford. *Encyclopaedia of Superstitions*. New York: Philosophical Library, 1949.

Reddall, Henry Frederic, ed. *Songs That Never Die*. . . . Boston: B. B. Russell, n.d.

Remlap, L T., ed. *The Life of General U. S. Grant . . . Together with His Trip Around the World*. New York: Loomis National Library Association, 1888. The author's name is apparently a pseudonym for Palmer.

Rogers, Howard Emerson. "Irish Myth and the Plot of *Ulysses*," *ELH: A Journal of English Literary History*, XV (December, 1948), 306–27.

Russell, George W. (A. E.). *The Earth Breath and Other Poems*. 2nd ed. London: John Lane, The Bodley Head, 1906.

——. *Homeward: Songs by the Way*. 4th ed. London: John Lane, The Bodley Head, 1908.

—— *Letters from AE*, ed. Alan Denson. New York: Abelard-Schuman, 1961.

Ryan, Stephen P. "Joyce's Father Cowley," *Notes and Queries*, IX (August, 1962), 305–6.

Scholes, Robert E. *The Cornell Joyce Collection: A Catalogue*. Ithaca, New York: Cornell University Press, 1961.

——, and Richard M. Kain, eds. *The Workshop of Daedalus: James Joyce and the Raw Materials for* A PORTRAIT OF THE ARTIST AS A YOUNG MAN. Evanston, Ill.: Northwestern University Press, 1965.

Schutte, William M. *Joyce and Shakespeare: A Study in the Meaning of* ULYSSES. New Haven: Yale University Press, 1957. This work is abbreviated *JS* in the list.

Sears, Minnie Earl, assisted by Phyllis Crawford. *Song Index: An Index to More Than 12000 Songs in 177 Collections Comprising 262 Volumes, and Supplement*. Two volumes in one. N.p.: The Shoe

String Press, Inc., 1966. Originally published in 1926; *Supplement* in 1934.

Senn, Fritz. "Cabbage Leaves," *James Joyce Quarterly*, II (Winter, 1965), 137–38.

——. "Esthetic Theories," *James Joyce Quarterly*, II (Winter, 1965), 134–36.

——. "Mullingar Heifer," *James Joyce Quarterly*, II (Winter, 1965), 136–37.

——. [Notes on *Ulysses*], *James Joyce Quarterly*, I (Summer, 1964), 64–65.

Shakespeare, William. *Shakespeare: The Complete Works*, ed. G. B. Harrison. New York: Harcourt, Brace and Company, 1948. This edition by Harrison generally follows the Globe text in scene divisions and line numbers.

Sharp, Cecil J., ed. *English Folk-Chanteys*. New York: H. W. Gray Co., n.d.

Sinnett, A. P. *Esoteric Buddhism*. 5th ed., annotated and enlarged by the author. London: Chapman and Hall, Ltd., 1885.

Skeat, Walter W. *An Etymological Dictionary of the English Language*. New ed., revised and enlarged. Oxford: Clarendon Press, 1909. This work was first published in 1879–82; I used the 1961 impression of the revised and enlarged edition.

Song Dex Treasury of Humorous and Nostalgic Songs. 2 vols. (called Parts One and Two). New York: Song Dex, Inc., 1956, 1963.

Songs of Many Wars from the Sixteenth to the Twentieth Century, ed. Kurt Adler. New York: Howell, Soskin, 1943.

Songs That Never Grow Old. New York: Syndicate Publishing Co., 1909.

Spaeth, Sigmund. *A History of Popular Music in America*. New York: Random House, 1948.

——. *Read 'Em and Weep: The Songs You Forgot to Remember*. Garden City, N.Y.: Doubleday, Page & Company, 1927.

——. *Weep Some More, My Lady*. Garden City, N.Y.: Doubleday, Page & Company, 1927.

Sparling, H. Halliday, ed. *Irish Minstrelsy, Being a Selection of Irish Songs, Lyrics, and Ballads*. London: Walter Scott, Ltd., n.d. [*ca.* 1888].

Spielberg, Peter. *James Joyce's Manuscripts & Letters at the University of Buffalo: A Catalogue*. Buffalo, N.Y.: University of Buffalo, 1962.

The Standard Jewish Encyclopedia. New, revised edition. Garden City, N.Y.: Doubleday and Company, Inc., 1962.

Steinberg, Erwin Ray. "The Stream-of-Consciousness Technique in

James Joyce's *Ulysses*" (unpublished Ph.D. dissertation, New York University, 1956; available on microfilm). Abbreviated in the list *SoC*.

Stevenson's Book of Quotations, Classical and Modern, ed. Burton Stevenson. 9th ed. London: Cassell and Company Ltd., n.d. [*ca.* 1958].

Sullivan, Kevin. *Joyce Among the Jesuits.* New York: Columbia University Press, 1958.

Sultan, Stanley. *The Argument of* Ulysses. Columbus, Ohio: Ohio State University Press, 1965.

Swift, Jonathan. *Polite Conversation,* ed. Eric Partridge. London: Andre Deutsch, 1963.

Thompson, Stith. *Motif-Index of Folk-Literature.* . . . Revised and enlarged ed. 6 vols. Bloomington, Indiana: Indiana University Press, 1955–58.

Thom's Official Directory of the United Kingdom of Great Britain and Ireland for the Year 1904. . . . Dublin: Alex Thom & Co., Ltd., 1904. Referred to in the list as Thom's *Dublin Directory* (1904).

Tindall, William York. *The Joyce Country.* University Park: Pennsylvania State University Press, 1960.

——. *A Reader's Guide to James Joyce.* New York: The Noonday Press, Inc., 1959. This work is abbreviated *RG* in the list.

Toomey, J. "Miscellaneous Song Index," (1957). This typescript work, compiled by the staff of the National Library of Ireland, indexes many of the paperback song books in their collection.

U.S. Library of Congress. *A Catalogue of Books Represented by Library of Congress Printed Cards Issued to July 31, 1942.* 167 vols. Ann Arbor, Michigan: Edwards Brothers, Inc., 1942–46.

——. *Supplements,* 1948——.

The Universal Jewish Encyclopedia. 10 vols. and Index. New York: The Universal Jewish Encyclopedia, Inc., 1939–44.

Variety Music Cavalcade 1620–1961: A Chronology of Vocal and Instrumental Music Popular in the United States, ed. Julius Mattfield. Revised ed. Englewood Cliffs, N.J.: Prentice Hall, Inc., 1962.

Visser, G. J. "James Joyce's *Ulysses* and Anglo-Irish," *English Studies,* XIX (April, 1942), 45–46; (June, 1942), 79–90.

Walsh, William S. *Handy-Book of Curious Information.* Philadelphia: J. B. Lippincott Company, 1913.

——. *Handy-Book of Literary Curiosities.* Philadelphia: J. B. Lippincott Company, 1892, 1925.

Walton's 132 Best Irish Songs and Ballads. [Dublin:] The Fodhla Printing Co., n.d.

Walton's Treasury of Irish Songs and Ballads. Dublin: Walton's Musical Instrument Galleries Ltd., n.d. [*ca.* 1947].

Ware, J. Redding. *Passing English of the Victorian Era: A Dictionary
of Heterodox English, Slang, and Phrase.* London: George Routledge & Sons, Ltd., n.d.

Weiss, Daniel. "The End of the 'Oxen of the Sun': An Analysis of the
Boosing Scene in James Joyce's *Ulysses,*" *The Analyst* (Northwestern University), No. IX (December, 1955), 1–16. The next
issue of this mimeograph publication included a "Commentary"
on Weiss's article, by various people (No. X, March, 1956, 10–18).

White, T. H. *The Bestiary: A Book of Beasts, Being a Translation from
a Latin Bestiary of the Twelfth Century.* New York: G. P. Putnam's Sons, 1954.

Wilde, Oscar. *De Profundis. . . .* London: Methuen & Co. Ltd., 1949.
With an introduction by Vyvyan Holland.

———. *The Portrait of Mr. W. H.,* ed. Vyvyan Holland. London: Methuen, 1958.

Willing's Press Guide and Advertisers' Directory and Handbook, 1905
[for 1904]. London: James Willing, Junr., Ltd., [1905].

Wilson, Colin, and Patricia Pitman. *Encyclopedia of Murder.* New
York: G. P. Putnam's Sons, 1962.

Wilson, T. G. *Victorian Doctor: Being the Life of Sir William Wilde.*
New York: L. B. Fischer, 1946.

Witt, Marion. "A Note on Joyce and Yeats," *Modern Language Notes,*
LXIII (December, 1948), 552–53.

Woods, Ralph L., ed. *A Treasury of the Familiar.* Chicago: Peoples
Book Club, 1945.

The World Almanac and Encyclopedia, 1905 [for 1904]. New York:
The Press Publishing Co., 1905.

Worthington, Mabel P. "Irish Folk Songs in Joyce's *Ulysses,*" *PMLA,*
LXXI (June, 1956), 321–39.

Wright, Joseph, ed. *The English Dialect Dictionary. . . .* 6 vols. London:
Henry Frowde, 1898–1905.

Yeats, William Butler. *The Variorum Edition of the Plays of W. B.
Yeats,* ed. Russell K. Alspach and Catherine C. Alspach. New York:
The MacMillan Company, 1966.

———. *The Variorum Edition of the Poems of W. B. Yeats,* ed. Peter
Allt and Russell K. Alspach. New York: The Macmillan Company, 1957.

INDEX

Songs that are better known by title than by author (e.g., "Love's Old Sweet Song") are listed under the title; songs by well-known authors (e.g., Thomas Moore, Stephen Foster) are listed under the author. Literary works are listed under their author.

Black fast, 152.1
Black forty-seven, the, 329.37
Black friars; *see* Dominican Order
Black's Guide to Killarney and the South of Ireland, 242.29
"Blacksmith of Limerick" (song), 296.41
Blacksod Bay, 328.2
Blackstone, Sir William, 100.8, 456.24
Blackwood, Sir John, 31.29, 573.30, 574.2
Blake, William, 24.9, 43.34, 391.18, 583.5, 587.16; "Ah! Sunflower," 391.21; "Auguries of Innocence," 33.38, 597.17; "Book of Los," 37.20; "Book of Urizen," 37.20; "The Chimney Sweeper," 589.28; "The Gates of Paradise," 48.7; "The Harvest Shall Flourish," 589.28; "I fear'd the fury of my wind," 391.19; *Jerusalem*, 21.13, 24.7, 25.20; "Let the Brothels of Paris be Opened," 205.41; *Milton*, 37.20, 37.21, 186.16; "Mock On, Mock On," 216.14; "My Pretty Rose Tree," 391.19; "O lapwing, thou fliest around the heath," 210.36; "The Proverbs of Hell," 24.9; "The Question Answer'd," 199.6; "The Sick Rose," 391.19; "Tiriel," 38.6; "To Nobodaddy," 205.41, 394.33; "A Vision of the Last Judgment," 24.7, 186.16, 587.14
Blavatsky, Mme Helena Petrovna, 140.30, 185.29, 185.38; *Isis Unveiled*, 185.29, 191.37; *see also* Theosophy
Bleibtreu, Karl, 214.9
Bloemfontein, 458.1, 748.43
"Blood libel," 108.30, 692.14
Blood of the Lamb, 151.11, 164.24
Bloody Bridge, 643.26
"Bluebeard" (nursery tale), 466.15
Bluecoat School, 182.37
Blumenbach, John Friedrich, 418.24
Blumenfeld, Ralph David, 137.27
B'nai B'rith, 487.8
Bobrikoff, General, 134.32
Bobs, Dowager Duchess of Manorhamilton, 536.29
Boccaccio, Giovanni: *The Decameron*, 45.31, 207.18
Boddham-Whetham, J. W., 47.35, 50.26
Bode, Johann Elert, 700.26
Bodkin, Matthew, 649.43, 654.29
Boehme, Jacob, 40.37; *The Signature of All Things*, 37.2
Boers, 163.10
Boer War (South African War), 162.40,

163.10, 187.22, 187.32, 205.4, 457.26, 458.1, 484.2, 596.14, 640.33, 722.15, 749.17, 762.20
Bohee brothers (minstrels), 443.18
Bohemian Girl, The (opera); *see* Balfe, Michael William
"Bold Traynor O" (song), 58.7, 281.38
Boniface (?), 427.2
"Bonsoir la Compagnie" (song), 427.6
Book of Ballymote, The, 331.40, 688.34
Book of Common Prayer, The, 96.14, 105.31, 114.28
Book of Howth, The, 688.34
Book of Kells, The, 520.22, 599.15, 688.34
Book of the Dun Cow, The, 688.34
Booth, General William: *In Darkest England, And the Way Out*, 436.29
Borgia, Cesare, 3.34
Borgia, Lucrezia, 3.34
Boucicault, Dion, 167.36; *Arrah-na-Pogue*, 297.13; *The Coleen Bawn*, 92.6, 297.14, 311.10, 426.19, 642.8; *The Shaughran*, 163.18
Bous Stephanoumenos, 210.19, 415.6
Boycott, Captain Charles Cunningham, 296.42
Boyd-Jones, E.; *see* Stuart, Leslie: *Floradora*
Boyle, William: *A Kish of Brogues*, 175.37
Boyne, Battle of the, 41.17
"Boyne Water" (song); *see* "Battle of the Boyne"
"Boys of Kilkenny, The" (song), 44.2
"Boys of Wexford, The" (song), 129.13, 285.2, 451.17
Bracegirdle, Anne, 370.16, 382.13
Braddon, Miss Mary Elizabeth: *Henry Dunbar*, 756.20
Brady, Joe, 304.30
Brady, Nicholas, 193.21
Branscombe, Maud, 370.16, 720.30
"Break It Gently to My Mother" (song), 7.23
Breakspear, Nicholas; *see* Adrian IV, Pope
"Break the News to Mother" (song), 7.23
Brehon Law, 323.6
Brian Boru (Brian Borohime), 45.12, 99.25, 296.36, 678.28, 679.5
Brigittine Order, 339.3
"Brothers and sisters had he none" (riddle), 708.4